AMERICAN TRAVELERS
ON THE NILE

AMERICAN TRAVELERS ON THE NILE

Early U.S. Visitors
to Egypt, 1774–1839

Andrew Oliver

*With best wishes to Gertrude
from Drew
August 16, 2015*

The American University in Cairo Press
Cairo New York

First published in 2014 by
The American University in Cairo Press
113 Sharia Kasr el Aini, Cairo, Egypt
420 Fifth Avenue, New York, NY 10018
www.aucpress.com

Exclusive distribution outside Egypt and North America by I.B.Tauris & Co Ltd., 6 Salem Road,
London, W2 4BU

Dar el Kutub No. 23473/13
ISBN 978 977 416 667 9

Dar el Kutub Cataloging-in-Publication Data

Oliver, Andrew
        American Travelers on the Nile: Early U.S. Visitors to Egypt, 1774–1839/
    Andrew Oliver.—Cairo: The American University in Cairo Press, 2014
        p.   cm.
        ISBN: 978 977 416 667 9
        Egypt—Description & Travel
        916.2

1 2 3 4 5   18 17 16 15 14

Designed by Adam el Sehemy
Printed in Egypt

Mais les vrais voyageurs sont ceux-là seuls qui partent
Pour partir; coeurs légers, semblables aux ballons,
De leur fatalité jamais ils ne s'écartent,
Et, sans savoir pourquoi, disent toujours : Allons!

But the real travelers are those who just go
To go; their hearts as light as balloons,
They never turn aside from their destiny,
And, without knowing why, say simply, "Let's go!"

Charles Baudelaire, *Le voyage* (1859), 17–20

CONTENTS

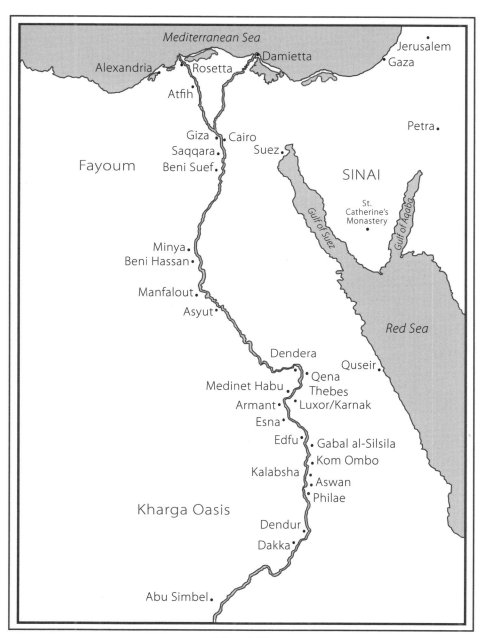

The Nile

ACKNOWLEDGMENTS

Over a period of some five years, a great many individuals and institutions provided assistance, information, and access to letters and diaries, and furnished photographs and permissions. I would like to acknowledge them in the order in which the results of their help appear in this book. The staff of the Library of Congress has been unfailingly helpful. In particular I owe thanks to Thomas Mann for his longstanding interest in my work. Electronic databases available at the Library revealed a wealth of information: travelers' initials became full names, passport applications provided dates of departure from the United States, newspapers carried accounts of their travels, and ships' manifests gave the names of those returning from abroad. I turn now to the individual chapters of this book.

Americans in Eighteenth-century Egypt: On two visits to the Massachusetts Historical Society in Boston, Jeremy Dibbell and other members of the staff made available to me the journal, notebook, and letters of Ward Nicholas Boylston as well as photocopies of two letters of Boylston's traveling companion, the young James Bowdoin. And I thank Elaine M. Heavy, Head of Reader Services, for permission to quote extensively from Boylston's diary. John W. Tyler of the Groton School, who had addressed the travels of Mr. Boylston before I had done so, read a draft of the chapter and offered useful suggestions. Janet L. Comey, curatorial research associate at the Museum of Fine Arts, Boston, provided information on Stuart's portrait of Boylston. To Wim Pijbes, general director of the Rijksmuseum, Amsterdam, and to Eveline Sint Nicolaas, curator in the Department of History at the museum, I owe permission to illustrate the 1771 group portrait of the Van Lennep family whom Boylston met in Smyrna. The original letters written to Thomas Jefferson by John Ledyard, the other American to visit Egypt in the eighteenth century, are owned by the New-York Historical Society, and I thank the staff there for letting me see them.

Mehmet Ali and His New Egypt: Jay G. Williams of Hamilton College made available to me a complete transcript of the diary of Edward Robinson, still owned by the Robinson family, on one page of which Robinson recounts seeing the Egyptian students sent to Paris in 1826 under the aegis of Mehmet Ali.

The American Navy and Trade in the Mediterranean: Cynthia Gilliland and Deborah T. Haynes of the Hood Museum of Art at Dartmouth College provided information on the ledger listing the souvenirs given to Dartmouth by Silas Dinsmore. On a visit to the Gilder Lehrman Institute of American History in New York, the staff brought out the recently acquired letter books of Thomas Appleton, United States consul in Leghorn from 1799 to 1824, in which the names of significant contacts appeared. At the Library of the American Philosophical Society, Charles Greifenstein and Earle Spamer provided a photocopy of Samuel Hazard's meteorological log. By generously providing selected scans of an anonymous journal kept on board a ship in the Mediterranean, a journal owned by the Houghton Library at Harvard University, Heather Cole and Emily Walhout allowed me to identify the author as Samuel Hazard.

Americans Return to Egypt: Christine Bertoni at the Peabody Essex Museum kindly provided a digital image of George Ropes' watercolor of *Cleopatra's Barge* and information as to where it has been published. Sarah Puckitt, collections information specialist at the Montgomery Museum of Fine Arts, arranged for photography of their portrait of Luther Bradish, while Pamela Bransford, registrar at the museum, furnished me with details on the provenance.

American Missionaries on Tour: I am grateful to the staff of the Burke Archives at Union Theological Seminary for making available to me during a visit to the library the Pliny Fisk papers in their possession. Danielle M. Rougeau, assistant curator of Special Collections & Archives at the Davis Family Library, Middlebury University, sent me digital versions of the diaries of Pliny Fisk in their possession. Jackie Penny, rights and reproductions coordinator at the American Antiquarian Society, provided a digital version of the single volume of the diary of Jonas King owned by the society.

The Eastern Question: Harvard Student Services provided a staff member to make copies of one of Pliny Fisk's journals owned by the American Board of Commissioners of Foreign Missions, now on deposit at the

Houghton Library at Harvard, microfilms of which are housed and available for inspection in Lamont Library. Paul Staiti of Mt. Holyoke College, author of the standard account of Samuel F.B. Morse as an artist, kindly steered me to the current owner of Morse's portrait of the Greek Boy.

The Lure of Egypt: Carolyn Yerkes at the Avery Library, Columbia University, brought out their set of sale catalogues of the library of Ithiel Town. Staff members of several libraries and historical organizations helped me determine the story of the first sets of *Description de l'Égypte* to come to the United States: Kate Wodehouse at the Providence Athenaeum; Barbara Doyle at Middleton Place, Charleston; Roy Goodman at the American Philosophical Society; Bruce Laverty at the Athenaeum of Philadelphia; Cornelia S. King at the Library Company of Philadelphia; Nancy Shawcross, curator of manuscripts in the library at the University of Pennsylvania; Gabriel Swift, reference librarian for special collections at Princeton; and Mary Warnement at the Boston Athenaeum. On the early education of Henry Oliver good information came from Bill Landis, archivist at Yale University Library, and from Linda Hocking at the Litchfield Historical Society. A photograph of the gravestone of Cornelius Bradford, located in Jerusalem, was made available by my friend and colleague Roger O. De Keersmaecker. The New-York Historical Society sent me photocopies of the two letters of Theodore Allen addressed to Rev. Samuel R. Johnson in which he gave an account of his tour to the Mediterranean with two colleagues. The Maryland Historical Society gave me access to the papers of Mendes I. Cohen about his Egyptian tour, and James Singewald, imaging services technician at the society, provided an image of the portrait of Cohen. My friend Allaire Brisbane Stallsmith brought to my attention the diary that she and her cousin Abigail Mellen edited of their great-grandfather Albert Brisbane, who considered going to Egypt while in Greece but did not do so.

The US Naval Squadron: Egyptian Curios and Civilian Passengers: At the National Archives in Washington DC, Charles W. Johnson and Chris Killillay were always on hand to lead me to log books of ships of the United States Naval Squadron in the Mediterranean. Debbie M. Rebuck, curator at the Dietrich American Foundation provided an image of West's painting *Lord Byron's Visit to the USS* Constitution. Harvard University Archives in Pusey Library made available a photocopy of the travel diary jointly kept by John T. Kirkland and his wife Elizabeth. David Dearinger and Patricia Boulos at the Boston Athenaeum arranged for a photograph of Horatio Greenough's bust of John T. Kirkland. At Mystic Seaport I owe thanks to the following for so willingly making available an image of a watercolor of Mehmet Ali in the album kept by Edward C. Young on board the USS *Concord:* Steve White, the director; Paul J. O'Pecko, vice president, Collections and Research; and Louisa Alger Watrous, intellectual property manager. Nancy Micklewright of the Freer Gallery of Art and Arthur M. Sackler Gallery helped me to understand the dress of the viceroy as shown in the watercolor. Through Timothy Young, curator of Modern Books and Manuscripts at the Beinecke Rare Books and Manuscript Library at Yale University, and Sara Azam, access services assistant, I obtained an image of the bear with the messenger boy on the *Concord* in a similar album of watercolors at Yale. Jennifer A. Bryan, head of Special Collections & Archives at the Nimitz Library of the United States Naval Academy in Annapolis, photocopied for me the diaries of two of the Patterson sisters, Eliza and George Ann. James W. Cheevers, curator at the academy, assisted with matters pertaining to Matthew Calbraith Perry, while Grant Walker provided an image of William Sidney Mount's portrait of Perry in their collection. The staff of the manuscripts room in the Library of Congress made accessible the papers of Commodore Daniel T. Patterson. Sara B. Zela of the Lamont Gallery at Phillips Exeter Academy located and arranged for photography of George Healy's portrait of Lewis Cass. Dr. William J. Schultz responded enthusiastically to my request for permission to illustrate the daguerreotype of Henry Ledyard in his collection.

Keepers of Diaries, 1833 to 1835: The reading of several important and unpublished journals was crucial to the writing of this chapter. First I wish to remember the kindness of the late L. Gordon Hamersley of New York and Sorrento, Maine. The name of the early nineteenth-century New Yorker, John W. Hamersley in the register of John Gliddon, the American consular agent in Egypt, prompted me to trace Hamersley's family, and I discovered that his descendants still lived in the New York area. In early 2006 I telephoned L. Gordon Hamersley and, after introducing myself, asked whether the family still possessed any memorabilia of their nineteenth-century forebear. After a pause, Mr. Hamersley replied, "a whole chest full, including a diary," and in the spring of 2007 he generously loaned me the diary. Over a two-year period I transcribed some eight hundred pages that covered western Europe, Russia, and the Mediterranean. I am also grateful for the continuing interest of his sons Nicholas and Gordon Hamersley in my work. Maria Castrillo, manuscripts curator at the National Library of Scotland, arranged to provide me with a copy of the letter written by Lady Hester Stanhope to William Dundas, one of Hamersley's traveling companions, as well as Dundas' notes on Jerusalem. Neilson Abeel of Portland, Oregon, whom I have known since we were ten years old, gave me an image of the daguerreotype of his great-grandfather J. Lewis Stackpole. The Scott Polar Research Institute in Cambridge, UK, offered space and time in their library to look at the pertinent pages in the diaries of Jane Franklin, who met several Americans on the Nile in 1834, among them Lewis Stackpole, Ralph Izard, and John Hamersley. Also thanks to Catherine Martin at the Cadbury Research Library at the University of Birmingham for arranging for photocopies of parts of the journal of the Rev. Johann Rudolph Theophilus Lieder (owned by the Church Missionary Society), who accompanied Jane Franklin on the Nile. Beth Moore of the Telfair Museums, Savannah, arranged for an image of William Brown Hodgson. The Huntington Library and Museum in San Marino, California, provided a typescript copy of the journal kept by Rittenhouse Nutt during his travels in Europe and Egypt with his father Rush Nutt, and the Mississippi Department of Archives and History (MDAH) in Jackson provided photocopies of letters written by Rittenhouse Nutt from Italy and Malta. Alanna J. Patrick of the MDAH told me that the original journal and other documents were owned as of 1995 by the late Mrs. Wesley G. Johnson (née Opal Russum), a great-great-granddaughter of Rittenhouse Nutt. With that information in hand, I contacted one of her sons, Gregory Johnson, who kindly introduced me to Woodbury Butler Gates, another descendant of Rittenhouse Nutt and the current owner of the journal, who in turn told me much about the family. In addition to his comments on an earlier version of the entire manuscript, Lawrence L. Berman, curator of Egyptian Art at the Museum of Fine Arts, Boston, provided helpful suggestions for the section on John Lowell, whose collection is now on exhibition there in the Egyptian Department. For permission to illustrate the watercolor portrait of John Lowell, on loan to the Museum of Fine Arts, Boston, I thank Mr. and Mrs. Ralph Lowell, owners of the work, and William A. Lowell, administrator of the Lowell Institute. Marta Fodor in the Department of Intellectural Property at the museum provided images of the watercolor and the two antiquities illustrated.

John L. Stephens and Fellow Tourists in the Mid-1830s: At the American Museum of Natural History in New York, Kristin Mable kindly provided information on the portrait of John L. Stephens owned by the Museum and located in the Department of Mexican and Central American Archaeology. The staff of the Winterthur Library in Wilmington copied the notebook kept by Richard Randolph during his travels, which belongs to the Joseph Downs Collection of Manuscripts and Printed Ephemera at the library. The South Carolina Historical Society in Charleston made available photocopies of the diary of Mary Allen, both the original manuscript and a typed transcript. Swarthmore College Peace Collection provided a digital image of the miniature of Horatio Allen. Patrick Casey of Blackrock, County Dublin, Ireland, owner of the diary of Sir Francis Hopkins, told me, to my regret, that while Mary Allen had mentioned him in her diary, he had not mentioned meeting the Allens in his. Stephen McAuliffe of Mount Auburn Cemetery in Cambridge, Massachusetts, copied for me the text of the inscription on the stone of Ambrose Stacy Courtis, whose body had been brought home from Greece where he had died.

Steamship Travel: András Riedlmayer, bibliographer in the Fine Arts Library at Harvard University, provided much useful information on the album of engravings done by Eugenio Fulgenzi, one engraving of which shows the harbor at Smyrna with two steamships, while Joanne Bloom, photographic resources librarian, forwarded a digital image of the engraving. The staff of the Harvard Theater Collection in the Pusey Library kindly photocopied for me the diary of the actor Edwin Forrest.

Professional Visitors: The Library of Medicine in Bethesda, Maryland, made available photocopies of the unused letters of introduction that Dr. Valentine Mott had obtained in France before traveling to Egypt. Mary-Jane Deeb, chief of the African and Middle Eastern division at the Library of Congress, and Fawzi Tadros brought out the manuscript of Abd al-Rahman's commentary on the *Aphorisms of Hippocrates* for us to inspect together and in which we found Valentine Mott's note of its source. Through Robert S Pirie I was introduced to Margaret Oswald Manning at New York Hospital and with her help Glenn Speigelman made a digital image of the portrait of Valentine Mott owned by the hospital. Lindsay Turley, manuscript and reference archivist at the Museum of the City of New York, made available on short notice the diary and passport of Henry P. Marshall, first US consul to Muscat.

Mills, Giraffes, and Skulls (and Even the Telegraph): Jessica Lepler of the Department of History at the University of New Hampshire, author of a recent publication on the Panic of 1837, kindly reviewed my comments on the financial panic, and in addition helped me with material on Aaron H. Palmer. The staff of the Bancroft Library at the University of California, Berkeley, let me have copies of Palmer's letters addressed to Mehmet Ali (Muhammad Ali) and George Gliddon, and one of William Kemble addressed to John L. Stephens, contained among the Stephens papers in the library. The Bancroft also furnished me with copies of letters of the Gliddons, father and son, written to various American business contacts. Charles Greifenstein and Earle E. Spamer of the American Philosophical Society facilitated the photocopying of the correspondence between George

R. Gliddon and Samuel George Morton of Philadelphia with respect to the collection of skulls in Egypt. Ann Fabian of Rutgers University, author of *The Skull Collectors: Race, Science, and America's Unburied Dead*, University of Chicago, 2011, helped me on matters of Gliddon and Morton. Joan Wood, a descendant of Alexander Marshall, one of the engineers sent to Egypt to help erect steam-driven equipment, shared with me her knowledge of Marshall's family. Neil Cooke advised me on the paragraph dealing with Burton's giraffe. Barbara De Wolfe, curator of manuscripts at the William L. Clements Library at the University of Michigan, Ann Arbor, and Janet Bloom on the staff there arranged to have made copies of letters relating to Benjamin L. Brown and Stebbins B. June and the giraffe trade.

Shall We Meet in Egypt?: Elizabeth Call, in charge of Special Collections at the Brooklyn Historical Society, kindly sent me a copy of the typescript of the diary of Susan Holmes. And Larry Weimer, project archivist at the society, took a close look at one passage of the original manuscript to confirm that the title of a novel of the period read by Susan Holmes on board the Danube steamer, rendered in the typescript as *Eugene Onegin*, was actually Bulwer Lytton's novel *Eugene Aram*, which made much more sense, since Pushkin's novel did not appear in French translation until the later 1860s and not in English until the end of the century.

Philip Rhinelander and His Friends: Jeanne Rhinelander, wife of the late John Rhinelander, a collateral descendant of Philip's uncle Dr. John Rhinelander, brought to my attention the miniature of Philip Rhinelander illustrated in an exhibition catalogue published by the Museums at Stony Brook in 1981. Christa Zaros, collections manager at the Long Island Museum of Amerian Art, History & Carriages, provided a digital image of the miniature, while Charles Miller, a member of the family that owns the miniature, graciously allowed it to be reproduced here. For information on John Caldecott, a remarkable but little-known scientist whom Rhinelander met in Cairo and again in quarantine in the Piraeus, I am grateful to Dr. Richard Walding, research fellow in the School of Science at Griffith University, Brisbane, Australia, who is preparing a biography of Caldecott, and to Dr. David Atkinson, a general practitioner in Whangarei, New Zealand, whose great-great-great-grandfather's sister (Sophia Rodgers) was Caldecott's second wife.

After 1839: Lauren K. Lessing of the Colby College Museum of Art told me much about the gouache-on-paper portrait of the family of Richard K. Haight at the Museum of the City of New York, which allowed me to understand to a much greater degree than before this remarkable work. Through Linda Thrift, head of the Office of Collections Information and

Research at the National Portrait Gallery in Washington, DC, I made contact with Jennifer Wilkerson, who enthusiastically provided helpful information on her great-great-grandfather Henry Abbott of Cairo and his collection of antiquities shipped in 1852 to New York and eventually sold to the New-York Historical Society; and in turn through her I met Deborah Abbott Hertlein, another descendant, who generously provided an image of the pastel portrait of Henry Abbott in her possession. Curtis Runnels, professor of archaeology at Boston University, who acquired for the Howard Gotlieb Archival Research Center at BU the set of works by Jean-François Champollion once owned by George Gliddon, kindly offered details about this remarkable set of works, as did Arthur Richter of Archaeologia Books in Oakland, California.

I was fortunate at the outset of this project to possess a relatively fine research library, in particular copies of the original accounts of some of the American travelers, including those of George Bethune English, George Rapelje, Pliny Fisk, George Jones (chaplain of the USS *Delaware*), John L. Stephens, Sarah Haight, the Rev. Edward Robinson, Dr. Valentine Mott, and the Rev. John D. Paxton, not to mention scores of European accounts of the period, ready access to which made the work move more quickly.

And other books came to my attention in the course of writing this book, including Ward Nicholas Boylston's own copy of William George Brown's late eighteenth-century travels, which I spotted in a New York City auction catalogue and was able to acquire. In Washington, John Thomson of Bartleby's Books brought to my attention and made available to me in 2008 one-and-a-half volumes of David Roberts, *Egypt & Nubia* (half of volume 2, all of volume 3), a fine colored copy of the folio edition once belonging to Joseph W. Drexel (1833–88), a founding trustee of the Metropolitan Museum of Art, and later owned by his daughter Lucy Wharton Drexel (1867–1944). In addition to stunning views of pharaonic ruins and Islamic monuments seen by many American travelers, it contains the image of the *Interview with the Viceroy of Egypt*, from which the illustration in this book is drawn. Briony Llewellyn, an expert on David Roberts, John Frederick Lewis, and other British artists–travelers in Egypt and the Near East, graciously responded with perceptive comments to my queries about the interview. In Paris, Paul Windey transferred to my possession several dozen volumes of the diplomatic correspondence and other archival material relating to nineteenth-century Europeans in Egypt, printed by the Imprimerie de l'Institut Français d'Archéologie Orientale for the Société de Géographie d'Égypte, beautifully bound in Egyptian leather and once owned by his grandfather, Simon Mani, in Cairo.

And in Cairo, at the American University in Cairo Press, where this book was published, I owe thanks to two individuals who helped oversee its transformation from a typescript to a book: Neil Hewison, Associate Director for Editorial Programs, and Nadine El-Hadi, Senior Project Editor.

Lastly I mention four individuals who have generously assisted me with the project. Deborah Manley of Oxford, a colleague at the Association for the Study of Travel in Egypt and the Near East, who has been immersed in nineteenth-century travel in Egypt far longer than I have, read an earlier stage of this text on which she made pages and pages of suggestions. Esther Ferington, whom I came to know through the Folger Shakespeare Library in Washington, DC, where she is an editor and I a member of the Board of Governors, commanded me to put order and forward direction to the narrative, and so it was done: "To hear is to obey," as the expression goes in the *Arabian Nights* (if only that were the case!). Jason Thompson, an authority on British and Near Eastern nineteenth-century history, offered a range of observations on the finished manuscript. And my friend Penny Du Bois, my most consistent critic, who has heard a thousand and one tales of my discoveries over breakfast and dinner, taught me to be sensible. It was she who brought to my attention Charles Baudelaire's *Les Fleurs du Mal*, the source of my epigraph.

INTRODUCTION

*A*merican *Travelers on the Nile* begins with the accounts of two New
Englanders who reached Egypt in the later eighteenth century. Yet
this is principally the story of the American experience in Egypt
and adjacent regions during the twenty-five-year period from the end
of the War of 1812 to the introduction of transatlantic steamship travel
and the invention of photography. News of the end of the War of 1812
reached the United States in early 1815, thereby reopening Europe
to American travelers (and the United States to European travelers).
Toward the end of this twenty-five-year period, in the spring of 1838,
steamships first crossed the Atlantic, facilitating tourist travel to every
location in Europe as well as the Mediterranean. These twenty-five years
saw many sorts of Americans visiting Egypt and the eastern Mediterranean: adventurers, missionaries on their way elsewhere, naval officers and
their civilian passengers, entrepreneurs seeking business opportunities,
and then of course, and in greatest numbers, American tourists: mostly
wealthy young men, graduates of East Coast colleges, traveling alone or
with colleagues, yet also a few married couples, and even one unmarried,
though chaperoned, young woman.

My interest in the subject of travel in the eastern Mediterranean
began with the purchase of one book in 1963, a single book, which in
time, developed into a library. Only after many years could I put a title to
the collection being formed, namely, the European and American redis-
covery of the lands of the Ottoman Empire. The first book was Richard
Chandler's *Travels in Greece* of 1776 acquired in New York City at Weyhe's
bookshop on Lexington Avenue. But this was by an English traveler, not
an American, and so it actually has little to do with the subject of this

1

present account. One of my first books by an American traveler to the eastern Mediterranean was John L. Stephens' two-volume *Incidents of Travel in Greece, Turkey, Russia and Poland* of 1838, which I acquired in 1968. Yet not until ten years later did an item come to my attention to suggest that I might have something to offer on the history of the subject. In March 1978, I purchased from the Argosy Book Shop in New York for one hundred dollars a 134-page manuscript account of travel in Greece and in Egypt, to Smyrna and to Constantinople in 1839, written by an American who at that time was totally unknown to me, namely the New Yorker Philip Rhinelander. It was the acquisition of that diary that has led over time to this book.

Yet collecting travel accounts was not a pastime separate from my professional interests. In 1960 I had joined the staff of the Metropolitan Museum of Art as an assistant curator in the Department of Greek and Roman Antiquities. Over the next ten years I had visited museum collections not merely in the United States but throughout Europe and the eastern Mediterranean. At the same time I had come to know the geography and landscapes that served as the settings for the range of eighteenth- and nineteenth-century Europeans and Americans who traveled there. One event in particular during my tenure at the museum sharpened my appreciation of American travelers in those regions. In 1968, the museum received from the Egyptian government, after several years of negotiation, the disassembled blocks of the Temple of Dendur, removed from its location at the edge of the Nile owing to the soon-to-be-rising water flooding the banks of the river behind the newly constructed Aswan Dam. The blocks were taken down-river to Alexandria and placed aboard the SS *Concordia Star*, an 800-ton load, for passage to New York City. At the museum they were laid out in a former outdoor parking lot below the windows of my office, which looked out onto Central Park, in a space the size of several tennis courts and covered, as if tennis courts, with an inflated polyethylene canopy. There, during an inspection of the disassembled temple (not long before a snowstorm collapsed the canopy, giving the blocks the appearance of a monument wrapped by Christo), I copied the inscriptions cut on the temple by nineteenth-century visitors on the Nile, including that of "Luther Bradish, 1821 of NY US." The name of Luther Bradish, brought home to New York City, brought home to me the reality of these travelers.

A year or so earlier, in 1967, David H. Finnie, then a legal counsel to the Mobil Oil Corporation, had published through the Harvard University Press his finely researched book, *Pioneers East: The Early American*

Experience in the Middle East. It was centered on the personality of the New York lawyer John L. Stephens, who had traveled in the region in 1836, and whose two best-selling accounts I acquired. In addition, Finnie surveyed the full range of American travelers, those who went to Greece, Turkey, Syria, Palestine, Egypt, and even Persia in the first half of the nineteenth century.

David Finnie's book became my guidebook. Among the appendices were two of particular interest: a bibliography of American travel accounts of the period, and secondly, a list of "all the American travelers who registered with John and George Gliddon, the first US consuls at Alexandria and Cairo, respectively." This list of fifty-eight travelers, from 1832 to 1842, was based on George Gliddon's *Appendix to "The American in Egypt,"* published in Philadelphia in 1842. In the course of time, I acquired virtually all of the books in the bibliography, and I began looking at the names of the Americans in the Gliddons' list. Some were relatively well-known individuals—not only John L. Stephens, but also John T. Kirkland, a former president of Harvard College, and Daniel T. Patterson, commodore of the Mediterranean Naval Squadron of the United States. Most others, however, were just names, and sometimes just last names.

In giving new life to these names and reviving their personalities, and discovering scores of other Americans who traveled to Egypt in this period whose names were absent from the list kept by the Gliddons (either because they came to Egypt before the Gliddons became consular officials or because they simply did not sign the registers), I have sought to explain why Americans visited Egypt as well as how they accomplished their journeys. Why indeed did they go? To what extent were they lured by the exoticism of the East or repelled and sent traveling by the banalities of their home life? The isolated quatrain quoted from Baudelaire's *Le voyage* offers only one answer. Elsewhere the poet asks whether *le voyageur* is fleeing a country gone awry, by which he probably means the suffocation of the modern world; or is fleeing the horrors of an upbringing and bad childhood; or is escaping a disastrous love affair. But regardless of the reason, what did the traveler find? Did the destinations live up to his (and also in this book her) fantasies? *Le voyage* is an ironic work whose theme, as one critic has said, "is the tragic disproportion between aspiration and reality."[1] It is fair to say, however, that many of the Americans displayed strong positivist feelings: they were traveling to expand their world, to get ahead, to witness firsthand the exotic, to bring back stories that would last a lifetime. How successful were these journeys? Alas, many times we simply cannot say whether they lived up to expectations. Since many of the travelers wrote accounts intended to be read by others, they avoided personal issues. Only two of these American travelers expressed private feelings, in large part because they had no intention of publishing their accounts, let alone having their diaries read by others.

We possess accounts of twelve Americans who traveled alone or with others in the Nile valley all the way from Cairo to Thebes or beyond in the 1820s and '30s, no one quite like another. Two appeared in book form in the nineteenth century; three more as letters published in newspapers of the period; while the remaining seven are unpublished manuscript diaries, two in public collections known for a long time, the remaining five, virtually unknown until now, and two of them still in private hands. Taken together, these twelve accounts tell a rich story of the American experience on the Nile. And they cover only those Americans who went as far south as Thebes. Many more accounts of Americans who never went beyond Alexandria and Cairo have come to light in recent years. They too give a full range of what Americans experienced in Lower Egypt, on their way around the eastern Mediterranean.

Where possible I have let the travelers tell their stories in their own words, with observations drawn from letters home, from diaries, and occasionally from published accounts. In some ways this sequence of accounts, actual or reconstructed (owing to the lack of primary sources), and the majority of them stemming from this twenty-five-year period, resembles a musical composition: theme and variations. The theme was the ideal or imaginary itinerary, one conceived before one actually arrived, which no traveler, however, actually completed. The travelers performed only the variations.

1 | AMERICANS IN EIGHTEENTH-CENTURY EGYPT

Ward Nicholas Boyston

> We put on our cloaks, wrapt ourselves up warm & drank a glass of aqua vita to prevent from taking cold from the change of air, & after resting a small space of time I began to mount to the top. . . . After near 3/4 of an hour hard labour reached the top from which is a delightful prospect of the country & the Nile for a great extent.[1]

So wrote the first American to visit Egypt, Ward Nicholas Boylston of Boston, who arrived in Alexandria in late 1774 and climbed the Great Pyramid at Giza at the end of December.[2]

Ward Nicholas Boylston was born Ward Hallowell in 1749, one of many children of Mary and Benjamin Hallowell (1725–1799). His father was a ship captain who, after a successful career, was appointed comptroller of customs at Boston in 1764. In 1770 he took a position on the American Board of Customs Commissioners. His mother was a Boylston, member of a leading family in Boston that had become wealthy by importing goods such as textiles, paper, tea, and glass from abroad. When Nicholas Boylston, one of Ward's uncles, lacking heirs, proposed in 1770 to leave him a generous legacy if he changed his surname to Boylston, the young man promptly did so (by royal decree). We know the faces of Ward's father and mother and of his mother's brothers and sisters through portraits painted by John Singleton Copley, but no likenesses exist of the young man.[3]

Early in 1771, young Ward Nicholas Boylston eloped with Ann, daughter of the prominent Patriot William Molineux, to New Hampshire where they were married by the chaplain on board HMS *Salisbury* in Portsmouth harbor.[4] On December 1 of that year their son Nicholas was baptized at the church in Brattle Square in Boston.[5] At some stage, as early as May 1771 to judge from newspaper advertisements, Boylston set up shop on King Street in Boston selling cloth imported from England.[6] That summer, on August 18, 1771, his rich uncle, Nicholas Boylston, died at age 56, and although the larger part of the estate went to Nicholas' brother Thomas, Ward still received £4,000.

This was a difficult period to be doing business in imported goods in Boston: the collapse (toward the end of 1770) of the merchants' agreement not to import goods from England led to a surplus. Despite easy credit offered by British suppliers, too many merchants were engaged in such business, and a newcomer also had to compete with long-established men such as John Hancock. Then, in mid-1772, a credit crisis in Britain obliged many British merchants to request repayment of loans.[7] To what extent that affected young Boylston is not known, but in any event (and clearly for another reason as we shall see), he placed notices in Boston newspapers in August 1773 announcing his intention to travel abroad and advertising the disposal at cost of the goods in his store.[8] Two months later, on October 12, he embarked on the *King of Naples* bound for Naples by way of Halifax. Boylston was twenty-six. He had one companion, the twenty-one-year-old James Bowdoin, known as Jemmy, a recent Harvard graduate and son of a wealthy political leader in Boston, the senior James Bowdoin. He left his wife and his son, not yet two, behind. In essence, he abandoned them. His marriage must have soured. Moreover, Boylston was a Loyalist, Ann's family were Patriots, not a good mix. If proof of difficult times were needed, on December 16, while Boylston and Bowdoin were still laying over at St. John's in Newfoundland before finally leaving on December 23 for Italy, a group of radical Patriots, including his father-in-law, boarded ships in Boston harbor and threw overboard thousands of pounds of tea.

While it was unusual for Americans to travel to Italy in these years, it was not unprecedented. In the fifteen-year period between 1760 and 1775, more than a dozen aspiring artists, medical students, and entrepreneurs, all with ample means, had traveled to England, France, and Italy in an unconscious reproduction of the itinerary of the well-born Englishman's grand tour.[9] The artist Benjamin West ventured abroad in 1760 with two Philadelphians, John Allen and William Shippen.[10] The Philadelphia physician John Morgan also started out in 1760 and in 1764 reached Rome and Naples with another Philadelphian, Samuel Powel.[11] In Italy Morgan and Powel met two more Americans, Thomas Palmer and John Apthorp. Palmer did what many British travelers had been

doing: He brought books home, six folios of the antiquities of Herculaneum and fourteen volumes of *Le Antichità Romane* by Piranesi, which he
presented to the Harvard College library in 1772, the first sets to enter
an American library.[12]

Americans, like their European counterparts, traveled with letters of
introduction to important persons in the cities they were to visit. In November 1773, when John Singleton Copley, the painter of so many portraits of
the Hallowell and Boylston families, was planning a trip to Italy—though
he would not leave until June 1774—two Americans who had previously
been there provided letters. Thomas Palmer wrote one for him to Sir William Hamilton in Naples, and John Morgan wrote others, including one to
Robert Rutherford, a merchant in Leghorn who could introduce Copley
in turn to Sir John Dick, British consul in Leghorn, and to Horace Mann,
resident in Florence.[13] Ward Nicholas Boylston and Jemmy Bowdoin also
carried letters of introduction to well-placed European residents. After
landing in Naples on January 22, 1774, they called on the British ambassador, Sir William Hamilton, and on their banker, George Tierney.

And like English travelers, Boylston and Bowdoin enjoyed the social
and intellectual life of Naples. They went to Teatro San Carlo to see the
opera *Alessandro nell'Indie*[14] and attended a masque ball sponsored by the
king of Naples. They dined on more than one occasion with Hamilton and
attended one of Lady Catherine Hamilton's harpsichord concerts. They
climbed Vesuvius and visited Portici to see the royal collection of antiquities from Herculaneum and Pompeii. Boylston kept a diary—which has
survived—in which we can read of their life in Naples and how, over the
next six months, he and Bowdoin traveled leisurely to Rome, Ancona,
Venice, Padua, Brescia, Milan, Parma, and Florence. There, in mid-June
1774, Bowdoin left Boylston to travel to London. Boylston, on the other
hand, went via Lucca to Leghorn. In this port city, to which ships of many
nations called, he took advantage of the traveler's network of connections:
he had a letter of introduction to Sir John Dick, the British consul.[15] He
dined with him one evening, after which they and other guests went on
board a Russian frigate commanded by Rear-Admiral Samuel Greig, a
Scotsman in service to the Russians.

A Russian frigate with a Scotsman as commander in port at Leghorn
requires some explanation.[16] Greig, together with other British naval
officers, had served in the Russian navy for five years, a period that first
saw the Russian fleet in the Mediterranean. In 1769 the Russians had
pursued Polish rebels into Moldavia and Wallachia, modern Romania,
after which, encouraged by France, the Ottoman sultan declared war on

Russia. The Russians responded by sailing part of their fleet, under British officers, from the Baltic to the Mediterranean to deal with the Turkish navy. After indecisive skirmishes in Greek waters and ports on the mainland and in the Aegean archipelago in early 1770, the Russians destroyed most of the Turkish fleet off Chesme in July of that year. Over the next several years, with intermittent engagements to keep the Turks in check and maintain an upper hand, Russian frigates cruised the eastern Mediterranean. They put into ports from the Peloponnesus to the island of Chios and further east reached Beirut in Syria and Damietta in Egypt. By 1774 hostilities were over, but the Russian fleet still maintained a presence in the region and continued to use Leghorn, as they had during the campaign, as a base away from home. When Boylston met Greig aboard his frigate he had been in Leghorn since February 1774, having sailed there from Kronstadt in Russia the previous November.

Once in Leghorn Boylston did something no other American had done: He decided to set forth to the East. His diary for July 6 reads in part, "Having provided ourselves with letters of recommendation . . . to the principal persons of the places we intended to visit we took leave of our friends expecting to embark . . . on board a Venetian [vessel] called the Bona Santa for Malta." He says "we," yet in no document does he ever name his companion. We know from other sources—discussed later in this chapter—that he was George Tasburgh, a recent widower, formerly married to Teresa Gage, sister of General Thomas Gage, then military royal governor of Massachusetts. Tasburgh was more than ten years older than Boylston and from a Roman Catholic family. The two travelers reached Malta on July 15. Continuing on, they passed Cape Matapan on July 24 and then spent ten days in the harbor of Myconos in August, waiting for a fair wind, which gave them a chance to fraternize with the officers of another Russian frigate stationed there.

In late August they reached Smyrna where they were "genteelly entertained" and enchanted by the consular representatives and expatriate European merchants to whom they seem to have had numerous letters of introduction. They presented themselves to the British Consul Anthony Hayes, to the Chancellor George Boddington, and to the French and Neapolitan consuls.[17] They dined on board the *Levant*, a British frigate of thirty-two guns, which would later be sunk by the Americans off Bermuda. They also dined with several resident merchants, among them David Van Lennep, the patriarch of the Van Lennep family, who had arrived in Smyrna as an eighteen-year-old around 1730 and now, in 1774, was married and had many children (plate 1).[18] William Maltass, another merchant, also entertained them; his beautiful daughter would make an unhappy marriage to George Baldwin, an English merchant and later consul in Egypt, but would also have her face and figure memorably painted in 1782 by Joshua Reynolds.[19] Visiting the Maltass family, Boylston was struck by the ladies who were dressed in the eastern manner—he provides descriptions of their clothes—very much as they are represented in the portrait of the family of David Van Lennep.

Leaving Smyrna they sailed to Cos, to Rhodes, and to Larnaca in Cyprus, where they passed nine days being entertained by the former British Consul John Boddington. From Larnaca they crossed to Tripoli and were put up at the local Jesuit community. From there they made an excursion to Baalbek, where they stayed with the secretary of the local emir. Returning to their ship, they passed Beirut and Sidon, going on to anchor near Acre from where they visited Nazareth. Then they went on to Hyffa to see Mt. Carmel and then sailed to Jaffa. In Jaffa they put themselves in the hands of the residents of the Latin convent, who provided them with proper clothes and advised them to negotiate with the local Bedouin to escort them to Jerusalem. On November 4, Boylston included the following observations in his diary:

> At 7 in the evening we arrived at Bethlehem Gate having rode 9 1/2 hours through rain & wet to the skin. Added to our misfortune we found the gate shut. The janissaries at their positions on the ramparts challenged us. Our guard assured we were two friars & begged to be admitted which [they] did in about a quarter of an hour. But the janissary when he found we were not friars made a difficulty but a piaster or two made matters easy. We [were] conducted to [the] Latin Convent & introduced to the president to whom we had letters of particular recommendation & rec'd with many friendly welcomes & after attended us to the [room they] had fitted up for our reception having been . . . advised of our coming by letters from Leghorn. Supped on fresh fish, boil[ed] eggs & served by 3 lay brothers who expressed great surprise at seeing an American.

Boylston and Tasburgh stayed in Jerusalem for nearly two weeks, at the end of which they received from the convent diplomas for having visited all the holy sites. On November 17 they returned to Jaffa to board a ship to take them to Alexandria.

At that point in Boylston's diary, three leaves are missing, that is, six pages of text. All that remains of the diary of Egypt is what Boylston wrote on the inside of the back cover of the marbled, cardboard binding. Two additional documents make up partially for the loss of these six pages: One is an account book given to him on December 30, 1774, by a contact in Cairo; the other is a twelve-page letter Boylston wrote to his mother from Genoa on June 15, 1775, on his way to London. Combining information from these three documents we know something about Boylston's time in Egypt.

Boylston and his companion spent little time in Alexandria on their arrival. Instead, as he expressed in the opening of his letter to his mother,

> I embraced the opportunity of joining a small caravan going to Cairo belonging to an English officer in the service of the Bey of that place. We went by land as far as Rosetta which is one of the pleasantest cities in Egypt. Here we found a Jerm of the Bey's ready to take us on board & to continue the remainder of the way to Cairo on the Nile. These Jerms are flat bottomed boats of about 50 feet long and 12 wide. Ours was about these dimensions with two masts and large sails manned by 30 men. One half of the deck was covered with a crimson cloth awning with a yellow fringe and a small cabin in the stern for women when any are on board. The deck was covered in handsome carpets and carried two swivel guns in the prow. Sailed well against the current which always sets to the sea & in many places very rapid. Besides we had a galley to attend us with 22 rowers. When the wind failed they towed us. Nothing could be more delightful than the prospect which this short voyage of 7 days afforded us. Villages and towns crowded with people, trees blooming, fields covered with grain and groves of palm trees loaded with fruit.[20]

Boylston had entered an ancient land; Smyrna and Jerusalem possessed antiquity but nothing like Egypt, and he saw the land before Napoleon's expedition of 1798 and the nineteenth-century reforms of Mehmet Ali would forever change the country. The name designating his river craft, *jerm*, could be taken as a symbol for the antiquity of Boylston's Egypt. *Jerm* is an old Arabic word that comes ultimately from a Greek word used in the Roman Imperial period.[21] The English officer, the swivel guns, and Boylston were modern; the *jerm* (at least its name) and everything else, including the customs and practices the young American would observe while in Egypt, were ancient, and ancient by as much as several millennia.

A glance at a map of the Nile Delta prepared fifty years earlier by the French traveler Paul Lucas shows the route along the shore from Alexandria to Rosetta and then the town-dotted banks of one of the two principal branches of the Nile leading south to Cairo. Two days after leaving Rosetta, Boylston and his companions stopped at Fuwa, the most significant town between Rosetta and Cairo, which owed its prosperity to being at the junction of the Nile and a canal that ran westward to Alexandria. That was in the old days. Now, although the canal was no longer navigable and would not be restored until the 1820s, the town had suffered. Yet it was still a fine place, and in Fuwa Boylston witnessed the time-honored eastern customs of hospitality and reciprocal gift giving.

The second day after our leaving Rosetta we stayed at a town called Foua. The governor immediately sent us an invitation to come to his house which we declined till pressed to come. He rec'd us with great civility & the usual entertainment of a Turkish visit as coffee & pipe was presented to each. He expressed a great satisfaction at seeing so many Europeans & urged our stay there for two days that [he] might have the pleasure of going with us to Cairo, but we represented to him our desire & the urgent business of the English officer who was chief engineer to the Bey of getting there as soon as possible, upon which he dropped the subject. On our return to our Jerm he sent us a present of three sheep, 100 eggs, 100 of rice, a pot of sherbet composed of sugar, lemons, water & juices, 100 green sugar canes & two large dishes of pilau, a dish much admired in the East, made of boiled rice & fowls with small seeds resembling our white beans. We in return sent him a clay bottle of Syrup of Capilare[22] & a small spy glass. The next day he renewed his favours by sending us a large pye and cake made of different kinds of seeds and confectionary. The wind coming fair about noon we saluted the gov. with a discharge of our two swivels and took leave.

In another town along the way they witnessed a wedding procession.

In front were musicians two and two by playing a kind of sackbut & pipes. Next the household furniture of the bride, cloaks or whatever she intended bringing her husband which consisted of two trunks, but whether full or empty I could not tell, two chairs or stools. . . . Next followed the bridegroom dress'd in the fashion of the country & next to him the bride accompanied by a number of women making a noise with their lips not unlike the gabling of a Turkey cock, which closed the parade and is esteemed by their greatest virtuosos as the perfection of musick.

Decades later, in the 1830s, the English orientalist Edward William Lane, long resident in Cairo, included in his landmark book on modern Egypt detailed descriptions of local weddings in which musicians lead the processions, playing wind instruments—Lane called them hautboys—and in which women walked along uttering cries of joy called *zagharit*, or ululation, a warbling sound made by moving the tongue rapidly to and fro in an open mouth.[23] Boylston may have been a trifle skeptical of the scene but at least he described it. Lane, on the other hand, offered sensitive and nonjudgmental descriptions of Egyptian weddings. His two-volume work would become one of the handbooks carried by a host of European and American visitors to Egypt.

Boylston was equally observant of the sights of Cairo, especially the street life. In the principal market located in one of the largest squares Boylston saw white and black slaves for sale, jugglers, and fortune tellers, and even naked saints seated in the midst of a square with seeming oblivious passersby taking not the slightest notice. Nevertheless he said that the city fell short of his expectations.

> The streets I found are more dirty & unpaved, the houses built round a court & few or no windows toward the street which are throng'd with beggars, cripples & blind. With respect to the latter I never saw so great a number in my life. . . . no Christian is allowed to ride anything better than a jackass & as it is almost impossible to pass thro' the narrow streets by reason of the continual throng of people, it became necessary for a stranger to hire one of these animals who have always a driver with them. They have no saddles but instead . . . a hard quilted cushion & no stirrups and as these poor creatures are some time so very small that they are hardly able to carry you that your feet drag on the ground & very often they lay down with you in the midst of a slough which I happen'd to experience more than once & should you happen to meet either the Bey or Bashaw or any principal officer either of church or state, let you be either in a pond of water or up to the middle in mire, you must immediately dismount.

Boylston was not alone in expressing these complaints. Virtually every subsequent European and American visitor to Cairo made similar comments.

This young Bostonian was the first of many Americans to visit the place where chickens were hatched in incubators. "It is perform'd by heating ovens of so temperate a heat as to come near to the natural warmth of the hen. 8 or 10,000 eggs are put into a large oven at a time, & in twenty-two days they produce chickens." Modern travelers since the sixteenth century had commented on the artificial incubation of eggs in Egypt; a reference even appears in Ben Jonson's play *The Alchemist* of 1610. In fact, the practice went back to antiquity.[24]

Like most travelers, he also visited Old Cairo. "Old Cairo is chiefly inhabited by a sect of Christians called Copts," he reported to his mother. "In a church belonging to the Copts in Old Cairo is [a] grotto in which they pretend the Holy family resided during their abode in Egypt,[25] and opposite to Old Cairo on a small island are steps which are on the banks of the river where it is said Moses was found by Pharaoh's daughter." The island was the island of Roda which he mentioned visiting in the one surviving page dealing with Egypt in his diary—to which we will come in a moment.

"While I was at Cairo I had an opportunity of seeing what few Europeans ever have, which is the going out of the Caravan for Mecca."[26] This spectacle seems to have impressed Boylston more than any other. The pilgrimage caravan, said to have been started in the reign of Sultan Baybars in the 1270s, left Cairo every year about the 23rd of the Muslim month Shawwal. This meant that in 1774 it would have left about December 28. The Muslim calendar shifts with respect to the western one, thereby placing the event 11 or 12 days earlier in each successive year. Ten years later, in 1784, the Polish traveler Jan Potocki witnessed the start of the procession on September 6.[27] Fifty years later, in 1834, when the English orientalist Edward William Lane observed the caravan and described it in great detail, it took place in early March, the festival having moved through the calendar nearly two years.[28] Boylston gave a rich description of the procession:

> It consists of 55,000 persons, 20,000 elegant horses, 3,000 camels besides mules and jackasses, 100 slaves well mounted, dressed in yellow with sabers and pistols, followed by 2 Beys of which there are 24 besides the chief Bey . . . . The next was a band of 250 soldiers called Taphagees followed by pilgrims on foot succeeded by 400 camels painted yellow with green pack saddles loaded with provisions, water & utensils for cooking.

Boylston observed well and must also have been in the company of resident Europeans who helped him to identify the participants. Edward William Lane, for instance, called attention to the irregular Turkish cavalry whom he calls "Tufekjees"—close to Boylston's spelling or pronunciation—and he noted that the camels were colored a dingy red with henna.[29] Boylston continued:

> A large body of troops guard the caravan & another of foot guards escorting almost 600 camels loaded as before. Then 4 Beys richer & more elegantly mounted than the first. The furniture of their horses was of gold & the horsing of cloth of gold of different colours ornamented with precious

stones. These were attended by 500 slaves very richly dressed . . . followed by . . . a number of Imams and Sharifs who are also orders of priests singing a hymn suitable to the occasion. Then followed 4 other Beys who were richly dress'd & mounted on most beautiful horses. The stirrups, bits & bridles were of gold. The horsing of cloth of gold in different shades set with diamonds, rubies, sapphires & other precious stones, which in the sun made a very glittering & brilliant appearance, hardly to be conceived.

Boylston finally described that part of the procession eagerly awaited by all of the onlookers:

A large body of janissaries joined by 300 slaves of the Basha of Cairo, who was also elegantly dressed & his horse richly caparisoned proceeded a led camel of the best & largest kind carrying on his back a pavilion covered with green cloth adorn'd with gold lace, streamers & ostrich feathers, containing the carpet, one of which kind is sent every year by the Grand Seignor to be laid over Mahamet's tomb . . . . At the approach of this the populace seemed to vie with each other in shewing adoration and respect to it. Those were sure of a Blessing who had been so happy as to have touched, either the pavilion or the camel with their handkerchiefs, turbans, or girdles which they afterwards rub over their faces & hands superstitiously believing it to be a charm against evil spirits, bad accidents & sickness.

The covered pavilion, known as the *mahmal*, was carried by a noble camel who thereafter was relieved of any burdensome duty.[30] In concluding his lengthy description of the procession to his mother, Boylston added:

After the pavilion came another body of guards, 2 Beys, a large guard of Janissaries in coats of mail & the remainder of the camels with a great number of pilgrims dancing and singing which closed the procession & took up to five hours in passing & was altogether the grandest sight I ever remember to have seen.

And finally, though he put it earlier on in his letter, Boylston reported to his mother that he went to Giza to see the Pyramids and the Sphinx. By chance the one surviving page of his diary relating to Egypt, written on the inside of the back cover of the notebook, describes his ascent of the Great Pyramid at Giza (a snippet of which was quoted at the outset of this chapter) and a visit to the Nilometer on the island of Roda, an excursion that he must have taken on December 29, 1774. Because it is all that is left of the Egyptian portion of the diary of the first American in Egypt, it should be quoted in full. It begins in mid-sentence:

... where we put on our cloaks, wrapt ourselves up warm & drank a glass of aqua vita to prevent taking cold from the change of air, & after resting a small space of time I began to mount to the top beginning over the entrance, but I soon found my error, the stones being so loose & covered with rubbish & found as made it extremely dangerous, so that I was obliged to descend & begin at the angle to the north east, where the steps are more entire & safer & after near 3/4 of an hour hard labour reached the top from which is a delightful prospect of the country & the Nile for a great extent.

After having satisfied ourselves with seeing this pyramid we went to the second which stands about 400 feet from it, but it is closed & neither does there any . . . happen [?] of its being ever opened & the outside is covered with polished granite so such joined [?] that it is impossible to ascend it. —— Near it are the ruins of a temple the stones of which are very large & close by it the celebrated sphinx of astronomical size, which is cut out of solid rock & is supposed to have been the sepulcher of Amasis. It has the head & breast of a woman and the body and legs of a horse & the tail of a lion, but only the head, breast, & back are to be seen the rest being covered with sand. It is at 27 high & across the breast 33 feet wide & 113 from the forepart of the neck to the tail. —— The other pyramids are not worth remarking after those already mentioned. From those you plainly see those of Saccara which are ten miles distance & it is I supposed the city of Memphis reached from those of Gize to those of Saccara, but it is entirely destroyed or covered over with sand being no other vestige remaining but the pyramids.

We returned to Gize about 4 o'clock in the afternoon & after making a short stay we returned to Cairo a little after sunset, having in our way stopt at the island of Roda which is opposite to old Cairo where is the mikias, the place where is kept the remarkable pillar for measuring the Nile, which is fixed in a deep basin on a level with the bed of the river, & so as the water to have a free passage thro' it. The pillar is placed under a dome with a Corinthian capital divided into measures for seeing the rise of the water & from the court which leads to the house is [sic] steps which descend into the site on which I was told Moses was found by Pharaoh's daughters.

30th & 31st returned several of . . . & took leave of our friends as we intended to leave this place in a few days.

The third document relating to Boylston's visit to Egypt is his account book, a relatively thick book for its size, not much more than five by three inches, but as thick as a finger, bound in thin green leather with gold stamped margins. There, on only a few of the pages, he gives sundry notes: expenses for the entire trip, a list of curios he bought, and the names of contacts in Egypt. We learn that in Cairo he went to the Citadel and to the baths (twice), and that he probably stayed in a Jesuit hostel. In Rosetta he must have stayed in a convent because he says he bought a present for the father. Other purchases included a mummy, five ostrich eggs, two wooden locks, a pair of balances, pieces of coral and petrified wood; also a present *(regalo)* for Mr. Maltass in Smyrna. His contacts are difficult to name because his cramped handwriting renders them nearly anonymous. One was a Jesuit in Cairo, whose last name might be Ginghimian. Though the Pope had suppressed the Society of Jesus in 1773, little more than a year before Boylston's arrival, some members of the order were allowed to live out their lives at their posts, those in Egypt under the protection of the French consul.

At the end of the account book are four lines I interpret as "Jaco's Iavaja & Co, Mer. in Cairo, Petro Massana, Giov. Massana," individuals whom I cannot otherwise identify. The names are Italian and it is reported that there were six Venetian commercial companies in Cairo in 1773, three of them Venetian Jews.[31] The names Boylston wrote are likely to refer to at least two of these merchant companies. Below their names he wrote "Rose of Jericho" and a misspelling *(Asiatica hirocantica)* of its Linnaean equivalent, *Anastatica hierochuntica*, a desert plant of the Near East. Elsewhere Boylston gives the name of the Venetian consul, Nicola Rigo (also known as Nicola il Conte Rigo), who held the position in Cairo from 1767 to 1778 and acted as consul in Alexandria from 1770 to 1774.

On the first page of the book is the statement: "The Gift of my friend Mr. John Antes of Cairo Dec. 30th 1774." Lower down on the page, after a list of purchases, he wrote, "Direct for J. Antes of Cairo to the Care of Sig. Alessandro del Senno at the Venetian Consuls at Alexandria." Boylston does not otherwise identify Antes beyond being a "friend." John Antes was born in Frederick, Pennsylvania, but had left America in 1764 for a town in Germany where he became a Moravian missionary. From 1770 to 1782 he served as a Moravian missionary in Egypt, and many years later, in 1800, he published an account of his experiences.[32] Some name him the first American in Egypt, but Antes stated in the introduction to his book, "I have always considered myself as an Englishman, my father having been naturalized and intrusted with offices in the king's service in America." This dovetails with the argument of Nicholas Biddle of Philadelphia who, while sailing from Naples for Sicily in 1806, sought to determine whether a fellow traveler was an American or an Englishman, and concluded, as he wrote in his journal, "education is much more decisive than birth."[33] Moreover, after leaving Egypt, Antes spent the rest of his life in England without returning to the United States and without leaving any American legacy. A similar potential ambiguity is displayed in the case of two young Americans, one from Boston, the other from New York, who left for England at the outbreak of the American Revolution owing to their families' Loyalist sympathies, and joined the British navy. After distinguished careers both found themselves as captains with Horatio Nelson off Egypt in August 1798 at the Battle of the Nile. Some modern historians call them Americans, but Americans of the day would have considered them British naval officers.[34]

At the time of Boylston's visit, the very start of the last quarter of the eighteenth century, European traders, consular representatives, and independent travelers in Egypt had to negotiate their business and affairs in the shadows of the two rival Mamluk beys, Murad and Ibrahim, who ruled the country largely independent of the sultan in Constantinople. The beys did not encourage European commerce, though they tacitly allowed travel in the Red Sea between Suez and India. Such traffic was officially opposed by the Ottoman sultan: the waterway was supposed to be the preserve of pilgrims to Mecca. Despite the lack of security for Europeans in Egypt, a number of French, British, and other foreign nationals were engaged in business there. In 1775 John Shaw, sent to Egypt by Warren Hastings, Governor of Bengal, negotiated a treaty with one of the Egyptian rulers allowing ships to sail to Suez at favorable rates of duty. George Baldwin, formerly a consul in Cyprus, had been briefly in Egypt in 1774. After the new treaty was achieved he returned to Alexandria from London in July 1775 to take up a position as unofficial agent for British merchants off ships at Alexandria and Suez, sending goods through Egypt. Baldwin would become consul-general in 1786, and was the first official British representative since Richard Harris, who had stepped down in 1757 after arranging for the Dutch to look after British affairs.[35] Carlo Rossetti, the Venetian consul, whom Boylston met, served as Baldwin's chargé d'affaires in Cairo. The French were more secure and had long had consular representation: at the time of Boylston's visit, Jean-Baptiste Mure had just become consul-general, in 1774; Jean-Paul Bories had been vice-consul in Alexandria since 1770.

Before leaving Egypt Boylston and Tasburgh surely spent some time in Alexandria (a stay of which we have no record) before setting out on their return trip to western Europe on board a hired ship. The route lay through the islands of Lampedusa and Malta to Leghorn, their original port of departure months earlier. In Leghorn the portrait painter John Singleton Copley saw him in early June, and wrote to his mother, "Mr. Boylston has been within a few weeks past at Leghorn after his return from Turkey."[36] By "Turkey" Copley meant the Ottoman Empire. Boylston then traveled to Genoa, Turin, Lyon, Paris, and the Austrian and French Netherlands, until he reached London on July 15, 1775.

In London Boylston met a number of fellow Bostonians. One of them was Samuel Curwen, an eighteenth-century Loyalist of Boston and Salem, who in the spring of 1775 had fled the coming revolution to live in England. An entry in Curwen's diary for July 29, 1775, reads "dined by invitation with Gov. H[utchinson] in company with Mr. Joseph Greene, Mr. Maudit, to whom I was introduced, and Mr. Ward Boylston, the latter gave us a very entertaining narrative of his march through Syria, Palestine and Egypt."[37] Hutchinson was Thomas Hutchinson, the last civilian governor of the Massachusetts Bay Colony, who, also fearing for his life, had left Boston for England a year before Curwen, in May 1774. Hutchinson kept his own diary in which he recorded the same dinner on July 29: "I went into the city to Mr. Mauduit's, who, with Mr. Jo. Greene, Mr. Curwen, and Mr. Boylstone, dined with us."[38] Hutchinson says nothing of Boylston's tour. His mind may have been on the recent news of the Battle of Bunker Hill. Curwen saw Boylston again on August 4: "I repaired to Mr. Ward Boylstones lodgings who very civily received me and showed us several curiosities, natural and artificial, he had brought from Egypt; the holy Land; Italy &c."

Hutchinson may have omitted specific mention of Boylston's eastern tour in his diary, but he does identify his traveling companion, whom Boylston fails to name. In the entry for August 28, 1775, only a month after Boylston's return, Hutchinson wrote, "Lord Gage [that is General Thomas Gage, Hutchinson's successor as governor, military governor, of Massachusetts] had got letters from his brother-in-law, Mr. Tasborough at Leghorn, the same that went to Jerusalem with Boylstone." Thomas Gage's sister Teresa, whom George Tasburgh (as the name is generally spelled) had married in 1755, died in August 1773, after some eighteen years of marriage.[39] This note of Hutchinson also suggests that Jerusalem was the principal destination of the two travelers and in the case of George Tasburgh, who was from a Roman Catholic family, a pilgrimage destination of some significance. In fact it is possible that Tasburgh was the organizer of the eastern itinerary and that he had asked Boylston to accompany him. In any event, Egypt was a logical add-on for both travelers, completing a circuit of the eastern Mediterranean.[40] The closing passage of Boylston's twelve-page letter to his mother offers some insight into his desire to travel:

> I am very anxious to learn from you the state of the family. Publick affairs make me pass many a melancholy hour & the want of a letter from my father quite distresses me. Traveling was no charm to dissipate my load of trouble. Go where I will that follows me & the only consolation is frail hopes; how soon they may be extinguished I don't know. I expect every moment to hear something dreadful from America. Every account which are mentioned in the papers seem but a prelude to it. But why should I trouble you with this subject. My pessimism betrays my heart & shows you what I wish to conceal from you, as it does not relieve me & only adds trouble to trouble, who have more to grapple with than I am able to conceive.[41]

The looming threat of revolution at home was exceedingly discouraging. In addition he was estranged from his wife and had left behind his infant son. After reaching England, Boylston, as a Loyalist, opted not to return to Boston and stayed on in London, where he remained for more than twenty years. There is no evidence, however, that he ever met his fellow American, John Ledyard, who set out from London in 1788 via Paris for Egypt.

John Ledyard

The life and travels of John Ledyard, whose name and visit to Egypt in 1788 form their own story, have merited several recent biographies covering his full career.[42] Egypt formed only the final chapter. Ledyard was born in Groton, Connecticut, in 1751, and attended Dartmouth College in Hanover, New Hampshire, in 1772. He sailed with Captain Cook on the latter's third voyage in 1776, witnessed Cook's death in the Sandwich Islands (now Hawaii), and published an account of the voyage. Ten years later, after having met Thomas Jefferson in Paris—he was the American minister to France—Ledyard traveled in 1786 and 1787 with several colleagues across Russia until the Empress Catherine the Great, fearing he would interfere with the fur trade, had him deported. By June 1788 Ledyard had returned to London. There he met with members of the African Association, newly formed under the aegis of Joseph Banks, one of the leading intellectuals of the day, and had received a commission to explore the interior of Africa.

Leaving London for Egypt, Ledyard had stopped in Paris, where he once again saw Thomas Jefferson, whom he had first met in Paris three years earlier. After a week in Paris, during which he met other Americans as well as Lafayette, Ledyard left for Marseilles with a letter of introduction to Stephen Cathalan, Jefferson's contact there. Despite misunderstandings with Cathalan—Ledyard seems to have been easily irritated—which Cathalan was at pains to explain in a letter to Jefferson, Ledyard obtained passage on a ship to the East.

On August 5 he arrived in Alexandria and on August 15 he wrote to Jefferson the first of three letters from Egypt:

> Alexandria at large forms a scene wretched and interesting beyond any other that I have seen: poverty, rapine, murder, tumult, blind bigotry, cruel persecutions, pestilence. A small town built on the ruins of antiquity—as remarkable for its base and miserable architecture as I suppose the place once was for its good and great works of this kind. A pillar called the pillar of Pompey, and an obelisk called Cleopatra's are now almost the only remains of great antiquity—they are both and particularly the former noble subjects to see and contemplate and are certainly more captivating from the contrasting desarts and forlorn prospects around them. No man of whatever turn of mind can see the whole without retiring from the scene with a "sic transit gloria mundi."[43]

On September 19, after reaching Cairo, Ledyard wrote again to Jefferson:

> I made the journey from Alexandria by water and entered the western branch of the mouths of the River Nile into the river. I was 5 days coming on the river to Cairo: but the passage is generally made in 4, sometimes in 3 days. You have heard and read much of this River, and so had I, but when I saw it, I could not conceive it to be the same—it is a mere mud puddle compared with the accounts we have of it. What eyes do travellers see with—are they fools or rogues. For heaven's sake, hear the plain truth about it: first, with respect to its size: plain comparisons in such cases are good: do you know the river Connecticut—of all the rivers I have seen, it most resembles it in size. . . . I saw three of the pyramids as I passed up the river, but they were 4 or 5 leagues off. If I see them nearer before I close my letter and observe any thing about them that I think will be new to you, will insert it. . . . The city of Cairo is about half as large as Paris and by the aggregate of my informations contains 700,000

inhabitants. You will therefore anticipate the fact of its narrow streets and will conceive it necessary also that the houses are high.[44]

In Cairo Ledyard met useful people, observed the inhabitants and their customs, investigating in particular the slave trade, and planned his trip to the interior. On November 15, in a third letter to Jefferson, he included these thoughts:

I have been at Cairo three months and it is within a few days only that I have had any certainty of being able to succeed in the prosecution of my voyage: the difficulties that have attended me have occupied me day and night . . . I have passed my time disagreeably here. Religion does more mischief than all other things. In Egypt it has always done more than in all other places. The humiliating situation of a Frank would be insupportable to me—but for my Voyage.[45]

It was his last letter. Late in the year 1788 or in early January 1789— the exact date is uncertain—after struggling to plan his journey with a group that would take him south, Ledyard died in Cairo without achieving his objective to explore Africa. Jefferson soon heard rumors of his death but only received final confirmation some time later. A letter from Thomas Paine to Jefferson in mid-June included the following account.

The letter which [Henry] Beaufoy [secretary] of the African Association received from Mr. [George] Baldwin the British Consul at Cairo . . . informs him—That a day was fixed for Mr. Ledyard's departure as he was prepared and seemed anxious to set off, but bad weather or other causes occasioned delay as happens to most caravans. Mr. Ledyard took offence at the delay and threw himself into a violent rage with his conductors which deranged something in his system that he thought to cure by an emetic, but he took the dose so strong as at the first or second effort of its operation to break a blood vessel. In three days he was suffocated and died. This account is confirmed by a letter from the Compte de Rosetti, the Venetian resident at Cairo, to Mr. Hunter, an English merchant who had lived in great intimacy with Mr. Ledyard from the time of their traveling together from Alexandria to Cairo to that of Mr. Hunter's departure for England. This letter is dated "Cairo 27th Jany. 1789" and tells Mr. Hunter that seventeen days ago poor Mr. Ledyard went to his eternal rest. He suffered himself to be transported with anger against the persons who had engaged to conduct him to Sennar because they delayed setting out on their voyage for want (as they said) of a fair wind. He was seized with a pain in his stomach occasioned by bile and undertook to cure himself, excessive vomiting ensued, in consequence of which he broke a blood vessel and died in six days.[46]

After his death in Cairo Ledyard's day-by-day journal was sent back to the African Association in London. Within a year Isaac Ledyard, his first cousin, had sought to retrieve it but was told that the journal was the association's property.[47] The journal was partially published in 1810 in the first volume of their *Proceedings*, and in these excerpts Ledyard provided additional comments about his experiences in Egypt, as for instance his trip on the Nile to Cairo.

> The view in sailing up the Nile is very confined unless from the top of the mast, or some other eminence, and then it is an unbounded plain of excellent land, miserably cultivated, and yet interspersed with a great number of villages, both on its banks and as far along the meadows as one can see in any direction: the river is also filled with boats passing and repassing—boats all of one kind, and navigated in one manner; nearly also of one size, the largest carrying ten or fifteen tons. On board of these boats are seen onions, water-melons, dates, sometimes a horse, a camel (which lies down in the boat), and sheep and goats, dogs, men and women. . . . Towards evening and morning they have music. Whenever we stopped at a village, I used to walk into it with my conductor, who, being a Musselman, and a descendant from Mahommed, wore a green turban, and was therefore respected, and I was sure of safety: —but in truth, dressed as I was in a common Turkish habit, I believe I should have walked as safely without him.[48]

On his first day in Cairo Ledyard wrote in his diary:

> From the little town where we landed, the distance to Cairo is about a mile and a half, which we rode on asses; for the ass in this country is the Christian's horse, as he is allowed no other animal to ride upon. . . . I arrived at Cairo early in the morning, on the 19th of August, and went to the house of the Venetian Consul, Mr. Rosetti, chargé d'affaires for the English Consul here. After dinner, not being able to find any other lodging, and receiving no very pressing invitation from Mr. Rosetti to lodge with him, I went to a convent. This convent consists of missionaries sent by the Pope to propagate the Christian faith, or at least to give shelter to

Christians. The Christians here are principally from Damascus; the convent is governed by the order of Recollects; a number of English as well as other European travelers have lodged there.[49]

In his diary and letters Ledyard had pointed to many of the striking features of ancient and contemporary Egypt noted by later American visitors in the early nineteenth century: the current state of Egypt in the context of her ancient ruins; the views along the Nile and its appearance compared to American rivers, usually the Hudson or the Mississippi, and in Ledyard's case the Connecticut River; the benefits of wearing Turkish clothes; the encounter with consular officials and missionaries; the obligation to ride asses; the slave markets; Pompey's Pillar and Cleopatra's obelisks in Alexandria, and the Pyramids.

Joseph Banks and Henry Beaufoy, secretary of the African Association, had the highest admiration for Ledyard. Paine reported to Jefferson (in his letter already quoted), "they considered him as falling a sacrifice to integrity and lament him with an affectionate sorrow. His manner of writing had surprised them as they at first conceived him a bold but illiterate adventurer. That man said Sir Joseph one day to me 'was all Mind.'" Earlier, when Banks had sent Ledyard with a letter of introduction to Beaufoy to be interviewed for the expedition, Beaufoy had commented, "Before I had learnt from the note the name and business of my Visitor, I was struck by the manliness of his person, the breadth of his chest, the openness of his countenance, and the inquietude of his eye."[50] John Ledyard was indeed a highly literate and stalwart explorer with few equals in his day.

European Travelers of This Period and Their Accounts
In the decades surrounding the visits of Boylston and Ledyard, Europeans explored many aspects of Egypt. Among the enlightened visitors in the twenty-five years prior to 1775, three made significant contributions to the European understanding of the region by their published accounts of travels or residences. Frederick Hasselquist (a pupil of Charles Linnaeus) traveled in 1750 and 1751 in Egypt and in the Holy Land and, although he died a year later in Smyrna, Linnaeus published his disciple's botanical observations with high praise.[51] The German surveyor Carsten Niebuhr was a member of a six-man scientific expedition sent to Egypt, Syria, and Arabia in 1761 by Frederick V of Denmark. After several years of travel in these regions and elsewhere in the East, he was the sole survivor, his five colleagues—a linguist, a botanist, a zoologist, an artist, and

a military officer—having succumbed to malaria and other diseases. He returned to publish two fine accounts with excellent maps of the regions he visited.[52] The diplomat James Bruce, having served as consul-general in Algiers since 1762, explored Egypt and Sudan from 1768 to 1773 with his draftsman Luigi Balugani, in the course of which he discovered the source of the Blue Nile and its confluence with the White Nile, all fully described in his celebrated five-volume account.[53]

Several Europeans who visited Egypt in the years between Boylston's and Ledyard's visits, 1775 and 1789, published accounts of varying significance.[54] Claude Savary, an Arabist, arrived in 1776 and, without apparently traveling south of Cairo, published an account of the country, largely on antiquities, much of it copied from others. John Ledyard dismissed his volumes, telling Jefferson, in one of his letters, "Burn them." François Baron de Tott, a French military officer stationed in Constantinople as adviser to the sultan, traveled to Egypt in 1778. With him came a French naturalist, Charles-Nicolas Sonnini de Manoncourt, whose trip was funded by the leading French naturalist of the day, Georges-Louis Leclerc, comte de Buffon. Constantin-François Chasseboeuf (whose nom de plume was Volney) traveled in 1783, probably under the sponsorship of the French Ministry of Foreign Affairs and produced a work widely cited by the Napoleonic expedition.

The twenty-three-year-old Swiss-educated Polish aristocrat Jan Potocki, a Knight of Malta and an officer in the Austrian army, visited Egypt in 1784 in the course of wide travels, accompanied by a fellow countryman, Józef Kownacki. Potocki published an account of his travels but would be little remembered today were it not for his later fantastic novel, *Manuscrit trouvé à Saragosse*. A portrait painted by Giovanni-Battista Lampi (c. 1788–1789 or 1804), and now in Lancut Castle in Poland, shows Potocki seated with a papyrus roll on his lap covered with hieroglyphic script, wearing medals of the Polish order of the White Eagle and the Russian order of Saint-Vladimir, an Egyptian bust near palm trees with an inscription on its pedestal taken from Herodotus, and in the distance, two pyramids. Egypt had made a strong impression on him, affecting not only this portrait but also his scholarly writings on chronology in the ancient world, in addition to parts of his novel.[55]

Three of these books, Bruce's *Travels to Discover the Source of the Nile* and Volney's and Savary's accounts (in English translations), were widely read in the United States. In New York City, for instance, the surviving ledger books of the New York Society Library (which reopened after the end of the American War of Independence) record the titles of the books charged by the members of the library. Between 1789 and 1792, the years covered by the first of library's bound ledger books, more than thirty readers charged the works of Volney and Savary, and some 125 readers took out one or more volumes of the five-volume set of Bruce's *Travels*.[56] Readers in Philadelphia and Boston must also have included Europeans' accounts of Egypt in their reading.

Boylston in London and His Return to Boston

Ward Nicholas Boylston published no account of his travels in the East. In England, however, where he lived for twenty-five years after his return from Egypt, first sitting out the American Revolution—he was a Loyalist—and then staying on in business, he became known as an expert on the region, and met and corresponded with people involved with things Egyptian and the East though there is no evidence that he ever encountered John Ledyard.

As soon as Boylston arrived in London, he recognized that he had stories to tell from his journal. As early as September 17, 1775, the American expatriate Samuel Curwen, whom Boylston met soon after arriving in London, wrote in his diary that Mr. Boylston "entertained us with reading a narrative of his travels through the Country of Palestine; which was very agreeable."[57] Some years later, Thomas Harmer (1715–1788), a minister and scholar who used observations in recent travel accounts to illustrate biblical passages, had access to Boylston's journal for this purpose. In the preface to volume three of the second edition of his work, which appeared in 1787, Harmer reported, "I also took a journey to London some time ago, expressly for the purpose of conversing with two persons on matter of this kind. The one was a very ingenious and friendly gentleman who visited the East in 1774: he very obligingly read over to me that part of his Journal which related to the Holy-Land and also communicated some other matters he recollected." A footnote names him: "W. Boylston, Esq. of London."[58] Among the various bits of information that Boylston conveyed to Harmer were observations on when the first rainfall occurred in Palestine the year he was there and the size of pigeons in the East. Knowledge of Boylston's journal seems to have circulated soon after his arrival in London.

Boylston also had dealings with Sir Joseph Banks. Banks had accompanied Captain Cook on his first voyage as a botanist, had been elected president of the Royal Society in 1778, and was now a leader in English intellectual circles. Among his endeavors was the African Association, of which he was a cofounder in 1788, and which that very year had sponsored

Ledyard's ill-fated Egyptian trip. In 1790, Samuel Breck, a young Philadelphian, in the course of an extended visit to London, recalled a conversation he had with Boylston in which Banks' name came up:

> I remember being at breakfast with him one day when a messenger came from Sir Joseph Banks to inform him that he had concluded to take an Egyptian statue, consigned to the care of Mr. Boylston, at the price of three thousand pounds sterling. The statue was very ancient but had lost its nose. The empress Catherine II of Russia had an agent in London ready to pay that sum if Sir Joseph should decline to do it. The gentleman purchased it, no doubt for the British Museum.[59]

Another instance of Boylston's association with Banks appears in a communication in 1793 to a learned society in London by Thomas Dancer, the chief botanist in the British colony of Jamaica: "I have for some time past, had the Acasia (or Mimosa) of which you sent me seeds, growing in the Botanical Garden [in Jamaica]. It was obtained from Sir Joseph Banks about four years ago." A footnote states: "Brought from Egypt by Mr. Boylston."[60]

Mention of acacia seeds brought from Egypt by Boylston should make us realize that the seemingly casual notation, "Rose of Jericho" with its Linnaean equivalent, in his slim Cairo notebook, was an indication of his broader botanical interests. And at least one more botanical specimen collected by Boylston lurks in the eighteenth-century record: the American expatriate Samuel Curwen reported that among the curiosities he had seen at Boylston's place in August of 1775 was "the locust supposed food of the Baptist one pod of which he presented to me."[61]

Boylston also displayed his reputation as one who knew Egypt in his contact with William George Browne. Browne, an explorer of independent means, traveled to Egypt and regions to the south, including Darfur, for three years in the early 1790s. On January 30, 1792, some three weeks after his arrival in Egypt, Browne wrote Boylston from Alexandria, reporting that he had been unable to meet with Joseph Banks and Henry Beaufoy, founding members of the African Association, to whom he had wanted to speak before he left, and adding many observations about his stay in Alexandria. The letter got passed on to Banks and is now among his papers at the British Museum. In 1799, after his return to London, Browne published an account of his journey, a copy of which he presented to Boylston with an inked dedication on the half title reading, "From the Author to Ward Nicholas Boylston."[62]

Boylston was still dining on his travels as late as 1794 when John Quincy Adams, newly appointed minister to the Netherlands, met him in London on October 25 on his way to The Hague.

Dined with Mr. Ward N. Boylston in Barnard's Inn, where he kept bachelors hall. . . . Our dinner was properly American, consisting of salt-fish and beef-steaks after the manner of our Country. Boylston is a little of the virtuoso as usual. Shewed us several curiosities in his possession. Gave us some of the genuine Water of the Nile, which was clear as crystal. . . . Boylston's conversation is entertaining. He has traveled into the Holy Land, and gave us quite an amusing account of his pilgrimage.[63]

In 1800 Boylston returned to Boston. By this time his first wife had died, and he had remarried and had two more sons.[64] Back home he became a benefactor of many local institutions. After some negotiations with Harvard College, he confirmed a bequest of his late uncle, Nicholas Boylston, to fund a professorship of Rhetoric and Oratory at the College, with John Quincy Adams as the first professor. Recent holders of the chair include the poets Seamus Heaney (1982–1996) and Jorie Graham. In 1802 he funded the Boylston Medical Library (now part of the Boston Athenaeum), and in 1817 he funded the Boylston prize for Elocution at Harvard, a prize still awarded. He gave the cranium of his mummy to Dr. George C. Shattuck who in turn presented it to the Warren Anatomical Museum, now part of the Countway Library at the Harvard Medical School, where it still is. In 1825, he commissioned Gilbert Stuart to paint his portrait, the original of which is in the Museum of Fine Arts, Boston and contemporaneous versions are now owned by Harvard University and the Massachusetts Historical Society.[65] The letter to his mother and his two-volume unpublished diary are owned by the Massachusetts Historical Society, located in Boston at 1154 Boylston Street. Though an expatriate in London for nearly twenty-five years, Ward Nicholas Boylston was in fact an American and the first American to visit Smyrna, Baalbek, Jerusalem, and Cairo.

2 | NAPOLEON AND THE FRENCH SAVANTS IN EGYPT

"**S**oldats, songez que, du haut de ces pyramides, quarante siècles vous contemplent."
(Soldiers, remember that from the heights of those pyramids, forty centuries look down upon you.)

Not mentioned in any Napoleonic document, this observation, frequently quoted, first appeared in the anonymous *Histoire de Bonaparte, premier consul* published in 1802.[1] Only later did Napoleon acknowledge the statement as his own. But the sentiment was surely there from the beginning. Napoleon's ill-fated but totally transforming invasion of Egypt, in 1798, brought his troops and his savants face to face with the country—not only with its myriad of inhabitants but, more lastingly, with its Pharaonic monuments. The published works of the savants—the scholars—who accompanied him radically changed the European perception of Egypt, bringing to the attention of the interested public Egypt's ancient monuments, her contemporary culture, and her fauna and flora. This and other publications contributed to increasing interest in the collecting of Egyptian art and antiquities among Europeans—especially among French, English, and Italians—and spurred both the experts and the merely curious to travel to Egypt and see the great monuments for themselves.

In June of 1798, Horatio Nelson had written to George Baldwin, by then no longer consul-general in Egypt but still resident there, expressing his fears of an imminent French invasion. And indeed, in the first days of July Napoleon began landing his troops in Alexandria, having evaded the British Mediterranean fleet.[2] Leaving a force in Alexandria, he then moved, after a week, east to Rosetta with 30,000 men, ill-equipped for the summer season, and proceeded up the Nile to Cairo, where, after initial setbacks, he defeated the Mamluk forces. The two Mamluk beys, Ibrahim and Murad, the longtime rival rulers of Egypt, fled, the former eastward into Sinai, the latter to the south, up the Nile. By July 24, the French were in control of Cairo. The French, with some 28,000 troops armed with artillery and muskets and fighting in infantry squares with bayonets, overwhelmed the Egyptians. At the beginning of August, however, the British fleet, under Horatio Nelson, surprised the French fleet in Abu Qir Bay and destroyed it, including Napoleon's flagship, the *Orient*. More than 1,700 French were killed. The commanding officer of Nelson's flagship, the *Swiftsure*, was Capt. Benjamin Hallowell, a Boston-born naval officer, who, as a Loyalist, had had to leave America and had joined the British navy;[3] he was the brother of Ward Nicholas Boylston (born a Hallowell), who had visited Egypt twenty-three years earlier.

In the same month, August 1798, one of Napoleon's generals, Louis Desaix de Veygoux, moved south from Giza with more than 2,500 men in pursuit of Murad Bey. General Desaix engaged Murad and his auxiliary troops, who had come across the Red Sea from Arabia and whom the French called "Meccans," in skirmishes and several pitched battles on the Nile; despite fearful loss of men and collateral damage to the local villages, the French ultimately prevailed. Yet Murad and his senior Mamluk staff vanished. The French progressed slowly up the Nile. By late December they were at Asyut, on January 24 they were at Dendera, on January 26 at Thebes, and by February 2 they had reached Syene (Aswan), where they stopped for more than a month. Nearby, on the island of Philae, a French sculptor later in the year carved an inscription on a wall of the Temple of Isis recording their victory over the Mamluks:

L'an 6 de la République,
le 13 messidor,
une armée française, commandée
par Bonaparte, est descendue
à Alexandrie.
L'armée ayant mis, vingt jours
après, les Mammelouks en fuite
aux pyramides,
Desaix, commandant la
première division, les a
poursuivis au-delà des
cataractes, où il est arrivé
le 13 ventose de l'an 7.

Les généraux de brigade
Daoust, Friant et Belliard,
Donzelot, chef de l'état-maior
Latournerie, Comm l'artillerie
Eppler, chef de la 21e légère.
Le 13 ventôse, an 7 de la République,
3 mars an de J.-C. 1799.
Gravé par Castex, sculpteur.

Generations of European and American tourists would copy into their diaries some, or all, of this inscription, usually incorrectly. And many would carve their own names nearby, though those considered too close were chiseled out in the 1830s.

When Napoleon landed in Alexandria in the summer of 1798, he brought with him his celebrated savants, a hundred and fifty artists and scientists, experts of many disciplines ultimately destined to survey every aspect of Egypt's ancient monuments, modern life, and fauna and flora.[4] After landing they had remained at Abu Qir for more than a month and had witnessed the destruction of the French fleet. The savants were drawn from the observatory in Paris, the Jardin des Plantes, the École des Ponts et Chaussées, the École Polytechnique, and other institutions. Three of them were senior professionals close to Napoleon: Claude-Louis Berthollet (1748–1822), Gaspard Monge (1746–1818), and Dominique Vivant Denon (1747–1825). Berthollet, a leading chemist, was a professor at the École Polytechnique. Monge, a mathematician, had been a professor at the École Normale and was one of the founders of the École Polytechnique. He had been with Bonaparte in Italy and had been in charge of selecting works of art, manuscripts, and scientific treasures to be brought back from Rome and other cities to Paris. Denon, an accomplished artist, had also had a distinguished career.

Denon received permission from Bonaparte to travel up the Nile with General Desaix. Over a period of nine months, he witnessed the horrors of the military campaign, theft, rape, senseless killing, noting in his published account, "Ô guerre, que tu es brillante dans l'histoire! Mais vue de près, que tu deviens hideuse, lorsqu'elle ne cache plus l'horreur de tes details!"[5] (War, how brilliant you shine in history. But seen close up, how hideous you become, when history no longer hides the horror of your details.)

Despite his disgust, or perhaps because of it, Denon wrote a sensitive account of his travels and made hundreds of sketches of the pharaonic ruins, especially those at Thebes. He sketched as he wrote. His passionate interest in recording the monuments did not mean that he understood their age or significance. One of the monuments he sketched and wrote about was an elaborately carved stone celestial zodiac forming the ceiling of one of the temple buildings at Dendera. "Le plancher très bas, l'obscurité de la chambre qui ne me laissait travailler que quelques heures dans la journée, la multiplicité des détails, la difficulté de ne pas confondre en les regardant d'une manière si incommode, rien ne m'arrêta." (The low ceiling, the dim light of the room that only let me work for a few hours a day, the great number of details and the difficulty of rendering them in these conditions, nothing stopped me.)[6]

In March 1799, while Denon was in Upper Egypt, a group of eight engineers under Pierre-Simon Girard, most of them in their twenties, was sent up river to assess the agricultural possibilities of the Nile. With them was the sculptor Jean-Jacques Castex who would carve the famous inscription at Philae. The engineers soon became more interested in the ancient monuments than with irrigation and, to the dismay of their leader Girard, received authorization to study the Egyptian ruins from a commanding general Auguste-Daniel Belliard (whose name is included in the Philae inscription). They met Denon and, acting on a tip from him, three of them—Prosper Jollois, Dubois-Aymé, and Édouard de Villiers—revisited Dendera in late May and drew the zodiac with even greater fidelity.[7]

Meanwhile, in February 1799, a month before this first group of savants left to go upriver, Bonaparte took part of his forces on an ill-advised mission across the Sinai Peninsula to counter a threat from a pasha headquartered at Acre and preparing to invade Egypt. By mid-March, after capturing al-Arish, Gaza, and Jaffa (where his men dishonored themselves by massacring prisoners), Napoleon reached Acre. There, lacking artillery, his troops could not take the fortress despite repeated attempts, and by late May he gave up and in early June returned to Cairo, having needlessly lost men through combat and disease.

Bonaparte was back in Cairo when Denon returned to Lower Egypt. After he had seen Denon's work and had spoken with him, he appointed two additional scientific groups in August 1799 to explore Upper Egypt, one led by Louis Costaz, the other by Jean-Baptiste-Joseph Fourier, each man in charge of a dozen professionals: astronomers, surveyors, engineers, architects, botanists, zoologists, health officers. They went as far south as Philae, meeting along the way at Esna in mid-September members of the first expedition now returning north. Among the places the savants visited in addition to Philae were Syene (Aswan), Kom Ombo, Gabal al-Silsila, Edfu, Esna, Armant, Luxor, Karnak, Medinet Habu, and Dendera, sites that would be stopping places for hosts of European and American travelers on the Nile in succeeding decades. On the side of one of the principal gates at Karnak they listed a *geographie des monumens*, that is the longitude and latitude of eight of the temples, from Dendera to Philae. The drawings and watercolors of these ruins done by François-Charles Cécile and Charles Louis Balzac, two accomplished artists with the second parties of savants, and by André Dutertre, who had gone up separately with the botanist Hippolyte Nectoux, are among the first accurate renderings of the great Egyptian monuments. At Philae, in September, members of the group led by Costaz had their names (together with those of Dutertre and Nectoux) carved in the temple, not far from the inscription done by Castex commemorating the victory over the Mamluks by General Desaix.

The French military presence in Egypt then slowly unraveled. In August 1799, as the second groups of two dozen savants were traveling south, Napoleon secretly fled the country, leaving General Kléber in command, and taking with him Vivant Denon and two other senior professionals, Berthollet and Monge. Kléber was assassinated in June of 1800. In late July 1801, the British landed 15,000 men at Abu Qir. By now, the French had lost 6,000 men. In August 1801, a combined Ottoman and British force compelled the French to surrender in Alexandria.

Tense negotiations followed between senior military officers of the French and the British, Generals Jacques Menou and John Hely-Hutchinson, about the fate of the antiquities assembled by the savants and in addition their notes and related collections, including extensive specimens of flora and fauna. Two English antiquarians, Edward Daniel Clarke and his companion William Richard Hamilton (secretary of Lord Elgin, then British ambassador in Constantinople), who were visiting Egypt on their own, were persuaded by the impassioned pleas of the leading savants, chief of whom was the zoologist Étienne Geoffroy Saint-Hilaire, that they should be allowed to retain their notes and scientific specimens. The pleas of the savants were successful. The British, on the other hand, appropriated all of the antiquities, the Rosetta Stone the most celebrated among them. But with great foresight the savants had recognized the significance of the Rosetta Stone for deciphering hieroglyphic script: before surrendering it they had made copies of the inscription, first by using the stone as if a lithographic block, which reproduced on a sheet the texts in white on a black background, and secondly by using it as if an engraved plate, which reproduced the text in black on a white background, in both instances with reverse images. At the end of September 1801, the scholars embarked for France. Not all of them: out of more than

150 who had come to Egypt, thirty had died. Some had been assassinated, others had died of the plague. The British left in the spring of 1803.

Napoleon's invasion left an extraordinary legacy. Detailed information about all aspects of Egypt began to become available in Europe and the United States. First of all, Denon, who had returned to Paris with Napoleon in late 1799, promptly arranged for his drawings and notes to be published; the two-volume work appeared in Paris in 1802.[8] Two-volume English translations in octavo format, minus most of the plates, were printed in London and New York as early as 1802 and 1803, bringing fresh information about Egypt to a wider public.[9] And indeed, he was recognized in America: in 1804, Denon (not to mention Napoleon) was elected to honorary membership in the New York Academy of Arts (later called the American Academy of Arts), established two years earlier through the efforts of Edward Livingston, mayor of New York, and his brother Robert R. Livingston, then US Minister in France. Years later, in 1826, when Denon's drawings were sold after his death, they were acquired by a collector from whom, in 1835, they passed in a quirk of fate to the British Museum where they are today.[10]

During this period, in 1822, a brilliant French scholar, Jean-François Champollion, succeeded in deciphering hieroglyphic script, basing his work largely on the inscriptions on the Rosetta Stone, not on the stone itself but on the printed copies of the text made by the French savants before it was handed over to the British. His decipherment finally and conclusively allowed Egyptian inscriptions to be translated, which gave new meaning to the great monuments along the Nile.[11]

The scientific endeavor of the savants, who had retained their papers and specimens, was published in the great *Description de l'Égypte*. This monumental work, which appeared in installments between 1809 and 1828, forever transformed the European and American understanding and appreciation of Egyptian antiquity. And not only antiquity: although five of the ten folio volumes concerned *Antiquités*, two were devoted to *État modern* and three to *Histoire naturelle*. The *memoirs* in the smaller text volumes devoted to modern Egypt and to its fauna and flora would bring naturalists of many disciplines to Egypt to follow up the researches of Napoleon's savants.[12] One thousand sets of *Description de l'Égypte* were printed: three hundred sets with plates colored in various degrees (two hundred printed on *papier vélin*, one hundred on *papier fin*), the remaining seven hundred printed on *papier fin* and uncolored, the four versions priced accordingly from 5,550 to 3,550 francs. In 1820, midway through the appearance of the volumes, a second edition, undertaken by the Paris

bookseller and editor Charles-Louis Panckoucke, appeared in installments between 1820 and 1830, with the text printed not in folio format
but octavo, twenty-four volumes bound as twenty-six. Like the first edition, one thousand sets were published. Both editions were marketed
through booksellers in Paris, and elsewhere in France and in Europe.[13]
An advertisement in one of the early volumes of the second edition listed
booksellers where purchasers could place subscriptions for the work: 22
booksellers in Paris, 139 in other French cites, and 64 in cities abroad.
One firm in Philadelphia was listed, *Carez et compagnie*, French spelling
for Mathew Carey, one of the country's leading publishers and booksellers.

Sets of the *Description de l'Égypte* soon reached select American libraries and architects. As early as 1822, volumes of the first edition were
being presented to the Harvard College Library by William H. Eliot,
class of 1815.[14] The Library of Congress purchased a set in 1830, and the
American Philosophical Society in Philadelphia acquired one in 1833.
Princeton University received a set of the second edition as a gift in 1836.
Three leading architects possessed the work in the 1830s: Ithiel Town
(1784–1844) of New York and New Haven, and Thomas Ustick Walter
(1804–1887) and John Haviland (1792–1852), both of Philadelphia. Some
of these sets and others are discussed in chapter 9.

And there is one additional legacy of Napoleon's presence in Egypt,
perhaps only a footnote, but a footnote with particular resonance for the
American appreciation of Egypt. When Napoleon left Egypt in August
1799, taking with him three of the savants, Monge, Berthollet, and Vivant
Denon, he had on board his ship a number of Egyptian antiquities. He
presented them to his wife Josephine, and for many years they were housed
at Malmaison, her chateau outside of Paris. Among them was a Twelfth
Dynasty brown quartzite statue of a seated man with a smaller standing
image of his wife incorporated into the block-like composition (plate 6).
After this sculpture was sold from Malmaison along with other items in
1816, it passed through three private collections, one French, one British,
one American, before being acquired in 1939 by the Brooklyn Museum,
where it can be seen today, "A souvenir of Napoleon's trip to Egypt."[15]

3 | MEHMET ALI AND HIS NEW EGYPT

fter the French and the British withdrew from Egypt, the country increasingly came under the rule of Mehmet Ali. Mehmet Ali was a Turkish-speaking Ottoman of Albanian background who came from Kavala in Albania (now northern Greece). He entered military service in Kavala where, on the death of his commanding officer, he married his widow and adopted her son (later Ibrahim Pasha in Egypt) as his own son. He next came to the attention of the authorities in Constantinople and was sent with a contingent of Albanians to oppose Napoleon's troops in Egypt, siding with the British at the Battle of Abu Qir in the summer of 1801. With the departure of the British, Egyptian troops increasingly looked to him as their leader and in 1806, after shrewd negotiations with the sultan in Constantinople, he obtained the pashalic of Egypt. The Mamluks, however, long the hereditary rulers of Egypt, opposed Mehmet Ali in his new role as pasha, and they persuaded the British to return to support them. In March 1807 the British landed in Alexandria from where they made two unsuccessful attempts to take Rosetta. Lacking real assistance from the Mamluks, and with only 5,000 men in the face of the superior forces of Mehmet Ali, who had the support of the French Consul Bernardino Drovetti, they lost hundreds of men and withdrew ignominiously from Alexandria in September 1807.

Mehmet Ali now set about securing his rule. For four years, after the defeat of the British, he had been skirmishing politically and militarily with the Mamluks without notable success. Then, in March 1811, under a pretext he invited more than sixty senior Mamluks to his palace and then, as they were about to depart on horseback, arranged to have them massacred in a narrow palace alley. In the immediate aftermath several hundred more were killed in the city and their houses pillaged. Those who escaped to Upper Egypt were chased and harried by the pasha's son Ibrahim. In addition, in mid-1811, pressured by the sultan in Constantinople, Mehmet Ali sent to Arabia a military force to purge Mecca and Medina of a fundamentalist Islamic sect, the Wahhabis (named after an eighteenth-century Muslim scholar Ibn al-Wahhab), which had taken control of the holy cities around 1803 and had refused to allow the Ottoman sultan's annual offerings to Mecca and Medina. The war dragged on until 1817 despite the capture of Jedda and Mecca in 1812, but was ultimately successful.[1]

With the elimination of Mamluk power and the suppression of the Wahhabis, Mehmet Ali now set about to modernize Egypt. He utilized expatriate French and British nationals and attracted others, including Italians and Germans, to develop medicine, education, industry and commerce, and to reform his military forces in Egypt. By introducing new commercial enterprises, establishing schools and medical facilities, and upgrading the military, the pasha sought to make himself and the country rich and to become independent from the sultan in Constantinople. It took the encouragement of the French consul, Bernardino Drovetti, and other senior officials, and the cooperation and employment of a wide range of Europeans to achieve his goals.[2]

The most ambitious public works project ordered by Mehmet Ali was the digging of the Mahmoudiya Canal (named after the reigning sultan in Constantinople) linking Alexandria with the Nile at the town of Atfih. This was a public works project on a scale of those undertaken by the ancient pharaohs. Alexandria lacked proper supplies of fresh water and in addition needed a more reliable waterway connecting it to Cairo owing to frequent interruption by bad winds of shipping through the port of Rosetta. First of all the dikes along the Mediterranean coastline, which kept storms from flooding the lakes and low-lying agricultural land, were improved. Work on the canal itself began in late 1817 after consultation with the sultan and under the supervision of a Turkish engineer who was aided by European specialists. The canal ran for eighty kilometers more or less along the line of an old canal dating back centuries.[3] In addition, a lake at the canal's terminus on the inland side of Alexandria was improved with proper walls and docking facilities to accommodate the boats using the canal. This work was accomplished under the supervision of the French architect Pascal Coste, who was also involved in other aspects of the canal's construction. By the time the canal and harbor were completed toward the end of 1819, about one in ten (some say as many as three in ten) of the some 300,000 men involved on the project are thought to have perished through accidents, hunger, and plague. Many European and American travelers went from Alexandria to Cairo via this canal and, having read the guidebooks, commented on the loss of life entailed in its construction. Yet despite subsequent talk of forced, so-called corvée labor, all of the laborers were paid. Difficulties, however, remained. The water was saltier than expected owing to the seepage of salt water from the bed of the canal. Second, sudden winds blowing across the canal would from time to time catch unwary crew by surprise and upset the boats, spilling passengers and cargo into the water. One of the first American travelers on the canal, in 1822, only three years after its completion, witnessed such an accident, as we shall see in a later chapter. Nevertheless merchants and travelers took advantage of the canal which usually saved time and worry in getting to Cairo.

Mehmet Ali also oversaw the construction of a range of industrial and commercial enterprises. An Englishman, Charles Brine, who had earlier worked in the West Indies, established in 1818 a sugar refinery at Radamon in Upper Egypt, which was later run by an Italian group. Around 1819, the Frenchman Louis Jumel helped to introduce Indian cotton, which was first grown at Heliopolis. Mulberry trees were planted for a new silk industry. Indigo was introduced from Syria in 1824. In 1825, merinos (sheep) were imported from Piedmont, and despite setbacks, the flocks increased and the wool improved. Rice was also introduced. Workers were imported for the new cloth manufacturing industries. But the efforts to import and maintain European and even American machinery to run these concerns foundered, in part owing to high taxes.

Education was also high among Mehmet Ali's priorities. A school, largely staffed by Italians, was established at Bulaq in 1821, where Lorenzo Masi from Livorno taught land surveying. In the pasha's college at Bulaq, a former Neapolitan Jesuit, Carlo Bilotti, taught mathematics, a Piedmontese named Scagliotti taught Italian, and a Maronite from Syria named Raffaele, who had studied in Europe, taught Arabic. A printing press was established there in 1822, the first in the Arab world. Many of the works were translations of European manuals on medicine and on military subjects. One of the more significant books to be issued was a two-volume Arabic edition of *The Thousand and One Nights*, published in 1835, apparently based on an eighteenth-century Egyptian manuscript.[4] The work cost one hundred piasters. This was beyond the reach of most Egyptians, and as a result European residents and travelers seem to have purchased most copies. No more than a dozen copies are recorded today.[5]

More important than the press and the schools was the program, begun in 1826, to send Egyptians abroad for training in a wide range of fields. Drovetti had recommended to Youssef Boghos, Mehmet Ali's secretary, that France, not Italy should be their destination, as a result of which between thirty and forty government officials and younger promising Egyptians were sent to Paris in mid-1826.[6] A young American scholar, Edward Robinson, visiting Paris for the first time in the summer of 1826, saw some of them in the gardens of the Tuileries:

> While there I saw the crowd all rushing to one point, & looking up, I beheld 7 Egyptians entering the garden in their oriental costume. They were a party of 30 who had just arrived & are put here by old Ali, the Pasha of Egypt, to go through a regular course of instruction in order to become teachers in their native land. These 7 were from 20 to 30 years of age; some of them had fine faces; others were of quite a sinister expression. They had splendid turbans; their dress was scarlet, a loose short coat or roundabout with loose sleeves; the huge trousers of the same; & morocco slippers. This was probably their gala dress. They marched with great gravity & seemed quite gratified at the notice of the throng.[7]

From 1826 into the early 1840s, some one hundred students went to France for study. Despite the pasha's professed disappointment after several years of the program, most scholars today recognize its importance: many of the students became senior Egyptian ministers.

Mehmet Ali also addressed public health and medicine. The pasha established quarantine at Alexandria and other Nile Delta ports for incoming visitors in 1813.[8] Health officials, many of them Italians and French, began a program of vaccinations against smallpox as early as 1822. Through emissaries Mehmet Ali recruited a young French doctor, Antoine-Barthélémy Clot, who came to Egypt in 1825 accompanied by some twenty European physicians to reorganize medical care for the army. This soon meant reorganizing medical care for the entire population. In 1827 Clot established a medical school where most of the medical instructors were French, with the addition of two Bavarians and a Spaniard. In 1830, a veterinary school was established and in 1836, under Mlle Palmyre Gault, a maternity school for midwives, which thrived, unique at the time in the Muslim world. Clot received the title Clot Bey in 1831 for not abandoning his post during the cholera epidemic of that year.[9]

To upgrade his military, Mehmet Ali also turned to Europeans. By 1817, two Italians, Giuseppe Forni and Giovanni Baffi, were engaged in the manufacture of gunpowder, for which a French engineer and architect, Pascal Coste, built a factory in 1820 on the very south end of the island of Roda, immediately adjacent to the ancient Nilometer.[10] The proximity of the factory would in time be fatal to the ancient dome covering the device measuring the height of the Nile. In 1819, after a turbulent career in the Napoleonic campaigns, the thirty-year-old Joseph Sève came to Egypt to help to train the new army. He converted to Islam and became known as Suleiman Pasha. In 1829 a Spanish colonel, Antonio de Seguera, helped to establish an artillery school at Tora. To replenish his ships lost at the Battle of Navarino in 1827 during the Greek War of Independence and to protect himself against the Turks, Mehmet Ali established a dockyard in Alexandria. In 1829 he recruited a French naval engineer from Toulon, Charles Lefebvre de Cerisy, to manage it.[11] About 1831, he purchased a British-built frigate, whose captain, the English naval officer John Prissick, stayed on in the service of the Egyptian navy. All of these improvements, "Western" in style, helped to make Egypt a region unique in the eastern Mediterranean. And in utter contrast to the eighteenth century under the Mamluks, Egypt became safe for travelers and thereby a special destination for European and American visitors.

There was a dark side to Mehmet Ali's innovations and reforms. They were for an elite, not for the ordinary Egyptian. Peasants, the *fellahin*, were taxed as never before. In addition, land owners were obliged to hand over to the state part of the produce of their land for which they were supposed to be paid a fair price. And much of their land now became state property. A cadre of police enforced the tax system. Punishments ranged from routine—the bastinado (flogging the soles of the feet)—to extreme (death). The pasha wielded ultimate authority: for major crimes, "a simple horizontal motion of his hand is sufficient to imply the sentence of decapitation," as the orientalist and cultural anthropologist Edward William Lane, long resident in Egypt, succinctly put it in his account of the customs of Egypt.[12] In addition, the slave trade managed under the pasha in the early decades of his rule was one of the more extensive in the world. By the late 1830s the number of slaves brought down river under terrible conditions by Turkish and even French traffickers from Sennar and Darfur in Sudan was in the range of 10,000 annually.[13] Travelers who visited the slave markets in Cairo and Alexandria expressed opinions of horror mixed with fascination. Only a few commented that southerners in the United States were engaged in equally horrifying acts involving chattel slavery. Young men throughout Egypt were conscripted in great numbers into the military. In attempts to avoid this duty, they frequently cut off one of their fingers thinking this would render them unfit to wield a rifle. British residents were well aware of the corrosive effects of the pasha's policies on the lives of ordinary Egyptians, but it was convenient to look the other way in order to preserve the institutions that gave a safe passage to India. Perceptive American travelers, while commenting on the safety of Egypt and the reforms of the pasha, also drew attention to the poverty and hopelessness to which so much of the population was reduced by the new regime of Mehmet Ali.

A few words should be added on the status of Christians and Jews in Egypt. In the period covered by this account, there were said to be some 150,000 Christian Copts in Egypt of whom only 10,000 lived in Cairo. Under Mehmet Ali they were well treated and even allowed, as most visiting Europeans were not, to ride horses; and they were exempt from military service. In contrast to the number of Christians, there were only 5,000 Jews in Egypt, most living in their own quarter in Cairo, in which there were said to be eight synagogues. Though held in contempt by Muslims, Jews were treated better in Egypt than in any other country of the Ottoman Empire and were left alone and were as well off or as poorly off as a great many of their fellow Muslim residents in Cairo.[14]

Francis Barthow

One who responded to the new Egypt was Francis Barthow, who settled in Egypt perhaps as early as 1810. Two seemingly conflicting versions exist of his origin. In one he was a naturalized American, also known as François Barthou, a Frenchman born in Saint-Domingue. The uprising of black slaves that began there in 1791 and led to an independent Haiti in 1804 witnessed an exodus of tens of thousand of refugees to East Coast cities of the United States in July 1793.[15] François Barthou may have been one of them. Another version calls him an American by birth, a native of Belleville, New York.[16] Some have considered him a renegade off one of the ships of the United States Mediterranean squadron, but it is more plausible to think of him as one who had arrived as an entrepreneur trading at Mocha on the coast of Yemen. Whatever his origin, he is surely the "Captain Bartou" seen by the traveler George Annesley running a brig between Suez and Mocha in 1805 and 1806. In volume two of Annesley's account he is named "Captain Barton," in volume three he has become Bartou, as if the sheets of volume two were proofread and text of volume three corrected before being printed.[17] In neither volume, however, does Annesley give his nationality.

In any event by this time Barthow was an expatriate. His presence in Egypt first became securely known when he accompanied two British travelers up the Nile in 1813, Thomas Legh and the Rev. Charles Smelt. In his published account of the trip, Legh wrote "on the 13th of January we sailed from the port of Cairo for Upper Egypt, having engaged Mr. Barthow, an American, who had resided many years in the country, to accompany us and act as our interpreter." Legh and Barthow carved their names on Egyptian buildings in the course of their Nile voyage.[18] The Swiss explorer Burckhardt saw "Captain Barthod" with Legh and Smelt coming down river on February 27.[19] Legh later described Barthow as one "who had traded many years in the Red Sea, spoke Arabic extremely well . . ."[20] That statement is the clue that reveals his route to Egypt, namely through the Red Sea, not the Mediterranean. Barthow must have been well recommended: two years later he accompanied the intellectual William J. Bankes and the Italian soldier Giovanni Finati to Nubia.[21] In coming to Egypt, Barthow joined Europeans of many nationalities who were seeking or responding to opportunities for advancement in the modernization of Egypt undertaken by Mehmet Ali, the new pasha.

Among Barthow's ventures was the trade in Egyptian antiquities. In the course of his Nile trip with Bankes he is reported to have brought downriver for him two sphinxes from Karnak.[22] Some years later in 1824, Barthow (then described as an American under the protection of the Austrian consul) made an agreement with Bernard Bienvenu de Clairambault, a career French diplomat in Alexandria, with Victor Besson, and with a Belgian shipowner, Jean-Baptiste De Lescluze, to send for sale in Europe a collection of antiquities he possessed.[23] It was acquired through a Dutch collector for the museum in Leyden. A few years later François Barthou, as the Dutch sources call him, was one of three representatives of Giovanni Anastasi in the sale of his antiquities to the museum in Leyden. In August 1827 he was in Livorno helping to negotiate the sale; several months later he traveled to Holland to deal directly with officials from the museum.[24] These were not his first ventures in this business. Even earlier, in 1818, Bernardino Drovetti (in political hiatus between two terms as French consul-general), reported in two of his letters that François Barthow (as he calls him) had sailed to Marseilles via Port Mahon in Minorca, though for reasons not explicitly stated by Drovetti and not known to me.[25]

4 | THE AMERICAN NAVY AND TRADE IN THE MEDITERRANEAN

The American experience in Egypt in the early decades of the nineteenth century cannot be separated from American contacts with other regions of the Mediterranean world. The earliest American involvement in the Mediterranean (apart from the travels of Boylston and Ledyard) was commercial in nature. After the Treaty of Paris in 1783, ending the American War of Independence, ships from ports on the eastern seaboard—Salem, Boston, New York, Philadelphia, Baltimore, and Charleston—resumed or initiated trade in Gibraltar, Malaga, and Barcelona in Spain, Marseilles in France, Genoa, Leghorn, and Naples in Italy, Palermo and Messina in Sicily, and Trieste at the head of the Adriatic. American consuls or consular agents were resident in most of these cities from as early as 1800.[1]

The Barbary Pirates and the American Navy

Trade in the Mediterranean was hazardous. Barbary corsairs preyed on shipping, even at times beyond the straits of Gibraltar in the Atlantic. After the War of Independence the British naval squadron in the Mediterranean no longer offered protection against the corsairs to American ships. To help resolve the problem of piracy, the United States had signed a treaty with Morocco in 1787, but similar treaties were not to be obtained from Algiers, Tunis, or Tripoli. American seamen had been imprisoned in Algiers as early as 1785; by 1793 the threat of capture had all but stopped American shipping in the region. Despite negotiations and payment of tribute, the situation was not to be resolved until the United States authorized the creation of its own navy in 1795. Before the arrival of naval vessels, the American government continued to pay tribute.

45

In April 1800, the armed frigate USS *George Washington* (a converted brig built by the Brown family of Providence and purchased from them by Congress in 1798) was taken to Philadelphia and loaded with stores and timber as tribute for the dey of Algiers. It sailed under the command of Captain William Bainbridge and arrived in Algiers in September 1800, the first American warship to enter the Mediterranean. But the dey humiliated Bainbridge by forcing him in turn to carry Algerian tribute, including wild animals, to the Ottoman sultan. Bainbridge sailed from Algiers on October 19, and by a ruse involving the pretense of lowering sail and firing a cloud-billowing salute, slipped through the Dardanelles without being stopped or sunk and safely reached Constantinople, where his Algerian humiliation was overshadowed by a surprisingly warm welcome. The frigate was the first American naval vessel to enter the port, as the British traveler Edward Daniel Clarke who was in Constantinople at the same time noted in his account.[2] Bainbridge invited him to dine on board where he joined a meal at which decanters of water and food of many continents were served. Clarke was on his way to Egypt where he would help negotiate the dispute between the British military and the French savants resulting in the savants' retention of their notes and specimens as mentioned in the chapter on Napoleon in Egypt (see chapter 2). The *George Washington* left Constantinople on December 30, 1800, returned to Algiers in mid-January 1801, and after a stop at Alicante in Spain, where Bainbridge took the French residents of Algiers who had been expelled by the dey, was back in the United States on April 19, 1801.[3]

One minor yet intriguing aspect of the voyage of the USS *George Washington* from Philadelphia to Algiers and Constantinople and back was the presence on board of a graduate of Dartmouth College, Silas Dinsmore (1766–1847). Dinsmore, after leaving Dartmouth where he was in the class of 1791, had taught for three years, had been commissioned a lieutenant in the Corps of Engineers in 1794, and had spent five years as a United States agent to the Choctaw nation of Indians. In 1800 he joined the Navy and as a purser was assigned to the *George Washington* when the frigate was in Philadelphia being prepared to sail for Algiers under Captain Bainbridge. Dinsmore surely had an opportunity to see Algiers and Constantinople while on shore leave during his tour. On July 15, 1801, some three months after the *George Washington* arrived back in the United States, he was discharged from the Navy.[4] He then resumed his career as a United States agent to the Choctaws. But there is more to the story. An 1810 inventory of Dartmouth College reports that a Mr. S. Dinsmore had presented to the college "two fragments of Pompey's Pillar from Alexandria in Egypt." Where did he obtain them? Not in Egypt. Additional entries in the inventory give a clue as to the source. Dinsmore also gave to Dartmouth a pair of shoes and fourteen Turkish canles [sic: either candles or canes] from Constantinople, as well as a Turkish lantern and three bowls of Turkish pipes.[5] He probably acquired his two stone fragments from a traveler he had met there who had brought them from Egypt. Pompey's Pillar, as noted in an earlier chapter, was the most prominent landmark of antiquity in Alexandria and a destination for seamen and tourists alike, some of whom are known to have chipped off pieces to take away.

The *George Washington* was the first warship to enter the Mediterranean; others would soon follow. In July 1801, three more American frigates, with Bainbridge in command of one of them, and a schooner reached Gibraltar, this time from Norfolk, Virginia. Over the next period of years, despite one major setback—the loss of the *Philadelphia* on an uncharted reef outside Tripoli in 1803 and the imprisonment of her crew—the Americans proceeded to blockade North African ports.[6]

One of the more memorable and decisive incidents of the extended American attempt to protect her shipping in the Mediterranean centered on William Eaton, who had been American consul in Tunis since about 1800. In 1804 he took the United States ship *Argus* to Alexandria in Egypt to initiate what would be a successful effort to restore Hamet, an ousted ruler who favored the Americans, to the throne of Tripoli (on the Barbary coast), and to implement negotiations favorable to the United States. After the expulsion of the Napoleon's French forces and withdrawal of British troops that had ousted them, Egypt was nominally back in the hands of the Ottoman Turks. But only the area around Alexandria and Cairo was secure. Elsewhere Albanian janissaries and Mamluk beys acted with impunity. Eaton landed in Alexandria with a Marine lieutenant, Presley Neville O'Bannon, and two midshipmen, George Mann and Eli Danielson, the latter Eaton's stepson. In Alexandria Eaton met the Turkish admiral and the acting English consul, Samuel Briggs, to whom he had a letter of introduction from Sir Alexander Ball, the governor of Malta and from whose firm, Briggs Brothers, he obtained funds and supplies. Then, on December 4, together with representatives of the British consulate, servants, and armed escorts, Eaton and his men proceeded by way of Rosetta to Cairo. There they met the British Consul-General Ernest Missett and the Turkish viceroy Kourschet Ahmet Pasha (or Ahmed Pasha Khorshid). During these meetings, in mid-January 1805, the viceroy presented a saber to Eaton intended as a gift for Isaac Hull, the captain of the *Argus*.

In a letter from Eaton to Hull, dated Rosetta January 14, he reported that "all the gentlemen with me received the same compliment."[7] Negotiations to secure the confidence and support of Hamet of Tripoli were successful, and they met up with him near Alexandria at Damanhur on February 5, 1805. The story of the subsequent epic trek across the desert to Derna, "to the shores of Tripoli," a well-known episode in the history of the United States Marines, has been told many times.[8] In the end, the imprisoned seamen were ransomed. Not until 1815, however, after the conclusion of the War of 1812 with the British, did the Americans inflict decisive damage on the Algerians and negotiate a final treaty of peace with the North Africans.

A final note on the sabers presented by the viceroy to the Americans. These were the famous Mamluk swords, around which much legend has developed. The story that Hamet presented one to Presley O'Bannon at Derna in gratitude for his services is the one that has become current but is not actually true.[9] The sword associated with O'Bannon which led to the adoption of the Mamluk sword as a military emblem by the United States Marine Corp was fashioned and given to him by the State of Virginia after his return.[10] The original sword presented to him by the viceroy in Egypt is lost. Yet two of the swords presented to the Americans in January 1805 are still extant: the one given to Isaac Hull, owned by a descendant of his brother, is on loan to the USS Constitution Museum in Charlestown, Massachusetts; and the one given to Midshipman George W. Mann is now in the United States Naval Academy Museum in Annapolis.

Merchants in Smyrna and Constantinople

Commercial ventures in the eastern Mediterranean and the Red Sea had begun as early as the later eighteenth century.[11] On December 27, 1796, two brothers, James and Thomas Handasyd Perkins (partners in their own firm), wrote from Boston to their cousin George Perkins in Smyrna. George Perkins, a Loyalist, had left Boston about 1775, just before the American War of Independence, to seek his fortune in Smyrna, joining a community of French, British, and Dutch firms that had been involved in Turkey since the earlier eighteenth century. The Perkins brothers wished to know whether an American brig would be favorably received in that port.[12] The answer must have been positive because in May 1797, the brig *Ann* of Boston was seen at Gibraltar, in from India and bound for Smyrna.[13] Years later, John Lee, member of the Levant Company, wrote to friends recalling that in 1797 he had been the first to cause the American flag to be flown on an American ship in Smyrna, namely on the *Ann* of Boston, under Captain Daniel Sawyer (or Savage), and that she had arrived from Tranquebar (a Danish port on the southeast coast of India) with a cargo of muslins, sugar, pepper, and more.[14] Her appearance in Smyrna may have persuaded Peter Abbott, member of an English family resident in Salonica and associated with the Levant Company, to write that very year to Rufus King, United States minister in London, asking about the possibility of American trade in colonial goods with the Ottoman Empire.[15]

In this same letter, Abbott reported to King that, in 1786 (some ten years before he was writing), a vessel flying the Stars and Stripes flag of the United States had sailed through the Dardanelles and had been welcomed in Constantinople. Abbott's reference to this voyage is confirmed in Thomas Jefferson's correspondence with contacts in Charleston, South Carolina. About April 1, 1789, Edward Rutledge wrote to Jefferson, then United States minister in Paris, wanting to learn prices for rice in Constantinople. He explained that a few years earlier, after the conclusion of the War of Independence in 1783, a member of the Ashby family of Charleston had sent, via Cowes in England, two cargoes of rice to Constantinople and had obtained a fair price. Now he wanted an update. It must have been one of these ships that Peter Abbott had seen or had heard about. Remarkably these two voyages were not even the first. Rutledge prefaced the "Trade with the Turks" section of his letter to Jefferson by saying, "Before the war, a Mr. Brewton . . . sent a vessel under the command of a Captain Carter to Constantinople and sold a Cargo of Rice to considerable advantage."[16] That statement is confirmed by newspaper reports of the day.

Yet there was no follow-up to these rice sales in Constantinople by South Carolina planters. Only with the arrival in Smyrna of the *Ann* in 1797 did American maritime trade with Turkey truly begin and have a prospect of long-term success despite threats of piracy, not only from Barbary corsairs but also from Greeks in the archipelago. Smyrna, the principal Ottoman port, required an official American presence, as Thomas Jefferson recognized. When a Philadelphia widow, Deborah Stewart, wrote to him in early April 1802 asking for help in finding a position for her eldest, twenty-one-year-old son William, who had been a godson of George Washington, Jefferson had found his man. Before the end of the month he nominated William Stewart to be consul in Smyrna, and on April 29 the Senate consented.[17] Stewart reached London in October and by April 1803 he arrived in Smyrna via Constantinople, where he had unsuccessfully sought recognition by the government. Writing to the secretary of state on April 25, 1803, he reported on his lack of status without an ambassador in the capital but also on the far-reaching significance of trade with Turkey.[18] Stewart's tenure was short: The Ottoman porte had not recognized the appointment, and he left in November, designating a British agent in his place.

Nevertheless, with or without consular representation, American traffic in Smyrna was beginning. In 1800, before Stewart's appointment, two ships had called at Smyrna (one of them the *Martha* from Salem discussed below), with cargoes of sugar and coffee; another came in 1801 (though it was lost at sea on the way home). Another came in 1804, a year after he left, and in 1805 at least seven. In 1806, David Offley, member of a Philadelphia firm that had been operating in Smyrna since 1805, arrived as a resident merchant. By now nearly a dozen American brigs a year were trading in Smyrna under the protection of the English Levant Company, exporting currants, figs, raisins, and opium. And now the Perkins brothers, who had made a fortune in the China trade, began to export opium and other goods from Smyrna, though they were never resident there. Constantinople also saw a few American brigs: In 1809 and 1810 four reached the capital.[19]

Trade between American ports and Smyrna, not to mention other Mediterranean ports, was not always straightforward—outward bound from an East Coast port to Smyrna with one cargo, homeward with another. An account of one of the first ships to reach Smyrna, preserved in its log, reveals the potential difficulties of such a voyage. In February 1800, John Derby and Benjamin Pickman of Salem shipped on board the *Martha*, a cargo of coffee and Cuban sugar to be sold in Gibraltar by her captain, John Prince, with orders to proceed to Canton to buy tea. Unable to market the cargo in Gibraltar, Prince sailed to Naples, and then to Leghorn, so as to trade in Genoa once the Austrians had seized the port from the French. But that was not to be: Napoleon's army defeated the Austrians at the Battle of Marengo, and Prince had to take the *Martha* elsewhere. He sailed first to Messina, where he sold a bit of his cargo, and only then eastward to Smyrna, arriving on April 25. He had a letter of introduction to the merchant George Perkins in Smyrna from Thomas Appleton, the US consul in Leghorn. There he sold and bartered his cargo for goat's hair, madder roots, opium, Turkish carpets, and dried fruits, as well as a large quantity of cotton. He was in port until December 30. After learning that the best market for cotton was Marseilles, he headed there, via Barcelona. Indeed, Captain Prince sold the rest of his cotton in Marseilles, and he took on board a variety of French clothes and notions. The *Martha* finally returned to Salem in October 1801. The log of the *Martha* is instructive in revealing the unpredictability of commerce in the region, though not all Mediterranean voyages were as roundabout as its was.[20]

American Merchants in Yemen

In the late eighteenth century, American ships, many from Salem, Massachusetts, began rounding the Cape of Good Hope to seek trading opportunities in India, China, and the East Indies. By the 1790s American ships had reached Calcutta, Bombay, and Madras in India (for rice, textiles, and even an elephant),[21] Canton in China (for tea and silk), and Manila, Batavia (modern Jakarta), and Sumatra (for pepper), often stopping at Île de France (Mauritius), which until seized by the British in 1810 was in French hands. About the same period, around 1800, American brigs began calling at Mocha in southern Yemen on the Red Sea to purchase coffee. The French and British had been conducting comparable business there for decades. Notable, for example, is the early-eighteenth-century account of Jean de La Roque in the region, in which coffee is one of the principal themes.[22] The first American ship to return home with a cargo of coffee from Mocha was the *Recovery*, owned by Elias Hasket Derby and captained by Luther Dana; it arrived in Salem, Massachusetts, in late October 1801, 118 days after leaving from Mocha. Three more Salem brigs were there between 1801 and 1803. In 1804 the number of American ships swelled to more than a dozen, eight of them from Salem. The exploits of one of them, the *America* from Salem, owned by George Crowninshield and captained by his nephew Benjamin, is told in the ship's log. Young Crowninshield arrived in Mocha in late November 1804, where he met the noted British traveler George Annesley (Lord Valentia) who, in his own magisterial account of his travels, mentions Captain Crowninshield and two other American ships in port at the same time.[23] The master of one of the two other ships he calls Captain Bancroft—this was Thomas Bancroft, master of the *Commerce*, also of Salem.[24] Benjamin Crowninshield purchased and loaded on board more than two thousand bales of coffee, left the port on January 21, 1805, and reached Salem on June 17, 1805, having been away nearly twelve months. Instead of off-loading his cargo in Salem, however, he sailed to Rotterdam to sell it there, and then proceeded on a second voyage to Mocha, reaching that port in late December 1805. Many other American ships sold their coffee not in the United States but in Smyrna, after rounding the Cape of Good Hope and sailing into the Mediterranean. That was safer and more expeditious than shipping the coffee overland from Mocha to Smyrna. American trade flourished in Mocha over the next fifteen years.

Alexandria

Trade with Egypt through Alexandria, however, was all but nonexistent. Howard Reed spoke of only one American ship in the first fifteen years of the nineteenth century. This was the brig *Pomona* of Newport which "freighted grain" from Alexandria to Marseilles in 1802. He provides no source for the information, but the phrase "freighted grain" is good nineteenth-century lingo, and American brigs were known to have sailed among western ports such as Alicante in Spain and Marseilles in France between 1797 and 1803. A run from Alexandria to Marseilles is plausible. Reed suggested that hostilities between France and England in the region, in the aftermath of Napoleon's campaign, might have given a vessel from a neutral country an advantage in a market now considered too risky by those who had previously had a monopoly. In addition to the *Pomona*, one other American ship appears in the record. Writing on January 30, 1812, to the Duc de Bassano, a minister in France, the French vice-consul in Alexandria, M. Saint-Marcel, included the information that "Un brigantin américain armé en courses et merchandises achetées à Malte pour compte du Pacha vient de mouiller en ce port."[25] Despite naming neither ship nor captain, Saint-Marcel provides incontrovertible evidence of an American merchantman in Alexandria in the early years of the nineteenth century.

Tourists Only as Far as Sicily

Americans came to southern France, to Italy, and to Sicily in the first two decades of the nineteenth century in search of culture, history, and adventure. They had no thought of proceeding farther east to Greece and Turkey. Sicily with her Greek ruins was as close as they got. Some of these visitors are well known through their letters and diaries; others are merely names, but virtually all were wealthy and could make use of social and diplomatic contacts.

Joel Roberts Poinsett

The twenty-three-year-old Joel Roberts Poinsett of Charleston, South Carolina, went to Paris in the fall of 1801, staying on through that winter and witnessing the reforms of Napoleon, the first consul, after the Peace of Amiens. In 1802 he traveled with an American friend from Paris to Rome, Florence, and Naples, and from Naples to Sicily.[26] There he and his companion landed in Messina, saw the ruins of Taormina, climbed Mt. Etna, went to Syracuse, took a brief trip to Malta and back, and traveled around Sicily visiting Agrigento and Palermo, after which they returned to mainland Italy. In the spring of 1803 Poinsett went on to Switzerland.

Near Coppet, on the shores of Lake Geneva, he was introduced by Robert R. Livingston, American minister in Paris, to the aging Jacques Necker and his daughter Madame de Stael and found himself on one occasion acting as interpreter between Livingston and Necker with the help of his daughter. That one encounter in Switzerland gives an indication of the connections enjoyed by well-placed Americans traveling abroad.

Washington Irving

The twenty-one-year-old Washington Irving set forth from New York in the spring of 1804 for a two-year tour of Europe.[27] He landed in Bordeaux, and traveled via Toulouse, Montpellier, Nîmes, Avignon, Marseilles, and Nice to Genoa. In Nice he met the Bostonian John Lowell (1769–1840), Harvard class of 1793, accompanied by his wife Rebecca, their daughter Rebecca Amory Lowell, and his wife's sister Mary Amory, on their way to Rome, Naples, and Sicily.[28] December 23, 1804, found Irving aboard an American brig, the *Matilda*, leaving Genoa for Sicily. He spent several weeks visiting Messina, Syracuse, and Palermo before crossing back in mid-March 1805 to the mainland, to Naples where he climbed Vesuvius and visited Herculaneum and Pompeii. Not only did he meet officers off American ships of the Mediterranean squadron, but in the space of one month in Sicily and Naples he met six American travelers from Boston, New York, and Virginia. In the shadows, behind Poinsett, Irving, and Lowell, whom we know from their perceptive journals, were clearly many others.

Greece, Turkey, and other regions of the Ottoman Empire were another matter. In the first twenty years of the nineteenth century, no American is recorded as traveling in the Holy Land, and only two are known to have reached Egypt, apart from William Eaton and his fellow naval officers in 1804. Few beyond the crews of American brigs trading at the port of Smyrna ventured to Greece and Turkey, and those who did were intrepid individuals.

Tourists in Greece and Turkey before 1820

Joseph Allen Smith of Charleston

The earliest known nineteenth-century American visitor to Turkey and Greece was the thirty-five-year-old Joseph Allen Smith of Charleston. Smith had gone abroad in 1793, passing through Portugal, Spain, and England to Italy, where he spent several years and where in 1797 François-Xavier Baron Fabre twice painted his portrait, one showing him contemplating the Arno, the other overlooking the Roman Campagna (plate 2).[29] Some years later, in May 1804, he arrived in Constantinople from Russia, Georgia, and Persia. Smith's latest travels were quasi-diplomatic in nature. His older, half-brother was United States minister in Lisbon, and he himself was traveling in Russia in part to explore the possibility of establishing diplomatic relations, meeting senior officials. He even dined with Tsar Alexander. In Constantinople, he stayed with the Russian minister, Count Andrei Italinski. From there, in the summer, he made a trip to Greece (apparently sailing on a Russian ship), to some of the islands, and then to the coast of Asia Minor. He was back in Constantinople in October, where he fell sick and stayed on until April 1805 before returning to Russia. Back in St. Petersburg, Smith arranged to have sent to Thomas Jefferson two publications on chronology in the ancient world, written by Jan Potocki, the Polish traveler and scholar who had visited Egypt in 1784. They were presentation copies to Jefferson, whom Potocki may have met in Paris, and are today in the Library of Congress in Washington, DC.[30] Smith left no detailed accounts of his travels in Russia and the Ottoman Empire; instead, we know the bare outlines of his itinerary and experiences only through a set of letters he wrote to Rufus King, United States minister in London (from 1802 to January 1805)[31] and a letter of April 1805 from Constantinople to the French Consul Louis-François-Sébastien Fauvel in Athens.[32]

When Joseph Allen Smith returned to western Europe, he found his fellow Charlestonian, Joel Poinsett, who had earlier been in France, Italy, and Sicily, intending to make a second trip, this time through Russia and its southeastern provinces and on to the eastern Mediterranean. In October 1806, Smith wrote letters of introduction for Poinsett to contacts he had made in Constantinople, Smyrna, and Athens.[33] Regrettably Poinsett had to abort the final stages of his trip. After visiting St. Petersburg and Moscow and even Baku and then Tiflis in Georgia, war between Russia and the Ottoman porte prevented him from reaching the Mediterranean.[34]

Nicholas Biddle of Philadelphia
In May, June, and July of 1806, the twenty-year-old Nicholas Biddle of Philadelphia, then serving as unpaid secretary to General John Armstrong, the American minister in Paris, traveled all over Greece. He had his portrait rendered in Paris in November 1805, shortly before he set out (plate 3).[35] Biddle arrived from Naples, Sicily, Malta, and Zante, and returned to Paris via Venice and Vienna. In Livadia (near Delphi), before reaching Athens, he met two British travelers who had arrived from Constantinople, Alexander Mackenzie, a recent graduate of Christ Church, Oxford, and his friend, John Palmer, then holder of the chair of Arabic at Cambridge.[36]

In Athens he toured the sites with the English classical scholar Robert Walpole and with Don Giovanni Battista Lusieri, the former agent to the British ambassador to Constantinople, Lord Elgin. He also met and dined several times with Louis-François-Sébastien Fauvel, the French consul, formerly an agent for the late eighteenth-century French ambassador to Constantinople, the comte de Choiseul-Gouffier. Biddle compared Lusieri and Fauvel, the two ambassadorial agents, and found Fauvel the superior man: "There is nothing more agreeable than to converse with a man of sense on a subject which he knows thoroughly. I experience this pleasure many times with Fauvel. An amiable Frenchman of the old school of manner, & perfectly acquainted with this country, which he first saw 25 years ago. . . ." Biddle himself was talented, well read in the classics, and was fascinated by Greek architecture.

Biddle's extensive diary in which he mentioned all of these encounters was not published in full until 1993. Toward the end of it he wrote,

> I shall always remember with pleasure my little tour in Greece. . . . I was tempted to go farther. I had determined on visiting Constantinople, & had dreamed of a still longer journey in Asia. I had many temptations to visit Smyrna, among which the principal was the hope of collecting informa-tion in order to extend our commercial relations in the Levant & in this way being useful to my country. But on the other hand my journey must have an end somewhere & unless I soon prescribe its limits I may wander until I am lost.[37]

John Hurd of Boston

In the spring of 1810 John R. Hurd of Boston was in Constantinople where he saw two of the first commercial brigs from the United States to reach that port, one of them the *Eleanor* of Baltimore. From there he trav-eled to St. Petersburg and reported his sightings to John Quincy Adams, the American minister who had just been appointed to the post the year before.[38] Hurd might have been the American who visited Smyrna from Ephesus in the winter of 1810 and who wrote an unsigned account of the tour published two years later in the Philadelphia periodical *The Port-Folio*, edited by Nicholas Biddle.[39] In any event, whoever the American was, he traveled there within a month or so of the visit to Smyrna and Ephesus by Lord Byron and his companion John Cam Hobhouse, a tour of Greece and Turkey during which Byron began *Childe Harold's Pilgrim-age*, recorded by Hobhouse in his published account and by Byron in letters to family and friends.[40]

The War of 1812

In June 1812 the United States declared war on Great Britain. The issues had been developing for a decade.[41] Foremost were the territorial disputes involving Canada and lands of the Indian tribes in the West, and it is along the borders of the United States and Canada that many of the significant military campaigns were to take place. In addition, and of greater significance for Americans involved in continental and Mediterranean trade, were the complications imposed on Americans by Napoleon's campaign against Great Britain. The British were contesting the right of merchant ships from the United States, a neutral country, to trade with France and were seizing ships on the high seas. At the same time the French, intent on disrupting trade with England, were seizing nominally neutral American ships in ports on the continent. It is estimated that between 1807 and 1812 the British and the French seized some nine hundred American ships. Directly related to Britain's war with France was the impressments of seamen. England, short on seamen owing to her naval campaigns against France, forcibly took seamen suspected of being former British sailors off American ships. After years of negotiation, the American Congress, responding to President Monroe, voted a formal declaration of war.

American shipping in the Mediterranean came to a virtual halt. In 1811 a dozen American ships called at Smyrna; in 1812, before the outbreak of war, another dozen. For the next two decades, not one. One story will illuminate the risks of Mediterranean shipping during the war. The twenty-eight-year-old Samuel Hazard of Philadelphia traveled as supercargo aboard the brig *Agent*, owned by Robert Ralston of Philadelphia and commanded by Captain Samuel Rowe. They sailed on March 14, 1812, before war was declared, bound for Smyrna, reached Gibraltar safely on May 6, and then went on to Malta. The next we know is that a French privateer, the corsair *Esperance*, captured her on June 23 off the Greek island of Serigo (now Kythera) and took her to Crete. Ultimately the *Agent* was released and sailed to Smyrna, where she and her seven-man crew sat out the war for the next three years, port-bound together with the brig *Ann* of Boston. Hazard was not idle. In June 1813 he visited Constantinople, and during his time in the environs of Smyrna, he investigated the wheat crop and collected samples. On one excursion he acquired a "marble foot of a colossal statue of Minerva" which he brought back to Smyrna on horseback. Not until July 6, 1815, did the *Agent*, still under the command of Captain Rowe, leave Smyrna for Philadelphia, with Samuel Hazard as a passenger, in convoy with the brig *Ann*, and escorted by the British frigate *Garland*. Hazard kept a detailed journal of the brig's capture and early days of detention, adding to it, after a hiatus of three years, a brief account of the first days of their homeward voyage from Smyrna. And separately he kept a summary meteorological account of part of the homeward voyage.[42] He presented the colossal marble foot to the Academy of Fine Arts in Philadelphia.

Ralph and Margaret Forbes of Boston
The difficulties of travel for Americans in these years can also be illustrated by the story of Ralph and Margaret Forbes of Salem and Boston who visited the Mediterranean in 1812. He was about thirty-nine, she thirty-seven.[43] Ralph Forbes had gone to Marseilles on business around 1810; in January 1811, his wife had left Boston with their two young boys to join him. Mrs. Forbes was a Perkins, a sister of James and Thomas Handasyd Perkins; James had once owned plantations in Saint-Domingue, both had made a fortune trading in China, and more recently they had entered the Smyrna market, where opium was the principal cargo, through their relative George Perkins. Putting the children in boarding school in Marseilles, Ralph and Margaret Forbes set off on a year-long excursion that took them to Italy, and apparently to the Barbary coast and to Greece and some of the Greek islands. Whether they made it to Smyrna to visit Margaret's cousin is not known. After returning to Marseilles and picking up the boys, they moved to Bordeaux for five months where a third son was born. On the way home in 1813, the British boarded two successive ships they had sought passage on from Bordeaux and Corunna in Spain; they finally eluded the British on the *Leda* from Lisbon to Newport, Rhode Island. Despite the bravado of the Forbes family and their ability to survive repeated capture at sea, the War of 1812 was clearly an inhibiting factor not only for American merchants but also tourists in the region.

By mid-1814, after some two years of war between the British and the Americans, which had severely curtailed commercial and private traffic across the Atlantic, both countries were anxious to end the conflict. Five American commissioners, headed by John Quincy Adams, who was then US minister in St. Petersburg, and their three British counterparts began meeting in Ghent in August 1814. After months of debate they finally negotiated an arrangement returning everything to a status quo ante bellum. The Treaty of Ghent, signed on December 24, 1814, ended the War of 1812, though most Americans did not learn of it until early February 1815. Americans and British were now once again free to travel across the Atlantic.

Edward Everett of Boston

Among the first Americans to take advantage of the peace to travel to Europe were Edward Everett and George Ticknor. They sailed on the Liverpool packet on April 16, 1815, intending to go on to Göttingen in Germany. Ticknor, Dartmouth College class of 1807, had briefly practiced law in Boston and now sought a new career. Everett, class of 1811 at Harvard, had just been appointed professor of Greek literature at Harvard and had been granted leave to study at Göttingen and to travel so as to prepare himself for the position. With them on board the packet were Mr. and Mrs. Samuel G. Perkins and their young son, Stephen H. Perkins, who was under Everett's supervision; also the two young sons of John Quincy Adams, on their way to St. Petersburg to see their father, then United States minister to Russia. On arrival in England they learned that Napoleon had escaped from Elba and was back in Paris, an event that delayed their departure for the continent. During the hundred days' delay they sought individuals who could advise them on a proposed visit to Greece. Among those they saw were Lord Byron and Henry Holland. Byron had been in Greece, Smyrna, and Constantinople in 1809 and 1810, Holland had visited Greece in 1812 and 1813, and from them Everett and Ticknor received letters of introduction to Ali Pasha, the semi-independent ruler of Ioannina in northwest Greece, and to Louis-François-Sébastien Fauvel, the French consul in Athens.[44]

Everett and Ticknor and the Perkins family left England for the Netherlands on June 30, twelve days after the Battle of Waterloo. They went on to Göttingen in early August, 1815, with the young Perkins boy, who was placed in school under Everett's charge. A year later, in 1816, John T. Kirkland, president of Harvard College, offered Ticknor the professorship of French and Spanish languages and literature. After accepting in 1817, he had to give up Greece. Instead, to help prepare himself for that position, he visited Spain in 1818, arriving there with a letter of introduction from Thomas Jefferson to George W. Erving, the American minister in Madrid, which enabled him to move with ease in Spanish society.

Two more Harvard graduates followed Everett to Göttingen, Joseph Green Cogswell, class of 1806, and George Bancroft, class of 1817, and they too considered joining him in Greece. But neither did so. In early 1818, when Everett visited Abbotsford to call on the novelist Walter Scott, his son Charles Scott asked his father for permission to join Everett in Greece but was refused. In the end, Everett teamed up with Theodore Lyman, another Bostonian. Before going they spent several months, from late 1818 to early 1819, in Rome. In February 1819, on the point of leaving Naples for Bari and Otranto and thence to Corfu and mainland Greece, they met the twenty-three-year-old Thomas Handasyd Perkins Jr., who had once been tutored by Everett, and they tried to persuade him to join them. But young Perkins declined, instead taking a cruise on the *Washington*, the flagship of the American squadron, then in Naples, at the invitation of Commodore Isaac Chauncey, his godfather.[45]

After spending April and May in Greece, visiting Ioannina, Meteora, Delphi, Thebes, Athens, Eleusis, Corinth, Argos, Sparta, and other sites, Everett and Lyman crossed the Aegean to Troy and then sailed up the Dardanelles to Constantinople.[46] Years later, in 1858, Everett recalled,

> walking in the delightful garden of the English embassy, I saw a trellis covered with a flowering vine in full bloom. I remarked to the ambassadress, who was present, that if we were not in Constantinople, that trellis would make me think I was at home; the flowers which clothed it so closely resembled those in our gardens. "They ought to do so,"—she replied, "It is the Virginia honeysuckle, which I brought with me from America and planted here."[47]

Her husband, Robert Liston, British ambassador to the Ottoman porte from 1812 to 1820, had served from 1795 to 1800 as minister to the United States.

On their way home, in London, in November 1819, Theodore Lyman, at the urging of Everett, purchased from the firm of Robert Barker and Robert Burford, panorama specialists, a panorama of Athens that had been exhibited in London in 1818. Lyman donated the panorama to Harvard College and it was first shown in Boston in 1821.[48] After returning to Harvard in 1819, Everett commissioned Gilbert Stuart to do a portrait, left unfinished at the artist's death (plate 4).

These early American travelers to Greece and Turkey, at least one looking at diplomatic possibilities, two of them keenly interested in classical antiquity, and others traveling out of curiosity as extensions of their business, provide the background for the earliest American visitors to Egypt. News of their travels circulated back home and would have served as an inspiration to those seeking opportunities to travel in Egypt and the rest of the Near East.

5 | THE EUROPEAN PRESENCE IN EGYPT FROM 1815 TO 1825

The first Americans to reach Egypt in the early decades of the nine-teenth century found a country in which Europeans had long played a role, as diplomats, merchants, scientists, and travelers. It is worth considering the European presence in Egypt in the decade from 1815 to 1825 so as to provide a context for the American experience. Four categories of Europeans of many nationalities, in particular French, British, and Italian, should be cited: first, semipermanent foreign residents who lived in Alexandria and Cairo as diplomats, who came to work for Mehmet Ali's new Egypt, or who came as merchants to engage in overseas business on their own accounts; second, research scientists seeking faunal, floral, and geological specimens as well as Egyptian antiquities; third, British officers and agents traveling via Egypt to and from India; and lastly, and in greatest numbers, tourists, many of whom also collected antiquities.

European Diplomats
As early as the late Middle Ages, the Venetians had established a consular presence in Egypt. By the seventeenth century the French had joined them; in the eighteenth century the British and the Dutch had set up consular offices, and by the decade under discussion, 1815 to 1825, representatives from Prussia, Austria, Russia, Sweden, Sardinia, and Spain, in addition to those countries already mentioned, could be found in Alexandria and Cairo. Principal among the diplomats were the French and British consuls and their assistants. Joseph Roussel was French consul from 1816 to 1819, Alexandre Pillavoine, acting consul from 1819 to 1821, and Bernardino Drovetti from 1821 to 1829. Drovetti had earlier been consul from 1803 to 1815 but had had to step aside with the restoration

of the Bourbon monarchy. Henry Salt, who had spent much time previously in Egypt and Abyssinia, was British consul-general from 1816 until his death in 1827. Peter Lee was consul in Alexandria from 1817 until his death in 1824. Travelers of many nationalities mentioned these diplomats and often received assistance from them.

Europeans Working for the Pasha's Enterprises
In an earlier chapter we drew attention to the scores of French, Italian, and British entrepreneurs who came to Egypt to engage in specific projects related to Mehmet Ali's modernization of the country. By way of example: Pascal Coste, a French engineer, was involved first in the Mahmoudiya canal and then in other projects. In 1817 two Italians, Giuseppe Forni and Giovanni Baffi, became engaged in the manufacture of gunpowder for the pasha's military. The Englishman Charles Brine established a sugar factory at Radamon in Upper Egypt in 1818. At the very end of the period covered, in 1825, the French doctor Antoine-Barthélémy Clot began his decades-long career in Egypt.

European Merchants
Mehmet Ali welcomed international business as conducive to modernizing Egypt. French and British firms predominated. As early as 1804, even before the era of Mehmet Ali, Samuel Briggs and Robert Thurburn were doing business in Alexandria. In 1819 they were joined by John Gliddon, who would become the American consular agent in 1832; he and his family had arrived from Malta. By 1826 eight other British firms were engaged in business in Alexandria. And by 1826 there were an equal number of French firms, but English-speaking visitors rarely mentioned them.

European Collectors and Researchers
Many Europeans saw opportunities to mount scientific expeditions. French, Italian, Prussian, and British explorers collected plants, prospected geologically, and acquired Egyptian antiquities. Snapshot views of the intentions and successes of some of these intrepid explorers will help illustrate the European activity in Egypt in the years preceding the first American experiences there in the nineteenth century.

In 1815, about the time Americans were resuming travel to western Europe after the end of the War of 1812, two scholars went up the Nile. Swen Frederick Lidman (1784–1845) was an orientalist and chaplain attached to the Swedish embassy in Constantinople. Otto Friedrich von Richter (1791–1816), a Baltic nobleman, was acting as his secretary. They stopped at Thebes and collected antiquities before going on to Nubia, where they observed and made extensive drawings and notes on the temples and antiquities.[1]

In September of that same year, the British traveler William John Bankes (1786–1855) set forth on the first of two excursions to Nubia. His companions were Giovanni Finati (a former soldier turned Muslim who was making the first of several excursions up the Nile),[2] Antonio da Costa (his Portuguese servant), an unnamed local interpreter, and François Barthow (the Saint-Domingue-born and naturalized, but now expatriate, American), whom we have mentioned in chapter 3. After studying Egyptian monuments as far south as Philae and Abu Simbel and acquiring some large-scale sculpture at Karnak, they were back in Cairo in mid-December.[3]

In January 1816 Frédéric Cailliaud (1787–1869), a French traveler who had come to Egypt in May 1815, made the first of many trips up the Nile. He was joined by Bernardino Drovetti, who had temporarily lost his position as French consul-general owing to the reestablishment of the Bourbon monarchy, and by Drovetti's interpreter, Joseph Rossignana, a deserter from Napoleon's army. They reached Thebes, Philae, and Wadi Halfa. After returning to Cairo Drovetti recognized Cailliaud's talents and introduced him to Mehmet Ali as an expert mineralogist competent to prospect in Upper Egypt and Sudan.[4]

Two years before Cailliaud had left for his first trip up the Nile, a young French sculptor, Jean-Jacques Rifaud (1786–1852), had arrived in Egypt, reaching Alexandria in January 1814. Bernardino Drovetti befriended him and introduced him to his colleagues, and making the right contacts, Rifaud was engaged to work for more than a year as an architect for the pasha. Then, in September 1816, together with Cailliaud (now on his second trip), Rifaud traveled for the first time to Upper Egypt. There he met Belzoni.

Giovanni Battista Belzoni (1778–1823) had set off for Thebes some months earlier, in June 1816, with his wife Sarah and with his longtime Irish assistant and servant James Curtin.[5] Belzoni was an Italian-born strong man who had performed in the circus in England before coming to Egypt in 1815. After failing to convince Mehmet Ali of the viability of a new water wheel, Belzoni was employed by the British Consul-General Henry Salt to bring downstream a colossal head and torso of a statue lying near what is now known as the Ramesseum at Thebes. By August 1816, Belzoni had moved it to the banks of the river, by the end of the year to Cairo, and by mid-January 1817, the colossus was aboard a ship in Alexandria.[6] Thus began years of feverish collecting undertaken by the British and French consuls-general.

In early 1817 two British naval officers, Charles Leonard Irby (1789–1845) and James Mangles (1786–1867) went up the Nile as far as the second cataract. They passed Dendera on the way up in May, were at Philae in June, and reached Abu Simbel in July. There they met Giovanni Belzoni who was up the Nile again, this time to clear the sand from the temple at Abu Simbel. With him was Henry William Beechey, Henry Salt's secretary. Irby and Mangles joined them for a month helping to oversee the clearing of sand, after which they returned downriver to Thebes to see the ruins there with Belzoni, who knew the site well. The two naval officers then returned to Cairo.[7] Belzoni stayed on at Thebes, and some months later made the momentous discovery in the Valley of the Kings of the tomb of the Egyptian pharaoh Seti I.

In December 1817 Comte Auguste de Forbin (1779–1841), newly appointed director of the Royal Museums in France, arrived in Egypt in the frigate *Cléopâtra* after a Mediterranean tour to collect antiquities.[8] Among those with Forbin was Pierre Prévost (1764–1823), a painter and designer of panoramas who, before he reached Egypt, had made painted sketches of Athens and Jerusalem, later to be enlarged as full-scale panoramas.[9] Also with Forbin was Louis Maurice Adolphe Linant de Bellefonds (1799–1883), a geographer and engineer. They traveled up the Nile in early 1818 visiting the ruins at Thebes and many other sites, and buying antiquities for the Louvre.

Forbin returned to France in April 1818. Prévost, who had added Cairo and Alexandria to his repertoire of sketches for panoramas, went home by way of Constantinople where he completed painted sketches of a fifth panorama. Linant, however, stayed on in Egypt—in fact for virtually the rest of his life, devoting his career to engineering projects including much later the Suez Canal. Linant now accompanied William Bankes on his second trip up the Nile between mid-December 1818 and mid-March 1819.[10] Joining Bankes, in addition to Linant, were Henry Salt, the British consul-general; Henry William Beechey, Salt's secretary and an artist who had been up river the previous year;[11] Jean Nicolas Huyot (1780–1840), an architect who had earlier been traveling in the Mediterranean with the Comte de Forbin;[12] Huyot's assistant, the artist Lachaise; Albert von Sack, a widely traveled Prussian nobleman and naturalist; and Alessandro Ricci, a young surgeon and artist.[13] Along the way they met other European travelers, among them, at Philae, David Baillie and his artist Charles Barry, two of the more than two dozen British travelers known to have been on the Nile that year. At Abu Simbel Huyot copied the hieroglyphs in two cartouches containing the names of pharaohs, which he later showed to Champollion and would prove to be significant in Champollion's decipherment of hieroglyphs.

Albert von Sack, who accompanied Bankes, had come to Egypt with Franz Christian Gau (1790–1854), a German-born, French-educated architect. Gau split with Sack shortly after their arrival in Egypt and made his own voyage up the Nile in 1818 and 1819, where he met the French architect Jean Nicolas Huyot, resulting in a grand folio publication three years later. Soon afterwards Gau became a naturalized French citizen.[14]

During this period the agents of Bernardino Drovetti and Henry Salt were excavating and taking downriver antiquities from Thebes and other sites on the Nile. Salt employed Giovanni Belzoni and Giovanni d'Athanasi (Greek-born excavator and collector).[15] Drovetti employed Jean-Jacques Rifaud, a serious scholar, and two adventurers, the Italian Antonio Lebolo and his French dragoman (interpreter) Joseph Rossignana. In Drovetti's behalf, Rifaud found major statues of pharaohs, Egyptian officials, and deities done in granite and dark stone at several sites at Thebes, principally Karnak. Most of them were purchased in 1824 from Drovetti by King Carlo Felice, Duke of Savoy and King of Sardinia for the collection in Turin that has now become the Museo Egizio. Rifaud carved his name and the date of their discovery, 1818, on more than a half a dozen of these statues.[16]

Among the many visitors to Egypt seen and assisted by Drovetti was the thirty-five year old Piedmontese aristocrat Carlo Vidua[17] who arrived at Alexandria in late December 1819 for a seven-month tour that took him as far south as Aswan. Vidua had been traveling in a private capacity in western Europe and Russia since 1818 and had the time, interest, and funds to do so. While in Egypt he assembled a modest number of small antiquities, including six wood *shabti*s from the tomb of Seti I. Later on Vidua was in a position to help Drovetti sell his important collection to the King of Sardinia.

Not all parties were specifically interested in antiquities. In the early 1820s, three groups of European naturalists explored the country. Christian Gottfried Ehrenberg (1795–1876) and Friedrich Wilhelm Hemprich (1796–1825), who had met in Berlin, came to Egypt in 1820 as two of several experts accompanying Menu von Minutoli (1772–1846), a Prussian army officer sent by the government on a scientific expedition. After a year they separated from Minutoli to conduct their own researches on plants, animals, and insects in the Nile valley, traveling in 1821 and 1822 as far south as Dongola.[18]

In 1822 the German naturalist Edouard Rüppell (1794–1884), accompanied by his colleague Michael Hey, also went up the Nile.[19] A third expedition of naturalists arrived in Alexandria in late 1822 under the direction of the Italian Giambattista Brocchi. They went up the Nile as far as Dendera and a bit beyond before taking a caravan to the Red Sea port of Quseir.[20] In succeeding years they traveled as far south as Sennar.

The British Passage to and from India

The standard way of reaching India from England in the early years of the nineteenth century was by ship around the Cape of Good Hope. The return trip was usually made using the same route, but a few officers went home from Bombay via Egypt and from Alexandria through the straits of Gibraltar. Among the first British officers assigned to India to have left a record of traveling through Egypt was George Augustus Frederick Fitzclarence (1794–1842), the eldest natural son of King William IV and his mistress Dorothy Jordan. He had gone to India in 1815 with the 24th Light Dragoons, and was aide-de-camp to Governor-General Lord Hastings. Fitzclarence arrived at Quseir on the Red Sea coast from Bombay in March 1818, crossed the desert to Thebes, and went down the Nile to Cairo. In the course of his travels he met the British consul Henry Salt and his agent Giovanni Belzoni.[21] The following year Sir Miles Nightingall took the same itinerary with his wife Florentia and two officers, captains John Hanson and Charlton Tucker. From late February to mid-April they crossed the desert from Quseir to Thebes, saw the ruins, and came down the Nile to Cairo and Alexandria.[22] In the next several years other British officers and men engaged in business in India followed the same route out or back, such as Digby Mackworth (1789–1852) of the Bombay 18th Light Dragoons, who arrived at Quseir with fellow officers on Christmas day 1821 and reached Cairo a month later;[23] Major-General Sir John Malcolm, senior British official of Central India, and his cousin John Pasley traveling home to England in January and February 1822;[24] and three British officers who arrived at Quseir with Joseph Moyle Sherer on March 3, 1823.[25] These are a select few who left accounts. Dozens, and then in the next decade, after 1825, hundreds of British officers passed through Egypt every year.

Tourists

In the early nineteenth century tourism was still a relatively new phenomenon. The word *tourist* in fact was only first used in the 1770s and was applied to English trippers in the Lake District and other visitors to the approachable regions of the Alps. In the period from 1810 to 1825 European tourists first visited Egypt. By way of example we can mention first a young French gentleman with diplomatic connections, traveling in 1816; and secondly, an Anglo-Irish family that reached Egypt in 1817 with servants and retainers. Their experiences will help demonstrate the way some European travelers reached Egypt just at the time Americans were first considering going there.

In March 1816, Ambroise Firmin-Didot (1790–1876), a twenty-six-year-old member of a notable French publishing family, eager to see the land of Homer, left Paris after arranging to be attached to the staff of the newly appointed French ambassador to Constantinople, the Marquis de Rivière: That would allow him to obtain the requisite documents to travel in the Ottoman Empire. He and the ambassador's secretary, the vicomte de Marcellus (who four years later would acquire the Venus de Milo for France), sailed with the marquis from Toulon on the frigate *Galatée*. They disembarked at the mouth of the Dardanelles to visit the site of Troy, after which they transferred to another ship for passage to Constantinople, owing to the prohibition against frigates sailing farther. On June 2 they arrived in the city, and on July 8, he and two young scholars whom he had met at the Palais de France, Guillaume Barbie du Bocage and Pierre Caussin de Perceval (who would become a leading orientalist), visited Broussa, across the Sea of Marmora. Then, on July 19, Firmin-Didot sailed for Smyrna, stopping again at Troy and also visiting Pergamon. After adventures in Smyrna he boarded the frigate *Galatée*, now bound for Alexandria with Joseph Roussel, the new French consul-general. From Alexandria on August 28 he went to Rosetta and then up the Nile to Bulaq, the port of Cairo on the Nile, and in Cairo he met the consular officials of many European countries. He declined an offer from Henry Salt, the British consul-general, to travel with him to Upper Egypt, limiting himself to the usual sight-seeing in Cairo. He left Egypt by way of Damietta, a port city in the Delta, and went by sea to Jaffa and Acre and then up to Jerusalem. Moving on to Syria, he called on Lady Hester Stanhope (about whom more in the next chapter) before returning to Constantinople via Cyprus, Rhodes, Halicarnassus in Asia Minor, Lesbos, and Cydonia. This, or a variation of it, was a route that would be followed by countless tourists in succeeding years. Firmin-Didot, among the first French tourists in Egypt, was a privileged traveler but perhaps no more so than many others. After returning to Paris he published, anonymously, a revealing account of his voyage.[26] Soon afterward he became head of the family-run printing firm, Firmin Didot Frères.

In the same year, 1816, the family of an Irish peer embarked on a Mediterranean excursion. This led to what might properly be considered the first party of tourists in Egypt. The Earl of Belmore, his family, his doctor (who kept an account), a tutor, and servants left Southampton on August 21, 1816, on board a 232-ton, fourteen-gun, two-masted schooner, the *Osprey*, manned by a crew of thirty-two. It was originally an American schooner, the *Madison*, taken prize by the British before the start of the War of 1812. They sailed to Gibraltar, Malta, Messina, and Naples, where they wintered for five months. Resuming their cruise in April 1817 they touched at Palermo, the Ionian islands (from where they made inland excursions), Athens, Zea, and Constantinople; and from there to Troy, Paros, Delos, Rhodes, Larnaca in Cyprus, Beirut, and Alexandria, where they arrived about September 7. They made an extended Nile journey reaching Philae on New Year's Day 1818. During their month-long stay at Thebes they were the first tourists to see the tomb of Seti I, just opened by Giovanni Belzoni. Within the ruins at Karnak, on the east bank of the Nile, they conducted their own excavations, helped by the Frenchman Jean-Jacques Rifaud. There they unearthed the remarkable black granite funerary boat of Mutemwia, the principal wife of Tuthmosis IV and mother of Amenhotep III, an object later presented by the Belmores to the British Museum.[27] Leaving Egypt they crossed the desert to Gaza, Jaffa, Jerusalem, and Damascus. They rejoined their ship on June 17 at Tripoli and made for Malta and Naples (where they sold the schooner) and returned home overland.[28] In succeeding years a great number of British tourists visited Egypt and ascended the Nile as far as Thebes or Philae, though few with as many retainers as the Belmore family.

In the decade from 1815 to 1825, there were many other parties of British, French, Italian, and Prussian travelers in Alexandria, Cairo, and the Nile valley. Reports of some of their exploits appeared in newspapers in the United States. The summary accounts in this chapter of the resident diplomats and merchants in Alexandria and Cairo, of travelers to and from India, and of research scientists and tourists on the Nile should help demonstrate the European presence in Egypt in the time when Americans, to whom we will now turn, first came in the nineteenth century.

6 | AMERICANS RETURN TO EGYPT

The Treaty of Ghent, ending the War of 1812, allowed transatlantic routes to be reopened for Americans seeking to visit western Europe. The new peace also gave an opportunity for them to extend their travels to the eastern Mediterranean lands such as Greece and Turkey. The two Bostonians, Edward Everett and Theodore Lyman, mentioned in chapter 4, were among the first to do so, but Egypt was not to be part of their itineraries.

A Gentleman of Boston

The first American tourist to visit Egypt in the nineteenth century was a Boston gentleman, name unknown, who stopped in Alexandria late in 1817, perhaps November, a year and a half before Everett and Lyman reached Greece. He had already been to Melos and Smyrna, traveling in all probability as a passenger on a merchant brig from the United States, and from Smyrna he visited Ephesus. We know that 1817 was the year he traveled because in one of his letters from Smyrna he speaks of the recent death (six weeks before his arrival in Smyrna) of Ciatip Oglou, the local ruler of Smyrna, who was treacherously strangled on orders of the sultan in August of 1817. His letters were published anonymously in New York in 1819 in a tiny book, measuring roughly five by three inches, in which nothing, however, is said about a visit to Egypt.[1] For that we must turn to the original publication of the letters, in serialized form in a newspaper, the *Boston Patriot*, beginning on March 3, 1818. There we read in the heading of the text the information that "the writer unfortunately died by the plague, on his passage from Alexandria, in Egypt, to Constantinople, in a Grecian vessel."

69

Who was he? Some libraries that possess the book identify the author as George Barrell, one of the three persons acknowledged in the introduction to a book by Henry A.S. Dearborn on commerce and navigation in the eastern Mediterranean published in 1819.[2] But that cannot be. Although Barrell was indeed in Smyrna in the early fall of 1817, he did not sail to Alexandria but rather for New York on board the brig *Aid* on October 8, together with William Turnbull, the owner of the vessel, and a fellow Bostonian, Orson Kellogg. Despite shipwreck at Sandy Hook at the entrance to New York harbor and the necessity to swim ashore, Barrell lived well into the nineteenth century, long after the author of these letters is known to have perished of the plague. As to the anonymous gentleman, we can add that he was educated: He speaks of reading Homer, he refers to the eighteenth-century British traveler and antiquarian Richard Pococke, and he writes with knowledge about the ruins of Ephesus. Was he known to any of the Bostonians studying in Göttingen? He has so far eluded identification.

The *Alligator* Episode

In August 1817, two years after Americans had resumed merchant activities in the Mediterranean following the peace ending the War of 1812, the polacre brig *Alligator* of Philadelphia, under Captain Farris, reached Alexandria, about the same time as the anonymous Bostonian.[3] This was perhaps the first American ship to come to Egypt since the brig mentioned in a report by the French consul in 1812. The *Alligator*'s visit and the alarming outbreak of the plague in Alexandria were communicated in an October report from Captain Bartholomew of the brig *Free-ocean* of Philadelphia, an account widely printed in East Coast newspapers in early December.[4] Meanwhile the *Alligator* took on a cargo of barley and sailed for Genoa. By the time it reached that port on October 24, Captain Farris and the first mate had died, after five days of illness. Under a new captain (Lock), the *Alligator* left Genoa about March first and arrived in New York 78 days later in mid-May, where knowledge of her itinerary caused her to be put into quarantine. So great was the fear of the plague that the public health official in charge, Dr. Benjamin de Witt, even brought the matter to the notice of Cadwallader D. Colden, the mayor of New York.[5] This was not an auspicious reopening of American trade in Alexandria, and no brig is known to have visited the port again until 1825.

Cleopatra's Barge

The year 1817 held promise of yet another American presence in Alexandria. In mid-January 1817 two newspapers, the *Boston Evening Gazette* and the *Salem Gazette*, ran a story about the proposed Mediterranean pleasure cruise of George Crowninshield's new ship, *Cleopatra's Barge*. This was the same family that had sent ships to Mocha.

> The elegant equipment of this vessel by Mr. Crowninshield for a voyage of pleasure, as it is an entire novelty in this country, has excited universal curiosity and admiration. . . . Cleopatra's Barge measures about 200 tons, and is modeled after one of the swiftest sailing ships which was ever driven by wind. . . . The intention of Mr. Crowninshield, we understand, is to proceed in the first instance to the Western Islands, thence through the straights of Gibraltar, and following the windings of the left coast of the Mediterranean, will touch at every principal city on the route, which will be, round the island of Sicily, up the gulph of Venice to Trieste, along the coast of Albania and the Morea, through the Grecian archipelago to the Dardanelles; if permitted by the Turkish authorities, he will proceed through the sea of Marmora to Constantinople, thence coasting along the ports of the Black Sea to the sea of Asov; he will return by way of the isle of Cyprus, upon the south side of the Mediterranean stopping at Acre, Jerusalem, and Alexandria, on his way, and sailing by the coast of the Desert to that of the Barbary states.

The newspaper accounts continue the proposed itinerary up the coast of Europe to St. Petersburg. The itinerary of *Cleopatra's Barge* may sound preposterous, but was it? American merchantmen had called at most of the ports listed. Moreover, about this time the Belmore family, whose tour was described in the previous chapter, made an extended tour in the eastern Mediterranean, including Egypt, and went up the Nile as far as Philae.

As for the American venture *Cleopatra's Barge*, George Crowninshield's magnificent hermaphrodite brig (that is, rigged square on the foremast and fore-and-aft on the mainmast), left Salem on March 30, 1817[6] (plate 8). George's brother Benjamin, secretary of the Navy, provided him with three hundred letters of introduction. After stopping in the Azores, the ship visited Tangiers, Gibraltar, Malaga, Cartagena (from where it raced with the frigate *United States* to Port Mahon, home port of the Mediterranean squadron), Barcelona, Marseilles, and by mid-July 1817, Genoa. She was a sensation everywhere, with thousands of visitors coming on board, many of them pilfering anything moveable and concealable. In Genoa, the German astronomer Franz Xaver Freiherr von Zach (Baron von Zach) visited the yacht. In an account published several years later, the Baron stated that it had already visited the archipelago, the

Dardanelles, the coasts of Asia and Africa. But he had misheard. Those were the regions *Cleopatra's Barge* was planning to visit after Genoa; the ship had not yet been eastward of Italy. After leaving Genoa it stopped at Leghorn (so as to visit Florence), Elba (where George purchased a pair of Napoleon's boots), and Civitàvecchia (from where they went to Rome for encounters with members of Napoleon's family). But then, instead of sailing toward Greece, Crowninshield turned westward, reaching Salem on October 3rd. Why did he not continue eastward? Fear of plague? The Belmore party had no qualms. Despite the lack of an explicit reason, there is ample testimony in the record to indicate that George Crowninshield had simply had enough. It was time to go home.

George B. English, Luther Bradish, and George Rapleje

These three accounts, one about a nameless traveler who died, the second about a plagued brig, the third about the unfulfilled cruise of Crownin-shield's *Cleopatra's Barge*, hardly reflect an auspicious return of Americans to Egypt in the early nineteenth century. During the next six years, however, from 1818 to 1823, six more Americans would lead the way to a more promising American encounter with Egypt. They could not have been more different from one another. The first, George Bethune English, a former naval officer with a degree from Harvard College and a background in theology, came as an adventurer. The second, Luther Bradish, a widower and lawyer, was rounding out an economic and diplomatic mission to Turkey with a trip up the Nile. The third, George Rapelje, a wealthy New Yorker, was extending a European grand tour for the fun of it. The other three, Pliny Fisk, Levi Parsons, and Jonas King, discussed in the next chapter, were young New England missionaries: Parsons coming to Alexandria for his health, Fisk escorting his invalid companion, King joining Fisk for a return visit a year later.

George Bethune English
George Bethune English arrived in Egypt in April 1818, less than a year after the ill-fated visit of the anonymous Bostonian. English, also a Bostonian, graduated with the class of 1807 from Harvard College. At first he studied law but then turned to theology. In 1811 he received from Harvard a master's degree in theology, and in 1812 he shared with Edward Everett the Bowdoin prize for his dissertation—a prize established by James Bowdoin. A year later he published a book skeptical of his religion, *The Grounds of Christianity Examined by Comparing the New Testament with the Old*, to which Edward Everett responded in 1814

with a decisive five-hundred-page rebuttal, *A Defense of Christianity against the Work of George B. English*. English replied ineffectively and, out-gunned, he left New England and moved briefly to Kentucky to serve as a tutor for a local family. Yet, once again he changed course and in February 1815 he was appointed a second lieutenant in the Marine Corps. He sailed to Havre from New York in June 1816 on board the US sloop of war *Peacock* as a Marine officer, escorting Albert Gallatin, President James Monroe's new minister to France. English made first lieutenant in April 1817 and served with the Mediterranean squadron, but was granted an extended furlough later that year, leaving his ship in Tunis. From there he went to Constantinople where he learned a little Turkish and subsequently traveled to Smyrna.

We know that he reached Egypt from Smyrna in early 1818 because the French consul-general, Joseph Roussel, included news of his arrival in an official dispatch to France dated April 27.[7] Roussel reported that English had a letter of introduction from the French minister in Constantinople, the Marquis de Rivière, and that he had housed him in Alexandria. Roussel added that English had had an interview with Youssef Boghos, the pasha's secretary, after which he had gone to Cairo. As an aside, Roussel said that "M. Bethune English est un jeune homme qui a des moyens, mais il s'exprime difficilement en français et ne sait que l'anglais." In another letter, two weeks later, Roussel reported that English had presented to the viceroy plans for a chariot with wheels equipped with blades, designed to throw terror and disorder among the enemy. The pasha was content to answer that he would have it studied by his engineers. A month later, on June 9, Roussel again mentioned English saying that he had become a Turk in Cairo, but that, owing to his education, it was not necessity that led him to apostasy. Roussel supposed rather that English wished to travel in the tracks of "Sheik Ibrahim, ce Suisse mort au Caire, il ya a pleusieurs mois," namely John Lewis Burckhardt who had died in Cairo in mid-October 1817. Burckhardt was the Swiss-born, English-trained Arabist who had traveled extensively in the East collecting manuscripts and had been in Egypt from 1814 to 1817. As for English, by early 1819 it had become general knowledge among his friends at home that he had become a Muslim. It is surprising that English had not obtained a letter from Robert Liston, British ambassador to the Ottoman porte from 1812 to 1820, to his counterpart Henry Salt, consul-general in Egypt. Earlier, from 1795 to 1800, Liston had served as minister to the United States and might well have been favorably inclined to lend his support to a visiting American.

According to American newspaper accounts of February 1819, English also proposed, unsuccessfully, his chariot to the Turkish military in Constantinople.[8] In Egypt a prototype was made, but nothing came of it. A footnote to a mid-nineteenth-century cyclopedia biography of Edward Everett, with whom English had had a war of words, states that his "scythe chariot was destroyed by an encounter with a stone wall in Cairo."[9]

In 1820—his whereabouts in 1819 are not reported but probably Turkey—with the help of Henry Salt, the British consul-general in Egypt, English was signed on by Mehmet Ali as an artillery officer to accompany his youngest son, Ismail Pasha, on a military expedition to Nubia. Egypt depended on the region for slaves, and Mehmet Ali had decided to pacify or eliminate the last of the Mamluks who had fled south to that region. By now English had taken the name Muhammad Effendi.

English kept a journal, later published, which opens in early October 1820 at Wadi Halfa on the second cataract where he met up with Ismail Pasha, in charge of the military expedition.[10] In it he reported that two Americans had joined him for the Nubian adventure: "I had with me two soldiers, one Khalil Aga, an American of New York, and the other Achmed Aga, a Swiss by birth but an American by naturalization."

Who was Khalil Aga, an American of New York? No printed source names him, yet at the time, in Alexandria, his true identity was known to the British residents. When Rev. Pliny Fisk arrived in Alexandria in January 1822, bringing with him his dying colleague, Rev. Levi Parsons—their story is told in the next chapter—Peter Lee, the British vice-consul in Alexandria told Fisk who he was, as we can read in Fisk's diary: "Mr. Lee also told of an American Captain, Mr. Donald, who came some years ago in distress, after a shipwreck, —at length became a Turk and also accompanied the army into Upper Egypt."

After a few days at Wadi Halfa, English became afflicted with the debilitating eye disease ophthalmia, which obliged him to remain behind as the Egyptian forces moved south. This caused him to miss the first part of the campaign, which was just as well, as it was horrifyingly cruel with troops wantonly mutilating innocent civilians. After recovering, English traveled south with his fellow Americans. Near Meroe in Sudan, on December 12, 1820, they met two British travelers, George Waddington and Bernard Hanbury, who considered them renegades, that is, Europeans or Americans "turned Turk."[11] Related to Salt's story about the former identity of Khalil Aga traveling with English—he recounted that Donald was a ship's captain—is a conversation reported by Waddington between himself and an acquaintance, an Italian, about American renegades: "One day, at Cairo, I saw pass by two Americans, dressed like common sailors (which they were) in a blue jacket and trowsers; and then, for eight or ten days, I saw no more of them. After that interval, I observed them again, dressed in red, with a white turban on . . . they have made Turks of themselves."

Continuing up the Nile above Meroe, English caught up with Ismail Pasha after a few days and obtained an audience with him in which he requested horses, camels, and the men of his contingent. After nine days, without honoring English's requests, Ismail Pasha moved on upstream on land following the course of the Nile. Lack of animals obliged English and his companions to proceed by boat upriver. A second, more positive interview with the pasha resulted in an invitation to accompany him over the desert to shorten the trek and to avoid the fourth and fifth cataracts. He was also furnished with two camels to retrieve his effects from his boat. One of them collapsed, however, apparently unable to carry a stone block with a Greek inscription that Khalil Aga had found for English in the ruins of a monastery on an island in the third cataract. In any event, English now joined Ismail Pasha overland while his two fellow Americans were to take the longer route along the course of the river. On May 24, 1821, English reached Halfa, near the future site of Khartoum, and on June 14 he and his contingent reached Sennar.

In the preface to his book, English writes that Domenico Frediani, Frédéric Cailliaud, and Pierre Constant Letorzec (whom he calls "Mr. Frediani, an Italian, and Messrs. Cailliaud and Constant") accompanied their camp to Sennar. Mehmet Ali had been persuaded by the French consul-general, Drovetti, to take Cailliaud, a mineralogist, to scout the likelihood of gold deposits.[12] Cailliaud also kept a diary, published in four volumes in 1826, much more expansive, with more detailed information on the natural history of the region and on Egyptian antiquities than can be found in English's account which, though not neglecting the monuments, is more devoted to anthropological observations of the people living along the Nile.[13]

Only one of the two American companions of English reached Sennar. English said that "Achmed Aga died on the Third Cataract, . . . of poison given him by a Greek in consequence of a quarrel." [It was actually the fourth cataract, not the third.] The culprit was a Smyrniot Greek (or Armenian), Dimitrio Botzaris, traveling with the Egyptian troops and the *protomedico* of Ismail Pasha. He seems to have been responsible for more than just the American's death, an event of which Cailliaud was also aware. Cailliaud reported in his own account that "Ibrahim perdit son premier médicin, qui mourut d'une fièvre inflamotoire: il était Génois, et se nommait Scot. Le pharmacien de ce prince eut plus tard le meme sort. Un Americain avait précédemment succombé. Le mort semblait vouloir tout moissonner autour de moi; déja six Européens n'existaient plus."[14] This was Cailliaud's only mention of an American. Nowhere does he name English. The Genoese doctor was Antonio Scotto. The pharmacist was Dr. Andrea Gentile, to whom Botzaris had owed a large sum.

After having reached Sennar, English himself was not in great health. Within a few days he requested permission from Ismail Pasha to return to Cairo, and after some hesitation he was allowed to leave. By summer's end English had returned to Lower Egypt where he and his companion Khalil Aga took refuge with Henry Salt, the British consul-general, to regain their health. September 21, 1821, found English traveling from Alexandria to Cairo on a canal boat with the eccentric but learned missionary Joseph Wolff (about whom more in a later chapter) with whom he had a long theological discussion. English stayed on in Egypt for several months, finally leaving for Malta on April 1, 1822, on board the brig *Dispatch*, Captain John Finley, in company with an American missionary, Pliny Fisk (whose journey in Egypt is described in the next chapter).

Khalil Aga, the former Captain Donald of New York, who seems to have remained in Egypt for many years, did not quite disappear from the record. Ten years later the American zoologist and medical doctor James E. DeKay, who had traveled with his brother Captain George DeKay to Constantinople in 1831 on board the corvette of his father-in-law, Henry Eckford (commissioned as ship builder for the sultan), heard that Khalil Aga was alive. DeKay wrote in the account of his Turkish experiences that "he is still in Egypt, where, I heard, that he is distinguished for his courage and good conduct."[15] But there is no mention as to how DeKay received this intelligence.

When English returned to Cairo, he showed his manuscript journal to Salt. And from a letter that Salt wrote a year later on September 22, 1822, to William Martin Leake, the topographer of Greece (who had actually been in Egypt in 1801), we learn, in Salt's own words: "I have forwarded the journal of an American, who travelled as a Mahomedan under the name of Muhammad Effendi, to Mr. Bankes, through Mr. Hamilton of the Foreign Office, which contains some interesting remarks, as far as Sennaar."[16] Complementing Salt's letter is one that English wrote to his father from Malta, on April 16, recalling first of all that he had last written him in June of 1820 before leaving for his expedition, and then proudly announcing that his journal had been sent to London for publication.[17]

The account of English's Nile exploits, *A Narrative of the Expedition to Dongola and Sennaar*, was indeed published in London in 1822, though with no indication of his authorship; instead, "by an American in the service of the Viceroy." Following the title page was a statement reading, "To His Britannic Majesty's Consul General in Egypt, Henry Salt Esq. my fatherly friend in a foreign land, this work is dedicated, with affectionate respect, by the author: and recommended to the kind care and patronage of John William Bankes, Esq. by his obliged friend and servant, Henry Salt." This would confirm that Salt had entrusted the manuscript (through Hamilton, he says) to Bankes. In the American edition, published one year later in 1823, English is named on the title page and mention of Bankes is omitted on the dedication page.

If we continue reading Salt's 1822 letter to Leake, we learn, in addition, "and I have also the journal of an American seaman, which I bought for about thirty pounds, who kept the course of the river all the way to Sennar. This I shall likewise soon be able to send to Mr. Bankes." He seems not to have done so. At any rate it was never published. It remained with Salt's papers, and was only recently discovered by Cassandra Vivian among his papers in the British Library.[18] The whole diary, clearly kept by the American who called himself Khalil Aga, covers the period August 26, 1820 to August 23, 1821. The account of the passage up the Nile through the fourth and fifth cataracts, which excited Salt, runs from February 21 to April 29.

After English returned to Boston, he wrote in January 1823 to Bernardino Drovetti, who had succeeded Roussel as French consul-general in Egypt. He said that he was still owed 2,200 piastres for his services to the pasha (withheld perhaps because he was absent from so much of the campaign), which he requested be deposited with Mr. Lee (Peter Lee, the British vice-consul in Alexandria).[19]

That was not the end of his Mediterranean career; English twice returned to the region. On the first return visit he left the United States in the fall of 1823 and arrived in Constantinople in early November with instructions from Secretary of State John Quincy Adams to sound out the Turkish authorities with respect to a commercial treaty. He left the city without achieving any results on February 1, 1824, and returned to the United States via Smyrna on the brig *Herald* at the end of April. On his second return visit, in the summer of 1826, he went as an interpreter for Commodore Rodgers on board the USS *North Carolina*, but once again, despite high-level conversations, no positive response was received from Constantinople. Back home English fell out of favor with Adams, and died in 1828.

Opinion is divided as to whether English truly adopted Islam, or did so only as an expedient. The French consul-general Roussel was of the latter opinion. And in fact one of his obituaries stated that "the charge of having turned Turk, which was generally spread abroad in this country and in Europe, he constantly denied."[20] More interesting to contemplate was his eccentric career. It is possible that he dreamed at an early age of adventure abroad even though he first studied in law and divinity. One friend said he displayed a Turkish scimitar in his Harvard College room. He told Joseph Wolff, whom he met on the Nile boat, that at college Voltaire was an influence. Years later, in 1865, George Ticknor, professor of French and Spanish languages and literature at Harvard in the 1820s and '30s, gave an appraisal of his merits and character during a eulogy for his recently deceased colleague Edward Everett, whose theological sparring with English in the late teens he was recalling:

> (George B. English), whom I knew personally, was a young man of very pleasant intercourse, and a great lover of books, of which he had read many, but with little order or well-defined purpose. He would, I think, have been a man of letters, if such a path had been open to him. A profession, however, was needful. He studied law, but became dissatisfied with it. He studied divinity, but was never easy in his course. His mind was never well balanced, or well settled on anything. He was always an adventurer, —just so much so in the scholarlike period of his life, as he was afterwards when he served under Ismail Pasha in Egypt, and attempted to revive the ancient war-chariot armed with scythes.[21]

Luther Bradish

In 1820, prior to the efforts of English in 1823 and 1824 to sound out economic possibilities with Constantinople and the commercial negotiations of Commodore Rodgers in 1826, President James Monroe had sent the thirty-eight-year-old New York lawyer Luther Bradish abroad on a similar scouting mission. Bradish, class of 1804 at Williams College in Massachusetts, was already a man of the world. After taking a law degree from Williams and briefly practicing in New York City, he traveled to the West Indies, South America, and Great Britain, returning to New York to serve as a volunteer in the War of 1812. In 1814 he married Helen Elizabeth Gibbs, daughter of Colonel George Gibbs, a friend of the novelist J. Fenimore Cooper whom Bradish also knew and would continue to know as a lifelong friend and correspondent.[22] Then, two years later, tragedy struck: In 1816, his wife and their child died.

During the next few years he sought to learn about commerce in the Mediterranean. He left the United States in late April 1820 on the USS *Columbus* furnished with a special passport and a second document, appointing him "agent for collecting such information in foreign countries, in relation to the commerce of the United States, as may prove useful and interesting to them," both signed by John Quincy Adams, secretary of state. After a preliminary cruise around the western Mediterranean with the Mediterranean squadron, Bradish arrived in Smyrna in October 1820 with the Bostonian Charles Folsom (Commodore William Bainbridge's private secretary) on board the USS *Spark*. They met with David Offley, the Philadelphia merchant and representative there, and then Bradish went on alone overland to Constantinople where he arrived October 23. On December 20 he wrote a lengthy letter to Adams expressing how chagrined he was that word of his secret mission had preceded him and then providing in some detail what might be involved in achieving a commercial treaty. Yet nothing came of the negotiations, in part because of the rebellion of the Greeks against the Ottoman Empire but more importantly owing to the opposition of European ministers to a United States diplomatic presence in Turkey.

Bradish left Constantinople in February bound for Alexandria and Cairo and furnished with letters of introduction, intending to keep his eyes open politically, but also acting as a tourist. He was seen at the Pyramids by Gawen William Hamilton, captain of HMS *Cambrian*, who reported this to the American missionary Pliny Fisk in Smyrna some months later. In fact Bradish carved his name on top of the Great Pyramid where it was still visible fifteen years later. We know that he visited Thebes because the French antiquarian Jean-Jacques Rifaud reported seeing him there. While on the Nile, probably between April and June 1821, he observed the French agent Jean-Baptiste Lelorrain cutting the celebrated "Zodiac of Dendera" out of the temple where Denon and other savants had made measured drawings of it twenty years earlier. Despite Lelorrain's apprehension that Bradish would report his surreptitious work to the authorities, he managed to get it loaded on a barge, sent downstream to Alexandria, and by July onto a ship bound for Marseilles. Within two years, an account of its removal and transfer to France circulated in an American periodical.[23] The zodiac, first installed in the Bibliothèque nationale in Paris, was transferred to the Louvre in 1919 and is now mounted on the ceiling in a quiet annex off the main Egyptian galleries, where a visitor can contemplate it without distraction.

Leaving Egypt, Bradish went across Sinai to Palestine. In Jerusalem he stayed at the Catholic convent and then, traveling to Syria, visited Lady

Hester Stanhope for two days, the first American to do so. We know this principally from stories told to Pliny Fisk, an American missionary in Smyrna, where Bradish stayed for more than a week in early September after leaving Syria. Lady Hester was the eldest child of the third Earl Stanhope and a niece and close friend of William Pitt, who as prime minister was unmarried and welcomed her presence as a hostess. In 1810, leaving England with her doctor Charles Meryon, her lover Michael Bruce, and a maid Anne Fry, and furnished with a handsome pension awarded her by her uncle William Pitt on his death in 1806, she traveled over the next several years to Athens (where she met Byron), Constantinople, Cairo, Jerusalem, and Damascus. In 1814 Michael went home and she settled with her doctor and a servant near Sidon. Meryon left in 1817, and his place was taken by Dr. Newberry (for only a year) and a former servant Elizabeth Williams.[24] About the time that Bradish saw her, in the summer of 1821, she was moving, or had just moved, from her first residence at Mar Elias to a more remote but splendid house in Djoun, where she would spend the rest of her life. As Pliny Fisk put it in his diary over a period of several days from September 8 to 11:

> When Mr. Bradish reached Saide he determined not to visit Lady Stanhope. Her residence is near Saide. At 12 o'clock at night a messenger arrived from her with a letter for Mr. Bradish from Lady Stanhope inviting him to visit her. He went and spent two days with her. . . . Lady Stanhope's residence is 1 ½ hours from Saide, & 5 hours from Beiroot. She has one female servant who came with her from England—a French secretary and French physician. Her other servants are Arabs. She has about 30 servants with her and perhaps 2 or 300 others in her employment. . . . She has travelled much, was in the plains of Palmyra in the time of a revolution there and was crowned Queen of Palmyra by one tribe of Arabs.[25]

If only we had Bradish's own account of his visit rather than knowing it second-hand from other sources. In any event several other Americans would visit Lady Hester Stanhope in succeeding years, some leaving fascinating accounts. From Syria, Bradish went to Smyrna and there, on September 3, he met the American missionary Pliny Fisk, who gave an account in his own journal, of the visit to Lady Hester Stanhope, and in addition highly entertaining and instructive facts and hints that Bradish gave about Egypt. On September 10, while in Smyrna, Bradish wrote to Richard McCall, United States consul in Barcelona from 1816 to 1825: "My letters to my friend Gouverneur[26] written from Gibraltar, Italy, Sicily, Constantinople, Egypt, and Palestine will have kept you pretty well informed of my rambles." Then, after recounting the conflict between Turks and Greeks and the potential diplomacy of the Russians, the British, and the Sublime Porte, he added

> I ascended the Nile thro' upper Egypt, Nubia until I passed the 2nd great cataract. It was not until my return to lower Egypt that I received intelligence of the altered state of things. This with the existence of the Plague along the Sea Coast from Alexandria to the eastern part of the Delta decided me to attempt to pass the Desert of Arabia by the Red Sea to Judea and Palestine. I therefore sent for the principal Sheiks of 12 of the Tribes of Bedouin Arabs of the Desert who contracted to take me safely thro' [the desert]. He and 3 other Sheiks with their families remained with the Vice Roy of Egypt, all of whose heads were to be taken off in case of any ill treatment to myself. Upon this engagement I departed from Cairo accompanied by an officer of the Vice Roy of Egypt, an Arab Sheik and 3 men of different tribes of the Bedouin . . . thus attended I entered the Desert.[27]

On September 16, Bradish left Smyrna for Constantinople and from there returned overland to Europe. He traveled extensively, to Vienna, Venice, Rome (for eight months), Scandinavia, St. Petersburg, and also spent much time in Paris. The American novelist Washington Irving, who had known him years before in New York, saw him on repeated occasions in Paris between August 1823 and August 1825, and Bradish is known to have attended the Fourth of July celebrations in Paris in 1823 and 1824.[28]

When Bradish returned to New York in early December 1825, he had been away more than five years. Back home he became a prominent New Yorker, served as lieutenant governor of the state from 1838 to 1840, and remarried in 1839, at which time he commissioned from his second cousin Alvah Bradish a portrait of his wife and himself (plate 27). In 1850 he became president of the New-York Historical Society, and during his tenure the society acquired the Egyptian antiquities assembled by the British "doctor" Henry Abbott in Cairo (see chapter 19).

Bradish had a companion during his travels in Egypt and adjacent regions, though he says nothing of him in what remains of his correspondence. A clue is given in an 1823 entry in the journal of an American mission, Rev. William Goodell. Goodell's original journals for his first years of missionary work in the East and Constantinople were destroyed in the fire that swept Pera in August 1831, but excerpts had already been published in *The Missionary Herald*. For the date November 14, 1823, we read: "Left Cyprus at seven o'clock this evening. As fellow-passengers, we now have one Turk, two Greeks, an Englishman who traveled in Egypt with our countryman Mr. Bradish, and two Armenians, a bishop and a priest, going with their servants to Jerusalem."[29] But Goodell fails to name him. The answer is given in Sarah Haight's 1840 account of the eastern tour she made with her husband Richard K. Haight in 1836. Reaching Beirut after leaving Egypt, they met the American consul there, Jasper Chasseaud, who reported that he had accompanied Bradish throughout the East.[30] Sarah Haight calls him a Greek from Salonica, but in fact he was a member of the extended Abbott and Chasseaud families, of English and French background, who had been engaged in business in Salonica since the late eighteenth century.[31] His uncle was Peter Abbott, British consul in Beirut since 1820; his mother was Mary Abbott. Peter and Mary were children of Jasper Abbott and Kiriaki Athanassi, hence Chasseaud's name—and Sarah Haight's notion that he was a Greek. Confirmation that Chasseaud traveled with Bradish is provided by graffiti on Egyptian monuments in the Nile valley, on the Ramesseum at Thebes, at Dendur, at Gabal al-Silsila, and at Abu Simbel, in which their names occur near one another with the date 1821. And if that were not enough, Pliny Fisk reported in his diary that when Bradish arrived in Smyrna in early September 1821, he was with "Mr. Chasseaud, the young man who traveled with him. In 1837, a year after the Haights saw him, Chasseaud wrote to Bradish seeking help in securing better compensation for his work as American consul and enquiring about the possibility of becoming a naturalized American.[32] In a postscript he added, "whenever I see Lady Hester Lucy Stanhope she always inquires very kindly after you." Some day we may discover Bradish's own account of his conversations with the Queen of the East.

George Rapelje

The third traveler in Egypt in this period, George Rapelje, spent five weeks in Alexandria and Cairo in April and May 1822 as a true tourist. Rapelje, a wealthy and well-connected lawyer and landowner, was a member of one of the oldest Dutch families in New York, his forebear Joris Rapalje (as the name was then spelled) having come to Manhattan in 1626.[33] Born in 1771, he was class of 1791 at Columbia College. He had traveled to the West Indies in 1793 and had visited England from 1795 to 1796. In 1798 he had married Eliza, a daughter of the Rt. Rev. Samuel Provoost, then Episcopal bishop of New York State, but they had no children. His wife's younger sister was married to Cadwallader D. Colden, who served as mayor of New York City from 1818 to 1821. Rapelje himself held no public office, perhaps owing to the eccentricity of his character.

In mid-March 1821, aged fifty, after advertising his country house in Pelham on Long Island Sound on long-term lease and leaving his wife in New York City, Rapelje went abroad for an extended European tour. He sailed on the *Albion*, a 400-ton packet built two years earlier. It was one of five ships then composing the Black Ball Line, the first line to offer scheduled service between New York and Liverpool, the very first run of which had been made by the *James Monroe* only two years earlier, in January 1818. This sailing occurred within three years of news of the Treaty of Ghent, ending the War of 1812, which allowed transatlantic passenger and freight service to be revived. Competitors soon joined the Black Ball Line. It is likely that the well-advertised luxuriousness of these new packets, scheduled "to sail on their appointed dates, full or not full," was one of the inducements for Rapelje to go abroad. The fare was forty guineas. Sailing with him on the *Albion* was a Mr. Haight from New York, namely the twenty-four-year-old Richard K. Haight who ultimately, fifteen years later in 1836, but not on this trip, would also visit Egypt. Rapelje and Haight traveled together through England, France, the Netherlands, Prussia, Switzerland, and Italy.

Parting from Haight in Italy, Rapelje left Naples for Messina and Malta in early January 1822, and in Malta he conceived of a plan to extend his tour to the East. From February to April 1822 he sailed through the Greek islands, stopping at Constantinople and Smyrna before reaching Alexandria. While in Egypt, and in fact, throughout his travels, Rapelje filled, or rather, overwhelmed his diary, which became a published account, with gossip about the British residents and travelers he met along the way.[34]

One of the travelers Rapelje encountered in Egypt was the Englishman John Madox, who in his own book described him as "an eccentric and curious man; his greatest delight seemed to be travelling with dispatches, dashing at everything, and running all chances, thereby sometimes getting into difficulties, which might have been easily avoided. The Turks, I think, once seized him and tied him to a tree."[35]

With Madox (whose name Rapelje spells as Maddox) George Rapelje saw many of the sights of Alexandria, and he is one of the first Americans to offer descriptions of the notable antiquities visible there, in particular Pompey's Pillar and Cleopatra's Needles. His diary for April 11 reads:

> I went with Mr. Maddox and visited the old city ruins, and saw Cleopatra's Needles, one standing, the other having fallen down by it, and it is very remarkable that it was not broken. The English were going to take it to London; but in my opinion, they will never be able to move it, being so

large. It is sixty-six feet long and seven feet square, and to appearance, solid red marble, covered on each square with Oriental, Egyptian, or other hieroglyphics from bottom to top; consisting of eagles, cows, owls and other unintelligible figures to which, I heard a key had lately been found, for the explication of all the Egyptian characters.

The two obelisks, both of red granite, had originally been set up about 1468 BC for the pharaoh Tuthmosis III at a temple in Heliopolis, a district now within modern Cairo, but in the nineteenth century well outside the city. They had been moved to Alexandria under the Roman Emperor Augustus in 10 BC to stand in front of the Caesareum, the temple of the deified Julius Caesar. They had nothing to do with Cleopatra but had acquired that name long before the nineteenth century. The fallen one was moved to the Thames embankment in London in 1877, the standing one to Central Park in New York City a few years later.[36]
Rapelje continued his tour of the city with Madox:

> We then went to the magnificent column long known as Pompey's pillar, which is seen from almost every part of Alexandria, and even approaching from the ocean, it is the first object which attracts the eye of the mariners. . . . It is the most beautiful piece of architecture I have seen; the propor- tion according to the most perfect science of the ancients; but at this day it would be thought bad taste to have so small a base. The proportions to an architect, I would venture to say are most exquisite; the inscription on it is illegible or unintelligible, notwithstanding what may be said to the contrary by antiquarians who spent a whole day to find our one character, which is said to compose the word Dioclesian.[37]

"Pompey's Pillar" is a monolithic column of red granite, more than 30 meters (98 feet) tall with a diameter of 2.70 meters (9 feet) at the base and an estimated weight of 285 tons. On top is a huge Corinthian capital. The name of Pompey was given it by early travelers seeking to link what they knew of Alexandrian history with its surviving monuments. During the Roman civil wars in the first century BC Pompey had fled to Alexandria after his defeat by Julius Caesar at the Battle of Pharsalus in Thessaly (Greece). Reality is different. A Greek inscription, barely visible on the base, first noticed in the mid-eighteenth century but only read more or less properly about twenty years before Rapelje's visit, records that the column was set up in a year equivalent to AD 291 and was dedi- cated by Publius, the prefect of Egypt, to the emperor Diocletian who had recaptured the city after a revolt. Holes on top of the Corinthian capital combined with an image of the monument on a Roman mosaic show conclusively that it once supported a statue of the emperor.[38]

Sailors off merchant ships, bringing ashore the right equipment, had successfully ascended the column since the later eighteenth century, as an illustration in the account of the British traveler Edward Daniel Clarke reveals.[39] The view published by Clarke, who was in Egypt in 1801, was taken from a watercolor made by the French antiquarian Louis-François-Sébastien Fauvel in 1789.[40] Fauvel watched sailors ascending the column. A kite was launched and once the kite's string was maneuvered over the top of the capital, the string was used to pull up a stout rope, and then the adventurous could climb the rope. Fauvel himself made the ascent. In 1798, some of Napoleon's savants had also reached the top. In the early nineteenth century, British naval officers continued to take up the challenge, and a week before Rapelje arrived in Alexandria, Captain Henry Smith of the English sloop of war *Adventure* had done exactly that. Other visitors complained that the officers would deface the column by painting their names and the names of their ships on the shaft in huge black letters.

In Alexandria, on April 17, Rapelje and Madox visited a warehouse where they saw some twelve mummies recently brought downriver from Thebes. Rapelje admired the freshness of the paintings on the wooden cases, and after a representative of the French consulate opened some of them for their inspection, he was struck by the strings of blue beads on one of the linen-wrapped mummies, specifically the network of blue faience beads, of exactly the sort covering some of the mummies of the late period that the museum in Leiden acquired from the Anastasi collection in 1828.[41] The two men learned that the mummies were to be exported to Trieste for sale, and could be had for between thirty and fifty dollars.

One day Rapelje had an interview with the pasha in the company of two Englishmen.

Mr. Sherman called on me, this morning, at seven o'clock, to go and see the Pacha of Egypt. Mr. Burton accompanied us. The latter gentleman being here by the Pacha's desire, as chemist, mineralogist, and botanist to his highness. We went to the palace along the sea, or bay shore, when we were in a few minutes ushered into the Audience Chamber, first passing through a large outer apartment. He sat at the upper end, near the corner of the chamber, and I suppose, cross-legged. His large cloth cloak, however, concealed or covered his legs and feet. He wore a large, beautiful, variegated, camel's hair turban; had a long beard, and mustochios, rather gray. He appeared about fifty, or more, and was smoking an immense long pipe, at least seven and a half feet long. The pipe was, indeed, a curiosity, adorned with silk, having two large silk tassels, hanging from the top part, a foot from the mouth-piece, and run down to about two feet from the bowl, which was highly gilt. The stem appeared to be set around with two or three rows of diamonds, and the bowl was resting on a silver saucer, about six or eight inches in diameter, on the floor. By his side there was an elegant green necklace of beads, of emerald; it lay on the broad sofa, together with a large precious stone snuff-box; a large handsome spy-glass, in order to see the ships coming in, or going out of the harbor.[42]

And Rapelje continued to describe the audience chamber and a bit of his conversation, through interpreters, in which he spoke about the lack of consular representation. They departed after sipping small cups of coffee.

At the end of his stay, on April 21, Rapelje took a boat, a *canjiah*, to proceed along the Mahmoudiya canal from Alexandria to Cairo. This was the canal that had been completed only two years earlier by hundreds of thousands of men under the authority of Mehmet Ali. Rapelje went in convoy with the Englishman James Burton, with whom he had seen the pasha. Burton had his own, larger *canjiah*, and two young men as companions.[43] The group stopped to admire Lake Mariout and farther along Lake Moeris, the shore of which was encrusted with salt. In the early evening the wind increased to such an extent that it capsized Burton's boat, and three others in the convoy, but spared Rapelje's boat, the crew of which, letting the sail fly, maneuvered it to the bank safely. Burton and his men were rescued but his supplies and papers sank. During the night, however, his attendants, who had been assigned by the pasha, retrieved his chests, as well as a thousand dollars in silver. Here was firsthand evidence of sudden winds, the principal problem of navigating the canal for the unwary boatman. Proceeding without further mishap they reached Atfih, the port on the Nile, and then went upriver to Bulaq, the port of Cairo.

In Cairo, on April 29, with another visitor to Egypt, Capt. Robert James Gordon of the Royal Navy, Rapelje set out to visit the Pyramids. Crossing the river, they stopped on the island of Roda intending to see the Nilometer, but lacking a permit were denied entry, the reason almost certainly being the immediate proximity of the gunpowder factory built just a few years earlier. Reaching the Pyramids, Rapelje did not ascend. Gordon invited him to accompany him to Thebes, but he declined because the weather was too hot. Captain Gordon, himself, left for Sudan, commissioned by the British African Association to find the source of the White Nile, but while near Sennar in September 1822, he died of fever.[44]

Rapelje left Cairo on May 7 and traveled overland to Gaza and to Jerusalem. From Jaffa he sailed to Beirut; on board, the eccentric English missionary Joseph Wolff encountered him. Rapelje did not relate their encounter but Wolff did so, to John W. Hamersley, an American he met years later in Malta. As Hamerlsey told the story in his diary, Wolff said that Mr. R. threw off all his clothes and paced the deck. Mr. W. expostulated with him. "I am a free and independent citizen of the United States," was the reply. "But," says Mr. W., "do the Americans walk about without their breeches?" Mr. R. would take out the picture of his wife and apostrophize it: "O, thou pattern of excellence, O, thou perfection of beauty." Who was more eccentric, Wolff or Rapelje?

In Beirut, on June 11, he "went to see the English consul, Mr. Abbott, who resided there. He had a daughter about eleven years old, and an Italian governess for her; his wife being dead." A succession of American visitors would receive the hospitality of Peter Abbott, consul since 1820 and now aged nearly fifty, and who in time would marry his Italian governess. Charles Colville Frankland of the Royal Navy, meeting Abbott four years later in August of 1827, found him married to an "interesting young Italian."[45] In fact Julia, Abbott's first daughter with his second wife, was born that very year. Rapelje also called on Lady Hester Stanhope, the second American to do so after the visit of Luther Bradish the year before, and heard her tales about her horses. Rapelje saw her companion and secretary Elizabeth Williams.

Rapelje returned by ship via Alexandria to Malta where in August 1822 he met Pliny Fisk and Daniel Temple, missionaries from Boston. In Malta, Rapelje picked up a ship to England. He arrived home in New York on December 11 on the *Cortes*, a packet belonging to another of the newly established transatlantic lines. Richard K. Haight, his traveling companion in Europe, reached New York on the previous run of the same ship, on August 5. The *Albion*, the packet they had shared on their outbound voyage from New York to Liverpool nearly a year and a half earlier; had been wrecked off the coast of Ireland in April 1822, with the loss of all the crew and all but one of the twenty-three cabin passengers.[46] "Floating palaces," the packets were called, and Neptune usually smiled on their crossings, yet over the years others besides the *Albion* were lost.

More than a decade passed before George Rapelje published the account of his travels, which gives us the first nineteenth-century account of an American in Alexandria and Cairo. He died a year after the book appeared, in 1835, leaving a million-dollar estate.

Egyptian Mummies

Rapelje's description of mummies recalls the stories of the first Egyptian mummies to reach the United States. In February 1823, less than a year after his visit to the mummy warehouse in Alexandria, the Smyrna firm of Jacob Van Lennep and Co. arranged to send to Boston on board the American brig *Sally Anne* a mummy with its painted wood case, shipped under the rubric *Egyptian Gum* to avoid spooking the crew. Jacob Van Lennep and his younger brother Richard had spent some time on business in the United States between 1807 and 1822, and the donation of a mummy obtained by them for Boston was one way of expressing their gratitude for American hospitality.[47] Part of the episode is explained in a letter written by Robert B. Edes, captain of the brig, and Bryant P. Tilden to Doctors Warren, Jackson, and Gorham of the Massachusetts General Hospital, where the mummy was destined to go. In this letter, published in the *Salem Gazette* in May shortly after the arrival of the mummy in Boston, Edes and Tilden quote a letter from the British consul in Alexandria, Peter Lee, who was related by marriage to the Van Lennep family in Smyrna—one of Peter's brothers, Edward, had married Hester Maria, a sister of Jacob and Richard Van Lennep. "I have procured you a Mummy, a capital one. —As no good ones, opened, were to be found at Cairo or this place I commissioned a person going to Thebes to select me one, and I am glad he succeeded in procuring you the best that has been seen for a long time." This mummy, the first to reach the United States, is still in the possession of the Massachusetts General Hospital.

Additional Egyptian mummies were to follow in the next several years, as careful scrutiny of local newspapers reveals. Two Massachusetts sea captains, Larkin Turner (of the *Caroline Augusta*) and Larkin T. Lee (of the *Fenelon*), each imported a mummy to the United States in 1824, the first arriving in February, the second in July. Captain Turner had obtained his at Trieste (where Rapelje said the ones he saw in 1822 were bound). Captain Lee had picked his up at Leghorn. Neither captain had ventured to Alexandria. Both mummies were encased in painted wood coffins. Captain Lee's mummy was opened and examined by two eminent American doctors, Samuel L. Mitchell and Valentine Mott (about whom more later). Captain Turner's mummy was likewise examined by medical authorities including John C. Warren of the Massachusetts General Hospital. In June of the same year Captain Clark brought "two mummies, fresh from Thebes, and of *undoubted* antiquity" on the brig *Peregrine* to Boston. A year later, in June 1825, a Philadelphia merchant, James L. Hodge, "received by the ship *America* an Egyptian mummy, which has been subject to the inspection of a number of physicians." Twenty years later Hodge deposited this mummy, with its case, in the Pennsylvania Academy of Natural Sciences, where it can still be seen.

On January 15, 1826, the brig *New Castle* under Captain Wilkinson arrived in Boston with "a very interesting collection of Egyptian Antiquites . . . received here in a vessel from Alexandria, which we understand were ordered to this country by the Pacha of Egypt. There are four Mummies."[48] Another newpaper reported that the brig had left Gibraltar for Boston on November 21, 1825, which would suggest that it had been in Alexandria in October or early November.[49] The Boston doctor John C. Warren examined these mummies also. Soon afterward all of the antiquities were offered for sale, and two of the mummies may have been among those purchased by the artist Ethan Allen Greenwood and shown in several New England towns in 1828.

In late 1825 or early 1826, the American artist Rubens Peale arranged to have sent to New York for Peale's Museum two mummies, said to be from near Cairo, which had been shipped from Egypt to Trieste and then onward to New York. They went on exhibition February 15 and were widely advertised in the *New York Evening Post*.[50]

In contrast to the mummies acquired by European collections in the 1820s, most of which soon entered public institutions where they are preserved to this day, the mummies shipped to the United States were treated as curiosities worthy of public exhibition for private commercial gain. Rubens Peale, for instance, by paying the Massachusetts General Hospital $650, obtained exclusive rights to exhibit their mummy for several months in different cities. Peale charged admission, as did those exhibiting most other mummies. In the end, suffering from such display, most of these mummies succumbed to the ravages of time. Only the mummy shipped from Smyrna by the Van Lennep firm to Boston, and now in the Massachusetts General Hospital, and the one shipped to Philadelphia in 1825, and now in the Academy of Natural Sciences there, have survived to this day.

7 | AMERICAN MISSIONARIES ON TOUR

Pliny Fisk and Levi Parsons:
Mission Postponed in Search of Health
The American Board of Commissioners for Foreign Missions (ABCFM), founded in 1810, sent its first overseas missionaries to India in 1813. Not until news of the end of the War of 1812 was received in early 1815 was it possible to contemplate missions in the Mediterranean. The first two missionaries to take advantage of the new peace were Rev. Pliny Fisk and Rev. Levi Parsons, classmates at Middlebury College in Vermont, and graduates of Andover Theological Seminary in Massachusetts. On Sunday, October 31, 1819, shortly before their departure each preached a farewell sermon in Boston, Fisk at the Old South Church, Parsons at the Park Street Church, in which they spoke of their yearning for Jerusalem and for the restoration of the Jews.[1] Modern historians often quote passages from their sermons emphasizing the focus on the Jews, while overlooking the language in the *Instructions* to Parsons and Fisk, delivered in the Old South Church on the same day by Samuel Worcester, secretary of the Prudential Committee of the ABCFM. Worcester asked them to keep two things in mind: what good could they do in Jerusalem and Judaea, and by what means—not only for Jews, but also for Arabs, Turks, Asiatics, and Europeans, of various countries and religions, Judaism, Paganism, Mahommedanism, and Christianity. And in addition, since their mission was to be centered in Smyrna in Turkey, not Jerusalem, Worcester said, with reference to Smyrna:

> There indeed you will be on Classick Ground, and whatever of contribution or of service you can afford to Literature or Taste, with fidelity to your

higher objects, will be interesting to many, and useful to the general cause. But however inspiring the scenes where Poets sung, and Sages mused, and artists displayed their enchanting skill; still more sacred, exalted, and affecting, will be the inspiration from those where Paul preached, and John saw his visions. . . . and on your journey, if you travel by land from the Lesser Asia to Palestine, many places and scenes and objects of deep interest will offer themselves to your notice and examination.[2]

With no idea that they would ever visit Egypt, Fisk and Parsons sailed from Boston on November 3, 1819, on the brig *Sally Anne*, and arrived in Malta in late December. By early January 1820, they were in Smyrna, their missionary destination where, over the next few months, they met the European residents. Parsons collected minerals for Frederick Hall, a professor he knew at Middlebury College, and he sent to Hall a pamphlet about the local Bible Society.[3] From May to October they were in the island of Chios to learn modern Greek. In November they visited the sites of four of the seven churches of the Apocalypse (in addition to Smyrna), namely Pergamon, Thyatira, Sardis, and Philadelphia, but missed Laodicea and Ephesus owing to Parsons' ill health. Along the way they observed ancient ruins and copied Greek inscriptions.

Not until after a year was a trip to Jerusalem undertaken, and then only by Parsons. He left Smyrna in early December 1820, armed with a Turkish firman procured by the British ambassador in Constantinople, with a letter of credit from an Armenian merchant, and with letters of introduction from the English and Russian consuls in Smyrna to their counterparts in Palestine. He sailed via Paphos in Cyprus and only arrived in Jaffa in February 1821. In Jerusalem he stayed several months with his Greek Orthodox hosts in excellent health, distributing gospels and tracts in several languages and touring the sites. He went to Jericho and the Dead Sea with two Englishmen, one of them Capt. Hamilton of the Royal Navy who had just arrived from Egypt.[4] Meanwhile, in April, during Parsons' absence, Fisk made a trip to Ephesus with three Americans: Thomas Langdon of Boston and his nephew Joseph who had just come to Smyrna in 1820, and George Perkins, a resident since 1775, who had encouraged his cousins, Thomas and James Perkins, to trade there at the beginning of the nineteenth century.

More importantly, while Parsons was away the Greek revolt broke out and the events in Smyrna, the random killing of Greeks by Turks and hearsay reports from elsewhere, are vividly recounted in Fisk's journal. This will be mentioned in the next chapter, which covers Americans and the Greek War of Independence.

Parsons left Jerusalem in early May, sailing via Paphos and Samos to Syra (Syros) where he stayed from July to November in ever-declining health. He returned to Smyrna in December in such precarious health that a local doctor and Fisk thought best to take him to Alexandria for a cure.

Fisk arranged accommodations for the two of them on the Austrian brig *Eliso* at a cost of $100 and they sailed on January 9. After a boisterous passage of only five days—but seasick the entire way—they arrived at Alexandria. Fisk delivered letters of introduction from Francis Werry (the British consul in Smyrna) and others to Peter Lee, the British consul in Alexandria, and Lee arranged lodgings for them at Mr. Gregg, a Catholic from Malta. Fisk also called on John Gliddon, a British merchant to whom he had a letter from Richard Van Lennep, and he met Mr. Schutz, a Dutch merchant whose sister, Mrs. P. Van Lennep, had written a letter of introduction. With Peter Lee's help Fisk engaged a physician, Dr. Morpurgo, to look after Parsons. Meanwhile Fisk encountered British naval officers and merchants and traveled about Alexandria, partly in the company of Selim, one of Mr. Lee's servants, to see the sights. Among these were Cleopatra's Needles and Pompey's Pillar, the latter monument readily visible from all points of the city and a landmark for sailors approaching and leaving port. In his diary Fisk wrote out the Greek inscription on the base of Pompey's Pillar based on the text copied by Hamilton in his book *Aegyptiaca*, and in his "Book of Extracts and Records" he did the same together with the text printed in the English translation of Chateaubriand's account of his visit to Alexandria in late 1806, noting the latter's restoration of the Greek text. Fisk gave his translation, with a footnote that the column is more ancient than the inscription.[5] But Parsons saw nothing. He lingered in their lodgings without recovering, despite almost daily visits by Dr. Morpurgo, and he finally died on February 10. Fisk wrote in his diary:

Early in the forenoon, Mr. Lee, the consul, called on me, and kindly offered to see that all necessary arrangements were made for the funeral. He said, that in this climate it was necessary to bury soon, to prevent putrefaction. On this account he thought it necessary that the funeral should be today. Four o'clock was accordingly appointed. All the English gentlemen resident in the place, six or seven in number, the captains of several English ships, and a great number of merchants, principally Maltese, attended the funeral. The consul walked with me next to the coffin, and the others, 60 or 70 in number followed in procession to the Greek convent, where the few English who reside here, bury their dead.[6]

Fisk was devastated at the death of his closest friend, but he persevered and continued to see friends. On February 13, for instance, at Peter Lee's house, where he had gone to post letters for Smyrna, he met Major-General Sir John Malcolm, a senior British official in India now returning to England where he enjoyed high-level contacts in the British government. Four days later, after preaching at Mr. Lee's house, he conversed with Sir John about missionaries in India and other matters concerning the church there. And Fisk continued to borrow books from Mr. Lee's library, among them Hamilton's *Aegyptiaca* and Belzoni's and Sonnini's travels, so as to learn about Egypt. On March 1, after paying $50 to the Greek monastery for the interment, $20 to Dr. Marpurgo for his services, and distributing any number of religious tracts to friends and contacts, Fisk left Alexandria and went up to Cairo. He compared the Nile along the way to the Connecticut River as it flows near Brattleboro, Vermont, as John Ledyard had done in 1788. He jotted personal thoughts in his diary, pouring out melancholy, yet at the same time making more hopeful observations:

> Three long solitary weeks have now passed since the death of Brother Parsons. I feel now more than ever that I am a pilgrim & a stranger on the earth. . . . Here a delightful moon and a gentle breeze in our favor. It is pleasant to stand on such an evening and look at the river and the country and think of the interesting events which the names of Egypt and the Nile are associated. On the banks of this river Moses was exposed and wonderfully preserved. Here I behold the land of Sesostris and the Pharaohs of the Ptolemies. Here God sent his plagues over Egypt and delivered Ismael. Here is the country of the pyramids and temples and catacombs and hieroglyphics.[7]

In Cairo Fisk discovered that the British Consul-General Henry Salt was upriver and so he delivered his letters of introduction from Francis Werry and Mr. Lee to Mr. Salavatore, acting in Salt's absence. In Cairo he found lodgings at the house of Jean-Louis Asselin de Cherville, a former French consul. And Fisk met Osman. Osman was a Scotsman, William Thompson, who was once a soldier in the British regiment that marched from Alexandria to Rosetta in April 1807 and was defeated there by the Egyptian forces. Those killed had their heads paraded in the streets, but those captured (with a few exceptions), instead of being enslaved, were released owing to the initiative of the French consul-general Bernardino Drovetti and the unusually magnanimous response of Mehmet Ali. Thompson, one of the exceptions, was enslaved, forced to turn Muslim (at least in name), and adopted the name Osman. As soon as Henry Salt became British consul-general in 1815, he persuaded the pasha to free him, and in response he began a long career as a dragoman in Salt's employ. But Thompson retained his adopted name.[8]

Pliny Fisk toured the sights of Cairo with Osman the dragoman. In his diary and in a letter to a Boston newspaper he spoke of the well of Saladin in the Citadel, the tombs of the caliphs, and the obelisk and sycamore tree at Heliopolis.[9] In Bulaq, the Nile port of Cairo, the pasha's Literary Institution, formed by Egyptians who had been sent abroad for a European education, impressed Fisk, and on March 11 he wrote in his diary:

> First called on Osman Effendi, one of the young who were sent by the Pasha to Europe for an education, who is now at the head of the Pasha's Institute. He spoke Italian very well, conversed about the school, printing press &c. . . . He is now employed in translating books from French and Italian into Arabic & Turkish. He showed me the library which consists of a choice selection on history, antiquities, math, philology, poetry, medicine, agriculture, the military arts, &c &c. . . . Went to the printing office. There are three presses, with a type foundery & types, French, Greek & Arabic.[10]

With Osman the dragoman as his guide, Fisk also visited the pasha's palace at Shubra, which had only just been completed, and wrote what is one of the first descriptions of the interior and of the gardens.

> The Palace is magnificent. The Pasha and all of his family being now in the city, we were permitted to visit the different apartments. The rooms are painted with much taste and elegance, the sofas are covered with rich velvet and adorned with several rows of fringes; there is one large, elegant room for the Pasha's wife and several for the other women; the divan is also large, and there are baths, and several smaller apartments. Instead of tables, chairs, bureaus, &c. &c. the rooms in which company is received are merely furnished with a sofa, which completely surrounds the room. The sleeping rooms are furnished with beds spread on the floor. . . . On the ground floor there is a large room with a fountain in the centre, which must be very cool and refreshing in the heat of the day. Adjoining the palace is a large garden, filled with fruit-trees, vines, aromatic herbs, flowers and delightful walks. In the garden is a circular kiosk, paved with pebbles of various colours, with a fountain in the centre, and seats around . . . . I have never before seen any thing which corresponded so well with the ideas which fancy forms of an oriental palace and garden. The display of wealth, of skill and taste, filled

me with a momentary admiration. But when I reflected that a multitude are here compelled to labour for the gratification of one, while they receive only the value of 6 or 8 cents per day at most, and are happy when they can get a piece of bread and an onion, or a watermelon for their dinner, I exclaimed, ah! Cruel despotism.[11]

On March 12, three English travelers arrived from Alexandria: John Madox, Captain Robert James Gordon, and a Captain Cupper, and they also lodged at Asselin's house. John Madox was the same British traveler who later met the New Yorker George Rapelje in Alexandria. On the following day, Fisk went to Giza together with Madox, Gordon, and Cupper, and with a Mr. Spurrier whom he had met earlier on, and with Osman, and all of them climbed the Great Pyramid.

We ascended the pyramid and found a level at the top of about 30 ft square. The view from this elevation was most singular & commanding around the base of the pyramid we saw rows of tombs & a little distance off the other pyramids & the sphinx. To the West an ocean of sand extending as far as the eye could reach, to the East the fertile fields which we crossed on our way, then the venerated Nile & beyond it other fertile fields, Cairo with its citadel & forts & hundreds of minarets & mount Mokattams stretching away through the opposite desert toward the Red Sea.[12]

Fisk left Cairo for Alexandria on March 22 together with John Madox and Captain Cupper. On April 1, he sailed from Alexandria on board the British brig *Despatch* together with the American adventurer George B. English; quarantined in the lazaretto in Malta, he had a trying conversation with him. In Malta Fisk met Rev. Daniel Temple, a missionary sent out by the American Board of Commissioners of Foreign Missions, who had only just arrived there for a long residence with his wife Rachel in February. And there, in Malta, George Rapelje, on his way home in August 1822, saw both Temple and Fisk.

Pliny Fisk and Jonas King, 1823: Missionaries as Tourists
In Malta, Fisk set about seeking a replacement for Parsons. He wrote to Jonas King whom he knew was in Paris. King, class of 1816 at Williams College in Massachusetts and class of 1819 at Andover Theological Seminary, had arrived in Paris on October 9, 1821, on leave from a newly appointed position of Oriental languages at Amherst College. He had gone to Paris to study Arabic at the École spéciale des langues orientales

vivantes with the venerable orientalist Baron Sylvestre de Sacy (1758–1838) and with the recently appointed Arabic scholar Armand-Pierre Caussin de Perceval.[13] How much Arabic he learned from them is open to question because he had to learn it through French and only after recovering from several months of sickness. In any event Fisk's letter altered his situation, and he soon raised funds through Sampson Vryling Stoddard Wilder, a well-connected American merchant from Massachusetts, resident in Paris, to undertake a three-year mission with Fisk. Having recently been made a member of the Société asiatique, he was able to obtain letters of introduction to consuls in Malta, Corfu, Aleppo, Beirut, and Egypt from the president of the society, the Duc d'Orléans. From the British ambassador in Paris he had a letter to the consul-general in Egypt. Through Mary Elliott he obtained a letter from William Wilberforce to Lady Hester Stanhope.[14] He was well armed.

Traveling via Lyon, Nîmes, and Marseilles, he reached Malta in the fall of 1822 and met up with Fisk. On January 3, 1823, King and Fisk left Malta for Egypt on the brig *Triune*. With them was the German-born, naturalized Englishman Joseph Wolff, a convert to Anglicanism via Roman Catholicism, well traveled and eccentric. Nine years later, the American Elizabeth Cabot Kirkland (about whom more later) would write:

[He is] a crazy sort of missionary in the East . . . not only crack brained, but the greatest sloven ever seen. I have been told that a lady at whose house he lodged burned the bed on which he slept, at his departure.[15]

After arriving in Alexandria on January 10, they met the French Consul-General Bernardino Drovetti, to whom King had a letter of introduction, and they visited Parson's grave. After ten days of distributing religious tracts and preaching (Fisk in Italian and Greek, Wolff in German and Hebrew, King in English and French), they sailed on a local boat called a *maash* to Rosetta. There they stayed in the house of the English vice-consul. They reported that since the opening of the Mahmoudiya canal the town had lost much of its business. Sailing upriver to Cairo, they found rooms at what they called the Frank Locanda and then called on the British consul-general Henry Salt, to whom King had a letter of introduction from Sir Charles Stuart, British ambassador to France. They also had extensive conversations with their Jewish, Coptic, and Roman Catholic brethren. Ancient Egypt was not neglected. On February 4 Fisk and King visited Giza, and King climbed the Great Pyramid, though the tourist aspect of his ascent was tempered by the fact that he preached a sermon when he gained the summit. Then, leaving Cairo on February 6, the threesome traveled up the Nile as far as Thebes on a trip that lasted several months, ostensibly to distribute Bibles and to meet the local Copts, which they did at Asyut and Akhmin and other towns on the way, but also to see the monuments of Thebes, their destination. Among the documents they carried giving them safe passage were letters of introduction from the Coptic patriarch and a letter to Ahmed Pasha, the governor of Upper Egypt from Mehmet Ali.[16]

Travelers tied up at Thebes for days at a time to do just what Fisk and King were about to do, that is, to see the ruins. Because of this the locality became a traditional meeting place for sightseers on the Nile. Fisk and King were the first Americans to write about these encounters. Arriving there on February 28, Fisk wrote "here we met two companies of travellers, one on their way to Aswan, consisting of a Polish nobleman whom we knew in Cairo, an Englishman, and a German, the other returning from Dongola & consisting of a Russian count and two Germans."[17] Who were they? Later in Jerusalem, Fisk wrote in his diary for June 9, "The Russian Count Medem, the German doctor Westphal & Barclay whom we knew in Egypt arrived today." But had Fisk seen them at Luxor or elsewhere in Egypt? The "Russian Count Medem" must be Peter von Medem (1801–1877), who is known to have been traveling at this time with Théodore de Lesseps (1802–1874) and Alexander von Üxküll (1800–1853). The trio, however, did not go as far south as Dongola, and moreover, according to Üxküll's diary, they did not stop at Luxor until March 10, several days after Fisk and his companions had left.[18] The "German doctor Westphal" whom Fisk saw in Jerusalem was the twenty-nine-year-old astronomer Johann Heinrich Westphal (1794–1831), who began a tour in Egypt in 1822. He may well have been at Luxor, accompanied by an Englishman named Barclay, on his way to Aswan. And the Polish nobleman with them was probably the Baron Renne whom Pliny Fisk reported seeing in Cairo on January 31, and probably to be spelled Baron von Roenne.[19]

But can the party returning from Dongola be identified? Yes, it was surely the group led by the twenty-five-year-old Gustav Parthey (1798–1872) of Berlin, later a philologist and Coptic scholar, who was traveling with count Cesarotti of C, doctor Longinus of M (localities not given in full), and a French servant, Joseph Grenier, acting as their cook, whom they had met in Rome.[20] They had left Joseph with their boat at Wadi Halfa while they had gone up country to Dongola. In the published account of the Nile trip, Parthey reported that on their return from Dongola they had encountered at Thebes three boats (whose occupants cannot be completely reconciled with those in Fisk's account), one with an Englishman and a German returning from Aswan, a second with a Russian and a Frenchman going upstream, the third with North American missionaries whose charge was to distribute handsome Arabic Bibles to the *fellahin*.[21] Count Cesarotti sounds Italian, not Russian, but the southern destination of Dongola from which they were returning makes the identification likely. Parthey went on to say that at some stage a caravan of camels, horses, and asses arrived overland from Quseir bringing British officers returning home from Bombay via Mocha and Egypt.[22] It was a busy time at Luxor.

Fisk adds that on that very first evening they also met "Mr. Rifaud, a Frenchman, who has been here several years engaged in researches." Jean-Jacques Rifaud, a French sculptor and antiquarian from Marseilles, had been conducting excavations in behalf of the French consul-general Bernardino Drovetti at Thebes for several years and would later produce an authoritative guide to Egypt as well as a five-volume account of his own work. He was now finishing his researches and would soon be leaving Upper Egypt.

Before Pliny Fisk and Jonas King arrived on February 28, 1823, the only Americans who had seen Thebes (apart from the expatriate Francis Barthow) were George English in 1820 and Luther Bradish in 1821. English had gone all the way to Sudan but was not traveling as a tourist; in his book he left no account of Thebes. Although Bradish was traveling as a sightseer his opinions of the monuments of Egypt are unknown because no diary of his trip is thought to have survived. Therefore in the letters and journal of Pliny Fisk we have the first surviving American description of the Pharaonic ruins at Thebes.

Fisk and his colleagues visited the Luxor temple on their first full day, March 1. He saw the two immense granite statues situated before the entrance gate, seated statues of Ramesses II, though he does not name the pharaoh. In front of them he saw the two obelisks, one of them later taken by French engineers to Paris and re-erected in the Place de la Concorde. The gateway was formed by two elongated towers with sloping sides and with a covered passage between them, which modern scholars call by the Greek word "pylon." They climbed to the top to admire the view. Within, after passing through the first courtyard, Fisk was struck by the two parallel rows of seven columns lining the passageway (the colonnade of Amenhotep III) leading to the second court, the peristyle court of Amenhotep III, and the sequence of colonnaded rooms beyond. He also commented on the piles of rubbish and the presence of mud huts used by the locals.

Two days later, Fisk, King, and Wolff visited the temple complex at Karnak, half an hour's ride north of Luxor. They had no idea of course, as we do now, of the extended building history of the suite of buildings, nor the identifications of the deities honored, Amun-Ra, his wife Mut, and their son Khonsu. But Fisk's account is sufficiently accurate for us to trace his route through the complex. They approached the ruins from the south, reaching it along an avenue of sphinxes (not all excavated in those days) that lined the road from Luxor to Karnak, a route you cannot completely follow today owing to the modern town. Some of the sphinxes had the body of a lion and head of a woman, others had rams' heads—though in many instances they had been knocked off. Fisk said that some of these sphinxes featured the image of a god—we now know it is a king—carved into the fronts of the statues. This avenue led to the leftmost of two pylons on the south perimeter wall. They were unaware that it was one of the last pylons to be erected at Karnak, though they might have noticed the lack of flanking towers for which only the foundations had ever been laid. Pylons complete with flanking towers and of greater antiquity gave access to the precinct elsewhere and, within the temples themselves, from one courtyard or building to the next. This gateway, put up in the third century BC by Ptolemy III Euergetes, is today considered one of the finest examples of Ptolemaic architecture remaining in Egypt.[23] It is one of the tallest at Karnak, more than 20 meters. Fisk guessed 70 feet.

Going through the pylon (now barricaded to prevent modern tourists from entering the complex on this side) they advanced between two rows of sphinxes, ten on each side, to the relatively small Temple of Khonsu, built under Ramesses III and Ramesses IV. Passing through the virtually intact first pylon of this temple—dating from the seventh century BC—they first entered a room with twenty-eight columns (Fisk said thirty), then through a doorway to a room with eight columns, beyond which they came out into the modern mud-hut village of Karnak where they said the dogs equaled the number of inhabitants.

In front of them and stretching far to the right were the immense walls and columns that formed the principal part of the complex, the Great Temple of Amun-Re. They entered on the side because the first space Fisk described was the huge hypostyle hall, the central attraction of the complex, begun under the pharaoh Horemheb (1323–1295 BC) and finished under Seti I (1294–1279 BC). He counted sixteen rows of huge columns, nine in each row. The central pair of nine columns, flanking the passage that led to the east end of the hall, were taller than the rest and had capitals now known as papyrus capitals. He noted that some of the ceiling was intact. Fisk then went out the pylon on the east side of this columned hall and at that point remarked that "before the east gate . . . were two pairs of obelisks." He rightly observed that at one time the obelisks stood in front of the pylon. Fisk noted that one of each pair was fallen and broken, the remaining two standing. One set is now known to have been erected by Tuthmosis I (1504–1492 BC), and the other by Queen Hatshepsut (1473–1458 BC). A fragment from the fallen one of Hatshepsut was retrieved in 1835 by the American traveler John Lowell and shipped to Boston (see chapter 11 and also plate 22A).

The three missionaries then backtracked to admire the pylon on the west perimeter wall of the precinct, to which another avenue of sphinxes provided access. This huge structure is also a relatively late construction at Karnak built at two successive periods, in the eleventh and fourth centuries BC.[24] Fisk noticed that it lacked hieroglyphics. He did not comment on the remains of the mud-brick ramps that allowed stonemasons to reach the upper courses. In his day they were present on the exterior but have now been removed. This is the modern entrance to Karnak where tickets are collected and where tour guides sometimes point out the inscription high up on the right-hand wall of the gateway carved by the French savants recording the latitude and longitude of the principal temples they saw on their way south to Thebes in 1799. The inscription is high up today because in those days the French who carved it would have stood on the accumulation of sand and rubbish that had not been excavated to its present level. Fisk may have seen the graffito but he did not mention it.

Having seen this gateway and flanking pylons, they went back and surveyed the suite of rooms east of the two pairs of obelisks, where Fisk mentioned one room where the roof was preserved supported by two rows of eight columns, and another space east of it with twelve columns. He mentioned statues but not their locations. They came out the east gate, another late construction of the fourth century BC, which lacked an avenue of sphinxes. They then went around outside the precinct wall to the principal south pylon, of fourteenth-century date, which, though he does not say so, was in ruins. While the gate's lintel was preserved, most of the stones of the flanking towers of the pylon had fallen. Beside the entrance Fisk saw an immense statue: He meant the surviving feet (and base with hieroglyphics) of the colossal quartzite statue of Amenhotep III, though he never named the pharaoh.[25] Rounding the base and remains of this statue, he entered the gateway in the pylon (today called the tenth pylon) and went through a sequence of three courtyards, each fronted by separate pylons, largely in ruins. There he saw several colossal statues without describing their positions; two of them, headless, flanked the doorway inside the tenth pylon, two more (of Tuthmosis II) at the eighth pylon. Along the way Fisk and King observed the great pond of water in the southeast corner of the precinct.

Fisk noted an avenue of sphinxes in front of this last pylon, sixty on each side, leading south to heaps of ruins and to a great number of statues. "We counted about sixty of Leo and Virgo," Fisk's way of describing the statues of Sekhmet, the Egyptian deity displaying the body of a woman and the head of a lion (see plate 22B). They were located in the precinct of the Temple of Mut, south of the main precinct at Karnak, east of the avenue of sphinxes leading from Luxor to Karnak. Fisk's description was not in fact so novel as it sounds. Giovanni Belzoni, in offering two statues of Sekhmet to his native city of Padua in March 1819, observed that they had the body of a woman and the head of a lion, adding that some people thought they represented the combined zodiacal signs of Leo and Virgo.[26]

Prior to Fisk's visit, several European travelers and agents, either with substantial personal resources or backed by their governments, had taken away dozens of the statues of Sekhmet.[27] Not until 1835, years after his visit, did an American traveler take possession of statues of Sekhmet: in that year the Bostonian John Lowell (whose visit is discussed in chapter 11) acquired two statues of Sekhmet (one of the two Sekhmets in Boston from John Lowell is illustrated in plate 22B), which he sent back to Boston and are now there in the Museum of Fine Arts. Fisk was probably unaware of this antiquities traffic.

Like most travelers to Egypt in those days, Fisk knew little of her history, but with a classical education and an enquiring mind, he took copious notes during the four hours he spent at Karnak. He even tried to calculate its dimensions, 520 paces east to west, roughly equivalent to its true dimensions in meters today. He called it the Temple of Jupiter, his translation of Diospolis (city of Zeus) as it was known, a rendering of City of Amun. He reported that the walls were very thick and generally covered with hieroglyphs but he never mentions the figured reliefs. Little of what he said, however, conveys the desolation of the site so apparent in watercolors of the 1830s and 1840s and daguerreotypes and photographs of the 1840s, 1850s, and 1860s, an uneven gravelly landscape with scrub growth, the sand piled to great depth against the granite walls and columns, and the ground pitted where the men of Giovanni d'Athanasi, Giovanni Belzoni, Jean-Jacques Rifaud, and other treasure seekers had dug for sculpture.

Despite the enthusiasm so evident in his appraisal of the ruins, Fisk recognized that his account had to be qualified. He ended by saying, "but as these walls and columns are now falling and perishing, so all human glory will soon fade and wither in the dust. But there is a Temple, whose columns shall never fall, and whose glory shall never fade . . ." and so on and so forth.

The next day they crossed over to the west side of the Nile and rode an hour to Qurna where "we stopped at the house of Mr. John Athanasius, to whom we had a letter from Mr. Salt. He is a Greek, and has spent several years at Thebes, making excavations, and searching for antiquities, in the employ of Mr. Salt. He lived sometime in a tomb, and then built a house over it which he now inhabits."[28] The Greek-born Giovanni d'Athanasi, as he was usually known (though often called Yanni, his name in Greek), worked for the British consul-general Henry Salt from 1817 to 1827, and then afterward in his own right. They were among the first travelers to note that Yanni had built his house over a tomb (a house regrettably bulldozed by the Egyptian antiquities service in May 2010). Yanni spent the day showing them the sites. As an additional guide, Fisk had with him a copy of William Richard Hamilton's 1810 publication *Ægyptiaca*, which he had borrowed from the British consul, Peter Lee, in Alexandria before setting forth, and to which he referred several times. They visited the tombs of the kings, reaching first the tomb of Seti I opened by Belzoni in 1817 only six years earlier, and there Yanni pointed out the place where his alabaster sarcophagus, soon removed to London, had been found. They also visited the Temple of Memnon, counting forty-seven columns still standing and the fallen broken statue; also the Temple of Isis, Medinet Habu, and the two colossi of Memnon.

Fisk did one other thing common among tourists on the Nile: He purchased some antiquities. Among the items that found their way from his estate to the Andover Newton Theological School were an alabaster jar and a painted wooden hawk, both acquired by Fisk at Thebes. In time they were transferred to the Peabody Museum (now the Peabody Essex Museum) in Salem, Massachusetts, where they can still be seen. Fisk may well have purchased them from Giovanni d'Athanasi. But these were souvenirs; Fisk and King were not collectors like the Belmore party of tourists (whose exploits are discussed in chapter 5).

Fisk also collected mineral specimens, following up what Parsons had begun, which he added to the collection from Asia Minor and elsewhere. He ultimately sent them to Frederick Hall, the professor with whom he and Parsons had studied at Middlebury College. Among those from Egypt were two stones from Karnak, a sample of a sarcophagus from one of the tombs of the kings at Thebes, a piece of one of the statues of Memnon, and a granite fragment from Alexandria, "given me by

Capt. Skinner, of an English brig, who had been on the top of Pompey's pillar, and broke it off himself."[29]

Fisk, King, and Wolff then started north to return to Cairo. Stopping at Dendera on March 6 to view the temple, Fisk remarked:

> It was from this temple that a Frenchman, about three years since, took away the Zodiac, which has excited so much interest among the learned. The walls, as usual, are covered with hieroglyphics, the mystical characters of the ancient Egyptians. Could we read these characters, we should no doubt derive much information about the ancient history, mythology, and customs of the country. Whether this knowledge will ever be attained, remains to be seen.[30]

Fisk was unaware of a recently announced discovery: At a meeting of the Académie des Inscriptions et Belles-Lettres held on September 27, 1822, and chaired by the classical scholar Bon-Joseph Dacier, Jean-François Champollion (who would not go to Egypt until 1828) read a paper, published a month later, in which he outlined the key elements that would lead him to decipher hieroglyphic script.[31] Two years later, in a second publication, Champollion fully revealed his understanding of the complex system he had deciphered.

Returning to Cairo on March 24, Fisk, King, and Wolff made the rounds of the European consuls, officials of the pasha, and their Jewish colleagues. In addition they were unexpectedly introduced to the admiral of the pasha's fleet, Ismail Djebel Akhdar, usually called Ismail Gibraltar, a name given to him after he sailed beyond the straits. He spoke French and Italian and a little English, having been to Europe to buy weapons for the pasha. The admiral spoke of having seen Luther Bradish during his visit to Egypt, an item of intelligence reported by both Fisk and King. King's own observations on their return visit to Cairo took the form of a letter to Mr. Wilder in Paris, his principal patron.[32]

On March 27 Fisk revisited the pasha's palace at Shubra together with King. In his letter to Wilder, King gave his own description:

> Early in the morning we went to Shoobry to see the Pasha's palace, gardens, Haram, &c. The garden is very fine and the pavilion superb. The Haram is splendid—has one large apartment for himself, and another for his wife, adjoining which are several smaller apartments for his concubines, of which he has perhaps three hundred. I also observed some small rooms which I was told were occupied by boys, and for purposes which

I should blush to name. I felt as though I were in Sodom and as though a tempest of fire and brimstone would soon come down from heaven![33]

Near the palace Fisk and King saw a giraffe:

We went to see a Camel-Leopard which was brought from Sennaar. An interesting animal. Its body is in size like that of a small horse but shorter. The neck and legs are considerably longer than those of a horse. Its head and neck are in form like those of a deer, its legs like those of a horse and its hoofs like those of an ox. Its skin is beautifully spotted, red and white. Its aspect is mild and gentle, its motions lively & gay & proud.[34]

Fisk and King were the first Americans, so far as we know, to see—or at least to describe—a giraffe.

On April 7, Fisk, King, and Wolff bade farewell to the British consul Henry Salt and started on their overland journey to Gaza with thirteen camels and their guide Mustapha, in a caravan that ultimately swelled to some seventy individuals, among them Arabs, Turks, Armenians, and Greeks. Jerusalem was their destination. After seeing everything in the holy city and in the neighboring countryside, they parted from Joseph Wolff and traveled together in Syria from June to September before returning to Jerusalem. In early July, in Sidon, King made use of his letters of introduction to Lady Hester Stanhope, including one from from Mr. Turnbull, English consul at Marseilles, and received an invitation from her dragoman to ride to her place.[35]

After his great mission to the East, sponsored by the Paris Missionary Society and by Mr. Wilder, King went home briefly to the United States. He then returned to the Mediterranean, to Greece, where he married a Greek, and prospered as a successful if contentious missionary in Athens until his death in 1869. Some two years after King's departure for the United States, Fisk developed a fever and died in Beirut on October 23, 1825. Two recent writers have declared, quite erroneously, that Fisk's health declined as a result of being struck in the arm by Bedouin bandits, but that episode took place outside Nazareth on May 12, months earlier, and though his arm was lame for a few days, there were no lasting effects.[36]

The Reverend Eli Smith in Egypt in 1826
In the following year, 1826, the Rev. Eli Smith, Yale class of 1821, visited Egypt. After Yale, Smith had gone on to graduate from Andover Theological Seminary in 1826, and on May 23 of that year left Boston bound

for Malta where he arrived on July 13, meeting up with his fellow missionary Daniel Temple. In early December 1826 he sailed to Alexandria. In a letter to the corresponding secretary of the ABCFM, Smith gave some account of his experiences in Egypt. "During the four or five days I passed in Alexandria, I lived in the family of the Rev. D[onald] Macpherson of the Wesleyan Missionary Society, and preached for him once in the hall of the British consulate, to an audience of between 20 and 30 English residents." In mid-December Smith went up to Cairo to stay with colleagues of the Church Missionary Society (an English organization) who had arrived in Egypt in September that year, namely five Lutheran clergymen from the seminary at Basle: Samuel Gobat, Christian Kugler, Theodore Müller, William Krusé, and John Lieder. All were just beginning the study of Arabic, and Smith joined them. "During my stay in that city, my time was employed in the study of Arabic." During this first time in Egypt—he would make two additional trips—he was conscious of what he considered the fanaticism of the Muslims. A Muslim-born woman married a Greek, and when it was discovered that she was an apostate, having converted to Christianity, she was drowned in the Nile. Her husband "saved his life by embracing the Mahommedan faith."[37]

After about six weeks, Smith and three of his Lutheran hosts, Messrs. Gobat, Kugler, and Müller, left Cairo on January 30, 1827, to travel overland via Jaffa to Beirut. In Alexandria and Cairo, Smith had worn Western clothes; now for the overland route through Sinai he adopted "oriental dress." In the short time he was in Egypt Smith can have learned only a little Arabic, but in Beirut, which was to be the base of his mission and where he would spend most of the rest of his life, he proceeded to master the language and after twenty years started work on his famous Arabic Bible.

David Van Lennep with his family in Smyrna in 1771. He and his wife Anna Maria (in quasi-
stern dress) are flanked by her father, Justinus Johannes Leidstar, and the family tutor (at the
right). The older children display their style and their talents. In 1774, on his way to Egypt,
e Bostonian Ward Nicholas Boylston was "genteelly entertained" by the Van Lenneps and
er expatriate European merchants.

2. Joseph Allen Smith of Charleston sketched by François-Xavier Fabre, overlooking the Roma
Campagna. In 1804 he went to Greece venturing where no American had gone before, a first
step in the Ottoman Empire toward Egypt. It is no coincidence that the pose is that of Goethe
in Tischbein's famous portrait: Fabre owned a sketch of the portrait.

The twenty-year-old Nicholas [Bi]ddle of Philadelphia, serving [as] secretary to the US minister to [Pa]ris, sat for this portrait in 1805 [sh]ortly before touring Greece.

4. Edward Everett of Boston, appointed professor of Greek at Harvard in 1815, began a four-year tour of Europe to prepare himself for the position. He reached Greece in 1819, returned to Harvard the following year, and commissioned this portrait (unfinished) from Gilbert Stuart in 1821.

5. *Description de l'Égypte*, the record of Napoleon's savants, impressed American architects, among them the New Yorker Alexander Jackson Davis, whose partner Ithiel Town owned one the first sets to reach the US. Davis drew on some of its plates for his 1830 restored rendering of the Temple at Armant, later demolished for building materials in the 1860s.

6. Egyptian quartzite statue of Senwosret Sunbefni (1836–1759 BC), brought home by Napoleon in 1799 and presented to his wife Josephine for her house at Malmaison outside of Paris. [The Brooklyn Museum acquired this 'Souvenir of Napoleon's trip to Egypt' in 1939.]

7. A fragmentary faience lion's head of Egypt's Persian period (525–404 BC), probably acquired in Alexandria by Frederick W. Moores, sailing master on the USS *Delaware*, and presented to the Boston Naval Library and Institute.

George Crowninshield of Salem took his private yacht, *Cleopatra's Barge*, on a cruise in
817 intending to circumnavigate the Mediterranean. But he never reached Alexandria, instead
turning home after port calls in Spain, France, and Italy.

The USS *Constitution* cruised the Mediterranean, exciting interest wherever she called. At Leghorn
1822, Lord Byron was rowed out to the ship in a longboat, standing and waving a red banner.

10. Matthew C. Perry, master commandant in the United States Navy, brought the Rev. John T. Kirkland, a former president of Harvard, and his wife Elizabeth Cabot to Egypt in 1832 as guests aboard the corvette *Concord*.

11. John T. Kirkland sat for this bust by the American sculptor Horatio Greenough, despite his wife's reservations, "it does not strike me that he has a head for a bust. His forehead is good but his nose is flat, and I am afraid that it will resemble the bust of Socrates, which is very ugly." Greenough proved her wrong.

12. Mehmet Ali paid a ceremonial visit to the *Concord*, while she was in port in Alexandria, dressed as we see him here in a watercolor by an artist member of the crew.

. Matthew Perry presented the pasha
h two bears he had received some
nths earlier in Russia. A young mes-
ger boy on board the *Concord* leads
e of them.

14. Mendes I. Cohen of Baltimore dressed *à la Turque* while in Egypt in 1832, during a five-year tour abroad. Unlike most American travelers to the East, he had himself portrayed so dressed when he returned home.

15. Commodore Daniel T. Patterson of the Mediterranean squadron, shown here while still a junior officer, visited Egypt with his family in 1834 off the US frigate *Delaware*.

16. The Hon. Lewis Cass, United States minister to Paris, visited Egypt with his family in 1837, traveling as guests on board the USS *Constitution*.

17. Henry Ledyard, a collateral descendant of the eighteenth-century American traveler John Ledyard, went to Egypt in 1837. In 1842, he became chargé d'affaires in Paris and is here shown in a daguerreotype of c. 1850 wearing his consular uniform, brought home as a souvenir of his Paris days.

18. J. Lewis Stackpole of Boston, class of 1824 at Harvard, visited Egypt in 1834 together with Ralph Stead Izard of Charleston. This daguerreotype of the early 1840s, attributed to Southworth and Hawes, shows an individual described by Oliver Wendell Holmes as, "a man of great intelligence, of remarkable personal attraction, and amiable character."

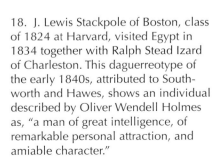

9. Horatio Allen, the first American to drive a steam locomotive in the United States, visited Paris in 1836 on his honeymoon where he commissioned this miniature portrait.

0. Diplomat William B. Hodgson was stationed in Algiers, until he joined the first American chargé d'affaires in Constantinople as dragoman in 1831. He left to take a fact-finding tour of Egypt and then resigned from the service in 1842 to marry a girl from Savannah, whom he had met in Paris and for whom this portrait was made.

21. John Lowell of Boston, who traveled to Egypt in 1835 with Swiss artist Charles Gleyre, one of the finest watercolorists of his day and painter of this portrait. During his Nile tour he assembled an impressive collection of Egyptian antiquities, which he sent home to Boston.

. Among Lowell's acquisitions from Egypt are: (A) a fragment of the fallen red granite obelisk
Hatshepsut (1473–1458 BC) at Karnak; and (B) a statue of the goddess Sekhmet, with the
dy of a woman and the head of a lion—hundreds lined avenues at Karnak and were eagerly
ght as trophies by diplomatic officials and by travelers.

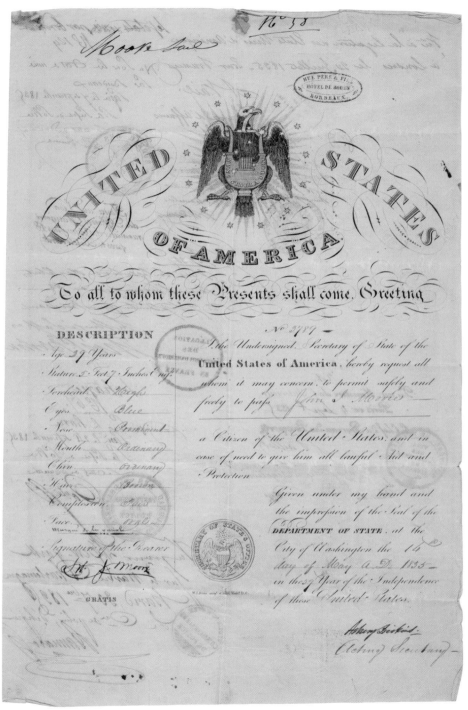

23. An American passport dated May 1835 shows an American eagle, charged with a lyre, and nine stars of the constellation Lyra, all encircled by thirteen stars of the original states. It was designed by John Qunicy Adams, secretary of state (1817–1825). The sheet opened to give ample room for consular stamps and, when not in use, was folded to fit into a small envelope.

. Two steamships, with side paddles and tall stacks displaying plumes of smoke, are visible this 1836 view of Smyrna. One steamer, probably the *Maria Dorothea*, flies the Austrian flag; e other, perhaps the *Crescent*, the British flag. Both ran service from Smyrna to Constantino- e, and American visitors to the eastern Mediterranean and Egypt took passage on these and any other steamers.

25. Dr. Valentine Mott, the most celebrated American surgeon of his day, sat for this portrait by Henry Inman in 1834 at the request of his colleagues before leaving for a European tour. On a subsequent trip abroad he visited Egypt.

26. Luther Bradish of New York, a thirty-eight-year-old widower, was sent to Constantinople in 1820 by President James Monroe and Secretary of State John Quincy Adams to seek a commercial treaty with the sultan. Unsuccessful, he followed up his duties with a trip to Egypt, Palestine, and Syria. This portrait was painted on the occasion of his second marriage in 1839.

27. Alexander Marshall, a New York engineer, sailed to Egypt in 1838 with steam-driven equipment for husking rice and pressing cotton seed, ordered by the American Vice-Consul in Cairo George R. Gliddon for the viceroy of Egypt. Before leaving, Marshall commissioned this portrait so that his wife and children would have something to remember him by.

8. This giraffe was presented by Mehmet Ali to Charles X in Paris in 1827. In 1838, giraffes nt from Alexandria were exhibited in New York.

29. Philip Rhinelander, a member of one of the wealthiest New York families of his day, probably had th likeness painted on graduating from Columbia College in 1834. In 1838 he began a European tour, like man rich college graduates, and extende it to Egypt the following year with several friends.

30. British officials interview the viceroy of Egypt and Consul-General Patrick Campbell is speaking. Seated with him are Thomas Waghorn, promoter of the postal service; the artist David Roberts, who made the sketch for this lithograph; Lieut. Goldsmith, commander of the steamer *Megara*; and perhaps the Rev. Henry Tattam, collector of Coptic manuscripts.

. Richard and Sarah Haight at home in New York in 1842, with their four children Lydia, Rich-
d, David, and Frances. They are gathered around a table laid out with a map of Asia; trophies
m their European travels are on display, a marble copy of Canova's *Three Graces*, and Greek
ses. Compare this family portrait with that of the Van Lenneps in Smyrna in 1771 (plate 1).

32. British-born Henry Abbott served as a physician to the Egyptian navy in the 1830s and moved to Cairo at the end of the decade, where he collected antiquities, entertained travelers and married and raised a family. In 1853 he came to New York to exhibit his antiquities, seeking to sell them to an American insitution, but returned to Egypt, unsuccessful. After his death they were sold to the New-York Historical Society.

33. George R. Gliddon, British born vice-consul of the United States in Cairo, became, like his father John Gliddon, American consul in Alexandria, a destination for American visitors to Egypt. In the 1840s he traveled widely in the United States, lecturing on the antiquities of Egypt, and while in Philadelphia he commissioned this lithographic portrait.

8 | THE EASTERN QUESTION

Americans and the Greek War of Independence

In the spring of 1821, one year after Fisk and Parsons had arrived in Smyrna, upward of twenty thousand Turkish men, women, and children were murdered by their Greek neighbors in communities across mainland Greece and in many of the islands.[1] The uprising was occasioned in part by the success in 1820 of Ali Pasha of Ioannina, who had ruled Albania and northwest Greece for some two decades, in maintaining his independence and rejecting Ottoman orders that year to submit to the sultan. The Ottoman government responded selectively but no less viciously to the Greek uprising and massacres by hanging the Greek Orthodox patriarch in Constantinople on Easter Sunday 1821, and summarily executing many other prominent Greeks across the country. In northern Greece, the Turkish authorities regained control. But Greeks besieged, took, and massacred Turkish populations in the Peloponnesus, in Navarino, Tripolitsa, and elsewhere. In Smyrna over a period of many weeks Turks took revenge by killing Greeks, casually shooting them on the streets or invading their houses and murdering the occupants. Similar killings took place in the islands of Cos, Rhodes, and Cyprus. In Smyrna, the American missionary Pliny Fisk, who would a year later travel to Alexandria with his dying colleague Levi Parsons, witnessed the random killings of Greeks by Turks. He wrote about the events to his friends in the United States and noted them day by day in his journal.[2] Parsons, coming from Jerusalem in the spring of that year, witnessed the seizure of Turks by Greeks off the ship on which he was traveling and heard about other horrors. Although each side was guilty of comparable atrocities, Europeans and Americans learned first of the

Turkish wrongs against the Greeks, only later about the equally horrifying Greek actions against Turkish civilians. The American traveler Luther Bradish spoke of the situation in his September 1821 letter to Richard McCall, already mentioned:

> The situation of Turkey, always bad, has greatly changed furthermore since my arrival within the Empire October last [1820]. All then was comparatively quiet and continued so as late as April. The revolt of Ali Pasha of Albania and the avowed disaffection of Service produced little effect in other parts of the Empire. But in April last [1821] a general revolt took place of all the subject Greeks in Moldovia, Walachia, the Morea and all the islands in the archipelago. The outrages committed by both parties in this revolution have been immense. . . . It has been literally a war of extermination. . . . There is a most melancholy example of this in the fine Province of Kalamaria and Salonica which contained upward of 50 flourishing Greek villages and which is now only a mass of Ruins. Not a solitary Hut remains to mark with spots where once stood considerable towns. The men were all either massacred or fled and the women and children without discrimination sold in captivity as slaves. Many of these have been bought for from $1–$150 each. . . . When I left Constantinople for Egypt in February every thing was quiet. . . . It was not until my return to lower Egypt that I received intelligence of the altered state of things.[3]

Despite reverses, the Greeks continued their revolt, nowhere more vehemently and tragically than on the island of Chios, or Scio, as it was then called. Chios was prosperous and enjoyed a high measure of independence under Turkish authorities. When the revolution broke out in mainland Greece, the Chiotes ignored it. In later March 1822, however, a band of Greeks from the island of Samos landed on Chios, destroyed some mosques, and besieged the citadel where the Turk had sought protection.[4]

On his way from Constantinople to Alexandria in March of 1822, the New Yorker George Rapelje witnessed the opening episode of the Chiote conflict. His diary entry for Saturday, March 30, begins:

> We passed along between the Island of Scio and the main land of Asia. There was great cannonading all day at the town of Scio; it was reported the Greeks had taken part of it, and were endeavoring to subdue it altogether. The most of it was in possession of the Turks.[5]

The next day, Sunday, March 31, he wrote:

We came within a few miles of the town of Scio, this morning, the can-
nonading still continuing. We saw a number of vessels of war of Scio; I
thought them Greeks. One of them bore down upon us, came up, hove to,
and sent her boat on board to see who was come. Three of our passengers
being Turks, I begged the captain to stow them away; and the steward put
them away in some small locker. If they had been seen, all our men said,
the Greeks would have instantly put them to death.[6]

Soon afterward, however, a Turkish fleet sailed from the Dardanelles and
in mid-April landed troops on the island. Mobs from the mainland joined
them and took revenge, slaughtering the Greek population. Those not killed
were sold as slaves, perhaps more than 40,000, mainly women and boys.

Greeks from other islands continued to harass the Turkish fleet. In the
night of June 18 and 19, 1822, Greeks maneuvered a fire vessel alongside the
Mansur el liwa, the flagship of the Turkish fleet on which senior officers were
celebrating the eve of the feast of Bairam, setting fire to it and blowing it up.
On that very night three ships of the United States Mediterranean squadron,
the frigate *Constitution*, the corvette *Ontario*, and the schooner *Nonsuch*, on
their way to Smyrna, were nearby and witnessed the explosion and aftermath.
David Geisinger, a lieutenant on the *Constitution*, wrote in his notebook:

At 2 o'clock this morning having charge of the deck saw an explosion
which was also seen by the officers of the watch in the direction of the
straits of Scio which we suppose to be one of the Turkish fleet. . . . Toward
evening spoke with an Austrian [vessel] who informed us that at the time
we saw the explosion—the Greeks sent two fire vessels among the Turkish
fleet—one of which grappled the Captain Pacha's ship, a 74—set fire to
her so effectually that she soon blew up with all on board.[7]

The day after, June 20, as the deck log of the *Ontario* reports, the American ships "passed a great many pieces of wreck & several dead bodies."
William Turk, surgeon aboard the *Ontario*, forwarded a brief account of
the cruise from Messina to Smyrna and back to Port Mahon to American
newspapers in which he wrote:

Horrible to behold! Our ship was surrounded with dead bodies and pieces
of a burnt wreck. We lowered down the boat, and turning some of the
bodies with a boat hook, discovered they were Turks.[8]

An officer on the *Constitution* wrote a similar account to local newspapers.[9] The ships reached Smyrna on June 24 but only stayed two days. Many Europeans and Americans responded to the events by setting out to help support the Greeks. Committees of Philhellenes were established in key cities of Europe, in particular German cities, and in the United States. Edward Everett, a professor of Greek literature at Harvard who had traveled in Greece with a fellow Bostonian, Theodore Lyman Jr., in 1819, helped to sponsor the appeal in Boston. John Izard Middleton of Charleston, South Carolina, then living in Rome, happened to be traveling in Greece in 1821; a year later he seems to have commissioned a German artist, Franz Ludwig Catel, to paint a small oil showing the battle between the Turks and the Greeks (now in the Gibbes Museum of Art in Charleston), which was soon exhibited in Philadelphia, thereby graphically bringing to Americans knowledge of the conflict.[10]

Volunteers came to Greece as early as November 1821. Among the hundreds arriving in Greece from western Europe was one American, George Jarvis. He traveled from Hamburg, where his father was a consular official, to Marseilles from where he sailed to Greece in 1822, and he remained there until 1828.[11] In 1824, Jonathan Peckham Miller, a New Englander, arrived at Messolonghi in November 1824 to join up with Jarvis.[12] Samuel Gridley Howe, with a medical degree from Harvard, came to Greece in 1825 for two years. Three years later, even before the outcome of the conflict, he published a classic account of what he knew and had witnessed.[13] John M. Allen of Kentucky, who went first to Smyrna in early 1825, was in Greece from 1826 to 1828.[14] Estwick Evans of Portsmouth, New Hampshire, arrived in Greece aboard the USS *North Carolina* in August 1825 and then went briefly to Smyrna.[15] But none of these philhellenes is known to have gone to Egypt. In fact, as we have seen, the only American visitors known to have been in Egypt in 1821, 1822, and 1823 were Luther Bradish, George Rapelje, and the three American missionaries Pliny Fisk, Levi Parsons, and Jonas King.

To help support the Turkish fleet, Mehmet Ali of Egypt contributed warships under the command of his son Ibrahim Pasha. For more than a year, the combined Egyptian and Turkish fleets sparred with Greek vessels at a variety of ports and waters around Greece, as if in a maritime game of chess.

About this time, July 13, 1825, the brig *Erin* of Boston, Captain Lawrence, was said to have arrived at Malta from Alexandria.[16] A few weeks later, on September 7, 1825, it was reported to have sailed back to Alexandria from Malta.[17] Early next year, on January 21, 1826, the *Erin* was stranded near Patras (western coast of Greece). One of the newspaper accounts added that the vessel had "been in the Egyptian service as a transport," another that it had "been in the Turkish transport service."[18] From this it would appear that it had been chartered to carry supplies, or perhaps even troops, from Alexandria to Greece to help the Ottoman forces combating the Greeks in the Morea. A letter from the French consul-general Drovetti to Baron de Damas, the French foreign minister, dated October 24, 1825, itemizes the nationalities and types of ships engaged in the war effort; augmenting the Ottoman, Algerian, Tripolitanian, and Egyptian vessels were twenty-eight European transports, among which there must have been the Boston brig *Erin*.[19]

In April 1826, Messolonghi (where Byron had lived, and had died in 1824) fell to the Ottoman forces, followed by Athens in August. The Greek holdouts on the Athenian acropolis surrendered in early June 1827. But the Ottoman successes were short-lived. About this time, certainly by mid-July 1827, the British effectively commanded the Greek fleet, and in accordance with a treaty signed in London that month, Britain, France, and Russia agreed to "secure the autonomy of Greece." In September 1827, Egyptians landed further reinforcements in the Morea. In mid-October 1827, the joint Turkish and Egyptian fleet was in Navarino Bay where, partly owing to lack of clarity in discussions among the Turkish, Egyptian, and European commanders, the combined British, French, and Russian ships inflicted overwhelming damage against the Ottoman vessels.[20] Independence was now assured for the Greeks.

During the war American ships of the naval squadron had remained neutral. Nevertheless, in the spring and summer of 1827, in the period leading up to the Battle of Navarino, and on several occasions the following year, American Greek committees in Boston, New York, and Philadelphia had arranged to send relief ships with food, clothing, and medical supplies to Greece. At least eight such shipments are documented.[21]

The Greek Boy

An enduring legacy of the American presence in the War of Independence was the group of Greek refugee children brought to the United States for education by merchants, missionaries, and philhellenes.[22] They were said to number some forty in all, of whom at least fourteen boys and one girl are known by name and later circumstances. Among them was an eleven- or twelve-year-old refugee from Thessaloniki, Christopher Evangeles, who had been living with his widowed mother in Smyrna. His early career in America is worth a mention because of his friendship with several young Americans who would later travel to Egypt. He left Smyrna on December 14, 1827, on the ship *Harriet* under Captain Russell E. Glover and arrived in New York on March 3, 1828. Peter L. Vandervoort, a twenty-year-old New Yorker, and two other young Americans, aged twenty-one and twenty-two, accompanied him on the *Harriet*.[23] In the year of his arrival the artist Samuel F.B. Morse painted his portrait in Greek costume for Peter Vandervoort, who had helped to bring him to New York.[24] And in this same year he served as the inspiration for William Cullen Bryant's poem, "The Greek Boy."

> And Greece, decayed, dethroned, doth see
> Her youth renewed in such as thee.[25]

The artist Robert W. Weir also painted him in Greek costume, a portrait bought by the New York banker Samuel Ward with whom Evangeles would later come to live. An engraving of Weir's painting by Asher B. Durand accompanied the first printing of Bryant's poem in 1828.[26]

We know much about Christopher, or Christy as he became known, because beginning in 1834 he kept a diary on the basis of which a fine appreciation has been written.[27] His sponsors sent him first to the Mount Pleasant Classical Institute in Amherst, Massachusetts; then, after moving to New York, he attended the University of the City of New York. Later, with financial support of the banker Samuel Ward with whom he was living, and with whose daughter Julia he formed a closed attachment, he entered Columbia College, graduating with the class of 1836. During this period he came to know a great many New Yorkers and had a sequence of female admirers. Then, on June 4, 1837, despite another love affair (with Sarah Douglass), Christy left for Greece and ultimately pursued a successful career as an educator on the island of Syra. Several of his Columbia classmates and New York friends would later meet up with him in Athens (where he had first gone to live after graduating from Columbia) on their way to Egypt (see chapter 18).[28]

American Diplomacy

The United States successfully maintained neutrality in Mediterranean politics during the decades of the 1820s and 1830s. Despite American humanitarian support of the Greek cause before 1830 and shipbuilding efforts for the sultan in Constantinople after that date, the American navy never became involved in the region militarily. The cruises of the

American fleet (normally stationed at Port Mahon in Minorca, the easternmost of the Balearic Islands) to the eastern Mediterranean, and even to Constantinople, were undertaken to protect American shipping from pirates and to serve as sight-seeing expeditions. American frigates were periodically moored in Smyrna harbor, as were ships of the British navy, not to take sides but to protect their own national interests. On Sunday, August 26, 1821, during the first summer of the conflict, the American missionary Pliny Fisk preached on board the frigate *United States*, then in Smyrna. In the very same month, as a London newspaper reported, three ships of the British navy "were lying at Smyrna for the protection of British interests in that quarter."[29]

Americans were completely absent in the Battle of Navarino in October 1827 in which combined European and Russian forces soundly defeated the Turkish and Egyptian squadrons. After the defeat of the Turkish and Egyptian fleet, the British and French ministers in Constantinople were recalled. In addition the Ottoman sultan closed the Bosporus to Russian shipping. Russia responded by attacking key positions in what is now eastern Bulgaria, and in the ensuing hostilities it overcame the defending Turkish forces. In the 1829 Treaty of Adrianople, Russia assumed control of the mouth of the Danube and initially at least the regions of Moldavia and Wallachia (modern Romania).

During the decade of the 1820s, the Americans had been seeking unsuccessfully to establish diplomatic relations with the Ottoman porte. But relations were otherwise good, merchant ships continued to trade in Smyrna and Constantinople, and American neutrality finally paid off. Now, in 1829, the administration of Andrew Jackson sent out a seasoned merchant, Charles Rhind of New York, to negotiate a treaty. After reaching Port Mahon he met up with James Biddle, the new commodore of the squadron, who had arrived there independently from the United States more than a month earlier on the frigate *Constellation*. Together they sailed on the *Java*, a frigate of the Mediterranean squadron, to Smyrna where Rhind left at once by himself for Constantinople. He arrived in the city in early February 1830 and with the help of Count Orlov of Russia, and despite adverse maneuverings of the British, he succeeded by April in negotiating for the first time a commercial treaty with the Turkish government. James Biddle, together with David Offley, the senior American merchant in Smyrna, went overland from Smyrna to Constantinople in May to sign the treaty. The United States Senate passed it in February 1831, and two months later in April, President Jackson appointed Commodore David Porter chargé d'affaires at Constantinople.

Ten years earlier, in 1820, Luther Bradish and Charles Folsom, acting for John Quincy Adams, secretary of state, had sought unsuccessfully to negotiate a treaty. George English had tried again in 1823 and 1826, the second time with Commodore Rodgers but without success, and Commodore William M. Crane and the Smyrna merchant David Offley had failed in 1828 and 1829, but at last the United States had succeeded. It was significant not just for American interests in Constantinople and Smyrna: now that there was formal representation at the Sublime Porte, a representative could some day—it took several years—be appointed in Egypt.[30]

Soon afterward Henry Eckford, an experienced shipbuilder from New York, recognizing an opportunity, sailed to Constantinople in his newly constructed corvette, the *United States*, which he intended to sell to the sultan. Captained by George C. DeKay, and with his brother James E. DeKay, a son-in-law of Eckford, also on board, the corvette arrived in August 1831, at the same time as the new chargé d'affaires David Porter arrived aboard the USS *John Adams*. Eckford was successful: the sultan purchased the corvette and commissioned Eckford to build ships at the arsenal. A crew of additional American shipwrights set out from New York for Constantinople. At this time, in 1832, with time on their hands, George C. DeKay and his brother James went to Smyrna, chartered a brig, *The Pilgrim*, and sailed to Beirut and Sidon, and from there they called on Lady Hester Stanhope and went on to Jerusalem. But they did not make it to Egypt.[31] Back in Constantinople, the master shipbuilder Eckford died in November 1832, probably of cholera, yet he was successfully succeeded by one of his American colleagues, Foster Rhodes. Rhodes was commissioned over the next several years to rebuild the sultan's fleet, severely depleted by the losses at Navarino Bay, in the same way that the French were engaged to rebuild the fleet of Mehmet Ali in Alexandria.

Greece, Egypt, the Sublime Porte, and the European Powers

In February 1832 representatives of the three protecting powers of Greece, namely Britain, France, and Russia, held negotiations in Constantinople with Ottoman officials to assure the independence of Greece, and through a subsequent treaty signed later in the year defined her border with Turkey. And through another agreement it was arranged for a Bavarian to assume the throne in Greece. In February 1833, Otho, the younger son of the Bavarian king, landed at Nauplion to become king, serving at first under three Bavarian regents, Count Joseph von Armansperg, the lawyer Georg von Maurer, and General Karl Heideck, with Karl

Abel as secretary. During this period Britain and France, though allied with Russia in advocating the independence of Greece, were anxious to support the Ottoman sultan in the face of potential Russian expansion.

Some of the European players involved in the so-called Eastern Question in this period are worthy of mention, not only owing to the significant roles they played in the politics of the region but because some of them were known and even called upon by American visitors. They included the prime ministers and foreign secretaries in London, Paris, St. Petersburg, and Vienna, and their representatives in Athens, Constantinople, and Alexandria, and in some of their respective capitals.[32] In London the Duke of Wellington was prime minister from 1828 to 1839, Charles Grey from 1830 to 1834; Lord Palmerston was foreign secretary from 1830 on. In Paris prime ministers after the Bourbon restoration and accession of Louis Philippe in 1830 included Victor de Broglie (1830) and Casimir Pierre Périer (1831–1832). Horace Sébastiani (who had served as minister to the porte from 1805 to 1807) was minister of foreign affairs from 1830 to 1832; Talleyrand was ambassador in London from 1830 to 1834. In St. Petersburg, the tsar was Nicholas I, his foreign minister Count Nesselrode; the tsar's ambassador in Paris from 1815 to 1835 was the Corsica-born Count Carlo Andrea Pózzo di Bórgo, and in London, Christopher Lieven with his flamboyant and accomplished wife, the Countess Dorothea Lieven. And last but not least, in Vienna there was Metternich. In Greece, representing the protecting powers, there were three foreign residents: Baron de Rouen, Baron Ruckmann, and Edward Dawkins (later replaced by Edmund Lyons). In Constantinople Britain had assigned Robert Gordon (as envoy), Stratford Canning (ambassador from 1825 to 1828), John Henry Mandeville (minister from 1831 to 1832), and beginning 1833, Lord Ponsonby (as ambassador). The Russian ambassador there was Butenov. The French were represented by Armand-Charles de Guilleminot, ambassador from 1824 to 1831; the Baron de Varenne, chargé d'affaires from 1831 to 1833; and Albin-Reine Roussin, ambassador from 1833 to 1830. The Austrian ambassador was Baron Stürmer. In Egypt the consuls-general of Britain were John Barker from 1829 to 1833 and Colonel Patrick Campbell from 1833 to 1839; of France Jean-François Mimaut from 1829 and the special envoy Boislecomte; and of Austria Prokesch-Osten. The British, the French, and the Russians also had their fleets at the ready, should they be needed.

Complicating the negotiations among the several parties to determine the future of Greece and at the same time maintain a strong Ottoman Empire were the expansionist policies of Mehmet Ali, the pasha of Egypt.

At the request of the sultan and apparently with the promise of territory in Greece, he had contributed forces to conquer Messolonghi in 1826, and he had sent ships to support the Turkish fleet. Mehmet Ali was in part compensated for the loss of most of the Egyptian fleet in Navarino Bay by being given the administration of Candia (the island of Crete). Nevertheless the pasha now decided to enlarge his empire by seizing Palestine and Syria. Ibrahim Pasha, his son, lay siege to Acre in late 1831. He took the city in May 1832 and advanced northward through Damascus and Aleppo into southern Anatolia itself. He defeated the Ottoman forces sent against him at Konieh in December 1832. Would the Ottoman Empire fall to the Egyptian forces? Competing views in European capitals debated the desirability of such an outcome, but ultimately western Europeans agreed that the Ottoman Empire should be preserved against Mehmet Ali. France, having moved into Algeria a few years earlier, in 1830, could not be counted on to provide military support; instead, despite the recently ended conflict between the Russians and the Ottomans in 1828 and 1829, the sultan called on Russia and its fleet entered the Bosporus in February 1833 and sailed to within sight of Constantinople. More than 5,000 Russian troops landed on the Asiatic shore to help forestall any assault by Egyptian forces. The Russian fleet remained in the Bosporus until July. A treaty was secured (the so-called Peace of Kutahya) in which Mehmet Ali retreated from Asia Minor proper but secured all of Palestine and Syria.[33] In May 1834, however, there were local revolts in Nablus, Jerusalem, and Hebron, which Egyptian forces under Ibrahim Pasha put down after several months with substantial loss of life and destruction of property.[34]

American Shipping in the
Eastern Mediterranean in the 1820s
During the 1820s, American merchant shipping prospered throughout the Mediterranean, including Smyrna, despite the constant threat of Greek pirates against brigs of all nationalities in the Aegean. At least a dozen American brigs called at Smyrna in 1821 and 1822, with the number rising to nearly twenty each year from 1823 to 1825. Many of these brigs returned year after year to Smyrna, a few even twice in one year, with predictable cargoes inbound and outbound. And during this period several American merchants came to Smyrna, joining David Offley of Philadelphia, who had been there since 1811.[35] The Bostonian John Langdon sent his son Joseph in 1820, while John's brother Thomas Walley Langdon came out about the same time; Thomas

returned in the 1830s, but young Joseph married a local girl (Lavisa Christine Gout) in 1830 and stayed for the rest of his life.[36] Oliver Clark and his wife Abigail Edes came from Boston in 1825 for a twelve-year residence. Griffin Stith of Baltimore arrived with his wife and ten-year-old son in 1826 and remained there with a growing family until 1838.[37] Charles Walley of Boston, a relative of the Langdons, came in 1827 and stayed for several years. The presence of these merchants demonstrates a flourishing American trade in Smyrna. That was not the case with Alexandria, where European shipping had long exercised exclusive coverage of the market and where there were no resident American merchants. American brigs would only go opportunistically, as indeed Captain Lawrence of the Boston brig *Erin* seems to have done to serve in the transport fleet of the Egyptians.

In the early 1820s shipping news of East Coast papers provide reports of another American brig bound for or coming from Alexandria. The earliest notice says that the brig *Fortune* of Boston, Captain Cutts, was to sail from Gibraltar for Alexandria in early November 1824.[38] Soon after came the report that the "brig *Fortune*, of Boston, sailed from Gibraltar Nov. 10th, for Alexandria, Egypt, having on board about 40 Spanish Constitutionalists."[39] (We know from other reports that the *Fortune* had been at Trieste on August 17, having come to the Mediterranean from Rio de Janeiro earlier in the year).[40] From later notices we can determine that the *Fortune*, now under Captain Jenney, returned to New York on July 25, 1825, from Marsala in Sicily via Gibraltar with a cargo of "Sicily Madeira Wine," and carrying from Gibraltar some members of the crew of the Baltimore schooner *Harriet*, wrecked off the Algerian coast a year earlier, who had been captured and enslaved by the locals until ransomed by the American consul in Algiers.[41] The *Fortune* then went on to its homeport, Boston, on August 12, and sold the wine there.[42]

There are many stories going on here, not the least of which concerns the Spanish Constitutionalists who, having formed a liberal form of government in Cadiz in 1812, were overthrown in 1823 by invading French forces and the return of an absolute king, and were now fleeing for their lives.[43] Taking them from Gibraltar to Alexandria was an opportunistic event for an American brig, not likely to be repeated. Spanish refugees did make it to Alexandria as we know from a separate source. In a report written to a French ministry by the French diplomat Baron de Boislecomte on July 1, 1833, he itemizes the foreign population of Alexandria: English, French, Greeks, etc, and among them Spanish, Italian, and German refugees, totaling forty.[44]

Here, together with these brigs making opportunitistic runs to Alexandria, belongs a letter written by "a gentleman formerly a resident of Philadelphia," to a friend in Philadelphia, dated "Alexandria (Egypt), July 1, 1826." Excerpts printed in newspapers later in the year include these observations:

> A desire to see the world in all its varieties, added to a species of romance for visiting the wondrous fertilizing Nile, pyramids, antiquities of the earliest people, Holy Land, and birth place of our Saviour, have been among the inducements that have led me to this quarter, bearing in mind also, not to return without some of the "filthy lucre." This City does not present many attractions—it is dirty—of rude architecture and surrounded by the ruins of its ancient greatness, literally verifying the prophecy of not one stone remaining upon another. The mixture of the people and languages make it a perfect Babel—and as the majority of the Franc or European population cannot trace their origin, to very noble ancestors, you must not consider it as highly chaste, refined or intelligent. With it I mix but little—the want of a fluent knowledge of Italian or French forming one barrier and, disinclination, another; the leisure from business is confined to our establishment, which is principally English—though a few interesting Donnas, somewhat of the character of your "Sicilian Nymph" might be selected from the Italian or Greek belles, but the number would be rather limited. The opening of trade between this and the United States is yet small, indeed nothing direct, yet capital might make a beneficial visit if not too anxious for an early return or disposed to go beyond the received limits of ordinary commercial operations.[45]

His final remarks betrayed the commercial aspect of the American spirit. I have no idea who he was, or whether in fact he was American or British.

9 | THE LURE OF EGYPT

American visitors to Egypt in the 1820s were unusual. We have told the stories of George Bethune English, Luther Bradish, and George Rapelje in 1820, 1821, and 1822; the missionaries Jonas King and Pliny Fisk, acting like tourists in 1823; and the brief stays of the missionary Eli Smith and an unnamed Philadelphian in 1826. Although there were doubtless others whose presence has gone undetected, their number was limited.

Beginning in 1829 and throughout the 1830s the story changes. There are several reasons. First, packets sailing between New York and English and French ports, regularly scheduled since 1823 and increasing in number since then, facilitated travel for Americans to western Europe and beyond. Within Egypt itself, the British sought to improve the hotels and transit within the country to facilitate their passage to India. Everything to do following the arrival at Alexandria of military officers and civilian officials bound for India, such as accommodations, travel to Cairo, opportunities for sight-seeing, and travel by caravan from Cairo to Suez, ultimately benefited all tourists. In 1839 an American traveler, Philip Rhinelander, whom we will meet in chapter 18, put it this way: "The expedition of Napoleon and the recent discoveries of their country-man Champollion, has excited [in the French] a strong interest in Egypt, while the overland passage to India has flooded the country with Englishmen, no fewer than eight hundred persons having crossed the desert to Suez within the last nine months." The numbers of passengers taking passage in steamers running from Suez to Bombay and other Indian ports, as published in journals, names in the hundreds, help to confirm the figure given by Rhinelander.

Second, more Americans were becoming aware of ancient Egypt. The decipherment of Egyptian hieroglyphs in the early 1820s by the French scholar Jean-François Champollion, which brought a new understanding to ancient Egyptian history, was widely reported in the United States. The American magazine *The North American Review* carried two articles in 1829 and 1831 in which Champollion's discovery was paramount.[1]

Champollion was significant in another respect. In 1826 he persuaded King Charles X to open galleries in the Louvre for the exhibition of Egyptian antiquities, where he himself became curator. In these galleries was displayed the major collection of antiquities purchased on Champollion's initiative that very year from the British consul-general in Egypt, Henry Salt, a collection that came to Paris to join Egyptian sculpture and smaller objects already assembled from other sources. And in these years in London the British Museum was expanding its own Egyptian galleries. There, in the new Townley Gallery, beginning in 1808, the Egyptian antiquities seized from the French in Egypt, including the Rosetta Stone and the sarcophagus of Nectanebo II, were displayed. They joined examples of Egyptian sculpture acquired from other sources in the closing decades of the eighteenth century. A major addition to these things came in 1823 with the acquisition of Henry Salt's first collection of monumental sculpture. Later, in the 1830s, the museum purchased more sets of antiquities, among them a third collection from Henry Salt (the second had gone to the Louvre) and the collection of Giovanni Anastasi, an Armenian merchant in Egypt.[2] American visitors to London and Paris could not have seen these newly installed Egyptian galleries in the British Museum and the Louvre without contemplating, though not necessarily fulfilling, a trip to Egypt.

Egyptian Revival and the *Description de l'Égypte*
The exhibition of antiquities was only part of the story. In addition, architects and craftsmen, particularly in England and France, began to use principles of Egyptian design in architecture and the decorative arts. Among the first was the architect of London's Egyptian Hall, an exhibition space built in Piccadilly in 1812, the Egyptianizing façade of which was based on drawings in Vivant Denon's book, *Voyage dans la basse et la haute Égypte*. No American visiting London would have missed it. It was here in 1821 and 1822, after the interior had been remodeled to give it an Egyptian look, that Giovanni Belzoni held his famous exhibition including a reconstruction of the tomb of pharaoh Seti I, which he had discovered in the Valley of the Kings at Thebes some years earlier. The building remained

standing until 1904. One writer has said, "The fame of the Egyptian Hall gave particular publicity to the taste for things Egyptian, and advanced the development of Egyptomania in all branches of the decorative arts."[3]

'Egyptian Revival' architecture, which originated in England and France in the first decades of the nineteenth century, soon spread to the United States. The illustrations of Egyptian monuments in the volumes of the first edition of *Description de l'Égypte*, the undertaking of Napoleon's savants, which appeared in volumes dated from 1809 to 1828 and was soon available in select American libraries and at least three private collections, were a potential source of inspiration for American architects. In 1831, under the guidance of Dr. Jacob Bigelow, a Harvard College professor of the Application of Science to the Useful Arts, the gateway and flanking porters' lodges at the entrance of Mt. Auburn Cemetery in Cambridge were constructed in Egyptian style. Bigelow, who served as architect, stated that the designs were "mostly taken from some of the best examples in Denderah and Karnac." He probably used the very first set of the *Description* to enter an American institution, namely the one presented to the Harvard College library over a period of several years beginning in 1822 by William H. Eliot, class of 1815, and cited in a publication about the library in 1830 as "a work, which, high as its value is at present, will no doubt be rendered more and more valuable by the inquiries now prosecuting into the wonders of Egyptian antiquities and art."[4]

New Yorkers would have been aware of the work of Alexander Jackson Davis who, as a young architect in the late 1820s and early 1830s, designed buildings in a range of styles, including Egyptian Revival. Like the Bostonian Jacob Bigelow, Davis knew the *Description de l'Égypte* as revealed in an elevation done in watercolor about 1830 of the Temple of Armant (also Erment or Hermonthis), based on an analysis of some of the plates (plate 5).[5] He had access to the set owned by his partner, Ithiel Town, who possessed an extensive library and had purchased his set in London in about 1828.[6] Davis designed a cemetery gate, a church, and a public institution (the American Institute of the City of New York), all featuring Egyptian façades, though none of them was executed. In 1835, Davis also submitted drawings in the competition for the Halls of Justice in New York in which the central portico on one side was to be in Egyptian style.[7]

Davis was not successful. In the end, the design of the English-born architect John Haviland (1792–1852), resident in Philadelphia, was selected for the Halls of Justice. The building, a combination of courts and prison built between 1835 and 1838, retained one entrance portico in Egyptian style, which gave to the building (no longer standing) its name,

"The Tombs" or even "The Egyptian Tombs." George Templeton Strong, fresh out of Columbia College, referred to it as "The Egyptian Tombs" in his diary entry of May 5, 1839.[8] Haviland surely drew on his own set of the *Description de l'Égypte*. He had acquired a set of the second edition in January 1835, as he recorded in his expense account ledger: "bought Panckoucke's Egypt . . . $250."[9]

The use by architects of the illustrations of ancient Egyptian monuments depicted in the *Description* was matched by the acquisition of the work and related publications by American libraries to satisfy their patrons' curiosity about Egypt in general. In 1829 the American Philosophical Society in Philadelphia elected as a member Edmé-François Jomard, the general editor of the *Description de l'Égypte*, and that very year Jomard presented to the society's library some of his publications. Among them were several text and folio parts of the original *Description* and six volumes of Jomard's text reprinted, in very limited number, in octavo format, with a folio volume of plates, by the Paris editor and bookseller Panckoucke in the 1820s as *Recueil d'observations et de mémoires sur l'Égypte ancienne et moderne*.[10] The library then set about to acquire a complete set of the *Description* and did so in January 1833, buying the volumes from John Vaughan, the librarian, who had gone to considerable effort to find a good set.[11]

Libraries farther south were also receiving the great French work. The Library of Congress, founded in 1800, burned by the British during the War of 1812 and then replenished, beginning with the library of Thomas Jefferson, was actively buying books in the 1820s and 1830s. The books were selected, not by the librarian, but by members of the joint committee on the library. Edward Everett, US representative from Massachusetts, became a member of the committee in 1825. Everett, a leading intellectual (discussed in chapter 4), had studied in Göttingen, had traveled in Greece, and had been a professor of Greek at Harvard, and to him should surely be given the credit for the acquisition of a set of the *Description de l'Égypte* in 1830 for $800.[12]

In 1830, the name of Henry Middleton (1770–1846) of South Carolina, minister to St. Petersburg from 1820 to 1830, appeared in the list of subscribers to the second Panckoucke edition of the *Description*.[13] After returning home Middleton offered his set to the American Philosophical Society in Philadelphia for $600 but was not taken up on the offer.[14] A few years later however, in 1834, he sold it for $500 to the Charleston Library Society, where it can still be found today.[15] Had it remained in his library at Middleton Place outside of Charleston, it would surely have been destroyed when much of the library was looted and burned in 1865 at the close of the Civil War.[16]

The most notable set of the *Description* to come to the United States in these early years is in the Providence Athenaeum. The Athenaeum acquired a set of the first edition in 1838, the very year the architect William Strickland completed a new building for the library. John Russell Bartlett (1805–1886), a Providence merchant, book lover, and acting director of the library then living in New York, arranged its acquisition through a London bookseller, and he raised the purchase price of $500 by subscription through ten wealthy friends of the library. The cost of the new building was $19,000, which gives an idea of the commitment made by Bartlett and his ten friends. Their distinguished set remains to this day (though in varying states of preservation from volume to volume) with its original red and gilded binding by Jean-Joseph Tessier ("relieur & doreur" to the Duc d'Orléans), whose engraved label is pasted inside the front cover of the first plate volume. The set had once belonged to Jules-Armand, Prince de Polignac (1780–1847), to whom it had been presented in 1830 shortly after he had been named minister of foreign affairs under Charles X. It was one of several sets presented at the suggestion of the general editor Edmé-François Jomard to senior government officials by the minister of the interior, at a time when some 340 sets remained unsold.[17] In the revolution of July 1830 Polignac fled, was then captured, imprisoned, and after several years amnestied in 1836, after which he went into exile in England. At some stage he parted with his set of the *Description*. In Providence Bartlett arranged for the construction of a chest-high wooden cabinet to house it, some nine by five feet, locally made and designed to resemble an Egyptian temple. In designing it, Bartlett consulted with the British artist Frederick Catherwood whom he had met in New York in 1838 where Catherwood had moved after spending years in Egypt drawing ancient monuments (see chapter 11).[18]

All told, at least eleven sets of the *Description de l'Égypte* reached American libraries or architects' collections prior to 1839,[19] and some of the illustrations served in the design of Egyptian Revival architecture in Cambridge, New York, Trenton, and Philadelphia. This range of interest in the United States for things Egyptian is indicative of the climate that, together with easier means of traveling abroad, led to a small but steady procession of Americans to Egypt seeking to extend their European experience. Now we will first consider those Americans who traveled in Egypt between 1829 to 1832, and then close with mention of a few who seriously considered going but for some reason did not make the trip.

Henry Oliver

Beginning in 1829, a never-ending succession of Americans had the determination and good fortune to reach Egypt. The first was Henry Oliver, a Baltimorean, who matriculated with the class of 1821 at Yale, but left in his junior year without graduating.[20] In 1821 he attended the Litchfield Law School in Connecticut, after which he spent years traveling. In February 1830 the Scottish doctor and traveler William Holt Yates, arriving from Malta, met him in Alexandria, after Oliver had finished his Nile tour and was about to leave Egypt, and Oliver recommended to Yates the dragoman he had engaged while in Egypt.[21] Little is known of Oliver's Egyptian visit. In Cairo he climbed the Great Pyramid: his name was noted at the top by another American traveler in 1834. And the fact that he had employed an experienced dragoman confirms a report that he ventured up the Nile as far south as Nubia. We know that he reached Thebes because he had his name cut on the right side of the first pylon at Luxor: H. OLIVER / U.STATES.[22] This itinerary suggests that he must have arrived in Egypt sometime in the second half of 1829. Was Oliver the "Gentleman in Egypt" who wrote a letter home in the fall of 1829, an extract of which was published in a Washington, DC, newspaper?

> There are seven learned Frenchmen here, who have been sent by the French Government, with the charge of translating and illustrating the hieroglyphics. Their head is the renowned Champollion, who reads hieroglyphics with as much readiness as his native language, and states that he finds all in the hieroglyphics that the Bible relates of Egypt. I have often seen these gentlemen, and hope to meet them in Cairo.[23]

These are surely words of an American, not a British traveler, destined expressly for an American newspaper. The extract seems not to have been reprinted from an account published in England.

In the months following his Egyptian trip, Oliver traveled through Palestine to Smyrna where he met the Rev. Eli Smith and Augustus Alvey Adee, a surgeon on the *Lexington*, one of the ships of the Mediterranean squadron, both of them fellow classmates at Yale. On April 12, 1830, Oliver set out on the week-long overland trip to Constantinople together with Eli Smith, and with Smith's colleague H.G.O. Dwight, who were bound ultimately for Armenia.[24] The threesome were followed a couple of weeks later by James Biddle, commodore of the Mediterranean squadron, and David Offley, the senior American merchant in Smyrna, the two officials charged to sign the commercial treaty negotiated by Charles Rhind,

Andrew Jackson's special envoy, as mentioned in chapter 8. Traveling with Biddle and Offley was Oliver's classmate the surgeon Augustus Adee, as well as Biddle's young cousin, John Biddle Chapman, a recent graduate of the University of Pennsylvania, who had come out to the Mediterranean with him months earlier. From Constantinople, Chapman reported in an unsigned letter to an American newspaper that Oliver had left the city for Odessa.[25] And Oliver may well have gone on to St. Petersburg, perhaps just in time to see the American minister Henry Middleton, who did not depart Russia after ten years at his post until later that summer.

Oliver had wanderlust and came from a family well endowed to support it. He was the second of three sons of Robert Oliver (c. 1759–1834), an exceptionally wealthy Baltimore merchant. All of them traveled abroad. His older brother, Charles (1792–1858), Princeton class of 1815, visited Rome in 1825 and was living in Paris in 1827. His younger brother, Thomas (1802–1848), also visited Europe in 1825. And Henry traveled. He must be the H. Oliver of Baltimore, returning to New York from Liverpool in early March 1824, evidence of an earlier trip abroad.[26] He is surely the "Oliver of Baltimore" sailing from New York for Havre in mid-October 1827, the start of a three-year trip that would include Egypt.[27] Before he left home in early fall 1827, "Henry Oliver, Esq." presented to Peale's Baltimore Museum two ethnographic items from Peru: a "walking dress and hood worn by the ladies in Lima," and a "silver breast pin, much resembling a teaspoon, worn by the inhabitants of Peru."[28] He appears to have been traveling in Spanish America in the period from mid-1824 to mid-1827. The year following his Mediterranean experiences found him traveling in Mexico and apparently again in South America. In addition to having wanderlust, he was considered by his family to need help. His father's will of 1834 appointed his brothers and his two brothers-in-law[29] to help take care of him. But Henry had died a year earlier, in 1833, in Mexico.

Cornelius Bradford

In Malta, before coming to Alexandria, Doctor Yates had met another American, Cornelius Bradford, with whom he decided to travel.[30] Bradford had arrived in Paris in June of 1825.[31] He was a nephew of Philip Hone (mayor of New York in 1825–1826), socially prominent, and a man of fashion. In 1826 he served as one of five members of the Committee of Arrangement for the Fourth of July party held under the auspices of the American minister at which Lafayette, whom he came to know, was the guest of honor.[32] On May 13, 1828, Peter Townsend, a doctor from New York studying in Paris (and who thought of coming to Egypt himself as we shall see at the end of this chapter), had met him at one of Lafayette's soirées, held every Tuesday: "Mr. Bradford as usual was also there, a very handsome young American."[33] In March 1829 Bradford had been appointed US consul in Lyon, succeeding J. Fenimore Cooper. Later that year he had traveled to Italy, and in Florence in October he had commissioned the American sculptor Horatio Greenough to do a plaster bust for which he paid a hundred dollars.[34] Greenough was also working on a plaster bust of John T. Kirkland, a former president of Harvard, who with his wife was also visiting Florence (see plate 11). In fact, Bradford traveled to Naples and Sicily with the Kirklands and then, upon their return to Naples, he went on to Malta.[35]

Regrettably there was another side to Bradford. An American naval officer, Charles Wilkes, on shore leave at Leghorn in 1830, visited Florence and heard the story from James Ombrosi, the Italian-born American consul resident in Florence.

When he could get me alone he was very communicative about his affairs and complained much of the manner he had been favored by Americans that brought him letters of introduction, borrowed money from him on drafts which had never been honored and had to be made good to the banks by him. One of the most remarkable was a Mr. Bradford, a nephew of Philip Hone of New York, who brought him letters from his uncle to aid him all in his power. Mr. Hone, he had been attentive to in Italy, and received his nephew, who also brought him letters from Paris intimating the wish he would receive his attention, that Bradford was engaged to be married to one of the daughters of Genl Lafayette and would return shortly to be married there on his way to the Southern parts of Italy. Although he, Bradford, had been but a short time from Paris, he represented himself as being out of money and showed the letters he had received from his uncles, & other documents in his possession, that Ombrosi did not hesitate to afford him the relief of $600, all the money he had & took his obligation on his uncle in the draft on New York. This Bradford journeyed to the far East, and swindled several Americans he met with, and among them Mr. Profr. ____ of whom he borrowed several hundred dollars. . . . I took from [Mr. Ombrosi] the draft, which Mr. Philip Hone had refused to honor, and made a statement of Mr. Ombrosi to Mr. Hone through my uncle [Charles Wilkes], the President of the Bank [of New York], which he presented to him. [Mr. Hone] regretted the circumstances, said he had paid so many bills of his nephew, & vowed he would not honour any more; but I believe he was induced by my uncle and finally sent the money.[36]

Bradford arrived in Alexandria with Yates in early February. Yates described him as animated, a gentlemen accustomed to polite society, and traveling out of curiosity. In an audience with Ibrahim Pasha in Alexandria, he displayed knowledge of the relative strengths of the sultan's and the pasha's arsenals, and the lack of American trade in the Black Sea as the obstacle to the establishment of diplomatic relations with the porte and by extension Alexandria. While in Alexandria Bradford must have met his fellow American Henry Oliver, but we have no record of their meeting.

Bradford and Yates set forth on the Nile from Cairo on March 11 in the company of two English travelers who had their own boat, George Robinson and William Maltass, the latter a member of an old Smyrniote family. Reaching Thebes, the two parties found another boat moored at the banks with two French travelers, Edmond de Cadalvène, *directeur du Service postal français* at Alexandria, and his companion Jules de Breuvery. Soon after their arrival, a fourth boat came in view with Mme Ida Saint-Elme. That was her adopted name. Born Maria Johanna Elselina Versfelt in 1776, her mother Dutch, her father Russian or Hungarian, she was also known as Elzelina Tolstoy van Aylde Jonghe. She had once been the mistress of several French officers, among them Marshall Ney. Her nom de plume was "La Contemporaine." She was adventurous. With her adopted son Leopold she had left Cairo on March 16, five days after Yates and Bradford in a *cangiah* lent to her by her old friend Joseph Sève, the French officer who had come to Egypt in 1819 to train the Egyptian army, had converted to Islam, and had assumed the name of Suleyman Bey.

Cadalvène and Breuvery wrote their own account of their Nile journey in which they offered a more caustic appraisal of Bradford:

Né sur les bords de l'Orénoque, avait sucé, avec le lait, cette idée de supériorité impérieuse que nourrissent les blancs américains contre les noirs et les hommes de couleur. Le reïs de sa conge ayant insolemment refusé de lui obéir, M. Bradford employa, pour vaincere sa résistance, la moyen auquel tout cède ordinairement en Égypte, et se jeta sur lui le bâton à la main.[37]

[Born on the banks of the Orinoco, he swallowed with his mother's milk the idea of superiority which white Americans hold about negroes and people of color. The captain of his *Cange* having insolently refused to obey him, Mr. Bradford tried to overcome his resistance by the standard means of Egypt, beating his hand with a stick.]

The two Frenchmen were not about to give an American traveler, a rarity in Egypt in the first place, his due. Americans, beginning with John Ledyard in 1788, compared the Nile to their own rivers, the Connecticut or the Mississippi. Perhaps the French travelers heard Bradford speak of the Hudson—he was a New Yorker—which prompted them to substitute their own outlandish river, the Orinoco. As for discipline, all Nile tourists, regardless of nationality, were encouraged to maintain the upper hand over their captains. Ida Saint-Elme also wrote an account, a detailed account, in six volumes, of her Egyptian experiences. She too recalled the encounter with other boats at Thebes and left her own impression of her fellow travelers. As a lady of the world in her early fifties she seems to have been more favorably disposed to Bradford.

> J'eus peine à reconnaître M. Robinson, qui s'était, ainsi que M. Cadalveine et son ami, déguisés en jubé et en turban, manie singulière des Européens, qui croient par là être plus respectés, tandis que l'habit français est le plus sûr porte-respect. L'Américain le sentait comme nous, car il était en simple costume de militaire en voyage. Il était fort bien de figure, et d'une taille avantageuse qui perdait quelque chose par une blessure au pied qui le forçait de boiter légèrement.[38]

> [I hardly recognized Mr. Robinson who, like M. Cadalvène and his friend, disguised *en jubé* and in a turban, a singular habit of Europeans, believe by so doing to be more respected, although the Frank dress surely carries more respect. The American thought like us, for he wore a simple military uniform. He was handsome and of commanding height though the strong impression he made was diminished by a wound in his foot which gave him a slight limp.]

She knew Robinson and Maltass because earlier in the year they had sailed together on the same ship from Smyrna to Alexandria. She never called Bradford by his name, only "the American," and she never mentioned Yates.

With their companions Robinson and Maltass, Bradford and Yates proceeded upriver to Nubia, reaching Philae, Abu Simbel, Wadi Halfa, and Abusir near the second cataract (where Bradford cut his name) before turning back to spend additional time at Thebes.[39] Back in Cairo they left Robinson and Maltass and traveled overland to St Catherine's monastery in Sinai via Suez. From Suez, on June 1, Bradford wrote a letter to a friend in New York, excerpts of which were published years later in a volume of *The Knickerbocker*:

I cannot resist the opportunity to date you a few lines from hence, while I trust you will look on as a remembrance not only of the interesting spot from which they are penned, but of the affectionate friendship of the writer. Our journey from Cairo to this place was entirely across the parched and sandy desert. We came on dromedaries, which are the same as camels, with the difference that they are early trained for more speedy travel. Our small caravan consisted of Doctor Y—, myself, Mahomet, our servant, and an Arab guide, all well armed, and five dromedaries. It would be difficult for me to convey to you with accuracy the dreariness of the route over which we traveled. Nothing but sand and sand-hills burning to the touch, and occasionally the bleached bones of some weary camel of a caravan, who had breathed his last during the tedious journey across the barren wastes. The town of Suez is a most desolate place; on one side the desert, on the other the waters of the Red Sea. It contains five hundred inhabitants, who are dependent entirely for every article of provision on Cairo and some of the small towns on the southern borders of the Sea. No shrubbery of any kind exists here. The land does not admit of the slightest cultivation; not even a solitary blade of grass is to be met with. Though I am very glad to have seen so celebrated a place as the Red Sea, I shall be heartily glad to get to civilized countries again. But few travelers have reached this spot. I am the third American who has ever gazed on the Red Sea, which overwhelmed Pharaoh and his hosts.[40]

In the guest book of the monastery at Mount Sinai Yates wrote, "Dr. William Holt Yates, of London, arrived at this convent, in company with Mr. Bradford, on the 5th of October 1829 [sic, meaning 1830], and left it on the 8th to go to Cairo, and thence to Syria. They have been exceedingly gratified with their sojourn to this interesting country."[41] After seeing Sinai, Bradford and Yates returned to Cairo, and then Bradford left Yates to proceed on his own to Jaffa via the seaport of Damietta. In Jaffa he stayed with the French consul and persuaded the consul's son to accompany him to Jerusalem. From Jerusalem he wrote a second letter to his friend, dated July 10, in which he gave a lengthy and lively account of the holy sites he had visited in and around the city. In it he said that he had "kept a complete journal of all the observations I have made since my arrival in the East."

Yates followed Bradford to Palestine several weeks later. When he arrived in Jaffa, about August 5, he met Breuvery, who had just arrived there overland from Suez and who told him the distressing news that

Bradford had died three days earlier in Jerusalem. Robinson left no account of the Egyptian portion of his journey, writing up only his subsequent travels in Palestine and Syria. In the opening pages of his two-volume work he reported that he sailed in early August from Damietta to Jaffa with Cadalvène, and that when the two of them arrived in Jerusalem a week later they too learned from Breuvery that Bradford had died. Robinson mourned for this spirited twenty-five-year-old who had seemed in such robust health only a few weeks earlier.

Yates says in his own account that he and three friends, presumably Robinson, Cadalvène, and Breuvery, arranged for a stone to be set up in the Latin cemetery where Bradford was buried, with the following epitaph. Yates gives the text:

> Memoriæ
> CORNELII BRADFORD
> Americæ Consulis Lugduni
> Galliarum, Bostoni orti
> virtutibus egregii anno XXV
> ætatis suæ in Sancta Civitate
> obiti 2do Die Augusti Anno Domini
> 1830
> Procul patria, familia, et amicis
> amici sui comitantes hunc
> exiguum et postremum pignus
> amicitiæ et doloris tribuere[42]

The Roman Catholic monks, in whose hospice he had died, did away with that inscription, substituting one of their own, stating that he had renounced his Protestant faith.[43]

> D.O.M.
> Hic jacet
> CORNELIUS BRADFORD EX AMERICÆ
> REGIONIBUS
> Lugduni Galliæ Consul Hyerosolomis tactus intrinsecus sponte
> Erroribus Lutheri et Calvini abjuratis
> Catholicam religionem professus synanche correptus
> E vita decessit IV. nonas Augusti MDCCCXXX Ætatis suæ XXV
> Amici merentes posuere
> Orate pro eo[44]

Most subsequent travelers who saw his grave knew that that was a false claim, and Yates even reported that one of the monks had later confessed to the falsehood.

The *New-York Spectator* carried a simple obituary in December: "At Jerusalem, Palestine, on the second day of August last, Cornelius Bradford, Esq. American Consul at Lyons, in France, formerly of this city." What happened to Greenough's plaster bust of Bradford? Unlike that of John Kirkland, which Greenough later did in marble and came to the Boston Athenaeum, there was no incentive to do the same for Bradford's, and now even the plaster has disappeared. Did any of his friends retrieve his diary? Or did the monks do away with that also?

Allen, Oakley, and Ferguson

In February of 1831, three American tourists visited Egypt. An American Episcopalian missionary, the Rev. John J. Robertson, saw them in Athens in late May on their way home. Writing to a friend, Robertson reported, "their names are Allen, Oakley, and Ferguson; the two former of Dutchess county, New York; the latter from Natchez, Mississippi. They have passed but a day or two here, to take a glance at the splendid remains of antiquity, on their return from a tour in Syria and Egypt."[45]

Allen was Theodore Allen of Hyde Park, New York; Oakley was Robert W. Oakley of Poughkeepsie; Ferguson is otherwise not known. Oakley had earlier in 1828 and 1829 traveled to Canton, China.[46] Both he and Allen were trained as lawyers and had been abroad for more than a year. On February 22, 1830, nearly a year before setting forth on the eastern Mediterranean legs of their tour, Allen and Oakley had celebrated George Washington's birthday as members of a party of fifty Americans gathered together in Rome under the aegis of the novelist J. Fenimore Cooper. There they would have seen Mr. and Mrs. John T. Kirkland, who had traveled to Naples and Sicily with Cornelius Bradford the previous year and would themselves visit Egypt in 1832. There also they would have met the American painter and inventor Samuel F.B. Morse, who more than a year later when he saw them again, said that all three, Allen, Oakley, and Ferguson, had been planning an excursion to the East.

We have some knowledge of their trip in Egypt and elsewhere in the Mediterranean through two long letters (now owned by the New-York Historical Society) written by Allen to the Rev. Samuel R. Johnson, rector of St. James Church, Allen's parish church in Hyde Park. The three young men arrived in Alexandria from Malta on January 30, 1831, and they left the city on February 5 to reach Cairo on February 12. Allen described this six-day boat trip by the canal to the Nile and up the Nile to Cairo with his two friends (whom he does not actually name) and their servants as one of the pleasantest experiences he had had during his stay abroad. On the 14th, two days after reaching Cairo, they rode out to the Pyramids and climbed the Great one. At the summit Allen fired a salute from his pistol, sang a stanza of "Hail Columbia" and "The Star-spangled Banner," drank a toast, and carved his name. In the first of his two letters he wrote, "I have today accomplished one great object of my eastern tour." In general he thought Cairo "disagreeable, vile, dirty, gloomy, and unpleasant." He saw nothing picturesque about streets so narrow that the balconies of the houses often met, or the sight of a camel with its load stuck between two houses on one of these narrow streets. On the 16th they left Cairo by the Nile and on the 20th arrived at Damietta where they promptly took passage in a brig bound for Joppa. This means they were in Egypt merely three weeks.

The only person they mention seeing (though Allen does not give his name) was the British consul-general (John Barker), from whom Allen reports hearing details about the Egyptian navy. The British merchant John Gliddon, resident in Alexandria, was not to be appointed United States consular agent until the following year.

After Egypt, Allen, Oakley, and Ferguson visited Jerusalem and Bethlehem, the holy sites of which Allen describes at length and with some skepticism, and then Ramah, Tyre, Sidon, and Beirut, where Allen says what a pleasure it was to meet the British consul (Peter Abbott) and two American missionaries, Isaac Bird and George Whiting. From Beirut they took ship for Constantinople, touching at Cyprus and Rhodes, and going ashore at Patmos and in the Troad to visit Troy and Alexander Troas. After visiting Constantinople they doubled back by ship to Greece. There, during a sight-seeing tour of Athens, they met the Episcopalian missionaries the Rev. John Hill and the Rev. John Robertson. The latter said in a letter of May 21 that he had met the threesome. By June 3 the three travelers were undergoing quarantine in Trieste.

Released from quarantine, they went to Venice where on July 12 Samuel Morse saw them again: "At noon had a visit from three American friends who left me in Rome last winter on a tour to Egypt, Palestine, Greece, and Turkey, Mr. Allen and Mr. Oakley from N. York and Mr. Ferguson from Natchez."[47] It would seem that soon afterward Allen and Oakley traveled separately from Ferguson. After spending several months in Europe, they arrived back in New York from Havre about October 20. From Venice Ferguson traveled with Morse for many weeks through Italy, to Verona, Brescia, and Milan, and on to Switzerland and Germany.[48] In Heidelberg in early September they went separate ways, Ferguson to Frankfurt, Morse to Paris. I have no record of Ferguson's homeward bound transatlantic passage.

Oakley died the following year. In 1834 Allen married Catherine, daughter of Luman Reed, a wealthy New York merchant and celebrated arts patron.[49] Ferguson remains elusive but his hometown makes one suspect that he was in Egypt not only to see the pyramids but also to observe the growing of cotton. Other planters, from South Carolina and Mississippi, and indeed from Natchez itself, later visited Egypt to obtain specimens of Egyptian cotton and also to witness the cultivation of rice.

The Obelisk from Luxor to Paris

Allen, Oakley, and Ferguson had left Egypt before the French brig *Luxor* arrived to retrieve an obelisk at Thebes. The idea of bringing an obelisk to Paris first circulated at the time of Napoleon's presence in Egypt, not one from Upper Egypt, but one of Cleopatra's Needles situated just outside the walls of Alexandria. One of those was upright, the other fallen but still intact. Both had been brought there from Heliopolis (near Cairo) early in the reign of the Emperor Augustus to stand before the Caesareum, a building dedicated to the cult of Julius Caesar. French and British officials had long coveted them, and in time, Mehmet Ali had agreed to cede one of them to France, the other to England. Jean-François Champollion, arriving in Alexandria in August 1828, made careful note of the two obelisks and then after other business, including an audience with the pasha, went up the Nile to Thebes. There he saw the two obelisks of Ramesses II in front of his temple at Luxor, and came to realize that one or both of them should go to France, not one of those in Alexandria. After intense discussions in Paris and in Egypt, Baron Isidore Justin Séverin Taylor arrived in Cairo in 1830 to negotiate the acquisition for France of one of the Luxor obelisks. It would be the first obelisk to leave Egypt since antiquity.[50]

The *Luxor* reached Alexandria on May 3, 1831, with a complement of officers and experts who, after a delay of some three months waiting for the river to rise, took the ship up the Nile to Thebes. Engineers from the École des Ponts et Chaussées, led by Jean-Baptiste Apollinaire Lebas, had been engaged to lower the westernmost of the two obelisks standing in front of the Temple of Ramesses II. First of all this involved the expropriation and demolition of private houses and the two large pigeon houses standing in front of the obelisks that figure so prominently in the 1799 watercolor of François-Charles Cécile and the drawing of J. Gardner Wilkinson done in the mid-1820s. The debris from these buildings would help to form a bed or platform on which the horizontal obelisk would come to rest. Lebas and his men were successful in lowering the obelisk (late October 1831), dragging it to the edge of the Nile, loading it on board (mid-December 1831), waiting out the winter until the next Nile flood, and transporting it down river to Rosetta (late August to early October 1832) and to Alexandria. Illustrations in several of the accounts, including that of Lebas, record the operation.[51] From Egypt the *Luxor* was escorted by a steamship, the *Sphinx*, to Cherbourg and Rouen, and from there the obelisk was taken up the Seine to Paris where it was re-erected in the Place de la Concorde in 1836.[52]

Back in Alexandria, of course, there were still two obelisks, one designated for the English, the other now no longer destined for France. One, the fallen one, would indeed go to London, to be re-erected on the embankment of the Thames, and the other, in 1880, would be shipped to New York City and be set up in Central Park near the Metropolitan Museum of Art. Americans should be grateful to Champollion for not choosing one of them.

Mendes Israel Cohen

Allen, Oakley, and Ferguson may have missed seeing the French, but one American, Mendes Israel Cohen, a wealthy Baltimorean, encountered them at Thebes. Cohen was midway through a leisurely Egyptian tour which was only one leg on what must have been the longer journeys taken by an American tourist in the nineteenth century. He had sailed from New York in mid-October 1829 bound for Liverpool, and reached Egypt in the spring of 1832 after some two-and-a-half years of travel in England, France, Switzerland, Italy, Turkey, and Palestine. Cohen was born in Richmond, Virginia, in 1796 where his parents had settled in the late 1780s after leaving England immediately following their marriage. At his father's death in 1803, his widowed mother moved with her seven children to Baltimore. In the War of 1812, Cohen, eighteen years old, served in the artillery, helping to defend Fort McHenry during its bombardment by the British. After the war he joined his family's banking firm J.I. Cohen Jr. & Brothers, representing the business for part of his career in New York. But in 1829, he retired and set off to travel.

After extensive travels in Europe and the eastern Mediterranean, Cohen arrived in Damietta from Jaffa. He was released from quarantine on April 11, 1832, and soon went to Cairo. Among his tourist destinations there were the Pyramids. On top of the Great Pyramid he saw cut into the stone the name of John T. Kirkland, a former president of Harvard College, and that of his wife, who were still in Egypt when he first arrived. Their story will be told in a later chapter devoted to the United States Mediterranean squadron: they had arrived on board a naval vessel, the *Concord*. He saw their names on the Pyramid, "as well as the names of several other Americans" (including perhaps those of Allen, Oakley, and Ferguson). Cohen did not meet the Kirklands, but he saw the British artist and architect Francis Arundale, who had arrived in Egypt on board the *Concord* with the Kirklands. Cohen expected to go up the Nile with him where Arundale intended to join the Scottish antiquarian Robert Hay (who had first come to Egypt in 1824) at Thebes. It is doubtful, however, that they actually joined one another for the Nile journey despite Cohen's comment in his diary: "I shall be accompanied by a Mr. Arundell [*sic*], an English architect, employed by Mr. Hay."[53]

In any event, from late April to mid-July Cohen was on the Nile, and from his diary we can trace his day-by-day itinerary. On May 12 he reached Thebes, where he met Hay and the French officers of the *Luxor* waiting until the river would flood; on May 21 he copied the Napoleonic inscription at Philae; May 30 saw him at Abu Simbel.

He carved his name on more than half a dozen monuments, including the temple at Dendur (now in New York City), the Temple of Isis at Philae, and the rock at Abusir. In modern times the French military and the savants had begun the practice with their respective inscription at Philae, but other members of Napoleon's expedition had left individual names on other monuments. The Americans Luther Bradish, Henry Oliver, and Cornelius Bradford had done the same when they were on the Nile, as had dozens of earlier British, French, German, and Italian travelers, usually with the year they were there. Americans often mentioned their country of origin and sometimes even their home city, as did Mendes Cohen. A modern cult of scholarship has flourished identifying the personalities behind the names. They were doing what many ancient Greek and Roman visitors to Egypt had been doing in antiquity since the sixth century BC. It has recently been reported, for instance, that three Greek mercenaries of the early sixth century BC carved their names on a leg of the statue of Ramesses at Abu Simbel adding their places of origin, Rhodes and two cities on the west coast of Asia Minor.[54] Other ancient travelers wrote epitaphs and even long verse inscriptions. Volumes of scholarly publications are devoted to the ancient inscriptions.[55]

On June 20, on his return visit to Thebes, Cohen noted in his diary that the French had lowered the obelisk and put it on board the *Luxor* waiting for the rise of the Nile, though he must have known that this work had actually been completed months before in November and December 1831. On June 22 at Medinet Habu (where he also carved his name), Cohen met the British scholar George Hoskins who was drawing antiquities, and two days later he visited the tombs of the kings with Hoskins and Arundale, and dined with Hay and his wife. While at Thebes and elsewhere in Egypt, Cohen collected Egyptian antiquities, the first American to do so in a serious way. At the end of June he resumed his trip toward Cairo, where he arrived about July 21 to meet George Gliddon. Then, until late August, he was in Cairo, Alexandria, and Cairo again, partly in the company of the English architect and draftsman Frederick Catherwood.

While on the Nile, Cohen, like most European travelers in Egypt, flew his national flag from his boat—an American flag made from material purchased for him by an Arab servant in Manfalout. It had thirteen paper stars. Back in Alexandria on August 6, Cohen called it "The first American Flag that ever appeared on the Nile, having been my National protection through Lower and Upper Egypt, Nubia & a distance of 1200 miles to the 2'd Cataract or Wady-Halfa. The extreme heat of the sun to which it was exposed has drawn the color." It survives to this day at The Johns Hopkins University, Baltimore.[56]

Cohen left Egypt via Suez in the company of "Signor Castro Gonsales, a Spanish priest missionary," and with Miles Ponsonby, the companion of George Hoskins on the Nile, whom he probably met at Thebes. Cohen was bound for Mt. Sinai and St. Catherine's monastery, and there he left his name in the guest book with the dates September 4 through 7, 1832.[57] He then returned to Jerusalem and went north on an extensive tour through Turkey outlined in a letter he wrote from Odessa some months later, printed in American newspapers.[58] From Odessa he went to Moscow, St. Petersburg, and Cracow; then to Vienna, Trieste, Venice, and into Germany. By now it was January 1834. He spent eighteen more months in western Europe, ending up in London. He reached home on August 27, 1835, having been away nearly six years. He is remembered today principally through his Egyptian collection, partly formed in Egypt, and partly purchased in London at the 1835 sale of the former British consul-general Henry Salt, which is now owned by the Johns Hopkins University,[59] and by a portrait he had done showing him in eastern dress, now owned by the Maryland Historical Society (plate 14).

John Gliddon, United States Consular Agent

When Mendes Cohen arrived in Egypt in the spring of 1832, John Gliddon, an English merchant who had lived in Alexandria for nearly fifteen years, had just been appointed consular agent for the United States. It was a good appointment as even the French consul-general Mimaut admitted in a letter of May 2, 1832, to Horace Sébastiani, the minister of foreign affairs in Paris: "Peu de temps auparavant, le gouvernement des États-Unis, qui n'avait jamais eu ici d'agent consulaire, en avait nommé un dans la personne d'un négociant anglais fort estimé."[60] At the same time, his eldest son, George Robbins Gliddon, was appointed consular agent in Cairo. John Gliddon was born in Exeter in Devonshire in 1784.[61] He and his wife Eleanor moved to Malta in 1811, where he became a merchant. In 1818 they went out to Alexandria. There within a short time he seems to have become well established within a community which by 1826, according to the English traveler Richard Madden, consisted of "nine English houses of commerce," Messrs. Briggs and Thurburn, Bell, Harris, Muir, Casey, Joyce, Schutz, Gliddon, and Hayes.[62] The American traveler George Rapelje used Gliddon as one of his bankers in 1822. George Gliddon, the eldest son, was born in England before the move to Malta; two daughters, Ellen and Emma, were born in Malta, and three more sons, Charles, William, and Henry, in Alexandria. Their mother took George, a sister, and another sibling to school in England in 1823, returning herself in 1825. George Gliddon returned to Egypt in 1827. Throughout this period, George Gliddon reported that his father "purchased for domestication such slaves as suited our family requirements," and that most of them were freed within a few years. After serving as a consular agent, John Gliddon was formally appointed consul in 1835, his son George in 1837. George maintained a registry for American visitors to sign from the time he was appointed consular agent in 1832 until 1842, the year his son George published the names in a work designed to rebut a charge of neglect leveled against his father by an uncharacteristically angry American and to show instead all of those visitors he had dutifully served.[63]

Virtually all American visitors, beginning in 1832 with Mr. and Mrs. John T. Kirkland of Boston (who were the first to sign the registry, and to whom we will turn in the next chapter) and the Baltimore traveler Mendes Cohen, paid tribute to their good services and their devoted attention to travelers' welfare. The Gliddons gave advice of every kind and introduced visitors to important contacts. Through them, many Americans, for instance, gained audiences with Mehmet Ali. In September 1833, John Gliddon's daughter Emma married Alexander Tod, a Scottish merchant who had been resident in Alexandria since 1829. After Gliddon's death in 1844, Tod would succeed him as American consul.

John Warren

About this time, a Mr. Warren, an American of quite a different frame of mind, first made his appearance in the East. On May 12, 1832 William Goodell, the American missionary in Constantinople, wrote in his diary that he had seen Mr. Warren, son of Dr. Warren of Boston.[64] Dr. Warren was John Collins Warren, the celebrated Boston surgeon and one of three doctors to receive the Egyptian mummy sent to Massachusetts General Hospital in 1823. Now, nearly ten years later, one of his sons was in the East. He was not J. Mason Warren, starting a three-year stint at medical training in Paris, nor was he Mason's younger brother Sullivan about to arrive in Marseilles to consider his future in life. Rather, he was Mason's older brother John, born in 1809, the errant one who would never have a career and was later described as a true son of Ishmael, with "his hand against every man and every man's hand against him." What he was doing in Constantinople is not known, apart from the fact that he was with a Mr. Christie whom Goodell also mentions. John Warren soon went to Smyrna where he boarded a brig, the *Cherokee*, bound for Boston, declaring himself "Dr" on the ship's manifest, and he reached home in July. The next we know of John he was again abroad, in Marseilles, in February 1833, where he met his brother Sullivan, still in Marseilles. Sullinvan wrote to his brother Mason in Paris that "John was only waiting for a fair wind to sail to Alexandria."[65] Did he go? The answer is yes, because his name appears in a list prepared by John Gliddon, the newly appointed consular agent for the United States, for the secretary of state of "visitors from the United States of America to the Port of Alexandria."[66] Later, from the port of Smyrna, sometime in September or October 1833, he again boarded a brig bound for Boston, the *La Grange*, this time calling himself a physician, and he arrived home on November 30. John's self-appointed titles, "Dr" in 1832 and physician in 1833, tells us poignantly how privately envious he must have been of his father and of his brother Mason whose medical careers were unattainable for him.

Several years later John was yet again abroad, traveling with Alexander Knox, Jr. of New York whom he had met in Naples in April 1837. Years later Knox remembered that "I embarked thence in company with John Warren, of Boston, on a trip up the Mediterranean to Smyrna, where I found a plague existing very badly . . . we had projected a trip to Egypt but John Warren got fearful and took the first vessel for Boston."[67] It would appear that John was seeking to embark on a second excursion to Alexandria. In 1841, some years after his return to Boston, he was committed to McLean Asylum—his father was one of the founders—where he would spend the rest of his life, allowed out for walks but never by himself lest he escape.[68] John's father, whom today we would consider cold and overbearing, disavowed him. After reading the records of John's life at McLean one modern psychiatrist remarked dryly that if he was not crazy when he was admitted, he was certainly crazy by the time McLean was through with him.

Americans Who Almost Went to Egypt
Let us now consider three Americans who considered going to Egypt but for various reasons did not undertake the trip.

James Fenimore Cooper
The novelist J. Fenimore Cooper came to Paris with his wife and children in 1826 and resided and traveled in Europe for seven years before returning home from London in September 1833. In 1828, after two years abroad, he wrote to a friend saying that he hoped to visit Greece, Palestine, and Egypt before returning home.[69] In June 1831 he conceived of a plausible way of doing this, as he explained in a letter from Paris to J.S. Skinner:

> I have had a strong wish to visit the whole Mediterranean coast before I quitted Europe. . . . I hope to be able to collect some five or six friends who will be willing to join me in chartering or purchasing a ship to make the voyage at our leisure and to bring back such articles of curiosity and interest as we may be able to collect. I think a year would be sufficient for the coasts of France, Spain, Italy, Greece, Constantinople, Jerusalem, Egypt, and the Barbary towns, so homeward without a quarantine—sailing and arriving in the spring. At present this is my day dream, though God knows whether it will ever be realized.[70]

Alas for posterity, he did not find time for the excursion.

Albert Brisbane
The young Albert Brisbane of New York State (1809–1890) came closer. In 1830, two years into a six-year stay abroad, after sailing from Trieste to Constantinople and back to Smyrna and Athens, he wrote, "I had intended to go to Egypt, but, finding no means of embarking for that country from

Greece, I resolved to turn my steps westward."[71] Brisbane soon afterward became a disciple of Charles Fourier and returned to the United States to become a leading utopian socialist.

Peter Solomon Townsend
Of greater interest than the attempts of Messrs. Cooper and Brisbane is the story of the New Yorker Peter Townsend. A graduate of Columbia College, Townsend had an 1816 medical degree from the College of Physicians and Surgeons. He had gone to Paris in 1828 with an interest in yellow fever, having written a book on the 1822 outbreak of the disease in New York. In Paris, Townsend visited all of the medical establishments and met the leading professionals in the field, among them Étienne Pariset who was also a yellow fever specialist. Pariset had been a member of a French commission sent to Spain in 1821 to study the disease there, and the two doctors had many conversations on the subject.[72]

They became such good friends that Pariset asked Townsend to join him on a trip to Egypt to study the plague. On March 25, 1828, Townsend wrote in his diary, "Mr. P. says there will be no difficulty about my being a foreigner—he will arrange all that with the government—our expenses to be paid which I told him was all I should ask." In addition, through Pariset, Townsend met Jean-François Champollion who, despite his fame at deciphering hieroglyphic script, had never been to Egypt and would now be accompanying them there. One evening, March 31, Townsend invited Champollion and Pariset and four other guests to dine with him at the Hotel l'Europe where he had been staying for two months. He seated himself between Champollion and Pariset.

> We did not retire into the sitting room until after 9 & the conversation at, as well as before and after dinner, particularly that of *Champollion* who took and kept the floor by universal consent and maintained it with a stream of uninterrupted eloquence rendered more impressive by his musical voice, his polished manner and brilliant elocution was the richest repast of antiquarian erudition I ever listened to.

On June 29:

> took breakfast with my friend Pariset at 8 o'clock and passed several hours with him. He is very anxious to have me accompany him to Egypt though he cannot arrange it so as to have me nominated on a commission. . . . He will procure a passage for me from the government in the

same vessel with him and that after our arrival we shall travel together. I consent to accept his kind proposal.

On July 17:

passed two or three hours with my friend Pariset who said he was rejoiced to see me for he wanted to inform me that Mr. Hyde de Neuville the minister of marine had personally assured him in conversation that the passage to Egypt should be granted to me and therefore that I must get ready as soon as possible to set out August 10 from Paris.

On July 30:

Mr. Darcet [Félix d'Arcet] one of the members of the commission who go out with Mr. Pariset called on me while I was out and left a note . . . to make arrangements relative to securing seats in the mail stage previous to our departure to join Mr. Pariset at Toulon.

But hearing doubts about the viability of the commission, Townsend was uneasy and on that very day decided not to go. Townsend's apprehensions were not unfounded. On August 4, "the expedition of Pariset had been countermanded which in fact I found confirmed in the *Courier Français* of this morning." Soon afterward, however, the Egyptian trip was back on but by then Townsend had returned to New York, having left Paris on August 12 and having sailed from Havre on the 17th.

Champollion and Pariset in Egypt

But we cannot leave Champollion and Pariset without saying a word of their travels that Townsend had the misfortune to miss. The two French scholars soon went to Egypt. Champollion, accompanied by an architect and four artists, among them Nestor L'Hôte, arrived in Alexandria on August 18. There he met a group of Tuscan counterparts—it was a joint expedition—led by Ippolito Rosellini, the first true Italian Egyptologist to visit Egypt. He was accompanied by an architect (his uncle Gaetano Rosellini), a naturalist (Giuseppe Raddi), and three artists. After making the Nile trip as far as Wadi Halfa, the two groups returned to Thebes where they lived for six months, viewing and sketching the monuments and acquiring antiquities. They were back in Alexandria at the end of September 1829. Champollion stayed on until early December, the others even later until early February 1830 before returning home. While in

Alexandria Champollion took the opportunity to purchase select objects from Giovanni Athanasi, the Greek-born agent and excavator for the British consul Henry Salt, whom many travelers, including Americans, knew as Yanni. Among his purchases was the extraordinary statuette of Karomama, which had been found at Karnak and is one of the finest Egyptian bronzes in the Louvre.[73] Champollion kept a journal and wrote letters to colleagues about the expedition.[74] L'Hôte kept his own journal and wrote letters to his family.[75] Rosellini also kept a journal and in addition published a magnificent set of volumes illustrating the monuments they had seen.[76] And after their return one of the Tuscan artists, Giuseppe Angelelli, painted a group portrait of all of the participants posed before the temple at Karnak.

Pariset reached Egypt shortly after Champollion had arrived. With him were five medical colleagues (most of whom Townsend had met in Paris), his widowed son-in-law Dumont, Félix d'Arcet, and three others, Guilhon, Bosc, and Auguste Lagasquie. Pariset and Champollion did not travel together but corresponded during their travels on the Nile, addressing one another by Egyptian names: Pariset was "Imouth," Champollion "Maïamoun." They did finally meet up in Cairo after their respective travels. Pariset submitted a report while he was still in Egypt to a learned journal and later published an account of his examination of the causes of the plague.[77] Lagasquie kept his own journal, which has only recently been published.[78] Had the American Peter Townsend been with them, I have no doubt that he too would have kept a fine journal as he had done during his months in Paris. And he might well have seen Henry Oliver, the Baltimorean mentioned at the outset of this chapter, who was also on the Nile in 1829.

10 | THE US NAVAL SQUADRON: EGYPTIAN CURIOS AND CIVILIAN PASSENGERS

The United States Squadron in the Mediterranean

We have briefly recounted in an earlier chapter the decision of the United States to form a naval squadron in the Mediterranean to protect American shipping from the predatory raids of the Barbary pirates. We mentioned the voyage of Captain William Bainbridge from Algiers to Constantinople in 1800, the exploits of the naval officer William Eaton in Egypt in 1804 seeking to restore to a throne in Tripoli a ruler favorable to the interests of the United States, and lastly the peace negotiated with the Barbary states in 1815 at the close of the War of 1812.

In 1815 the United States sought a permanent naval base in the Mediterranean and after some negotiations found haven at Port Mahon on the Spanish island of Minorca. Summer cruises in the early years after 1815 were limited to the western Mediterranean, to Malta, Naples, Messina, Syracuse, and other ports. The first venture to the eastern Mediterranean took place in October 1820 when the US sloop *Spark*, under Captain William L. Gordon, put in to Smyrna with the Americans Luther Bradish and Charles Folsom on board, on their way to negotiate, unsuccessfully as it turned out, a treaty with the Ottoman porte. The next year, in late August and September, the US frigate *United States* was in Smyrna, as reported in the unpublished journal of the American missionary Pliny Fisk; twice Fisk went on board to preach.[1] A year later the squadron's cruise began with a highlight in Leghorn. There, on May 22, 1822, Lord Byron visited two of the ships.[2] Commodore Jacob Jones invited him on board the frigate *Constitution* after which Captain Wolcott Chauncey asked him to see the corvette *Ontario*. The deck log of the *Ontario* reports: "at 4 PM fired a salute of seventeen guns in consequence of a visit from Lord Byron and manned the yards." The American artist William Edward West, then living in Italy, had also gone on board the *Constitution*. He later portrayed the scene, showing the frigate at anchor, topsails displayed, with Byron dressed in top hat and waving a red banner as he stood in one of three dories approaching the ship (plate 9).[3] After continuing their cruise in Italian waters, stopping at Naples and Messina, the *Constitution* and the *Ontario*, together with the schooner *Nonsuch*, reached Smyrna in mid-June where they stayed, however, only two days. Off the island of Chios in the eastern Aegean they observed the results of hostilities between Turkish and Greek communities, the wreckage of the Turkish flagship, and bodies in the sea. In succeeding years, ships of the squadron made Smyrna one of their normal ports of call, often escorting merchant brigs through the Greek archipelago.

The First Encounter of the Squadron and Egypt
No ships of the United States Mediterranean squadron in these early years, from 1815 on throughout most of the 1820s, ever went to Alexandria. Nevertheless, two American naval officers attached to ships of the squadron are known to have acquired Egyptian antiquities prior to 1820, in this case *shabti*s. *Shabti*s were funerary figurines made of faience, stone, or wood, placed in tombs and intended to perform eternal duties for the deceased. Where did those acquired by the two naval officers come from? The story is not straightforward and is worth looking at in some detail. In 1949 John D. Cooney, curator of Egyptian art at the Brooklyn Museum, drew attention to one Lieut. Tanner who had formed a collection of nearly a dozen painted wood *shabti*s bearing the cartouche of the pharaoh Seti I:

> In 1823, Lt. T. Tanner presented to the Peabody Museum of Salem, Massachusetts [then the Museum of the East India Marine Society], a collection of Egyptian antiquities which includes about two dozen ushabtis of Seti I. They are of wood, with incised inscriptions, the entire surface covered with opaque black varnish, and are of interest here primarily because Tanner must have obtained them from Giovanni Belzoni, the excavator of the tomb of Seti I at Thebes in 1815, which sets an approximate date for the formation of the collection. Tanner probably went up to Thebes where he bought the ushabtis from Belzoni and also acquired other pieces now in Salem bearing the vague attribution "from a tomb at Thebes."[4]

A few observations about this statement: first, the records of the Peabody Museum (now the Peabody Essex Museum) refer to Tanner as Lt. Thos. Tanner; second, Belzoni discovered the tomb of Seti I in

October of 1817, not 1815; and third, can it be that Tanner ever visited Egypt? Naval records indicate that the first ship of the Mediterranean squadron to call at Alexandria did not do so until 1829. And there is more to the story. Museum records reveal that a Capt. Crane, USN, gave to the East India Marine Society in 1824, one year after the date of Tanner's gift, a blue faience *shabti*, said to have been found in Upper Egypt in 1818, that is, soon after the discovery made by Belzoni.

I have been unable to identify an American officer with the rank and name of Lieut. Thos. Tanner,[5] but Captain Crane was a well-known figure, namely William M. Crane (1776–1846), who came to the Mediterranean in July 1815 on board the USS *Independence* and stayed on first as captain of the *Erie*, and second, in 1818, as captain of the *United States*. He was in Port Mahon on the *United States* on January 3, 1818, and then cruised to Syracuse, Messina, Leghorn, Tunis, Algiers, Malaga, Leghorn, and Tunis a second time, Melos in the Aegean, the gulf of Aegina in Greece, and, from early December to early March, Messina. He and his ship left Gibraltar in late March 1819 and returned to Hampton Roads on May 22. In the spring of 1823 he was appointed commander of the Navy Yard and Station at Portsmouth, New Hampshire. Here he probably came into contact with the East India Marine Society in nearby Salem to which he gave the *shabti* that he must have acquired in one of the ports visited during his cruise on the *United States*.

The opening of the tomb of Seti I was a remarkable event. Although the tomb had been disturbed in antiquity, Belzoni was the first to enter it in modern times. The wall paintings are magnificent and copies of them, which he displayed in London's Egyptian Hall at Piccadilly some three years later in 1821, caused a sensation.[6] The alabaster sarcophagus was still present and Belzoni managed to extract it and get it to London. There, after being turned down by the British Museum as being too expensive, it was purchased by Sir John Soane and is today a chief attraction in the museum that bears his name in London.[7]

Scattered around the tomb were some seven hundred mummy-shaped statuettes known as *shabti*s or *ushabti*s, in painted wood and faience, not all of them intact. Like the sarcophagus, they seem to have been Belzoni's to dispose of, even though he was working nominally for the British consul-general Henry Salt. Somerset Lowry-Corry, the 2nd Earl of Belmore, and his party of relatives and servants, his chaplain, and his doctor—their Mediterranean tour has been mentioned—visited the tomb in November 1817, only a few weeks after its discovery, surely the first tourists to do so, and acquired at least five faience *shabti*s found there. A descendant sold them at Sotheby's in 1972, and they are now dispersed.[8] Traveling on the Nile with the Belmore party was Henry Salt, the British consul-general, and he too acquired *shabti*s of Seti I. They were included in two collections of Egyptian antiquities he formed over the next several years, one collection bought by the British Museum, the other by the Louvre.[9] The Italian traveler, Carlo Vidua, who went up the Nile as far as Abu Simbel in late winter and early spring of 1820, acquired six wood *shabti*s of Seti I; these are now in a museum in his home town of Casale Monferrato.[10] A few years later the Scottish antiquary Robert Hay, who first went to Egypt in late 1824 and formed a large collection of Egyptian antiquities, acquired seven more wood *shabti*s from the same tomb. After Hay's death in 1863, his son sold the collection and many of the objects, including ten *shabti*s, passed through a London dealer, Rollin and Feuardent, to a Boston collector, Samuel Way, whose son, C. Granville Way, presented them in 1872 to the Museum of Fine Arts in Boston.[11] The British traveler John Madox, visiting Thebes in early October 1823, reported that "an immense quantity of small wooden mummies about a foot in length, and varnished" were still to be found in the tomb.[12] Hundreds of the wooden *shabti*s of Seti I, as well as some of faience, having followed their own eccentric routes of commerce, are to be found today in collections of Egyptian antiquities throughout western Europe and the United States.[13]

Major collections of Egyptian antiquities were being formed at this time to be sold to European institutions. Three such collections passed through Leghorn (Livorno) in Italy on their way to their ultimate destinations. Bernardino Drovetti, a Piedmontese with an assumed French nationality who had served in Napoleon's Egyptian campaign and had stayed on to collect antiquities, shipped his first collection, which had been some five to ten years in formation, to Leghorn in 1821 (the same year he was appointed consul-general of France); from there, it was purchased by the King of Sardinia and went to Turin. Henry Salt shipped his second collection to Leghorn, care of his brother-in-law Pietro Santoni (husband of Salt's younger sister) to await sale. There, with Jean-François Champollion overseeing negotiations, the Louvre acquired it in 1826. Salt's first collection had been shipped directly to England in 1821 where it was purchased by the British Museum.[14] Giovanni Anastasi, the Alexandrian merchant of Armenian extraction, sold his second collection via Leghorn to the museum in Leiden in 1828, the same year he was appointed consul-general of Norway and Sweden. Smaller collections also found their way out of Egypt. Tourists of the day said that good antiquities found in Thebes were quickly sold downriver in Cairo and

Alexandria and therefore could easily have found their way into other Mediterranean emporia, such as Leghorn where, as we have seen, several collections had been shipped for sale. Officers in the US Navy, such as Captain Crane and the elusive Lieutenant Tanner, would have had opportunities to purchase exotic Egyptian curios in selected ports in the course of a Mediterranean tour. The deck log of the *United States* shows that twice on his 1818 tour Captain Crane put in to Leghorn; there, in all likelihood, he acquired his *shabti*.

William M. Crane returned to the region in 1828 as captain of the *Delaware* and as Commodore of the Mediterranean squadron. His principal mission was to serve as one of the commissioners seeking to negotiate a treaty with the Ottoman porte to allow American shipping into the Black Sea. American warships, as we have recounted, had long been cruising in the Mediterranean, at first of course, at the beginning of the century, in the western reaches to extinguish the threat of Barbary pirates, later throughout the region to protect shipping against Greek pirates and to carry officials on diplomatic missions. Yet their principal mission was to protect shipping, and since shipping to Alexandria was virtually nonexistent, no warships had seen the need to visit Egypt. The rarity of American merchantmen in Egypt was made clear in a newspaper account of early 1830, listing the nationality of vessels reaching Alexandria in 1829. The total was 909, of which 361 were Austrian, 200 English and Ionian, 185 Sardinian, 44 French, and the remaining 119 from other nations or regions;[15] only one was American, namely the brig *Smyrna*.

The *Warren*, Charles W. Skinner, in 1829

Indeed, the first ship of the Mediterranean squadron to visit Alexandria, the US sloop *Warren* under Captain Charles W. Skinner, arriving in July of 1829, was escorting the *Smyrna* to protect it against Greek pirates. The *Smyrna* was from Boston, its captain was Seth Sprague of Marshfield, Massachusetts. The *Warren* had previously patrolled the sea lanes in the Greek archipelago. Two years earlier, men from the *Warren* and the schooner *Porpoise* had landed and burned ships and houses in Mykonos and Andros, hideouts of Greek pirates, in reprisal for attacks on American shipping. On arrival in Alexandria the captain of the port came on board "with the usual complements, offers of assistance, and an assurance that any equal number of guns would be returned to any salute the captain of the *Warren* might fire." The *Warren* exchanged twenty-one-gun salutes with the shore battery.[16] Then, together with three lieutenants, the surgeon and purser, and two midshipmen, and accompanied by the Danish consul (Daniel Dumreicher), Skinner went ashore and was received at the palace by Mehmet Ali. Skinner conversed with him in Italian through the pasha's Italian interpreter. They also had an audience with his son, Ibrahim Pasha, whom they invited on board the *Warren* the next morning. Ibrahim Pasha spent three hours examining the sloop. He was accompanied by the ministers of the army and the navy (the latter Osman Nourredin) as well as senior French naval officials, one of whom the American report called "Mr. Cheerisy," American spelling for Louis-Charles Lefebvre de Cerisy, who had come to Alexandria from Toulon in March 1829 to manage the new dockyard. Ibrahim Pasha drank coffee using sugar and a spoon, ate white American crackers, and accepted a glass of wine, reports of which amazed the Franks in town. Later a party of officers rode to Rosetta where they drank and bathed in Nile water, and Captain Skinner rode with the Danish and Sardinian consuls to see Pompey's Pillar, one of the tourist landmarks in Alexandria. Disregarding whatever contacts George Bethune English may have had with Mehmet Ali in 1818 and the early 1820s, this was the first official encounter of Americans with the pasha of Egypt. More familiar and more distinguished naval officers would follow Skinner's lead in the 1830s and 1840s, but none would excite the admiration of the Egyptians and European residents of Alexandria as did this first visit.

Not until 1832 would another ship of the United States squadron visit Alexandria, and in the intervening period several Americans came to Egypt: Henry Oliver in the second half of 1829, Cornelius Bradford in 1830, and Messrs. Ferguson, Oakley, and Allen in 1831. There was no contact between these travelers and United States naval vessels.

The *Concord*, Matthew C. Perry, and the Kirklands in 1832

In late March 1832, the US naval officer Matthew Calbraith Perry, commander of the corvette *Concord*, sailed into the harbor at Alexandria (plate 10). A year earlier, in June 1831, the frigate *Constellation* had planned to cruise from the Aegean to Palestine and Egypt, but had aborted the itinerary owing to the threat of cholera in the seaports it was to visit.[17] Now, in early 1832, the cholera had subsided and Perry had no qualms about Egypt. On board were four passengers who had joined the *Concord* on March 15 at Malta: Jane Franklin (the wife of Sir John Franklin, an explorer who had already achieved fame looking for the Northwest Passage in northern Canadian waters); Francis Arundale, a young British artist on his way to join Robert Hay (the British topographer of Egyptian ruins); and an American couple in the final year of a three-year European residence, the sixty-two-year-old John T. Kirkland, a Unitarian minister and president of Harvard College from 1810 to 1828 (plate 11), and his wife, Elizabeth Cabot Kirkland (aged forty-seven), whom he had married relatively late in life, in 1827.[18] Mrs. Kirkland was the daughter of George Cabot (1752–1823), US senator from Massachusetts from 1791 to 1796 and a prominent Federalist in American politics. Lady Franklin had proposed a Mediterranean trip to them the previous year, in part so that she could visit her husband on diplomatic duty in Corfu, and now they were jointly pursuing it.

March 27 was the first full day the *Concord* was in Alexandria, and on that day the four passengers landed to find local accommodations, their belongings following them. Lady Franklin had a servant and masses of baggage including five trunks, three carpet bags, and a side saddle. The Kirklands traveled relatively lightly, but they still had two trunks, one bundle of bedding, one carpet bag, one hat box and hat, two umbrellas, one writing case, one cloth cloak, one silk cloak, one shawl, and a great coat, not to mention food: sugar, honey, butter, tea, figs, and drink—cases of champagne, madeira, marsala, and sherry, and six bottles of brandy (carefully itemized in the deck log of the *Concord*). With them was their Arab servant, Achmet, almost certainly engaged in Malta.

The Kirklands left several accounts of their visit. John T. Kirkland recorded their stay in a brief letter to Thomas Handasyd Perkins printed in a Boston newspaper, in which he described Alexandria as "a place quite well worth visiting."[19] He also left a partial record of their tour in a diary preserved in the Harvard University Archives at the Pusey Library. But this diary is written in two hands, one neat and accomplished, the other shaky and uncertain. The former, representing the major part of the diary, is surely that of Elizabeth Kirkland, the latter that of her husband. The shaky hand recalls a comment by Theodore Dwight Woolsey, 1820 graduate of Yale (and later president of Yale), who met the Kirklands in Rome in 1830, while he was in Europe studying Greek. He said in a letter, "I helped Mr. Kirkland in his sight-seeing in Rome, as he was nearly helpless and desirous of seeing everything, yet forgetting it all the next day."[20] Elizabeth Kirkland also recorded their experiences in Europe and in Egypt in a comprehensive and entertaining series of letters now owned by the Massachusetts Historical Society.[21] From these letters and from the Kirklands' joint diary, we know much about their visit to Egypt.

The deck log of the *Concord* and Perry's personal letter book record events on board the ship during the week in Alexandria. The ship had a sequence of visitors and many of the officers went for a shore excursion.

The newly appointed American consular agent John Gliddon came aboard March 27 with a seven-gun salute. In addition several Europeans in the service of the Egyptian fleet paid a visit, among them "Capt. Prissick, an Englishman, commanding a man of war in the Pasha's service, dressed *a la mode de Turk*." On March 28 the Egyptian admiral paid a visit receiving a fifteen-gun salute. On March 29 nine junior officers of the *Concord*, among them lieutenants John Marshall and James H. Ward, left the ship and rode donkeys along the coast to Rosetta.[22] The next day three senior officials visited the *Concord*, the secretary of foreign affairs to the pasha, the secretary of interior affairs, and the Turkish ambassador from Constantinople.

On April first, as the deck log notes, Perry "sent the bears as a present to the Pacha." It was customary to exchange gifts in these parts, but this was indeed an unusual gift for Matthew Perry to have presented to the pasha. Perry had received them as a gift from the court of the Tsar in St. Petersburg where he had been with his ship seven months earlier in August 1831, seeking to deliver a new American minister to Russia. In a watercolor done by Edward C. Young, a young Marine sergeant on board, we see one of the bears, standing on his hind legs, in the keeping of a young messenger boy of the *Concord* in a white sailor's outfit, when the animal was still small enough to handle (plate 13).[23] In return for the bears, "the Pasha made Capt Perry a handsome present of a beautiful shawl for Mrs. Perry, also one for Capt. Kennedy's wife," as Mrs. Kirkland put it.[24] Perry wrote to John Gliddon saying he had no qualms about accepting the shawls because they were a reciprocal gift and in any event were not intended for the officers.

The high point of the port stay was the visit of Mehmet Ali and his suite early in the morning on April 2. The officers of the *Concord* who had left the ship for their excursion to Rosetta had returned at eight the previous evening. Captain Perry had invited Lady Jane Franklin and John and Elizabeth Kirkland, who had remained in Alexandria for the week, to come aboard to witness the event. "At 8:30 the Viceroy of Egypt visited the ship." Joining him were selected officials, among them Boghos Bey, the Armenian-born chief adviser to the pasha, and Suleiman Aga, the last of the Mamluks, yet still a favorite of Mehmet Ali.[25] The crew manned the yards and cheered. Lady Franklin noted that upon seeing two ladies in western dress the pasha at first hesitated but then reconsidered and approached. Elizabeth Kirkland reported that he saluted them by putting a hand to his breast and inclining his head. Another watercolor done by Edward C. Young on the *Concord* shows him as he appeared on the occasion of his visit, dressed in a shirt (*gömlek*) tucked into his full loose trousers (*shalvar*), and over his shirt a jacket, all in green. He wore a colored sash under his jacket, a white turban, and red leather shoes. A ceremonial sword was slung from his shoulder (plate 12).[26] On departing he was again cheered and received a twenty-one-gun salute.

It is apparent from correspondence between John Gliddon and Matthew Perry that the pasha intended to present sabers to Perry and his officers. Perry, however, had scruples about accepting them but John Gliddon said that it would be offensive to refuse them. After discussion with the Ward Room officers, Perry relented. In the evening of April 3, the day before their departure, ten gilt-handled Egyptian sabers, one for each officer, were delivered to the ship. Perry composed a letter to Commodore James Biddle—obviously intended as a letter of record to be delivered some weeks later—in which he reported that he had retained the sabers subject to Biddle's orders or those of the secretary of the Navy. The officers clearly coveted them and did not forget them. Among the many items that Lt. John Marshall mentioned to his sister Mary in a letter he wrote from Marseilles later in the year, on September 2, were the swords: "If Congress decides to give us the swords presented to the officers of this ship by the Pasha of Egypt, I wish father to get mine, and to have it put away until my return."[27] But where are they today?

Later on Perry requested reimbursement from the US government for the extra expenses he had incurred in carrying out these official duties and received $1,500. For helping to arrange the visit John Gliddon received thanks from Youssef Boghos, chief interpreter and minister of foreign affairs to Mehmet Ali:

> Honored Sir, His highness the Viceroy, my illustrious sovereign, charges me to express to you the peculiar satisfaction which he experienced in his visit to the corvette Concord, belonging to the great nation so worthily represented by your honored self, and for which his highness has always cherished sentiments of sincere esteem and admiration.[28]

On April 3, the day before the *Concord* sailed, the Kirklands set off on their own excursion to Rosetta. There they stayed overnight in a house lent to them by John Barker, the British consul-general (appointed after the death of his predecessor Henry Salt), before setting forth the next day on the Nile for Cairo. They remained in Egypt for a month. Elizabeth Kirkland said that in Cairo they stayed in the house of one of the Galloway brothers, two English engineers superintending manufactures for the pasha:

We are most comfortably situated, and kindly treated at Mr. Galloway's. The eldest brother Mr. Thomas Jefferson Galloway has been eight years in the Pasha's service. He is lately married to a Miss Beckwith, daughter of a gun-smith in London, she is a pretty woman and well educated. She ought to be much in love with her husband to give up the comforts of an English home and sojourn in Egypt. We left them in Alexandria, but the other brother George Washington has been our host. You will perceive that the father of these gentlemen is a great admirer of our republic, and a noted radical in England.[29]

In Cairo the Kirklands visited the Citadel, and rode out to Giza, "with Osmin the Scotch renegade spoken of in the 'Modern Traveller' for our cicerone." Osman, as he is usually called, was the Scotsman William Thompson, who had been a soldier in a British regiment that was defeated by Egyptian forces at Rosetta in April 1807, was captured, and obliged to became a Muslim, at least in name. He was freed by the British consul-general Henry Salt in 1815. The American missionary Pliny Fisk had met him in 1822 and had toured Cairo with him. Now it was the Kirklands' turn. With Osman, the Kirklands lodged in one of the catacombs at Giza for the night and rose at sunrise to ascend the Great Pyramid. Elizabeth Kirkland went up, he did not, but she arranged with Mr. Coster, a gentleman staying with the Galloways, to carve all their names on top anyway.

With the exception of the Pyramids, the Kirklands seem to have been more impressed by the new Egypt of Mehmet Ali and his European advisers and by expatriate British residents and travelers than by ancient ruins, as we read in the diary.

The day we left Cairo we visited the Pasha's palace and gardens at Shoubra cultivated somewhat in the English style. . . . We saw on the same day Mrs. Col. Light who has just returned from Thebes in the Mameluke dress, a very remarkable woman. . . . Very masculine in mind and achievements, but soft feminine manners. She is said to have made considerable proficiency in hieroglyphics, she smokes with great skill, shoots, knows all the ropes of a ship so that she can direct the sailors in the absence of the captain. . . . But the usual observances of female life she sets at nought, thinks nothing of coming from Thebes without any of her own sex in the boat with Capt Bowen, a fine, handsome dashing almost impudent looking fellow in the Turkish dress, to whom she occasionally says, "Only think of that Jack." It is said Col. Light and she are not very happy together, that though she is very fascinating to others she is not particularly interesting to him. I should like to have seen more of her.[30]

So would many of us. Mrs. Colonel Light was the beautiful Mary Bennet, an illegitimate daughter of the third Duke of Richmond, who had come out to Egypt with Colonel William Light in 1830. In 1832, about the time Mrs. Kirkland met her, Colonel Light left her, and in 1836 he moved to Australia where he founded the city of Adelaide. Mary later had three children with Captain H.A. Bowen to whom she gave the surname Light. Her journal describing her work at Thebes and elsewhere on the Nile is said to survive.[31]

Back in Alexandria Robert Thurburn, from the firm of Briggs and Co., provided the Kirklands "with every luxury," and they saw again Captain John Prissick, whom they had first met when he came on board the *Concord* at the outset of their visit to Alexandria. He was a British naval officer who had come to Egypt in command of a British-built frigate purchased by the pasha in the previous year. And they acknowledged the help of John Gliddon, who they knew had been recently appointed consular agent of the United States. Elizabeth Kirkland wrote in the joint diary that "Mr. Wellesley, son of the Marquess, Captain Melville, and Major Ovans dined with us at several places" (she does not specify where) and that they "had come from India overland, they were 25 days from Bombay to Cossier [Quseir] in the steamer, 7 days across the desert from Cossier to Thebes." We know from another source that they had left Bombay on the British steamer *Hugh Lindsay* on January fifth; they had come down the Nile in early February. I cannot identify Melville. Ovans was Major Charles Ovans of the European Regiment, Bheel agent in Candeish, who had been granted a furlough. Gerald Wellesley was the most prominent. His father Richard had been governor of Madras, governor of Bengal, and finally commander in chief in India; his uncle was the Duke of Wellington. Gerald was one of five children. His mother Hyacinthe, a French actress, was only married to Richard in 1794 after all the children had been born. She was separated from Richard in 1810 and died in 1816, nearly eight years after Gerald had gone out to India. Later, in 1825, his father married a wealthy American widow, Marianne Caton Patterson, whom the Kirklands had sought to meet in London when they were there in 1830 but were regrettably unable to do owing to her indisposition.[32] Following a successful and financially rewarding career in India, Gerald had resigned as the East India Company's resident at Malwa (Indore) and was now returning home through Egypt. Sadly, he fell sick in Belgrade after departing from Constantinople and died in England in July 1833, aged forty-one, leaving, as his family learned for the first time on reading his will, an Indian mistress and three children.

Surely, in settings devoid of the constraints of London and continental society, John and Elizabeth Kirkland explored subjects beyond the ordinary with Gerald Wellesley and with the other Englishmen they met in Egypt; and surely their conversations were enlivened by cases of sherry, madeira, and champagne.

After a month in Egypt the Kirklands left Alexandria in an Austrian brigantine bound for Jaffa, together with Lady Franklin and with Coster, a good linguist, whom they had engaged to accompany them as interpreter. And from Jaffa they all went to Jerusalem. A letter from John Kirkland (written perhaps with the help of his wife), published some years later in an American periodical, gives some account of their visit to Jerusalem and onward journey to Rhodes, Smyrna, and Constantinople.[33] They returned to Vienna, partly on horseback via Belgrade.

The *Delaware* and Daniel T. Patterson in 1834

Two years later, from mid-July to August 10, 1834, two more ships of the Mediterranean squadron, the US frigate *Delaware* and the schooner *Shark*, called at Alexandria, one of the more significant ports of call on a six-month cruise round the Mediterranean. The shore party destined for Cairo comprised the largest number of Americans yet to visit Egypt at one time: Commodore Daniel T. Patterson, his wife and three daughters, and his two sons (the elder a midshipmen, the younger a captain's clerk, both on the *Delaware*), and twenty additional officers from the two ships, all named in the ships' deck logs, among them midshipmen James Lawrence Heap, the twenty-two-year-old son of Samuel D. Heap, the American consul at Tunis; and David Dixon Porter, the twenty-one-year-old son of Commodore David Porter, chargé d'affaires at the American legation in Constantinople.

We are well informed about the excursion owing to the wealth of published and manuscript accounts. The chaplain of the *Delaware*, the Rev. George Jones, made Egypt the first third of his book.[34] Lieutenant David R. Stewart and passed midshipman Samuel T. Gillett, both of the *Delaware*, and an unnamed officer of the *Shark* wrote letters to US newspapers. David Porter wrote a letter to his father, and Harriet Patterson, the commodore's eldest daughter, wrote up the visit of the ladies to the harem, which was copied in Stewart's account and reprinted elsewhere.[35] In addition, her two younger sisters, Eliza and George Ann, kept journals.[36]

Commodore Patterson had made his name as a young naval lieuten-ant together with the future president Andrew Jackson in the Battle of New Orleans in December 1814 and January 1815, the closing encounter between the Americans and the British in the War of 1812. Soon afterward he was promoted to captain. In 1813 he had married George Ann Pollock and in time had had three daughters and two sons born between 1813 and 1820 in New Orleans. About 1820 he had had his portrait painted by John Wesley Jarvis, well known for having painted other naval heroes, showing Patterson as a strikingly handsome man in his uniform (plate 15).[37] Now, in 1834, the Pattersons were taking what could be considered a family cruise, the men on duty, the women accompanying them. Young midship-men and lieutenants would not have objected to the presence of the three Patterson girls, aged 15, 20, and 21, who by all accounts had inherited the good looks of their parents.

With the help of John Gliddon, the American consular agent in Cairo, this party of twenty-six Americans plus servants traveled to Cairo, first navigating the Mahmoudiya canal in four boats, one for the Patter-sons, another for the lieutenants, a third for the midshipmen, the fourth, a small one for George Jones and the surgeon Dr. Turk, whom the ward-room officers declined to have on their boat. At Atfih, the junction of the canal and the Nile, they changed to three larger boats, cangias, and Jones and Dr. Turk were invited to join the Pattersons in theirs. Nov-elty greeted them every day. David Porter wrote to his father that the hours flew by like music, the passage of three days seeming like so many hours. On arrival at Bulaq, the Nile port of Cairo, on July 20, they were welcomed by John Gliddon's son, George R. Gliddon, the American con-sular agent in Cairo, not only with an English-style coach (said to have been presented to the pasha by the Russian tsar) drawn by four beauti-ful grays for the ladies, but with a cavalcade of thirty richly caparisoned Arabian horses for the officers to ride the several miles into the city. Previously Europeans had not been allowed to ride horses, only donkeys, and on this occasion one of the two doctors, who disliked spirited horses and rode a donkey instead, was treated by the Egyptian attendants as a servant and rode at the rear in the dust. On arrival in Cairo, George Gliddon turned over for their week-long stay his own house of which the *Delaware's* chaplain George Jones gave a fine description. Accord-ing to Jones, a long passageway from the street gave access to Gliddon's three-story, courtyard house. The house formed three sides of the court, a wall, beyond which was an outer yard or garden, the fourth side. The first (ground) floor was for servants and storage. The second floor had offices, the kitchen, and the dining room, the last ornamented with fine woodwork, and with a raised section at one end furnished with carpets and cushions suitable for smoking Turkish pipes after dinner. On the third floor was what we would call the principal living room and the sleeping apartments. There was space for all the officers and the ladies. Lieutenant David R. Stewart served as caterer for their stay.

On successive days the party from the *Delaware* and *Shark* visited the tombs of the caliphs, the new factories, the garden and palace of Ibrahim Pasha on the island of Roda, the slave market and the bazaars, the Citadel, the arsenals, cannon foundry and cotton mills, the tombs of the Mamluks, and the mausoleum built by Mehmet Ali for himself. David Porter thought they were rushed and said that the commodore was anxious to get back to the ship. Nevertheless, along the way Daniel Patterson managed to acquire a copy of *Notes on Hieroglyphics*, a detailed study of the cartouches of the rulers of Egypt prepared by the British officer and antiquarian Major Orlando Felix and published in lithographic form in Cairo in 1830.[38]

Their trip to the Pyramids on July 24 became a caravan of eighty persons, including servants and escorts, on camels, donkeys, and horses, with a carriage for Mrs. Patterson. Almost all climbed the Great Pyramid, even the three Patterson girls; Eliza described the preparations, the early morning trip, and the ascent in her journal:

That night we did not sleep at all. I retired at 11 but all the animals, dromedaries, horses, mules and donkeys, say nothing of the Arabs themselves, had been brought to Mr. Gliddon's so as to be ready as the baggage was to be loaded on before we were up. They made such a dreadful noise that scarcely no one in the house closed their eyes. At 2 o'clock we rose and at 4 most of the party were on their way. . . . The distance was only 10 miles and we walked our horses the whole way so as not to fatigue ourselves at all previous to ascending the pyramids. . . . We seated ourselves beneath this stupendous work, the Pyramid of Cheops and wonder of the world . . . we remained in silent contemplation interrupted now and then by the acclamation of "My God, what calm!" We had all assembled and were each provided with two Bedouin Arabs to assist us up. You can imagine what a train we formed, 27 of us, most with 2 guides. . . . My two guides each grasped an arm not in the most gentle manner. They seemed to think I was made of the iron substance they were themselves. They actually pulled me up 3 or 4 immense steps of 3 to 3 and ½ and 4 feet high by my arms alone, supporting the whole body by them. The pain was so great for I really thought my arms would have given way. Then I screamed, I pulled from them, pushed them away, but all would not do. They minded me no more than they would have done a piece of stick which they had been ordered to carry up to the summit of the pyramid as such they really seemed to consider me. . . . It was no matter whether I got up . . . dead or alive. Finding I could not prevail over them to leave me, I called one of the officers near me and begged him to make them relinquish their hold. He succeeded by the aid of a stick he had in doing so and then I went up by making them give me their hands and assisting me in that way only when I could not climb myself. In about 20 minutes we reached the summit. It was some minutes before I was able to speak after I got up, had some water and a few moments rest restored me. Some played cards, some dated letters, whilst the rest of us were busy inscribing our names. I had my name cut deep in the stone. Each of the officers wrote a letter until it was finished. We remained there about an hour . . . . We saw some names we knew, Lady Franklin's. Mrs. Kirkland's, Miss Gliddon's. We were the second American ladies on the pyramid. Mrs. Kirkland was the first.[39]

On the top David Porter, burned by the sun but not minding the heat, began his letter to his father. Later, within the Pyramid, inside the suffocating principal chamber, the youngest girl, Georgy, fainted, and married officers—no bachelors—had to be found to carry her out. Also, within the Pyramid, an English midshipman of the Indian navy, Mr. Quandborough, traveling with three colleagues on his way to India, dislocated his shoulder after a fall. Dr. Turk, the surgeon, was able to reset it.[40] July 27, the sabbath, was a day of rest.

On the last day the Americans sought to return the favors shown them by George Gliddon by giving him a party in the form of a picnic at Shoubra, the pasha's palace on the Nile outside the city. Joining them was the Scottish botanist James Traill, who had recently arrived in Egypt as successor to the Luxembourgeois botanist Nicolas Bové, to oversee the gardens at Roda and at the pasha's palace at Shoubra. Also accompanying them was the superintendent of the pasha's military school at Tora, the English-speaking Spanish officer Antonio de Seguera, and his wife. Their two daughters brought guitars and amidst jasmine, oleanders, and roses sang Spanish songs for the ladies and the officers. Wine flowed and there was dancing. "At sunset the Spanish ladies took their leave, and we to our boats, Mr. Gliddon accompanying us as far as the head of the Delta, where, as he left us, we gave him three cheers." By this time it was three o'clock in the morning.

At dawn they stopped to take a tour of a public works project being undertaken by the pasha, namely the barrage being built at the apex of the Delta. When completed it would help control floodwaters along the Rosetta and Damietta branches of the Nile in a way to irrigate cultivable land. In his book the chaplain George Jones provided a schematic drawing of the project provided by the chief engineer in charge of the project, Mons. Linon, as he called him. This was Maurice Adolphe Linant de Bellefonds, who had first come out to Egypt in 1818 and would stay on for years in the service of the pasha and his successor, ultimately becoming one of the chief engineers during the construction of the Suez Canal. Now, in late July 1834, he was three months into the barrage project.

In Linant's tent near the work, the Americans met Barthélemy Prosper Enfantin, also known as Le Père, the thirty-eight-year-old leader of the Christian socialist group the Saint Simoniens, whose members had come from France to Egypt in late October 1833 to engage in good works.[41] Enfantin was eccentric but shrewd, and he had a substantial following. Joining him in Egypt were more than fifty of his disciples, many of them engineers who like him had been educated at the École Polytechnique, but also doctors, agricultural experts, military instructors, artists, and musicians. Linant de Bellefonds was not actually a member of the group but was serving as chief engineer with the assistance of engineers who had accompanied Enfantin. Upon arriving in Egypt, Enfantin and his entourage had been well received by the French consul Jean-François Mimaut, who had assisted him in gaining an audience with Mehmet Ali. Enfantin had proposed a canal through Suez, but Mehmet Ali had forbidden that project, concerned that it would promote competition with his own trade through Alexandria and Cairo. Instead he proposed the barrage that would regulate the flow of water in the Nile Delta. George Jones was told that 10,000 men were at work— Eliza Patterson said only 7,000—that despite the appearance of corvée labor they were being paid, and that Linant was seeking to provide as best he could for their welfare.

In January of 1835, some five months after the visit of the Americans, an outbreak of the bubonic plague severely hampered this and other projects in Egypt. To escape being struck down, Enfantin, many of his followers, and other Europeans fled Lower Egypt for several months to Luxor. Nevertheless, by 1836, ten of the Saint Simoniens had died, including some of the key French engineers at the barrage. For this and for other reasons the project was abandoned, and Enfantin and most of his surviving followers soon returned to France. Yet Enfantin left a legacy: Some of the senior doctors and military instructors remained in Egypt as senior officials, and his proposal of a canal through Suez was not forgotten.

Back in Alexandria, on August 3 the shore party of officers and the Pattersons saw the sights of the port, but it must have been something of an anticlimax. Commodore Patterson and as many officers as could be spared from their duties on board the two ships assembled in the city on August 4 for an audience with the pasha. Mehmet Ali and his suite had made a ceremonial visit to the *Delaware* on July 23, while the commodore was in Cairo; now the Americans were returning the gesture. Pleasantries were exchanged and coffee and sherbet were served but Commodore Patterson, expecting more, thought he had been received *sans cérémonie*. A few days later, on August 10, the *Delaware* and the *Shark* sailed from Alexandria. In 1829 and 1832, officers of the *Warren* and the *Concord* had met the pasha and had ventured along the shore to Rosetta. Now a substantial party of officers and passengers had gone all the way to Grand Cairo and had seen the Pyramids.

Not all of the American officers of the *Delaware* and the *Shark* had gone to Cairo; some had had to stay with the ship in Alexandria. By contrast, at their next port of call, Jaffa, time allowed all of the officers and midshipmen to form two parties and to visit Jerusalem in sequence. That was not the case in Egypt, where, given the time available, only half of the officers could visit Cairo. In Egypt, however, those who remained behind must have been given an opportunity to go ashore for at least a day's visit in Alexandria.

One of those who surely visited Alexandria was Frederick W. Moores. This enterprising and educated officer had started his naval career as sailing master of the *Lexington* from mid-1827 to late 1829, but then took a leave from the navy. He returned to Hampton Roads in Virginia from Smyrna in Turkey as a passenger on the US Ship *Delaware*.[42] And with good reason: he was a married man. Rejoining his family he turned around and sailed from Boston bound for Smyrna with his wife Harriet Hathaway—whom he had married about 1820—and their three children, age nine, seven, and five. On May 30, 1830, they arrived in Smyrna for an extended stay. Soon afterward, Griffin Stith, an American merchant from Baltimore, resident in Smyrna, wrote home saying, "We have very lately (by the arrival of the *Smyrna* from Boston) received an accession to our circle of Americans by the arrival of Mr. & Mrs. Moores and three children."[43] And about the same time, Richard Jones Offley (son of David Offley, a leading American merchant, formerly of

Philadelphia and long resident in Smyrna) wrote to his sister-in-law Catherine H. Offley in Trieste saying, "Our American company has received quite a reinforcement with the arrival of Mr. Moores, Mrs. Moores and children three."[44] The Moores family had clearly made an impression. Frederick Moores was not inactive. In December 1830 he joined the Scottish doctor William Holt Yates (then returning home from Egypt via Syria and Asia Minor) and the Rev. F.V.J. Arundell, the British chaplain at Smyrna, for a trip inland. Moores helped to measure the magnetic deviation of compasses near the acropolis of Magnesia, as reported in both Arundell's and Yates' subsequent accounts.[45] In late 1831 the Moores went home, and within about a year Frederick Moores was assigned to the *Delaware*. But did his family join him on the cruise of the *Delaware* in 1834? The record does not say.

In 1834, at the conclusion of his 1833–1834 tour of duty on the *Delaware*, sailing master Moores presented to the Boston Naval Library and Institute some miscellaneous items picked up during his shore excursions, including the upper arm of a female statue from Baalbek and some things from Jerusalem. Did he collect anything in Egypt? Among the antiquities transferred from the Boston Naval Library to the US Naval Academy Museum in Annapolis in 1921, then to the Peabody Museum in Salem in 1923, and finally to the Brooklyn Museum in 1948, is the lower part of a faience drinking horn in the form of a lion, dating from the Persian period in Egypt (c. 525–404 BC) (plate 7).[46] We cannot know for sure whether Moores was the source of this object but he is the most likely candidate. That it came from Egypt, however, is certain: Four comparable objects in faience passed to the Louvre in the mid-nineteenth century from the collection of Antoine-Barthélémy Clot (known as Clot Bey), the leading French physician in Egypt.[47]

But a footnote is necessary on the festivities and the intellectual pursuits of the officers. Not all was as seemly as appeared in the stirring newspaper accounts. Competition and private needs among the officers led to darker acts. The following year in August 1835, David R. Stewart, a senior lieutenant on board the *Delaware* who had been chosen to ride beside the commodore on their way from Bulaq to Cairo and who had served as caterer to the officers while they were housed at George Gliddon's residence, had an argument with a fellow lieutenant, Thomas Turner, after a visit to Agrigento in Sicily. Turner, who had a grievance against Stewart, called him a liar and challenged him to a duel. The next day, on the beach, Turner mortally wounded Stewart. He died the next day.[48] And that's not all. Many officers seem to have known that lieutenant Owen Burns, who had gone to Cairo with others off the *Shark*, had had a habit of compelling the ship's boys to frig him at night in his cabin. He was called to account in a court of inquiry held on board the USS *Potomac* in Naples harbor the following year, and after testimony from several parties, and despite efforts of fellow officers to sweep it under the rug, Commodore Patterson ordered Lieutenant Burns to be publicly reprimanded.[49] And there was one further tragedy. A year and a half after the visit to Egypt, on February 15, 1836, as the *Delaware* neared port in Norfolk, Virginia, Harriet Patterson, who had written up the excursion to the harem in Cairo, died after a long illness.

But in time, one happy event came to pass as a result of the cruise. One of the midshipmen, the twenty-one-year-old David D. Porter, son of the chargé d'affaires at the American legation in Constantinople, had been struck by the youngest Patterson girl, George Ann, known as Georgy, and she by him: Five years later, in 1839, they were married.

The *Constitution*, the *United States*, the *John Adams*, and the *Shark* in 1836

Four ships of the squadron, the frigates *Constitution* and *United States*, the sloop *John Adams*, and the schooner *Shark* visited Alexandria in 1836, but only briefly, from October second to the sixth. They had previously called at Greek, Syrian, and Palestinian ports; from Beirut most of the officers had visited Baalbek, and from Jaffa they had gone to Jerusalem. In Alexandria, on October 4 Mehmet Ali and his suite went aboard the *Constitution*, and on one of the days in port the ships' commanding officers, Jesse D. Elliott, Jesse Wilkinson, Silas H. Stringham, and William Boerum, went ashore to visit Mehmet Ali at his palace, but nothing is known of their experiences. It is likely that John Gliddon, the American consul, made all the arrangements: Earlier in the year the US consul in Gibraltar had written Gliddon telling him to expect their visit.[50] The deck logs of the fleet are laconic, as usual, with the exception of the statement that on October third two seamen from the *John Adams*, George Martin and James Spencer, deserted from one of the cutters sent ashore. From another source we know that the pasha presented to Jesse Elliott, through John Gliddon, a number of ceremonial swords, one of which was handed on to a lieutenant on board the *Constitution*, George F. Pearson, and that two years later the navy was writing to Pearson clearly opposed to his retention of the saber.[51] This reminds us of the hesitation displayed by Matthew C. Perry of the *Concord* at accepting a set of swords from Mehmet Ali when he was in Alexandria in 1832.

The *Constitution*, Jesse D. Elliott, the Hon. Lewis Cass, and Henry Ledyard in 1837

The Cairo excursion of the Pattersons and officers off the *Delaware* and the *Shark* was repeated in September 1837 when Commodore Jesse D. Elliott from the US frigate *Constitution* returned to Alexandria. On board was Lewis Cass, who had served with Elliott in the War of 1812 on Lake Erie, had been governor of Michigan Territory for many years (1813–1831), and secretary of war (1831–1836) under President Andrew Jackson, and was now the newly appointed United States minister to France. With him was his wife and their four children, Mary, Lewis, Matilda, and Isabella, ranging in age from seventeen to twenty-five (their eldest daughter Elizabeth had died in 1832 in the cholera epidemic); also with him was his aide, James Henry Prentiss, a graduate of West Point in 1830 and now a captain in the US Army,[52] and his secretary, Henry Ledyard, a graduate of Columbia College in 1830 and now a lawyer. All except Prentiss had sailed from New York to Havre in October 1836 on the packet ship *Quebec*. Before boarding the *Constitution* in Marseilles in May 1837, Elliott had written to Cass advising him of servants, the appropriate dress for the ladies in Arab countries, and amenities on the ship for their enjoyment. Once on board, the Cass party had visited Florence, Siena, Rome, Palermo, Malta, Athens, Smyrna, Troy, Constantinople, Delos, Syra, and Crete before arriving in Palestine.[53] The commodore and the Cass family rode from Jaffa to Jerusalem, they swam, or floated, in the Dead Sea, and they rode up to Damascus and Baalbek. We know something of this trek from the account of Edward Clifford Anderson, a twenty-two-year-old midshipman, published many years later.[54] From Sidon, they traveled inland to call on Lady Hester Stanhope.[55]

Egypt was one of the last stops on the itinerary. Earlier in the year, in March, Commodore Elliott had written to John Gliddon, the United States consul in Alexandria, announcing that Lewis Cass and his family would be aboard his ship on a tour of inspection.[56] Forewarned, Gliddon arranged shore visits for the commodore, his officers, and the Cass family. With his interpreter and minister Boghos Bey in attendance, Mehmet Ali received them in the palace of his son just outside the city. After seeing Alexandria, the Americans sailed on the Mahmoudiya canal to Atfih and then upriver on the Nile, which Cass compared to the Missouri River, to Bulaq. There, repeating the honors shown to Commodore Patterson and his entourage three years before, a cavalcade of horses and carriages met them and took them into Cairo where they found quarters in a house furnished by the pasha. During their short stay they visited the usual sights: the slave market, the workshops of Mehmet Ali, the military school, and the Citadel. In addition they had an audience with Ibrahim Pasha, Mehmet Ali's son. Outside Cairo, they went to Memphis, Saqqara, the tombs of the caliphs, Heliopolis, and Giza where they climbed and entered the Great Pyramid.

There were two groups of sightseers: on the one hand the ship's officers, and on the other hand Lewis Cass, his family, and his entourage. Among the lieutenants known to have been on board (namely Oscar Bullus, Henry A. Steele, Henry Darcantel, Percival Drayton, Bushrod W. Hunter, and William S. Ringgold), some must have gone ashore in Egypt. We can be certain that Lieut. Percival Drayton of South Carolina (1812–1865) did so: a year later he presented to the American Philosophical Society in Philadelphia an Ibis mummy and four *shabti*s, two of wood, two of ceramic. And some of the midshipmen must also have gone ashore and to Cairo. We know that two midshipmen and the surgeon accompanied the commodore and the Cass party to Jerusalem and elsewhere in Palestine and Syria, namely Edward Clifford Jones, John W. Bryce, and Dr. Daniel C. McLeod. And in Cyprus, Lorenzo Warriner Pease, the American missionary stationed there, wrote in his diary that several young officers called on him, among them Lieut. Percival Drayton and Midshipmen Rodgers, Hunt, and Woolsey: namely Eugene E. Rodgers, Montgomery Hunt, and Melancthon Brooks Woolsey, all in their early twenties.[57] Many of these officers and others besides must have gone to Cairo.

No member of the Cass party can have missed the excursion to Cairo. One person in particular, Henry Ledyard, had a compelling reason to see Egypt: John Ledyard, the eighteenth-century world traveler from Connecticut who had died in Cairo in 1788, was a first cousin of Henry's grandfather, and the family had retained an interest in the "traveler's" life. Dr. Isaac Ledyard (a brother of Henry's grandfather) had intended to write a biography but never did so. Instead Jared Sparks, a young New England historian, drawing on material collected by Isaac Ledyard that had been handed down in the family, including the letters that Ledyard had written to Jefferson, which the old doctor had retrieved from Jefferson, published the first biography of John Ledyard in Boston in 1828. Henry was already attending Columbia College and must have seen the book. Despite the death of his father before he was born, Henry received a fine education. Moreover his mother's father, Henry Brockholst Livingston, was a justice of the Supreme Court of the United States and so he grew up in enlightened company. For his commencement at Columbia College on August 3, 1830, he composed "An Oration on the Character and Writings of Lord Byron." After briefly practicing law in New York, he was hired by Lewis Cass to serve as secretary of the legation, and in that way found himself accompanying the minister on the cruise of the *Constitution*.

The cruise around the Mediterranean came to an end and Lewis Cass and his entourage returned to Paris. In late June of 1838, Cass and his family, and presmuably his aide and his secretary, went to London to witness the coronation of Queen Victoria. And also in 1838 Cass met the young American painter George P.A. Healy, then living in Paris, and he asked Healy to paint his portrait (plate 16).[58] This was one of the first of the many fine portraits Healy executed in Paris and gives us the best image we possess of Cass at this time.[59]

Later in the same year Henry Ledyard and his colleague at the embassy, Captain James H. Prentiss, returned together from Havre to New York on the packet *Louis Philippe*, arriving on October 20, 1838, Henry bearing diplomatic dispatches. Ledyard's visit to New York was temporary. In early May the following year he returned to Paris with his long-widowed mother and on September 19, 1839, he married Matilda Francis Cass, one of the daughters of the minister. When Cass resigned his position in 1842, Henry Ledyard became chargé d'affaires, a post he held for two years. About 1850, after returning home, Ledyard had a daguerreotype done showing him in his consular uniform (plate 17).[60] And he kept another uniform: In 1858, at a costume ball in Washington, Ledyard, then a resident of Detroit and having briefly served as mayor of the city, "sported a genuine Egyptian uniform of the pattern worn by the troops of Mehemet Ali," a memento he must have carefully saved from his youthful adventures in Egypt.[61]

During the cruise Commodore Jesse D. Elliot collected things of quite a different order: memorabilia and trophies he had in mind to present to friends and institutions back home. These included Arabian horses (one from Jericho and four from Damascus), two column capitals from Caesarea, an Egyptian mummy (presented to Dr. James H. Miller, president of Washington Medical College in Baltimore), and a caravan of donkeys.[62] For the animals and relics, space had to be found on the ship, on deck, or below, however inconveniencing it might be for the officers and crew (and contributing ultimately to charges against the commodore that led to a court martial). One officer complained that instead of muzzles of cannons visible at the gun ports were heads of braying donkeys.

Most notable, or at least best remembered today, among the trophies brought home were two Roman marble sarcophagi (recently found near Beirut), which were dragged to the shore with help of hundreds of the ship's crew using block and tackle, and hoisted aboard the *Constitution*. Elliott thought that they would "be appreciated by the antiquaries and the learned of our country." On his return Elliott presented one to Girard College near Philadelphia, and some years later he offered the other to President Andrew Jackson for use as his tomb. But Jackson politely declined to be buried in a sarcophagus that had once served, so it was then thought, as the sarcophagus of the Roman emperor Alexander Severus. In 1845 it was presented to the Smithsonian Institution. In 1955 the one given to Girard College was transferred on permanent loan to Bryn Mawr College.[63] Some of these episodes are mentioned in the somewhat disorganized summary Jesse D. Elliott gave of the whole excursion.[64]

The shore excursions by the ships' officers, at least fifty in all from 1829 to 1837, recall a passage in an essay that Matthew C. Perry (captain of the *Concord*) helped his brother-in-law Alexander Slidell write, in which it was said that the Mediterranean was "an admirable school" for naval officers because it afforded the opportunity to acquire culture "by visiting a thousand sites crowned by the pure monuments of a classic age and consecrated by undying associations."[65] With these officers were the Kirklands, the family of Commodore Patterson, and the entourage of Lewis Cass, traveling in style on ships of the US Mediterranean fleet as privileged tourists. Most Americans made their own way. Over the period covered by these first visits of ships of the United States squadron to the port of Alexandria, from 1829 to 1837, some twenty-nine other Americans are known to have visited Egypt on their own.

11 | KEEPERS OF DIARIES: 1833 TO 1835

Eli and Sarah Smith

> Mr. Smith and I took a walk at sunset, the air being mild, and the clouds brilliant. The foliage of the distant grove of palm trees gave surpassing beauty to the scene.[1]

In 1826 the Rev. Eli Smith had visited Egypt and had since then traveled as far as Persia with his American colleague Rev. H.G.O. Dwight. He had returned to the United States in June 1832, and in 1833 had married Sarah Huntington, a well-to-do woman from Connecticut. Newly married, Eli and Sarah Smith arrived in Alexandria in December 1833 with their servant Ahmed, who was dressed in Turkish trousers and wore a red cap with a blue tassel. They had sailed from Malta on the brig *Gran Bretagne* together with an English traveler, Charles Rochfort Scott, and two of the latter's friends. Rochfort Scott tells of the crossing in the published account of his travels.

> The weather, calm and cloudless as we sailed slowly out of the beautiful harbour of La Valetta, soon afterwards became wet and tempestuous; and for four days and nights, our little vessel was tossed to and fro by a sea that, excepting in the Gulf of Lyon, I scarcely expected to have encountered in the Mediterranean, and which completely drenched every thing that was not under hatches. Fortunately, myself and two friends had secured the main-cabin for our own use, where, speaking by comparison, we were tolerably free from inconvenience on the score of salt water . . . . Our patron [the captain], a staunch Romanist—as most Maltese are—implored St. Antonio and all the protectors of salt water travellers to intercede for

167

us and allay the fury of the pitiless element. Finding his prayers unavailing, he told me, in accents of despair, that he greatly feared then inclemency of the weather and obduracy of the saints were occasioned by his having been so imprudent as to receive an American Methodist Missionary on board. This gentleman, with his wife and attendant, was snugly boxed up in a "state cabin" six feet by four, and totally unconscious of danger, and was flattering himself with the hope (the wind being perfectly fair) of a speedy termination to this maritime purgatory.[2]

All landed safely on Christmas day, 1833, and went their separate ways. Over the next several days Eli and Sarah Smith saw the usual sights in Alexandria, as he recorded in his diary. One day he wrote an unusually perceptive account of the appearance of the city from the vantage of Pompey's Pillar.

The Pillar, at which we had been aiming, stands upon a slight eminence, and the sky being delightfully serene, we enjoyed much the prospect from its base. Looking northward toward the city, its minarets were to be seen rising behind the tops of palm-groves, moving like crests of ostrich feathers in the gentle breeze. Farther onward to the verge of the horizon stretched the blue waters of the Mediterranean. On the left of the city bristled a forest of masts from the western harbor; and nearest to us on the same hand were some thirty or forty windmills, spreading their motionless arms to court the sleeping wind. To the right, and behind us, almost as far as the eye could reach, was spread out the lake Mareotis; a beautiful sheet of water, reflecting with the brilliancy of a mirror the rays of the mid-day sun. By the side of us stood the pillar pointing to times gone by, to the recollection of which the scene before us owed nearly all its interest.

They also went to the Greek convent to revisit the grave of Levi Parsons, who had died in Alexandria in 1822, and whose grave Smith had seen on his first visit to the city in 1826.

At my former visit to this convent seven years ago, I found in the pavement of the inner court, under the arcade, a slab of marble with an inscription pointing out the grave of Parsons. Now no trace of such a monument appeared. We were conducted into an open burying ground to search for it, but could find it nowhere. . . . The pavement had evidently been recently relaid, and as the convent received an income from the sale of burial places, the monument had doubtless been removed, that the place it occupied might be sold again.[3]

On December 29, the Smiths dined with the American consular agent John Gliddon where they met an American gentleman from Salem, Massachusetts, whose name they do not give but who is surely the J.C. Dodge named in John Gliddon's list of American visitors to Alexandria in this period, namely John Crowninshield Dodge, a young merchant who made several voyages to Mediterranean ports.[4] On another occasion they met Jane Franklin, who had arrived in Alexandria about the same time, on her second visit to Egypt. Lady Franklin described Rev. Smith as "rather a priggish and self-conceited looking man, small and thin, sharp and clever-looking with a true Presbyterian cut about him."[5] But Lady Franklin was not given to describing any strangers favorably.

Sarah Smith left her own observations of their visit to Alexandria in her journal and letters. In the evening of December 30, she wrote:

> Mr. Smith and I took a walk at sunset, the air being mild, and the clouds brilliant. The foliage of the distant grove of palm trees gave surpassing beauty to the scene. Unlike other trees, when viewed from a distance, their outline is distinct but graceful. Pompey's pillar, in its simple beauty, rose behind their elegant clusters. We stood upon a slight elevation, just as the sun dipped his last lines below the horizon; when a discharge of small guns, from the fleet in the harbor, was heard, followed by the evening tattoo. Immediately we perceived the flags of the minarets hoisted, and from a small door on the south side towards Mecca, which opens into a gallery near the top, appeared the criers, whose voices we distinctly heard, as they resounded through the soft air of an Egyptian evening.[6]

They left Alexandria on January 15 (without having gone to Cairo) on an Austrian trabaccolo (an Adriatic coasting vessel), the *Pomo*, bound, via Larnaca in Cyprus, for Beirut. Eli and Sarah Smith had enjoyed their brief visit to Egypt. They were well lodged, they enjoyed the attentions of the Gliddons, and they were on their honeymoon.

John W. Hamersley

On January 19, 1834, four days after Eli and Sarah Smith left Alexandria, John W. Hamersley arrived in Egypt following six months of travel. Hamersley was class of 1826 at Columbia, with a master's degree from the university in 1829, and he had made a previous trip to Europe, from early October 1831 to late February 1832. His brother, Gordon, was at that time secretary at the United States legation in Paris.

On this second trip Hamersley kept an extensive diary. The evidence that Hamersley was ever in Egypt used to rest solely on the presence of his name in the register of John Gliddon, the American consular agent in Egypt. Now, as explained in the introduction, we have had access since the year 2007 to his eight-hundred-page diary covering his travels in western Europe and the Mediterranean. Hamersley's narrative begins in Brussels in mid-June 1833 and carries him through Prussia, Sweden, Finland, and Russia, to Constantinople, and on to Egypt, Palestine, Syria, Greece, and Italy. His unpublished diary gives us the first full surviving account of an American in Egypt and on the Nile. The unpublished accounts of Theodore Allen and Mendes Cohen are earlier but restrained and Allen did not go up the Nile. Only the letters of Elizabeth Cabot Kirkland (whose visit to Egypt with her husband John T. Kirkland was described in the previous chapter) bear comparison, but the Kirklands limited themselves to Alexandria and Cairo.

On reaching Alexandria, Hamersley underwent two weeks of quarantine in a lazaretto recently established by Mehmet Ali. Quarantine was deemed essential because a ship from Constantinople had arrived on which bubonic plague had broken out.[7] Hamersley says that some twenty-one in a lazaretto specially set aside for them had already died. Notified of his arrival, John Gliddon, the American consul, did what he could. Hamersley and some of his fellow travelers were allowed, after exchanging their clothes for others provided from the shore, to pass the days in the pasha's baths on the Porto Vecchio, in a process called *spoglio*, that is, discarding one's clothes.

With him were two English gentlemen, Messrs. Somerville and Walsh, whom he had met in Constantinople and with whom he had shared passage to Alexandria. He never gives their first names, yet remarks that Somerville was a Cambridge man. The only Somerville at Cambridge who would have been of the right age and was not married in the 1830s was Henry Somerville who matriculated at Caius College in July 1825.[8]

Like many Americans traveling alone Hamersley had an incentive to meet, dine, and see the sights in the company of other foreigners. And like all travelers he arrived with letters of introduction to useful people, including letters from Theodore Allen of Dutchess County, New York, who had been in Lower Egypt, Palestine, and Syria just three years earlier, and from Mendes Cohen, the Baltimore traveler, whom he had seen in St. Petersburg. In Alexandria he met the Gliddons and was periodically entertained by them, finding their daughter, who had been educated in England, very pretty. He conversed with the celebrated Swedish doctor and naturalist Johan Hedenborg, who was collecting bird, insect, and fish specimens. He met Dr. James Laidlaw, an expert on cholera, active in Alexandria throughout the 1830s. He went to a local wedding ceremony with Édouard Lavison, a French diplomat and chancellor and dragoman to the Russian consulate in Alexandria who had lived in Egypt since 1828, and he saw him on other occasions also. And he met the Russian consul himself, Colonel Alexander Duhamel, who had only recently arrived in Egypt. He enjoyed the company of Captain John Prissick, an English naval officer in the service of the pasha, whom the Kirklands had met two years earlier. He saw the *Jem*, the yacht of Henry Beresford, the third Marquess of Waterford, moored in Alexandria harbor. He met a host of other visiting British travelers, among them Messrs. Sproule, Wilmer, and Martin, and Colonels Needham and Forbes. Wilmer was Bradford Wilmer (Christ's College, Cambridge, 1831), who was traveling with Robert Curzon, the celebrated manuscript collector.

One day Patrick Campbell, British consul-general, made arrangements to present Hamersley and some of his friends to Mehmet Ali, but Campbell (whom Hamersley thought was full of etiquette and humbug) did all the talking, which annoyed him. He wanted his own audience and finally obtained it through George Gliddon, the American consular agent, resulting in a personal conversation with the pasha.

On March 3, toward the end of his stay in Cairo, Hamersley and his companions Somerville and Walsh witnessed one of the great public events of the city:

the grand procession of the carpet going to Mecca. This carpet is sent by the Pacha every year to be thrown over the tomb of the Prophet in place of the old one which is supposed to be worn out by the kisses of the faithful. It is carried with great pomp and circumstance the whole distance. We started from our hotel at 6 o'clock in the direction of the citadel. The shops were all shut, the streets crowded, very few Franks were seen and right enough they were to keep out of the way. In this pious occasion the fanaticism of the Mohammedans is screwed to the highest pitch and by many a sly blow at Christian dogs as my skull can testify do they demonstrate their love of the Prophet. . . . Mobs of boys would with palm sticks split at the top, headed by stout desperate men forced themselves through the crowd, giving the unlucky Franks the alternative of giving backshish (money) or getting a flogging. . . . At length, the cries of the multitude announced the processing. Some majestic camels covered with cloth ornamented with various shells and embroidery, their heads decked with ostrich feathers, led the van. The Pacha's band with a regiment of Arabs followed in good order. Now came flags, standards, and horsemen. Camels covered with cloths of gold supporting pennants of every colour and strange oriental emblems and devices. A four wheel closed carriage bore the bed of the chief. Ever and anon came bands of dervishes clapping their hands, singing and turning round, accompanied by the national instrumental music, most of which were common copper vases covered with parchment which they beat with a bone. The while all the women were howling to give encouragement to the Hadgis. Now came the grand nemches [?] which was headed by music, chiefly the kettle drum. On stately camels a large carpet of silk made into the form of a tent was guarded by files of soldiers and Jannissaries with sticks to prevent the crowd from touching it. Being considered holy, every one rushed to touch it at the expense of a blow but an Arab woman near us with a most commendable fearlessness seized it in her hand and succeeded in kissing it. The sacred lamps covered with silk closed the procession.[9]

1834 was the year that the British Orientalist Edward William Lane was composing his book on the modern Egyptians, and it must have been this very procession that formed the background for the observations in his book.[10] Hamersley never met him.

On March 7, Hamersley, with his two friends Somerville and Walsh, started upriver to see the great monuments. By March 22, after bypassing many sites, which they would see on the way downriver, they reached Thebes where they stopped only briefly before proceeding to Armant. André Dutertre, one of Napoleon's savants, had sketched the temple at Armant in 1799, and his view and images by a fellow artist were reproduced in the *Description de l'Égypte*. Around the year 1830, using Dutertre's published view, the American architect Alexander Jackson Davis made a splendid restored elevation in watercolor of the façade of this temple (plate 5). In the decades after Hamersley was there, the building was photographed at least three times: in 1849, by Maxime Du Camp who was traveling with Gustave Flaubert; in 1852, by Félix Teynard; and in 1857, by the British topographical photographer Francis Frith.[11] These are the only pictorial records of the building because it was pulled down between 1861 and1862 to build a sugar factory. Hamerlsey said that the temple itself was nearly intact, and that the walls in front were covered with hieroglyphs and with representations of men and animals: cats, ibises, serpents, wolves, and so on.

A change of wind, now from the south, persuaded them to return from Armant to Luxor. They admired the temple and the reliefs on the great pylon and they marveled at the one remaining obelisk. Somerville had seen the other in Corfu on its way to France.

On March 24 they were at Aswan and Philae. There, Hamersley met Lady Franklin who had come to Alexandria two years earlier and now, on a return visit, had ventured up the Nile. She was traveling with Johann Rudoph Theophilus Lieder, a German-born missionary who had been sent to Egypt by the Church Missionary Society of England in 1826.[12]

On March 27, in the temple at Dakka (a Ptolemaic temple, dismantled and moved forty kilometers upstream in the mid-1960s during the construction of the high dam) they encountered the determined fifty-three-year-old Margareta Charlotta Heijkenskjöld—Hamersley misheard and misspelled her name Heiskinskioll—a Swedish lady traveling alone. Famously traveling alone and with a name no one could spell correctly. The young American poet Henry Wadsworth Longfellow knew about her in Naples in April 1828, referring to her as "Eichenshoult or whatever her name is—the Swedish woman."[13] In 1833, before her Nile trip, Heijkenskjöld took passage on the *Francisco Primo*, the first passenger steamer in the eastern Mediterranean (discussed in chapter 12), where she was listed as Mme la comtesse Heikeinfied of Stockholm.[14] Hamersley found her in the temple, sketching. Somerville had met her in Naples, which may have eased the introductions. Her determination was evident in what she told Hamersley: On one occasion, to persuade her crew to continue traveling, she had had to fire her pistols. In early July 1834, shortly after leaving Egypt, she fell sick in Palestine and died.[15]

On April 4 they reached Wadi Halfa and the second cataract, the farthest south they would go. The next day they walked to Abu Simbel. On April 6 they turned north, stopping for Somerville and Walsh to revisit Dakka—Hamersley stayed on board because his feet were sore from so much walking—and then farther downriver they saw the temple at Dendur, a temple dating from the time of the Roman emperor Augustus that was dismantled in 1963 and presented by the Egyptian government to the Metropolitan Museum of Art. On April 8 they visited the temple at Kalabsha, also Augustan, and also dismantled in the 1960s, but not sent abroad, merely re-erected downstream. From there they walked to Philae. Continuing north they saw the temples at Kom Ombo and Edfu, and the tombs at El Kab, and finally returned to Thebes.

At Thebes, after touring the temple at Karnak, Hamersley met "Mr. Dundas of Scotland, county of Perth. Had spent fifteen years in India, a magistrate &c., had taken a route in Europe something similar to my own. He had lost most of his clothes by his boat upsetting, but his money and 'batterie de cuisine' the most important part of a man's outfit, had been saved." This was William Dundas (1796–1842) who had spent many years in the Bengal Civil Service, and had gone home to Scotland some years earlier. He was now extending a European grand tour like Hamersley to include Egypt, and he joined the trio for the rest of their tour in the East.

While visiting the colossi of Memnon, on the west bank, Hamersley saw "Mr. Yani," namely Giovanni d'Athanasi, the agent of the late British Consul-General Henry Salt, who showed him the exact spot where two colossal red granite sphinxes had stood, which he had removed in March 1829 and taken downriver for sale to a Russian diplomat (Count Andrej Mouravieff). The French artist Nestor L'Hôte had witnessed their removal and has left us a sketch of the operation.[16] Hamersley said that he had seen them in St. Petersburg. In the St. Petersburg portion of his diary, written in the fall of 1833, he reported that they were in the courtyard of the Academy of Arts and Sciences, and that they had been purchased of Mr. Barker (the British consul) in Alexandria. They now sit on pedestals on the banks of the Neva.[17]

Hamersley was back in Cairo on May 1, having been on the Nile seven weeks. Now he toured Ibrahim Pasha's garden on the island of Roda with James Traill, the Scottish botanist recently appointed head gardener. He visited the Nilometer at one end of Roda; special permission was required because the gunpowder factory nearby had exploded some years earlier, destroying the superstructure of the building.[18] He met Messrs. Gosset and Costigan, the first, according to Hamersley, a member of the provincial parliament of Jersey, the second a witty and well-read Irishman. Gosset was John Gosset who later acquired a mummy at Thebes which, on his death soon afterward in Paris, his father gave to the new museum on the Island of Jersey. Costigan was Christopher Costigan who the next year explored the river Jordan and the shores of the Dead Sea but fell sick and died after returning to Jerusalem.[19] In Alexandria, Hamersley again dined at the Gliddons where this time he met a Mr. Montague and William Henry Bartlett, the British topographical artist. The former was invited to accompany Mrs. and Miss Gliddon to Beirut. The latter was to join Hamersley on his tour of Palestine and Syria.

On May 23, 1834, "a young gentleman now on his tour through the old world" wrote a letter to the editors of the *New-York Gazette* (printed in October), in which he summarized the political and commercial situation in Egypt. The writer must have been Hamersley, who is known to have left Alexandria for Palestine the next day.

Egypt, under an enlightened ruler, "ploughed by the sun-beams only," would be one of the most productive countries of the world. No security, however, is given to industry, no satisfaction to justice—each man is at liberty to cultivate what quantity of land he pleases, but the whole crop becomes the property of the Pacha, who allows the fellahins small pittance as will barely support existence. The natural consequence is, that but a small portion of land is under cultivation, and very little attention bestowed upon it. While the Pacha is thus killing the goose to get the golden eggs, the European merchant grows rich by his double profit, first by buying the produce, and secondly by making payment in European manufactures and productions. The Pacha . . . sells rice, cotton, indigo, hemp, wheat, and receives in return timber, large cannon, anchors, and machinery of all kinds.

Other American tourists encountered international travelers but few spoke of them as did Hamersley in his diary. You might almost have thought that Egypt was a stage set for great conversations with newly found friends. At the same time, however, Hamersley saw and clearly took in the monuments of ancient Egypt and the enterprises of modern Egypt. With at least two guidebooks in hand, *The Modern Traveller* and Rifaud's *Tableau de l'Égypte*, he wrote detailed accounts of what he saw.

Hamersley left Alexandria for Jaffa on a seventy-ton goletta named the *Achilles*. With him were his Nile companions, Messrs. Somerville, Walsh, and Dundas, his Maltese servant Antonio, and the artist Bartlett. At Jaffa they stayed with the British Consul Damiani. There they met the American missionary William Thomson, a graduate of Princeton Theological Seminary who had gone to Beirut in 1833 and who had recently moved with his wife to Jerusalem. He brought them up to date on the political and military situation in the region.[20] Two years earlier, in 1832, Egyptian forces had seized Palestine and Syria from the Ottoman sultan and had retained control of the region after tense negotiations with Constantinople. In May 1834, just before Hamersley left Egypt, Nablus, Jerusalem, and Hebron had revolted against Egyptian policies, and Mehmet Ali had sent his son Ibrahim Pasha to put down the rebellion. This was the situation Hamersley and his companions encountered. In Jaffa they visited the camp of the Egyptian army, and on June first they even gained an audience with Ibrahim Pasha. They missed Jerusalem because of the military campaign but saw Carmel and Acre. In a letter Thomson wrote to *The Missionary Herald*, he reported on June 2 that "Four English gentlemen and an American called at Jaffa yesterday. They desired to visit Jerusalem and thought of accepting the invitation from the Pasha to go up with the troops, but finally gave up the plan and passed on to Acre."

After arriving at Acre, Somerville, Walsh, and Dundas decided to go by boat to Beirut while Hamersley and Bartlett and the servant Antonio opted to travel overland to Tyre and Sidon. Reaching Sidon Hamersley and Bartlett made arrangements to call on Lady Hester Stanhope at her remote estate, an encounter that deeply impressed Hamersley, because that portion of his journal recounting their meeting became the only part of his journal that he later revised and published.[21] Bartlett was at first turned away, being an Englishman, and had to spend the night in a hovel, but Hamersley changed Lady Hester's mind, and the next day, even though he was English and an artist, Bartlett was allowed to meet her. Bartlett wrote up his own account of the trip, including the visit to Lady Hester Stanhope, in which he mentions Hamersley, though not by name.

> My American companion, on whom I was now exclusively dependent for society, was a very creditable sample of the sons of the West; but he possessed two of their peculiar characteristics in a prominent degree, that of going a-head, and that of bragging as to the infinite superiority of everything transatlantic . . . . The American girls were the handsomest in the world; the ponies beat all creation in a trotting match; the houses in New York were far finer than those in London; even the pumpkin, or, as he would have it . . . pünkin pies of America were unequalled by any other earthly delicacies attainable in England. . . . I listened, and sunk into insignificance, and as my fellow traveller had been long enough in the East to grow a beard, allowed him to take precedence, and make all the necessary arrangements.

After they had seen Lady Hester, Bartlett added, "My American friend, who to do him justice, was really a handsome fellow, had met with her unqualified approval."[22]

During their conversations Lady Hester recalled two Americans who had called on her: One was "Com. DeKay," namely George C. DeKay who had skippered the shipbuilder Henry Eckford's corvette from New York to Constantinople in 1831, and then in 1832 had chartered with his brother James a brig and sailed from Smyrna to Beirut and Sidon, and after visiting Lady Hester in midsummer 1832, had gone on to Jerusalem.[23] The other was Mendes Cohen, also in 1832, who she said had a long beard and whom she did not know to be a Jew until he had left. In turn, Hamersley mentioned to Lady Hester the names of his other traveling companions, Somerville, Walsh, and Dundas, and also Montague, who had traveled directly to Beirut with Mrs. and Miss Gliddon. Dundas, being Scottish, intrigued her, in part because she thought him to be related to the late Lord Melville (Henry Dundas), and the next day, June 10, she wrote and invited him to visit her, suggesting that he bring along Mr. Montague. Dundas' reply is not preserved, but Hamersley's diary gives us the gist of it: Dundas said that, "he was not a relative of the Melville family, but if her ladyship wished to see him he would be very happy to call on her." In Lady Hester's second letter she suggests a date and says that she looks forward to receiving him.[24]

Hamersley continued his travels: to Beirut, to Smyrna, where he dined with British naval officers with the fleet stationed there, and to Greece, and westward to Malta. In Malta in November he saw a Mr. Dodge of Boston, lately returned from Egypt, who must have been John C. Dodge, not of Boston but of the nearby town of Salem.[25] And he went to Sicily where he climbed Mount Etna, and finally to Naples where he ran into many American tourists. There, before reaching Rome, his two-volume diary comes to an end. He remained in Europe until the spring of 1836, returning home only in late April of that year. Back in New York, where he became a leading lawyer, he retained an interest in the eastern Mediterranean, giving soirées for his friends in which he retold stories of his travels.[26]

J. Lewis Stackpole and Ralph Stead Izard, Jun.

When Hamersley first arrived in Alexandria, he heard that two other American travelers, whom he had seen earlier in Constantinople in late November, had just been there and had left for Cairo. They were J. Lewis Stackpole and his younger traveling companion Ralph Stead Izard, Jun. of Charleston; they had arrived in Alexandria in late December 1833.

Lewis Stackpole was a well-educated Bostonian. His father, William, was class of 1798 at Harvard, and Lewis also went to Harvard, entering in 1820 at age thirteen. Two years later, in 1822, his parents, who had moved to Louisville, Kentucky, died of yellow fever in the great epidemic of that year. Stackpole went to Samuel Ripley, who ran a school in Waltham (near Boston), saying he would have to withdraw, but Ripley offered to pay his bills. At Harvard Commencement on August 25, 1824, Stackpole delivered "A Literary Inquiry" on "The Influence of Johnson as a Critick in His Own Times and at the Present Day."[27] The annual meeting of the Phi Beta Kappa society, of which Stackpole was a member, had as its honored guest at dinner that week General Lafayette who was touring the United States. Upon graduation Samuel Ripley forgave Stackpole's indebtedness, commenting that "no young man ought to start life saddled with a debt."[28] Stackpole then studied law, received an LL.B. from Harvard in 1828, was admitted to the bar in Boston in January 1830, and repaid his debt to Ripley. Within a few months his article on "Customs and the Origin of Customary Law" appeared in a leading legal periodical.[29] In May he joined the New England Guards as a lieutenant.

Some time afterward Lewis Stackpole left the United States for an extended European residence. On July 9, 1831, he was one of 110 Americans at a meeting in Paris for the benefit of the Polish nation, chaired by the novelist J. Fenimore Cooper.[30] At the Congress of Vienna in 1815, Poland had been partitioned among Russia, Prussia, and the Hapsburg Empire, and in 1829 Tsar Nicholas I had been crowned King of Poland. Late in November 1830, Polish officers in Warsaw had staged a revolt against the oppressive policies of the tsar, and the revolution had spread among many levels of society. Despite attempts by the leading Poles at negotiations, the Russians had moved troops into Polish territory. During the conflict many Europeans and even Americans raised funds for the Polish patriots. In Paris Lafayette was one of the leaders of the cause, even though he missed the July meeting at which Stackpole was present. Lafayette corresponded with Fenimore Cooper and contributed funds alongside the Americans. But to no avail. After months of fighting the Russians took Warsaw in September 1831, and in October the remaining Polish troops crossed into Prussia to avoid surrendering.

The next year and a half in Stackpole's life is a blank. Then in March, 1833, the twenty-nine-year-old Ralph Waldo Emerson met Lewis in Rome and saw the sights with him and with William Pratt, both classmates at Harvard with Emerson's brother Edward: "Glad I was amidst all these old stumps of past ages to see Lewis Stackpole, as fresh and beautiful as a young palm tree in the desert." From Rome Emerson wrote to his brother William on April 21, "Let me not forget to name among the Americans Lewis Stackpole whom it was charming to see & who is gone to Naples & to Constantinople."[31] In Italy Stackpole is likely to have met up with the eighteen-year-old Izard who was traveling after having finished his education in Europe.

Ralph Stead Izard, Jun., originally of Weymouth and Milton, Prince George's Parish in South Carolina, was only one year old when his father died in 1816. His mother died not long afterward in 1819, leaving Ralph and his older sister Anne orphans. But the family was extended and wealthy, and Ralph and his sister were apparently taken care of by one or more of their several surviving aunts, sisters of their late father.[32]

In 1803, twelve years before Ralph was born, one aunt, Elizabeth, had married Thomas Pinckney, Jun., son of the United States minister to England, with whom she had two children, Elizabeth and Rosetta Ella. (Rosetta would later marry her first cousin Ralph Stead Izard, Jun.). In 1806, another aunt, Mary (1780–1858), had married John Julius Pringle Jr. of Charleston, though after a year of marriage and one son, her husband had died. Two more aunts, Patience and Rosetta, were also around. One or more of them must have been responsible for bringing up young Ralph and his sister. Ralph Izard is said to have completed his education abroad presumably in the late 1820s and early 1830s, during which time he surely saw some of his relatives who were traveling. Among them was his aunt Mary Izard Pringle who was in Europe in 1829 with her son John Julius Izard Pringle (1808–1858); Mary and her son spent at least half of that year in Rome where, like many American visitors, they had their portrait painted.[33] Later, in October 1833, after many years of widowhood and just at the time Ralph Izard Jun. must have met Lewis Stackpole, Mary Pringle married Joel Roberts Poinsett, who as a young man in 1802 had traveled in Italy and Sicily, and who now was prominent in United States politics. Ralph Izard Jun. came from a family well connected in the United States and accustomed to travel in Europe.

No diaries by Stackpole or Izard recording their Mediterranean travels are known to have survived. The meager knowledge of their Egyptian tour must be culled from diverse sources. Where they first met in Europe is not recorded, but we know that they made their way to Constantinople in the fall of 1834 where Hamersley saw them in late November. In Cairo, like Hamersley, they had an audience with Mehmet Ali. We know this from an 1837 letter from H.M. Rutledge of Nashville to Ralph's uncle, Joel R. Poinsett (his aunt Mary's second husband who had recently been appointed secretary of war in Martin van Buren's cabinet), preserved in the Historical Society of Pennsylvania, in which Rutledge mentioned the audience and stated that Izard was improved by his foreign travels. And like Hamersley they met the Gliddons. Not only do their names appear in the consular register, but on February 4 Lady Franklin met them at Gliddon's house in Cairo. Earlier she had seen them at the palace of Ahmed Pasha, one of the newly constructed, quasi-European architectural demonstrations of position erected by important officials surrounding Mehmet Ali.

Stackpole and Izard preceded Hamersley up the Nile. He met up with them on March 26 at Thebes in Upper Egypt where they were traveling in the company of another boat with two French travelers. Hamersley noted in his diary that Stackpole and the French travelers displayed marks of smallpox, despite having been vaccinated, but that Izard had escaped. Lady Franklin encountered them about the same time at Kalabsha. Like Hamersley, she noted that with the exception of Izard they had contracted smallpox, but that only the faces of the French were pitted, and not that of Stackpole. Elsewhere in her diary Lady Franklin wrote "that they had taken a slave boat at Cairo, one which had been brought down river, and that was infected with smallpox. [The] captain's son had died on board."[34] She added that on getting sick they had turned back to Cairo but then, recovering, had again proceeded upriver. These observations recall a passage in the book of a later American traveler in Egypt, Sarah Haight (about whom more later): "I remember being informed by two American gentlemen in Paris that they both contracted the smallpox from their boat, which they learned had been used to transport a cargo of black slaves from Abyssinia to Cairo."[35]

Stackpole and Izard reached Wadi Halfa. When Lady Franklin saw them at Kalabsha, they were returning from that ultimate destination. Hamersley saw their names carved on the rock overlooking the second cataract; their names are still visible at Abu Simbel.[36] Weeks later, on April 20, the French animal trader Reboul, on his way to Sudan to purchase giraffes with his colleague Georges Thibaut, encountered Stackpole and Izard above Minya, as they were within a few days of Cairo. In his diary Reboul said that they spoke a little French and were traveling en suite with another boat with two Parisians, one of them the "Comte de Baral," probably Joseph-Napoléon-Paul de Barral (1806–1850); the other a "monsieur Poupilier," the latter surely the twenty-four-year-old Charles Poupillier of Paris, who like Stackpole and Izard, cut his name at Abu Simbel.[37] The two Americans invited the four Frenchmen aboard their boat for lunch, one course of which was quail they had recently shot.[38] After leaving Egypt, Stackpole and Izard and monsieur Poupillier, who was still traveling with them, met up again with Hamersley, this time in Rhodes in late July.

A year elapsed before they returned home. In late May Lewis Stackpole may well have attended the marriage of his younger sister, Roxana, in London, to her first cousin Frederick Dabney. In the late summer or early fall of 1835, he visited Dublin where George Ticknor, who had shortly before resigned his professorship at Harvard and was traveling with his wife and family, met him. Izard and Stackpole returned together to New York in early December 1835, and within a month Stackpole had presented to the Boston Society of Natural History mummies of a crocodile, a hawk, and an ibis.[39] With Stackpole and Izard on the packet ship *Normandie* from

Havre was John Lothrop Motley, a young Bostonian who had been study-ing at Göttingen and Berlin and who had been traveling with Stackpole and Izard in the months before their return. Motley and Stackpole had become the greatest of friends and were destined to marry the Benjamin sisters a few years later. Motley would become an accomplished histo-rian in the course of the nineteenth century. Stackpole was also a noted figure who died relatively young, in a freak train accident. Oliver Wendell Holmes described him as "a man of great intelligence, of remarkable per-sonal attractions, and amiable character."[40] A daguerreotype, perhaps by the firm of Southworth and Hawes, done in the early 1840s and owned by a descendant, shows a handsome man with sideburns, beard below the chin, and no mustache, a face fitting Holmes' words (plate 18). Accounts of his travels, not yet located, would be of great interest.

William B. Hodgson

In Rhodes, in late July, Hamersley, Stackpole, and Izard encountered a fourth American traveling quite by chance in that region, namely Wil-liam B. Hodgson, the outgoing dragoman of the United States legation in Constantinople. He was on his way to Egypt with an Anglo-Irishman, a Mr. Goff.[41] The lead-up to Hodgson's Egyptian trip is worth a digres-sion.[42] Hodgson, who had previously served in the consulate in Algiers, was posted to Constantinople in 1831 to serve as interpreter, and arrived there in August aboard the USS *John Adams* together with the newly appointed chargé d'affaires David Porter. Over a two-year period Hodg-son's relations with the exceptionally difficult David Porter soured, and in mid-November 1833, it actually came to blows, not with David Porter himself but with his son David Dixon Porter, a midshipman on the USS *Delaware*, then in the harbor at Constantinople. Hodgson had been a guest on board the ship for dinner and, after being taken ashore in the ship's boat by the young Porter, he was assaulted by the young man in return for alleged trouble he had given his father. By extraordinary coin-cidence, John W. Hamersley, the New Yorker whose visit to Egypt has been described, had also dined on the *Delaware* that very night, and after being taken ashore with Hodgson by young Porter, witnessed the whole episode and provided a blow-by-blow description in his diary. Hamersley returned with Hodgson and young Porter to the *Delaware*, confirmed the veracity of Hodgson's account, and wrote in his diary that Commodore Patterson had the young Porter arrested. He was never punished, but Hodgson was reimbursed for the destruction of his cloak, which, Hamer-sley said, "was literally torn from his back."

In any event, the upshot of this episode was that Hodgson's position as dragoman was ultimately withdrawn, though his service with the Department of State survived. He arrived in Alexandria in late August 1834 charged to explore commercial and diplomatic opportunities with Mehmet Ali and other officials. After three weeks of quarantine he contacted John Gliddon, who arranged two interviews with Mehmet Ali and Boghos Bey, the minister of foreign affairs.

A small merchant commerce is already opening between Alexandria and the U. States. The enterprising firm of Isserverdens Stith & Co. of Smyrna have engaged in this trade and a shipment made by them from New York of Lignum Vite mahogany and other articles has arrived here for the Pasha's arsenal. I have also been told confidentially that he himself offered to sell his opium crop to an American citizen upon adventageous terms, which was only declined on account of that gentleman's position.

While in Alexandria he encountered two American travelers, father and son, from Natchez, Mississippi, Rush and Rittenhouse Nutt, to whom we will turn in a moment. Hodgson then traveled to Cairo where he met George R. Gliddon, and through him he had an interview with Habib Effendi, the lieutenant governor:

He entertained me with a long description of the international commerce of the country. Our conversation was held in Turkish and his expressions of pleasure for that circumstance was flattering to me. It is singular he said that you from the New World should have taken the rare pains to study my language. From Cairo I proceeded up the Nile as far as the sugar refinery of Radamon in latitude 28° 15' north and I visited the intermediate cotton factories of Benisoueif, Minyer and Malacoi.[43]

Hodgson left Egypt in November, returning home via Malta and England, arrived in New York from Liverpool about March 1, 1835, and soon filed the last of several diplomatic reports to the secretary of state.[44]

Rush and Rittenhouse Nutt
Dr. Rush Nutt of Natchez, Mississippi, and his son Rittenhouse Nutt, whom William B. Hodgson (the former dragoman in the American legation in Constantinople) met in Alexandria, were coming to Egypt to survey the cultivation of cotton, to obtain handfuls of cotton seed, and to travel on the Nile. The doctor was about fifty-three, his son about

twenty-three. As a young man Dr. Nutt had studied medicine at the University of Pennsylvania with Benjamin Rush, after which, in tribute to his mentor, he had shortened his given name from Rushworth to Rush.[45] He named one of his sons Rittenhouse after the well-known eighteenth-century mathematician and scholar of Philadelphia David Rittenhouse.

Father and son sailed from New York for Havre on the packet ship *Utica* on May 1, 1834. It was the doctor's second attempt to reach Egypt; he had left New York a year earlier, in May 1833, had gone as far as Marseilles, but owing to sickness had returned home via Havre and New York (where he arrived in late August). This time he brought his son. Fellow passengers on the *Utica* included Daniel Brent, US consul in Paris, and his nephew John Carroll Brent; also Frederick de Peyster Jr., his wife, and three children, one of whom, John Watts de Peyster, kept a brief account of their trip.[46] Rittenhouse Nutt kept a full journal, the earlier part in the form of letters, the latter part in the form of day-to-day entries, from the time they landed in France to their southernmost destination in Egypt.[47]

After landing they went by diligence from Havre to Paris: "The French diligence is similar to our stages and are drawn by six horses. The roads were uncommonly fine, and there seemed to be much of the 'go ahead spirit in the drivers,' who kept the horses in a gallop." In Paris, together with the American consul Mr. Brent and his nephew, they visited the Jardin des Plantes and marveled at the live animals and birds from many quarters of the globe: "The giraffe, the elephant and ostrich of the east meet the llama, the puma and condor of the west. Indeed the collections are so complete, that should there be another deluge like that in ancient times, Noah the Second might here find every species necessary for the supply of his ark."

After visiting many other sights in Paris, they set off for southern France. The Nutts traveled overland to Lyon, and then by Rhone steamer from Lyon to Avignon, and then again overland to Aix and Marseilles. There the young John W. de Peyster who had been with them on the transatlantic crossing wrote of Dr. Nutt:

> At Marseilles he said he was going to the East, that he would assume the Turkish dress and habits, and pass himself off for a Mohammedan. Dear father [that is Fredrick] innocently asked him if he could speak Turkish or Arabic; Nott [*sic*] as naively answered, "Not a word."[48]

From Marseilles the de Peysters went by steamer to Italy, while Rush and Rittenhouse Nutt went by diligence from Marseilles to Florence via Nice, Genoa, Leghorn, and Pisa. They met the de Peysters again in

Rome, where they signed the consular register together.[49] Rittenhouse filled his journals with accounts of their sight-seeing, augmenting it with information derived from his guidebook, *Stark's Italy.* In Naples Rittenhouse climbed Mount Vesuvius, and in Sicily he ascended Mount Etna. Finally, in late August 1834, after visiting Syracuse and Agrigento, father and son reached Malta.[50] There they met Ralph Izard and Lewis Stackpole, now on their way back to Europe from the Mediterranean. The Nutts left Malta in the evening of September 7 for a week-long passage to Alexandria.

> On the 15 of September, the spires of the Turkish mosques of Alexandria were in sight. Never shall I forget my emotions when I landed on the shores of Egypt. Everything that met the eye was new and strange. Had I been transplanted to another planet, the changes could not have been greater. Surrounded on all sides by red Egyptians with strange dresses, strange language, beards six inches long, and pipe stems six feet, all smoking as if we had dropped down from God knows where.[51]

The morning after they arrived, the janissary of John Gliddon, the American consul, brought them a bundle of English newspapers, and during their stay in Alexandria they had "the pleasure of meeting with two Americans—Mr. Brown, who wished to introduce our Cotton Gin into Egypt, and Mr. Hodgson, former Secretary of our Legation to Constantinople." "Mr. Brown" was Charles Brown of New York, whom John Gliddon names in his list of Americans visiting Alexandria in this period.[52] "Mr. Hodgson" was, of course, William B. Hodgson, the former dragoman at the American legation in Constantinople. In a newspaper account (*New-York Spectator*, April 27, 1835), three unnamed Americans are quoted as seeing the Nutts on their arrival in Alexandria and saying that the doctor and his son were intending to make a "geological *reconnoissance* of the Delta and the valley of the Nile, so far as the second cataracts." Two of the anonymous Americans might have been Messrs. Brown and Hodgson, the third perhaps Mr. Mayo of South Carolina, mentioned elsewhere in the same *New-York Spectator* article as having been in Egypt that year, but about whom nothing more is known.

In the company of Mr. Brown and Mr. Gliddon's janissary, they saw the sights of Alexandria: Pompey's Pillar, the pair of obelisks, the catacombs, and the bazaar, and after two days they left for Cairo. Along the way Rittenhouse observed the growing of cotton, the only American traveler other than William B. Hodgson to do so.

The crop is not so abundant, but instead of one as we had been accustomed to, two or even three crops are annually grown on the same piece of ground. . . . The cotton is sown in drills as we do in America, and suffered to remain instead of being thinned out, or scraped, to use the southern term . . . . The stalk has but few branches pointing upwards, and not more than 2½ or 3 feet high. The bolls are now opening; the leaf, seed and fibers are the same as the Sea Island, which we grow in the Southern parts of America. In gathering, they pull the bolls or pods from the stalks, take them to their houses, and extract the cotton at their leisure.

In Cairo Rush and Rittenhouse Nutt engaged a Maltese dragoman, Paolo Nuozzo, and they hired a boat with a crew of thirteen. They started up the Nile on September 26, and as they went, Rittenhouse day by day observed the crops cultivated on the banks of the river. He wrote perceptively about what he saw in his journal, but not a word was noted about Pharaonic ruins. On October 6 they passed Thebes, and the next day, a day's sail above Thebes, they encountered Christopher Costigan and John Gosset, whom the New Yorker John Hamersley had seen earlier in the year in Cairo, and who were now coming downstream from Dongola. Both father and son Nutt had fevers, and Rush Nutt was suffering from the painful eye infection ophthalmia. In this situation and on the advice of Gosset and Costigan (the latter also afflicted with ophthalmia), they returned with them to Thebes and took up residence in one of the houses built by the French during the removal of the obelisk. With Costigan and the elder Nutt laid up, Gosset and Rittenhouse Nutt explored ancient Thebes.

Once Mr. Gosset and myself, being a short distance from the house, our servant ran to us nearly out of breath saying that our companions were going to fight. We had not the least idea of such a catastrophe taking place, yet wishing to hear the dispute, crept guiltily up to the door. There they sat opposite on their restive divans, their eyes bunged to, their faces in the direction they supposed one another to be, both talking at the same time, and gesticulating with all the vehemence of a member of the French chamber of deputies.

This encounter, despite strong differences of opinion between Costigan and Rush Nutt, combined with a two-week stay in Thebes, revived their spirits and improved their health. They lived fairly well, procuring vegetables from a local garden, in which there were also a few figs, acacia, and small lime trees, besides a few stalks of cotton. Ever interested in the cultivation of cotton, the Nutts took seeds of the plant they found there and concealed them in an empty ostrich egg so as to remove them unobserved from Egypt. (In fact family tradition says that they took a total of eight ostrich eggs full of cotton seeds.)[53]

Finally, leaving Costigan and Gosset, who continued downstream, the Nutts resumed their passage south as far as Abu Simbel, where they arrived November 7. There, Rittenhouse Nutt's account of Egypt breaks off, and nothing else is known of their travels in Egypt, except that after returning to Cairo they remained there through Christmas, with enough time to visit the Pyramids.

The next we know of their travels comes from a letter that Rittenhouse wrote from Jerusalem in late February 1835 to his grandmother, Mrs. David Ker, his mother's mother.[54] He said that they had left Egypt on December 29 and had reached Jerusalem after an eighteen-day camel ride across the desert. Rittenhouse admitted that he "felt a degree of awe . . . in visiting the objects of pilgrimage in Jerusalem particularly in kneeling before the supposed tomb of Christ notwithstanding the ridiculous mummery of Latin priests." There, in January 1835, as we know from another source, Dr. Rush Nutt sought to treat the dying American medical missionary Asa Dodge, and in late February he helped to bury Dodge on Mount Sion. In this same burial ground they saw the grave of the young New Yorker Cornelius Bradford, who had died in Jerusalem in 1830.[55] The American missionary Lorenzo Pease met them in Cyprus in early March as they were about to depart for Tripoli.[56] In Smyrna, in May, they joined the New Yorker John L. Stephens and traveled with him by steamer to Constantinople. From Stephens we have a brief sketch of Rush Nutt:

> He was about 55, of a strong, active, and inquiring mind. . . . He possessed all the warm high-toned feelings of the Southerner, but had a thorough contempt for the usages of society and everything like polish of manners. . . . Notwithstanding his impracticabilities as a traveller, I liked the Doctor.[57]

After seeing the sights of Constantinople, at times with Stephens, they returned to Smyrna. "With great regret," Stephens wrote, "I took leave of Dr. Nutt and his son, who sailed the same day for Smyrna." Back in Smyrna Rush Nutt decided to go home, directly, and took passage without his son on a brig sailing for Boston. In Smyrna, Thorowgood S. Stith, the seventeen-year-old son of the resident Baltimore merchant Griffin Stith, met the doctor and mentioned him in a letter he wrote to his uncle in mid-June 1835:

There is a Dr. Nutt, a planter from Mississippi, who has been traveling some time in Egypt; he goes home passenger in the *Padang*. Perhaps you will meet with him. He is about 60 or 65 and has young children at home. He has a son with him who will return by way of Europe, a regular backwoodsman. They say he (the father) is to publish a book when he arrives at home, which will contain much curious matter, something quite original, he is an original himself. What a curious idea, that of traveling for a man of his age.[58]

The *Padang* left Smyrna on June 13 and reached Boston on August 25, 1836, a run of seventy-three days. Rush Nutt had seven fellow passengers: Mrs. Purdie (a young Bostonian, née Ellen Pratt, who had married a British merchant from Smyrna and was now returning to visit her parents); her two-year-old son Charles; and her servant Ellen O'Neale. In addition there was Homan Hallock, a printer to the American missionaries, returning home after working in Smyrna for several years; two mechanics (perhaps former employees of Foster Rhodes, the shipbuilder in Constantinople); and lastly Edmond F. Bradlee, age twenty-one, described as a gentleman. And the doctor must have had with him, as ballast, the "enormous boxes of earth and stones" as John L. Stephens described them, presumably to help serve as evidence for the age of the earth, one of his key interests. And also with him, carefully packed and padded, must have been the ostrich eggs full of cotton seed. Rittenhouse Nutt, now on his own, would have taken a relay of steamers from Smyrna to Athens and Malta and on to Marseilles. He sailed from Liverpool on the packet ship *Ajax* in October, and arrived in New York on November third.[59]

Back home later in the year, Rush Nutt contributed a piece on cotton in Egypt and adjacent regions and the age of trees in the eastern Mediterranean to an issue of *The New Orleans Bulletin*.[60] It reveals how interested he was in the landscape. In Egypt, for instance, he "was curious to know how long the Sycamore of Heliopolis had existed in that demolished city, as it was stated to him that Joseph and Mary, on reaching Egypt, sat under this tree, and drank water of a neighboring well." Most tourists saw this tree. John Hamersley, for example, says that he was "brought to the tree under which tradition says that the Virgin Mary took refuge. It is certainly a tough old tree but then again this is rather a tough story. It is an Egyptian sycamore fig tree. I send home some leaves." Rush Nutt sought to determine how long the tree might have been there. He knew that sycamores and other species put forth new sprouts from a decaying old stump and by measuring the size of the circle of more recent growth around the center he calculated the age (by what means I do not know) at more than eighteen hundred years. It certainly was old; the English traveler George Sandys saw it in the early seventeenth century at which time it was already venerable.[61] In his *Egypt & Nubia* the British artist David Roberts gave a good idea of its appearance a few years after Hamersley and the Nutts saw it.[62] Rush Nutt died within a few years after his return. His other son, Haller, to whom Rittenhouse had written several letters describing the Mediterranean trip, succeeded his father as a planter and in time came to own some 43,000 acres of land and eight hundred slaves. In 1859 he engaged the Philadelphia architect Samuel Sloan to build one of the great southern plantation houses. Known as Longwood, this octagonal mansion of "Oriental Revival" style is based on the design of an oriental villa published by Sloan in his 1852 book, *The Model Architect*.[63] It could well have been chosen by Haller in the recollection of his father's and brother's descriptions of buildings in Cairo. The exterior, including the onion-dome cupola, was largely completed at the outbreak of the Civil War in 1861, but then lack of labor obliged Nutt to abandon finishing the house except for the interior of the ground floor. The upper floors have never been completed. Even in its unfinished state, however, the mansion stands as a major tourist attraction in Natchez.[64]

John Lowell

The last American known to have traveled to Egypt before the introduction of scheduled steamship travel in the Mediterranean was the Bostonian John Lowell. John was the son of a noted American entrepreneur, Francis Cabot Lowell who, together with two colleagues, had introduced the water-powered loom into the New England textile industry in 1813. Upon his father's premature death in 1817, John had inherited a considerable fortune.[65] He married well, but in late 1830 his young wife died of scarlet fever and within a year and a half his two daughters died of the same disease.

Shattered, Lowell sold his houses, put his affairs in the hands of a cousin, and in late November 1832 set off from New York for an extended European tour. He landed in Havre and after living for months in Paris and London, he toured cities in Belgium, France, and Italy. In Florence he commissioned a statuette of Venus Victrix from Horatio Greenough, who some years before had done a bust of the former president of Harvard, John T. Kirkland. Lowell reached Rome in early spring 1834. There, having decided to engage an artist to accompany him on the eastern legs of his travels and to record pictorially what he saw, he sought the advice of Horace Vernet, head of the French Academy. Lowell hired one of two recommended by Vernet, namely the twenty-six-year-old Swiss artist Charles Gleyre whom he described in a letter to a cousin,[66] "very plain, a little melancholy, very diffident, of gentlemanly and delicate motions, and according to Vernet a most accomplished artist. He paints in water-colors, Vernet says, better than anybody he knows, is excellent in landscapes and perhaps still better at costumes and portraits." Vernet was correct.

Lowell and Gleyre set off on their eastern tour in early spring 1834.[67] After visiting Naples (April), Sicily (May), Malta (mid-June), western Greece (July), Athens (August), Smyrna (October into early November), and Constantinople, Lowell turned his attention to Egypt. In Constantinople he chartered a Greek brig, the *Bellerophon*, and set sail on December 9, 1834. After a detour to Rhodes, they arrived in Alexandria on December 27, 1834, where they must have missed encountering Rush and Rittenhouse Nutt by a matter of weeks if not days. Released from some two weeks in quarantine, Lowell and Gleyre met a host of well-placed Europeans: He had letters of introduction to John Gliddon, the United States consular agent; to Reinlein the Dutch vice-consul; and to Schutz, the Dutch consul-general. In Cairo on January 24 he and several others visited Ibrahim Pasha, who had just returned, three days earlier, from his Syrian campaign. On the 28th he dined with Patrick Campbell, the British consul-general. On other occasions he met Bernardino Drovetti (the former French consul-general) and Lieutenant Colonel Varin (the French officer in charge of the cavalry school). On February 10 he dined at the house of Joseph Sève (also known as Suleiman Pasha) where he met the leader of the Saint Simoniens, Barthélemy Prosper Enfantin. Lowell thought Père Enfantin had "the physiognomy of a rogue," that he had "a particularly restive eye," and that "the other young men are well bred penniless mortals, the dupes of their own passions & of the seductive doctrines" of their leader.

Lowell also encountered reports of a serious outbreak of bubonic plague.[68] He said that "the European residents have all put themselves in quarantine in their respective houses." Some Europeans, however, responded by moving to Upper Egypt. Edward William Lane, the British Orientalist, whom Lowell would meet, was one of them. Lane made plans as early as January 4 to travel south and he left on the 8th for a five months' stay at Thebes. Meanwhile, and seemingly disregarding the dire threat of the plague, Lowell and Gleyre were in Cairo visiting the usual sights including the Pyramids. From the top of the Great Pyramid on February 12, Lowell wrote to a friend:

The prospect is most beautiful. On the one side is the boundless desert, varied only by a few low ridges of limestone hills. Then you have heaps of sand and a surface of sand, reduced to so fine a powder, and so easily agitated by the slightest breeze, that it almost deserves the name of fluid. Then comes the rich, verdant valley of the Nile, studded with villages, adorned with green date trees, traversed by the Father of Rivers, with the magnificent city of Cairo on its bank, but far narrower than one could wish, as it is bounded, at a distance of some fifteen miles, by the Arabian desert and the abrupt calcareous ridge of Mokattam. Immediately below the spectator lies the city of the dead, the innumerable tombs, the smaller pyramids, the Sphinx, and, still farther off, and on the same line, to the south, the pyramids of Abou Seer, Sakarà, and Dachoor.[69]

Lowell then hired a *canjiah* and went up the Nile. On February 15 he passed Colonel Duhamel, the Russian consul, going in the same direction. He reached Luxor in early March, without any effects of the plague but not without enduring fevers, migraines, and bodily sores. To sleep he says he resorted to laudanum. At Thebes on March 4 Lowell met Edward William Lane, the British Orientalist. In the course of his conversation, "I mentioned to him that we had heard he was Moslem. He said that was very ridiculous. But that he passed easily for such and had even had himself circumcised. He said that without this he should have found it impossible to pursue his studies & researches in the Arabic language." Lowell also met John Gosset, an Englishman from the Isle of Jersey, whom John Hamersley and Rush Nutt and his son had seen the previous year. Lowell and Gleyre stayed for a month at Thebes, both of them sick with dysentery and the eye disease ophthalmia.

At Thebes, despite bouts of illness, Lowell added to his collection of Egyptian antiquities. On March 14, Lowell wrote: "I visited the Typhonium (that is the Mut precinct at Karnak) yesterday and ordered two statues of the goddess with a lion's head to be brought to the boat." Later, on March 23, he reported that "I rode to Karnac today to see an immense block of granite that the shekh & some 50 men are slowly transporting to the boat. It is a fragment of an enormous block of red Syanite granite forming part of what perhaps constituted a sanctuary to a little temple in that immense pile of buildings at Karnac." This five-foot-tall block is now recognized as coming from the sanctuary of one of the Macedonian successors of Alexander the Great, namely Philip Arrhidaeus, a building designed to house the sacred boat of the god Amun-Re, now reconstructed but then partially in ruins.[70] In addition,

Lowell acquired from Karnak two fragments from the fallen red gran-ite obelisk of the Eighteenth Dynasty queen Hatshepsut, one fragment more than three-and-a-half feet tall showing the queen herself (plate 22).[71] Also thought to have come from Karnak is a colossal, two-and-a-half-foot-tall, red granite head of the pharaoh Ramesses III. These sculptures were more significant than any in the collection of the Bal-timorean Mendes Cohen. Lowell also purchased a stuffed crocodile, nearly ten feet long, and in early May he sent them downriver by boat to Cairo. Gleyre made a splendid series of architectural studies, among them watercolors showing the Avenue of the Sphinxes at Karnak and the interior of the Temple of Amon. At some stage of the journey he rendered Lowell in eastern dress (plate 21).

Sailing north in April they backtracked to Abydos and Asyut from where they trekked across the desert to the Khargeh Oasis, spending a week in May at the oasis. This was an unusual destination for Europeans. The French explorer Frédéric Cailliaud was the first European to visit the site, in July 1818.[72] The French Consul-General Bernardino Drovetti was there in 1819, Sir Archibald Edmonstone, Capt. Henry Hoghton, and the Rev. Robert Master in 1819,[73] and George Hoskins, Robert Hay, and Frederick Catherwood in the fall of 1832.[74] Lowell was the first American to visit the oasis.

Back on the Nile they again went south and returned to Luxor on June 10 where they saw nine Frenchmen, among whom must have been Messrs. Barral, Fortin, Portalis, Artaud, and Delon, some of them Saint Simoniens, who had fled plague-ridden Lower Egypt in April with Pros-per Enfantin for the presumed safety of the south. All of the Europeans who had fled south were indeed wise to do so. It has been estimated that as many as 75,000 people died in Cairo that year, 1835, about one third of the population.

Then, despite illness but not suffering from the plague, Lowell and Gleyre continued south. They reached Edfu on June 12, Philae on June 22, and Abu Simbel on July 15. In October, near Meroe in Sudan, they met the Swedish naturalist and doctor Johan Hedenborg, whom Ham-ersley had seen the year before in Lower Egypt. Lowell and Gleyre reached Khartoum in October or November 1835. There they parted. Gleyre stayed in Khartoum for nearly a year before returning to Cairo and eventually to Marseilles and Paris. Lowell went overland to the Red Sea and took a local sailing vessel to Mocha, where on January 23, 1836, he boarded the British steamer *Hugh Lindsay* for Bombay.[75] He arrived there in early February, but within a month, on March 4, 1836, he died.

Lowell kept an extensive account of his entire European and eastern tour. His diary exists in two versions: One, a copy with blank sections, is on long-term deposit from the Lowell family in the Egyptian Department of the Museum of Fine Arts, Boston, together with the letters he wrote to friends.[76] The other version, the original, is on deposit from the Lowell family at the Boston Athenaeum. His legacy as a Bostonian: the princely sum of nearly $240,000 to endow the Lowell Institute, designed to sponsor popular and scholarly lectures, given annually to this day. His legacy as a traveler in Egypt, twofold: first, the forty cases of antiquities, not to mention the stuffed crocodile, which arrived in Boston in mid-December 1835, shortly before his death. In 1875, the Lowell family presented nine pieces of monumental sculpture to the Museum of Fine Arts, Boston, including, in addition to the sculptures and reliefs from Karnak already mentioned, a magnificent head of an anthropomorphic basalt sarcophagus. And, secondly, the watercolors and pencil drawings of sites and people commissioned from his traveling companion Charles Gleyre, the originals of which are all on deposit in the Museum of Fine Arts, Boston.

So far as I know, Lowell was the only American to engage an artist while touring the Mediterranean in this period. Artists had traveled with Europeans but not Americans. Prominent among artists engaged by European scholars and travelers in the time just before Lowell's trip were the Frenchmen Nestor L'Hote (1804–1842), Adrien Dauzats (1808–1869), and Prosper Marilhat (1811–1847).[77] L'Hote was one of several artists who accompanied Champollion to Egypt in 1828, staying on into 1830. Dauzats accompanied Baron Isidore Justin Séverin Taylor, who had been furnished by the French government with presents for Mehmet Ali and charged with negotiating the acquisition of the Luxor obelisk. They arrived in the spring of 1830. Marilhat was hired by the Austrian botanist K.A.A. von Hügel to accompany him and the French naturalist Polydore Roux of Marseilles on an extended tour to the East. Marilhat arrived in Egypt in October 1831 with Hügel and Roux and stayed on after the two scholars had left. He himself left Egypt in 1833 on the boat taking the Luxor obelisk to France. All three artists produced hundreds of drawings, some of them details of Egyptian architecture, others topographical landscapes and genre studies. Selected drawings were worked up later as oil paintings for the annual salons and other purposes. A comparison of their work with that of Charles Gleyre justifies Horace Vernet's appraisal of Gleyre as one who painted in watercolors better than anyone he knew.

Two Brigs from Boston Reach Alexandria

In the same year that Lowell traveled in Egypt, 1835, two American brigs from Boston called at Alexandria, perhaps the first to do so since the *Fortune* and *Erin* in 1824 and 1825. From a letter sent to John Forsyth, United States secretary of state, by John Gliddon, and from snippets of information published in the marine columns of local newspapers, it is possible to learn something of their voyages. On July 28, 1835, N. Pendleton, captain of the *Alexander*, having been cleared from Boston for Gibraltar on June second, reached Alexandria with a cargo of Spanish cigars, herring and other fish, New England rum, sperm oil candles, white and brown sugar, and what is unusual, sets of furniture, namely chairs, couches, tables, and wash stands. She left the port on August 13 with a cargo of antiquities and specimens of natural history, bound for Rhodes and Smyrna (where she loaded an additional cargo of fruit and sponges), and ultimately for Boston where she arrived in mid-December. On December 21 the *Boston Courier* reported, "The *Alexander* brings about forty packages of Egyptian Antiquities, three Egyptian Mummies and a stuffed crocodile." Whose antiquities? Surely those collected by John Lowell, which he had sent downriver to Alexandria as he went south with Gleyre. Before leaving Egypt, Lowell must have arranged through his Boston contacts to have the *Alexander* call for them.

The second brig arrived in Alexandria on August 25, two weeks after the departure of the *Alexander*. William D. Phelps, captain of the *Regulator*, had left Boston in September (destined for Tenerife, the largest of the Canary Islands), and had reached Egypt after a preliminary stop in Malta, where he off-loaded part of his cargo. In Alexandria, he had a letter to Rossetti, the Tuscan consul-general, through whom he managed to sell to the pasha the remainder of his cargo, the nature of which is not known. While in port he and his first and second mates, Martin Adams and James Warden, arranged to load five hundred bags of salt from lake Mariotis as ballast. The return itinerary took them to Smyrna where they took on board a cargo of wool, opium, gum Arabic, senna, and sultana raisins before setting forth for Boston on October 12, but the brig never reached port: Off Plymouth on February 4, 1836, she was shipwrecked on a sandy shoal and was a total loss. How lucky that Lowell's antiquities were shipped on the *Alexander*.[78]

12 | TRAVELING IN EGYPT

Within the first five years of the 1830s, the pattern of American visitors to Egypt had largely been established. But before looking at what arrangements were made about hotels, documents and letters of introduction, guidebooks, guides, funds, dress, food, and health in Egypt, let us first consider travel to Egypt in the overall context of American travel to western Europe.

Travel in Europe

The numbers of Americans traveling to Europe in the early decades of the nineteenth century are not easy to determine, but some attempt can be made based on maritime and consular records. According to French records quoted in a recent study of American tourists in France, 678 Americans registered in the hotels and pensions of Paris in 1825, 847 in 1826, and by 1830 perhaps 2,000 arrived in Paris.[1] During the 1830s the figures grew substantially. How many of them made it to Italy? On February 22, 1830, 49 Americans gathered in Rome to celebrate Washington's Birthday.[2] The total for the whole year surely approached one hundred. Consular records of the United States with the Papal States offer more figures for Rome, from mid-1824 to mid-1826 and then from mid-1833 to mid-1836, partially comparable to the Paris figures, and a least a useful guide.[3] Twenty-eight Americans registered at the consulate in the second half of 1824, approximately 49 for 1825, and 28 for the first half of 1826; then 95 for the period from July through December 1833; 100 for the whole of 1834; 121 for the whole of 1835, and 160 for the first half of 1836. A guess that between 5 and 10 percent of the Americans visiting France reached Rome would be plausible. Many went on to Naples, a much smaller percentage to Sicily, and as we will see, only a fraction to the eastern Mediterranean. But Americans were only a fraction of English-speaking tourists in Italy. One writer has estimated that in the 1830s some 5,000 British visited Rome annually.[4]

In the 1820s and 1830s Americans usually spent more than a year abroad, longer if they traveled to the Mediterranean. Before the introduction of steamer service from New York to Havre, Liverpool, and London in 1838, more than two months of that time was spent getting there and back. The voyage by sailing packet from New York and other American ports to Europe took more than a month on the outward trip, up to six weeks on the homeward one. Steamer travel reduced that to little more than two weeks and allowed a set schedule, little dependent on weather. In any event a month was needed to cross the Atlantic in both directions.

There was no one European itinerary, but a typical one would include, after the landing at Havre, passage by horse-drawn coach to Paris via Rouen. Not laid until the 1840s, after the period covered in this account, was a rail line between Havre, Rouen, and Paris. A visit to Paris might be followed by a trip down the Rhone to Marseilles, by coastal boat to Leghorn or Civitàvecchia (the port of Rome), followed by weeks in Florence, Venice, Rome, and Naples, Naples being the focus of obligatory excursions to Pompeii and Vesuvius. Some travelers then sailed to Malta (Sicily was often excluded) and on to various Mediterranean localities. Passage to Alexandria and then by boat up the Nile to Cairo and then to Thebes may have been the most exotic venture sought by travelers, but it was an optional leg of a Mediterranean tour, which also included days or weeks in Malta, Greece, Palestine and Syria, and Smyrna and Constantinople. Many travelers, European and American, made the Mediterranean circuit without ever reaching Egypt.

A return to western Europe from the Ottoman capital prior to the establishment of steamships in the mid-1830s involved going overland by horseback through Bulgaria to Vienna. Once regular steamer service was established, you could travel to the mouth of the Danube and then by a relay of steamers upriver to Vienna. To complete the circuit, tourists visited Munich, Dresden, Berlin, and other cities in Prussia if they had not seen them before setting out for the south. More adventurous Americans, even at an early period, ventured to Scandinavia and Russia. Sometimes the trip was done in the reverse order, but if Egypt was to be included in the itinerary, the counterclockwise approach was preferred because travelers coming to regions of the Ottoman Empire, including Egypt, from Europe, Malta, and Greece avoided quarantine. Arrival in Alexandria from

Constantinople and Smyrna, on the other hand, entailed a week or more of medical incarceration. Whatever the circuit, all travelers had to undergo quarantine when returning to Europe, in Piraeus, Malta, or some place between Constantinople and western Europe.

Travel within the Mediterranean was dependent on securing passage on commercial sailing ships, which often entailed lengthy delays. Steamship travel in the eastern Mediterranean (covered in chapter 14) was not introduced until the second half of the 1830s. American travelers, like their European counterparts, arrived in Egypt by two routes. Some came overland from Syria and Palestine, crossing Sinai to Cairo. More usually, however, they arrived by sailing ship to Alexandria. Most sought passage on a commercial brig, sailing from Malta, the Greek island of Syra, Smyrna in Turkey, or from Beirut. A small number of wealthier Americans were in a position to charter their own ships.

Passports and Letters of Introduction
Most American travelers in the eighteenth and nineteenth centuries carried passports, though American law did not require them to do so. The early nineteenth-century passport was a folio-size, engraved document, boldly displaying the heraldic device of the United States and the words, "To all to whom these Presents shall come, Greeting. I, the Undersigned, Secretary of State of the United States of America, hereby request all whom it may concern, to permit safely and freely to pass [name] a Citizen of the United States and in case of need to give him all lawful Aid and Protection" (plate 23). On the left side was a description of the bearer including age, height, and features such as the color of eyes and hair, and his signature. On the lower right, adjacent to the seal of the United States, were the date it was issued and the signature of the secretary of state.[5] The most prominent feature, at the top of the document, which drew the attention of foreign officials who might not be able to interpret anything else on the passport, was the heraldic device, an eagle, framed by the words "United States of America." The eagle had a lyre at its breast with ten stars of the constellation Lyra in the field, and was encircled by thirteen larger stars, signifying the original states. John Quincy Adams (the future president) had designed the image and, as a member of the Massachusetts legislature, had used it as early as 1802. Later, as secretary of state from 1817 to 1825, he had it placed on passports beginning about 1822.[6] The folio paper was folded over, leaving the engraved image and text on the face and providing blank space inside the fold for endorsements by consular officers such as the American legations in London and

Paris, and foreign customs and police officials. The National Archives in Washington, DC, possesses passport applications written by or in behalf of many of the travelers discussed in this book.[7]

Jurisdictions within the United States could also issue passports. By way of example the Commonwealth of Massachusetts and the City of New York issued passports for travel abroad. In 1831 the Commonwealth of Massachusetts issued a passport "to permit *Mr. Charles Larkin* . . . a citizen of our Commonwealth going to *Smyrna and elsewhere* to pass safe and freely, without giving, or permitting to be given to him, any hindrance" and so on. Larkin's name and his destination were written in spaces left blank.[8] The passport is signed by Levi Lincoln, the governor, and by Charles Larkin. On March 7, 1838, the City of New York issued a passport, signed by the mayor of the city, Aaron Clark, to Henry P. Marshall, a young twenty-four-year-old merchant, about to embark to take up a position as first US consul to Muscat (Oman) and whose story is told in chapter 15.[9] Even though Marshall was representing the United States, his passport was issued by the city where he did business. And many other such passports exist.

Upon reaching Egypt travelers had to apply for a firman, that is, a document written in Arabic or Turkish granting the bearer the right to travel in the country and affording protection under the pasha. Some guidebooks of the period included model language that the traveler could insist on to assure a properly worded document.

Most Americans also carried letters of introduction to contacts who could help them with accommodations and otherwise make their life agreeable and sociable. Ward Nicholas Boylston, the first American in the East, had letters to people along his itinerary. So too did virtually all of the Americans who reached Egypt in the early decades of the nineteenth century. Travelers carried letters from friends at home to consular officials in western Europe, who in turn provided them with letters for ongoing legs of their journeys. In the case of one traveler, Valentine Mott (discussed in chapter 15), those letters of introduction that he did not use—that is, addressed to individuals whom he was not able to meet—are preserved. In them we can read the kind of language used.

Guidebooks

The first popular description of the region, *Egypt, Nubia, and Abyssinia*, two volumes, London, 1827, appeared in the series *The Modern Traveller: A Popular Description, Geographical, Historical, and Topographical of the Various Countries of the Globe*, edited by Joseph Condor. It was not so much a guidebook as a compilation of extensive quotations, often translated, of what others had already said about the country, including the rule of Mehmet Ali, with added commentary where appropriate. The New Yorker John L. Stephens had a copy with him during his 1836 Nile trip. He also had an English translation of Volney's account of Syria and Egypt, first published in 1787. Before and even after the availability of *The Modern Traveller*, tourists would carry older accounts of Egypt, like that of Volney, or the published works of more recent visitors, such as Robert Richardson's *Travels along the Mediterranean* that recounted his tour as a physician with the Earl of Belmore and his family, including their encounter with Belzoni in late 1817 at the newly found tomb of Seti at Thebes.[10]

Available within a few years of the *Modern Traveller* was a guide by Rev. Michael Russell, *View of Ancient and Modern Egypt: With an Outline of Its Natural History*, Edinburgh, 1830, or the American edition, published in Harper's Family Library, New York, 1831, the latter with a special insert warning the reader not to be misled by the disparaging remarks made against the achievements of the French savants. In 1839 the New Yorker Philip Rhinelander carried a copy of the Edinburgh edition of Russell (see chapter 18). Or you could select Jean-Jacques Rifaud, *Tableau de l'Égypte, de la Nubie et des lieux circonvoisins: ou itinéraire à l'usage des voyageurs qui visitent ces contrées*, Paris, 1830, which appeared the same year in German, *Gemälde von Egypten, Nubien und den umliegenden Gegenden*, to serve the growing number of German tourists. Russell said in his introduction, "the object of this volume is to present to the reader, in a condensed form, an account of all that is known about Egypt, both in its ancient and in its modern state." But Russell had never been to Egypt and his book contained no handy tips to the traveler. He drew his account from the principal published authorities, quoting ancient authors and modern travelers such as Shaw, Volney, Denon, Belzoni, Hamilton, Carne, and Richardson. Rifaud, on the other hand, had spent years in Egypt, beginning in 1814, and had worked at Thebes from 1817 to 1823 with a team of French and British antiquarians. His publication was based on his own research and experience in Egypt and contained, besides descriptions of the countryside and monuments, general instructions for the traveler. An appendix of more than fifty pages, *Vocabulaire des dialects vulgaires de la Haute-Égypte*, contained useful words and phrases, in two columns, French on the left, Arabic in Western characters on the right. In 1833, the New Yorker John Hamersley purchased a copy of Rifaud's guide in Constantinople before setting sail for Alexandria, and he also had with him the *Modern Traveller*.

Topography of Thebes, and General View of Egypt: Being a Short Account of the Principal Objects Worthy of Notice in the Valley of the Nile, . . . *With Remarks on the Manners and Customs of the Ancient Egyptians and the Productions of the Country, &c, &c* appeared in London in 1835. This was the first edition of John Gardner Wilkinson's work on Egypt. The author, a Harrow and Oxford man, was drawn to antiquity early on, and after Oxford spent much of a year in Naples with the classical scholar William Gell. In 1821 he went to Egypt where he lived until 1833, becoming fluent in Arabic, and visiting, sketching, and making notes on virtually every important monument in the Nile valley to the extent that he grew to be recognized as the British Egyptologist of the day.[11] Wilkinson's attention to detail made *Topography of Thebes* a landmark publication on ancient Egypt. Moreover it was illustrated with eight engravings drawn from Wilkinson's extensive repertory of sketches. Owing to its success, his publisher, John Murray, issued an enlarged and up-to-date two-volume version in 1843.[12] The publisher then commissioned Wilkinson to condense this to a one-volume format, which appeared in 1847 as Murray's *Hand-book for Travellers in Egypt*, a guide frequently reprinted. A ten-page appendix in the 1835 edition offered helpful tips to the tourist about servants, provisions, books to bring, and how to plan for a trip to the Pyramids and a journey to Thebes. There was also a sixteen-page "English and Arabic Vocabulary." In the 1843 and 1847 editions, Wilkinson provided extended sections, nearly 200 pages in the 1843 edition, on transportation, quarantine, hotels, money, dress, boat travel in the country, servants, and provisions, as well as the scholarly appraisal of the history and monuments found in the 1835 edition, all based on his years of experience in the country. The guide gave full schedules, charges, and regulations for people and cargo on most of the steamship lines. First-class passage on the French packet from Civitàvecchia via the Greek island of Syra to Alexandria cost 380 French francs; to bring your dog, ten francs extra. To ship a giraffe from Alexandria to Malta, £15 s15. Now travelers knew what to expect.

Funds

Independent travelers carried convenient quantities of gold and silver coins and letters of credit, as we learn from their accounts. A letter of credit was issued by one's bank to one or more other banks, requesting that the corresponding bank advance funds to the bearer of the document and vouching for his solvency and reputation. In Alexandria in 1822, George Rapelje had a letter of credit from the firm of Kerr, Black & Co. to Messrs.

Gliddon, Brothers & Co. In Cairo, Rapelje went to a Mr. Delavaratore with a letter of credit from Gliddon in Alexandria.[13] In the early 1830s Mendes Cohen used the Boston firm of Samuel Welles in Paris, and Rothschild in Egypt. John W. Hamersley says he visited "Mr. Cunningham my banker" in Constantinople. In Alexandria he called on Mr. Gauthier (of the French firm Gauthier and Pastré), agent of Messrs. Barings, who gave him letters of credit on his house in Cairo. Later, in Greece, Hamersley said that he had trouble with bills at Napoli (Nauplion) because Messrs. Barings had no banker there. In addition, many travelers carried cash in the form of silver and gold coins. Gold coins included the French twenty-franc piece. It is likely that upon arrival in Alexandria they converted their cold cash into the form of credit with local bankers, to avoid having such valuables with them on a Nile trip.

Hotels

After arrival at Alexandria and negotiation with the donkey boys at the landing stages, hotels were available in the city. In Alexandria in 1822, George Rapelje "put up at a miserable place, called the Maltese Hotel, kept by a French woman," but soon changed to the Greek Hotel kept by a Spaniard.[14] In 1833 Eli and Sarah Smith stayed in a boarding house there kept by an English lady.[15] A year later Hamersley stayed at the Three Anchors Hotel. Two of his friends stayed at the Aquila d'Oro, run by an Italian and located on the quay of the quarantine harbor with a splendid view. In his 1843 guide Wilkinson recommended L'Hotel d'Europe and L'Hotel d'Orient in Alexandria. The former, until 1842, was Hill's Hotel. Moving on to Cairo, Wilkinson recommended Hotel d'Orient; formerly first choice had been Hill's, also called the Eastern Hotel. The Giardino or French Hotel was "cheaper, but it has no very good rooms." George Rapelje stayed there in 1822 and reported, "put up at the French or Garden Hotel, and miserable enough it was."[16] In 1836, John L. Stephens stayed at the Locanda d'Italia.

Dress

Travelers often adopted local dress when they arrived in Egypt, but how a European dressed in Egypt was debated at the time and has remained a subject of interest.[17] On his arrival in Cairo in 1821 Gardner Wilkinson, who went on to write the preeminent nineteenth-century guide to the country, was taken to buy Turkish clothes. In the first edition of his guide, published in 1835, though written several years earlier, Wilkinson said that were the traveler to "inquire if the Turkish dress is necessary, I answer, for a voyage in Upper Egypt it is by no means so; for Qaherah [Cairo] it is convenient from not attracting notice; and for a journey in the Desert, as to the Oasis or Berenice, it is indispensably necessary."[18]

In his 1843 version of the guide, he rephrased his comments: "If the traveler inquires whether the Turkish dress be necessary, I answer, for Upper Egypt, it is by no means so, for Cairo it is convenient from not attracting notice either of dogs or men."[19]

Ten years earlier, about the time Wilkinson was first composing his work, the English officer C. Rochfort Scott, who had arrived in Alexandria in 1833 on the same ship from Malta with the American missionary Rev. Eli Smith, had this to say:

> With respect to a travelling dress, the Turkish, or rather Nizam, which is a variation of it, is that which is generally recommended; but, I must confess, that after some personal experience in the matter, I would strongly advise travellers to save themselves the expense of buying, and the bore of wearing this cumbersome attire.[20]

Yet many travelers surely bought Turkish clothes merely to dress the part, and they took them home. In 1830, about the time the Americans Henry Oliver and Cornelius Bradford were in Egypt, Sir Baldwin Leighton arrived there from Naples, Greece, Cyprus, and Palestine. Three years later, his wife, an accomplished watercolorist, painted him dressed head to toe in a Turkish outfit, reclining at home in Shropshire, with his dog and an Ottoman sword on the floor by his side, and their first child, Frances Christina, in the arms of a nanny in the doorway.[21]

Food

As for food, George Rapelje in Alexandria in 1822 wrote as follows: "Living, as to meat and vegetables, well. I found a good dish of tea or coffee, in the Italian or French style." On leaving Cairo for Suez he took along "provisions of bread, cheese, and some Bologna sausages, and had some limes and oranges which I found very grateful by squeezing them in water, and adding some sugar."[22]

In 1834 Hamersley gives a sample menu on board the Nile boat he shared with two English companions: for breakfast: "café au lait, tea, toast, omelet, butter, honey and orange marmalade and whatever cold fowl and tongue there is. For dinner: soup, pilaf, roast meat, cheese, oranges and coffee. At night: milk, tea, sugar, biscuits." Two years earlier, Mrs. Kirkland complained about the quality of the meat. In 1836 John L. Stephens wrote that the outfit for his Nile voyage with his dragoman Paolo Nuozzo was not very extravagant: "two tin cups, two pairs of knives and forks, four plates, coffee, tea, sugar, rice, macaroni, and a few dozen of claret."[23] Wildfowl shot along the way would supplement the staples. Once at Philae, they had "Irish stew," mutton and potatoes, both roasted and boiled. Leaving Cairo for his journey across the desert, Stephens packed "bread, biscuits, rice, macaroni, tea, coffee, dried apricots, oranges, a roasted leg of mutton, and two of the largest skins containing the filtered water of the Nile."[24] Hector Horeau, a French traveler, leaving Cairo to go upriver the following year in 1837, reported that his basic provisions were biscuits, rice, dried fruit, cheese, sugar, and spirits; he would purchase other eatables en route.[25] A clergyman, George Cheever, traveling in 1838 found the oranges very good, and said that on the Nile they could procure fresh milk, eggs, and butter.[26] Many travelers also lived on chicken and eggs.

A fashion of dining experienced by only a few Americans in this period was related by Eliza Patterson, one of the daughters of Commodore Patterson whose family was in Cairo in 1834 (described in chapter 10). After touring the pasha's palace with two ladies, one of them the wife of a Turkish colonel, the other the sultana herself, Mrs. Patterson and the three girls, Harriet, Eliza, and Georgy, paused for lunch. Eliza recounted the meal in her diary:

By this time it was 12 o'clock, when she asked us at what hour we wished to dine, we told her at any hour she chose. In a few minutes we were led down stairs to the fountain chamber we had first entered where we found a small round table holding six plates set out. The top was a round slab of glass, resting on a small wooden stand. Here a girl handing one to me, handed us each a silver basin while she poured from a silver pitcher . . . water over our hands. Another handed us an embroidered towel to wipe our hands. After this operation we sat down and then a fine white towel beautifully embroidered in gold was passed over the left shoulder and under the opposite arm in order to preserve our clothes. The first dish on table was roasted lamb— everything was served in the handsomest style on finest china, knives and silver forks &c. I felt very much inclined to dine off the lamb, being very good, but Ma, who remembered when Papa had told us about dining with a Turk once, and having forty dishes of meal brought on table separately, said, "recollect the forty dishes," upon which I instantly let drop my knife and fork. Dish after dish came on, first meat, then sweets, then fish, and if we had one dish of fish on table we had ten. We were finally so sick tasting all these dishes, for we were obliged from politeness to taste everything. At first they helped us very largely as they do themselves, I suppose, but seeing we only tasted, they became far sparing and merely gave us a taste. They removed the dishes and brought them in rapid succession, till two or three times I thought I would have to leave the table. I was so sick. Imagine the mixture of sweets, fish, and meat, 39 dishes were brought on. The last was watermelon and we enjoyed it for til the latter part of dinner we had not been able to procure some water. . . . At three o'clock we rose from table when we again underwent the operation of washing our hands.[27]

Guides and Security

Travelers engaged servants and/or guides to accompany them on their tours. George Rapelje had an Arab who spoke English followed by a Portuguese guide who spoke Arabic and English.[28] Henry Oliver recommended to William Holt Yates the dragoman he had engaged for his Egyptian journey, a Cairene whose name according to Holt was Mohammed Abdini.[29] In December 1833, Eli and Sarah Smith brought with them a Turkish servant, Ahmed, from Malta, dressed in loose Turkish trousers and with a red cap.[30] A year earlier, in April 1832, the Rev. John T. Kirkland and his wife Elizabeth Cabot Kirkland had with them in Alexandria, and presumably during their entire Egyptian stay, an Arab servant named Achmet, similarly dressed. Perhaps they too had brought him from Malta.[31] Rush Nutt and John L. Stephens employed the same Maltese dragoman (interpreter), Paolo Nuozzo, who continued to serve foreign visitors well into the 1840s.[32] In 1836, Sarah and Richard Haight engaged a dragoman, Giovanni, at Odessa, and a cook, François, at Smyrna, both of whom accompanied them throughout the East; they also had Selim, an Arab boy who helped in minor matters.[33] Most travelers carried firearms, but probably more for sport than for protection. When Allen, Oakley, and Ferguson rode out to visit the Pyramids in 1831, Allen reported, "I had my daggers buckled on, my pistols stuck in my belt, & my [double-barreled shot] gun flung at my back & with all this armament I was mounted on a donkey." John L. Stephens purchased a double-barreled shotgun in Cairo.[34] But the guns were not so much for protection as for sport. Tourists shot ducks, geese, and pigeons which they ate—Allen said he bagged between forty and sixty on the journey from Alexandria to Cairo—and upriver tourists also shot at crocodiles, which seemed not to notice.

Health

Diseases in Egypt and elsewhere in the Mediterranean included the two potentially fatal ones of plague and cholera. Travelers were also subject, if not vaccinated, to the disfiguring (and sometimes fatal) effects of small-pox. In addition, if they were not prudently abstemious, they ran the risk of syphilis with its long-term chronic effects. Ophthalmia, the painful and debilitating, though curable, eye disease was particularly associated with travel on the Nile. Dysentery could affect travelers anywhere.[35]

In Egypt, public health officials had introduced quarantine early on in the nineteenth century to combat outbreaks of plague and cholera. A laza-retto (the name came from the Italian word *lazzaretto*, derived from the sick beggar Lazarus in Luke 16:20) was established at Alexandria for trav-elers coming from ports in the eastern Mediterranean, though not Greece. Lazarettos also existed in Syra, Hydra, the Piraeus, and Malta, not to men-tion Trieste and other European ports, for travelers coming from Egypt.[36]

Plague—bubonic plague—an old disease, circulated among rodents and their fleas and was communicated to humans through flea bites. Symptoms included swollen glands, hence the adjective *bubonic*, and high fever. The disease was highly fatal. The plague was known in Egypt as well as the rest of the Mediterranean world in the seventeenth and eighteenth centuries and recurred with particular virulence in 1834 and 1835.[37] The best method to avoid the plague was to leave the place where it was occurring, which for many Europeans and upper-class Egyptians in Cairo meant going up the Nile. Alternatively you could shut yourself in your house to the extent feasible.

Cholera was a relatively new disease and first struck Egypt in 1831, apparently introduced by pilgrims returning from Mecca, to where it had been brought from India. An isolated outbreak had occurred earlier in Muscat (modern Oman) and in regions of Syria in 1822 and 1823 but had not spread. The 1831 cholera epidemic caused well over 100,000 deaths in Egypt and then swept western Europe and the United States causing tens of thousands of additional fatalities.[38] Since it was not known in the earlier nineteenth century that cholera was transmitted through water contami-nated with feces from those already sick, there were no prohibitions about drinking water, and the disease was easily spread. In Egypt, the French doctor Antoine-Barthélémy Clot, who received the title Clot Bey by not abandoning his post during the epidemic, recognized that cholera was infectious but not contagious. You could not contract the disease simply by being in contact with an individual stricken with it. You had to drink infected water or consume some other contaminated substance.

Smallpox was widespread in Egypt in the early decades of the nineteenth century, but both Mehmet Ali and the French doctor Antoine-Barthé-lémy Clot (not yet awarded the title Bey by the pasha) were responsible for effective immunization programs in the 1820s.[39] Two methods were used, inoculation (sometimes called variolation) and vaccination. The first involved transferring a small bit of smallpox matter to an opening in the skin of the person to be protected who got a mild case but recovered and was then immune; the second involved infecting the individual with cowpox, a milder disease that caused no serious effects and rendered the person immune from smallpox. The first method, the older of the two, was practiced in Europe and the United States early in the eighteenth century, partially as a result of the publicity given by Lady Mary Wortley Montagu, wife of a British consul at Constantinople, who had survived smallpox herself and had had her own son inoculated when they were in Constantinople in 1718.[40] In the United States inoculation was first performed in Boston in 1721, at the urging of Cotton Mather, by Zabdiel Boylston (1679–1766), a great-uncle of Ward Nicholas Boylston, whose travels to Egypt are described in the first chapter of this book.[41] The second method was discovered and recommended by the English doctor Edward Jenner in 1796. Safer, it soon superseded the older method, and was first practiced in the United States in 1800 in Cambridge, Massachusetts, by Dr. Benjamin Waterhouse of the Harvard Medical School. Aware of Jenner's work and being encouraged by Thomas Jefferson, Waterhouse began by vaccinating his own children. The only American known to me who contracted smallpox in Egypt in the early nineteenth century was J. Lewis Stackpole, who, despite having been vaccinated, caught a mild case while on his Nile boat in 1834 and recovered without disfiguring spots. But the disease could not easily be dismissed. In the summer of 1831, William Meredith, a traveling companion of Benjamin Disraeli and who was engaged to his sister, caught what at first seemed a mild case after traveling to Thebes, but tragically died of it in Cairo.[42]

The eye disease ophthalmia afflicted several American travelers on the Nile, among them George Bethune English, Rush Nutt, and John Lowell. All were slowed up by the ailment but all recovered.

No American, to my knowledge, contracted syphilis in Egypt in the early nineteenth century. The classic case was that of Gustave Flaubert who, when he was traveling in Egypt with Maxime Du Camp in 1849 and 1850, had sexual relations with any number of women during the Nile journey and suffered the effects of syphilis for the rest of his life.

What we would today call patent medicines were widespread. Laudanum—tincture of opium—had been taken for decades as a pain-killer for all kinds of ailments by children as well as grownups. Over-used it could become addictive, as the English poet Coleridge discovered. European and American visitors commonly carried laudanum in Egypt. In his diary John Lowell, for one, reported taking laudanum while on the Nile. In addition to laudanum, Gardner Wilkinson recommended in an appendix to his guide book, *Topography of Thebes*, other items for the medicine chest, among them sulphate of zinc and ipecacuanha.[43] To help cure ophthalmia, an application of sulphate of zinc in rose-water was recommended, or nitrate of silver in rose-water. To help cure dysentery it was recommended that you take an emetic of ipecacuanha (an extract from the root of a plant in the madder family native to Brazil and first used in Europe in the seventeenth century), and a concoction consisting in part of rhubarb.

13 | JOHN L. STEPHENS AND FELLOW TOURISTS OF THE MID-1830S

The perfect freedom from all restraint, and from the conventional trammels of civilized society, forms an episode in a man's life that is vastly agreeable and exciting. Think of not shaving for two months, of washing your shirts in the Nile, and wearing them without being ironed. . . . You go ashore whenever you like, and stroll through the little villages, and be stared at by the Arabs, or walk along the banks of the river till darkness covers the earth; shooting pigeons, and sometimes pheasants and hares, besides the odd shots from the deck of your boat at geese, crocodiles, and pelicans. And then it is so ridiculously cheap an amusement. You get your boat with ten men for thirty or forty dollars a month, fowls for three piastres a pair, a sheep for half or three quarters of a dollar, and eggs almost for the asking. You sail under your own country's banner . . . . From time to time you hear that a French or English flag has passed so many days before you, and you meet your fellow-voyagers with a freedom and cordiality which exists nowhere but on the Nile. These are the little every-day items in the voyage, without refer-ring to the great and interesting objects which are the traveller's principal inducements and rewards, the ruined cities on its banks, the mighty temples and tombs, and all the wonderful monuments of Egypt's departed great-ness. Of them I will barely say, that their great antiquity, the mystery that overhangs them, and their extraordinary preservation amid the surrounding desolation, make Egypt perhaps the most interesting country in the world.[1]

So wrote John L. Stephens, one of the best-known American travel-ers in this period, commenting on the pleasures of being on the Nile. Stephens was one of a succession of Americans from Boston, New York, Philadelphia, Baltimore, and Charleston who took extended grand tours to Egypt and the eastern Mediterranean in the second half of the 1830s. Most were young college graduates, but some, like Stephens, were lawyers; others were doctors, clergymen, and merchants in search of business opportunities. A few were married couples. There were no unattached women.

John L. Stephens

John L. Stephens, born in 1805, was educated at private schools in New York, entered Columbia College in 1818, and graduated with the class of 1822. From 1822 to 1824 he studied law at Tapping Reeve's Law School in Litchfield, Connecticut. But before practicing law, he set off on an excursion to the Midwest in 1824 with his cousin, Charles Hendrickson, the son of his mother's sister Mary. They reached Cincinnati, and then went down the Mississippi River to New Orleans before returning home. After this adventure Stephens was admitted to practice as an attorney in March 1827 and joined the law office of George W. Strong in New York City.[2]

Then in 1834, ostensibly on doctor's advice to cure a throat infection, Stephens decided to go abroad. He sailed from New York on the packet ship *Charlemagne* in November 1834, bound for Havre, but left the ship in England and visited London first. From there he went on to France and Italy. In Naples he met a fellow New Yorker, Dr. Marinus Willett,[3] whose brother, Edward, also a lawyer, was married to one of Stephens' sisters. Dr. Willett was on his way to see the American missionaries in Greece. Stephens, Willett, and a Scotsman whom Stephens at first calls M, only later Maxwell, reached Greece in February 1835.[4] Parting from Willett and Maxwell who returned to Europe, Stephens went on alone to Smyrna and Constantinople; there he postponed his trip to Egypt owing to reports of the bubonic plague, which had overwhelmed Alexandria and Cairo beginning in January, and went instead to Odessa, Moscow (on the fourth of July), St. Petersburg, Warsaw, and Cracow. Returning to western Europe, he again went south and with the plague gone, arrived in Egypt via Malta before Christmas, December 1835.

In Malta Stephens had engaged Paolo Nuozzo, a native of the island, to be his dragoman—that is, interpreter—and guide. Stephens had first met him in Smyrna in May when he had been in the service of two fellow Americans (namely Rush and Rittenhouse Nutt) and had been impressed by him. Paolo had served as guide and interpreter for other European parties before the Nutts and Stephens, including Gerald Wellesley and his two companions with whom Elizabeth and John Kirkland had dined in Egypt in 1832.[5] Stephens said that Nuozzo called Wellesley the son of the Duke of Wellington whereas he was actually a nephew. He was still serving as a dragoman on the Nile as late as 1844 when he carved or had his name carved with that date at the Ramesseum in Thebes.[6]

Immediately after landing in Alexandria, Stephens called on the American consul, John Gliddon, and while he was with him,

> an English gentleman came in—a merchant in Alexandria—who was going that night to Cairo. Mr. Gliddon introduced us; and, telling him that I too was bound for Cairo, Mr. T. immediately proposed that I should accompany him, saying he had a boat and everything ready, and that I might save myself the trouble of making any preparations and would have nothing to do but come on board with my luggage at sundown.

Traveling alone, as his fellow New Yorker John Hamersley had done nearly two years earlier, Stephens was clearly receptive to company and took him up on the offer. Who was Mr. T? We can deduce that he was Sidney Terry of the firm of Briggs & Co. in Alexandria. Then, still having daylight, Stephens and Nuozzo rode out to see Pompey's Column and Cleopatra's Needles, reckoning that they could see the other sights on their return.

In the evening they joined Terry and set off up the Mahmoudiya canal, toward the Nile. They started in company with Thomas Waghorn, a former officer in the Royal Navy turned entrepreneur, now seeking to set up a postal service between England and India via Egypt and the Red Sea instead of around the Cape of Good Hope. This involved hiring boats for the canal and the Nile, and arranging rest houses, guides and routes for camels and horses across the desert from Cairo to Suez. Waghorn had arrived in Alexandria in late November and had already made one trip to Cairo escorting the mail. Now he was on a second run from Alexandria to Cairo. At the junction of the canal with the Nile, both parties changed boats. At first they had a favorable north wind, but as it swung to the south Stephens was stalled. But not Waghorn; with his own boat and stout rowers, he went on ahead determined to deliver the mail. Stephens was the first of many Americans to meet Waghorn.

Arriving at Bulaq, the port of Cairo, five days later, Stephens and his friend breakfasted, as he wrote, "with Mr. T—, the brother-in-law of my friend, an engineer in the pachas' service, whose interesting wife is the only English lady there." The second Mr. T. was Peter Taylor. He and Terry were married to the Friend sisters, Sarah and Mercy, who had come out to Alexandria with their parents years before.

In Cairo Stephens saw George Gliddon, who arranged an audience with the pasha, and they visited the usual tourist sites. Then Stephens and Nuozzo set forth on their Nile journey. The date was January 1, 1836. Passing the towns of Minya, Manfalout, Asyut, and Djiddeh, they reached Gheeneh on January 18, and there they stopped to see the temple of Dendera. The wind had been against them, progress had been slow, and Stephens was cold, circumstances that colored his impression of his first Egyptian temple: It disappointed him in comparison with the classical ruins of Athens. They went on, passing by Thebes (to be seen on the descent) to Gabal al-Silsila, to Aswan, and through the first cataract to their destination and furthest southern point, Philae.

Philae struck Stephens as no other site, beginning with the rocks and islands in the river on the approach, memorably captured in photographs by Francis Frith some twenty years later. The Temple of Isis at Philae is the only monument of Egyptian architecture that appealed sufficiently for Stephens to describe it: the colonnade that led to the gate and the twin pylons with figures of Isis twenty feet tall. He also remarked on the ancient Greek and Latin inscriptions, on the inscription recording the French military presence, and on the inscription left by Cornelius Bradford, below which he cut his own.

At Aswan, Stephens met Robert Thurburn, the British consul at Alexandria—he mentions his position and calls him Mr. T.—who after eighteen years in Egypt was making his first journey up the Nile, accompanied, as Stephens reports, "by his daughter, who had reigned as a belle and beauty in the ancient city of Cleopatra, and her newly-married husband."[7] At first glance there is something amiss with this statement because in 1836 Thurburn's eldest daughter was eighteen, the twins, only sixteen, and they were not married until the 1840s. But Thurburn had a stepdaughter, Rosina, daughter of his wife Mary by her first husband, Pierre Anthony Pellegrini de Tibaldi, who was poisoned by Mehmet Ali in 1812 because he opposed the massacre of the Mamluks. In 1813, Thurburn had married Tibaldi's widow, becoming stepfather to her four children, one son, three daughters. Rosina was then eight. Now she was thirty and had just married John W. Larking, who, after Thurburn's resignation as consul in Alexandria in 1839, would succeed him. Stephens was quite taken with Thurburn, "so much so," he says "that at Thebes I gave him the strongest mark of it a man could give, I borrowed money of him; and I have reason to remember his kindness in relieving me from a situation which might have embarrassed me."

Philae was as far south as Stephens went. Coming downstream he stopped briefly to see the temple at Edfu (which he visited by moonlight and featured in his published account with an illustration derived from a watercolor by the French artist Charles-Louis Balzac reproduced in *Description de l'Égypte*) and the one at Esna. In mid-January he reached Thebes with its great temples at Luxor and Karnak, and ruins and tombs of the pharaohs on the west bank. In his popular book Stephens' description of Luxor and Karnak seems to have been done largely from memory and from a reading of Richardson's published account of the Belmores' visit some twenty years earlier. Not only does he quote Richardson at one point in his description of the Karnak temple, but he reports, erroneously, that three obelisks were standing (not two as was the case), repeating Richardson's similar error. Stephens was clearly struck by some of the ruins but he admitted they were not his strong suit: They provide merely a background for his observations of the local Egyptians, his musings on life so far from home, and his encounters with other European visitors.

At Luxor Stephens met a party of English travelers who had arrived in Egypt shortly before he had. Charlotte and Richard Rowley were on their honeymoon—they had been married on June 24, 1835—and were traveling with Charlotte's brother William Shipley-Conwy and a friend, Henry Ker Seymer. They had gone to Cairo, but once there, instead of proceeding up the Nile, had gone to Suez, Sinai, down the Red Sea to Quseir, and across the desert to the Nile. They were now on their way to Khartoum and Sennar. Stephens never names them, but what is given in excerpts of their own diaries published in the late 1990s[8] matches his description of them and his summary of their itinerary:

> The party consisted of four, a gentleman and his lady, he an honorable and heir to an old and respectable title, a brother of the lady, an ex-captain in the guards, who changed his name and resigned his commission on receiving a fortune from an uncle, and another gentleman, I do not know whether of that family, but bearing one of the proudest names in England. They were all young, the oldest not more than thirty-five, and, not excepting the lady, full of thirst for adventure and travel. I say not excepting the lady; I should rather say the lady was the life and soul of the party.[9]

They were not the first honeymooning couple to travel the Nile. At least two British couples had spent their honeymoons on the Nile in preceding years. On September 6, 1830, Lieutenant James MacKenzie, adjutant in the 8th Bengal Light Cavalry, had married Napier Louisa Johnston, daughter of Col. Francis J.T. Johnston, commanding the 8th Light Cavalry—namely his boss's daughter—after which they set off to visit Egypt. Their names are carved at Medinet Habu: "Napier MacKenzie / JM VIII B Cav / March"; hers is at Karnak: "Napier Louisa MacKenzie."[10] On January 19, 1831, William Nathaniel Peach married Hester Elizabeth, daughter of John Barker, the British consul-general; they too, to judge from a graffito visible at Medinet Habu, "W. Peach / May 1831," took their honeymoon on the Nile.[11] The first American couple to include the Nile on a honeymoon, Horatio and Mary Allen, did not do so until a year after Stephens' visit.

Stephens had one dinner with Charlotte and Richard Rowley, her brother, and their friend. They were seated around a table set on canteens under a tent with a mattress on each side for seats and talked until late in the evening.

> To them I am indebted for the most interesting part of my journey in the east, for they first suggested to me the route by Petra and Arabia Petræa.... It was ... a glorious evening; a bright spot that I love to look back upon, more than indemnifying me for weeks of loneliness. I sat with them till a late hour; and when I parted, I did not feel as if it was the first time I had seen them, or think that it would be the last, ... but I never saw them again.[12]

Stephens also met another English couple, Mr. and Mrs. S., who had followed him up the Nile and who traveled some of the way back with him, enjoying their company in part owing to the fine Dalmatian chef Michel they had with them.

Back in Cairo in early March, recalling the advice he had received from the English foursome at Thebes, Stephens crossed Sinai via St. Catherine's monastery (where he wrote comments in the guest book)[13] to Petra, becoming the first American to visit the site. He recorded his visit there by writing his name alongside those of the few earlier European travelers who had preceded him. Not long afterward the Rowley party also left their names in the Khazna at Petra. Nearly a hundred years later, while visiting Petra in 1930, Alan Pryce-Jones, writer and book review editor, saw the four names of the Rowley party and imagined a conversation he had with them which takes up some ten pages of his travel journal, *The Spring Voyage*.[14] Can we imagine their dinner conversation with Stephens at Thebes? Perhaps it remains waiting to be read in their unpublished diaries.

From Petra Stephens went on to Jerusalem, where he saw the memorial to the young American Cornelius Bradford, to the Dead Sea, where he saw the boat used on the ill-fated surveying expedition by Costigan (whom John Hamersley had met two years before), and to Beirut, where he heard of the death of John Lowell (whose travels in Egypt are described at the end of chapter 11). He returned to the West on an Austrian steamer via Alexandria. In the course of his travels he took advantage of business and political opportunities. He became involved in the giraffe trade, and when he returned to New York in early September 1836 on board the *Hibernia*, he was carrying dispatches from David Porter, the chargé d'affaires at the Sublime Porte. Back home he worked up his diaries into two two-volume works that became the best selling travel accounts of the day: *Incidents of Travel in Greece, Turkey, Russia, and Poland* and *Incidents of Travel in Egypt, Arabia Petræa, and the Holy Land*, the latter reviewed by Edgar Allan Poe in the *New York Review* of October 1837.[15]

Stephens' legacy, however, amounted to more than the two published accounts of his European experiences, and it is worth mentioning the British artist and architect Frederick Catherwood, who would help make his real reputation.[16] On two occasions Catherwood had visited Egypt and adjacent regions and had covered much of the same ground that Stephens had. He was first in Egypt in late 1823 and 1824 as one of four British architects working together, studying and making measured drawings of ancient monuments at Luxor. He visited Egypt again in the summer of 1832 on which occasion he and two other British architects, Francis Arundale and Joseph Bonomi, were working for Robert Hay, a well-to-do Scottish antiquary whom he had first met on his way home from his first trip. The Baltimore tourist Mendes Cohen met him in mid-August 1832 when they found themselves traveling together from Alexandria to Cairo. For nearly a year Catherwood sketched monuments in the Nile valley, in the course of which he made drawings of Thebes (later to be enlarged by Robert Burford and shown in London and New York as a panorama).[17]

In August 1833, together with Arundale and Bonomi, Catherwood left Cairo for Mt. Sinai, Jerusalem, and Syria. In March of 1834 he married Gertrude, the daughter of Peter Abbott, the British consul in Beirut. The New Yorker John W. Hamersley met them in June 1834 at Baalbek where Catherwood had gone with Bonomi to make sketches for a panorama. Hamersley, who says that Catherwood had already made one of Algiers and Jerusalem, observed them "working on their panorama under square white umbrellas supported on poles. They had chosen an elevated situation. They draw it in pieces which are to be amplified 200 fold. It is going to New York after the Londoners are tired of it." Hamersley considered the twenty-one-year-old Mrs. Catherwood who had "her carpet amid the ruins" to be the most interesting person of the party. Two years later, in the spring of 1836, before returning to New York, Stephens met Catherwood in London during a showing of Robert Burford's painted panorama of Jerusalem worked up from Catherwood's drawings made shortly before Hamersley had met him at Baalbek.[18] Burford had already shown Catherwood's view of the great temple of Karnak and the surrounding city of Thebes in 1835.[19] Soon afterward, in June, Catherwood came to New York with his family to lecture on Egypt and the Holy Land. Several years later, when Stephens was appointed consul to Guatemala, he asked Catherwood to accompany him as an artist to Chiapas and Yucatan. That experience and the published accounts and illustrations of the great Mayan ruins they found in the jungles made lasting names for both of them.[20]

Stephens' reputation would have prompted the portrait now owned by the American Museum of Natural History in New York showing him with a full beard and intent expression, probably painted in the early 1840s. The portrait came to the museum in 1945 from George Gordon Hammill (1870–1966), husband of Margaret Willett Boardman, who had inherited it from her parents Daniel and Margaret Boardman. Margaret Boardman was the youngest daughter of Edward M. Willett and Amelia Ann Stephens, the younger sister of John L. Stephens.

The Haights and the Allens

The same year, 1836, saw the arrival of two married couples traveling, like the Kirklands, as tourists: Mr. and Mrs. Richard Kip Haight and Mr. and Mrs. Horatio Allen. We have good records of their trips because the women of both parties, Sarah Haight and Mary Allen, kept accounts of their journeys, and Sarah Haight published hers in 1840. The Haights were in Egypt from February to mid-April; the Allens were there at the end of the year, from November 27 through January 1837.

Messrs. Haight and Allen were not recent college graduates, but experienced and talented men. Richard Haight, known as Dick, was from a family of exceptionally successful New York merchants and had previously traveled in 1821, partly on business, to England, France, Austria, and Italy with his fellow New Yorker George Rapelje (whose own trip to Egypt has already been described). He had traveled abroad again in 1826. Horatio Allen, younger brother of Theodore Allen who had reached Egypt in 1831, was a graduate of Columbia, class of 1823, and had become a civil engineer. He was involved in canals and railroads, and in 1828 was commissioned by the Delaware and Hudson Canal Company to go to England to purchase iron track and steam engines. He acquired four engines, one from Foster, Rastrick & Co. of Stourbridge, three from

Robert Stephenson of Newcastle. On arrival in New York they were assembled by the West Point Foundry in lower Manhattan, and in 1829 Allen made a test run of the one from Foster & Rastrick, called the *Stourbridge Lion* owing to the face of a lion painted on one end the boiler. It was the first steam locomotive driven in the United States.

Richard and Sarah Haight and Richard Randolph

The Haights, who had been married for several years, had sailed from New York for London on July 20, 1834, with their young daughter Lydia, then about six, and a servant. Sarah was pregnant when she left New York and gave birth to a son, Richard, some time after arriving in Europe. They had spent the winter of 1835 in a luxurious apartment on the Place Vendôme in Paris, entertaining frequently.[21] Some time later, probably in June 1835, minus their daughter and newborn son whom they left in Paris, they were in Vienna, intending to travel to the East via the Danube and Constantinople, but hearing "confirmation of rumors of the plague raging there," they postponed that portion of their trip. Instead they spent six months traveling in Europe and in Russia during which time Sarah kept a diary or letters published three years later in installments in the *New-York American*, and later assembled in 1916 by their son Dr. David L. Haight.[22]

In Leipzig, on July 16, 1835, they met Richard Randolph, a Philadelphia merchant who had been abroad for more than a year. In 1820, at age twenty-nine, Randolph had married Elizabeth Ely, four years his junior.[23] Some time afterward he had bought a house in New Hope, in Bucks County, Pennsylvania, known as Cintra, named after the castle of Cintra near Lisbon. About a decade later, in October 1831, his wife had died of yellow fever.[24] There were no children. Within three years of her death the widowed Randolph had conveyed Cintra to his brother-in-law by a deed dated March 11, 1834, and less than a month later, on April 9, he had applied for a passport to travel abroad.[25]

When Randolph met the Haights in Leipzig, he decided to keep in a notebook an account of their joint expenses to which he added his own personal expenses later on in Europe.[26] After leaving Leipzig they went to Berlin, then to the Netherlands (August), and doubled back to Hamburg from where they went to Denmark, Norway, and Stockholm (September); and then east to St. Petersburg (October) and Moscow (November). They reached the Ottoman capital from Odessa in late December. Then, sailing via Smyrna, they arrived at Alexandria on February 10, 1836. Randolph was about forty-five, Richard Haight about thirty-eight, his wife Sarah ten years younger.

Sarah Haight's account of the Mediterranean part of their tour took the form of letters of which two versions were worked up. The first version, addressed to the *New-York American*, was copied among several newspapers at intervals in October and November 1836, some installments under the byline of "Correspondence of the *New-York American*," others "By a Lady."[27] The second version, attributed to "A Lady of New York," appeared in the *Daily National Intelligencer* from July to October 1839 and is identical to the text of the two-volume book she published in 1840,[28] perhaps seeking to capitalize on John L. Stephens' highly successful *Incidents of Travel*. The matter-of-fact and straightforward language of the first version (the installments of which are not called letters) is quite different from the worked-up flowery prose interspersed with poetry published four years later.

From Alexandria the Haights and Mr. Randolph sailed along the canal and up the Nile to Cairo. In a letter published in American newspapers, dated February 26, 1836, signed "By a Lady," Sarah Haight told the story of their approach to Cairo, its narrow streets, and the projecting and overhanging nature of the upper storeys. She moved right on to their visit to the Pyramids, accompanied by the American consular agent George Gliddon and some other gentlemen.

> On arriving near the spot, we were beset by crowds of Bedouin Arabs, who live in the villages near by, and serve as guides; they are wretched looking people, but they are truly necessary evils, particular to those who wish to ascend. I very bravely commenced making the attempt, but succeeded in going only about two-thirds of the way, which was more owing to the fears my husband entertained for my safety, than to my own timidity, although I must acknowledge it appears to me a very hazardous undertaking; but so great was my desire to stand on "the summit of this most ancient and mighty monument of man's power and pride," that I think I would have succeeded but the entreaties of Mr. ——— for me to descend.[29]

A few days later the party began their voyage on the Nile. By mid-March they had reached Thebes and from there, on March 26, she wrote another letter (addressed, "My dear Mrs. B.") in which she reported that at Philae, near the famous French inscription, she had seen the name of C. Bradford of New York, and that,

> of another American gentleman, since dead, whose name I gazed upon with peculiar feelings. It is now nearly nine years since I met him on Lake Ontario: he had but a short time previous returned from this country; and

so enthusiastic was the account he gave me, that ever after I felt a desire
to visit it, and have ocular demonstration of what he related; and thus far
I have not been disappointed.[30]

Who was this other American, since deceased? If Sarah Haight's
memory was correct, that person had been at Philae in 1827, but no
record exists of an American on the Nile then. The closest is the unnamed
Philadelphian writing from Alexandria on July first, 1826. Another candidate is Henry Oliver who was on the Nile in the fall of 1829. I have no
doubt that some day he will be identified.

Returning to Thebes, they now saw the monuments there, including
the temple at Luxor, with its one remaining obelisk. In the first version
of her letters Sarah wrote, "In front of the propylon stands one of the
two beautiful obelisks which guarded the entrance; the other some time
since took its departure for Paris, where I saw it lying in a barge." In the
published version this became, "Look up, and behold the towering walls
of Luxor above our head, with its aspiring obelisk, ready in anger to dart
at the sun for not having annihilated, at a stroke, the barbarous Gaul who
so lately robbed it of its mate."[31] She knew what would sell.

The Haights and Mr. Randolph returned to Cairo on April 10. They
left Alexandria around April 26, bound for Beirut, carrying a letter of
introduction from John Gliddon to the American missionary Eli Smith.[32]
From Beirut they visited Damascus in mid-June and were back in Beirut
at the end of the month. Leaving Syria they returned to Europe via
Constantinople (August), Athens (September), and Trieste (October),
reaching Paris by December first. They came home separately the next
year: Randolph reached New York via London on May 23, 1837. Mr.
Haight arrived back on June 22, 1837, Mrs. Haight with her two children,
in mid-September.[33] They had been away three years.

Egypt meant much to the Haights and to Randolph. After returning
home, Messrs. Haight and Randolph both joined the Egyptian Society of
Cairo, which had been founded in mid-1836. Sarah Haight devoted half
of her book to their experiences in Egypt and Richard retained a lifelong
interest in Egyptology. Randolph left no account, at least none is known
today, but he surely remembered his time in Egypt. Among the long list
of items purchased by him after his return to Europe, there are listed
in his memo book (in addition to engravings, writing equipment, and
clothes of every description, including clothes for a lady), a map of Egypt
(purchased in Paris for 26 francs) and in London on March 15, 1837, at
the very end of his trip abroad, for nine shillings, "Copy of Koran."

Horatio and Mary Allen, and Mrs. Simons

Horatio Allen and his wife Mary were traveling on their honeymoon with Mrs. Allen's widowed mother, Mrs. James Dewar Simons. Horatio was thirty-four, Mary twenty-nine, her mother about fifty. He had met his wife, daughter of the late Rev. James Dewar Simons, in Charleston where he had moved in 1829, after his famous test run of the *Stourbridge Lion*, to become chief engineer of the South Carolina Railroad; he oversaw the construction of the Charleston & Hamburg Railroad, considered when completed in 1833 to be the world's longest. Horatio and Mary were married in November 1834, and some six months later, in May 1835, the family group left New York for Liverpool.

Mary kept a diary of their whole tour.[34] The Allens toured England from mid-June to mid-November, then spent the winter of 1835–1836 in Paris (the diary skips from late November to early March). In Paris, Horatio Allen had his portrait painted, a miniature on ivory, by the French artist Amélie d'Aubigny (plate 19).[35] And in Paris they met up with Christian Edward Detmold (a German-born engineer who had worked with Allen on the Charleston & Hamburg Railroad) and his wife Phoebe. In the spring the Allens and Mrs. Simons left Paris for a lengthy tour through Belgium, the Netherlands, Germany, and Switzerland. At Brienz in Switzerland they met Henry Wadsworth Longfellow and went across the lake with him to see the falls of Giessbach.[36] The next day Longfellow helped them to buy the right kind of blank notebooks in which they could dry plant specimens.

The Allens reached Constantinople in October 1836 via Vienna and the Danube steamships, and there they met John Porter Brown, nephew (and interpreter) of the chargé d'affaires, David Porter. Porter accompanied them on a tour of the city. One Sunday they attended divine services at the house of the American missionary William Goodell, who, in his own journal (preserved in the Library of Congress), records that he met them. On October 3 they boarded the steamer *Maria Dorothea* for Smyrna where they were met by John B. Adger, a missionary from Charleston whom Mary Allen might have known from years before, and they saw much of him. On October 11, they left for Athens. With them on the boat was Sir Francis Hopkins, who had gone out to Persia in 1835 with Henry Ellis, the new British ambassador to the shah, and was now returning home to Dublin.[37] In Athens, assisted by the American missionary Jonas King, they found rooms in the Hotel de France just being vacated by Prince Pückler-Muskau. Leaving Athens they went first to the island of Syra, where they were entertained by the American missionaries, and then chartered a small sailing vessel for Alexandria.

It was a roundabout voyage to Alexandria, not direct from Syra but via Patmos, so they did not arrive until the end of November. After the usual excursions around Alexandria with John Gliddon and meals with him and his son-in-law Alexander Tod, they went to Cairo. Again they saw the usual sites including the gardens at Roda and the pasha's retreat at Shubra. One day the Allens trekked to the Pyramids. There they met Giovanni Battista Caviglia (1770–1845), the Genoese-born former sea captain who had come to Egypt in 1816 eager to conduct antiquarian research.[38] A self-styled Englishman—his home port had been Malta—Caviglia came to know the British Consul-General Henry Salt who had helped to sponsor the first of many years of impressive discoveries he made at the Pyramids and the Sphinx. Now, twenty years on, Caviglia was at the end of his career; he left Egypt for Paris the very year the Allens saw him.

The Allens dined with Thomas Waghorn (the English naval officer who helped to develop the route across the Egyptian desert from Cairo to Suez for the post and for people going to India) and his wife, and on another occasion visited the Citadel with them. John L. Stephens had met Waghorn on the canal boat from Alexandria to the Nile at the end of December 1835, but Sarah Haight made no mention of him in her letters of 1836. In late 1836, when the Allens met him, Waghorn was experimenting with a railway from the Mokattan mountains—overlooking Cairo—designed to bring stone from quarries there to the Nile for the purpose of building a barrage in the Delta. Although Mary Allen says nothing in her diary, surely her husband Horatio, a great railway entrepreneur, conversed with Waghorn about railways.

Leaving Cairo on December 22, they proceeded up the Nile, reaching Thebes on January 6, 1837. "At Gournou [Qurna] we met Lord Lindsay's boat which had preceded us a short time. We afterwards saw several boats each with its own flag, and met many parties of visitors in the ruins." In his own account, Alexander Crawford (Earl of Lindsay, 1812–1880), traveling with William Wardlaw Ramsay, does not mention an encounter with the Allens.[39]

That very day they visited the ruins at Karnak. They admired the hypostyle hall with more than one hundred columns, covered with figures and with painted capitals. They walked past the two obelisks and took their dinner "in the granite sanctuary restored by Alexander. Its walls are sculptured and painted. On what remains of the ceiling are stars upon a blue ground." This was the small structure now known as the sanctuary of Philip Arrhidaeus. At the end of the day they rode their donkeys along the avenue of sphinxes to Luxor where their boat awaited them. The next day they visited Luxor and then from January 9 to 11, they saw all of the monuments and the tombs on the west bank.

The Allens did not make it to Philae. The farthest south they went was the temple at Edfu, which they saw in the early evening of January 14. After climbing to the top of the pylon, Mary Allen wrote, "we looked down upon the temple which I believe is considered the most perfect in Egypt as regards its general remains . . . but that it is sadly filled up with dirt and rubbish and Arab huts, which are also built upon the roof." Gardner Wilkinson, author of the guidebook *Modern Egypt and Thebes*, drafted in the 1830s, wrote that "the whole of the interior is so much concealed by the houses of the modern inhabitants, that a very small part of it is accessible."[40] The drawing by the French artist André Dutertre, done in 1799 and used for *Description de l'Égypte*, shows the Arab mud brick structures in front of the pylon and on top of the temple. By the 1850s and 1860s, when the first photographs were made, they had been cleared.

The family returned to Cairo stopping at many towns along the way. They left Alexandria on a British steamer bound for Malta on January 30, 1837. Mrs. Allen said that the departure was delayed until an English family from India, the Turtons with their children and goats, had arrived. Thomas Edward Mitchell Turton, a barrister at the Supreme Court of Calcutta, had sailed from Bombay with his wife, six children (the eldest nine, the youngest one), and servants late in 1835. The family arrived in early January on the coast of the Red Sea at Quseir from where they crossed the desert to Keneh on the Nile and thence to Cairo and Alexandria. No Americans were traveling with small children at this time, but the Turtons reported no difficulty in doing so. And in fact English family excursions on the Nile (though not with very young children) date back to the celebrated tour of the Belmores in 1817, nearly twenty years earlier.

After transit through Malta, the Allens returned to Italy where they stayed until June. They arrived back in New York from Liverpool on December 4 on the packet ship *Roscoe* by which time they had a two-month-old child. The Allens moved to New York and in the spring of 1838. Horatio Allen joined John Jervis, a colleague with whom he had worked earlier in 1829 assembling the first steam locomotive in the United States. Now he would be a principal engineer in the Croton aqueduct project designed to bring water from upstate to New York City.[41]

"Mr. Dorr and Mr. Curtis"

In the winter, and perhaps into early spring of 1836, the same season that Stephens and the Haights were on the Nile, several more Americans extended a grand tour to include Egypt. But unlike Stephens, the Haights, and the Allens, they have left no known accounts of their travels. Instead, what little we know of their experiences must be gathered from various sources, one of which is the published account of an English traveler. In Athens in early July 1836, this traveler, George Cochrane, wrote of the encounter:

> Made the acquaintance of an English and two American gentlemen; the former, Mr. George Booth, and the latter, Mr. Dorr and Mr. Curtis. . . . they had proceeded from Paris, through Germany, Moldavia, and Wallachia, and had resided some time in Constantinople. Thence they went to Bagdad, Smyrna, Jerusalem, and visited Lady Hester Stanhope. Thence to Alexandria, Cairo, the Pyramids, back again to Alexandria; afterwards to Tunis.[42]

Dorr was James Augustus Dorr of Boston, Harvard College class of 1832. Passenger lists show that he sailed from New York on the ship *South-America* for Liverpool in mid-February 1833. What is known of his travels is limited. He surely spent time in Paris because in early January 1833, as he was about to sail for Europe, Nathaniel Bowditch wrote a letter of introduction (now in the Massachusetts Historical Society) for him to his son Henry Ingersoll Bowditch, who had gone to study medicine in Paris after receiving a medical degree from Harvard in 1832. But not until nearly two years later, early 1835, can we again locate Dorr, this time in Rome, where he registered with the American consul.[43] A year later, in 1836, he was indeed in Egypt: his name appears in Gliddon's consular register.

No mention of Curtis is in Gliddon's register or in the passenger list of Dorr's ship leaving New York. Yet Curtis is identifiable. His name was actually Ambrose Stacy Courtis (not Curtis). He was born in Marblehead, Massachusetts, in 1775, was married in 1808, and in time had at least five children. He later lived for a while in Salem, and then in the early or mid-1820s moved to Boston. Courtis was a self-made man, without a college education, who "by his probity, industry, and intelligence," as one report said, prospered in business, one aspect of which involved the importation of textiles of every description.[44] Despite the lack of higher education, he was strongly interested in science and literature. In 1829 he had become a shareholder of the Boston Athenaeum, a private library, still the finest of its kind in the United States.

In 1834, more than a year after Dorr had traveled abroad, Courtis, now a man of substantial fortune and aged 59, gave up his business in order to travel. He sailed from New York for Liverpool in early August 1834 on the ship *Orpheus*. After arriving in England he displayed his interest in science and support of learned institutions by purchasing a solar microscope with achromatic lenses from Dollards of London, which he presented to the Boston Society of Natural History. By December of that year, 1834, he was in Rome where he too registered with the American consul.[45] Where and when he met up with Dorr is not known, but Rome is a good guess, not only because they registered with the consul within a month of one another, but because the Englishman Cochrane who saw them in Greece said that they had been traveling together about two years. Sarah Haight saw Courtis in Constantinople in January 1836, and afterward in Smyrna.[46] From there Cochrane said that Dorr and Courtis had gone to Jerusalem (with a visit to Lady Hester Stanhope), to Alexandria, and to Cairo.

In Greece, from July sixth to tenth 1836, Cochrane, Dorr, and Courtis, joined by Mary Baldwin and by Elizabeth and Frederica Mulligan, sisters of Mrs. John Hill, wife of the American missionary (all three women teachers at the Hills' school), rode to Marathon, Porto Rafti, and Sounion. Less than a month later, on August second, Cochrane met the threesome again in Nauplion just after they had arrived from Sparta and Tripolizza.[47]

Courtis would not return home to Boston. In late August a correspondent in Athens forwarded to a friend in Malta news about the United States Mediterranean squadron and other Americans who he knew were in Greece. The Athens witness wrote:

We have here at this time Mr. Richard K. Haight, of New York, and lady, and Mr. Randolph of Philadelphia, in quarantine, just arrived from a long journey in the Eastern countries. Mr. Dorr, of Boston, and Mr. Courtis, of Boston, are at Naples [i.e., Nauplion]: the latter, I regret to add, is so ill that I have no hope of his recovery.[48]

Soon afterwards Dorr wrote to a friend in Boston:

I have been delayed about six weeks in this fortress [at Nauplion], in order to take care of my excellent deceased friend and traveling companion, Mr. Ambrose S. Courtis, of Boston. He died here, on the 27th August, in my arms, without a groan, or struggle, after a long illness (a gastute [*sic*] and nervous fever) during which, I am happy to say, he felt but little bodily pain. I bear testimony to the pure and honorable character of my departed friend, a man more innocent of all evil, it has never been my good fortune to meet. Just, upright, virtuous, benevolent, he commanded the respect, and won the esteem of all who knew him.[49]

Courtis was sixty-one. The disease Dorr described was probably typhoid. The New York traveler Sarah Haight, who had been in quarantine in Athens, saw his grave in Nauplion and remarked that he was the same "Curtis" whom she had seen earlier (January of 1836) in Constantinople and later in Smyrna.[50] In his will Courtis left substantial sums to the Massachusetts General Hospital, the Boston Athenaeum, the Massachusetts Horticultural Society, and the Boston Society of Natural History, bequests that remained largely intact despite being contested by his children.[51] In 1840 Courtis' remains were brought home from Greece and buried in Mount Auburn Cemetery in Cambridge, Massachusetts.[52]

James McHenry Boyd

After Courtis' death Dorr met another American who had visited Egypt, James McHenry ("Henry") Boyd. Boyd was a Baltimorean and a graduate of Yale, class of 1831, who, as a twenty-two-year-old in the spring of 1834, began his own two-year European tour. Most of his trip, apart from the beginning and end of the trajectory and two sightings along the way, is a blank. In late May 1834 he applied for a passport, and on June 11th he sailed for Liverpool with his parents on the packet ship *George Washington*. He appears on the passenger list as H. Boyd, H for "Henry," from McHenry (his middle name, and his mother's maiden name). The family made their way to Italy, and there, in Naples, in late December John W. Hamersley encountered them. With the Boyds were Hamilton Murray and William T. Whittemore, two young New Yorkers Henry's age, who had sailed with them from New York and had traveled with them to Italy. Hamersley also saw in Naples Charles Elliott Scoville, one of Boyd's Yale classmates, who had sailed from New York about the same time. On one of the many occasions when the boys joined one another for dinner in Naples, Hamersley could well have encouraged Boyd, a classical scholar, to extend his travels to Syria and Egypt.

More than a year passed before he reappears in the record, first in the United States consular records with the Papal States in early 1836.[53] Then in May 1836 on his way from Damascus to Palestine, he was seen by the Haights, traveling with two European companions, one English, the other Italian.[54] Boyd went on to Egypt, where he would not have arrived before late May or early June, and where he signed the American consular register. Nothing is known of his Egyptian experience. Later he met up with Dorr who now, after the death of his companion Courtis, would have been traveling alone. The two returned to New York on May 13, 1837.

Henry Boyd embarked on a diplomatic career, and by 1846 was serving as secretary and acting chargé d'affaires in the American legation in London. He died accidentally of a self-inflicted gunshot wound in 1847.[55] Dorr became a New York lawyer, formed a distinguished book collection, and translated from the French a work on Louis Bonaparte (*Napoleonic Ideas*).[56] Despite what we know about Dorr, Courtis, and Boyd, we lack records of their experiences in Egypt. Yet there is hope. A newspaper stated that while on the continent, Courtis wrote letters to the *Register*, perhaps the *Boston Register and Recorder*.

A New Yorker in 1837

Some American travelers to Egypt in this period remain anonymous. A New Yorker arriving in Egypt in the late fall of 1837 by way of Malta has yet to be identified.[57] From Cairo, on November 10, 1837, he wrote a letter to a fellow New Yorker that was published in the January 30, 1838, issue of the *New-York Daily Express*. In addition to saying the usual things about Cairo and observing that the steamship *Atalanta* was now running regular service between Bombay and Suez (she had begun in September), he added this noteworthy item:

> I fortunately reached here just in time to witness a scene of extraordinary gaiety and feasting. It is called the Feast of the Circumcision, and has lasted for the last eight days. On this occasion nearly two thousand children, including sons of Pachas and men the highest offices of the government, have been circumcised. The ceremony, or operation, was performed in the most public manner, and subject to the gaze of the crowd. At the palace, hundreds of camel loads of provisions were cooked for the thousands and thousands that attended. Fireworks of the most brilliant description were set off, and a large amount of money distributed to the crowd. All has been music, dancing, &c.

This was a remarkable celebration. The only other celebration of this kind in the early nineteenth century took place in the first week of December 1829, as we know from a letter of John Barker, the British consul-general, and from a notice in a newspaper of the period.[58] The festival on that occasion celebrated the circumcision of two sons of Mehmet Ali, and one of Ibrahim Pasha, his son, with days of fireworks and the release of prisoners from jails in Alexandria and Cairo. The newspaper said that "only two foreigners mixed with the Musselman guests—the consul-general of Sweden, and Mr. Briggs, an English merchant. Most of the European ladies were dressed in male attire."

Although many Europeans in Cairo must have witnessed the week-long 1837 event, only one other seems to have written about it, and in such a way as to confirm the accuracy of the American's description, namely Thomas Waghorn, the British postal and transport entrepreneur, who by this time had been appointed a deputy consul in Egypt. In one of his periodic letters to an English newspaper, *The Morning Chronicle* of London, the issue dated November 15, Waghorn wrote:

> Cairo has been the scene of greater gaiety, pastime, and feasting than was ever before remembered by its oldest inhabitants: this lasted from the 3rd to the 10th [of November]. It may be more properly called the feast and revels of circumcision: there were in all eight children, sons of Mohamed Ali Pacha, of his son Ibrahim, of his grandson Abbas Pacha, and of his nephew Ibrahim Pacha, the younger, to be circumcised after the revels were over, with 1,500 children of the lower classes. . . . Camel loads of meat, &c. of every description were continually going there for consumption; one hundred cooks were employed, money was thrown away, and £30,000 is said to have been spent. There was the Turkish and Egyptian music, with the bands of the three regiments with European instruments; fireworks of beautiful description . . . . The English in Cairo from India were especially delighted, and expressed their wonder and admiration at the magnificence of the scene. Sixty thousand blank cartridges were fired from a cavalry brigade of guns in the vicinity of the palace, during the eight days.

Henry McVickar and John Bard

On November 20, 1837, two young New Yorkers, Henry McVickar, or Harry, as he was known, and his first cousin John Bard, sailed from New York bound for Havre for a European tour that would also take in Egypt. McVickar, age twenty-one, had just finished Columbia, class of 1836. Bard, eighteen, had been privately tutored. He came from a successful old New York family: His grandfather, Dr. Samuel Bard (1792–1821), was one of the founders of the New York College of Physicians; his father William Bard had recently established the New York Life Insurance and Trust Co.[59] McVickar's father, John McVickar, had married Eliza Bard, sister of William, John Bard's father, and was professor of moral philosophy at Columbia College, a position he owed in part to his father-in-law. John McVickar had proposed the trip, and he had made the application for their passports. A year earlier he had even thought of accompanying Harry and his older brother Samuel Bard McVickar to Palestine, but Bard McVickar, as he was known, was in poor health and died in August 1837.[60]

Now, despite the death of his son Bard and reversals of the family's fortunes, severely depleted by the economic panic of 1837, Professor McVickar was determined to give his son Harry this experience. He furnished him and his cousin with letters of introduction to notable figures in Europe, including the poet John Kenyon (1783–1856), through whom the two boys probably met Elizabeth Barrett (Kenyon's distant cousin) and Robert Browning, and also, surely, Sir Robert Inglis, the noted English politician, whom McVickar had long known. When the New Yorker John Hamersley, on his way home from his own Egyptian travels, dined on board a ship of the British squadron at Vourla near Smyrna in late August 1834, Inglis was one of his fellow guests. Inglis told him that he had just written a "scolding letter" to Mr. McVickar [namely John McVickar] to the effect that he had not sent him any Americans. Four years earlier, when McVickar was in England, Inglis had written him, saying "send us such friends as yourselves from your country, you are better than any treaties of peace." Harry McVickar and John Bard were surely charged with paying a call on Inglis.

With respect to the Egyptian leg of their trip, little is known except for their names in the consular records kept by John Gliddon, McVickar's name cut on the top of the Great Pyramid at Giza,[61] and at the mortuary temple of Ramesses III at Medinet Habu,[62] and mention of both of them in a diary kept the following year by a fellow New Yorker and Columbia graduate who employed the same guide they had had on the Nile. The order of their names in the consular record suggests that they were in Egypt between January and May 1838, and given the date of their departure from New York, late November 1837, it must have been late April or May. Months later, in March 1839, John Bard was in Rome where he met a fellow New Yorker, Susan Holmes, who herself had been in Egypt in January of 1839. Bard joined Miss Holmes and her friend Frances Butler for several outings in Rome and in Naples, and even returned with them to New York from Havre on August 22, 1839. McVickar was not with them and I do not know how he reached home. Extensive McVickar and Bard papers exist; some day young Harry's diary and that of John may surface to tell more of the story.

14 | STEAMSHIP TRAVEL

The American in Cairo, mentioned in the previous chapter, writing to his friend in New York on November 10, 1837, described how the existence of British steamer service from Malta to Alexandria had prompted him to change his plans and visit Egypt.[1] It was a timely observation. Steamer service throughout the Mediterranean transformed the way tourists and others could travel by offering speed, schedules, and reliability, which permitted more timely planning of itineraries, all contributing in the 1830s and 1840s to an increasing flow of Americans and Europeans to the eastern Mediterranean.

Passenger service by steamer in the western Mediterranean was inaugurated in 1824. In that year a Neapolitan steamship, the *Real Ferdinando* (built in Glasgow), began a run from Naples to Palermo and Messina, and occasionally to Malta. European travelers took to the service. In May 1828, for example, Capt. C.C. Frankland of the Royal Navy, two fellow officers, and a fourth traveler went on her from Malta to Naples via Messina.[2] In March 1833, Ralph Waldo Emerson took her from Messina and Palermo to Naples.[3]

The first steamers to reach the eastern Mediterranean were not passenger vessels. In 1826 the British sent out the *Perseverance* and the *Enterprise*, two steamers, to augment their regular naval fleet in Greek waters. More promising was the *Swift*, an English steamboat that left Smyrna in May 1828 for Constantinople. An English traveler, Charles MacFarlane, boarding her in Gallipoli, described her arrival in the capital, with astonished crowds lining the shore to observe this first steamer in Constantinople making way against the wind and the current. But she was soon purchased by the Armenian head of the mint (with one or two other wealthy residents contributing funds) for 350,000 piastres and presented to the sultan to augment his fleet.[4] The following year, another steamer, the British-built *Hylton Joliffe*, which had served the Naples–Palermo trade, was sold to the sultan. The very first steamer to arrive at Alexandria in Egypt was likewise not a passenger vessel. In 1832, the French government sent out the *Sphinx* to accompany the *Luxor*, which was bringing back to France the Luxor obelisk, now in the Place de la Concorde.

Not until 1833 did a steamer designed to carry passengers reach the eastern Mediterranean. In April of that year, a Neapolitan steamship, the *Francisco Primo* (*François Premier*), left Marseilles bound for Constantinople. Her inaugural voyage was advertised in American newspapers in January 1833, with the price of passage listed at "from sixty to eighty-five guineas according to the part of the boat occupied . . . including breakfast, dinner, coffee and wine while the vessel is at sea," but there were no American takers to the offer.[5] The voyage seems to have been in the air for more than a year: In a letter of July 15, 1830, to Peter Augustus Jay, J. Fenimore Cooper wrote, "It is thought that a steamboat will run next summer between Naples and Constantinople! The quarantine is the one great embarrassment to the intercourse."[6] The *Francisco Primo*, the first proper passenger steamer to venture into the eastern Mediterranean, had on board the crown prince of Bavaria and a galaxy of rich and titled personages from at least ten European countries, among them the Swedish lady Margareta Charlotta Heijkenskjöld whom John W. Hamersley later saw on the Nile.[7] The ship reached her destination. An English traveler, John Auldjo, boarded her in Constantinople for the return voyage.[8]

Two years later, in April 1835, surely owing to the glowing reports of returning tourists of the splendid sights in the Mediterranean, an American company based in New York proposed a cruise to Italy and the eastern Mediterranean. The advertisement in the April 16 issue of the *New-York Spectator* read as follows:

PLEASURE TRIP—A company has been formed in this city called the Yacht Association, who have purchased a fast sailing ship of 400 tons, a vessel of the first class, to be dispatched to the Mediterranean about the middle of next month, for the purpose solely of a pleasure excursion. She is to sail hence for the coasts of Italy, Egypt and Syria, where the party will have opportunities of visiting Leghorn, Florence, Rome, Naples, Vesuvius and Pompeii, the Nile as far [as] the pyramids, Jerusalem and Damascus; after which if the season is not too far advance, it is proposed to visit

Smyrna, Athens, pass through the Grecian Archipelago, touch at Malta, and return to the United States in the Autumn.

The expedition will be placed under the command of an officer in the U.S. Navy, whose intimate acquaintance with every part of the Mediterranean eminently qualifies him for the responsibilities here proposed; he has very recently returned from a cruise, in which he visited the coasts of Spain, France, Italy, Egypt, Syria and Greece, and is an experienced seaman and navigator. Terms for each passenger $200 per month, for which sum stores, beds and bedding, of the best kind will be furnished. Servants one third the price.

The number of passengers is limited to forty, and the agents are Tinkham and Hart, of No. 97 Pine street.

But this was a brig, not a steamer. Not until 1838 would steamers cross the Atlantic; sail was still the only way to get there. The introduction in 1834, however, of European steamers operating on established schedules in the eastern Mediterranean made the success of such an American venture unlikely. In any event I find no record that the cruise ever took place.

Seeking to expedite travel and the shipment of mail between England and India, British entrepreneurs were the first to consider steamship travel for Egypt and were proposing the venture in print as early as the mid-1820s.[9] In 1830 the British began offering service between Falmouth, Gibraltar, and Malta, with an additional run from Malta to Corfu, a British possession. The *Meteor*, the first steamer to make the run, was soon followed by others. By 1835 service was extended from Malta to Alexandria for the India traffic. Once a month the Malta-to-Alexandria steamer made a trip to Beirut. Three of these steamers were the *Blazer*, the *Hermes*, and the *Volcano*, names evoking speed and the fire of the engines. At the same time, in 1830, another group inaugurated a run between Bombay and Suez with the *Hugh Lindsay*. The anonymous American who arrived in Alexandria in 1837 learned that the British had put into service a second steamer from Suez to Bombay, namely the *Atalanta*, supplementing the *Hugh Lindsay*. In fact, two British steamers were added in mid-1837, the *Atalanta* and the *Berenice*.

On November 1, 1834, the *Maria Dorothea*, built by the Danube Steam Navigation Company (Donaudampfschifffahrtsgesellschaft), an Austrian company founded by two Englishmen, left Trieste, where she was built, with a British captain, John Ford, for Smyrna and Constantinople, to inaugurate weekly service between those two cities. Within a year, two more steamers connected Constantinople, Smyrna, and the Piraeus, the *Crescent* and the *Levant*, the latter, captained by Benjamin Ford (John's brother), initially running between the Piraeus and Smyrna until a dispute with the Greek government forced it off that route. A description of the service soon appeared in an English-language guidebook to travel in the region.[10] And within a year an illustration of the harbor of Smyrna by a local engraver, Eugenio Fulgenzi, showed two of the steamboats, both rigged as schooners, side paddles visible on their port sides, smoke billowing from their tall stacks, one flying the Austrian flag, the other the British (plate 24).[11]

In September 1835 a group of travelers in Smyrna persuaded Captain Ford to take them in the *Levant* to Rhodes, Beirut, Jaffa, and Alexandria, so that they could easily visit Damascus, Jerusalem, and Cairo in the short space of two or three weeks. After an advertisement in the *Smyrna Gazette* to gain additional passengers for "a grand and novel excursion" the *Levant* left on September 13 with a range of tourists, including Charles G. Addison, who, in his published account of the first legs of the cruise, reported that "our party . . . appears composed of travellers from all parts of the world; some from Egypt, some from America, and two have just arrived from Liverpool."[12] In a newspaper report, Rev. Josiah Brewer, an American missionary stationed in Smyrna, repeated that the "vessel has lately gone on a business and pleasure excursion to Syria, Rhodes, Beyroot, Jaffa, Alexandria, &c."[13] The travelers from America are not identified.

Did the *Levant* make it to Egypt with her passengers? She did. We know this from the account of two Americans from Philadelphia, Henry Wikoff and Edwin Forrest (already a star of the American stage), who arrived in Smyrna in late October 1835, having come from St. Petersburg, Moscow, Odessa, and Constantinople. They were intending to go on to Egypt by way of the Syrian coast, and not wishing to entrust themselves to some foul Greek sailing vessel, were delighted to encounter the captain of the *Levant* who had just returned from these parts to Smyrna. But Ford absolutely declined to make the trip again. As Wikoff said in his published account:

Nothing would induce him to make the tour we proposed. He had just come from those very places, he said, and what with quarantines, dirt, disease, and endless annoyances, he had "supped full of horrors," and return to them he would not. Both Forrest and myself did our best to overcome his scruples, and plied him briskly with golden arguments. We offered him at last 3000 dollars to make the trip suggested, but money and entreaties both failed.

Instead, going on board the *Levant*, they went with Captain Ford to Piraeus.[14]

Six months later, in April 1836, a French entrepreneur, Louis Benet, launched the *Phocéen*, a 330-ton steamer, and advertised a pleasure cruise around the Mediterranean: Marseilles, Algiers, Tunis, Malta, Navarino, Smyrna, Constantinople, Athens, Malta, Palermo, and back up the coast of Italy.[15] Three thousand francs, meals included. An American from Vermont, Fanny W. Hall, who published a two-volume account of her travels in 1840, describes the luxurious accommodations when she took passage on the first legs from Marseilles to Genoa, Leghorn, and Civitàvecchia in May and June 1836.[16] With her were her brother Fredrick Hall and his wife; he had been a professor at Middlebury College in Vermont but had moved to the Columbian College (now George Washington University) in Washington, DC. She reported that there were about twenty-five gentlemen on board intending to do the whole itinerary. The coast of Palestine and Alexandria were not included.[17] The voyage was not repeated because the following year in Marseilles the sultan arranged to purchase the *Phocéen* for his navy, renaming her the *Peyk-i Sevket*.[18]

By 1836 the French ministry of finance had funded ten steamers of approximately 620 tons for the Administration des Postes to cover three Mediterranean routes. Their names evoked literature and history of the region: *Dante, Eurotas, Leonidas, Lycurgue, Mentor, Minos, Ramsès, Sésostris, Scamandre, Tancrède*.[19] They were operated by the postal administration and commanded by officers of the French navy. The first route ran between Marseilles, Leghorn, Civitàvecchia, Naples, and Malta; the second between Malta, Syra, Smyrna, and Constantinople; the third between Piraeus, Syra, and Alexandria. Seven of the ten ships, built to the same design, had four officers, a crew of thirty-two men, and carried up to twenty-six passengers. Among the amenities on each boat were a ladies' salon, a small stock of books, and a piano. American tourists reported traveling on all of them. One of them is shown in a vignette in Hector Horeau's *Panorama d'Égypte et de Nubie* of 1841.

The Austrian Lloyd Steam Navigation Company (Die Dampfschifffahrtgesellschaft Österreichischer Lloyd), a publicly held company whose chief shareholder was Baron Salomon Rothschild, launched new steamers in 1837.[20] The *Arciduca Ludovico* made its first run from Trieste to Constantinople in May of that year and was soon joined by three more steamers. The American biblical archaeologist Edward Robinson took passage on the *Giovanni Arciduca d'Austria* from Trieste on December first 1837, disembarking at the Piraeus.[21] By 1838 the company ran steamers from Piraeus to Syra (the *Baron Eichhof*) and from Syra to Alexandria (the *Fürst Metternich*), and from Syra to Constantinople (the *Mahmoudie*). For passengers traveling from Vienna to Constantinople, another Austrian company, the Donaudampfschifffahrtsgesellschaft, offered service on the Danube in relays from Presburg to Galatz. From Galatz, from June to August, the *Ferdinando Primo* ran to Constantinople at two-week intervals; in 1838 the schedule was lengthened to be earlier and later in the season, and by this date service on the Danube was extended to Vienna and above Vienna to Linz. Lastly, the Russians had been running two steamers between Odessa and Constantinople since 1833.

The days of having to negotiate passage in the Mediterranean on commercial sailing ships, involving unpredictable schedules and uncertain service, were over. Transatlantic steamship travel for Americans was not far behind; service began in 1838 between New York and Liverpool and other European ports. In the spring of that year the *Sirius* and the *Great Western* arrived in New York harbor within a week of one another. A new era had begun.

15 | PROFESSIONAL VISITORS

Not all travelers to Egypt in the 1830s were purely tourists. In addition to the single young men and occasional married couples seeking to extend the grand tour for their own enlightenment, two groups of visitors visited Egypt as part of a tour in the East in the capacity of professionals: one group biblical scholars, the other medical doctors. And lastly there was a young man appointed US consul to Muscat (Oman).

Rev. Edward Robinson, Biblical Archaeologist

Edward Robinson arrived in Alexandria on New Year's Day, 1838, determined to see Cairo and the great monuments of the Nile valley before crossing the desert to Mount Sinai and on to Palestine and Syria to study the land of the Bible. His scholarly life had prepared him for the venture.[1] In 1818, two years after graduating from Hamilton College (in New York State), Robinson had married Eliza Kirkland, the youngest sister of John Thornton Kirkland, president of Harvard College, a woman much older than he was—she was 39, he was 24. Eliza had died within a year leaving him a large farm, which he tended while working on an edition of the *Iliad*. This led him in 1821 to Andover Theological Seminary in Massachusetts where he embarked on a new scholarly career. In 1826 he had gone abroad to study in Paris, Göttingen, Berlin, and Halle, in the course of which he met a range of young fellow Americans also studying and traveling abroad. In Halle in 1828 he had married Therese Albertine Louise von Jakob, an accomplished young woman in her own right and the daughter of a professor at the university there.[2] He had returned with her to Andover in mid-1830 as professor of sacred literature. While

235

there in 1832 he had discussed the prospects of a trip to Palestine with Eli Smith, a former pupil at Andover and now a missionary visiting the United States from Beirut. Smith had visited Lower Egypt in 1826 and was to do so again briefly with his wife on their honeymoon in 1833. But the trip would have to wait. For the next three years Robinson lived in Boston where he had moved for his health.

The opportunity came in 1837 when Robinson accepted a position at Union Theological Seminary in New York with the understanding that he could travel abroad for several years. Now, finally, at the age of forty-three, he set off with his wife, two children, and a female servant for the trip to the East that he and Smith had discussed some five years earlier. In mid-July 1837 they sailed from New York on the packet *England* for Liverpool with some twenty fellow passengers, among them the naturalist and artist John James Audubon with his newly married son John W. Audubon.[3] After a brief European tour, Robinson left his family in Germany and set off by himself to Trieste to make the long-awaited expedition with the expressed intention of compiling material for what was to become the preeminent nineteenth-century reference book on biblical archaeology.

On December 1, in Trieste, Robinson met, by chance, two younger clergymen, Rev. James Adger of Charleston and Rev. George B. Cheever, a controversial pastor of Salem, Massachusetts.[4] Adger, fourth of nine children of a wealthy Charleston merchant, was twenty-four; Cheever, class of 1825 at Bowdoin College, thirty. Cheever had sailed from New York in November 1836, and had traveled in Europe for a year before meeting Robinson. Adger had sailed from New York in late July 1837 with his mother and two of his sisters, perhaps intending to reach Smyrna where one of his brothers, John, was stationed as a missionary.[5] On January 1, 1838, after several days in Athens, the three clergymen arrived in Alexandria on the Austrian steamer *Prince Metternich* from Syra.

> The moment we set foot on shore, we needed no further conviction, that we had left Europe and were now in the oriental world. We found ourselves in the midst of a dense crowd, through which we made our way with difficulty,—Egyptians, Turks, Arabs, Copts, Negroes, Franks; complexions of white, black, olive, bronze, brown, and almost all other colours; long beards and no beards; all costumes and no costume; silks and rags; wide robes and no robes; women muffled in shapeless black mantles, their faces wholly covered except for peep-holes for the eyes; endless confusion, and a clatter and medley of tongues, Arabic, Turkish, Greek, Italian, French, German, and English, as the case might be.

That was Robinson's observation. The American Consul John Gliddon, to whom they had a letter of introduction, gave them the usual assistance, but his son George was absent from Egypt on his prolonged visit to the United States.

All three went up the Nile. Robinson and Cheever kept notes, Robinson's published in the opening section of his three-volume *Biblical Researches*,[6] Cheever's in the form of expansive observations in a series of letters, beginning in Athens, to an American weekly, the *New-York Observer*. Nothing is known from Adger's pen.

They left Cairo in late January and after only a few days on the river, before reaching Manfalout, they encountered black slaves, on which Cheever devoted several passages in his letters.

> We have passed a boat today loaded with slaves. The cargo seemed to be mostly young girls and boys, and they were chattering as if on a party of pleasure; but in two or three days they will form a portion of the revolting hideous spectacle in the slave mart in Cairo. They were crowded in the open body of the vessel, but without chains, and in paradise compared with the floating hell of a slaveship for the supply of Christian markets. . . . We have passed a second boat, completely laden with slaves, almost entirely women, and exceedingly black. Further up the river, at a short distance below Thebes, on the bank in front of the village of Gheneh, we found a spectacle of misery and dreadful degradation, in a crowd of between two and three hundred slaves, most of them females, all young, and very many of them mere children. They were scattered in groups upon the ground, sitting or lying in the dust, some of them employed in bruising grain for bread. They were on the way to the great slave mart in Cairo.[7]

Interspersing his remarks on slavery Cheever quoted from the account of an Englishman, the Rev. William Jowett, who had traveled on the Nile nearly twenty years earlier in 1819[8] and had observed the slave trade.

Cheever was not the first American to write about the traffic of slaves in Egypt, and since he wrote passionately, it is worth digressing for a moment to examine the subject. The Haights, the Allens, and John L. Stephens, among other Americans, visited the slave market in Cairo, but today their remarks sound quite dispassionate. In addition, the Allens saw a cargo of slaves at Qena, as had Cheever. Mary Allen, a southerner, whose mother, Mrs. James Dewar Simons, was traveling with them, owned slaves back home in Charleston, South Carolina, had this to say in her diary on January 15, 1837:

Several slave boats on their way down the river to dispose of their slaves at Cairo, had stopped here, and the merry negroes were cooking their supper on shore. They appeared to be left very much to themselves so seemed quite happy. Most of them were female children, and girls: they were stolen from Darfour. Their skins were black as jet; they wore very little clothing and their hair divided into small locks, full of hair grease. We walked among them and they offered us a pretty little girl to purchase.[9]

Rittenhouse Nutt, a member of a major slave-owning family in Natchez, Mississippi, wrote about a cargo of slaves he and his father saw at Aswan on November 1, 1834, two years before the Allens' tour and four years before Cheever's:

I saw a group of beings surrounded and closely watched by their masters, the Arabs—caught in Sennaar or some of the upper countries bordering the Nile, and undergoing the taming and fattening process, to render them saleable as slaves in Cairo or Alexandria. They looked something like men and women, but so wild, so lean and haggard that had I come suddenly upon one of them in the Mississippi swamps, or even in the streets of Natchez, would most assuredly taken to my heels. . . . They are fattened on dates, a handful three times a day—tamed by the lash and mild treatment alternately. The boys are transformed into Eunuchs on account of their being more faithful slaves than those who are suffered to retain their natural formation. . . . My God! said I, was it for the retaining of these creatures in their wild and ignorant condition that the Slave Trade was abolished by all Christendom? Is it more humane to take charge of these miserable Africans, to feed and clothe them or to let them drag through a starving, brutish life in their own country? Is it more Christian to bring these wretches into Christendom where the lights shall be shown them, and their souls cultivated, or suffer them to remain in darkness, or go down to hell or oblivion? I have reflected much on this subject, and have come to the conclusion that the slave trade more advanced the cause of Christ than all the Missionaries that ever left the shores of Great Britain or America.[10]

The Rev. George B. Cheever expressed a different view in one of his letters.

Will slavery continue here, as it has done in other lands, long after the introduction of Christianity, or will the teachings of the gospel, as interpreted by the practice and example of the churches which send forth missionaries to the heathen, at once and effectually abolish this cruelty? Will it be stamped, universally, as a sin against God and man? If it is allowed at home, it cannot be effectively rebuked abroad.[11]

Robinson, Adger, and Cheever arrived in Thebes on February 7 and stayed until the morning of the 11th, during this period visiting all the ruins including the tomb of Seti I opened by Giovanni Belzoni in 1817. On the way downriver they visited Dendera and Beni Hasan and were in Cairo again on February 28. Around Cairo they saw the usual sites: the island of Roda with Ibrahim Pasha's gardens and the Nilometer, Heliopolis with the obelisk and sycamore tree, the Great Pyramid which they entered and climbed, seeing American names carved at the summit, followed by Saqqara and Memphis.

In Cairo, the Rev. Eli Smith joined Robinson by prearrangement from Smyrna for the overland trek across Sinai to Jerusalem. On March 12 they left the city, provided with rice, biscuit, coffee, tea, sugar, butter, dried apricots, tobacco, and charcoal, armed with a pair of muskets, a pair of pistols, a firman from the pasha, and a letter of introduction to Saint Catherine's Monastery and accompanied by two servants and by attendants with three dromedaries and five camels.

Cheever stayed on in Egypt for another three weeks, during which time he visited the pasha's boys' school and one of the frigates in Alexandria. Also in Alexandria he encountered a newly found statue of a pharaoh, in two pieces, head and shoulders in one part, torso in the other, but missing the legs, which had been "discovered by Mr. Gliddon in a recent visit to Tanis in company with Lord Prudhoe." Gliddon told Cheever that he intended to send it to America as soon as he could find a convenient opportunity. Cheever added that he thought Gliddon intended to present it to the museum of the American Board of Commissioners of Foreign Missions.[12] But where is this statue today? Cheever then went on by steamer to Smyrna, Brusa, and Constantinople, followed by additional time in western Europe. He returned home from Malaga in Spain in early June 1839.[13]

Meanwhile, reaching Jerusalem on April 14, 1838, the day before Easter, Robinson, Smith, and Adger joined a group of American missionaries who had assembled for their annual meeting in the holy city.[14] On their third day in the city, they visited the several Christian cemeteries—Armenian, Greek, Latin, and American—just south of the Zion gate and the Armenian convent. There in the Latin convent Robinson saw the grave of the American traveler Cornelius Bradford, whom he had known in Paris nearly a decade before.[15] Like others he expressed skepticism over the alleged deathbed conversion of Bradford to Roman Catholicism. Over the next many weeks they made extensive surveys of the city and its surroundings.

In Jerusalem they also met the Rev. John D. Paxton and his family who had arrived ten days after they had, on April 25, from Beirut. After seeing the city they were intending to go on to Egypt. Paxton was not a missionary but a Presbyterian minister traveling as a tourist. He had once had a parish in Cumberland, Virginia, and was first married in 1822. In 1827, his wife died leaving a year-old son, who in turn died of scarlet fever at the age of five in 1831. He moved to Kentucky and married again, but his second wife died not long afterward of cholera.[16] Twice widowed and nearly fifty, Paxton needed a change, and as a man of some means he went abroad in October 1834 on an extended tour to England, France, and Italy, continuing on to Malta, Greece, and Turkey, finally arriving in Beirut in June 1836.[17] There he teamed up with the local missionary community and met and married Martha Dodge, the widow of Dr. Asa Dodge, the medical missionary whom Dr. Rush Nutt had sought to treat and had helped to bury in Jerusalem in early 1835.

After a month in Jerusalem touring the sites, Paxton and his family sailed from Jaffa to Alexandria, arriving on June 1, but were obliged to spend three weeks in quarantine. On the way to Cairo, Paxton compared the Nile to the Ohio at Cincinnati. In Cairo they met German missionaries and members of the Church Missionary Society who had just returned from Abyssinia. They visited Giza where Paxton alone ascended the Great Pyramid, after which the whole family had lunch in the shade of the Sphinx. The Paxtons were the first Americans to travel in Egypt with very young children, namely Mary and Martha Dodge, aged five and three, the two daughters of Martha and the late Asa Dodge.

Meanwhile Robinson, Smith, and Adger crisscrossed the Holy Land, gathering material for Robinson's book. By early July they were in Beirut. There, on July 8, they boarded the British steamer *Megara* for Alexandria, where they remained on board, in quarantine, until they could transfer to a French steamer on the 17th bound for Syra and Smyrna. After a week in Smyrna with missionary friends, Robinson went to Constantinople. Eli Smith caught up with him there in mid-August, and together they took the relay of steamers up the Danube to Vienna where they arrived September 13. Despite the serious illness of Robinson and three of his traveling companions, he recovered in Vienna and was reunited there with his family.[18] Robinson went to Berlin where over the next two years he transformed his notes into his famous book. Smith went to Leipzig to have an Arabic font cast for the Smyrna press.

Adger, who had traveled with Robinson and Smith everywhere in Palestine except the excursions to Gaza and to Wadi Musa, missed his brother in Smyrna; John had gone with his family to meet another brother and their father in England, where James himself arrived in September. He returned to the United States on the *British Queen* from London in late July 1839. With him was Eli Smith. James Adger was the silent partner of this trio of travelers: not a letter, nor any other record of his experiences abroad is known from his hand. All we have is a comment that his brother John, the missionary, made when they met in London: "my brother James, having just arrived from his travels in Egypt." This suggests that the Egyptian leg of his travels was the most memorable.[19]

Dr. Valentine Mott, Surgeon

In late May and June of 1838, about the time the Paxtons were in Egypt, two doctors from New York and two young men, one a New Yorker, the other from Kentucky, visited Alexandria and Cairo. The leader was the fifty-year-old Valentine Mott, the most celebrated surgeon in America. He had an 1806 medical degree from Columbia College (soon to be renamed the New York College of Physicians and Surgeons) and had studied for several years in England with Astley Cooper, a leading London surgeon, after which he had been appointed to the chair of surgery at Columbia College. Mott's European tour, which led to his excursion to Egypt, was not his first trip abroad since his student days in England. Earlier, in February 1835, he had sailed for London with his wife and two of his older children, Louisa and Valentine junior. Joining the family to London and Europe on the first tour in 1835 was Dr. John W. Schmidt Jr., one of Mott's former students. Shortly before leaving New York, Schmidt and several other medical colleagues had persuaded him to sit for his portrait by Henry Inman, a portrait now owned by the Society of the New York Hospital (plate 25).[20] After traveling in northern Europe, Mott reached Italy early in 1836, probably with his family, although only his name appears in the consular list in Rome.[21] He returned with his family to New York about June 1, 1836. On the second trip, which began in late 1836 (and would lead to Egypt), Mott came to Paris with his wife and this time all nine of his children, then between the ages of sixteen and three. In Mott's 1842 published account of his travels, these two separate ventures abroad are recounted as a seamless narrative without any indication of his return to New York between them.[22] But United States passport records and ships' passenger lists help to clarify the dates of his travels.

Now, on his second family trip, after having made Paris his base for a year, he left his family and set off for the Mediterranean. With him were Dr. William Henry Jackson, who had received a medical degree from the New York College of Physicians and Surgeons in 1835, and Mott's faithful German servant Henry. William Jackson was the fourth of five children of the Rev. John Frelinghuysen Jackson, the fourth generation of his family to live in the New York area and one of the more celebrated pastors of the day in the Dutch Reformed Church.[23] His father had recently died, in 1836. Jackson would have gone to Paris as a graduate of the College of Physicians and Surgeons to further his studies with French medical specialists, as dozens of young American doctors, recent graduates of medical schools at Harvard, the University of Pennsylvania, and Columbia, had been doing in the 1820s and 1830s.[24] He left New York for Paris by way of Liverpool on October 11, 1837. Once in Paris, he might have considered traveling to Rome, as many American medical students were doing, but he probably had had no intention of going as far as Egypt, until persuaded to do so by Mott.

Joining Mott and Jackson were two young men, Samuel Waring, age twenty-three, of New York, and Dudley M. Haydon, age twenty-one, from Kentucky. Waring had sailed from New York on October 27, 1837, bound for Havre. Haydon, whose passport was issued March 7, 1837, had left Philadelphia on or around April 23 for Liverpool on the packet ship *Pocahontas*, together with three others from Kentucky (George Kirkland and Mr. and Mrs. William Lang). In some way Jackson, Waring, and Haydon met up with Mott in Paris and formed a group for their Mediterranean tour, Dr. Jackson as a younger colleague of Mott in the way that Dr. Schmidt had been in northern Europe several years earlier, Waring and Haydon coming along for the ride. Evidence that Haydon was with them is provided by a letter of introduction written to Rev. Messrs. Goodell, Homes, and other American Missionaries at Constantinople by the Rev. Robert Baird from Havre on March 18, 1838, as he was awaiting passage to New York:

My dear Brethren, Allow me, in leaving France for a visit to our country, to commend to your kind regards Mr. Haydon & his traveling companions. Dr. Mott, who is one of them, must be known to you by reputation. Any attentions to them will be most grateful to me.[25]

Traveling via Marseilles and Malta, the foursome went to Athens where they saw all of the archaeological ruins and met the Rev. and Mrs. John Hill, the Americans who ran the famous school there. They also called on the American missionary Jonas King: "he wrote for us several kind letters of introduction to the East; among others, one to the governor of Jerusalem, and another to that eccentric lady, Hester Stanhope." King had called on Lady Hester Stanhope years earlier, in 1823.[26]

Mott, Jackson, Waring, and Haydon finally reached Alexandria, and were delighted to see in the harbor an American brig from New York, flying the "star-spangled banner." She was the *Carroll* from New York, whose captain and passengers we will meet in the next chapter. In Alexandria the four Americans saw the usual tourist sites, and all four signed Gliddon's consulate register. In Cairo one of the quartet (unnamed in a brief newspaper account of their trip but perhaps Waring) dressed *à la Turque* and slipped into one of the mosques. They visited the island of Roda with its English-style gardens and were entertained there by the Scottish gardener, James Traill, who had come out to Egypt four years earlier to superintend the gardens of Ibrahim Pasha, Mehmet Ali's son. Traill offered the Americans sherry, fruits, and cake. They visited Giza, but there, owing to a bad heart, Mott declined the opportunity to climb the Great Pyramid. His young friend Waring did so, however, and carved all their names, or at least their initials, at the summit. At the catacomb of the birds near Saqqara, Mott took away a fourteen-inch-tall, unopened ceramic jar, said to contain a bird mummy. The obelisk at Heliopolis impressed them more than the standing one in Alexandria; Mott considered the nearby sycamore to be a fig tree.

Mott and Jackson sought out as many senior medical officials as they could, something no other American visitors had done, and since Mott was a well-known surgeon, his name opened doors. Moreover, Mott had letters of introduction from American and French officials in Paris to their contacts in Egypt and elsewhere. The letters they were not able to use, including three from Ferdinand de Lesseps (French consul in Egypt from 1833 to 1837), are preserved among Mott's papers at the Library of Medicine in Bethesda, Maryland. One of Lesseps' was addressed to the French physician Clot Bey, whom they missed seeing because he was away in Syria. On the other hand they did meet the Bavarian surgeon Dr. Franz Pruner who had come out to Egypt in 1834 and who now undertook to show the four Americans all of Cairo's medical facilities. They visited the newly established civil hospital with its attendant maternity school for midwives, under the care of a French professor. Mott was impressed with the medical school, connected with the military hospital and staffed in part by Europeans. There the group met a French professor, dressed as an Egyptian gentleman, who later, at his house, showed Mott a large folio volume of Avicenna "in the original Arabic." This got Mott to thinking that he wanted to acquire for himself "an original copy of Avicenna and a work of the other great Arab apostle in medicine, Rhazes," but such manuscripts were not to be had. Instead, and perhaps even more significantly,

> was I honoured in a most distinguished manner, by the presentation from my much-valued friend, Dr. Pruner of a manuscript copy of the *Aphorisms of Hippocrates* in royal octavo size, of exquisite penmanship, almost like copperplate, and in admirable preservation. A note appended to it, in Dr. Pruner's own handwriting, calls it *"The Aphorisms of Hippocrates, commented on by an Arabic physician, Abderrahman, the Son of Ali, the Son of Abi Saadek. The manuscript is judged by the famous sheikh Mohammed Aiad e Thanthaoui, to be from three to four hundred years old."*[27]

Mott had earlier presented to Pruner a fine set of medical instruments.

Then owing to the presence of the plague and cholera and the threat of two weeks of quarantine, Mott, Jackson, Waring, and Haydon abandoned their plans to visit Jerusalem and Syria and to call on Lady Hester Stanhope. Instead they steamed directly to Smyrna and then went on to Constantinople, where they remained until July 20. Leaving the city Mott and Jackson took the relay of steamers through the Bosporus, the Black Sea, and the Danube for Vienna. By September 1838 they had returned to Paris, their starting point some five months earlier. Waring stayed on in the Mediterranean and Haydon probably joined him. They had no professional or family reasons to draw them back to Paris. On February 22, 1839, Waring was in Leghorn, where he met a fellow New Yorker, who had just been to Egypt with friends. He arrived back in New York on May 8, 1839, on the steamship *Liverpool*. Dudley Haydon stayed on for yet another year in Europe, returning to Boston from Liverpool on the *Caledonia* about October 2, 1840.

After returning to Paris, Valentine Mott wrote a report on the incidence of disease and the practice of medicine in Athens, Alexandria, Cairo, Smyrna, and Constantinople that was published in *The American Journal of Medical Sciences* in August 1839.[28] But he seems to have stayed on with his family in Paris. Not until early May 1841 did he and his wife and their nine children return to New York.[29] His colleague William Jackson had already returned, two years earlier, in mid-April 1839, on the steamship *Great Western*.

Valentine Mott's Arabic Manuscript
We cannot leave Valentine Mott without asking about his Arabic manuscript. A select number of British visitors in these years were keenly

searching for biblical manuscripts, and in particular Coptic manuscripts, but the acquisition of any manuscript in Egypt by an American in the 1830s was exceptional.[30] With this in mind it would be good to know what happened to Mott's copy of the commentary by Abd al-Rahman ibn Abi Sadiq on the *Aphorisms of Hippocrates*. On his death in 1865, his widow purchased a brownstone at 64 Madison Avenue near 27th Street and there established the Mott Memorial Library, making available to the public his collection of some four thousand medical volumes.[31] In 1890 the library was combined with the library of the New York State Medical Association, but within ten years the library saw less use. In 1912, the building on Madison Avenue was sold.[32] By that time many, if not all, of the books seem to have been dispersed, including apparently the Arabic manuscript. To this day there are books on the antiquarian book market bearing the stamp of the Mott Memorial Library.

But what about the Hippocrates? In searching for the manuscript, I found illustrated on the website of the Near Eastern collections of the Library of Congress in Washington one page of a copy of the Arabic commentary by Abd al-Rahman ibn Abi Sadiq on the *Aphorisms of Hippocrates*.[33] But was it Mott's copy? After arranging to see the book with the staff of the library, proof that it was indeed Mott's manuscript became evident in the form of a note pasted inside one of the covers which reads in part, "Cairo the I June 1838. Presented to the most honourable Doctor Mr. Mott by his most humble servant Dr. Pruner head-physician of the central hospital at Cairo." Acquisition records indicate that the New York and Paris book dealer Kirkor Minassian, who had come into possession of the manuscript at some unknown date, sold it in 1941 to the Library of Congress, where it has been ever since.[34]

The Hippocrates is not the first Arabic manuscript to have entered an American collection. William B. Hodgson, whose exit from Constantinople and brief sojourn in Egypt in 1834 were described in chapter 11, had earlier, in 1826, been posted to the consulate in Algiers, there to assist the American consul, William Shaler, and to learn Arabic and Turkish. Over the course of several years Hodgson acquired both locally and in Paris some three hundred manuscripts in Arabic, Turkish, and Persian, and in 1830 he brought them to Washington where, as we can read in newspaper accounts of the day, they were exhibited at the Library of Congress.[35] But they did not remain in the United States. Four years later, in 1834, Hodgson sold most of them to the British Museum.[36]

It may be no coincidence that in this period another American stationed in the Mediterranean sought out manuscripts of this description.

In 1835 William B. Llewellyn, the consular agent in Salonica, acquired from a local individual a collection of twenty-two Arabic, Turkish, and Persian manuscripts, which he arranged to send to the United States through David Porter, the chargé d'affaires in Constantinople. Llewellyn presented the manuscripts to the US Naval Lyceum in New York.[37] The Lyceum transferred them to the US Naval Academy Museum in Annapolis in 1892, and that institution in turn placed them on long-term loan to Harvard College in 1919, and formally gave them to Harvard in 1931. They are now at Houghton Library.[38]

The only other comparable manuscripts to have entered an American collection in the early nineteenth century are the six Greek texts of the Evangelists, Acts and Epistles, a church father, and another writer, dating from the tenth to fourteenth centuries, that Edward Everett, professor of Greek Literature at Harvard, acquired in Constantinople in 1819: "Just as I was leaving Constantinople, I heard from Mr. Cartwright, the British consul-general, of a few Greek manuscripts, belonging to the family of a Greek prince in decay, which were offered for sale." Everett presented them to the college on his return in 1820, and they too are now in the Houghton Library at Harvard.[39]

Henry P. Marshall, US Consul to Muscat

In February 1838 President Martin van Buren appointed the twenty-four-year-old New Yorker Henry P. Marshall, a member of the firm of Scoville & Britton, East India traders, to be United States consul to Muscat—present day Oman. In March, Marshall received a passport from the City of New York signed by the mayor, Aaron Clark, and not long afterward, in mid-March, he sailed from New York on the packet ship *Pennsylvania*, bound for Liverpool, together with one of his firm's principals, Lloyd L. Britton.[40] Over the next three months (as we know from his diary)[41] he proceeded to the East via London, Falmouth, Lisbon, Cadiz, Gibraltar, and Malta. On May 9 he reached Alexandria where he signed the registry of the American Consul John Gliddon. After quick excursions to Pompey's Pillar and Cleopatra's Needles, he took the canal and Nile boats to Cairo and from there without any sight-seeing he crossed the desert to Suez and sometime shortly after May 17 took passage to Bombay. Not until late September, after spending several months in India, did Marshall visit Muscat, and then for only about ten days.

But toward the end of the year he returned from Bombay to Marseilles via Suez and Alexandria, intending to return home to New York by one of the transatlantic packets. His name appears among the list of passengers on a run of the British steamer *Berenice*, which left Bombay on December 5, 1838, and arrived at Suez on the 22nd of the month.[42] With seven of his fellow passengers he crossed the desert to Cairo, Marshall riding a horse, not a donkey, and along the way they noticed rocks of petrified wood. In Cairo Marshall found that George Gliddon, the American consul, was absent, but he arranged through Mr. Waghorn (the British agent for travel through Egypt) for his party of eight to stay at Gliddon's house.

Over the next several days, Marshall, now with more leisure time, proceeded to see the sights he had missed on the way out to Bombay: the palace at Shubra, the Citadel, the gardens of the island of Roda, and of course the Great Pyramid, which he and his companions climbed. They also dined with the British doctor Henry Abbott, who told Marshall that his sister was married to one of the Browns of Brown Brothers & Co. in New York.[43]

In early January 1839, Marshall returned to Alexandria, and on January 8 he boarded the French government steamer *Sesostris* for Syra, the first leg of his return to Europe. His passport, issued not by the United States of America but by the City of New York, and signed by the mayor (also preserved in the Museum of the City of New York), is stamped and signed by five officials showing the dates of his itinerary from Alexandria to Marseilles.[44] The American consul, John Gliddon, signed it in Alexandria on January 7, 1839, with an indication that he was bound for Malta on the French steam packet. In Malta, after a twenty-day period of quarantine, his passport was signed on February 6, and in Civitàvecchia (the port of Rome), it was signed at the French consulate on February 9.

But once in Marseilles, Henry Marshall learned from a report in an American newspaper and from letters that his firm of Scoville & Britton had sent a brig to Bombay for him and that he had to return to India. And so reluctantly he made arrangements to do so. On February 21, his passport was signed by the American consul in Marseilles, Daniel C. Croxall, as well as by the Commissaire Central de Police, the former indicating passage to Malta and Alexandria, the latter writing, "pour aller à Alexandria voie de mer." Events recounted in chapter 18 of this book reveal that Marshall took a steamer back to Civitàvecchia and on to Malta, and from there he boarded the steamer to Syra, together with several American tourists, one of whom, in turn, mentions meeting him, so as to return to Alexandria and points east.

16 | MILLS, GIRAFFES, AND SKULLS (AND EVEN THE TELEGRAPH)

In the fall of 1836, John Gliddon, the British merchant serving as American consul in Cairo, sent to the United States his son, George Robbins Gliddon, US consular agent in Cairo. A principal reason, though not the only one, was to help oversee the acquisition of steam-driven machinery for the pressing of cottonseed into oil and husking of rice that had been ordered by Mehmet Ali. By this date, at Rosetta, there already was a steam-driven rice mill of British manufacture, but the pasha seems to have become interested in obtaining American equipment.[1]

The pasha's awareness of American machinery for the processing of cotton went back at least two years. In mid-September 1834, during one of their first days in Alexandria, Rush and Rittenhouse Nutt (father and son) from Natchez, Mississippi, met a fellow American, one "Mr. Brown, who wished to introduce the cotton gin into Egypt." Subsequent comments in the son's diary suggest that Brown was not a new arrival: Rittenhouse said that Brown had already become well acquainted with "the mode of doing things in Egypt." Nutt's mention of Mr. Brown's endeavor squares, more or less, with a comment made by George Gliddon in his essay on the cotton of Egypt published some years later, that "as far back as 1832, Whitney's saw gin was exhibited to the pasha in person, but though admired, it was not purchased."[2] Brown was surely the American demonstrating the gin to the pasha; Gliddon, writing more than five years later, got the date wrong by two years.

In any event, George Gliddon was now traveling with the intention of fulfilling the pasha's aroused interest in American equipment. Starting out from Alexandria in late September 1836, together with one of his younger brothers, William, they went first to Constantinople where they met the

American couple Horatio and Mary Allen on their way to Smyrna, Athens, and Egypt.[3] The Gliddon brothers then went to Smyrna where, in mid-October, they boarded the brig *Odeon* bound for New York.[4] They arrived at Newport, Rhode Island, on January 24, 1837, after having spent nearly a month off the coast of New England in severe weather.[5] The only other passenger was William T. Mann of Boston. Six years earlier in 1831, when the Havre packet carrying Alexis de Tocqueville and his friend Gustave de Beaumont was obliged to put into Newport instead of New York owing to contrary winds, the two French travelers and their fellow passengers took the Long Island Sound steamer to New York.[6] George and William Gliddon probably did the same; they reached New York four days later on January 28 and soon afterward wrote to their father saying that they had safely arrived.

The brothers spent most of their time in New York City, Philadelphia, Washington, and Boston, remaining in the United States into March 1838. In New York the Gliddons sought out Americans who had recently traveled to Egypt, namely John L. Stephens, John W. Hamersley, and Richard and Sarah Haight. George Gliddon told Stephens about the Egyptian Society of Cairo, newly established some six months earlier, in July 1836, and its intention to form a library and have rooms where resident members and travelers from abroad could meet. Stephens printed the by-laws of the society as an appendix to his account of travels in Egypt.[7] And the Gliddons met other New Yorkers of position and society, among them Francis Griffin and Frederic Bronson (both lawyers), the Misses Stephens (presumably sisters of John L. Stephens), Mrs. Sands, and Miss Ward. Miss Ward was probably Julia Ward, daughter of the banker Samuel Ward, who had befriended the Greek refugee from Smyrna, Christy Evangeles.

In May 1837, Theodore Dwight, first corresponding secretary of the American Lyceum in Philadelphia, presented a communication in George's name on the recent formation of the Egyptian Society in Cairo.[8] Gliddon himself was in Philadelphia at some point and met Richard Randolph, whom he had seen several years earlier in Egypt with the Haights. He also traveled to Washington, DC, in connection with his forthcoming consular appointment where, among others, he met the Secretary of the Treasury Levi Woodbury. In October 1837, "by and with the advice and consent of the Senate," Gliddon was formally appointed US vice-consul in Cairo, and in late December the Secretary of State, John Forsyth, sent to him in New York for use in Cairo, an American flag, a seal, and the arms of the United States.[9] At some stage he purchased from Samuel Colt one of his new rifles with a rotating breech for 127 dollars, a firearm we would now call a revolver, manufactured in Paterson, New Jersey, and only first patented in 1836. We know that he went upstate, because two years later, when a New Yorker met him in Cairo, George remarked that he had been to the Adirondacks.

In early November 1837, while in New York, George Gliddon received a letter from the thirty-nine-year-old Samuel George Morton, a physician and physical anthropologist in Philadelphia, asking whether Gliddon could provide him with a set of ancient skulls from Egypt.[10] With degrees from the Pennsylvania Medical College and the Medical School at the University of Edinburgh, Morton was well trained and highly regarded. In Philadelphia he was practicing medicine and lecturing on anatomy at the College of Physicians, and had become director of the Academy of Natural Sciences. Since 1830 he had been collecting skulls from many parts of the world through the efforts of friends and colleagues. Morton had been drawn to the pre-Darwinian debate over the unity of mankind: multiple species and creations (polygenesis) or a single species and creation (monogenesis). In connection with this he was making precise measurements of Native American crania (from all of the Americas) to determine their volumes and the relationships of the groups from which they were taken. The results of this work would appear in 1839 in his *Crania Americana*, a prospectus for which Morton sent to Gliddon. Morton was now seeking to expand his research to cover wider populations and was writing to Gliddon as one who could responsibly collect a set of skulls from Egypt. Gliddon agreed to oblige Dr. Morton, and we will return to that later in this chapter.[11]

George Gliddon's principal mission, of course, had to do with the pasha's interest in American machinery, and at the outset of his visit to New York he met Aaron H. Palmer, president (and sole employee) of the "American and Foreign Agency," who was the original American agent for the machinery ordered by Mehmet Ali.[12] Palmer had been corresponding with John Gliddon about financial arrangements as early as August 1835. And he had written to the pasha in January 1836, giving an estimate obtained from American manufacturers for equipment for the pressing of cottonseed oil and the husking of rice, in the amount of some $36,000. In October 1836 Palmer had received from John Gliddon a letter stating that authorization had been received from Mehmet Ali to proceed with the order, and that he was sending his son George to New York with a letter of credit from the House of Messrs. Isaac Nicholson in London. Thus notified, Palmer placed advertisements in local newspapers and periodicals for millwrights, engineers, and other experts to accompany the equipment to Egypt and oversee its management.[13] George Gliddon met with Palmer soon after arriving in New York, bearing the pasha's order, though without the letter of credit, which was not received until May.

Connected with the mission to acquire machinery was a related project, namely a request from Mehmet Ali to analyze samples of coal, a large box of which Gliddon had brought with him from Egypt. Some years earlier, after the Egyptian conquest of Syria, a mining engineer from Cornwall, James Bretell, had gone out to Lebanon to oversee the extraction of coal from deposits in the mountains just east of Beirut. The British were exporting coal from Newcastle to resupply steamships at Alexandria and Suez, but Mehmet Ali wanted his own sources for Egyptian projects. But the Syrian coal, as it was called, proved to be of uncertain quality and according to European engineers in Egypt who were using it, it was ruining their equipment. The pasha wanted confirmation. George Gliddon arranged for Professor James Renwick of Columbia University and engineers at the West Point Foundry to test it. All agreed that it was of terrible quality.[14]

In the spring of 1837, shortly after George Gliddon's arrival in New York, a general credit crisis, now known as the Panic of 1837 even though its effects lasted for several years, convulsed the United States. The causes (which have been debated for decades by historians) involved, in part, the accumulation of silver in American banks, the increasing issuance of paper money by the banks, the rise in the price that people paid the government for land in the West, as well as the rise in the prices of cotton and other staples exported by the United States, all against a background of imbalance of payments abroad. At the same time, buyers of federal land in the West were required to pay in hard currency, not paper, thereby draining local banks of specie reserves. British banks lost confidence in American paper financial instruments, and a sudden tightening of British credit extended to US firms helped to bring on panic in March. In May there was a run on New York banks, which responded by suspending payment in specie owing to inadequate reserves. Businesses and banks failed, both before and after the suspension of payments, and the fortunes of many were depleted.[15]

Not surprisingly the so-called Panic worked in favor of George Gliddon by lowering prices. According to Palmer, George Gliddon was able to place an order in June of that year for the equipment with the West Point Foundry, located on the Hudson, upriver from New York City in the town of Cold Spring opposite West Point, for the sum of $29,000, considerably less than the original estimates. Palmer stated that George Gliddon made the contract with the foundry in two versions, one, which Palmer called the bona fide contract, in the amount of $29,000, the other, which was to be submitted to the pasha, in the amount of $36,275. The latter, according to Palmer, was his original estimate, inclusive of commissions, insurance, freight, and so on.

The relationship between Palmer and Gliddon, and ultimately it seems between Palmer and everyone who dealt with him, deteriorated in the course of the business. Palmer was imperiously irascible and litigious. According to Palmer, and we only have his side of the story, in the form of three letters that he subsequently wrote to the pasha in March 1838, the course of events just recounted and those that follow have been reconstructed.[16] By early 1838, if not earlier, Gliddon had had enough of Palmer. On February 19 Palmer sent Gliddon a bill for his commission of $1,486 with a snippy covering note. Gliddon's counter-offer, according to Palmer, was $1,000, whereupon Palmer accused him of duplicity and breach of faith, saying that he was entitled to a full 5 percent commission. Palmer reported that Gliddon backed down and said that the 5 percent deal was put in writing.

The three letters that Palmer addressed to the pasha, two dated March 6, one March 10, were attempts to blacken the names of the Gliddons in the eyes of the pasha. Among the things that Palmer told him in the first was that George Gliddon, so he had been told, had made about $3,000 on the exchange (from sterling to dollars) owing to fluctuating exchange rates stemming from the financial panic, and that in addition, he and his father, the consul in Alexandria, would pocket the difference between the two contracts ($36,275 and $29,000), another $7,275, for a total of $10,275! By now Palmer suspected that the West Point Foundry officials were in collusion with Gliddon. He also blamed an alleged delay in shipping the machinery to Egypt on Gliddon, who he said should not have done other business in the United States at the same time. In the second of the three letters—this one forwarded through N.M. Rothschild & Sons—he revealed that back in August 1835 John Gliddon had requested a private commission of 10 percent of the total contract. In an aside he added that his firm had survived the panic brought on by "overtrading, the spirit of speculation, and the impolitic fiscal measures pursued by our Federal Government." In the third letter he stated that he was suing Gliddon for his full commission. He also said that the original estimate, $36,275, had been obtained from the firm of Codwise and Bailey, Manufacturers and Refiners of Cotton-seed Oil in New York, that he had introduced Gliddon to Mr. Codwise, who had expressed an interest to go to Egypt as superintendent of the mills.

George Gliddon received copies of the letters, which he passed along to William Kemble, president of the West Point Foundry. Some months later Kemble showed them to Francis Griffin with a covering note dated October 3, 1838:

> At Mr. Gliddon's request I enclose copies of sundry communications from Mr. Aaron H. Palmer to the Pasha which he would request you to examine & advise what course should be pursued. My own view, however, is that nothing in law should be done, as the fellow is too cunning to commit himself. The 2 sets of bills, altho nothing wrong was intended, would give him just cause for pretty sound strictures. While a letter now to the Pasha stating facts that the Am[erican] & Foreign Agency is a mere title & another name for Aaron H. Palmer will put things in their true light, & close all further correspondence with his highness.[17]

Aaron H. Palmer got nowhere with his letters to the pasha, who had long admired the Gliddons, but apparently three years later he was still around. In a long letter of July 8, 1841, from George Gliddon to Francis Griffin, one of his principal New York contacts, George asked, "Where is that infernal Blackguard Aaron Haight Palmer? What a d__d rascal he is, as I some day may have the satisfaction of telling him. Do you know that he has again written to his friend Mohammed Ali, offering all sorts of American machinery."

Now to return to the story of the mills. In November 1837, the West Point Foundry completed work on the coal-fired and steam-driven machinery, and William Kemble, president of the foundry, secured the men to manage it. The principal was Alexander Marshall, an engineer from New York who had previously worked with steamboats. Marshall was a man of substance with a sound reputation. Born in Glasgow in 1797, he had come to the United States with his parents and siblings around 1810, was married in 1819, and by the time of this Egyptian venture had a daughter and five sons, the eldest eighteen, the youngest only a year. Before he set sail, William R. Hamilton, a fellow Scotsman and an accomplished artist, painted his portrait, which is still in the family (plate 27).[18] With Marshall were two other engineers, John P. Bee and Charles Palmer. William Kemble helped to obtain their passports, which they received on January 14, 1838,[19] and George Gliddon arranged shipment of the machinery and passage for the men to Alexandria on the brig *Carroll*, under Captain Josiah Simpson. The brig sailed from New York on March 19, 1838, with the three engineers. Joining them was Dr. George W. Codwise, a surgeon in the US Navy who was going to Egypt "for scientific purposes," and overseeing the group was George Gliddon and his brother William. A New York paper noted their departure.

> The brig *Carroll* . . . is freighted with machinery of American manufacture, and carries out a company of Americans, who have entered into an arrangement with an agent of the Pasha of Egypt for the establishment of mills for husking rice, and for the expression of oil from cotton seed. Various attempts have already been made, both by French and English mechanics, to bring into operation mills of this description; but through defects in the machinery their projects have invariably proved abortive. At length Mehemet Ali resoved to try the mechanical genius of America; and hence the present expedition has been fitted out, and, we are happy to add, with every prospect of success.[20]

The *Carroll* reached Gibraltar about April 23 and the group went ashore. There they met Henry P. Marshall, the young New Yorker who had been named consul to Muscat and was on his way to Bombay via Alexandria and Suez. All of the Americans were entertained by the American consul, Horatio Sprague. The *Carroll* finally arrived in Alexandria on May 21, 1838, and sometime in the next ten days or so was seen in the harbor by the American doctor Valentine Mott and his companions on their arrival in Egypt (discussed in chapter 15). In due course, after interviews with the pasha and his aides to discuss terms, Alexander Marshall and his men, under the aegis of an Egyptian agent, proceeded to Rosetta where they would set up the mills. How did Marshall and his men fare in Rosetta and elsewhere in Egypt? We know a little of Marshall's experiences through a letter he wrote his wife in which he says that in Rosetta he was assigned to a one-room house and had a local woman taking care of his needs, and she would wash the place down inside and out each day because the sand flies were so terrible.[21] Yet he and his men surely had time to see more of Egypt than Alexandria and Rosetta. They must have gone to Cairo where they could not have missed climbing the Pyramids. They may even have ascended the Nile to Thebes. Marshall is reported to have brought home a mummy and other small items of local manufacture.

And we know something of them through reports of visitors to Rosetta. On May 17, 1839, a year after their arrival in Egypt, a Scottish clergyman Andrew Bonar, passing through Rosetta with several colleagues, saw them:

We visited a rice mill which is in the course of erection; and found that the principal workmen were four Americans employed by the Pasha. They were very happy to meet with us, and invited us to their lodging. One of them begged us to leave any English books which we could spare, as they had read over all their store. They said they kept the sabbath every week, for when engaging with the Pasha, he allowed them this privilege, that they might take either their own Sunday or the Mahometan Friday for rest.[22]

And, according to a report in *The Times* of London, Mehmet Ali himself visited the mills in September 1839.[23] With American reports on the quality of the pasha's Syrian coal decisive, they were surely burning coal from Newcastle. About the same time, Pierre Nicolas Hamont, who had come to Egypt to set up a veterinarian school and who later transformed his observations on a range of enterprises in Egypt into a published account, visited Rosetta and had this to say about the rice mills:

En 1839, j'ai vu le nouvel édifice corrigé, perfectioné et monté. Tandis que j'étais à Rosette, il a opéré pour la première fois, tout était au mieux. Le riz déposé par en enfant dans une large caisse en bas, était enlevé par des espèces de godets, puis porté et versé dans les mortiers sans aucon secours étranger. Les battues se faisaient avec régularité. Chaque partie de l'échaffaudage fonctionnait avec une précision, une vitesse remarquable. L'ensemble d'un travail aussi complexe, aussi délicat, excitait l'admiration des assistants. On se trouvait heureux de pouvoir dire: j'ai sous les yeux, ce qu'a fourni de plus étonnant, la conception des hommes; puis, réfléchissant que les fellahs allaient encore s'emparer de cette innovation, d'avance on la condamnait à la nullité. J'ai vu l'ingénieur en chef, et je l'ai félicité sur le magnifique établissement qu'il donnait à l'Égypte. Il a reçu mes compliments en riant; ses alenteurs riaient aussi, "Monsieur, me dit-il, j'ai rempli ma mission, je vais partir; mais cet établissement est perdu. Les Arabes sont incapables de le diriger; leur intelligence est trop bruite, elle n'est pas en rapport avec ces créations; il y a trop loin de l'une à l'autre.[24]

In 1839 I saw the new device, revised, perfected, and assembled. While I was at Rosetta, it ran for the first time, and everything was at its best. The rice, deposited by a child in a large container down below, was raised up by kinds of cups, then carried and poured out into mortars without any outside help. The beatings worked with regularity. Each part of the structure functioned with precision, with remarkable speed. The totality of a work so complex yet so delicate, excited the admiration of the assistants. One found oneself happy to be able to say, "I have before my eyes the most stunning product of man's invention"; then, realizing that the *fellahin* would eventually take possession of this innovation, foresee its eventual demise. I saw the head engineer, and I congratulated him on the magnificent device that he had given to Egypt. He received my compliments with a laugh, even his companions laughed. "My dear sir," he said, "I have fulfilled my mission, I am about to leave, but the establishment is lost. The Arabs are incapable of running it; their intelligence is too crude, too distant to these inventions; the one is miles away from the other."

Monsieur Hamont also saw the equipment imported by the Americans to obtain cotton seeds.

Les mêmes Américains ont construit des manéges pour obtenir des semences de coton, l'huile qu'on en retire en Amérique. J'ai vu ces manèges. Les ingénieurs eux-mèmes contestaient leur utilité. La graine du coton égyptien est plus petite, plus séche, que celle du même abrisseau en Amérique, elle contient moins d'huile.

The same Americans have constructed some machines to extract from cotton seeds the oil that is extracted in America. I have seen these machines. The engineers themselves disputed their utility. The grain of Egyptian cotton is smaller and drier than that of the same plant in America, it contains less oil.

In the end the Americans lasted not quite three years in Egypt. Monsieur Hamont visited Rosetta again in late 1841.

Le samedi 11 décembre 1841, je me trouvais à Rosette. Les ingénieurs américains étaient partis dans le mois de septembre de la même année, et avaient pour succesiers: 1 un Italien que ne savait ni lire ni écrire. Cet homme, ancien calefat à Alexandrie, faisait des baquets dans la tannerie de Rosette sous M. Rossi; il remplaçait l'ingénieur en chef; 2 un Maltais éleveur de cochons à Rosette, était l'ingénieur en second; et on leur a adjoint un autre Maltais vieux, impotent, qui vendait de l'eau-de-vie et des cigarres.

Saturday December 11, 1841 found me once again at Rosetta. The American engineers had left in the month of September of the same year, and had as successors, first, an Italian who knew neither how to read or write. This man, former calefat at Alexandria, used to make buckets in the tannery of Rosetta under monsieur Rossi; he has replaced the head engineer; and secondly a Maltese breeder of pigs in Rosetta, he was the second engineer. And joining them was another old Maltese, useless, who used to sell booze and cigars.

The Americans had indeed left, and at least two of them much earlier in the year than September. Writing on July 8, 1841, to Francis Griffin, one of the New Yorkers he had come to know on his American trip several years earlier, George Gliddon, in London since mid-May, began a long letter by reporting that Marshall and Palmer—namely Alexander Marshall and Charles Palmer, two of the engineers—had arrived in London on June 17, and that Marshall would personally carry his letter to New York.[25] It is likely that Marshall and Palmer had left Alexandria by one of the steamers, French or English, to Syra or Malta, had gone on to Marseilles, and ultimately to London. They must have left Egypt no later than mid-April, leaving their machinery to its fate. They would now be returning to New York. There Alexander Marshall would once again see his wife and six children, including his youngest who was now a boy of four, who would have known his father only from the portrait painted the year before he left.

In the same letter to Francis Griffin, George Gliddon asked if Codwise had returned to New York. Codwise had also left and in March 1840 he presented to the Lyceum of Natural History in New York a "print of hieroglyphics, taken from a rock on the banks of the Nile: the impression was produced by first moistening the paper, and then pressing it forcibly against the face of the rock."[26] If only we knew more of the exploits of Dr. Codwise in Egypt.

Giraffes: From Sudan to Broadway

The brig *Carroll*, which had brought the husking and pressing machinery, the three American engineers, and the surgeon from the US Navy, would not return empty. Several sources provide details. Copies of letters from John and George Gliddon, also preserved among the papers of John L. Stephens in the Bancroft Library at the University of California, Berkeley, explain part of the story. Before leaving New York for Alexandria, George Gliddon had signed a contract (dated December 15, 1837) to import giraffes from Egypt to New York with Francis Griffin, John L. Stephens, Frederic Bronson, and John W. Hamersley. They were shareholders in the New York Zoological Institute, a fancy name for the menagerie owned by Messrs. June, Titus, and Angevine, forerunners of

P.T. Barnum. In letters of mid-July 1838 to Francis Griffin (one copied to Stephens, Hamersley, and Bronson), John and George Gliddon said that the *Carroll* was returning from Alexandria to New York with a cargo of 1,900 *ardab*s of linseed (an *ardab* equaling a bit more than five and a half bushels or 125 kilos). They also reported that on board were two giraffes and three Egyptians, namely Mustafa Hode, janissary of the US Consulate, and Ali and Abdella, animal handlers.

Constantinople, London, Paris, and Vienna were the first cities to receive these exotic animals, sent as diplomatic offerings. In early 1824 the pasha presented to the sultan a giraffe that had been brought downriver by his son Ibrahim from Sennar and kept for nearly a year at his palace outside of Cairo at Shubra. This was the giraffe seen by the American missionaries Pliny Fisk and Jonas King in late March 1823. Although the ship carrying it from Alexandria to Constantinople had been shipwrecked off the Dardanelles, the giraffe, together with twenty-one Arabian horses traveling with it had been saved, and it had proceeded overland to the capital to be admired by multitudes.[27] Two years later, in late 1826, the pasha presented female giraffes to British and French royalty (plate 28).[28] In February, 1827, the Bostonian Andrew Bigelow saw one of them in the basement of the armory in Malta, awaiting shipment to England.[29] In October the same year, J. Fenimore Cooper, then in the second year of a long residence abroad, saw the other in the Jardin des Plantes in Paris, ending his description with the observation that "the creature appears formed of the odds and ends of other animals."[30] In 1828 Mehmet Ali sent a fourth giraffe by way of Trieste to Francis II in Vienna but it lived for less than a year in the menagerie at Schönbrunn Palace.

In 1833, the English traveler James Burton—whom we encountered in chapter 6 traveling in 1822 with his companion, a fellow Englishman Charles Humphreys, and with the New Yorker George Rapelje on the canal from Alexandria toward Cairo—was still in Egypt. Now, in November 1833, Burton was about to ship a giraffe from Alexandria to Leghorn and from there to England, to the Zoological Society for display in Regent's Park in London.[31] But the giraffe died between Leghorn and southern France.

In 1834, about the time of the death of Burton's giraffe, the Zoological Gardens of Regent's Park commissioned a French animal trader, Georges Thibaut, to collect giraffes in the Sudan.[32] On the way south he and his companion M. Reboul met the two Americans J. Lewis Stackpole and Ralph Izard (mentioned in chapter 15). After more than a year, in the summer of 1835, they brought downriver from Dongola four giraffes, which left Alexandria in the fall and wintered over in Malta.[33] The giraffes reached London in May 1836 on a Manchester steam vessel, with Thibaut and his attendants, three Nubian and one Maltese, the whole menagerie featured in several periodicals of the day.[34] Two years later, in July 1838, Ellen Wayles Coolidge, granddaughter of Thomas Jefferson, who was in London with her husband, had this to say about the giraffes she saw in the Zoological Gardens of Regent's Park: "I am charmed with the beauty of the Giraffes—a beauty so peculiar—The grace of their movements is also of its own kind. They give one new ideas of what is graceful & beautiful, departing from all the old standards & conventions—Glimpses of new forms of creation. They might be creatures of another planet."[35]

The American traveler Sarah Haight saw two sets of giraffes in early 1836. In a letter of February 26, 1836, written from Cairo (but not included in the second version of her letters published in her 1840 book) she reported: "we saw five young giraffes . . . which are destined for the United States, and will soon take their departure. . . . They were taken not far from Sennaar."[36] Haight's statement is confirmed by a report in a London newspaper: "Mr. J. Vaissiere . . . is about to forward to New York five superb giraffes, some of which were collected by himself in a journey which he made to Claubat, in Abyssinia."[37] Despite what Sarah Haight had heard and what was reported in the newspaper, these giraffes were not shipped to New York. Where they went I do not know, unless they are the same that Sarah Haight had seen on the lawn of their hotel in Alexandria (only four now) "lately arrived from Abyssinia on their way to the Zoological Garden of London."[38] She meant the Surrey Zoological Garden at Walworth, which was to be a rival of the one in Regent's Park. As soon as word was received in London that a first shipment of giraffes was on its way, the owner of the Surrey Garden sent one J.E. Warwick to acquire another group of giraffes. They embarked at Alexandria on May 9, 1836, soon after Sarah Haight had seen them, for a two-month voyage to London, as told in *The Saturday Magazine* for September 3, 1836, and elsewhere.[39]

The two giraffes that Gliddon was sending to New York on the *Carroll* were not even the first to reach the United States. Someone else had already been sending giraffes to New York, namely the firm of Welch, Macomber & Weeks, which had imported two shipments of giraffes from the Kalahari, shipping them from Cape Town. Two giraffes arrived in the spring of 1837,[40] two more in June 1838. Philip Hone, a former mayor of New York, went with his wife to see the latter pair soon after they went on show, as he reported in his diary for July 3: "*Giraffes.* Two of these beautiful animals are being exhibited in a lot on Broadway below Prince Street; the place is handsomely fitted up, and great numbers of persons pay their respects to the distinguished visitors. The giraffes or cameleopards, as they are called (I like the first name best), were taken by one of our Yankee brethren in the interior of Southern Africa. They are the only survivors of eleven who were taken, and have been brought to this country at great expense, I went with Catherine yesterday to see them."[41]

Elsewhere in the correspondence preserved among the Stephens papers John Gliddon mentions a charter party on board the *Carroll*, which helped to defray expenses of the passage to New York. What did he mean by charter party? A passage in the last of the letters of the Rev. John D. Paxton leads us to the answer. On the way back to Alexandria from their excursion to Cairo Paxton reported that

> The vessel in which we took passage to Atfi had two giraffes on board, destined for the United States. We did not see them until we went on board the boat. . . . They were under the special care of a mustapha or janissary of the U.S. Consul, who had engaged to accompany them to the United States. He had with him two Arabs, for the twofold purpose of waiting on himself and taking care of the giraffes.[42]

Paxton's published letters fail to record the means of his return home from Alexandria, but in his memoirs published in 1870 he says that he took passage on the *Carroll* under Captain Simpson.[43] And, in fact, immigration records preserved in the National Archives state that he arrived in New York on October first, seventy-seven days from Alexandria on the brig *Carroll*. According to these records, with him and his wife and her two children, Mary and Martha Dodge, was an infant daughter of nine months, Martha Paxton, nowhere mentioned in Paxton's account! Also on board were two twenty-one-year-old boys, not part of the Paxton family: William E. Snowden and William Ellis, the former in a cabin, the latter on deck. That was the charter party. Gliddon fails to mention any of them by name, nor does Paxton record two giraffes on the seventy-seven day voyage from Alexandria to New York. He says only that it was "a long time to be confined on board a small trading vessel." The two sets of minds were too far removed from one another to appreciate their respective interests.

Ellis is not otherwise known. William Edward Snowden, one of four children raised by an enterprising widow, attended Trinity School in New York and graduated with the class of 1838 at Columbia.[44] Newspaper accounts of the commencement exercises note that he was absent by permission.[45] One is tempted to speculate that he traveled to Egypt knowing that two other New Yorkers, John Bard and Henry McVickar, the latter a member of the class of 1836 at Columbia, whom he surely knew, would be making the tour that very year also. And it is possible that he sailed to Egypt on the outward-bound leg of the brig *Carroll*. Regrettably we know nothing of his travels apart from the fact that he returned home from Alexandria in mid-July aboard the *Carroll* together with the Paxtons.

The *Carroll* arrived on October first and the giraffes were delivered to the New York Zoological Institute, which went about renovating a building on Chestnut Street to exhibit them with their other animals. Sadly, one of them died in early November.[46] A few weeks later, on November 18, 1838, John L. Stephens, who had traveled to Egypt in early 1836, and who was one of the shareholders—along with Francis Griffin, John W. Hamersley, Frederic Bronson, and others—in the giraffe speculation, applied for a passport for the forty-year-old Benjamin F. Brown. Stephens said that Brown was about to sail on the *Great Western*, on which he indeed took passage for Bristol about November 26. He was to collect additional giraffes for the Zoological Institute of New York, the corporate name of which was June, Titus, Angevine, & Co. He took with him a letter (from the institute) dated November 19 to George Gliddon (a copy of which, unsigned, is preserved today in the Brown papers at the Clements Library at the University of Michigan, Ann Arbor) reporting the death of one of the two giraffes recently sent to New York, spelling out the financial terms for Gliddon's participation in securing additional giraffes, and mentioning the encouragement of Messrs. Stephens, Griffin, and Hamersley in the venture. Stebbins B. June, also associated with the Zoological Institute, had already left New York for London on the packet ship *President* five months earlier in July. Brown arrived in Egypt no later than very early February 1839, June surely sometime before. Mustafa and the two Arab grooms who had accompanied the giraffes to New York in the summer of 1838 arrived back in Alexandria, via Marsala and Malta, on February 5.

After George Gliddon's return from New York in May of 1838, he went about seeking to secure a new set of giraffes for the Zoological Institute. We know that he possessed one a year later (in early May 1839) because around that time Mr. and Mrs. Cator, an English couple returning from India, saw a giraffe in Cairo, in the care of George Gliddon, "previous to its embarkation for America," as they quaintly put it.[47] Gliddon kept the giraffe, which he had purchased from the French doctor Clot Bey, well fed and in good health for more than a year until others could be found to justify a ship's voyage to New York. Thwarted in their efforts of procuring additional giraffes at competitive prices locally, Brown set off south on April

23, 1839, to Dongola to catch them in the wild. He took along with him a Maltese dragoman, Jeffrey, and two servants, Deri and Haroum, all found by Gliddon, as well as Gliddon's Colt revolver (to impress the locals), which Gliddon had sold him for virtually nothing more than the purchase price.

June, meanwhile, traveled up the Nile to Wadi Halfa as a tourist and was back in Cairo on June 30. There he fell sick and was laid up for a month, after which he went to the Holy Land for a short tour. Six months later, he traveled again up the Nile as far as Aswan, this time with a party of American tourists, namely James and Louisa Cooley and Stephen Olin, president of Middlebury College in Vermont and a recent widower. In his own published account Olin said that, "Mr. June . . . has been nearly a year in Egypt, and [has] acquired considerable knowledge of the language, as well as of the habits and dispositions of the Arabs."[48] At this same time George Gliddon made a trip up the Nile with the English merchant and antiquities collector Anthony Charles Harris, leaving Cairo on December 12. At Aswan, on February 5, they met June, Olin, and the Cooleys and traveled with them to Thebes, splitting up on February 13.

June returned to Cairo with his American party on February 21. Gliddon and Harris made it back to Cairo on March 3, by which time they had made a remarkable discovery at Amarna, namely a twenty-five-foot-tall inscription of Akhenaten, one of the so-called boundary stelae, carved on a rock face just east of the site, near the passageway leading to the royal tomb.[49] Brown, after an absence of more than a year, finally returned to Cairo on April 26 with three giraffes. Two French travelers, Dr. Gassier and Amadée Ryme, had encountered him and his dragoman, Jeffrey (whom they called Geffrey-Boni), as he was returning with his giraffes, the first time in Dongola in the Sudan on February 11, 1840, the second time at Aswan on March 30.[50]

June's letters from Alexandria to Benjamin Brown in Cairo, in April and May of that year, recount the difficulties of finding a suitable vessel at an affordable price to make the passage from Alexandria to New York with giraffes. But he was finally successful. In late May, Brown and June, the four giraffes (the three that Brown had captured and the one that Gliddon had been boarding), together with three gazelles not mentioned in Gliddon's correspondence, went aboard the British brig *Helme*.

Also placed on board were nine cases of human skulls, which Gliddon had been assiduously and quietly collecting for the Philadelphia physician and physical anthropologist Samuel George Morton ever since his return from New York to Egypt in late 1838. Partway through the project, on March 31, 1839, Gliddon had written to Morton:

Many a chuckle have I had with my Snake Hunter . . . at the success of our ruses, spite of the vigilance of Priests, Shiekhs, Guards, and Families to abstract skulls from Convents, Tombs, Sanctuaries, and Mummy Pits, especially as we required to keep our operations secret. . . . the collection is the envy of many medical residents and scientific travelers at Cairo who wonder how the devil it was managed.[51]

Gliddon shipped 143 skulls in all, from Saqqara, Abydos, Thebes, Philae, and elsewhere, including fifteen skulls contributed by the French doctor Clot Bey, all carefully listed in an accompanying document together with itemized charges in the amount of $141. Gliddon consigned them (with a covering letter to Dr. Morton) to Francis Griffin, president of the West Point Foundry from whom he had ordered the rice and cotton mills for the pasha.[52] The *Helme* set sail on May 26, and on August 15, 1840, seventy days out of Alexandria, reached New York with June and Brown shepherding their exotic menagerie to the New York Zoological Institute, and with the skulls consigned to Mr. Griffin for Dr. Morton.

The giraffe venture had not been easy and had proved to be exceptionally trying for George Gliddon. Under the influence of Cooley, who detested George Gliddon, June turned against the Gliddons, and his letters of April and May to Brown are full of slights against them. Moreover, June and Brown wanted George Gliddon to secure a rhinoceros owned by the pasha and complained among themselves, when this proved impossible, that Gliddon was not sufficiently acting in their behalf. Brown, older by some seven years, disliked Gliddon, but Gliddon was the key to his success, knowing better than most Europeans in Egypt "how cats jump." Gliddon's disappointment with Brown and June, revealed in a seven-page letter to Francis Griffin, recounting the whole venture and written just after the departure of the *Helme* from Alexandria, rings truer than Brown's and June's petty disdain of Gliddon.

Morse's Telegraph: From Paris to the Pasha

Mellen Chamberlain met the American painter and inventor Samuel F.B. Morse in the summer of 1838 in Paris. Morse was demonstrating his newly devised electromagnetic telegraph to the praise of François Arago, a French astronomer and member of the French legislature, who explained its principles before a joint session of the Académie des sciences and the Académie des beaux-arts. It was an invention on a par with the photographic process announced early the next year by Louis Daguerre, whose invention was likewise explained before the two Academies by

Arago.[53] Chamberlain was a Vermonter, then about forty-three years old, a graduate of Dartmouth College in Hanover, New Hampshire, class of 1816, a lawyer and businessman, and a recent widower who had decided to travel.[54] He had left New York on June 16 on the packet *Emerald* bound for Havre. With him were Samuel Gilman Brown, graduate of Dartmouth College and recent principal of the Young Ladies High School in Andover, Massachusetts, and Brown's friend, Isaac McLellan, a young lawyer, amateur poet, and a recent graduate of Bowdoin College in Brunswick, Maine.

Impressed by the demonstration of Morse's telegraph in Paris and apparently having previous experience in marketing new inventions, Chamberlain signed a contract with Morse on September 12, witnessed by Brown, to demonstrate and sell the apparatus in geographical regions outside of Morse's range of interest.[55] Chamberlain's territory covered countries of the Mediterranean including Egypt. Before the three arrived in Paris, Chamberlain probably had little idea he would meet Morse; he simply took advantage of an interesting prospect.

In select correspondence preserved among the Morse papers, Chamberlain says little about his residence and travels in Europe, and nothing about Egypt.[56] In a letter written many years later to Morse, Samuel Brown gave a bare outline of the trip with Chamberlain and McClellan via Florence and Athens to Egypt.[57] McLellan, however, wrote a full account of their whole trip in two series of letters published in the *Boston Courier* the year following his return to the United States, describing Paris in detail, the trip south to Egypt and Syria, and his return with Brown through Italy.[58] The details offered in these two sets of letters provide a reasonably coherent account of their travels. After the summer and early fall in Paris, Brown and McLellan left the city in late October for Italy, finally reaching Florence. There, on November 30, Chamberlain joined them for a demonstration of the telegraph at the Royal Museum of Physics. They then sailed via Leghorn and Malta for Greece.

The last of McLellan's first set of letters, and some passages in Brown's later letter to Morse, record their experiences in Greece and in Egypt.[59] In Athens, where they spent more than two weeks, they showed Morse's invention to the American missionaries Jonas King, John H. Hill, and Nathan Benjamin. Just before leaving the city they had an audience with King Otho and his queen and their many attendants at the royal palace where Chamberlain again demonstrated the invention. On the steamer, en route to Alexandria, the three were joined by the Willingtons, a Charleston family (discussed in the next chapter), and two young men, William

Bennett and Charles R. Swords. Bennett was also from Charleston and apparently a family friend of the Willingtons. Swords was a New Yorker, a graduate of Columbia College, class of 1829, and had sailed from New York for Liverpool on June 2, 1838.

In taking the steamer from Greece to Egypt, McLellan said that "our determination to visit Egypt had been rather a hasty one; but in Paris we heard so much of a tour in the East from Gen. Cass and family, Dr. J., Mr. C., and others, that we concluded to make the tour."[60] They arrived in Alexandria on January 14, 1839 and stayed in the Eagle Hotel (that is, the Aquila d'Oro) where the Willingtons and Messrs. Swords and Bennett also put up. After seeing the usual sights they made preparations to leave for Cairo:

> Hired a servant to attend us, who could speak the French, Italian, Arabic, Greek, and a little English. I shall not soon forget honest Nicolo. Procured provisions sufficient to last us until we should reach Cairo—such as bread, ham, chickens, potatoes, macaroni, rice, and a plentiful supply of dishes, cooking apparatus, &c.[61]

They left Alexandria on January 17 and arrived in Cairo on the 23rd where they found another Italian-run hotel. On the 25th they rode out to the Pyramids and ascended the great one, and over the next several days they saw the usual tourist attractions. On the 30th, they accompanied the Willingtons and Messrs. Swords and Bennett to the Pyramids for a second visit. On February 1, McLellan wrote that he and his party had decided not to ascend the Nile. A subsequent letter, which can only have been written by Chamberlain himself, from Constantinople on April 15, relates that they went downriver from Cairo to Damietta, across the desert to Gaza and Jerusalem, on to Tyre, Sidon, and Beirut.[62] Mrs. Willington said that Swords and Bennett accompanied them across the desert to Jerusalem. Brown (in his letter to Morse written years later) adds that from Beirut, where they also demonstrated the telegraph, they doubled back by steamer to Alexandria where they had a final demonstration of the apparatus. Then Chamberlain, Swords, and Bennett took the steamer to Constantinople via Smyrna, while Samuel Brown and Isaac McLellan, who had been traveling with Chamberlain since they left New York for Paris, now went their own way. They left Alexandria about March 24 for Malta and from there they went on to Italy for an extended stay. At last they would now have a chance to use a letter of introduction written for them by Henry Wadsworth Longfellow, shortly before they had set off, to George Washington Greene, United States consul in Rome, a city they had skipped on their way south.[63]

17 | SHALL WE MEET IN EGYPT?

Nine Americans visiting Egypt in 1839 had sailed on the same packet ship, the *Siddons*, from New York to Liverpool in May the previous year. Four of the nine were rich young college graduates intent on taking the grand tour. In addition, the publisher of a Charleston newspaper was traveling with his wife and daughter. And lastly, there was a nineteen-year-old young woman from Brooklyn: she was traveling with a couple (he in his early forties, she in her early thirties) and a fifteen-year-old sister of the married woman. The Brooklyn girl would come to Egypt with the gentleman, who would leave his wife and her young sister behind in Europe. Out of the thirty-nine passengers on the *Siddons*, one-quarter of them traveled as far as Egypt. There were surely conversations during their passage to Liverpool about their respective itineraries over the coming year and the possibilities of extending their European tours to meet in Egypt.

Several other Americans traveling in Egypt that year were there on business, as we learned in the previous chapter: Benjamin Brown and Stebbins B. June had been commissioned to capture giraffes; Mellen Chamberlin, accompanied by two New England college graduates, Samuel G. Brown and Isaac McClellan (traveling as tourists), had come to demonstrate Morse's newly invented electromagnetic telegraph to the pasha. In addition, an agent of the American Bible Society stationed in Smyrna paid a brief visit, and several other single wealthy gentlemen rounded out the number. The growth of American visitors to Egypt in the course of the decade is striking. In 1830 two Americans are known to have been in Egypt; in 1839 the number was at least thirty.

In addition to the surviving correspondence of the animal hunters and the letters to newspapers of the threesome promoting the telegraph, the accounts of six other travelers survive: Three wrote letters to hometown newspapers, and three kept diaries. In this and the next chapter we will discover what the letters and diaries reveal about these Americans and the Egypt they witnessed.

Aaron Smith Willington,
Publisher of the Charleston *Courier*

Aaron Smith Willington, whom Chamberlain, Brown, and McLellan met on the steamer from Syra to Alexandria, was the fifty-eight-year-old longtime publisher of *The Courier* of Charleston, South Carolina, the newspaper to which his wife wrote an extended account of their Egyptian adventures. Mrs. Willington's report to *The Courier* takes the form of excerpts from her daily diary covering nearly three weeks, from January 19 to February 9.[1] The Willingtons, like many tourists of the period, had arrived in Alexandria from Europe and Greece, in their case via Rome, Naples, Messina, Malta, and Athens, having left the United States for Liverpool on May 1, 1838. They were traveling with their daughter Harriet and they traveled in style. Describing their departure from Alexandria on January 19, Mrs. Willington wrote:

> We . . . made a formidable appearance, having three camels laden with our baggage, bedding, furniture, stores, &c. and our party mounted on six donkeys, each with an Arab driver, the whole procession led forward by an enormously fat Janissary, with his broad sword at his side, and his silver headed stick of office in his hand; his presence being necessary to have us pass the Custom House without trouble. He was a dark copper colored man, with immense mustaches and beard, and, with his Turkish turban and dress, his look commanded obedience, particularly from those under his control. Arriving at our boat, Vicenza, our cook, and Antonio, our house servant, and I ought to say, man of all work, soon made our cabin comfortable, arranged our beds, set the table, and gave us a very nice dinner of cold ham, chicken, &c. which we all enjoyed, being in good spirits, and having fine appetites.[2]

As noted earlier, Charles Swords and William Bennett had come with them from Athens and had accompanied them to Cairo. Mrs. Willington remarked on the Nubian slaves, the unfamiliar dress of the locals, the degree to which they were objects of attention, the appearance of the fields beside the Nile, the blindness in one eye of many of the boys and even men, the fleas that attacked her daughter. In Cairo,

George Gliddon, the American consul, sent a carriage to collect them from the landing stage at Bulaq:

> I suspect that Mr. G's carriage is the only one in the city, and a curious affair it is; the shape is something like a jersey wagon, wheel and body painted white, and it is very small, drawn by a beautiful pair of Arabian horses, a white coachman in the Frank dress, and two Nubian attendants in the Turkish, one to run by the side, the other in front to clear the street, and make a passage for the vehicle, which the people all appear afraid of encountering.

While in Cairo they went to the usual tourist sites. Mr. Willington and Harriet climbed the Great Pyramid and went inside, Mrs. Willington declined. Concluding her entry for Tuesday, January 29, Mrs. Willington wrote: "After spending a pleasant day, we returned to a late dinner, and sat down, nine Americans in number, having met four here—the largest number, I am told, that have ever assembled in Cairo at one time." She said that a few days later Swords and Bennett "made up their minds to go to Jerusalem with the American gentleman we met here." She was referring to Chamberlain.

In addition to the pyramids, Mrs. Willington said that they visited the tombs of the caliphs and ascended one of the minarets; rode to see the obelisk at Heliopolis and the tree under which Mary and Joseph were said to have rested, one of the classic tourist traps; visited the Citadel, the palace, and the royal mint, and "Joseph's Well," supposedly dug by Saladin. In the palace Mrs. Willington admired the divans on which one sat. Outside of Cairo they visited Ibrahim Pasha's palace and on the island of Roda his gardens. They went to the chicken farms where for centuries eggs had been hatched in special heated areas. One day she wrote:

> In company with two very pleasant English gentlemen—one of them a physician, who has resided here some years and has adopted the costume of the country, and who gave us many anecdotes of the habits of the people—we went ten miles into the Desert to see a petrified forest, where we found the trees lying in all directions and the ground strewn with them, broken into chips by the hand of time. After collecting as many specimens as we could conveniently bring away, out servants unpacked the baskets with which they had provided themselves, and we made an exellent dinner, our donkey ride having given us famous appetites.

The physician, whom she does not name, was Henry Abbott, who had recently moved to Cairo after some seven years of service with the pasha in the Egyptian navy, and was seen by several American travelers to Cairo in the later 1830s.

On the day after, George Gliddon escorted them to the house of a distinguished Levantine family where they were politely received and offered coffee, in small cups without saucers and with no milk. They noticed that the lady of the house walked on elevated shoes, twelve inches off the floor, and that she wore a crescent of diamonds on her forehead that Mr. Gliddon said had cost ten thousand dollars. She dressed Harriet in an elegant costume and even painted the rims of her eyes black, after which the brother of the lady, who spoke French, complimented her on her new appearance.

The next day, together with the Levantine lady and a Mrs. Keer (or Keir) with her maid, and escorted by their man Antonio, Mrs. Willington and Harriet visited the women's baths. Antonio remained outside. The large dressing room had an elevated marble fountain under an open dome, and canopies around the perimeter in which to disrobe. Mrs. Willington witnessed what she could, seated Turkish fashion on a Turkey carpet. Mrs. Keer and Harriet went into the bath, a vapor bath with clouds of steam, wrapped in blue mantles which they discarded on entering. Many of their fellow bathers had brought their children who chatted, laughed, and cried to no end. After two hours they "came out, as red as beets, each wrapped in large white mantles, a towel round the neck and shoulders, embroidered at the ends in gold, and a Turkish turban made of another, richly embroidered in gold and colors." Harriet reported that they had scrubbed her with the fibers of the date tree, covered her with almond paste, head and all, and then poured basins of warm water over her. She also had her toenails dyed with henna. Finally, before dressing, their Levantine friend served sherbet. That evening George Gliddon came over and was impressed by the account.

In her last dated journal entry, February 9, Mrs. Willington said that they did not have the time to go up the Nile or visit the Holy Land, and that they would return by way of Smyrna, Constantinople, the Danube, and Vienna. But Mr. Willington became indisposed and instead they returned via Malta and Rome, the way they had come to Egypt. In Alexandria, before leaving, they met William Young, third son of Rear-Admiral William Young of the Royal Navy, who was returning home from business in India and had arrived in Suez on the steamer *Atalanta* on January 20. Soon afterward, while in quarantine (location not stated but surely Malta), their daughter, Harriet Elizabeth, fell in love with him. They reached Rome sometime in April and then returned to Paris. There, on July 22, in the chapel of the British embassy, Harriet married William: she was eighteen, he was thirty.[3] On November 2, all four arrived in New York on the steamer the *Great Western*. For some reason they submitted alternative given names to the agent in charge of the list of passengers on the ship's manifest. Aaron Willington became Andrew, his wife Sarah became Clara, his son-in-law William became Jonathan, Harriet Elizabeth became Sarah.[4] In the British embassy in Paris, Willington had become Wellington. Perhaps that gave them the idea. They were clearly enjoying themselves.

"Mr. L. and Miss H."

Mrs. Willington mentioned another American group whom she knew must have been making a trip on the Nile and whom they hoped to see but did not. On January 23 on the Nile between Atfih and Cairo she reported:

> Our boat was hailed, and enquiry was made if we were Americans, and if Mr. W. was on board? . . . My husband went out immediately and ordered our boat to lie to, the other appeared to be making preparations to send some one on board. . . . After waiting some time, we found, much to our disappointment, the stranger had disappeared; a most provoking circumstance as we have been expecting to meet Mr. L. and Miss H. of New York, who are on their way from Upper Egypt to Alexandria, and now feel convinced it was they that hailed us.

Mr. L. and Miss H. of New York were Nathaniel Littlefield and Susan Holmes. On May 1, 1838, Littlefield had sailed from New York for Liverpool with the Willingtons.[5] With him were his wife Henrietta; her youngest sister, fifteen-year-old Frances Butler; and a twenty-year-old friend, Susan Holmes, youngest of four daughters of Obadiah Holmes (1790–1869), a New York merchant. Leaving his wife and sister-in-law in Europe, Nathaniel made the Mediterranean journey with Susan, using the clockwise itinerary. An English traveler, Adolphus Slade, met them among the passengers on the relay of Danube steamers from Vienna to Constantinople in mid-October 1838. Toward the end of that leg of the trip, Slade wrote that he heard Mr. Littlefield say, as the mist dissipated on their approach to Constantinople, "Well, . . . this *is* finer than New York."[6] The American missionary Jonas King (who himself had traveled up the Nile with two companions in 1823) saw them in Athens.[7] After leaving Egypt, Nathaniel Littlefield fell sick; he died at Leamington in England on August 18, 1839.[8] This was a second loss for Mrs. Littlefield. Some months before she and her husband had left New York on their European tour, their own seventeen-year-old daughter Mary had died.[9] This probably accounted for their wish to travel in the first place, and with two young women.

These meager snippets from a variety of disparate sources are all that we would have of their tour except for a quirk of fate. The manuscript diary of Susan's European and Mediterranean travels, quietly given to the Brooklyn Historical Society in 1968 by one of her great-grandsons, Hugh P. Brinton, reappeared to public view when it was catalogued on the society's website in 2006.[10]

Susan's account is one of the better diaries written by an American traveling abroad in this period, in part because it covers her entire trip from start to finish. Taking the form of a diary and letters to her sister Kate, it begins on May 1, 1838, the day she and her friend Frances and the Littlefields sailed from New York, and ends on July 31, 1839, just before she and Frances arrived home. Between those two dates, she recorded her own thoughts and her impressions of western Europe and the East in what amounts to more than 135 single-spaced typed pages, as transcribed in modern times. She called it "Letters from a Wanderer."

Before reaching Egypt, Susan, the Littlefields, and Frances Butler made a European tour. After landing at Liverpool they traveled to Chester, Shrewsbury, Cheltenham, Oxford, and then to London. In London they met English friends, went shopping, and saw the sights, museums, and the major churches, and even the giraffe in the Zoological Garden, all with her friend Frances Butler. Susan also sat for a miniature portrait.

Those were the least of the reasons they were in London. On June 28 she witnessed the festivities surrounding the coronation of Queen Victoria. "It was one of the most novel, interesting, grand and imposing spectacles that I have ever witnessed. And a long day it was, too, for we went out at 7 a.m. and did not return home except for tea til one o'clock the next morning." She wrote it up the next day in a long letter to her sister Kate, which is also preserved. This is not the place to recount her impressions except to say that she had a good view of the Queen: "Her appearance is decidedly pleasing. She is graceful and dignified without being haughty, has a sweet smile and still not at all pretty. There is quite a likeness between her and Harriet Willington, which has been very generally noticed here."

From London the foursome went to Antwerp and Brussels. In Brussels she said to herself, "My hopes of getting to Greece and Constantinople (not Jerusalem) are waxing brighter, if an unfortunate war between Turkey and Egypt does not prevent." They went on to Waterloo, Liege, Aix-la-Chapelle, Cologne, Wiesbaden, Mainz, Frankfurt, Carlruhe, Homberg, Zurich, and Lucerne. Now it was August and on the 20th she wrote to Harriet Willington hoping to meet her and travel together. At Lake of Brigatz, Susan met a Mrs. Phillips, wife of an officer of the East India Company, "who had just returned from Egypt and said the difficulties of traveling there, the plague, etc. are much exaggerated."

They then traveled to Bern, Thurn, Fribourg, Brunnen, Zurich (again), to Ragatz, and then over the pass in the snow to Italy and to Lake Como and Milan. Now it was early September. Then on to Brescia, Chiari, Verona, Vicenza, Padua, to Venice, and from Venice to Trieste and to Vienna.

Vienna was the departure city for their tour to the East, which only Susan Holmes and Nathaniel Littlefield were to take. It is now apparent from her diary that he was not escorting her: She was taking him. In Vienna they met Mr. Muhlenberg, the American minister there. And on October 1, she met Eli Smith, the American missionary who had arrived two weeks earlier with Edward Robinson by the Danube route from Constantinople after their celebrated survey of Palestine. He spoke pessimistically of plague, but Susan was not to be dissuaded.

From Vienna they rode an hour to Presberg to catch the Danube steamboat. Among the passengers who made the full journey with them to Constantinople were Baron Bartolomäus Stürmer, the Austrian internuncio to the porte, who spoke English; the Baroness (Parisian-born); and Mr. Isfording, an attaché of the legation; also Madame Ruthvin ("a French lady who does not at all take with us"); and three Englishmen, Col. Knox, Mr. Barton, and Mr. Llandachen.[11] She failed to mention Adolphus Slade who was traveling with Col. Knox of the guards and had mentioned Mr. Littlefield's comment on approaching Constantinople. Near Orsova the passengers transferred to the steamboat *Pannonia*. Susan had been reading Walter Scott novels but on board she found a copy of Bulwer Lytton's three-decker 1832 novel *Eugene Aram*. At Braila they changed steamboats again, now to the *Ferdinand*. She played chess with the Baron, who beat her. That was before the steamer entered the Black Sea and rolled so much that the "poor Baron was lying on the floor, vowing that he should die soon." Susan, however, was a good sailor; even the captain complimented her. In the morning of October 4 they approached Constantinople.

I was awakened with the tidings that we were about to be entering the Bosphorus, and that I must hasten to come on deck. I rose and hastened to dress myself quickly, and truly it was a sight that I would not have lost for a very great deal. If we should see nothing else in Constantinople itself, the view we have had today, of the Bosphorus and the approach to the city, would amply repay us for the trouble and exertion. . . . To meet the Ambassador was a caique, lined in red satin, with 8 or 10 rowers whose jackets were trimmed in gold braid.[12]

After a visit of two-and-a-half weeks, they left on October 23 by steamboat for Smyrna. They were the only passengers so they had the "gentlemanly pleasant captain" to themselves. In Smyrna they saw the missionary Rev. Daniel Temple, who had arrived in 1834, after some ten years' residence in Malta, and had remarried after the death of his first wife and two of their four children. They also met "Miss Danforth, who is engaged in teaching a very flourishing school . . . and Miss Brayton, an American also, governess in an English family here," whose parents had known Mr. Littlefield. She showed them "the interior of a handsome Smyrna house."

In late August 1835, the American missionary Josiah Brewer, resident in Smyrna since 1830, had sailed to New York, taking with him his five-year-old daughter, but leaving his wife with their two youngest children in Turkey. He returned nearly a year later, in early June 1836, with his daughter, and now accompanied by a nephew, Eliot Brewer, and a young woman of Pittsfield, Massachusetts, Martha Partridge, coming out to help take care of the children. Also on board was Agnes A. Brayton. She was to have joined the school of the American missionary Rev. John Robertson on the island of Syros but, by the time Susan Holmes saw her in the fall of 1838, she had become a governess to an English family in Smyrna. And, as already stated, Susan saw yet another single woman, Salome Danforth, also of Pittsfield, who had sailed separately from Brewer but had come to teach in his school.[13] Yet where Susan was bound, Egypt, American missionaries had never set up a post (though English missionaries had done so), and no single American women ventured there to embark on a vocation, whether to take care of children in an American household or to teach in a missionary school. In a way Susan was the first single American woman to reach Egypt, for even though she was traveling with a family friend, an older man who was nominally her protector, she possessed independence.

On October 30 Susan Holmes and Nathaniel Littlefield took the French Steamer *Rameses* through the archipelago to the island of Syra. There they met the American missionary Elias Riggs, who told them that his Episcopalian colleague John J. Robertson, to whom they had a letter, was just about to depart for Egypt. The lazaretto looked awful and they managed to persuade the English Consul, Richard Wilkinson, to obtain a small sailing craft for them, "smaller," said Susan, "than any of our North River sloops, perhaps the size of the lifeboat of the *Siddons*" (their transatlantic packet). Into this they squeezed with their fellow passengers Messrs. Brennan, Stone, Dambricourt, and Gibson. They dined on macaroni and eggs. They had fine weather until rounding Cape Colonna, after which a gale and rain buffeted them, reducing the "ignorant captain" to give up all hope, implying that they might have to abandon ship. Susan put on a life preserver. Mr. Littlefield "collected as much gold as he could conveniently carry." But the danger passed and they landed.

In Piraeus they were quarantined from November 5 to 15, during which time the tedium was relieved by repeated visits from a sequence of European and American residents of Athens, the missionaries Jonas King and Nathan Benjamin, the missionary school teachers Rev. and Mrs. John H. Hill (who brought them a copy of John L. Stephens' *Incidents of Travel* to read). Susan was unable to persuade John Hill to accompany them to Egypt. Other visitors were Miss Baldwin of Virginia and Miss Mulligan, the latter a sister of Mrs. Hill, and both of them assistants at the school. They were fulfilling the same function in Athens as Salome Danforth was doing in Smyrna. They also saw Christy Evangeles (a Greek refugee from the War of Independence who had gone to Columbia College in New York and had now returned to Greece), and the Scotsman George Finlay (the future historian, to whom they had letters) and his Greek wife. After their release from quarantine, they saw sites in and around Athens, and they called on the venerable Petro Mavromichalis, one of the heroes of the Greek revolution, with whom they exchanged "pretty speeches" about the bonds of Greeks and Americans.

On November 19 they took the French steamboat *Lycurgus* for Alexandria where they docked on November 24. With them probably were the French traveler M. Dambricourt and the three Irish gentlemen, Messrs. Brennan, Stone, and Gibson. Later on in Egypt, Dombricourt and Gibson joined an English artist from Bristol, William James Müller, on a tour of the Nile during which Müller made a series of remarkably fine watercolor sketches, which might even serve to illustrate Susan Holmes' account.[14]

For five days in Alexandria, the American Consul John Gliddon, his wife, and his two daughters entertained Mr. Littlefield and Susan Holmes. They saw Pompey's Pillar and Cleopatra's Needles, which Susan recognized from illustrations. And "they rode to the sea-shore and visited the new palace with is being built for Mohammed Ali. Some of the furniture very splendid and tasty."

Then, in company with our Irish traveling companions (Messrs. Brennan, Stone, and Gibson?) and two servants, one of them an Arab girl for Susan, they set off on the Mahmoudiya canal. Waiting at Atfih for the Nile boat on December 2, they "had quite a long visit with Dr. Robertson who had just come down river." Robertson had requested (or had been urged) to take a rest cure in Egypt, at the stage in his career when he was transferring his missionary duties from Syra to Constantinople.[15] Robertson is unlikely to have gone farther south than Cairo; he was in Egypt no more than a month.

Reaching Bulaq they rode the mile and a half into Cairo, took rooms in a hotel, and were called on by George Gliddon. Over the next several days they saw many of the usual buildings and gardens, but one day, December 11, was "a day never to be forgotten—an era in my life—for I have seen the Pyramids. I have stood on their summit and have penetrated their dark and mysterious recesses and chambers and I now feel I have indeed seen one of the wonders of the world." She made the excursion with a Captain MacPherson and Mr. Brennan. Susan was determined.

An Arab seized hold of each of my hands and almost before I was aware of it, I found myself suspended in mid air, alone with the Arabs. Mr. Littlefield and Capt. MacPherson had given up the attempt. Mr. Brennan was far above me, but my Arabs seemed inclined to take all possible care of me, and in about 20 minutes I found myself on the pinnacle of the far-famed Pyramid. The view from the summit is singular, but not remarkable for beauty. The most pleasing feature is the meeting of the sands of the desert and the rich green fields, the former looking much like the sea, dashing its waves against the shore. . . . Near what is at present the base but what was once only a third of the distance is the entrance to the Pyramid, and here commenced with me the real difficulty. Preceded by guides and torches we entered the aperture and first went down a narrow inclined plane and then groped through a passage so low we were obliged to bend nearly double. This brought us to the lower chamber which contained nothing but the dust of the ages. We then climbed up a steep ascent with another narrow passage, but here we were brought to a stand, as Mr. B. assured me I could proceed no farther. I told him I was not going back until I had seen the whole. My Arabs seemed to enter into my spirit, so one of them kneeled down, another placed me on his back, while a third took hold of my arms and hauled me up. Another long slanting passage was traversed, another low alley crept through, and soon we found ourselves by the side of the empty sarcophagus, which alone remained to tell that here a king had found his last resting place. The dust and heat were suffocating and when we came out, hardly even our dearest friends could recognize us, so completely covered were we with the dust.[16]

After seeing Cairo they were to cross the desert via Mt. Sinai to Palestine, and at the outset of their visit in the city, George Gliddon was making the usual arrangements. Intelligence received however "obliged us to give up Mt. Sinai and Petra and content ourselves with the route to Gaza." Camels proved difficult to get on time, and then Mr. Littlefield was half sick on their sofa, and after a visit from the doctor, they decided against Syria, much to Susan's regret, and determined instead to go to Thebes.

On December 21, they received a call from Dr. Henry Abbott, whom many visitors saw during their visit to Cairo, after which Susan manufactured an American flag.

Spent the whole afternoon and evening in a new species of handiwork—manufacturing a flag of my nation, but the star-spangled banner we love, is certainly very pretty and I do love it very much, yet I could not help wishing there were more stripes and fewer stars, as the latter were very hard to make, but no American flag can Cairo produce.

They were on their way by December 23. On the 28th they met two Englishmen they had come to know in Cairo, on their way to superintend a sugar plantation for the pasha, and with them they visited the works. January 1, 1839, was "the first New Years' Day I ever spent away from home." They reached Thebes on January 8, but only stayed until the 10th before heading downriver. They returned to Cairo on the 21st.

On the way from Cairo to Atfih on January 23, they "passed a boat which I am sure contained the Willingtons, as on hailing them we were told they were Americans but they did not seem to understand that we wished to stop or who we were, and as they had a good wind they were soon so far ahead that we could not overtake them. It was a sore disappointment to me, as in this far distant land the sight of a familiar face would indeed be refreshing." Indeed it was the Willingtons because that was the very moment when Mrs. Willington thought that they had passed a boat with "Mr. L. and Miss H."

They were back in Alexandria on the 25th and sailed on the steamer *Hermes* on the 28th bound for Malta. Among their fellow passengers was

Lady Grant, widow of the late governor of Bombay, and her four little children.[17] Also on board was Mrs. Waghorn, whom Susan had come to know well in Cairo. In Malta they were again quarantined, for two weeks, from February 2 through 15. This pointed up a disadvantage of a clockwise tour that included Egypt, namely two periods of quarantine.

Leaving Malta they reached Leghorn on February 21 and were there reunited with their family and friends. The next day Susan received "calls from Mr. De Forrest and Mr. Warring, Americans, the latter of whom has been dwelling in the East, but has seen neither Thebes nor Jerusalem . . . . Found it very pleasant to talk over reminiscences of the journey." "Warring" was Samuel Waring, the same young man who had traveled with Drs. Valentine Mott and William Jackson to Egypt the previous year. He had not returned with them to Paris but had spent additional time in the East.

They left Leghorn March 7 and arrived in Rome on the 9th where they spent some three weeks seeing every monument in and around the city: every church, every gallery, every Roman ruin. In Rome they met Mr. and Mrs. Butler, not the parents of Frances Butler and Mrs. Littlefield, but the thirty-five-year-old Charles Butler and his wife Eliza, friends but not relatives (at least not near relatives), who were in Italy with their six-year-old son Ogden and thirteen-year-old nephew William, all of whom are mentioned by Susan.[18] On March 13, two Americans, Mr. Heard and Mr. Bard, invited Susan and Frances to ascend to the top of St. Peter's. On their way up, "some gentlemen who had just come down, gave a dreadful account of it, said they would not have attempted it if then had known how bad it was, etc. Would we attempt it or would we not? was then asked. Most certainly was the reply. Should a young lady who had been to the top of the Pyramids hesitate about the ball of St. Peters? Certes not, so on we went." Bard was John Bard who had been traveling in Europe and Egypt with Henry McVickar, but was now going his own way.

April 4 found them on the road to Naples. In Naples they saw repeatedly "Gov. Troop," namely the Honorable Enos T. Throop, the American envoy in Naples. Heard and Bard were there also and they jointly made a visit to the museum to look at bronzes and ornaments from Pompeii. Heard invited them for an ascent of Vesuvius. Several days later at their lodgings Susan remarked in her diary:

> In walked Messrs Heard and Bard, our expected Vesuvius escorts, who very coolly announced that they had given up their intention of going to Mt. Vesuvius! Was ever such unparalleled impudence, such cold-blooded butchery of our feelings heard of! Not one emotion of regret at our

disappointment did the hard-hearted wretches seem to experience—not one word of apology did they made. Coolly and calmly they informed us they were not going. Not one word did we make in reply.

April 15, the day they were to have gone, was cloudless, a perfect day to climb Vesuvius, but she and Frances were "beauless," as she put it, until she asked Mr. Littlefield whether John (apparently a servant of the Littlefields) could escort them. It was agreed upon and so they climbed Vesuvius with him, in an ascent she compared to that of the Pyramid. After reaching home, Susan wrote, "And now let our recreant knights act on their own option about the ascent. We are independent of them, and rejoice in the fact, and this time I think have fairly the laugh against them."

Leaving Naples around April 17, they went to Florence, then north into Switzerland and into France and entered Paris via the park at Fontainbleau on June 12. Her diary ends, not with Paris, of which she records only the first two of many days, but with brief daily accounts of shipboard life on the packet ship *Silvie de Grasse* from Havre to New York. With her was Frances Butler, but not the Littlefields, who had gone to England. She mentions Miss Botton, Miss Bowen, and a Mr. Gordon who threatened two duels, one with Mr. Richards (which she put a stop to by informing the captain), another with John Bard, who was also on board, which came to nothing. On Sundays one of the two bishops on board, McGill of Philadelphia or Purcell of Cincinnati, said Mass for the Catholics. She and her friends "had a pitched battle with a French lady and her faction, who being jealous of our aristocracy as they call it, do everything in their power to annoy us."

From Susan's diary it is evident that she was not only determined to do everything but possessed the strength of character to carry out her wishes. And she was talented. While in Frankfurt, for instance, she wrote:

We were very much amused when we first traveled on the Continent, by my being taken for the Madam of the party. . . . I always addressed the servants, as I was the only one that could speak French fluently. I have found my French extremely serviceable to me and now the experience the "worth of the money" which dear Father has expended upon it for me.

Her diary also reveals that the coronation of Queen Victoria at the outset of her trip and her many weeks in Rome, Naples, and Florence were of greater significance than Egypt, except for the Pyramid. Writing letters home to her two sisters and, even more important, receiving letters from home were of the greatest importance, particularly when she was traveling duo with Mr. L. She had to fight back tears when none were waiting for her at the usual places. In Italy she realized that a year of touring was enough. In Leghorn, on May 6, about to start for northern Italy and Paris, which they had bypassed at the outset of their travels, she wrote, "Packed a trunk this morning to send home and had some idea of putting myself in it."

We learn that she met the Willingtons in New York a few days before they sailed for Liverpool, and that she had communicated with them at least five times in Europe in vain attempts to meet up and travel together. Susan received at least two letters from Harriet while in Italy. She may have seen them in Paris but she left France before Harriet's wedding. Missing the Willingtons in Egypt contributed, I believe, to her vague sense of disappointment (apart from her memorable day at the Pyramids) in her several weeks there. The continuing uncertainty of Mr. L.'s health cannot have helped.

Simeon Howard Calhoun, Native of Boston

Two travelers in these earlier months of 1839 had not been passengers on the *Siddons* bound from New York to Liverpool in May of 1838. One of them was an American clergyman, Rev. S.H. Calhoun, who arrived in Alexandria in mid-February from Syra. The American consular list of Americans visiting Egypt, quoted by George Gliddon some years later, says he was from South Carolina.[19] But that is a mistake. The phrase "South Carolina" has slipped down from the Willingtons' entry above where it would have properly referred to Charleston. Simeon Howard Calhoun was born in Boston, one of many children of a merchant there, was graduated from Williams College in western Massachusetts in 1829, and was ordained a minister in Springfield, Massachusetts, a few years later.[20] He never set foot in South Carolina. Calhoun applied for a passport as a "native of Boston" in early November, 1836, and sailed on the *Metamora* bound for Smyrna from Boston in mid-November as an agent of the American Bible Society. With him on board was the Rev. John J. Robertson, an Episcopal missionary who had first been in Greece in the early 1830s and was now returning from leave in the United States; and there were three other passengers, Charles R. Lincoln, printer for the American missionaries in Smyrna, his wife Lucretia, and George M. Soule of Boston.[21]

Over the next several years Calhoun wrote letters to the *Springfield Gazette* and other papers about his experiences in Smyrna, Constantinople, Athens. Now from Egypt he wrote additional letters, recording his brief time in Alexandria and Cairo before he set forth overland for Jerusalem in early March. One passage alone is worth quoting because in it Calhoun described something few others had done, namely a visit to a royal house in Alexandria.

> The palace and gardens of one of the sons of Mehmet Ali. Some of the rooms in the palace are beautifully furnished in French fashion. The young prince's library, at least that part of it which I saw, was composed principally of French books, among which I opened Voltaire's works, in more than sixty volumes. Thus is the arch-infidel, after his death, disseminating his corrupting sentiments among the Mohammedans.[22]

Missionaries might have despaired, and others been pleased. George B. English, who had read Voltaire as an undergraduate at Harvard and who had gone up the Nile in 1820, would have been amused. The set might have been the seventy-five-volume Paris edition by Baudouin frères of 1825–28.[23] Whether or not, it was one of the fruits (though now dried) of Mehmet Ali's enterprise beginning in 1826 to send promising young Egyptians to Paris to be educated. What happened to the prince's library? Was it destroyed in the British bombardment of Alexandria in 1883? Or did it survive into the twentieth century to become part of King Farouk's library, and perhaps be dispersed at the sale of his belongings after he was overthrown in the 1950s?

Before leaving Alexandria for Cairo, Calhoun borrowed from John Gliddon, the American consul, an American flag for his boat on the canal and on the Nile. Along the way he noted, in contrast to the apparent poverty of the inhabitants, how rich and green the land was, "the barley full in head, the wheat just heading, the flax in bloom, the clover rank, and the beautiful date tree shading the whole plain." In Cairo, he was welcomed by George Gliddon. He met the missionaries Johann Lieder and William Kruse, and on another occasion he went to Giza to climb the Great Pyramid and explore its inner recesses. On March first he dined with the Lieders where he met Alexander Tod (the son-in-law of John Gliddon), the Rev. Henry Tattam (the collector of Coptic manuscripts), and Tattam's stepdaughter Eliza Platt.[24] Some days later Calhoun left Cairo with Dr. John Forbes (1802–1899) of the Scottish Church for Jerusalem, arriving there in late March via Gaza. By mid-April he was in Nazareth, having traveled to the Dead Sea and many places in between. He reached Beirut and from there went by steamer back to Alexandria, where on May 17 he took the steamer for Syra and Smyrna.

A Nameless American Tourist in May

The second of these two travelers was a young American who wrote six letters published in a weekly, *The New-York Mirror*, between August 8 and October 17, 1840. He remains anonymous. From his first letter, which begins as he is leaving Alexandria on the canal on May 5, 1839, we know that he had arrived there by steamer from Syra, probably some time in late April. On the Nile from Atfih to Bulaq he encountered several English officers he had met on the steamer from Syra. In Cairo he teamed up with a gentleman from Milan for the Nile trip south, and the two left the city on May 12 with their dragoman Hassan and a crew of eight. By May 23, they neared Dendera. On May 28 they were at Edfu. Near Aswan on June 1 they met an Italian and a German on their way downriver from Cordofan and Sennar, and after hearing fascinating descriptions of hippopotamuses, giraffes, ostriches, Sennar horses and elephants, rhinoceroses, and Abyssinian women, regretted not having made plans while in Cairo to have traveled farther south.

On June 6 they stopped at Esna where the Almehs, the girls who danced and sang in exotic costumes and had been exiled from Cairo in 1834, entertained them.

> One of these, Sophia, renowned for her beauty and much for her musical talents, had on some occasion given personal offence to Abbas Pacha, governor of the capital; and in consequence she, with many of her companions, had been banished to this place, where they occupy a house at the entrance of the town. . . . We were desirous of calling upon these ladies and listening to some specimens of their art, and consequently directed the reluctant Mohammed to go and obtain their permission. This being conceded, we repaired to the house, accompanied by our dragoman to interpret for us. . . . The one who immediately riveted out attention was Tibi Damiatia, called the Queen of the Almehs. She is large and tall, her figure being one which is considered perfection among the orientals, and beautiful anywhere. . . . She was walking on the terrace smoking a Narguileh, which a slave carried behind her. We were courteously received, and shown into an adjoining chamber, where, seated on the divan, and smoking our chibouques, we entered into conversation through the medium of Mohammed. At the same time we took note of the costume of Tibi, which was very beautiful. She wore immense trowsers of pale green silk elegantly figure; a corsage of embroidered muslin, unbuttoned at the neck; with a skirt divided into four depending from it; over this a rich embroidered jacket. About her neck and over her forehead a great

variety of jewels and ornaments; long pendants in her ears. Her hair was braided in innumerable tresses, which fell from under a red velvet calotte embroidered with gold. From her neck were suspended by a silver chain numerous amulets to preserve her from the evil eye, sewed in little bags ornamented with silver spangles. . . . There were several others present, but none so remarkable in her appearance as Tibi. But soon Sophia entered, and excited even greater admiration in us. Her costume was the same as that of Tibi, with the addition of a long white veil descending from the head to the feet, which, when she laid aside, we perceived a face of singular beauty. Her features are Italian; her complexion a Parisienne might envy; and her eye of that peculiarly oriental form the ovale allonge, its brilliancy artificially heightened by the kohl with which the lids are tainted at their edges. They now proceeded to favor us with an exhibition of their musical talents, and sang several Arabic poems. They sang the music, which was of a melancholy cast, and all in the minor mode, with a great deal of feeling and expression, each singing a strophe alternately. . . . We lost a great deal in not understanding the words. Their voices were chiefly remarkable for sweetness and flexibility, rather than for compass or power. . . . After a prolonged visit we took our leave, much gratified.[25]

Here the account breaks off. No letters survive giving the rest of his Nile account, and nothing lets us identify this young man who seems closer in spirit to a French traveler than the usual American.

18 | PHILIP RHINELANDER AND HIS FRIENDS

O n the packet ship *Siddons* with the Willingtons, the Littlefields, and Susan Holmes were four young men who would visit Egypt that same season, Philip Rhinelander, John I. Tucker, Samuel H. Whitlock, and Andrew L. Ireland, all of New York. But before we trace their Mediterranean adventures, we should consider who they were.

Philip Rhinelander was born in 1815, son of Philip and Mary Rhinelander. His father was a descendant of Philip Jacob Rhinelander (1686–1737?) from Bad Duerkheim in the Rhineland-Palatinate who had come with his family to Philadelphia in 1727, and by the time of his death was living in New Rochelle. His mother was Mary Hoffman, daughter of Judge Josiah Ogden Hoffman, and younger sister of Matilda (fiancée of Washington Irving) who had died in 1809 before marrying Irving. In April 1818, Philip's sister Mary was born, and five months later their mother died at age 22. In 1830, when Philip was fifteen, his father died and the will provided for two guardians: Frederick William Rhinelander, one of their uncles, and Ogden Hoffman, their late mother's brother. Another family member who would have been in a position to help was John R. Rhinelander, also an uncle, and professor of medicine at the Columbia College of Physicians and Surgeons. He may have helped Philip enter Columbia College in 1831, then located in southern Manhattan, opposite City Hall Park, to join twenty-two other members of the class of 1834. At some point, perhaps on graduating from Columbia, he had his portrait painted—an oil-on-paper miniature—showing him well dressed, wearing glasses, with a mustache and a light beard (plate 29).[1] By this time, yet another uncle, William C. Rhinelander, was helping to manage his affairs. Some of the family money came from sugar and commerce with Havana;

other funds were in real estate. Philip was co-owner of two houses, one on Broadway worth a substantial sum. What he was doing in the four-year period between leaving Columbia and embarking for Europe is not known. And no record of an application for a passport exists.

That is not the case for Messrs. Tucker and Whitlock. The National Archives of the United States preserve their passport applications addressed to the secretary of state, John Forsyth, one written by William Whitlock Junr on April 12, 1838, for his son, Samuel H. Whitlock, the other written by Fanning C. Tucker on April 14 for his son.

> My son, John Ireland Tucker, and another young gentleman, his companion, Mr. Saml. Whitlock, both of this city, are about to embark for Europe & will probably leave here in the packet of the 1st of May. As they will need passports—may I beg the favour of your causing them to be furnished, under cover to me? I will give herewith a description of their persons &c. In addition to this, I am very desirous of obtaining a letter for them to our minister in London & in Paris; and were it not for your uniform urbanity & kindness, I should not dare to express a hope that you would honour me with one. If it be, at all, incompatible with the rules which govern in these matters—I will have only to regret that I have unintentionally presumed too far. I will take leave to add that they are young men of agreeable manners, of unexceptionable character, & not likely to do discredit to their friends or their country; and that my son will be most happy to take charge of any commissions which you may be pleased to entrust to him. They are both recent graduates of Columbia College, & go abroad with the object of improvement, as well as of passing a year or so agreeably. I beg pardon for this troubling you and am, with great respect, Dear Sir, Your obt. servant

Both Tucker and Whitlock had graduated from Columbia College, class of 1837, three years behind Philip Rhinelander. Their fathers, Fanning Tucker and William Whitlock, were men of substance. Some years earlier, in 1832, Whitlock senior had founded a line of packet ships serving Havre, comprising the *Albany*, the *Duchesse d'Orleans*, and others. Earlier, in 1824, when young Sam was only a boy of about five, his father had volunteered the 95-foot *Cadmus*, in which he owned a controlling interest, to bring the Marquis of Lafayette, his son, his secretary, and his valet from Havre to New York, after President Monroe had issued a formal invitation. When Lafayette was greeted in New York by the greatest outpouring of ships and spectators ever yet seen in the port, Whitlock was one of the men of the hour.[2] As for Tucker's father, one report said,

This is truly a "tall" good fellow in every sense, being near seven feet in his shoes, as is plain to all men's view, sings an admirable song, and patronizes music and the opera, drives a fine team, and in short is a first rate gentleman, living as a gentleman should, and showing that one can be such without neglecting even the severer engagements of business and the counting room. For where is the better and richer merchant than he among the whole catalogue of shippers?[3]

Before seeing his son off, Fanning Tucker told him to "keep a journal of everything you see and hear. Let this be done every day. Do not postpone it from day to day with the hope of posting it up at the end of the week."

Andrew Lawrence Ireland, about ten years older than Tucker and Whitlock, had entered Hamilton College but had left before graduating with the class of 1827. He became a lawyer and served as a colonel in the New York State militia. When his father, John Ireland, a widower, died in 1836, he and his two older brothers and two older sisters inherited handsome fortunes, and it gave him the impetus to travel.[4]

The departure from New York on May 1, 1838, was quite an event. The diarist George Templeton Strong, just finishing Columbia College, gave a lively description.

All our class wanted to go down to the *Siddons* and see John Hone off, so one or two of us went in and got leave of absence for the class after the first hour. . . . The crowd was outrageous, for there were three packets to go and the *Sirius* besides, and there were lots of passengers, tearful friends, spectators, and loafers. Two thirds of Columbia College were on the wharf amid the jam, besides many of the last Senior class to see Tucker and Whitlock take their departure.[5]

Five ships left New York harbor that day, the *Sirius*, the first steamship to cross the Atlantic, which had arrived from London the previous week and was now returning; and four sailing ships, the *North America* and the *Siddons* for Liverpool, the *St. James* for London, and the *Utica* for Havre.[6] Rhinelander, Tucker, Whitlock, and Ireland sailed on the *Siddons* for Liverpool together with the Willingtons, the Littlefield party, Andrew S. Hamersley (one year behind Rhinelander at Columbia College, and first cousin of John Hamersley who had gone to Egypt in 1834), and George Strong's classmate John Hone and John's two sisters Emily and Maria.

John Hone's uncle, Philip Hone, former mayor of New York in 1826 and 1827, and keeper of a diary ever since he left office, had these comments on the arrival of the first two steamships to cross the Atlantic, the *Sirius* and the *Great Western*. He wrote them on April 23, 1838, the day the *Great Western* followed the *Sirius* into New York harbor.

> The passengers on board the two vessels speak in the highest terms of the convenience, steadiness, and apparent safety of the new mode of conveyance across the ocean. . . . Our countrymen, "desirous of change and pleased with novelty," will rush forward to visit the shores of Europe instead of resorting to Virginia or Saratoga Springs; and steamers will continue to be the fashion until some more dashing adventurer of the go-ahead tribe shall demonstrate the practicability of balloon navigation and gratify their impatience by a voyage over, and not upon, the blue waters in two days, instead of as many weeks.[7]

Three-and-a-half weeks after their departure from New York, Rhinelander, Tucker, Whitlock, and Ireland landed at Liverpool on May 25. And from there, like the Willingtons, the Littlefields and Susan Holmes, and doubtless most of the other passengers on the *Siddons*, they must have made for London to witness the processions and festivities on the day of the coronation of Queen Victoria. But none of them, to my knowledge, except for Susan Holmes, left a surviving record of that event.

A great many Americans traveled to England to witness the coronation of Queen Victoria, among them, as we have seen, the passengers on the *Siddons*. Another New Yorker, who later met up with Philip Rhinelander and his friends in the Mediterranean, may also have gone to London at this time. This was Henry Augustus Cram, born in 1818 and the same age as Tucker and Whitlock. The second of five children of Jacob and Lydia Cram, Henry had graduated from Princeton in 1837 and had a law degree from Harvard. His father, from an old New England family, had become a wealthy New York distiller and moved in educated circles. Henry's older sister (Ann Louise) had married the English actor John Kemble Mason in March 1838, on the occasion of which, as a newspaper report observed, "Mr. Cram has, we understand, very handsomely presented the happy pair with a *cadeau* to the tune of $10,000, to enable them to make the tour of Europe in style, and to be present at the coronation of her most sacred majesty Queen Victoria."[8] Henry Cram may well have sailed for England about the same time, so also to be present at the festivities surrounding the coronation, though neither passport application nor record of his passage on a packet is preserved.

Once in Europe, John Tucker did indeed keep a diary as his father had recommended, but the excerpts from it, which were published more than a hundred years ago—sadly the original is missing—record events only in Egypt and Turkey.[9] Philip Rhinelander also kept a diary, which has survived and, more importantly, covers in detail the full and rich Mediterranean portion of their tour, from the time he and his friends left Civitàvecchia (the port of Rome) in Italy on their way to Malta and Athens to the time they arrived months later in Constantinople.[10]

Rhinelander boarded the French steamer *Minos* at Civitàvecchia on February 24, 1839, bound for Malta. With him were Tucker, Whitlock, and Ireland, and also a Mr. Seymour from Georgia. The four New Yorkers had been traveling for a year after reaching London and before boarding the steamer in the Mediterranean, but we know little of their itineraries and activities. The late nineteenth-century biographer of Tucker says that he lived part of the time in Paris to study French and take singing instruction and part of the time in Italy to learn Italian. From hints in Rhinelander's diary, we know that prior to traveling in the East he (and presumably the others) had visited London, Paris, Venice, Rome, and Naples, and at one point he reports, in remarking on the departure of their servant Antonio, that Antonio had accompanied some of them from Paris. When they boarded at Civitàvecchia, they met Henry P. Marshall, who was returning to Bombay after an aborted trip from India to Marseilles. In his own diary Marshall mentions all five men by name, and he went on to say "Of course New York and its inhabitants were often subjects of conversation and comparisons were drawn between society and thought at home and on the continent. Col. Ireland could talk of nothing to a foreigner but the United States and he made himself the laughing stock."

On the next leg of their trip, on the French steamer *Lycurgus* from Malta to the Greek island of Syra (February 28 to March 4), Rhinelander mentions in his diary some of his fellow passengers, among them Henry P. Marshall whom he describes as "a young man and very agreeable." He also saw John Lutzo: he was a self-styled Greek prince—his family a Hospodar of Wallachia—returning from London as a representative of the Court of Athens to the coronation of Queen Victoria—together with his wife, son, two daughters, and a French governess. There were Prussians, Russians, and Germans as well as English on their way to India, perhaps as many as forty passengers in all. Rhinelander was mortified that so many Americans traveled in ignorance of other languages. One of the passengers, whom he at first mistook for an Englishman, was a Prussian who spoke Russian, French, Italian, English, Turkish and his own native tongue. "The time which we devote to the acquaintance of the dead languages which are soon forgotten," Rhinelander observed "they give to learning modern tongues. . . . It is no uncommon thing to hear Shake-speare and Byron quoted by the misnamed Russian bears."

Stopping in Syra, already a steamship hub, Rhinelander, Tucker, Whitlock, and three Americans companions (but not Henry Marshall) took another French steamer, the *Mentor*, back to Athens. With them were most of the other passengers, including John Lutzo returning from Queen Victoria's coronation with his family, and two English ladies, sisters, the Misses Walsh, "pious, accomplished, zealous, devoted Chris-tians," whom Henry Marshall had been asked to escort from Marseilles and whom he now turned over to the Rev. John Hill, the American mis-sionary stationed in Athens, who had come to Syra to collect them and take them on to Athens where they would teach in his school. Only nine passengers, including Henry Marshall, went on to Alexandria.

In Athens the six Americans met Christopher Evangeles, the same American-educated Greek boy who had called on Susan Holmes while she was in quarantine in Piraeus the year before. Evangeles had been brought as a twelve-year-old refugee from Smyrna to New York by Peter Vandervoort and Russell E. Glover, a ship's captain. He had com-pleted his education at Columbia, graduating a class ahead of Tucker and Whitlock, who knew him, as did everybody including Susan Holmes, as Christy. In 1836 he had returned to his homeland. Rhinelander and his friends spent the better part of a week touring the sights with their Greek-born former classmate. He says that as a troop of six Americans they visited the school established by the American missionary the Rev. John H. Hill who had come with his wife to Athens about 1830, and whom they would have met on board ship from Syra to Athens. By this time Mr. Seymour of Georgia seems no longer to have been with them, instead a Mr. Fleming of South Carolina. The sixth American must have been the New Yorker Henry Augustus Cram (mentioned above), who probably joined them in Malta. The boys also saw Petro Mavromichalis, who asked about Dr. Mott and Miss Holmes. The latter had clearly made an impression on the Greek hero, and probably on Rhinelander as well: They had sailed together on the *Siddons*.

Years later, in 1854, on a visit to New York, Christy included in a news-paper article a seemingly minor event he remembered during his days with the boys in Athens but one which clearly meant much to him; it con-cerned Tucker, who Christy knew had later become an Episcopal priest.

A minister of the Gospel, the Rev. Mr. J. Tucker. He and I were boys together. In a book he borrowed from me at Athens, when he was leaving

Athens, he placed twenty francs in gold. As soon as he left I found out the gold piece. I was going to run after him to give it back to him, but I felt very hungry and I kept it.[11]

Then, on March 10, the six Americans returned to Syra where they changed steamers for Alexandria. At this point Rhinelander wrote in his dairy that with the nonarrival of the Malta boat in Syra he would not receive his letter of credit and therefore was on his way to Egypt without funds, and that much against his principles he would have to borrow them. From another source we know that his bankers, from whom he was expecting a letter of credit, were Welles & Co. in Paris, and that more than a week later, after reaching Cairo, he indeed borrowed just over a thousand francs from Andrew Ireland at one-half percent interest per month.

Landing in Alexandria on March 15, 1839, they faced the usual raucous greeting of boys and men pressing on them the use of their donkeys, which they accepted and rode to the Hotel d'Europe "situated in the grand square, a large open space surrounded by fine buildings generally occupied by consuls, whose several flags displayed present quite a gay appearance." Wandering through the narrow, crowded streets, they marveled at the exotic locals, then went out to see Pompey's Pillar and Cleopatra's Needles. Rhinelander had his hair cut and bought a tarbouche, a red cap of cloth with its tassel of blue silk, under which he would wear a white skullcap. From John Gliddon they hired an eight-man *canjiah*, with its two great triangular lateen sails, to take them along the Mahmoudiya canal to Atfih and up the Nile to Bulaq, the port of Cairo. To signal their nationality they acquired or had made an American flag and fired a salute as they raised it on the mast. Rhinelander reported that their party now consisted of seven persons and two servants. He says that two more had joined them since they had left Italy: One was Henry Cram (who was with them in Athens), the other a Mr. Betancourt from Cuba (probably Manuel de Betancourt), otherwise not known.

In Cairo Rhinelander and his friends met George Gliddon "who seems to remember with pleasure his sojourn in America. He spoke of it with feelings of joy, and took pride in showing us the memorials of the country which he had collected, his rifles, pictures of our steamers, and our public buildings, horns from a deer of Elm Lake." In Cairo he also purchased "several suits of Turkish clothes which are to be worn on the Nile." And he bought a gun. They "went to the citadel to see some elephants presented to the Pacha, which had been sent to him by the honorable East India Company." From Gliddon they chartered a forty-ton riverboat, the *Americana*, the same one that the Haights had taken two years earlier. For provisions they laid on rice, macaroni, coffee, pickles, fruit, and more, not omitting tobacco. Along the way they would buy chickens, eggs, and pigeons.

At that point, passing up the opportunity to sail south toward Thebes on the Nile, Ireland and Betancourt departed, having seen enough of Egypt, taking with them the servant Antonio who, as we said, had been with them since Paris. And by this time, the young American consul to Muscat, Henry P. Marshall, was about to leave Suez for Bombay, the second time he had made the trip eastward, and the third time he had crossed the Indian Ocean. After leaving Rhinelander and the other Americans in the harbor of Syra, he went directly to Egypt, arriving on March 6, and after ten days in Alexandria and in Cairo where he revisited some sites and saw new ones, he left for Suez. There, on March 19 while waiting for the steamer, he met a group of Europeans who had also crossed the desert from Cairo for Suez but were not bound for India: the Rev. Henry Tattam (collector of Coptic manuscripts) and his stepdaughter, Eliza Platt (although he does not name them); the Rev. John Lieder and his wife; Alexander Tod (a Scottish merchant who had married John Gliddon's daughter Emma in 1833); and Emma's sister, still a Miss Gliddon. Also with Tod was a Mr. Roberts of Alexandria, but not David Roberts, the artist. Tod and Roberts were to return to Cairo; the rest were to go to Sinai. Henry Marshall sailed to India on the English steamer *Berenice* on March 24.

Rhinelander and His Friends on the Nile

And from Cairo, on the very same day, March 24, Rhinelander and his four companions set off up the Nile. And as in Athens, Alexandria, and Cairo, Rhinelander filled his diary with observations and thoughts. Opposite Beni Suef he wrote, "I lay on deck this evening till a late hour watching Orion and the Pleiades." The next day he changed out of his western clothes.

> I now put on for the first time my costume which I had bought in Cairo. It is the Nazim or regenerated dress of the Turk. It consists of wide pants gathered round the waist in thick folds, which hangs a little below the knees, from thence downward they are tight fitting close to the leg, like a gaiter. These for coolness I wear of white linen. My vest is of rich silk and over this is worn a large jacket with sleeves open to the elbow. Around my waist is wound a sash of crimson silk which passes round and round in

many folds, it being six yards in length. In this I bear my arms, pistol and knife. On my head I wear the tarbouche, and on my feet are the double Turkish slippers, the inner of yellow, the outer of red morocco. Thus arranged I wander on the banks or in Arab villages, staring and stared at. I might almost pass for a real Turk, were it not for my specs.[12]

After Manfalout he observed:

In the evening we passed a boat bearing the French flag. In passing we talked Nile with her passengers. It is pleasant to meet here in Africa those who speak a language that we have heard before. In Egypt among Arabs and Turks even a Frenchman seems a countryman.

About his visit to the Temple of Esna on April 3 he wrote:

A door was opened and I was literally entranced, so totally unexpected was the scene of grandeur which broke upon me, a grand chamber in which rose twenty-four columns, of great size and perfect preservation, covered with hieroglyphics, the capitals of each one different from its neighbor. . . . At no time during my whole travels have I felt such emotions of admiration and astonishment as on that first view of the portico of the temple at Esna. Now are equaled all my expectations. I have reaped the fruits of my long journey.

At Philae, after copying the first part of the inscription of the French, Rhinelander wrote:

Let not travelers talk of the dangers and difficulties of a voyage upon the Nile, when an army marched even into Nubia, and in the face of enemies. The surface on which this inscription appears has been smoothed, all hieroglyphics removed, and above the historical record appears the following: *Le page d'histoire ne doit pas etre salee.* Whether this refers to the obliterated hieroglyphics or to the French inscription I know not.

It was actually directed at the European and American tourists who wrote their names too close to the great inscription. An Englishman, Eliot Warburton, on the Nile in early 1843, also quoted the inscription and recalled that John L. Stephens said in his book that he had cut his name close to the French inscription. Warburton went on to say that a subsequent French traveler had eradicated it, and had written the warning just quoted.[13]

At the temple at Edfu on the way downriver, Rhinelander and one of his companions had an adventure.

We set out to return to our boat alone and wandering over fields their uniformity unbroken by a single tree we lost our way and wandered for about two hours not knowing whither to direct our steps. While traversing the plain we were suddenly arrested by someone who called loudly upon us. We looked round and saw seated on a fast donkey a dark looking arab, dress in rich costume with robe of silk and streaming turban, and bearing before him on the pommel of his saddle, a most suspiciously ugly gun to which he pointed most significantly, gradually approaching near to us and continuing his address in Arabic. I grasped by my Nubian club and waited patiently for the issue of this scene. He halted within a few yards of us, and with a grim smile raised his gun, and pointing it towards us, showed us suspended from the muzzle a fine fat hare which had just shot and which he wished us to purchase. We declined however unable to bargain in Arabic. We then separated peacefully he galloping towards the town and we continuing the search for our boat. I was disappointed at this result. Every circumstance had promised an adventure, and then so quiet a conclusion was so bad. If one cannot be robbed or murdered why should one leave Italy for adventure, even in that civilized country there is more danger than in barbarous Egypt.

Nearing Karnak along the avenue of sphinxes "at the extremity of the avenue rises the most sublime propylon in Egypt, the most graceful and well proportioned, covered with the most delicate sculptures, forming a meet approach to the grandeur beyond." Within the hypostyle hall with its 134 columns he mused:

Seated on a fallen fragment of the roof, I passed some time wrapped in wonder at the scene around, and in musings on Old Egypt and her kings, on the people and the monarchs who have left these stupendous memorials of their power and greatness.

Downriver at Asyut, he wrote:

We were most fortunate in the cook whom we hired in Cairo. He possesses in an eminent degree the art of producing variety from sameness; our meals consist of chickens, pigeons and eggs. Our Sundays varied by eggs, chickens, and pigeons. The immense quantities of the eatables which we have consumed is almost incredible.

After leaving Egypt Rhinelander itemized their expenses on the Nile, in particular their food: 822 eggs, 180 chickens, 60 pigeons. In addition they bought twenty-six pounds of butter, milk, onions, bread, thirty or so melons, coffee, oil, salt, spice, ten pounds of sugar, two sheep for the crew, charcoal, and a goose.

Back in Cairo on April 27 the five young men saw all the tourist sites starting with the Great Pyramid. On that first day or shortly afterward, Rhinelander met John Caldecott (1801–1849), astronomer royal to the Rajah of Travencore, who was traveling to England to purchase new scientific apparatus to take back to India. He had landed at Quseir on April 12, had crossed the desert to Thebes, and had come downriver just a few days behind the Americans. Rhinelander said he had measured the height of the Pyramid with Wollaston's Thermometrical Barometer.

Over the next two weeks the Americans visited Heliopolis, the Citadel, the mint, the city of the tombs (as he called them), including that of the family of Mehmet Ali, the Mosque of Sultan Hasan, the menagerie of the pasha with its rhinoceros, the slave market, the pasha's railroad, his stables, the military school at Tora, the egg hatchery, the cavalry school, the convent of the Greeks in Old Cairo, the gardens at Shubra. Both Rhinelander and John Tucker described the visit to the egg hatchery, which Ward Nicholas Boylston of Boston had seen some 55 years earlier in 1774. Tucker wrote in his diary:

> To get into them, we crept through a small hole, and found ourselves in an extremely warm and "fleay" place, a chamber about 20 feet long and five side. On one side were ovens or small chambers, in which eggs were deposited; some were bursting the shell, others not so far advanced. On the other side of the passage were chickens just hatched, others three or four weeks old. They manufacture 4000 a month, and are employed all the year with the exception of four months. The chickens are all small, as is the case with the eggs in Egypt.[14]

They also "rode out to the Tombs of the Mamluke Sultans," as Rhinelander called them, and he must mean some of those of the northern cemetery.

> They rise from the desert with dome and minaret in all the richness of Eastern architecture, profuse in ornament. They are from a distance strikingly beautiful, but a nearer approach exhibits a roughness either original or the effects of time. . . . We entered several. . . . The holy of holies

containing the tomb of the founder was closed to the infidels. Through a gilded grating we saw its single tomb of marble covered with gold and hung round with lamps. The pavement of the inner chamber was of tessellated marble. The view from the top of one of the most lofty minarets was next to that of the citadel, the most beautiful that I have seen comprising the Nile and pyramids beyond & on the other side the rich valley bounded by desert sands.

They had a séance with the magician and they saw the newly formed Egyptian library, courtesy of Henry Abbott, an Englishman and former physician in the pasha's navy who had moved to Cairo and would form a notable collection of Egyptian antiquities (discussed a greater length in chapter 19). With 'Dr.' Abbott they also had a Turkish-style dinner.

A small round table about 18 inches in height was placed in the centre of the room, and upon it were placed napkins, bread, and glasses for eight persons. A servant bore round a basin holding our hands over which water was poured upon them. These lavations over we clustered around the table seating outselves on cushions or divans. Soup was then brought in, the bowl being placed in the middle of the table. From this common reservoir we all helped outselves by means of wooden spoons, each one putting his spoon into the bowl. Various dishes were then introduced in succession, from each of which, with our fingers we conveyed the morsals to our mouths. . . . The order of the courses, in number about fifteen, was all confusion, sweets, fish, flesh, and fowl were introduced with no fixed plan, the only established regulation being that soup shall begin and end the meal. The skill shown by our host, carving the fowls was astonishing, without knife or fork. He used nature's instruments, and taking them in his hands, separated each joint most accurately and gracefully. . . . Our meal finished, water was again handed round, then the Chibouk and coffee concluded the entertainment. I was much pleased with this feast of reason and of soul. The guests brought close together are sociable and inclined to merriment.

Of all the sites and buildings they saw Rhinelander was most taken with the Mosque of Sultan Hasan, built in the thirteenth and fourteenth centuries and one of the masterpieces of Mamluk architecture in Cairo. Rhinelander was also struck by how courteously they were treated.

Among the changes which a few years have wrought in Egypt none is more remarkable than that which has opened the mosques to Christians. . . . No more is now asked than is required in every Christian church. We allow no one to enter a church with covered head and the Musselman applies the same restriction to the feet, his indeed being the most sensible regulation, its object being to prevent any dust or dirt being brought into their chapels. . . . That cleanliness is the only object is proved from the manner in which one of my companions gained admission. He unfortunately wore fashionable Paris trousers, which with their fastened straps forbade the removal of his boots . . . but men in attendance at the door, Musselman sextons, brought clothes which they wrapped about his feet and he enjoyed the same privileges as we in our stocking feet.

Rhinelander carefully described the interior, not omitting what was in poor repair.

Passing the threshold we found ourselves in a large paved court, open to the sky in the centre of which rose a fountain covered. One half of this court, that toward Mecca was laid with matting and here were several Musselmen at their devotions . . . this portion of the court was covered with a roof, from which were hung innumerable lamps. Its eastern wall was covered with numerous inscriptions in Arabic, verses from the Koran . . . . Adjoining to this court, which composes the body of the mosque, the part open and free to all, is the holy chamber containing the sepulcher of the Sultan, the founder of the building. You enter through large doors of bronze, richly inlaid with gold and silver. The room is square in form and large. In the centre a railing encloses the holy tomb, above which are hanging sacred banners and warlike trophies. A large copy of the Koran is placed upon the tomb. The apartment has once been brilliant with all the richness of Saracenic taste, but now is a mere wreck of former splendour. The pavement . . . has become uneven from the effects of time, and the elaborate Gothic or Saracenic ornaments which once adorned each of the corners, where the ceiling meets the wall, [the so-called stalactite pendentives] have been despoiled of their rich covering of silk, and show only the mouldering framework of wood. The walls too have been discolored and through the now glassless windows numberless pigeons enter. . . . This has been one of the most interesting objects that I have seen in Cairo.

In the evening on May 11, the five young men left Cairo to return north, and on May 14 they reached Atfih on the Nile and transferred to a craft on the Mahmoudiya canal.

Philip Rhinelander and his four friends were back in Alexandria on May 15. Unable to get rooms at the Hotel d'Europe where they had stayed when first in the city, they "found accommodations at Mr. Hill's establishment which is pleasantly situated without the city among palms and flowers." An English couple, returning home from India via the Red Sea port of Quseir and the Nile, found them there. Their published account is anonymous but they must have been Peter Cator and his wife, he a barrister working in India. "The Pasha was an object of particular interest to a party of young American gentlemen who left our hotel in the morning in the hope of seeing his highness in divan."[15]

On May 16 Rhinelander wrote in his diary:

Mehmet Ali is now in Alexandria, but as our stay is short we cannot be presented. We expected however that we might obtain at least a sight of him. He usually holds divans every morning and we hope by mixing with the crowd in the ante chamber to see the great man, but the divan was finished for the day when we reached the palace. We however saw him seated in a window giving audience to one of the European Consuls. He is a venerable old man, with a flowing grey beard. He is aged sixty-seven. The palace is extensive, and situated on the harbour.

The British artist David Roberts was present at an audience with the pasha that took place four days later, on May 20. His later lithograph complements Rhinelander's observation (plate 30). The palace opens on to the harbor full of ships. Mehmet Ali is seated on a divan in the sunlight with a hookah pipe. Facing him are Patrick Campbell, Her Majesty's consul-general; Lieutenant Thomas Waghorn, promoter of the postal service; David Roberts himself in civilian dress; and Lieutenant Goldsmith, commander of the steamer *Megara*. The next figure, also in civilian dress and face partially hidden, cannot be positively identified: perhaps John Pell (traveling with Roberts); or John A. Dunlop, just arrived from India; or the Rev. Henry Tattam, a collector of Coptic manuscripts. Standing at the rear is Alfred S. Walne, a surgeon and vice-consul of Cairo. Among those behind the pasha in eastern dress are Boghos Bey, the first minister; Artin Bey, the interpreter (the interview was conducted in Italian through him); Seyd Bey, Admiral of the fleet; Abbas Bey, governor of Cairo; and Linant de Bellefonds, the French explorer, architect, and engineer who had first come out to Egypt in 1818 and was now working for the pasha. Seated on the ground is a scribe, surely belonging to the court, taking notes.[16] Coffee is about to be served. On the day that Rhinelander caught a glimpse of the pasha, he and his four friends would have been outside, below the balustrade, just out of sight.[17]

On May 16, Rhinelander "shipped to Smyrna, thence to be sent to America, all the curiosities which I have collected during my stay in Egypt." These included a Nubian club, spears, a shield of crocodile skin, and the complete dress of a Nubian damsel with all her jewelry. On May 17, the five Americans went on board the French steamer *Leonidas* bound for Syra. Tucker said that also on board, among the forty-five passengers, was "a Mr. Calhoun, a missionary." He, of course, was Simeon H. Calhoun, agent of the American Bible Society who, having completed his tour of the Holy Land, had come from Beirut to Alexandria in order to return to Smyrna. Rhinelander added that with them was Antoine Barthélémy Clot Bey. Clot Bey was the French medical officer appointed surgeon-in-chief by Mehmet Ali in 1823 and given the title Bey in 1831. "He has quite a menagerie, consisting of a noble lion, a gazelle, an ibex, birds of various kinds, &c."[18]

After reaching Syra, the five young men opted for the better lazaretto in Piraeus than that in Syra to pass many days of quarantine, just as Nathaniel Littlefield and Susan Holmes had done some months earlier on their way to Athens. There, as Rhinelander wrote, "all the English and American prisoners have formed a club, and having hired a saloon we take our meals together . . . . we have persuaded a restaurateur and a servant to put themselves in quarantine to wait on us during the day." Among the English with them was John Caldecott, astronomer royal to the Rajah of Travancore, whom they had seen in Cairo. Clot Bey was not with them, having traveled from Syra to Malta to undergo quarantine there.

Confined to the lazaretto and with time for contemplation, Rhinelander wrote on May 26 some of the few remarks that expressed his own feelings.

Can man ever be perfectly happy? I who have every earthly blessing, still feel in my soul a longing after something still unpossessed, and this is Sympathy. I have health and you and a wealth of competence, light spirits and a glad heart, but still I enjoy all this alone. There is no heart, here at least, which beats in unison with mine, none that shares my pleasures. These are all my own alone, and even at home it is much the same. Even there I suffer from the absence of any motive for exertion and pass my days in listlessness and inactivity. Where there are none to praise or blame, man knows not his own powers.

After ten days of quarantine, they returned to the island of Syra and took passage on the French packet *Scamandre* for Smyrna. Upon landing Rhinelander noted, "This being Sunday, flags were flying from all the Consulates, and here my eyes were gladdened by the sight of my country's banner, the stars and stripes, which floated from the consulate." They stopped at the house of the American consul, David W. Offley—Offley had just succeeded his father, David Offley, longtime consul, who had died the previous year—and they admired the beautiful Greek girls. During the space of a week Rhinelander and his friends met several American missionaries and visited the local sites, but they did not venture as far as Ephesus.

From Smyrna, they sailed by the Austrian steamer, the *Maria Dorothea*, to Constantinople. Rhinelander described the passengers:

> The number of first class passengers is small, but with deck passengers we are laden down. Every part of the deck is covered with them. . . . Among this crowd are representatives from the four quarters of the globe, a motley crew, Citizens of the United States, from America; Austrians, Greeks, Portuguese and Poles from Europe; Nubians and Egyptians from Africa; Turks, Armenians, Indians, and the Syrian Maronites from Asia.

On June 10 they steamed into the Sea of Marmora and there Rhinelander, who was clearly aware of the political issues of the region, observed the sultan's fleet:

> Passed part of the fleet of the Sultan under sail towards the Dardanelles, probably with the view of joining the rest of the naval power at Gallippoli [*sic*], and thence to put to sea and chastise the refractory pacha of Egypt. This portion of the fleet consists of three ships of the line, three frigates, four smaller vessels, and two steamers. The giant ship *Marmoudie*, said to be the largest in the world, sailed in this division; one of the frigates which was noticed by all, conspicuous from its beauty and grace was built by Mr. Rhodes, the American successor of Eckford.[19]

The sultan's fleet had left Constantinople the day before, bound for the Dardanelles, to await orders to sail to Egypt. The fleet ultimately did leave for Alexandria, but instead of chastising Mehmet Ali, defected to him.[20]

Once in Constantinople the Americans crossed from where they landed to Pera, the European quarter, and found quarters at the Hotel of Madame Roboli opposite the ruins of the French legation, which together with the British and Dutch embassies had burned in the great fire of early August 1831. Now, in 1839, the rebuilding of the French embassy had just gotten underway.[21] During their stay in Constantinople, Rhinelander and his friends went to a Turkish theater, ascended the Galata tower to see the view, visited the Byzantine monuments, and took a caique across the Bosporus to Scutari, where they witnessed a performance of the howling dervishes. They saw the aging sultan as he was rowed up the Bosporus in a twenty-four-oared caique to a mosque, and heard a band play the sultan's march composed by Giuseppe Donizetti, brother of the opera composer. They witnessed a launch of a cutter designed for the sultan by the American Foster Rhodes and after the ceremony dined with him, and later went aboard a steamer also recently designed by Rhodes; in the pantry they were surprised by champagne glasses but learned that sparkling wine was not forbidden by the Qur'an. In the suite of Prince George of Cambridge, a grandson of George III and cousin of Queen Victoria, and with Lady and Lord Carnarvon (Henry Herbert, 1800–1849) they visited Hagia Sofia. They spent time in the bazaars and dined well. On one of their last days they encountered another party of Americans, the Rev. Dr. Charles Lowell traveling with his wife and youngest daughter.[22] They had spent the winter in Rome, and were now on their way to Rhodes, Cyprus, Damascus, Beirut, and Egypt. All told, Rhinelander and his friends spent nearly three weeks in the great city.

"Dreadful Accident on the Danube"

Meanwhile, before the end of April, during the time that Rhinelander and his friends were still on the Nile, Ireland and Betancourt had reached Constantinople. There they encountered Messrs. Chamberlain, Swords, and Bennett, who were about to travel to Vienna to obtain better equipment for the magnetic telegraph, since a first demonstration to the sultan had been unsatisfactory. McLellan and Brown were no longer with them, for they had gone their own way from Alexandria to Malta.

Betancourt, Ireland, Chamberlain, Swords, Bennett, and other passengers left Constantinople May 6 on board the *Ferdinando Primo*, the first of a relay of steamers toward Vienna. The steamer route led up the Bosporus, into the Black Sea to the mouth of the Danube, and up the Danube to Orsova where there was an obligatory ten-day quarantine. Freed from quarantine at Orsova, the fifteen passengers and nearly ten servants boarded a barge early in the morning of May 14 to continue upriver to Drenkova. That afternoon, as the craft was towed by horses around a bend in a treacherous stretch of the river, it failed to respond to the helmsman, veered away from the bank, and capsized to float keel upward. There were only five survivors: Betancourt of Cuba, Ireland and Swords of New York, Bennett of Charleston, and one other, apparently the commander of the vessel. As the upturned craft was swept downstream, they managed to swim to the keel and hang on for half an hour before being rescued. Among those who drowned was Mellen Chamberlain, whose body, found in his cabin, was identified from the name engraved on his watch; also the dragoman of the Austrian embassy at Constantinople; and Chevalier Steinberg, the Austrian consul at Salonica; in addition two British officers returning home on furlough from India, who had landed at Quseir on the Red Sea and had traveled down the Nile, namely Captain M. Joseph and Lieutenant Duncan Pirie;[23] and, it must be said, all of the servants.

Bennett described it in a letter dated May 18, Orsova (where they had been put back in quarantine!), addressed to the *Charleston Courier*. The United States Consulate in Vienna submitted a formal report to Washington dated June 16, 1839, based on the accounts of Bennett and Swords, which gave additional information. The report stated that Chamberlain's body "was interred in the church yard of the village called Szinica. A collection of £12 sterling was made in order to erect him a monument which sum was deposited in the hands of the British consul, General Robert Gilmour Colquhoun, Esq., from Bucharest, who was just then in quarantine." An obituary of Chamberlain was published in an American newspaper in August.[24] Egypt was safe compared to this. The wreck was visible to Danube travelers for nearly two years.[25]

Rhinelander and His Friends Leave for Vienna

Leaving Constantinople on July first, a month-and-a-half after the Danube disaster, Rhinelander and his friends took the relay of steamers up the Bosporus, along the Black Sea coast to the mouth of the Danube, and up the river to Orsovo for quarantine, and from there, on to Vienna. With them for much of the way were two young Englishmen, Messrs. Thring and Rawnsley.[26] There is no mention in the surviving portions of Tucker's diary that they learned of the accident that befell their former traveling companions, but it seems hard to believe that they did not witness the wreck and learn from those they encountered on the way what had happened.

Arriving in Vienna on August 5, they did business and toured the city, though Tucker and Rhinelander were sick with chills and headaches. They both summoned physicians. On the ninth Tucker said he had such a headache that the chambermaid had sat up all night applying ice to his head every five minutes, and they were no better in the next two days. Tucker wrote the following in his diary for August 11:

> At nine o'clock Rhinelander was much better; at two o'clock he was much altered for the worse; he became extremely enervated and ill. The physician was sent for. He was much astonished when he saw his patient, and hurrying into my room, with his face flushed, asked, "Is he a Catholic?" At first, I did not perceive his meaning, but afterwards I soon perceived that my poor friend was just hovering between life and death. At four o'clock, he was still much more enervated; another physician was called in. The disease had changed to cholera, and poor Phil's life was despaired of. We inquired for a Protestant clergyman: in this gay city, no one was to be found, who spoke English. One of our English friends, Thring, kindly volunteered to read the "Service for the Visitation of the Sick," in which my poor friend entered with much interest. I was anxious to leave my bed, and visit my sick friend, but was forbidden. He sent me messages to his friends, which I was obliged to commit to Cram, in consequence of my inability to write. He lingered until nine o'clock, in great agony and anxious for death. He said "he was happy" and that "he loved his sister." At nine o'clock, he calmly died away.[27]

He was buried in Vienna two days later. Once again the American consul in Vienna, J.G. Schwarz, had to write to the Honorable John Forsyth, secretary of the Department of State.

> In my last report [number] 17, I naturally expressed the hope of it being the last announce[ment] of a death, but alas, I have to make other such sad notices. A young hopeful citizen, Mr. Philip Rhinelander, of New York, age 24. . . . This young man was seized with a fever during his passage on the Danube from Constantinople. The sickness was a species of cholera. His traveling companions informed me that a sister of the deceased was lately married to a Mr. John A. King, Jr. in New York. On 15th August I wrote the sad news to Mr. King, Jr. whose reply confirmed the relationship. . . . Among the rather disorderly papers was an account book by which it seems that Messrs. Welles & Co. of Paris were still indebted to him 8631 francs, 25 cts., besides interest. On the other hand the said account book showed him to be indebted to Andrew L. Ireland . . . in the loan of francs 1004, and 32 cents for eight months, from 23d March 1839, at one-half percent, interest per month.[28]

That was the sum Rhinelander had borrowed from Ireland in Cairo just before they separated. And it was in a second letter written to the secretary of state (this time Daniel Webster) that we learn that Philip was co-proprietor, presumably with his sister Mary, of two houses, one of which on Broadway was said to have been valued in excess of $100,000.[29] The American consul in Vienna also spoke of Philip's writing desk on which, we must suppose, he wrote his diary.

19 | AFTER 1839

A fter Rhinelander's death in Vienna, his companions were stunned. Tucker wrote:

> I cannot think of one pleasant hour, but that I recall to mind the friend
> who has been taken from us. But he died happy: this should be to all
> sufficient consolation. . . . With what pleasure we had all looked forward
> to Vienna! The amusements we had set apart to add to our pleasure—what
> are they now to us? It is so unexpected! In Egypt we looked for sickness
> and danger, but at Vienna we expected to find nothing but amusement. We
> have been so intimately associated since we left America, that I feel as if I
> had lost a near relative—it makes such ravage in our little party![1]

But they pulled themselves together and continued traveling, to Linz,
Salzberg, Berchtesgaden, and Munich, where they arrived September 1.
There Tucker's diary stops. The boys returned to New York, Fleming and
Cram on December 9, 1839, Whitlock and Tucker on April 14, 1840.

John I. Tucker graduated in July 1844 from the Episcopal Theological
Seminary in Chelsea in New York (now General Theological Seminary),
and was ordained an Episcopal priest. He then became deacon in charge
of a small parish in Troy, New York, and in succeeding years played a
leading role in introducing choral music into the liturgy of the Episcopal Church. Tucker went abroad again in 1850 and 1851 revisiting many
places in France and Italy he had seen on his first trip in 1838. He died
unmarried in 1895.[2]

Henry McVickar, who had been John Bard's traveling companion
in Egypt, also attended the Episcopal Theological Seminary in New

York, one class behind Tucker. McVickar was one of four students accused in 1844 and 1845 of promoting Romanism in the fashion of the more Roman Catholic ideas of the Oxford Movement, and though he remained an Episcopalian he withdrew from the seminary.[3] Despite that he was called to serve in several churches in upstate New York, among them a missionary church at Lake George, before his early death in 1851.

And remarkably, a third traveler to Egypt, William Edward Snowden, class of 1838 at Columbia, who had visited Egypt that very year and had returned from Alexandria with the family of the Rev. John Paxton on the brig *Carroll* bringing giraffes to New York, also entered Episcopal Theological Seminary in New York. But owing to poor health he left after a year and went south to North Carolina where he became chaplain to the family of Mrs. Joseph H. Skinner. In 1842, soon after being ordained to the priesthood by the Bishop of North Carolina, he married a daughter of Mrs. Skinner. In the course of his life Snowden had at least eight children, and served for forty years as rector of a sequence churches in South Carolina, Maryland, Connecticut, and New York State.[4]

We are well informed about Cram, one of the companions of Rhinelander, Tucker, and Whitlock, in part through the diary of George Templeton Strong, the same writer who had seen Tucker and Whitlock off on the packet ship *Siddons* from New York in May 1838. With a degree from the Harvard law school, Cram joined Strong at his father's firm. On June 9, 1840, Strong wrote:

> We're to have a new "student" (in the technical sense of the term), that distinguished individual Mr. Augustus Cram: son of that respectable boiler of the devil's teapot, old Cram the distiller. He's going to be a great bore, I'm afraid; however, he has probably addicted himself to the law merely as a gentlemanly way of doing nothing, and we probably shan't be troubled with him for more than half an hour per diem after the first fortnight. He's a graduate of Princeton, and the reputation he bore there was that of a very talented, lazy, conceited, overbearing puppy. . . . He's a traveled gentleman withal—recently returned from the grand tour of Constantinople, Mesopotamia, and Chinese Tartary besides, for ought I know; and when he got back, he said he thought New York "quite too contracted." The infatuated youth seems to be making desperate efforts to raise a moustache, but I doubt the ultimate success of the project.[5]

But observe Strong's comments four months later, on October 2:

Cram, I think, is not the despicable character I supposed him to be. Notwithstanding his moustache, his distingué air, and the exquisite cut of his coat, he is decidedly intelligent, very well informed in matters that can be drawn from books, and what is a rarer merit, he has gathered knowledge for himself by traveling with his eyes open.[6]

Henry Cram was married in 1849 to Katherine Sergeant, with whom he had seven children, and he became a leading trial lawyer in the city. In July 1869, Strong gave his final appraisal of Cram, on the occasion of his colleague's father's death.

Died old Jacob Cram at eighty-seven, a remarkable old codger who would have made an admirable study of a Silenus. A notable distiller in his day . . . he doubtless leaves a million or so at least. So H.A. Cram, who comes in for a quarter, will doubtless give up legal practice altogether. He's already very rich, but I regret to say that prosperity has developed his bad traits and made him insufferable, purse-proud, arrogant, and dictatorial, and lavish in evil speaking beyond all example. He describes every man he don't like, and he likes but few, as being simply an unmitigated brute, scoundrel, thief, and pirate, and generally *knows*, sir, yes *knows*, what he's telling you to be true—that he ought to be in the State Prison for fraud or rape or perjury. These views he likes to set forth in rather impassioned dinner-table harangues, as if he were practicing for his next jury.[7]

That may be reflected in the portrait of Cram painted by John Singer Sargent in 1893, the year before his death.[8] Two of his children later became great friends of the novelist Edith Wharton, near to whom they lived in western Massachusetts.[9] In 1986 the old Cram estate at Highwood, next to Wharton's, was purchased by the Boston Symphony Orchestra and added to Tanglewood, the site of the summer music festival.

Samuel Whitlock also became a lawyer and also joined George Templeton Strong's father's firm, about the time that Cram did so. On June 12, 1840, Strong wrote, "Whitlock is going to enter the office! He'll do very well if he isn't spoiled by his travels."[10] Some ten years later, in February 1850, he married Jeannette Emmet McEvers.[11] Their son, Bache McEvers Whitlock, was born in June 1852. Four years later, on May 18, 1856, Strong wrote, "Samuel Whitlock is dangerously ill at Staten Island with remittent fever." Two days later he added:

Samuel H. Whitlock is to be buried on Thursday, the first of that happy hopeful dozen of law students who took the world so easily and found my father's office so pleasant a rendezvous. Sad to think of Sam Whitlock's past nonchalant gaiety and good nature with Cram and Pete Strong . . . . Sadder to remember his enviable vigor and enterprise, walking, leaping and climbing years ago when we were together at Catskill.[12]

Strong did not forget him. On June 27, 1873, he wrote:

At 68 Wall Street this morning. Young Bache McEvers Whitlock there, having just entered as a student. He is poor Sam Whitlock's eldest son; he inherits his father's kindly pleasant manner, and I regret to say, a little of his mamma's deafness. He and Johnny [George's own son] are studying law in the very same office in which their respective papas had a good time together as law students some thirty-three years ago.[13]

All that was before Messrs. Cadwallader, Wickersham, and Taft joined to give their name to what has become the oldest continuously running law firm in New York.

And Philip Rhinelander was not forgotten. While he was abroad, his sister Mary had married John A. King Jr., whose grandfather Rufus King had been US minister in London, whose father, John Alsop King, would become governor of New York State in 1856, and whose uncle, Charles King, would serve as president of Columbia College from 1849 to 1863. Philip had had an oil miniature done some years earlier, probably on graduating from Columbia, and after his death his sister put it in a mourning frame (plate 29).[14] The eldest child of Philip and Mary King, Mary Rhinelander King, inherited many of the family possessions. When she died unmarried in 1909, she left at least two family portraits to the New-York Historical Society: a miniature watercolor on ivory of Matilda Hoffman (Philip Rhinelander's aunt who had been engaged to Washington Irving but died in 1809), and an oil on canvas of John A. King senior by John Trumbull.[15] But not the miniature of Philip Rhinelander, which seems to have belonged to William C. Rhinelander, one of Philip's uncles, and descended through his heirs and is still owned by a Rhinelander descendant. Philip's sister Mary is likely to have kept his diary, which was probably sent home from the consulate in Vienna to her husband, the executor of Rhinelander's estate, but that document left the family, probably early in the twentieth century and reappeared in the New York book trade in 1978; it is now in my collection in Washington, DC.[16]

The survivors of the Danube disaster, the three Americans, Bennett, Ireland, and Swords, and the one Cuban, Manuel de Betancourt, also continued traveling and made their way separately back to New York. Betancourt arrived in New York from Havre on July 29, 1840, but beyond that I have not been able to trace him. Nor have I been able to trace William Bennett, the young man from Charleston.

Andrew L. Ireland had attended Hamilton College but had left before graduating with the class of 1827. Before traveling he had inherited, together with his two brothers and two sisters, a considerable fortune when his widowed father died in 1836.[17] In the late 1850s or early 1860s, he purchased Isola Bella, an island in front of Scarron village near the Adirondack region of upper New York State. "Ireland [was] a wealthy gentleman of New York, who went there in search of health, and who spent large sums of money in subduing the savage features of the island, erecting a pleasant summer mansion upon it, and in changing the rough and forbidding aspect of the whole domain into one of beauty and attractiveness."[18] He died in 1873.

About Charles R. Swords, the fourth survivor of the disaster, we are better informed. After reaching Vienna he went on to Italy. Isaac McLellan, still traveling with Samuel Brown, met him in Milan on July 18. Swords had been with them in the East. "We were rejoiced to see our old friend Swords here. He gave us an interesting account of his travels, after leaving us in Egypt—his visit to Constantinople and up the Danube—and the disastrous accident which befell his party. He is traveling with an agreeable party, a Mrs. Shaw and daughter, the latter a very pretty and pleasing little girl."[19] They saw him and the Shaws several days later in Como and made arrangements to go over the pass with them into Switzerland. In mid-October 1839, Swords returned to New York from Havre on the packet ship *Erie*. Some years later he married Sarah Willis and had three children, Lydia, Mary, and Charles Robert, born between 1860 and 1872.[20] The family lived in New York City and had a residence in Hudsonville, New York. He became a trustee of Columbia in 1870, and died in 1881.

Samuel G. Brown and Isaac McLellan also soon returned home to resume their careers. McLellan continued to practice law and write poetry and became an expert on fishing.[21] Samuel G. Brown returned to the United States on the steamer *Great Western*, arriving March 7, 1840. Some months earlier, in late 1839, he had been appointed professor of oratory and belles-lettres at Dartmouth College, where his father, now deceased, had been president. He retained that position until the later

1860s, and then, from 1867 to 1881, he served as president of Hamilton College in New York State.[22]

John Bard, who had traveled with Henry McVickar in 1838 and had met Susan Holmes afterward in Rome and Naples, returned to New York on the same ship with her and with Frances Butler. More than a decade later he married Margaret Johnston, from a wealthy family, which made him financially independent. The New York diarist George Templeton Strong was not charitable in his appraisal of this match. On January 15, 1849, he wrote, "Miss Johnston is engaged to John Bard: a fashionable fool purchased with the profits of thirty years' successful ironmongery."[23] In 1853 they bought a Hudson River estate, Blithewood, and renamed it Annandale. Soon afterward, in 1860, John Bard founded St. Stephens College, designed to provide education for young men destined for the Episcopal ministry, and provided it with much of the land that belonged to his family.[24] Still located in Annandale-on-Hudson, St. Stephens was renamed Bard College in 1934 and thrives today.

Of the later life of Dudley Haydon, who traveled with Valentine Mott in 1838, we have only snippets. In 1849, he averted being involved in a duel with Dr. David W. Yandell. That same year he was one of several delegates from Desha County to a convention in Memphis. On December 14, 1854, he married Anna Gillespie at "Hollywood" in Adams County, Mississippi, which became their residence. Their oldest son died there in June 1863. In the Civil War he was a major attached to the staff of General Albert Sidney Johnston of the Confederate Army whose death he witnessed during the Battle of Shilloh in 1862, as reported in the Natchez Courier. He was still alive in 1885 when he gave an interview to the Memphis Daily Appeal of April 12, on recollections of General Johnston. In the bibliography of a recent biography of General William Preston, it is stated that the Houghton Library at Harvard possesses papers of Dudley M. Haydon.[25] We would like to know more because he was the first of many Americans from Kentucky to visit Egypt over the next decades.

Susan Holmes, who had been traveling with Nathaniel Littlefield in Egypt, reached New York with Frances Butler on August 22, 1839, without knowing that her traveling companion would die in Leamington. Less than a year later, in May 1840, she married Alexander Hamilton Bishop, Yale class of 1830, pastor of the First Reformed Church of Astoria. They had two children, Gilbert Livingston Bishop and Susan Holmes Bishop, who are shown together in a daguerreotype of about 1854 owned by the Library Company of Philadelphia.[26] In 1847, much too young, Susan died, aged 31.

Susan's dear friend Harriet Willington had married William Young. In Paris Mr. Willington had offered Young a job at his newspaper, the *Charleston Courier*. Back home, however, he came to realize that his son-in-law's views on slavery would not sit well with the paper's readers; as a result he purchased in 1848, in his son-in-law's name, the New York *Albion*, an Anglo-American newspaper where William Young became editor and remained so for nearly two decades.[27] For William and Harriet Elizabeth, Egypt and even more so quarantine in Malta must have evoked wonderful memories.

Nor must we forget Henry P. Marshall, the young US consul to Muscat, who had met Rhinelander, Tucker, Whitlock, and others on board the French government steamers to Malta and Syra in February 1839 as he was on his way back to Bombay so as to return from there to New York. Marshall reached Bombay in April 1839 without mishap. And there in Bombay he boarded the *Archibald Gracie*, the brig sent out by his firm Scoville & Britton, and after months sailing around the Cape of Good Hope and across the Atlantic reached New York on November 28, 1839, nearly a year later than he had expected to return home. His last diary entry reads, "God be praised." He later joined the Seaman's Bank for Savings where he worked until his death in 1888.

The continuing interest in Egypt of one traveler, namely Richard K. Haight, contributed significantly to American knowledge of the Nile and the monuments lining its banks. He collected important publications relating to Egypt, among them the great work *I Monumenti dell'Egitto e della Nubia* by Ippolito Rosellini, a leader of the Franco-Tuscan expedition to Egypt in 1828, published in several volumes beginning in 1832. In a report on Rosellini's death in 1843, the obituary writer states that only three copies of this great work were known to be in the United States: "One, the first imported, belongs to the library of R.K. Haight Esq., of New York."[28] And Haight's interest in the region manifested itself in other ways. The merchant Philip Hone, a former mayor of New York (1826–1827) and keeper of a famous diary, says that Mr. Haight went to a ball on February 29, 1840, dressed as a Turk.[29]

Not long afterward, perhaps in the year 1842, the Haights commissioned a family portrait (plate 31).[30] There we see Richard and Sarah with their four children, Lydia, Richard, David, and Frances, gathered around a table in the library with a map of Asia displayed on it. Selected trophies from their European travels are displayed in the room, a marble copy of Canova's sculpture of the *Three Graces* in a niche between bookcases, and Greek vases, perhaps acquired in Naples, perched on top of the bookcases.[31]

About 1849 all their possessions were moved into a new Italianate mansion on the corner of Fifth Avenue and 15th Street.[32]

Richard Haight's most important contribution to American knowledge of Egypt was his continuing contact with George R. Gliddon, the former American consular agent in Cairo. Gliddon came to the United States in January 1842 and over the next several years gave courses on Egypt to large audiences in East Coast cities: New York, Boston, Philadelphia, Baltimore, Washington, Richmond, Charleston, and Savannah. Haight was one of Gliddon's sponsors in these endeavors and even made his books on Egypt available for his use. The second time Gliddon spoke in Boston, in the winter of 1843 and 1844, the Lowell Institute, endowed by John Lowell who had traveled in Egypt in 1835, sponsored his set of thirteen lectures. Each year there were four lecturers; this was the fifth year they were given. At some stage Gliddon commisioned a portrait by the Philadelphia artist Matthias S. Weaver, reproduced as a lithograph, showing him in formal consular dress (plate 33).

One other Englishman living in Egypt decided to try his luck in America, in this case by presenting to the public his collection of Egyptian antiquities—with the idea of eventual sale. The year was 1852, the man was Henry Abbott. Abbott had come to Egypt about 1830 with the title of physician in service to the son of the viceroy of Egypt, Ibrahim Pasha, treating sailors in the Egyptian fleet. As early as 1834 he was known to American naval officers off ships of the US squadron in Alexandria.[33] About 1838 he had moved to Cairo, and there he had met and entertained several American travelers mentioned in this book, among them Susan Holmes, the Willingtons, Henry P. Marshall, and Philip Rhinelander and his friends. In August 1840 Abbott had married an Armenian woman born in Turkey, apparently of some wealth, and by the early 1850s he had three children. Over a twenty-year period he had been assembling a notable collection of Egyptian antiquities, and now he seems to have decided to turn his collection into an endowment for his family's benefit. New York rather than London was the place to go and with good reason. In the late summer of 1828, some two years before Henry Abbott reached Egypt, his parents and his siblings, aged twenty-one to six, had moved from England to New York.[34] And in 1830 his sister Mary Ann had married the New Yorker Stewart Brown, a member of the banking firm of Brown Brothers. In New York Henry Abbott would be received.

Abbott is said to have arranged to ship his antiquities through the port of Suez owing to potential problems with Egyptian authorities had he sent them from Alexandria.[35] The shipment arrived at the port of Boston and was forwarded to New York.[36] He himself traveled to England and after sailing from Liverpool on the steamship *Arctic*, arrived in New York on September 6, 1852.[37] His great Egyptian collection was put on exhibition at the Stuyvesant Institute on Broadway in January 1853, and soon afterward, and perhaps for display with the antiquities, the artist Andrew Morris produced a colored pastel portrait of Henry Abbott in eastern dress, reclining on cushions within a tent, some antiquities near his feet, the tombs of the caliphs visible in the distance.[38] His collection attracted many visitors, and in late November fifty-four notable New Yorkers attached their names to a document urging that an institution acquire it.[39] Among them were four gentlemen who had traveled in Egypt prior to 1840, namely Luther Bradish, Horatio Allen, George B. Cheever, and Valentine Mott, and another fourteen who had traveled since then, in the 1840s and early 1850s.

Despite the enthusiasm there was no institutional buyer, and disheartened, Abbott returned to Egypt. There he went back to raising his family and in fact had two more children, and over the next several years he continued to receive American visitors. In 1859 he died, and a year later the New-York Historical Society, whose president at this time was Luther Bradish, acquired the collection for $53,000 from his estate.[40] In 1863 the American artist Thomas Hicks painted a version of Morris' portrait of Abbott for the Historical Society showing him seated in eastern dress on a red-cushioned divan as if in the desert and with a revised vision of Egypt in the background: a camel caravan, the Sphinx, and the Pyramids.[41] He looks contented as he smokes his hookah pipe. It is a good way to remember him (see plate 32).

During this period in the 1850s, George R. Gliddon was engaged in a wide range of activities. He did much more than give lectures, and his career is a subject in itself which has been told elsewhere.[42] His last venture, arranged through a colleague, the archaeologist and entrepreneur Ephraim George Squier, took him in April 1857 to Honduras to serve as an agent of the Honduras Inter-Oceanic Railroad Company. Alas, he contracted yellow fever and died in Panama in November of the same year.

After George Gliddon's death in Panama, Richard Haight obtained from his estate a collection of books and pamphlets by Jean-François Champollion given to Gliddon by Champollion's brother in Paris in the early 1840s. Haight presented them to the New-York Historical Society in 1860. In the later twentieth century, the Historical Society unaccountably sold them, and after passing through two booksellers, they were acquired in 2003 by Boston University; there they can now be found in the Howard Gotlieb Archival Research Center.[43] In 1863, E.G. Squier, who had engaged Gliddon to come to Central America in the first place, arranged for his remains to be sent from Panama to the publisher J.B. Lippincott in Philadelphia and there, fittingly, since Gliddon so aspired to act like an American, if not actually be one, they were interred in Laurel Hill Cemetery, in a spot marked by an inscribed marble tablet topped by a bold relief of a winged Egyptian sun-disk.[44]

The lectures given by George Gliddon and the exhibition of Henry Abbott's Egyptian antiquities in New York, combined with the success and reliability of steamship travel, and the stories brought home by recent travelers, contributed to the increase of American tourists to Egypt. By the 1850s at least a hundred Americans, if not twice that number, visited the Nile each year. Most of them never knew the difficulties and hardships endured by the first Americans in Egypt.

ILLUSTRATION CREDITS

1. The family of David Van Lennep in Smyrna. Oil on canvas by Antoine de Favray, about 1771. The Rijksmuseum, Amsterdam (SK A 4127).
2. Joseph Allen Smith in the Roman Campagna. Oil on canvas by François-Xavier Fabre, about 1797. Musée Fabre, Montpellier, bequest of François-Xavier Fabre 1837, 837.1.156.
3. Nicholas Biddle. Wash drawing done by an unknown artist in Paris, October 1805. Biddle family collection.
4. Edward Everett as a young man. Oil on canvas by Gilbert Stuart, 1821. The Massachusetts Historical Society, Boston. Courtesy of the Massachusetts Historical Society.
5. Study of the Temple of Armant. Watercolor, ink, and graphite on paper by Alexander Jackson Davis, about 1830. The Metropolitan Museum of Art, Harris Brisbane Dick Fund, 1924 (24.66.445).
6. Egyptian quartzite statue of Senwosret Sunbefni, c. 1836–1759 BC The Brooklyn Museum, New York. Charles Edwin Wilbour Fund, 39.602.
7. Fragmentary faience rhyton (drinking horn), Egyptian, Persian period, 525-404 BC The Brooklyn Museum, Gift of the Peabody Museum, 48.29.
8. *Cleopatra's Barge.* Watercolor and gouache by George Ropes, 1818. Peabody Essex Museum, Salem, M 8255. Gift of Mrs. Francis B. Crowninshield.
9. Lord Byron's Visit to the USS *Constitution.* Oil on canvas by William Edward West, about 1822–1824. Dietrich American Foundation, Philadelphia.
10. Captain Matthew C. Perry. Oil on canvas by William Sidney Mount, 1834. United States Naval Academy Museum, Annapolis, 41.10.6.
11. John Thornton Kirkland. Marble bust by Horatio Greenough, 1830–1831. The Boston Athenaeum, Boston, acquired 1832, UH 77.

12. Mehmet Ali, the viceroy of Egypt, in ceremonial dress. Watercolor by Edward C. Young, 1832. G.W. Blunt White Library, Mystic Seaport. Miscellaneous volume 464, page 31.

13. Messenger boy of the *Concord* with a pet bear. Watercolor by Edward C. Young, 1832. Beinecke Rare Book and Manuscript Library, Yale University, Gen Mss vol. 541. Gift of Susan Howe in honor of Peter H. Hane (Yale 1957), 2010.

14. Mendes Israel Cohen. Oil on board by an unknown artist, 1830s. The Maryland Historical Society, Baltimore, bequest of Mrs. Harriet Cohen Coale, 1947, 22.2.1

15. Commodore Daniel Todd Patterson. Oil on canvas by John Wesley Jarvis, c. 1820. Chrysler Museum of Art, Norfolk, Virginia, 65.34.6.

16. Lewis Cass. Oil on canvas by George P.A. Healy, 1838–1840. The Lamont Gallery, Phillips Exeter Academy, Exeter, New Hampshire, presented by the children of Lewis Cass.

17. Henry Ledyard. Daguerreotype, c. 1850. Collection of Dr. William J. Schultz.

18. J. Lewis Stackpole. Daguerreotype attributed to Southworth and Hawes, early 1840s. Collection of Neilson Abeel, Portland, Oregon.

19. Horatio Allen. Miniature, oil on ivory by Amélie d'Aubigny, c. 1836. Current location not known. Image courtesy of the Swarthmore College Peace Collection.

20. William B. Hodgson. Watercolor on ivory by Ernest Joseph Angelon Girard, 1842. Telfair Museums, Savannah, Georgia. Gift of Mr. and Mrs. William K. Wallbridge, 1959.4.

21. John Lowell Jr. Watercolor on paper by Charles Gleyre, 1835. On deposit from the Lowell family at the Museum of Fine Arts, Boston. L-R 9.65.

22A. Red granite fragment of the fallen obelisk of Hatshepsut from Karnak. Museum of Fine Arts, Boston, 75.12. Gift of John A. Lowell and Miss Lowell in 1875.

22B. Granodiorite statue of the goddess Sekhmet from Karnak. Museum of Fine Arts, Boston, 75.7. Gift of John A. Lowell and Miss Lowell in 1875.

23. American passport issued in May 1835. Author's collection.

24. View of Smyrna harbor showing the *Maria Dorothea* and another steamboat. Engraving by Eugenio Fulgenzo, 1836. Harvard University, Fine Arts Library.

25. Dr. Valentine Mott. Oil on canvas by Henry Inman, 1834. Society of New York Hospital, New York.

26. Luther Bradish. Oil on canvas by Alvah Bradish, c. 1840. Montgomery Museum of Fine Arts. Gift of Mrs. B.B. Comer, 1942.17.

27. Alexander Marshall. Oil on canvas by William R. Hamilton, 1838. Private collection.

28. The giraffe presented by Mehmet Ali to Charles X in Paris. Watercolor and gouache on paper by Nicholas Hüet, 1827. The Pierpont Morgan

Library and Museum, New York, 1994.1. Purchase on the Sunny Crawford von Bülow Fund.

29. Philip Rhinelander. Oil on paper by an unknown artist, perhaps 1834. Collection of the children of Mr. and Mrs. Charles Duncan Miller. Image courtesy of the Long Island Museum of American Art, History & Carriages.

30. Interview with the viceroy of Egypt, Alexandria, May 1839. Lithograph by Louis Hague, 1849, after an 1839 sketch by David Roberts. Author's collection.

31. The family of Richard K. Haight. Gouache on paper, c. 1842. The Museum of the City of New York. Bequest of Elizabeth Cushing Iselin, 74.97.2.

32. Henry Abbott. Oil on canvas by Thomas Hicks, 1863. The Brooklyn Museum, gift of the New-York Historical Society, 1948, 48.191.

33. George R. Gliddon. Lithograph by Matthias S. Weaver of Philadelphia, c. 1842. Author's collection.

NOTES

Introduction
1   Martin Turnell, *Baudelaire: A Study of His Poetry* (London: Hamish Hamilton, 1953), 82.

Chapter 1
1   From Ward Nicholas Boylston's diary owned by the Massachusetts Historical Society.
2   Some historians have named John Ledyard, who reached Alexandria in 1788, as the first American to visit Egypt. I for one did so in *Beyond the Shores of Tripoli* (Washington, DC: Washington Society of the Archaeological Institute of America, 1979), as did David H. Finnie, *Pioneers East: The Early American Experience in the Middle East* (Cambridge, MA: Harvard University Press, 1967), 137, and Gerry D. Scott III in Nancy Thomas, ed., *The American Discovery of Ancient Egypt* (Los Angeles: Washington Society of the Archaeological Institute of America and Los Angeles County Museum of Art, 1995), 37.
3   Carrie Rebora and Paul Staiti, eds., *John Singleton Copley in America* (New York: Harry N. Abrams, 1995), fig. 52 (Ward's mother Mary), cat. no. 33 (his aunt Rebecca), fig. 187 (his uncle Thomas), cat. nos. 31–32 (his uncle Nicholas), and cat. no. 30 (his grandmother Sarah Boylston). Copley also painted his father Benjamin Hallowell. On the family see William Bentinck-Smith, "Nicholas Boylston and his Harvard Chair," *Proceedings of the Massachusetts Historical Society* 93 (1981), 17–39.
4   Margaret Green Devereux, *The Land and the People* (New York: Vantage Press, 1974), 125.
5   *The Manifesto Church: Records of the Church in Brattle Square, Boston, with Lists of Communicants, Baptisms, Marriages and Funerals, 1699–1872* (Boston: The Benevolent Fraternity of Churches, 1902), 187.

6 Advertisements began appearing in Boston newspapers in May 1771.

7 John W. Tyler, *Smugglers and Patriots: Boston Merchants and the Advent of the American Revolution* (Boston: Northeast University Press, 1986), 139–69.

8 *The Boston News-Letter*, August 23, 1773; *Boston Post Boy*, August 23, 1773.

9 Arthur S. Marks, "Angelica Kauffmann and Some Americans on the Grand Tour," *The American Art Journal* 12 (1980), 5–24.

10 Jules David Prown, *Art as Evidence: Writings on Art and Material Culture* (New Haven: Yale University Press, 2001), 281–82.

11 Sarah Jackson, ed., *A Journal of Samuel Powel (Rome 1764)* (Florence: Studio per edizioni scelte, 2001).

12 Robert O. Parks, ed., *Piranesi* (exhibition catalogue) (Northampton: Smith College Museum, 1961), 52–54, nos. 117–22. Letter accompanying the gift: Josiah Quincy, *The History of Harvard University* (Cambridge, MA: John Owen, 1840), vol. 2, 487–88, 595.

13 *Letters and Papers of John Singleton Copley and Henry Pelham 1739–1776* (Boston: Massachusetts Historical Society, 1914), vol. 71, 204–209.

14 Libretto by Pietro Metastasio, music by Niccolo Piccinni (the second version), first performed on January 12, 1774, the birthday of King Ferdinand IV.

15 On whom see Ilaria Bignamini and Clare Hornsby, *Digging and Dealing in Eighteenth-century Rome* (New Haven: Yale University Press, 2010), vol. 1, 263–64.

16 Russians in the Mediterranean: R.C. Anderson, *Naval Wars in the Levant 1559-1853* (Princeton: Princeton University Press, 1952), 277–307; Sebag Montefiore, *Prince of Princes: The Life of Potemkin* (London: Weidenfeld and Nicholson, 2000), 84; Robert K. Massie, *Catherine the Great: Portrait of a Woman* (New York: Random House, 2011), 376.

17 Hayes, a British merchant, was consul from 1762 until his death in 1794. Boddington (1706–1800) was chancellor of the Levant Company, a position comparable to that of secretary. The French consul, Claude-Charles de Peyssonnel (1727–1790), a distinguished traveler and scholar, served in Smyrna from 1765 to 1779.

18 The portrait of David Van Lennep and his family, now in the Rijksmuseum, Amsterdam, is attributed to the French artist Antoine de Favray and to the year 1771, the last year the artist was in Constantinople on a nine-year visit: Stephen Degiorgio and Emmanuel Fiorentino, *Antoine Favray (1706–1798): A French Artist in Rome, Malta and Constantinople* (Valetta: Fondazzioni Patrimonju Malti, 2004), 111–15, fig. 3.9. I thank Eveline Sint Nicolaas of the Rijksmuseum, Amsterdam, for permission to illustrate the portrait and for kindly providing information on its provenance (email of November 29, 2011).

19 The original is in the Compten Verney Art Gallery, Warwickshire, ex Lansdowne collection and Sotheby's London, July 1, 2004; Reynold's studio copies: Christie's, London, November 26, 2003 (withdrawn), ex William

Randolph Hearst; and New York, The Metropolitan Museum of Art, 1906, ex Earl of Charlemont and the Blodgett family.

20 This quotation and others, with the exception of his climb of the pyramid, come from Boylston's letter to his mother owned by the Massachusetts Historical Society.

21 The Arabic tradition: The Arabic word stems from a late Greek word found in Greek papyrus texts of the Roman period and in the sixth-century Byzantine writer Procopius: *American Journal of Philology* 4 (1883), 200; J.R. Rea in *The Classical Review* 19 (1969), 91–92; and the references under διέραμα in P.G.W. Glare and A.A. Thompson, *Greek-English Lexicon, Rev. Suppl.* (Oxford: Clarendon Press, 1996).

22 *Syrup of Capillaire*, a sweet herbal remedy, made in the eighteenth century from the Adiantum or maidenhair fern *(Adiantum capillus-veneris)*, water, sugar, and honey.

23 Edward William Lane, *An Account of the Manners and Customs of the Modern Egyptians: Written in Egypt during the Years 1833, –34, and –35, Partly from Notes Made during a Former Visit to that Country in the Years 1825, –26, –27, and –28.* 5th ed., Stanley Poole, ed. (London: John Murray, 1860), 163, 174.

24 *The Alchemist*, 127–28: "That you should hatch gold in a furnace, sir, / As they do eggs in Egypt!" Aristotle, *Historia Animalium* 559b 1; Pliny, *Natural History* x.75.

25 The eighth-century church of Abu Sarga or St. Sergius.

26 The Swedish botanist Hasselquist had seen it in 1750: Frederick Hasselquist, *Voyages and Travels in the Levant: In the Years 1749, 50, 51, 52* (London: L. Davis and C. Reymers, 1766), 77–83. The Danish explorer, Carsten Niebuhr, together with the five scientists traveling with him, had witnessed it in 1762 but the account of his travels was not published until 1774.

27 Jean Potocki, *Voyages en Turquie et en Egypte, en Hollande, au Maroc*, Daniel Beauvois, ed. (Paris: Fayard, 1980), 90–92.

28 Lane, *Manners and Customs of the Modern Egyptians*, 480–87.

29 Lane, *Manners and Customs of the Modern Egyptians*, 484.

30 Jacque Jomier, *Le Mahmal et la caravane égyptienne des pelerin de la Mecque (XIIIe–XXe siècles)* (Cairo: Institut française orientales, 1953); Venetia Porter, ed., *Hajj: Journey to the Heart of Islam* (Cambridge, MA: Harvard University Press, 2012), 140.

31 Information kindly provided by Maria Pia Pedani of the Dipartimento di Studi sull'Asia e sull'Africa Mediterranea, Venezia (email of January 30, 2012).

32 John Antes, *Observations on the Manners and Customs of the Egyptians, the Overflowing of the Nile and Its Effects with Remarks on the Plague and other Subjects* (London: John Stockdale, 1800). Those interested in Antes' experience in Egypt should consult the fine chapter devoted to him in Cassandra Vivian, *Americans in Egypt, 1770–1915: Explorers, Consuls, Travelers, Soldiers, Missionaries, Writers and Scientists* (Jefferson, NC: McFarland, 2012), 9–23.

One argument advanced for his being an American is a letter he wrote to Benjamin Franklin in 1779 in which he calls attention to the country where he was born. I would argue on the other hand that Antes knew how to ingratiate himself to Franklin.

33 R.A. McNeal, ed., *Nicholas Biddle in Greece. The Journals and Letters of 1806* (University Park: The Pennsylvania State University Press, 1993), 51.

34 Boylston missed by one or two years an opportunity to meet Edward Wortley Montagu, the errant son of Lady Mary Wortley Montagu, who lived the life of a renegade in Egypt between 1763 and 1773. Some of his papers are in the Stanford University Library (Special collections M 0279). His portrait, painted by George Romney in Venice in 1775, formerly owned by the Earls of Warwick, and for some years on loan to the Metropolitan Museum of Art, was sold at Sotheby's in London on July 9, 2014, Old Master & British Paintings Evening Sale, lot 45.

35 On Baldwin and the situation in Egypt at this time see Rosemarie Said Zahlan, "George Baldwin: Soldier of Fortune?" in Paul & Janet Starkey, eds., *Travellers in Egypt* (London: I.B.Tauris, 1998), 24–38.

36 *Letters & Papers of John Singleton Copley and Henry Pelham*, 330.

37 Andrew Oliver, ed., *The Journal of Samuel Curwen, Loyalist* (Cambridge, MA: Harvard University Press, 1972), vol. 1, 40.

38 Peter Orlando Hutchinson, *The Diary and Letters of His Excellency Thomas Hutchinson, Esq.* (London: Sampson Low, Marston, Searle & Rivington, 1883), vol. 1, 499.

39 Some records give the date as 1775, but obituaries confirm a date in August 1773, e.g., *The London Magazine* 42 (August 1773), 412. George Tasburgh was traveling shortly after her death. A portrait of her is at the Gage family house, Firle Place, East Sussex.

40 One other point: Tasburgh's brother-in-law, Thomas Gage, was married to Margaret Kemble whose father, Peter Kemble (1704–1789), had been born in Smyrna, son of an English merchant there. Although Peter Kemble had left for England in 1712 for his education and had moved to New Jersey in 1730, his children, among them Margaret Kemble Gage, may well have retained an interest in Smyrna, or at least things Turkish. In 1771 Margaret posed for John Singleton Copley wearing pseudo-Turkish dress, admittedly modish at the time but in her case perhaps reminiscent of family background: Rebora and Staiti, *John Singleton Copley in America*, 286–92, cat. no. 67; Carrie Rebora Barratt, *John Singleton Copley and Margaret Kemble Gage: Turkish Fashion in 18th-Century America* (San Diego: Putnam Foundation, 1998); for the style, also see Marcia Pointon, "Going Turkish in Eighteenth-century London: Lady Mary Wortley Montagu and her Portraits," in *Hanging the Head: Portraiture and Social Formation in Eighteenth-century England* (New Haven: Yale University Press, 1993).

41 Boylston's letter to his mother, owned by the Massachusetts Historical Society.

42 James Zug, *American Traveler: The Life and Adventures of John Ledyard, the Man Who Dreamed of Walking the World* (New York: Basic Books, 2005); Bill Gifford, *Ledyard: In Search of the First American Explorer* (New York: Harcout, Inc., 2006); Edward C. Gray, *The Making of John Ledyard: Empire and Ambition in the Life of an Early American Traveler* (New Haven: Yale University Press, 2007). Still readable is Helen Augur, *Passage to Glory, John Ledyard's America* (Garden City, New York: Doubleday, 1946). The first biography was that of Jared Sparks, *The Life of John Ledyard, the American Traveller: Comprising Selections from his Journals and Correspondence* (Cambridge, MA: Hilliard & Brown, 1828). For his Egyptian experience see Anthony Sattin, *The Gates of Africa: Death, Discovery, and the Search for Timbuktu* (New York: Harper Collins, 2005).

43 Julian P. Boyd, ed., *The Papers of Thomas Jefferson* (Princeton: Princeton University Press, 1956), vol. 13, 516–17.

44 Boyd, *Papers of Thomas Jefferson*, vol. 13, 595.

45 Julian P. Boyd, ed., *The Papers of Thomas Jefferson* (Princeton: Princeton University Press, 1958), vol. 14, 180–82. All three letters are in the New-York Historical Society, the gift of John Ledyard Vandervoort in 1879.

46 Julian P. Boyd, ed., *The Papers of Thomas Jefferson* (Princeton: Princeton University Press, 1958), vol. 15, 198–99. Paine's letter is in the Library of Congress.

47 W. Bernard Peach, ed., *The Correspondence of Richard Price*, vol. 3 (Durham, NC: Duke University Press, 1994), 302–303.

48 "Mr. Ledyard's Communications," *Proceedings of the Association for Promoting the Discovery of the Interior Parts of Africa* (London: W. Bulmer and Co., 1810), vol. 1, 24-46.

49 "Mr Ledyard's Communications," 26–27.

50 Henry Beaufoy in *Proceedings of the Association for Promoting the Discovery of the Interior Parts of Africa*, vol. 1, 18.

51 English translation: Frederick Hasselquist, *Voyages and Travels in the Levant*.

52 On the expedition see Thorkild Hansen, *Arabia Felix: The Danish Expedition of 1761–1767* (London: Wm. Collins Sons and New York: Harper & Row, 1964); F. Nigel Hepper and I. Friss, *The Plants of Pehr Forsskal's 'Flora Aegyptiaco-Arabica' Collected on the Royal Danish Expedition in Egypt and the Yemen 1761–63* (Kew, UK: Royal Botanic Gardens, 1994), 1–25.

53 See Paul Hulton, F. Nigel Hepper, Ib Friis, *Luigi Balugani's Drawings of African Plants: From the Collection Made by James Bruce of Kinnaird on His Travels to Discover the Source of the Nile 1767–1773* (New Haven: Yale Center for British Art, 1991).

54 A summary list of these travelers' publications is given by John von B. Rodenbeck in Jason Thompson, ed., *Egyptian Encounters*, Cairo Papers in Social Science 23, issue 3 (2002), 104ff.

55 Fernando Mazzocca et al., eds., *Un ritrattista nell'Europa delle corti: Giovanni Battista Lampi 1751–1830* (Trent: Provincia autonoma di Trento: Servizio

beniculturali, 2001), 212–13, no. 23; François Rosset and Dominique Triaire, *Jean Potocki* (Paris: Flammarion, 2004), illus., 248–249. Sylvia Peukert, "Jan Potocki und das alte Ägypten im universalgeschichtlichen Denken um 1800," *Zeitschrift für Ägyptische Sprache und Altertumskunde* 136, no. 1 (2009), 57–83.

56   Nina Root, "The Eighteenth-century Society Library," *The New York Society Library, Notes* 17, no. 3 (Fall 2010). A digital version of the Library's First Charging Ledger (1789–1792), with lists of readers and books, is available online: www.nysoclib.org/ledger

57   Oliver, *The Journal of Samuel Curwen*, vol. 1, 69.

58   Thomas Harmer, *Observations on Divers Passages of Scripture . . . by Means of Circumstances Incidentally Mentioned in Books of Voyages and Travels into the East* (London: J. Johnson, 1787), vol. 3, preface, v.

59   H.E. Scudder, ed., *Recollections of Samuel Breck, with Passages from His Note-books (1771–1862)* (Philadelphia: Porter and Coates, 1877), 158.

60   *Transactions of the Society Instituted at London for the Encouragement of Art, Manufactures, and Commerce*, vol. 11 (1793), 206.

61   Oliver, *The Journal of Samuel Curwen*, vol. 1, 43.

62   W.G. Browne, *Travels in Africa, Egypt, and Syria, from the year 1792 to 1798* (London: T. Cadell, junior and W. Davies, 1799). This very copy was sold by a Boylston descendant at auction in New York in December 2009, and is now owned by the author: Bonhams, *Books, Maps and Manuscripts, Historical Photographs*, December 15, 2009, lot 5254.

63   Charles Francis Adams, ed., *Memoirs of John Quincy Adams, Comprising Portions of His Diary from 1795 to 1848*, vol. 1 (Philadelphia: J.B. Lippincott & Co., 1874), 51–52.

64   *Bulletin of the Public Library of the City of Boston* (1921), 308.

65   *American Paintings in the Museum of Fine Arts*, Boston (Boston: Museum of Fine Arts, 1969), vol. 1, 260, vol. 2, 97, ill.; Andrew Oliver (1906–1981), Ann Millspaugh Huff, Edward W. Hanson, *Portraits in the Massachusetts Historical Society* (Boston: Massachusetts Historical Society, 1988), 18-20. The version at Harvard College was originally presented by Boylston to the Boylston Medical Society in 1825 and later, in 1936, given by the Society to Harvard: Laura M. Huntsinger et al., *Harvard Portraits: A Catalogue of Portrait Paintings at Harvard University* (Cambridge, MA: Harvard University Press, 1936), 26.

Chapter 2

1   *Histoire de Bonaparte, premier consul, depuis sa naissance jusqu'à la paix de Lunéville* (Paris: Chez Barba, 1802). And one of Napoleon's premier savants, Dominique Vivant Denon, included a version of the expression in his *Voyage dans la Basse et la Haute Égypte pendant les campagnes du général Bonaparte* also first published in 1802: "Allez, et pensez que du haut de ces monuments quarante siècles nous observent" (Paris: Editions Gallimard, 1998), 71.

2   Napoleon in Egypt: Henry Laurens, *L'expédition d'Egypte 1798–1801*, nou-
     velle édition (Paris: Édition du Seuil, 1997); Juan Cole, *Napoleon's Egypt:
     Invading the Middle East* (New York: Palgrave Macmillan, 2007); Philippe
     Mainterot, ed., *"Du haut de ces pyramids..." L'Expédition d'Égypte et la nais-
     sance de l'égyptologie (1798-1850)* (Lyon: Fage éditions, 2013).
3   James H. Stark, *The Loyalists of Massachusetts and the Other Side of the Ameri-
     can Revolution* (Boston: James H. Stark, 1910), 283–84; Carlos Gilman
     Calkins, "American Admirals in the British Navy," *United States Naval
     Institute Proceedings* 35 (1909), 701–709; *Oxford Dictionary of National Biog-
     raphy* (Oxford: Oxford University Press, 2004), vol. 10, 41–43 (under Sir
     Benjamin Hallowell Carew). One other "American" naval officer served in
     Nelson's fleet, Ralph Willett Miller, who was born in New York in 1762. As
     Loyalists his family lost their property at the outbreak of the Revolution,
     at which time he was sent to England and joined the navy in 1778. Captain
     of HMS *Theseus* at the Battle of the Nile, he was later killed in an accident
     aboard his ship off Jaffa in 1799.
4   *Il y a 200 ans, les savants en Égypte* (Paris: Éditions Nathan, 1998); Yves Lais-
     sus, *L'Égypte, une aventure savante avec Bonaparte, Kléber, Menou (1798–1801)*
     (Paris: Fayard, 1998); Charles Coulston Gillispie, *Science and Polity in
     France: The Revolutionary and Napoleonic Years* (Princeton: Princeton Univer-
     sity Press, 2004), 557–600; Nina Burleigh, *Mirage: Napoleon's Scientists and
     the Unveiling of Egypt* (New York: Harper, 2007).
5   Denon, *Voyage dans la Basse et la Haute Égypte*, 168.
6   Denon, *Voyage dans la Basse et la Haute Égypte*, 279.
7   Edouard de Villiers du Terrage, *L'expédition d'Égypte: Journal d'un jeune
     savant engagé dans l'état-major de Bonaparte (1798–1801)*, Présentation et
     dossier d'Alain Pigeard (Paris: Cosmopole, 2001), 114–23.
8   Dominique-Vivant Denon, *Voyage dans la Basse et la Haute Égypte, pendant
     les campagnes du général Bonaparte*, 2 vols. (Paris: P. Didot l'aîné, 1802).
9   The New York edition: Vivant Denon, *Travels in Upper and Lower Egypt,
     during the Campaigns of General Bonaparte in that Country* (New York: Heard
     and Forman, 1803).
10   Exhibition catalogue: *Dominique-Vivant Denon: L'oeil de Napoléon, Paris,
     musée du Louvre 20 octobre 1999–17 janvier 2000* (Paris: Réunion des
     Musées Nationaux, 1999), 116–27.
11   Richard Parkinson, *Cracking Codes: The Rosetta Stone and Decipherment*
     (Berkeley: University of California Press, 1999); John Ray, *The Rosetta Stone
     and the Rebirth of Ancient Egypt* (Cambridge, MA: Harvard University Press,
     2007). Andrew Robinson, *Cracking the Egyptian Code: The Revolutionary Life
     of Jean-François Champollion* (Oxford: Oxford University Press, 2012).
12   Charles Coulston Gillispie, "Scientific Aspects of the French Egyptian
     Expedition 1798–1801," *Proceedings of the American Philosophical Society* 133
     (1989), 447–74.

13   Yves Laissus, *Jomard: Le dernier Égyptien 1777–1862* (Paris: Fayard, 2004), 102, 185–87. In 1830 the exchange rate was about 5 francs, 25 centimes per dollar. Paul-Marie Grinevald, "La *Description de l'Égypte.* Trente ans de travaux. 1798–1802–1829" in *"Du haut de ces pyramides..." L'Expédition d'Égypte et la naissance de l'égyptologie (1798–1850)* (Lyon: Fage editions, 2013), 78–93.

14   [Edward Everett], *The North American Review*, October (1823), 236, footnote; Alfred Claghorn Potter, *Descriptive and Historical Notes on the Library of Harvard University* (Cambridge, MA: Library of Harvard University, 1903), 28.

15   Brooklyn Museum, Charles Edwin Wilbour Fund, 39,602, from the collections of the comte de Pourtalès-Gorgier, Lord Amherst, and William Randolph Hearst: John D. Cooney, "A Souvenir of Napoleon's Trip to Egypt," *The Journal of Egyptian Archaeology* 35 (1949), 153–57; Sophie Descampes-Lequinne and Martine Denoyelle, eds., *De Pompéi à Malmaison, les Antiques de Joséphine* (Paris: Musée du Louvre éditions, 2008), 178, no. 64.

Chapter 3

1   See M. Sükrü Hanioglou, *A Brief History of the Late Ottoman Empire* (Princeton: Princeton University Press, 2008), 12–13.

2   See the chapter, "The Transformation of Egypt during the Reign of Mehemet Ali: Drovetti's Contribution," in Ronald T. Ridley, *Napoleon's Proconsul in Egypt: The Life and Times of Bernardino Drovetti* (London: The Rubicon Press, 1998), 202–47.

3   Alan Mikhail, *Nature and Empire in Ottoman Egypt: An Environmental History* (Cambridge: Cambridge University Press, 2011), 242–90, an account using Ottoman sources. A plan made by the French architect Pascal Coste around 1821, just after its completion, shows the route of the canal: Dominique Jacobi, ed., *Pascal Coste, Toutes les Égypte* (Marseilles: Éditions Parenthèses, 1998), 87.

4   This was the text used by the distinguished English orientalist Edward William Lane (1801–1876), long resident in Cairo, for the first translation directly from Arabic into English of these celebrated stories. Jason Thompson, *Edward William Lane 1801–1876: The Life of the Pioneering Egyptologist and Orientalist* (London: Haus Publishing, 2010), 401–40. On the Bulaq edition see Jean-Claude Garcin, *Pour une lecture historique des Mille et Une Nuits: Essai sur l'édition de Būlāq (1835)* (Aix, Marseilles: Actes Sud, 2013), esp. 15–23.

5   Antiquariat Inlibris, *A Selection of Books, Autographs and Manuscripts* (Vienna, 2012) 88, no. 50, in which it is reported that fewer than ten copies are currently recorded. The only copy in the United States is in the Beinecke Library at Yale; it came from the Bibliotheca Lindesiana, and was acquired by Alexander Crawford, Lord Lindsay at Bulaq in 1836: *Letters on Egypt, Edom, and the Holy Land* (London: Henry Colburn, 1838), vol. 1, 59–60.

6   Alain Silvera, "The First Egyptian Student Mission to France under Muhammad Ali," *Middle Eastern Studies* 16, no. 2 (1980), 1-22; Ronald T. Ridley, *Napoleon's Proconsul in Egypt*, 206–14.

7   Diary entry of Sunday, August 13, 1826; owned by the Robinson family; transcript made available to the author by Jay G. Williams of Hamilton College. Robinson visited Egypt in 1838 on his way to Palestine on a topographical survey which, when published, would make his reputation as the preeminent biblical archaeologist of the day.

8   LaVerne Kuhnke, *Lives at Risk: Public Health in Nineteenth-Century Egypt* (Berkeley: University of California Press, 1990), 33–44; Ridley, *Napoleon's Proconsul in Egypt*, 214–20; Mikhail, *Nature and Empire in Ottoman Egypt*, 234–36.

9   Gerard N. Burrow, "Clot-Bey: Founder of Western Medical Practice in Egypt," *The Yale Journal of Biology and Medicine* 48 (1975), 251–57.

10   Patrice Bret, "Gunpowder Manufacture in Cairo from Bonaparte to Muhammad 'Alî: Adaptation, Innovation and the Transfer of Technology, 1798–1820," in Brenda J. Buchanan, ed., *Gunpowder, Explosives and the State: A Technological History* (Aldershot and Burlington, VT: Ashgate, 2006), 206–29 (218–23).

11   Paul de Mautort, "Corresondance de Charles Lefebvre de Cerisy, Créateur de la Marine Egyptienne, avec Louis-Charles Beaucousin-Deligières 1829–1835," Société d'Émulation d'Abbeville, Bulletin Trimestriel, 1922, 141–79.

12   Edward William Lane, *Manners and Customs of the Modern Egyptians*, Stanley Poole , ed. (London: John Murray, 1860), 110.

13   R. Mowafi, *Slavery, Slave Trade and Abolition Attempt in Egypt and the Sudan 1820–1882*, Lund Studies in International History (Malmö: Esselte Studium, 1981), 32–35.

14   Lane, *Manners and Customs of the Modern Egyptians*, 529–56. Michael B. Oren (Israel's ambassador to the United States from 2009 to 2013) judges the treatment of Jews in Cairo to have been much worse than was noted by many nineteenth-century observers. See Michael B. Oren, *Power, Faith, and Fantasy: America in the Middle East 1776 to the Present* (New York: W.W. Norton & Co., 2007), 154.

15   Jeremy D. Popkin, *You Are All Free: The Haitian Revolution and the Abolition of Slavery* (Cambridge: Cambridge University Press, 2010).

16   Mendes Cohen, a traveler from Baltimore who met him in Alexandria on August 2, 1832, tells that story, as reported in Cohen's diary in the Maryland Historical Society (see chapter 9). And more is given by Cassandra Vivian in her chapter on Barthow in *Americans in Egypt, 1770–1915: Explorers, Consuls, Travelers, Soldiers, Missionaries, Writers and Scientists* (Jefferson, NC: McFarland, 2012), 56–72.

17   George Annesley (Viscount Valentia), *Voyages and Travels to India, Ceylon, the Red Sea, Abyssinia, and Egypt* (London: William Miller, 1809), vol. 2, 410, 423–24, 426, and vol. 3, 340–44.

18 Michel Dewachter, "Graffiti des voyageurs du xixe siècle relevés dans le temple d'Amada en Basse-Nubie," *Bulletin d'Institut Français d'Archéologie Orientale* 69 (1971), 139–41.

19 John Lewis Burckhardt, *Travels in Nubia* (London: John Murray, 1819), 16.

20 Thomas Legh, *Narrative of Journey in Egypt* (London: John Murray, 1816), 33, 110–11.

21 William J. Bankes, ed., *Narrative of a Journey in Egypt and the Country Beyond the Cataracts*, vol. 2 (London: John Murray, 1830), 72; Patricia Usick, *Adventures in Egypt and Nubia: The Travels of William John Bankes (1786–1855)* (London: The British Museum Press, 2002), 31.

22 See Cte de Forbin, *Voyage dans le Levant* (Paris: Imprimerie Royale, 1819), 423, quoting a report from an Egyptian journal of the period, *Courrier du Mont Mokatam*, 18 février 1818.

23 Baudouin van de Walle, "Jean-Baptiste De Lescluze, négociant et armateur brugeois (1780–1858)," *Annales de la Société d'Émulation de Bruges* 97 (1960), 154–229, esp. 199–204; summarized in *Biographie nationale, publiée par l'Académie royale des sciences, des lettres, et des beaux-arts de Belgique*, vol. 32 (1964), 432–40, at column 437.

24 R.B. Halbertsma, *Scholars, Travellers and Trade: The Pioneer Years of the National Museum of Antiquities in Leiden, 1818–40* (London: Routledge, 2003), 100, 102, 106.

25 Sylvie Guichard, *Lettres de Bernardino Drovetti consul de France à Alexandrie (1803–1830)* (Paris: Maisonneuve & Larose, 2003), 294, 301.

Chapter 4

1 One of the American representatives was Thomas Appleton, United States consul in Leghorn (Livorno) from 1799 to 1824. His letter books, containing copies of more than one thousand letters he sent out during this period, have recently been acquired by the Gilder Lehrman Institute of American History, housed at the New-York Historical Society. When analyzed, the correspondence should provide a rich view of American commercial activities in the region in the early decades of the nineteenth century.

2 Edward Daniel Clarke, *Travels in Various Countries of Europe, Asia and Africa* (London: T. Cadell and W. Davies, 1812), vol. 2, 59–61.

3 H.A.S. Dearborn, *The Life of William Bainbridge, Esq. of the United States Navy*, James Barnes, ed. (Princeton: Princeton University Press, 1951), 18–40.

4 Captain Dudley W. Knox, ed., *Naval Documents Related to the Quasi-War between the United States and France: Naval Operations from December 1800 to December 1801* (Washington, DC: Government Printing Office, 1988), 326.

5 *Treasures of the Hood Museum of Art* (Hanover: Dartmouth College, 1985), 32. It is possible that the one remaining fragment from Pompey's Pillar still in the collection of Dartmouth College is that presented by Frederick Hall in 1838 (as related in chapter 7 on missionaries), and not one of the two given

by Silas Dinsmore before 1810. In any event the rest of Dinsmore's souvenirs have gone astray. His gifts are cited in a 1975 summary of a 1921 typed copy of the 1810 ledger. I am grateful to Cynthia Gilliland and Deborah T. Haynes of the Hood Museum of Art for giving me details of this document.

6   Glenn Tucker, *Dawn Like Thunder: The Barbary Wars and the Birth of the U.S. Navy* (Indianapolis and New York: The Bobbs-Merrill Company Inc., 1963); Ian W. Toll, *Six Frigates: The Epic History of the Founding of the U.S. Navy* (London: W.W. Norton, 2006).

7   *Naval Documents Related to the United States War with the Barbary Powers* (Washington, DC: United States Government Printing Office, 1939), vol. 5, 278. Letter in the Hull–Eaton correspondence owned by the American Antiquarian Society.

8   Louis B. Wright, Julia H. Macleod, *The First Americans in North Africa: William Eaton's Struggle for a Vigorous Policy against the Barbary Pirates, 1799–1805* (Princeton: Princeton University Press, 1945); Tucker, *Dawn Like Thunder*, 371–413.

9   See BGen Edwin H. Simmons, USMC (Ret), "O'Bannon's Sword?" *Fortitudine. Newsletter of the Marine Corps Historical Program*, vol. xiv (summer 1984), 3–9.

10 Now in the United States Marine Corps Museum in Quantico.

11 Howard A. Reed, "Yankees at the Sultan's Port: The First Americans in Turkey and Early Trade with Smyrna and Mocha," in Jean Louis Bacqué-Grammont and Paul Dumant, eds, *Contributions à l'histoire économique et sociale de l'Empire ottoman* (Leuven: Éditions Peeters, 1983), 353–83.

12 Thomas G. Cary, *Memoir of Thomas Handasyd Perkins: Containing Extracts from His Diaries* (Boston: Little, Brown and Company, 1856), 282–83.

13 *Gazette of the United States*, July 5, 1797.

14 *The Army and Navy Chronicle*, vol. 4 (1837), 43; *The Sailor's Magazine, and Naval Journal*, vol. 10 (1838), 128–29, both quoting letters from John Lee.

15 State Dept Archives, misc. letter xxiv; Reed, "Yankees at the Sultan's Port," 359.

16 Julian P. Boyd, ed., *The Papers of Thomas Jefferson*, (Princeton: Princeton University Press, 1958), vol. 13, 13. Miles Brewton (1731–1775) was a Charleston planter. William Carter was captain of a brig, the *Friendship*, which first sailed in the spring of 1772, to Cowes and Bremen, but not to Turkey: George C. Rogers Jr. et al., eds., *The Papers of Henry Laurens* (Columbia, SC: University of South Carolina Press, 1980), vol. 8, 322. Evidence of a pre-war rice sale in Turkey appears in newspaper accounts, e.g., the *Connecticut Courant* of Hartford for May 26, 1772: "*Constantinople (Turkey) February 3*. We have a great quantity of rice here. The Carolina rice sells for ten paras (*about 18d. sterling*) a bushel, more than the finest Egyptian or Italian rice, notwithstanding its long passage." Newspapers also stated that a *Friendship*, under a Captain Carter, was captured by an

Algerian galley on her way from Leghorn to London in the fall of 1771 and was then released by a British man of war: *Pennsylvania Gazette*, February 27, 1772; but that *Friendship* must be an earlier brig of the same name. The story is still obscure. There is no mention in Leila Sellers, *Charleston Business on the Eve of the American Revolution* (Chapel Hill, NC: University of North Carolina Press, 1934).

17 Barbara B. Oberg, ed., *The Papers of Thomas Jefferson* (Princeton: Princeton University Press, 2010), vol. 37, 204, 290, 324, 348.

18 Mary A. Hackett et al., eds., *The Papers of James Madison*, Secretary of State Series (Charlottesville: University Press of Virginia, 1998), vol. 4, 547–48.

19 Reed, "Yankees at the Sultan's Port," 369; Jacques M. Downs, "American Merchants and the China Opium Trade, 1800–1840," *Business History Review* 42, no. 4 (1968), 418–42.

20 The story of the *Martha* is told by James Duncan Phillips ("The Ship *Martha*'s Shopping Trip in the Mediterranean in 1801," *The American Neptune* 5 (1945), 43–63) and also summarized by Phillips (*Salem and the Indies: The Story of the Great Commercial Era of the City* (Boston: Houghton Mifflin, 1947), 228–29). A copy of the letter to George Perkins dated June 25, 1800, is preserved in the letter books of Thomas Appleton owned by the Gilder-Lehrman Institute of American History, New York.

21 Brought by Jacob Crowninshield in his ship *America*. The log was kept by Nathaniel Hathorne (father of Nathaniel Hawthorne who added a *w* to his name). G.G. Goodwin, "The First Living Elephant in America," *Journal of Mammalogy* 6 (1925), 256–63.

22 [Jean de la Roque], *Voyage de l'Arabie Heureuse . . . dans les années 1708, 1709, & 1710: Avec la relation particuliere d'un Voyage fait du Port de Moka à la cour du Roy d'Yemen, dans la seconde Expedition des années 1711, 1712 & 1713* (Paris, 1716). Modern reprint: (Besançon: Éditions La Lanterne Magique, 2008).

23 George Annesley (Viscount Valentia), *Voyages and Travels to India, Ceylon, the Red Sea, Abyssinia, and Egypt* (London: William Miller,1809), vol. 2, 207–209.

24 D. Hamilton Hurd, *History of Essex County, Massachusetts, with Biographical Sketches of Many of Its Pioneers and Prominent Men* (Philadelphia: J.W. Lewis & Co., 1888), vol. 1, 83.

25 Édouard Driault, *Mohamed Aly et Napoléon (1807–1814)* (Cairo: L'Institut français d'archéologie orientale pour La Société Royale de Géographie d'Égypte, 1925), 166.

26 J. Fred Rippy, *Joel R. Poinsett, Versatile American* (Durham, NC: Duke University Press, 1935), 10–15.

27 Nathalia Wright, ed., *Washington Irving, Journals and Notebooks*, vol. 1 (Madison: The University of Wisconsin Press, 1969).

28 Ferris Greenslet, *The Lowells and Their Seven Worlds* (London: Ernest Benn Limited, 1947), 101–14. The Massachusetts Historical Society possesses their 1804 diaries.

29 Fitzwilliam Museum, Cambridge (PD16.1984), and Musée Fabre, Montpellier: Maurie D. McInnis and Angela D. Mack, eds., *In Pursuit of Refinement: Charlestonians Abroad 1740–1860* (Charleston: University of South Carolina Press, 1999), 134–37, nos. 19 and 20. The latter shows him seated in the pose of Goethe in the Roman Campagna painted by Johann Heinrich Wilhelm Tischbein in 1787, and in fact Fabre owned a finished pen-on-paper sketch by Tischbein of this very subject, now also in the Musée Fabre: *Apollo*, January 1989, 22. On his travels see E.P. Richardson, "Allen Smith, Collector and Benefactor," *American Art Journal* 1 (1969), 5–19; and R.A. McNeal, "Joseph Allen Smith, American Grand Tourist," *International Journal of the Classical Tradition* 4 (1997), 64–91.

30 *The Writings of Thomas Jefferson*, vol. 11 (Washington, DC: The Thomas Jefferson Memorial Association of the United States, 1904), 177, a letter of March 28, 1807 to Levett Harris, the American consul in St. Petersburg.

31 Preserved in the New-York Historical Society. George C. Rogers Jr., "Letters from Russia, 1802–1805," *South Carolina Historical Magazine* (1959), 94–105, 154–63, 221–27.

32 Preserved in the Bibliothèque nationale de France, département des Manuscrits, ms. fr. 22873, f. 9 r/v. Alessia Zambon kindly made the text available for me. See also, Alessia Zambon, *Aux origines de l'archéologie en Grèce. Fauvel et sa méthode* (Paris: Institut national d'histoire de l'art, 2014), 44.

33 Preserved in the Pennsylvania Historical Society, the letters are addressed to André Italinski, Russian Envoy in Constantinople, M. Giraud and Robert Wilkinson in Smyrna, and Louis-François-Sébastien Fauvel and Giovanni Battista Lusieri in Athens.

34 Charles L. Chandler, "The Life of Joel Roberts Poinsett," *Pennsylvania Magazine of History and Biography* 59 (1935), 1–31, esp. 15.

35 Nicholas B. Wainwright, "Nicholas Biddle in Portraiture," *Antiques* (November 1975), 956, fig. 1.

36 On Palmer (1769–1840), see Michael E. Martin, "Two Cambridge Orientalists on Athos," *Byzantine and Modern Greek Studies* 26 (2002), 149–77.

37 R.A. McNeal, ed., *Nicholas Biddle in Greece: The Journals and Letters of 1806* (University Park: The Pennsylvania State University Press, 1993), 193–94.

38 Worthington Chauncey Ford, ed., *Writings of John Quincy Adams* (New York: The Macmillan Company, 1914), vol. 3, 442–44.

39 "Journal of a Tour through Asia Minor," *The Port-Folio* 8 (1812), 13–16.

40 J.C. Hobhouse, *A Journey through Albania and Other Provinces of Turkey in Europe and Asia, to Constantinople, during the Years 1809 and 1810* (London: James Cawthorn, 1813). Leslie A. Marchand, ed., *Byron's Letters and Journals*, vol. 1 (Cambridge, MA: The Belknap Press of Harvard University Press, 1973), 225–27. A son of Erasmus Darwin had made the same trip to Ephesus

six months earlier, in July 1809, having arrived in Smyrna from Malta on an American schooner, the *Dolphin*: Francis Sacheverell Darwin, *Travels in Spain and the East 1808–1810* (Cambridge: The University Press, 1927).

41 Donald R. Hickey, *The War of 1812* (Urbana: University of Illinois Press, 1989), 5–18.

42 The journal is in the Houghton Library at Harvard: MS Am 1028. The meteorological account is in the American Philosophical Society in Philadelphia: no. xii under 551.5 M 56. See also Thomas R. Hazard, *Recollections of Olden Times: Rowland Robinson of Narragansett and His Unfortunate Daughter; With Genealogies of the Robinson, Hazard, and Sweet families* (Newport, RI: John P. Sanborn, 1879), 247–49. Samuel Hazard, "On Smyrna Wheat," *Memoirs of the Philadelphia Society for Promoting Agriculture* 4 (1818), 52–54.

43 Robert B. Forbes, *Personal Reminiscences*, 2nd ed. (Boston: Little, Brown, and Company, 1882), 12; Sarah Forbes Hughes, ed., *Letters and Recollections of John Murray Forbes* (Boston and New York: Houghton, Mifflin and Company, 1899), vol. 1, 38–39.

44 On their time in England, see [George S. Hilliard, ed.], *Life, Letters, and Journals of George Ticknor* (Boston: James B. Osgood, 1876), vol. 1, 48–69.

45 Augustus Thorndike Perkins, *A Private Proof Printed in Order to Preserve Certain Matters Connected with the Boston Branch of the Perkins Family* (Boston: T.P. Marvin & Son, 1890), 69.

46 Everett kept a diary, still unpublished, owned by the Massachusetts Historical Society. For summaries of the tour, see "Memoirs of Edward Everett," *Proceedings of the Massachusetts Historical Society* 38 (1903), 99–101; and Paul Revere Frothingham, *Edward Everett, Orator and Statesman* (New York: Houghton Mifflin, 1925).

47 Edward Everett, *Orations and Speeches on Various Occasions* (Boston: Little, Brown, and Company, 1859), vol. 3, 627.

48 R.A. McNeal, "Athens and Nineteenth-Century Panoramic Art," *International Journal of the Classical Tradition* 1, no 3 (1995), 84, 8n; Caroline Winterer, *The Culture of Classicism: Ancient Greece and Rome in American Intellectual Life, 1780–1910* (Baltimore: Johns Hopkins University Press, 2002), 66–67.

Chapter 5

1 Sergei Stadnikow, "Otto Friedrich von Richters Forschungsreise in Unternubien im Jahre 1815: Auszüge aus dem Tagebuch," *Mitteilungen für Anthropologie und Religionsgeschichte* 15 (2000 [2003]), 125–61; Indrek Jürjo and Sergei Stadnikow, "Brief aus Ägypten: Otto Friedrich von Richters wissenschaftliche Reise in Ägypten und Unternubien im Jahre 1815." 2008, http://archiv.ub.uni.heidelberg/de/propylaeumdok/volltexte/2008/86.

2 William J. Bankes, ed., *Life and Adventures of Giovanni Finati* (London: John Murray, 1830).

3   Patricia Usick, *Adventures in Egypt and Nubia: The Travels of William John Bankes (1786–1855)* (London: The British Museum Press, 2002), 31–52.

4   Philippe Mainterot, *Aux origins de l'égyptologie: Voyages et collections de Frédéric Cailliaud (1787–1869)* (Rennes: Presses Universitaires de Rennes, 2011), 27–32.

5   Stanley Mayes, *The Great Belzoni: Archaeologist Extraordinary* (New York: Walker and Company, 1961); Marco Zatterin, *Il gigante del Nilo: Storia e avventure del Grande Belzoni, l'uomo che svelò i misteri dell'Egitto dei faraoni* (Milan: Mondadori, 2000); Ivor Noël Hume, *Belzoni: The Giant Archaeologists Love to Hate* (Charlottesville: University of Virginia Press, 2011).

6   Deborah Manley and Peta Rée, *Henry Salt: Artist, Traveller, Diplomat, Egyptologist* (London: Libri Publications Limited, 2001), 82–99.

7   Charles Leonard Irby and James Mangles, *Travels in Egypt and Nubia, Syria, and Asia Minor; During the Years 1817 & 1818* (London: T. White and Co., 1823).

8   Pascale Linant de Bellefonds, "The Journey of the Comte de Forbin in the Near East and Egypt, 1817–1818," in Charles Foster, ed., *Travellers in the Near East* (London: Stacey International, 2004), 107–33.

9   Bernard Comment, *The Painted Panorama* (New York: Harry N. Abrams, 2000), 30–47; Antoine Gautier and Louis du Chalard, "Les panoramas orientaux du peintre Pierre Prévost (1764–1823)," *Orient, Bulletin de l'association des anciens élèves et amis des langues orientales, Institut National des Langues et Civilisations Orientales* (June 2010), 85–108. His painted sketches of Constantinople are preserved in the Louvre.

10   Marcel Kurz and Pascale Linant de Bellefonds, "Linant de Bellefonds: Travels in Egypt, Sudan and Arabia Petraea (1818–1828)," in Paul and Janet Starkey, eds., *Travellers in Egypt* (London: I.B.Tauris, 1998/2001), 61–69.

11   Patricia Usick, "Berths under the Highest Stars: Henry William Beechey in Egypt 1816–1819," in Paul Starkey and Nadia El Kholy, eds., *Egypt through the Eyes of Travellers* (Durham: Astene, 2002), 13–24.

12   Pierre Pinon, "L'Orient de Jean Nicolas Huyot: Le voyage en Asie-Mineure, en Égypte et en Grèce (1817–1821)," *Revue du monde musulman et de la Méditerranée*, no. 73–74 (1994), 35–55.

13   Daniele Salvoldi, "Alessandro Ricci's Travel Account: Story and Content of his Journal Lost and Found," *Evo* 32 (2009), 113–19, lincei.academia.edu.

14   On Gau see Harry Francis Mallgrave, *Gottfried Semper: Architect of the Nineteenth Century* (New Haven: Yale University Press, 1996), 18–19.

15   Jean-Jacques Fiechter, *La moisson des dieux* (Paris: Édition Julliard, 1994).

16   Silvana Cincotti, "Les fouilles dans le Musée: la collection égyptienne de Turin et le Fonds Rifaud," *Cahiers de Karnak*, 14 (2013), 279–285; Fiechter, *La moisson des dieux*. See also, the review by R.T. Ridley in *Journal of Egyptian Archaeology*, 82 (1996), 244–46.

17   Cesare Balbo, ed., *Lettere del Conte Carlo Vidua*, vol. 2 (Turin: Giuseppe Pomba, 1834); Michel Dewachter, "Le voyage nubien du Comte Carlo Vidua (fin Fevrier–fin Avril 1820)," *Bulletin de l'Institut français d'Archéologie orientale*, 69 (1970), 171–89; Gian Paolo Romagnani, ed., *Carlo Vidua viaggiatore e collezionista (1785–1830)* (Città di Casale Monferrato: Assessorato per la Cultura, 1987).

18   D.B. Baker, "C.G. Ehrenberg and W.F. Hemprich's Travels, 1820–1825, and the Insecta of the *Symbolae Physicae*," *Deutsche entomologische Zeitschrift* 44 (1997), 2, 165–202.

19   Edouard Rüppell, *Reisen in Nubien, Kordofan und dem peträischen Arabien* (Frankfurt am Main: Friedrich Wilmans, 1829).

20   Giambattista Brocchi, *Giornale delle osservazioni fatte ne'viaggi in Egitto, nella Siria e nella Nubia* (Bassano: A. Roberti, 1841–1843).

21   Lieutenant-Colonel Fitzclarence, *Journal of a Route Across India, through Egypt, to England* (London: John Murray, 1819).

22   [John Hanson], *Route of Lieutenant-General Sir Miles Nightingall, K.C.B., Overland from India* (London: T. Baker, 1820).

23   [Digby Mackworth], *Diary of a Tour through Southern India, Egypt, and Palestine, in the Years 1821 and 1822* (London: J. Hatchard and Son, 1823).

24   John Malcolm, *Malcolm. Soldier, Diplomat, Ideologue of British India. The Life of Sir John Malcolm (1749-1833)* (Edinburgh: John Donald, 2014), 457–58.

25   [Joseph Moyle Sherer], *Scenes and Impressions in Egypt and in Italy* (London: Longman, Hurst, Rees, Orme, Brwon, and Green, 1825).

26   [Ambroise Firmin Didot], *Notes d'un voyage fait dans le Levant en 1816 et 1817* (Paris: Typographie de Firmin Didot [1826]).

27   Robert Richardson, *Travels along the Mediterranean, and Parts Adjacent in Company with the Earl of Belmore during the Years 1816–17–18* (London: T. Cadell, 1822), 152–53.

28   Peter Marson, *Belmore: The Lowry Corrys of Castle Coole 1646–1913* (Belfast: Ulster Historical Foundation, 2007), 127–62.

Chapter 6

1   *Letters from Asia: Written by a Gentleman of Boston, to a Friend in that Place* (New York: A.T. Goodrich & Co., 1819).

2   Henry A.S. Dearborn, *A Memoir on the Commerce and Navigation of the Black Sea, and the Trade and Maritime Geography of Turkey and Egypt* (Boston: Wells and Lilly, 1819).

3   A polacre brig was a three-masted vessel carrying a square sail on the mainmast and lateen sails on the fore- and mizzenmasts.

4   E.g., *Commercial Advertiser*, New York, December 5, 1817, and *City of Washington Gazette*, December 8, 1817.

5   *The New-York Columbian*, May 20, 1818.

6   Francis B. Crowninshield, ed., *The Story of George Crowninshield's Yacht Cleopatra's Barge on a Voyage of Pleasure to the Western Islands and the Mediterranean 1816–1817* (Boston: privately printed, 1913); David L. Ferguson, *Cleopatra's Barge: The Crowninshield Story* (Boston: Little, Brown, and Co., 1976), 88–118.

7   Édouard Driault, *La formation de l'empire de Mohamed Aly de l'Arabie au Soudan (1814–1823)* (Cairo: L'Institut français d'archéologie orientale du Caire pour la Société royale de Géographie d'Égypte, 1927), 102.

8   E.g., *The Alexandria Herald*, February 5, 1819.

9   Evert A. Duyckinck and George L. Duyckinck, eds., *Cyclopaedia of American Literature* (New York: Charles Scribner, 1856), vol. 2, 170n.

10   George Bethune English, *A Narrative of the Expedition to Dongala and Sennaar* (Boston: Wells and Lilly, 1823).

11   George Waddington and Barnard Hanbury, *Journal of a Visit to Some Parts of Ethiopia* (London: John Murray, 1822), 114–15.

12   Michel Chauvet, *Frédéric Cailliaud: Les aventures d'un naturaliste en Égypt et au Soudan 1815–1822* (Saint-Sébastien-sur-Loire: Édition ACL-CROCUS, 1989). Philippe Mainterot, *Aux origines de l'Égyptologie: Voyages et collections de Frédéric Cailliaud 1787–1869* (Rennes: Presses universitaires de Rennes, 2011).

13   Frédéric Cailliaud, *Voyage a Méroé, au fleuve blanc, au-delà de Fâzoql dans le midi du royaume de Sennâr, a Syouah et dans cinq autres oasis; fait dans les années 1819, 1820, 1821 et 1822*, 4 vols. (Paris: Imprimerie Royale, 1826–1827).

14   Cailliaud, *Voyage*, vol. 2, 320.

15   [James E. DeKay], *Sketches of Turkey in 1831 & 1832* (New York: J. & J. Harper, 1833), 488n. On DeKay see David M. Damkaer, *The Copepodologist's Cabinet: A Biographical and Bibliographical History*, Memoirs of the American Philosophical Society (Philadelphia: American Philosophical Society, 2002), vol. 240, 206–13.

16   J.J. Halls, *The Life and Correspondence of Henry Salt, Esq. F.R.S. &c. His Britannic Majesty's Late Consul-General in Egypt* (London: Richard Bentley, 1834), vol. 2, 210.

17   *Essex Register*, Salem, Massachusetts, July 6, 1822.

18   Cassandra Vivian, "Khalil Aga: A Lost American on the Nile," in Deborah Manley and Diane Fortenbury, eds., *Saddling the Dogs: Journeys through Egypt and the Near East* (Oxford: ASTENE and Oxbow Books, 2009), 81–91; and Vivian, *Americans in Egypt, 1770–1915: Explorers, Consuls, Travelers, Soldiers, Missionaries, Writers and Scientists* (Jefferson, NC: McFarland, 2012), 79–94.

19   Silvio Curto and Laura Donatelli, eds., *Bernardino Drovetti Epistolario (1800–1851)* (Milan: Cisalpino-Goliardica, 1985), 242.

20   *The Rhode Island American*, October 7, 1828.

21 George Ticknor, *Remarks on the Character of the late Edward Everett, Made at a Meeting of the Massachusetts Historical Society, January 30, 1865* (Boston: J.E. Farwell and Company, 1865), 10.

22 Frank E. Bradish, "Luther Bradish," *Memorial Biographies of The New-England Historic Genealogical Society* (Boston, 1894) 5, 268–76; James Franklin Beard, ed., *The Letters and Journals of James Fenimore Cooper* (Cambridge, MA: The Belknap Press of Harvard University Press, 1960), vol. 1, 38, 39, 130, 154, 221, 286.

23 M. Lelorrain, "A Journey in Egypt," *The Atheneum*, February 1, 1823; Edward Everett, review of *Notice sur le Zodiaque de Denderah*, par M.J. Saint-Martin, Membre de l'Institut, Paris 1822, in *The North American Review* (October 1823), 233ff. For a full account of the Zodiac, see Jed Z. Buchwald and Diane Greco Josefowicz, *The Zodiac of Paris* (Princeton: Princeton University Press, 2010).

24 Lorna Gibb, *Lady Hester: Queen of the East* (London: Faber and Faber, 2005).

25 From Pliny Fisk's manuscript diary at Middlebury College.

26 Surely Samuel Laurence Gouverneur (1799–1865), class of 1817 at Columbia, son of Nicholas Gouverneur and Hester Kortright, whose sister Elizabeth was married to President James Monroe. Young Gouverneur became a secretary to Monroe and married his daughter (and his own first cousin) in March 1820.

27 Letter in the New-York Historical Society.

28 *The Eclectic Magazine*, vol. 60 (September 1863), 111–14; Walter A. Reichart, ed., *Washington Irving: Journals and Notebooks; Volume III, 1819–1827* (Madison: University of Wisconsin Press, 1970). Fourth of July: *National Advocate*, August 28, 1823; *Daily National Intelligencer*, September 13, 1824.

29 Mention of Bradish is omitted in the entry for that date published in Goodell's memoirs many years later: E.D.G. Prime, *Forty Years in the Turkish Empire: Or Memoirs of Rev. William Goodell, D.D.* (New York: Robert Carter and Brothers, 1876), 77.

30 [Sarah R. Haight], *Letters from the Old World* (New York: Harper & Brothers, 1840), vol. 1, 297.

31 Despina Vlami, "Entrepreneurship and Relational Capital in a Levantine Context: Bartholomew Edward Abbott," *The Historical Review* 6 (2009), 129–57.

32 Letter of September 9, 1837, among the Bradish papers at the New-York Historical Society. Chasseaud had become a secretary for Lady Hester Stanhope by 1830 and therefore had many opportunities to see her. In 1832 he was appointed US consular agent in Beirut, and in 1835 he was appointed American consul there.

33 James Riker Jr., *The Annals of Newtown, in Queens County, New-York: Containing Its History from its First Settlement* . . . (New York: D. Fanshaw, 1852), 268–80.

34	George Rapelje, *A Narrative of Excursions, Voyages, and Travels Performed at Different Periods in America, Europe, Asia, and Africa* (New York: West & Trow, 1834).
35	John Madox, *Excursions in the Holy Land, Egypt, Nubia, Syria, &c. Including a Visit to the Unfrequented District of the Haouran* (London, 1834), vol. 1, 129. On the travels of Madox see John H. Taylor, "John Madox: A Diligent Traveller and his Scattered Legacy," in Diane Fortenberry, ed., *Souvenirs and New Ideas: Travel and Collecting in Egypt and the Near East* (Oxford: Oxbow Books, 2013), 179–91.
36	P.M. Fraser, *Ptolemaic Alexandria* (Oxford: Oxford University Press, 1985), vol. 1, 24–25 and notes.
37	Rapelje, *Narrative of Excursions*, 296.
38	Jean-Yves Empereur, *Alexandria Rediscovered* (New York: George Braziller, 1998), 100–109; Fraser, *Ptolemaic Alexandria*, vol. 2, 85–89.
39	Edward Daniel Clarke, *Travels in Various Countries of Europe Asia and Africa* (London: T. Cadell, 1814), vol. 3, frontispiece, drawn by Fauvel, the French diplomat and scholar, who visited Egypt in 1789 and 1792. The feat was first achieved by British sailors in 1777 as related in Eyles Irwin, *A Series of Adventures in the Course of a Voyage up the Red-Sea, on the Coasts of Arabia and Egypt* (London: W. Davies, 1780), 370–72.
40	Two versions are known. One, the source of Clarke's illustration (in *Travels in Various Countries*), is in the Thomas Hope collection in the Benaki Museum in Athens: L. Beschi, "Nuovi disegni di L.S. Fauvel nella collezione di Thomas Hope," in Francesco Prontera, ed., *Geografia storica della grecia antica: Tradizioni e problemi* (Rome: Laterza, 1991), 24–45, fig. 7. The other has been in the Paris art market: Galleries Georges Petit, Paris, *Catalogue des Aquarelles et Dessins de l'École Française du xviiie siècle, Composant la Collection de M.J. Masson*, 7 mai 1923, lot 75; and recently, Vente Boisgirard et Associés, Paris, 19 octobre 2011, lot 25. Alessia Zambon of Paris brought the first version to my attention. On Fauvel in Egypt see Alessia Zambon, *Aux origines de l'archéologie en Grèce. Fauvel et sa méthode* (Paris: Institut national d'histoire de l'art, 2014), 32–33.
41	Maarten J. Raven and Wybren K. Taconis, *Egyptian Mummies: Radiological Atlas of the Collections in the National Museum of Antiquities at Leiden* (Turnhout: Brepols, 2005), 120–38, figs. 10.1, 11.1, 12.1, 14.1, 15.1.
42	Rapelje, *A Narrative of Excursions*, 299–300.
43	Burton (1788–1862), Trinity College, Cambridge, was hired as a mineralogist but stayed on for many years as one of the first Egyptologists. His companions must have been Charles Humphreys, his secretary, and Vicenzo, their servant: Neil Cooke, "The Forgotten Egyptologist: James Burton," in Paul and Janet Starkey, eds., *Travellers in Egypt* (London: I.B.Tauris, 2001), 88–89.
44	John O. Udal, *The Nile in Darkness: Conquest and Exploration 1504–1862* (London: Michael Russell, 1998), 241.

45 Charles Colville Frankland, *Travels to and from Constantinople in 1827 and 1828* (London: Henry Colburn, 1829), vol. 1, 333.

46 Carl C. Cutter, *Queens of the Western Ocean: The Story of America's Mail and Passenger Sailing Lines* (Annapolis: United States Naval Institute, 1961), 152–53.

47 Mentioned in a website, *The Van Lennep Genealogy Smyrna Branch*: http://www/levantineheritage.com/pdf/The_Van-Lennep_Genealogy_Smyrna_Branch.pdf. Jacob Van Lennep, born 1769, is one of the young children near their mother in the Van Lennep portrait (see plate 1). Richard Van Lennep was born ten years later, in 1779. On his first trip to Boston in 1807, on board the topsail schooner *Tryal*, Richard Van Lennep kept a sketchbook that was recently in the maritime collection of J. Welles Henderson: J. Welles Henderson and Rodney P. Carlisle, *Jack Tar: Maritime Art & Antiques, a Sailors Life* (Woodbridge, Suffolk, UK: Antique Collectors' Club, 1999), 149. The sketchbook did not figure in the sale of Henderson's maritime collection: Northeast Auctions, Portsmouth, New Hampshire, August 16, 2008.

48 *Boston Evening Transcript*. Announcement of the Sale in the *Boston Commerical Gazette*, January 30, 1826.

49 *Aurora and Franklin Gazette*, Philadelphia, December 29, 1825.

50 The story of mummies entering the United States before 1900 is the subject of a recent book: S.J. Wolfe with Robert Singerman, *Mummies in Nineteenth-Century America: Ancient Egyptians as Artifacts* (Jefferson, NC: McFarland & Company, Inc., 2009).

Chapter 7

1 Pliny Fisk, *The Holy Land: An Interesting Field of Missionary Enterprise; A Sermon Preached in the Old South Church, Boston, Sabbath, Oct. 31, 1819, Just before the Departure of the Palestine Mission* (Boston: Samuel T. Armstrong, 1819); Levi Parsons, *The Dereliction and Restoration of the Jews: A Sermon Preached in Park-Street Church Boston, Sabbath, Oct. 31, 1819, Just before the Departure of the Palestine Mission* (Boston: Samuel T. Armstrong, 1819).

2 S. Worcester, *Instructions from the Prudential Committee of the American Board of Commissioners for Foreign Missions, to the Rev. Levi Parsons and the Rev. Pliny Fisk, Missionaries Designated for Palestine; Delivered in the Old South Church Boston, Sabbath Evening, Oct. 31, 1819.*

3 *Société pour l'avancement de la connaissance Chrétienne en Turquie, et dans le Levant etablie à Smyrne*. A copy of this pamphlet in my possession, inscribed *Prof. Frederick Hall. Smyrna Feb. 10, 1820*, is probably the very copy sent to Hall by Parsons.

4 Gawen William Hamilton, captain of HMS *Cambrian*, seen later by Fisk in Smyrna.

5 Fisk's "Book of Extracts and Records" is preserved in the Burke Library of Union Theological Seminary, part of the Columbia University Library.

The inscription appears on pages 74–75. F.A. de Chateaubriand, *Travels in Greece, Palestine, Egypt, and Barbary, during the Years 1806 and 1807* (London: Henry Colburn, 1811), vol. 2, 221.

6   Letter to the ABCFM, Feb. 10, 1822, *The Missionary Herald*, July 1822; Alvan Bond, *Memoir of the Rev. Pliny Fisk, A.M. Late Missionary to Palestine* (Boston: Crocker & Brewster, 1828), 181–82.

7   Fisk's manuscript diary at Middlebury College.

8   Jason Thompson, "Osman Effendi: A Scottish Convert to Islam in Early Nineteenth-Century Egypt," *Journal of World History* 5, no. 1 (1994), 99–123.

9   Letter to the *Boston Recorder*, reprinted in the *Religious Remembrancer*, Oct. 5, 1822.

10 Quoted from Fisk's diary at Middlebury College. A version is in a letter to the ABCFM from Malta, May 9, 1822; Bond, *Memoir of the Rev. Pliny Fisk*, 208–209.

11 Letter to the editor of the *Boston Recorder*, reprinted in the *Religious Remembrancer*, Oct. 5, 1822. Not in Bond's *Memoir of the Rev. Pliny Fisk*. For the palace at Shubra as it is today see Shirley Johnston with Sherif Sonbol, *Egyptian Palaces and Villas: Pashas, Khedives, and Kings* (New York: Abrams, 2006), 20–22.

12 Fisk's manuscript diary.

13 F.E.H. Haines, *Jonas King: Missionary to Syria and Greece* (New York: American Tract Society, 1879), 46–64. Francina Eglée Hannah Haines, daughter of S.V.S. Wilder, based her account of King on his journals addressed to the Paris Missionary Society under whose auspices he was traveling in the East, and on letters addressed to Wilder, and to his daughters, Electa, Francina, and Vrylina. One journal, containing copies of a diary and letters, devoted to Cairo (the return visit after the Nile journey), Sinai, and Jerusalem, was given to the American Antiquarian Society by her great-grandson, Lawrence Alan Haines, in 1982.

14 Haines, *Jonas King*, 68–74. The French traveler Ambroise Firmin-Didot had met Caussin de Perceval in Constantinople in 1816 where Caussin was studying Turkish.

15 "Letters by Mrs. John T. Kirkland," *Proceedings of the Massachusetts Historical Society. Second Series*, vol. 19, 1905 (Boston, 1906), 490.

16 "Journal of Messrs. Fisk and King, in Upper Egypt," *The Missionary Herald*, November 1823; Bond, *Memoir of the Rev. Pliny Fisk*, 240–50, but omitting most of the description of Karnak. Two copies of the journal kept by Fisk during their time in Egypt exist: one, belonging to the American Board of Commissioners for Foreign Missions, is on deposit at the Houghton Library at Harvard; the other is owned by Middlebury College.

17 Bond, *Memoir of the Rev. Pliny Fisk*, 247, and Fisk's manuscript diary.

18 Richard Hill, *A Biographical Dictionary of the Sudan* (London: Frank Cass and Company Limited, 1967), 212. On Üxküll see Sergey Stadnikov, "Die Wanderungen des deutsch-baltischen orientreisenden Alexander von Üxküll

in Ägypten und Nubien 1822–1823," *Göttinger Miszellen* (1995), 71–92. Both Üxküll and Lesseps carved their names at Abu Simbel and at other places.

19 Wolff saw him also: "Extracts from the Journal of Mr. Wolff," *The Religious Miscellany Containing Information Relative to the Church of Christ* (Carlisle: Fleming and Geddes, 1823), vol. 2, 179.

20 Joseph Grenier cut his name with the date 1823 in the Kiosk of Trajan at Philae.

21 Gustav Parthey, *Wanderungen durch Sicilien und die Levante. Zweiter Theil. Das Nilthal* (Berlin: in der Nicolai'schen Buchhandlung, 1840), 494.

22 Probably Moyle Sherer and his three companions who arrived at Luxor on March 8 from Quseir: [Joseph Moyle Sherer], *Scenes and Impressions in Egypt and in Italy* (London: Longman, 1825).

23 Dieter Arnold, *Temples of the Last Pharaohs* (Oxford and New York: Oxford University Press, 1999), 166–67, fig. 112.

24 Arnold, *Temples of the Last Pharaohs*, 34–35, fig. 7, and 115–17, fig. 72. The central gate was probably constructed under Sheshonq I (945–924 BC), while the flanking pylon towers, left unfinished, probably date from the reign of Nectanebo I (c. 379–361 BC).

25 Arielle P. Kozloff, Betsy M. Bryan, Lawrence M. Berman, *Egypt's Dazzling Sun: Amenhotep III and his World* (Cleveland: The Cleveland Museum of Art, 1992), 47, fig. II.6.

26 Stanley Mayes, *The Great Belzoni: Archaeologist Extraordinary* (New York: Walker and Company, 1961), 236.

27 As early as 1760, the Italian naturalist Vitaliano Donati had removed one, now to be found in the Museo Egizio in Turin: Alberto Siliotti, ed., *Viaggiatori Veneti alla scoperta dell'Egitto* (Venice: Arsenale Editrice, 1985), 71–72. At the very end of the eighteenth century, the French savants under Napoleon had retrieved one intact statue and fragments of others only to have them confiscated by the British and sent to London in 1802. The British traveler William Bankes took two in 1815; he later sold them to the Duke of Devonshire and they are still to be found at the family house in Chatsworth: Patricia Usick, *Adventures in Egypt and Nubia: The Travels of William John Bankes (1786–1855)* (London: The British Museum Press, 2002), 51 and 195. In 1817, the Anglo-Irish Earl of Belmore acquired two, which were later, in 1843, acquired by the British Museum. In the very year that Fisk and King were at Thebes, the British Museum acquired from the British consul-general Henry Salt six seated and standing Sekhmets from Karnak among any number of sculptures that had been excavated for him in preceding years by Giovanni Belzoni: Stephanie Moser, *Wondrous Curiosities: Ancient Egypt at the British Museum* (Chicago: The University of Chicago Press, 2006), 96–98, figs. 4–7a and 4.7b. Peter A. Clayton, "A Pioneer Egyptologist: Giovanni Battista Belzoni, 1778–1823," in Starkey and Starkey, *Travellers in Egypt*, 43–44. Belzoni himself, as we have just

mentioned, presented two to the city of Padua; they are now in the Museo
Civico agli Eremitani: Siliotti, ed., *Viaggiatori Veneti all scoperta dell'Egitto*,
85. The Museo Egizio in Turin acquired from the French consul-general
Bernardino Drovetti twenty Sekhmets, excavated for him in 1818 by
Jean-Jacques Rifaud, whom Fisk and King met on first reaching Luxor.
The French government made up for their loss of a complete Sekhmet,
confiscated by the British in 1799, by obtaining in 1818 others from the
Comte de Forbin, director general of French museums, who in turn had
acquired them from Giovanni Belzoni. Later, in 1826, the Louvre acquired
at least one from Henry Salt's second collection: Marc Etienne, *The Louvre
and the Ancient World* (Atlanta: High Museum of Art, 2007), 60–61. Seven
others, from the collection of John Barker, British consul-general in Egypt
from 1829 to 1833, were sold anonymously at Sotheby's in London in
March, 1833, and after passing through two English private collections
were acquired in 1915 by the Metropolitan Museum of Art in New York:
Albert M. Lythgoe, "Statues of the Goddess Sekhmet," *Bulletin of the
Metropolitan Museum of Art* 14 (1919), 3–22; Gerry D. Scott III, "A Seated
Statue of Sekhmet and Two Related Sculptures in the Collection of the San
Antonio Museum of Art," in Sue H. D'Auria, ed., *Servant of Mut: Studies
in Honor of Richard A. Fazzini* (Leiden: Martinus Nijhoff Publishers, 2007),
223ff. Lythgoe, followed by Scott, reported that they came from the collec-
tion of Henry Salt, but John H. Taylor of the Department of Ancient Egypt
and Sudan at the British Museum, made me aware that John Barker (not
Salt) was the consignor to the 1833 sale at Sotheby's.

28 Bond, *Memoirs of the Rev. Pliny Fisk*, 251.
29 Bond, *Memoirs of the Rev. Pliny Fisk*, 377 (a letter to Professor Hall at Mid-
    dlebury); and Frederick Hall, "Notice of Oriental Minerals," *The American
    Journal of Science and Arts*, January 2, 1838, 254–55. The minerals were pre-
    sented to Dartmouth College where Hall had gone to teach.
30 "Journal of Messrs. Fisk and King, in Upper Egypt," *The Pittsburgh
    Recorder*, January 2, 1824; Bond, *Memoirs of the Rev. Pliny Fisk*, 254.
31 Jean-Paul Champollion, *Lettre à M. Dacier, . . . relative à l'alphabet des hiéro-
    glyphs phonétiques employés par les égyptiens pour inscrire sur leurs monuments,
    les titres, les noms et les surnoms des souverains grecs et romains* (Paris: Firmin
    Didot Père et Fils, 1822).
32 A copy of which is preserved in a volume of King's journal owned by the
    American Antiquarian Society.
33 King's manuscript journal at the American Antiquarian Society.
34 Fisk's manuscript diary at Middlebury College.
35 Haines, *Jonas King*, 128–30; diary of Pliny Fisk at Middlebury College, 101.
36 Hilton Obenzinger, "Holy Land Narrative and American Covenant: Levi
    Parsons, Pliny Fisk and the Palestine Mission," *Religion & Literature* 36
    (2003), 263; Michael B. Oren, *Power, Faith, and Fantasy: America in the*

Middle East, 1776 to the Present (New York: W.W. Norton, 2007), 96. Fisk kept a diary from June 22, 1824, into 1825, preserved today in the Burke Library at Columbia University.

37   "Letter from Mr. Smith to the Corresponding Secretary," *The Missionary Herald*, November 1827.

Chapter 8

1   William St. Clair, *That Greece Might Still Be Free: The Philhellenes in the War of Independence* (London: Oxford University Press, 1972), 1–12; Douglas Dakin, *The Greek Struggle for Independence 1821–1833* (Berkeley: University of California Press, 1973), 57–60.

2   Fisk's journal covering February 17 to May 10, 1821, owned by the ABCFM, is on deposit in the Houghton Library at Harvard University. Middlebury College owns the subsequent volume, covering June 1 to August 17, 1821.

3   Owned by the New-York Historical Society.

4   St. Clair, *That Greece Might Still Be Free*, 78–81.

5   George Rapelje, *A Narrative of Excursions, Voyages, and Travels Performed at Different Periods in America, Europe, Asia, and Africa* (New York: West & Trow, 1834), 286–87.

6   Rapelje, *Narrative of Excursions*, 287.

7   "Notes of a cruise on board the United States Ship Constitution, kept by Lieutenant David Geisinger, 12 May 1821—9 April 1824," manuscript in the Maryland Historical Society; R.C. Anderson, *Naval Wars in the Levant 1559—1853* (Princeton: Princeton University Press, 1952), 487.

8   *Albany Argus*, November 12, 1822; *Daily National Intelligencer*, November 18, 1822.

9   *Saturday Evening Post*, September 14, 1822; *American Mercury* (Hartford), September 16, 1822.

10   Maurie D. McInnis and Angela D. Mack, eds., *In Pursuit of Refinement: Charlestonians Abroad, 1740–1860* (Charleston: University of South Carolina Press, 1999), 162–63, no. 36.

11   Stephen A. Larrabee, *Hellas Observed: The American Experience of Greece 1775–1865* (New York: New York University Press, 1957), 95–107; George Georgiades Arnakis, ed., *George Jarvis: His Journal and Related Documents* (Thessaloniki: Institute for Balkan Studies, 1965).

12   Larrabee, *Hellas Observed*, 107–12; St. Clair, *That Greece Might Still Be Free*, 336–40.

13   Samuel G. Howe, *An Historical Sketch of the Greek Revolution* (New York: White, Gallaher & White, 1828).

14   Larrabee, *Hellas Observed*, 123–28; James F. Hopkins, ed., *The Papers of Henry Clay*, vol. 5 (Lexington, Kentucky: The University Press of Kentucky, 1992), 10.

15 Larrabee, *Hellas Observed*, 134–41; *The Boston News-letter, and City Record*, February 18, 1826: Evans returned to Boston from Smyrna as a passenger on the brig *Sally Anne*.

16 *Boston Commercial Gazette*, October 27, 1825. More than a year earlier, in December 1823, it had been undergoing repairs at Trieste: *Salem Gazette*, February 17, 1824.

17 *Aurora and Franklin Gazette*, Philadelphia, December 17, 1825.

18 *Boston Commercial Gazette*, June 12, 1826; *Connecticut Herald*, June 20, 1826; *National Gazette and Literary Register*, June 15, 1826.

19 Édouard Driault, *L'expédition de Crète et de Morée (1823–1828): Correspondance des consuls de France en Égypte et en Crète* (Cairo: L'Institut français d'archéologie orientale du Caire pour La Société Royale de Géographie d'Égypte, 1930), 94–95.

20 C.M. Woodhouse, *The Battle of Navarino* (London: Hodder Stoughton, 1965).

21 Larrabee, *Hellas Observed*, 148–75.

22 Larrabee, *Hellas Observed*, 157, 165, 177, 179, 181.

23 The *Harriet's* manifest in United States immigration records names Vandervoort's two companions: Daniel Jepson and W.J. Whiting. See also the *Baltimore Patriot*, March 4, 1828, where Jepson's name is David, Whiting appears as Whitney, and Evangeles is Angelo and is said erroneously to be a refugee from Chios.

24 Paul J. Staiti, *Samuel F. B. Morse* (Cambridge: Cambridge University Press, 1989), 131–32, pl. X.

25 First published in 1828. William Cullen Bryant, *Poems* (Boston: Russell, Odiorne and Metcalf, 1834), 133–34.

26 Reproduced in *The Talisman for MDCCCXXIX* (New York, 1828); *The Art Quarterly* 20 (1959), 365, fig. 1, and p. 368. A later state, done about 1835 when Evangeles was at Columbia, is illustrated in Charles Henry Hart, *Catalogue of the Engraved Works of Asher B. Durand Exhibited at the Grolier Club* (New York, 1895), 93, no. 215. The original, sold to Philip Hone after Ward's death in 1839, is lost.

27 John Gregoriadis, "The Greek Boy," *Modern Greek Studies Yearbook* (Minneapolis: University of Minnesota), vol. 10/11 (1994/1995), 603–27. See also Constantine G. Hatzideimitriou, Christodolos M. L. [Evangeles] Evangelides (1815–1881): "An Early Greek American Educator and Lobbyist," *Journal of Modern Hellenism* 21–22 (2004–2005), 205–38, concerned largely with his later visit to the United States in 1854. The New-York Historical Society possesses his diary.

28 By the time he left Columbia, "Christy" had acquired two additional names: class records list him as Christodoulos Leonidas Miltiades Evangeles.

29 "Ship News," *Morning Post*, London, January 29, 1822.

30 The story of the treaty is told in James A. Field Jr., *America and the Mediterranean World 1776–1882* (Princeton: Princeton University Press, 1969), 141–53.

31 Phyllis DeKay Wheelock, "The Levant Journal of Capt. George C. DeKay," *Lands East* 1, no. 9 (1956), 19–23 and no. 10, 20–26.

32 Charles W. Webster, *The Foreign Policy of Palmerston 1830–1841* (London: G. Bell & Sons, Ltd., 1951), vol. 1.

33 Georges Douin, *La première guerre de Syrie*, vol. 1: *La conquête de Syrie (1831–1832)*; vol. 2: *La Paix de Kutahia (1833)* (Cairo: Société royale de géographie d'Égypte, 1931).

34 For the full story of the Eastern Question in these years see Frederick Stanley Rodkey, *The Turco-Egyptian Question in the Relations of England, France, and Russia, 1832–1841* (Urbana: University of Illinois, 1924; repr. New York: Russell & Russell, 1974); Vernon John Puryear, *France and the Levant: From the Bourbon Restoration to the Peace of Kutiah* (Berkeley: University of California Press, 1941; repr. Archon Books, 1968); Alexander Bitis, *Russia and the Eastern Question: Army, Government, and Society 1815–1833* (Oxford: Oxford University Press for the British Academy, 2006).

35 David Offley's letters from Smyrna to his sister in Philadelphia were put on the market by a descendant shortly before 2010 and are now widely dispersed.

36 On the Langdons see Tom Rees, *Merchant Adventurers in the Levant: Two British Families of Privateers, Consuls and Traders 1700–1950* (Stawell: Talbot, 2003).

37 Letters written from Smyrna by Griffin Stith are preserved among the Dallam papers at the Maryland Historical Society.

38 *Columbian Sentinel*, Boston, December 8, 1824.

39 *Columbian Sentinel*, Boston, January 13, 1825.

40 *Baltimore Patriot*, March 29, 1824.

41 *Daily National Intelligencer*, Washington, DC, August 18, 1825 (picked up from the *New York Gazette*).

42 *Boston Commercial Gazette*, August 15, 1825.

43 Raymond Carr, *Spain 1808–1939* (Oxford: Clarendon Press, 1966), 129–46.

44 Georges Douin, *La Mission du Baron de Boislecomte: L'Égypte et la Syrie en 1833* (Cairo: L'Institut français d'archéologie orientale du Caire pour La Société Royale de Géographie d'Égypte, 1927), 109.

45 For example, *Maryland Gazette and State Register*, Annapolis, November 9, 1826; *Charleston Courier*, November 10, 1826.

Chapter 9

1 Henry Wheaton, "Egyptian Antiquities," *The North American Review* 29 (1929), 361–88; Edward Everett, "Hieroglyphics," *The North American Review* 32 (1831), 95–126.

2 Stephanie Moser, *Wondrous Curiosities: Ancient Egypt at the British Museum* (Chicago: University of Chicago Press, 2006), 65–170.

3 Jean-Marcel Humbert, Michael Pantazzi, and Christiane Ziegler, eds., *Egyptomania: Egypt in Western Art 1730–1930* (Ottawa: Publication Division of the National Gallery of Canada, 1994), 273–74. On Belzoni's exhibition

at the Egyptian Hall, see Susan M. Pearce, "Belzoni's Collecting and the Egyptian Taste," in Cinzia Sicca and Alison Yarrington, eds., *The Lustrous Trade: Material Culture and the History of Sculpture in England and Italy, c.1700–c.1860* (Leicester: Leicester University Press, 2000), 191–210.

4   Benjamin Peirce, ed., *A Catalogue of the Library of Harvard University in Cambridge, Massachusetts* (Cambridge, MA, 1830), vol. 1, xi.

5   Amelia Peck, ed., *Alexander Jackson Davis, American Architect 1803–1892* (New York: The Metropolitan Museum of Art, 1992), color plate 26; *Description de l'Égypte, ou Recueil des observationss et des recherches* (Paris: Imprimerie Impériale, 1809), vol. 1, plates 91–94.

6   *Important notice to all colleges, state, and other public libraries, athenaeums, & other institutions . . . of rare and valuable books . . . Ithiel Town, now of New York, will proceed immediately to have his whole library & collection disposed of, at private sale* (New York, 1842), 4: "Bonapart's Egypt, 23 vols, a copy presented to one of his generals." The University of Southern California in Los Angeles now owns Ithiel Town's set.

7   Peck, *Alexander Jackson Davis*, color plates 1, 27 (the Halls of Justice), 32.

8   Richard G. Carrott, *The Egyptian Revival: Its Sources, Monuments, and Meaning—1808–1858* (Berkeley: University of California Press, 1978), 146–92. Richard A. Fazzini and Mary E. McKercher, "'Egyptomania' and American Architecture," in Jean-Marcel Humbert and Clifford Price, eds., *Imhotep Today: Egyptianizing Architecture* (London: University College London Press, 2003), 135–59; Allan Nevins and Milton Halsey Thomas, eds., *The Diary of George Templeton Strong* (New York: The Macmillan Company, 1952), vol. 1, 104.

9   Carrott, *The Egyptian Revival*, 113–15, 54n, and p. 165, pls. 107, 110. Papers of John Haviland in the Library of the University of Pennsylvania, vol. 4, p. 93. Another Philadelphia architect, Thomas Ustick Walter (1804–1887), designer of a debtors' prison in Egyptian style in the early 1830s (Carrott, *The Egyptian Revival*, 118, fig. 105), owned a set of the first edition of the work. In 1841, temporarily bankrupt, he sold it to the Carpenters' Company in Philadelphia (where it still is) for $300.

10   "Donations for the Library," *Transactions of the American Philosophical Society*, vol. 4, new series (1834), 480. Sadly, volume one is lost. Lehigh University and the American Oriental Society at Yale also possess sets of this work (Yale's set missing volume one).

11   *Early Proceedings of the American Philosophical Society* (Philadelphia, 1884), 630: "Denon's Egypt procured by Mr. Vaughan, to be purchased from him. Special vote of thanks to Mr. Vaughan for the pains he has taken in relation to Denon's Egypt." The *Description* was often called "Denon's Egypt" in those days.

12   New York Post, ca. April 20, 1830; *Catalogue of the Library of Congress in the Capitol of the United States of America, December 1839*, Washington, DC, 1840, 512–13. This set was destroyed when the congressional library, then at the Capitol, burned in December 1851.

13 *Description de l'Égypte*, 2nd ed. (Paris, 1830), vol. 18 (3e partie), 21: "Middleton (de) envoyé extraordinaire et ministre Plenipotentiaire des États-Unis d'Amérique, près la cour de Russie, St.-Pétersbourg."

14 Letter from Middleton to Henry Vaughan of the APS dated April 13, 1831.

15 *Niles Weekly Register*, July 12, 1834.

16 Harriott Cheves Leland and Harland Greene, eds., "Robbing the Owner or Saving the Property from Destruction," *The South Carolina Historical Magazine* 78 (1977), 92–103.

17 Yves Laissus, *Jomard: Le dernier Égyptien 1777–1862* (Paris: Fayard, 2004), 261, 8n: a letter of February 19, 1830, to Polignac in the Bibliothèque de Versailles.

18 Christopher Monkhouse, "A Temple for Tombs: The Egyptian Elephant Folio Cabinet in the Providence Athenaeum," *Furniture History:. The Journal of the Furniture History Society* 26 (1990), 157–64 (brought to my attention by Kate Wodehouse, collections librarian at the Providence Athenaeum). Jerry E. Mueller, ed., *Autobiography of John Russell Bartlett (1805–1886)* (Providence: John Carter Brown Library, 2006), 18, fig. 3.

19 Other sets: the New York Mechanics' Institute, which maintained a library, a museum, and offered courses after its founding and incorporation in 1831 and 1833, owned a copy of "Napoleon's Great Work on Egypt" as early as 1837 if not earlier, which was said to have been "purchased at a cost of eight hundred dollars," *New-York As It Is in 1837* (New York: J. Disturnell, 1837), 110; *Catalogue of the Library of the Mechanics' Institute of the City of New York* (New York, 1844), 15, nos. 312–20, and p. 63, stating the cost. The present-day Library of the General Society of Mechanics & Tradesmen no longer possesses this set. The Philadelphian merchant, Matthew Newkirk (1794–1868) presented a set of the second edition in 1836 to the University of New Jersey (now Princeton), where it is still located.

20 Letter to the author from Bill Landis, archivist, Yale University Library, October 2, 2008; *Proceedings of the Class of 1821, at their meeting held Yale College, August 19, 1846, with a summary of the record of the class, from 1821 to 1846* (New Haven, 1846), 15; Margaret R. Leavy, "Looking for the Armenians: Eli Smith's Missionary Adventure 1830–1831," *Transactions of the Connecticut Academy of Arts and Sciences* 50 (1992), 197–275, at 205.

21 William Holt Yates, *The Modern History and Condition of Egypt* (London: Smith, Elder and Co., 1843), vol. 1, 65–66.

22 Roger O. De Keersmaecker, *Travellers' Graffiti from Egypt and the Sudan, XII: The Luxor Temple* (Mortsel, Antwerp, 2011), 97.

23 *Daily National Journal*, Washington, DC, October 10, 1829.

24 "Extract of a letter from the Rev. H.G.O. Dwight, American missionary at Smyrna," *The Religious Intelligencer*, October 2, 1830; "Mr. Brewer's Journal (for April 12th)," *The Religious Intelligencer*, November 27, 1830.

25   Letter of May 25 to the *New York Journal of Commerce*, c. September 1830.
26   *The National Advocate*, March 13, 1824; on the packet ship *New York*.
27   *New York Spectator*, October 19, 1827; on the packet ship *Queen Mab*.
28   *Baltimore Gazette and Daily Advertiser*, October 1, 1827.
29   Margaret (1790–1856) had married Roswell L. Colt in 1811; Emily had married Robert Morgan Gibbes.
30   Yates, *Modern History and Condition of Egypt*, vol. 1, 13.
31   *Aurora and Franklin Gazette*, Philadelphia, May 18, 1825; on the packet ship *Cadmus*.
32   *Daily National Intelligencer*, Washington, DC, August 17, 1826. He also assisted in the arrangements for the 1828 celebration: *Eastern Argus*, Portland, September 9, 1828.
33   Rosen, ed., "An American Doctor in Paris in 1828: Selections from the Diary of Peter Solomon Townsend, M.D.," *Journal of the History of Medicine*, vol. 6 (1951), 233.
34   Nathalia Wright, *Horatio Greenough, the First American Sculptor* (Philadelphia: University of Pennsylvania Press, 1963), 82; Nathalie Wright, ed., *Letters of Horatio Greenough American Sculptor* (Madison: University of Wisconsin Press, 1972), 49, 6n; 59, 5n.
35   James Franklin Beard, ed., *The Letters and Journals of James Fenimore Cooper* (Cambridge, MA: The Belknap Press of Harvard University Press, 1960), vol. 1, 403.
36   William James Morgan, David B. Tyler, Joe L. Leonhart, and Mary F. Loughlin, eds., *Autobiography of Rear Admiral Charles Wilkes, U.S. Navy 1798–1877* (Washington, DC: Naval History Division Department of the Navy, 1978), 95. Wilkes, who wrote his 2,800-page manuscript in 1871, long after the events, relying on diaries and memory, reported that his conversation with Ombrosi took place in 1820, during his first visit to Florence, but of course it belongs to the year 1830.
37   E. de Cadalvène and J. de Breuvery, *L'Egypte et la Turquie, de 1829 à 1836* (Paris: Arthus Bertrand, 1836), vol. 2, 63.
38   [Ida Saint-Elme], *La contemporaine en Égypte* (Paris, 1831), vol. 3, 175–76.
39   Yates, *Modern History and Condition of Egypt*, vol. 2, 480.
40   *The Knickerbocker*, "Editor's Table," vol. 25 (1845), 358–59.
41   Marie-Joseph de Geramb, *Pélerinage à Jérusalem et au Mont Sinaï, en 1831, 1832 et 1833* (Paris, 1836), vol. 3, 235 (there written in French as translated from the English).
42   Yates, *Modern History and Condition of Egypt*, vol. 1, 467. English translation: In memory of Cornelius Bradford the American consul to Lyon in France, originating from Boston, of excellent virtue; he died at the age of 25 years in the Holy City on the second of August in the Year of Our Lord 1830, far away from his country, his family and friends. His accompanying friends bestowed on him this poor and last pledge of their friendship and grief.

(I wish to thank Dr. Goren Proot, Curator of Rare Books at the Folger Shakespeare Library, and Dr. Jeanine De Landtsheer of the Katholieke Universiteit, Leuven, for this translation.)

43   [John L. Stephens], *Incidents of Travel in Egypt, Arabia Petræa, and the Holy Land* (New York: Harper & Brothers, 1838), vol. 2, 225; Edward Robinson, *Biblical Researches in Palestine, Mount Sinai and Arabia Petræa: A Journal of Travels in the Year 1838* (Boston: Crocker & Brewster, 1841), vol. 1, 338. The stone, still extant, is illustrated in De Keersmaecker, *Travellers' Graffiti from Egypt and the Sudan, X: The Temple of Kalabsha, The Temple of Beit el-Wali* (Mortsel, Antwerp, 2011) facing page 38. The stone carver misspelled several words that I have tacitly corrected here.

44   Keersmaecker, *Travellers' Graffiti from Egypt and the Sudan, X*, facing page 38. English translation: To our Lord, Good and Mighty. Here lies Cornelius Bradford from the United States of America, consul at Lyon in France, struck in Jerusalem by the Lord, he abjured the errors of Luther and Calvin and in his heart and spontaneously professed the Catholic faith. Affected by an inflammation of the throat, he died on the second of August 1830 at the age of 25. His worthy friends bestowed this memorial. Pray for him. (Courtesy of Dr. Goren Proot).

45   Letter printed in the *Connecticut Courant*, November 29, 1831.

46   *New-York Spectator*, October 6, 1829, returning, five months from Canton.

47   Digitized diary for Monday, July 12, 1831, http://lcweb2.loc.gov/cgi-bin/ampage?collId=mmorse&fileName=059/059004/059004page.db&recNum.

48   Edward Lind Morse, ed., *Samuel F.B. Morse: His Life and Journals* (Boston: Houghton Mifflin Company, 1914), vol. 1, 395–402.

49   Ella M. Foshay, *Mr. Luman Reed's Picture Gallery: A Pioneer Collection of American Art* (New York: Harry N. Abrams, 1990), 24 (portrait of Catherine Reed).

50   In the late first century BC the Emperor Augustus had taken two from Heliopolis to Rome; in the fourth century AD the Emperor Constantine had brought one (and perhaps two) from Karnak to Alexandria, and his son Constantius had taken it to Rome; later in the century the Emperor Theodosius had taken a second obelisk from Karnak (perhaps already brought to Alexandria earlier in the century) to Constantinople.

51   Léon de Joannis, *Campagne pittoresque du Luxor* (Paris: Chez Mme Huzard, 1835); Apollinaire Lebas, *L'Obélisque de Luxor* (Paris: Carilian-Gœury et V. Dalmont, 1839).

52   See Robert Solé, *Le grand voyage de l'obélisque* (Paris: Édition du Seuil, 2004); [Benjamin Weiss], "Napoleon, Champollion, and Egypt," in Brian A. Curran, Anthony Grafton, Pamela O. Long, and Benjamin Weiss, *Obelisk: A History* (Cambridge, MA: Burndy Library, 2009), 229–55.

53   Diary and letters owned by the Maryland Historical Society.

54   Charlette Roueché in the *Times Literary Supplement*, July 15, 2011, 32.

55 E.g., André et Étienne Bernand, *Les inscriptions grecques et latines du colosse de Memnon* (Paris: Institut Français d'Archéologique Orientale, 1960).

56 Andrew Oliver Jr., *Beyond the Shores of Tripoli* (Washington, DC: Washington Society of the Archaeological Institute of America, 1979), cover.

57 de Géramb, *Pélerinage à Jérusalem*, vol. 3, 236.

58 *New York Evening Post*, December 1833, copied in the *Boston Courier*, December 23, 1833, and the *Maryland Gazette*, January 2, 1834.

59 See e.g., Gerry D. Scott III, catalogue entries in Nancy Thomas, *The American Discovery of Ancient Egypt* (Los Angeles: Los Angeles County Museum of Art, 1995), 79–81.

60 Georges Douin, *La première guerre de Syrie: La conquête de Syrie (1831–1832)* (Cairo: Société royale de géographie d'Égypte, 1931), vol. 1, 181.

61 Wendy Norman, ed., *The Gliddons in London, 1760–1850: A Family Record by Anne Gliddon* (Wellington, NZ: Steele Roberts, 2000).

62 R.R. Madden, *Travels in Turkey, Egypt, Nubia, and Palestine in 1824, 1825, 1826, and 1827* (London: Henry Colburn, 1829), vol. 1, 214.

63 [George Gliddon], *Appendix to "The American in Egypt"* (Philadelphia: Merrihew & Thompson, 1842), 28–30; David H. Finnie, *Pioneers East: The Early American Experience in the Middle East* (Cambridge, MA: Harvard University Press, 1967), 281–85.

64 Diary in the Library of Congress.

65 Russell M. Jones, ed., *The Parisian Education of an American Surgeon. Letters of Jonathan Mason Warren (1832–1835)* (Philadelphia: The American Philosophical Society, 1978), 110.

66 National Archives, Record Group 84, vol. 36, Cairo, Egypt, letter of 23 October 1834.

67 *United States Supreme Court Records and Briefs, October term 1892* (Washington, 1892), 422–43.

68 Alex Beam, *Gracefully Insane: Life and Death inside America's Premier Mental Hospital* (Cambridge: Perseus Books, 2001), 39–44.

69 Beard, *Letters and Journals of James Fenimore Cooper*, vol. 1, 245.

70 Beard, *Letters and Journals of James Fenimore Cooper*, vol. 2, 111–12.

71 Redelia Brisbane, *A Mental Biography with a Character Study* (Boston: Arena Publishing Company, 1893), 131; Abigail Mellen and Allaire Brisbane Stallsmith, eds., *The European Travel Diaries of Albert Brisbane 1830–1832: Discovering Fourierism for America* (Lewiston, NY: Mellen, 2005).

72 George Rosen, ed., "An American Doctor in Paris in 1828. Selections from the Diary of Peter Solomon Townsend, MD," *Journal of the History of Medicine*, vol. 6, Winter 1951, 64–252, from which the quotes from Townsend's diary are taken.

73 J. Yoyotte, "Les Adoratrices de la IIIe Période Intermédiaire, à propos d'un chef-d'oeuvre rapporté par Champollion," *Bulletin de la Société française d'égyptologie*, no. 64 (1972), 31–52; Elizabeth Delange, "The Complexity of

Alloys: New Discoveries about Certain 'Bronzes' in the Louvre," in Marsha Hill, ed., *Gifts for the Gods: Images from Egyptian Temples* (New York: The Metropolitan Museum of Art, 2007), 38–40, fig. 19.

74 Jean-François Champollion, *Lettres et journaux écrits pendant le voyage d'Égypte*, H. Hartleben, ed. (Paris: Christian Bourgois, 1986).

75 Diane Harlé and Jean Lefebvre, eds., *Sur le Nile avec Champollion: Lettres, journaux et dessins inédits de Nestor L'Hôte; Premier voyage en Égypte—1828–1830* (Orléans, Caen: Éditions Paradigme, 1993).

76 G. Gabriele, ed., *Giornale della spedizione letteraria toscana in Egitto negli anni 1828–29* (Rome: Tipografia Befani, 1925); Ippolito Rosellini, *I monumenti dell'Egitto della Nubia, disegnati dalla spedizione scientifico-letteraria Toscana in Egitto: Distribuiti in ordine di materie, interpretati ed illustrati*, 1832–1844; Marilina Betrò, ed., *Lungo il Nilo: Ippoloto Rosellini e la Spedizione Franco–Toscana in Egitto (1828–1829)* (Florence and Milan: Giunti, 2010).

77 "Rapport sur les Travaux de la Commission médicale d'Égypte" par M. Pariset, *Revue médicale française et étrangère*, vol. 3 (August 1829), 201–28; Étienne Pariset, "Mémoires sur les causes de la peste et sur les moyens de la détruire," *Annales d'hygiène publique et de médecine légale* 6 (1831), 243–312.

78 *Hégoa* no. 26–27, 2006–2007: *Médecine et géographie dans la première moitié du XIXe siècle: Du raisonnement médical au questionnement géographique; Le récit des voyages d'un touriste-médecin, Auguste Lagasquie* (Pau: CNRS et l'université de Pau, 2007).

Chapter 10

1 Owned by the ABCFM; on deposit in the Houghton Library at Harvard College. The deck log of the *United States* for the year 1821 is not owned by the National Archives.

2 Leslie A. Marchand, ed., *Byron's Letters and Journals* (Cambridge, MA: The Belknap Press of Harvard University Press, 1979), vol. 6, 161–65.

3 Theodore E. Stebbins Jr., ed., *The Lure of Italy: American Artists and the Italian Experience 1760–1914* (New York: Harry N. Abrams, 1992), 328–29. Collection of the Dietrich American Foundation, Philadelphia.

4 John D. Cooney, "Acquisition of the Abbott Collection," *The Brooklyn Museum* (1949), vol. 10, 19.

5 One should mention a Lieutenant Thomas Tanner, an English naval officer active in the Indian Ocean and the Persian Gulf in this period. In 1817 he was commander of the Honorable Company's cruiser *Psyché* off Bahrain: "Remarks on the Passage to Bahrain," *The Asiatic Journal* (1818), 464–66. In 1825 he was promoted to captain. But can he have been the man who presented Egyptian curios to the Peabody Museum? If he ever had any *shabti*s, perhaps he traded them with a Salem merchant at Mocha.

6 Marco Zatterin, *Il Gigante del Nile: Storia e avventure del Grande Belzoni, l'uomo che svelò i misteri dell'Egitto dei faraoni* (Milan: Mondadori, 2000),

143–58; Daniela Picchi, ed., *Tutte le anime della Mummia: La vita oltre la morte ai tempi di Sety I* (Siena: Protagon editori, 2009), 75–91.

7   Tim Knox, *Sir John Soane's Museum London* (London: Merrill Publishers Limited, 2008), 108–109, figs. 102–104.

8   Sale catalogue Sotheby's London, December 4, 1972, lots 110–13. The finest of them reappeared at auction in Paris in 2012: Hôtel Drouot, Paris, 24 octobre 2012, Thiery de Maigret: Antiquités égyptiennes, Collection Charles Bouché, lot 26.

9   For faience *shabti*s from Salt's collection, see Florence Dunn Freidman, ed., *Gifts of the Nile: Ancient Egyptian Faience* (Providence: Museum of Art, Rhode Island School of Design, Thames and Hudson, 1998), 94 and 194, no. 48 (illustrating one in the British Museum).

10   Gian Paolo Romagnani, ed., *Carlo Vidua viaggiatore e collezionista (1785–1830)* (Città di Casale Monferrato: Assessorato per la Cultura 1987), 38.

11   Albert M. Lythgoe, "Report of the Curator of the Egyptian Department," *Museum of Fine Arts Boston, Twenty-seventh Annual Report, for the Year 1902* (Cambridge, MA, 1903), 93–96; 72.4091, .4100-1, .4111–4, .4116, Res.7232, Res.72.72.

12   John Madox, *Excursions in the Holy Land, Egypt, Nubia, Syria, &c. Including a Visit to the Unfrequented District of the Haouran* (London: Richard Bentley, 1834), vol. 1, 280.

13   Jean-Luc Bovot, *Les serviteurs funéraires royaux et princiers de l'Ancienne Égypte* (Paris: Réunion des Musées Nationaux, 2003), 80–168, with lists.

14   Deborah Manley and Peta Rée, *Henry Salt: Artist, Traveller, Diplomat, Egyptologist* (London: Libri Publications Limited, 2001), 243–45.

15   *Rhode Island American*, Providence, April 13, 1830.

16   Full account in the *Columbian Gazette*, December 1830, picked up by other newspapers.

17   E.C. Wines, *Two Years and a Half in the Navy* (Philadelphia, Carey & Lea, 1832) vol. 2, 229; Charles Lee Lewis, *Admiral Franklin Buchanan* (Baltimore: Norman, Remington Company, 1929), 66.

18   On Kirkland see Bernard Bailyn, "Why Kirkland Failed," in Bernard Bailyn et al., eds., *Glimpses of the Harvard Past* (Cambridge: Harvard University Press, 1986), 19–44.

19   *Boston Daily Advertiser*, late August 1832, picked up by other papers.

20   Theodore S. Woolsey, *Theodore Dwight Woolsey: A Biographical Sketch* (New Haven: Yale Publishing Company, 1912), 57–58.

21   "Letters of Mrs. John T. Kirkland," *Proceedings of the Massachusetts Historical Society, second series, vol. xix, 1905*, (Boston, 1906), 440–504.

22   The other seven officers were William McMurtrie (purser), James M. Green (surgeon), midshipmen John Rodgers, Dominick Lynch, James Alden Jr., and Oliver H. Perry, and Joseph William Jenks (Amherst class of 1829; chaplain, schoolmaster, linguist, and interpreter).

23 Samuel Eliot Morison wondered whether they had been brought on board at Kronstadt where the *Concord* called near St. Petersburg the previous August and that they had now grown too big to handle: Samuel Eliot Morison, *"Old Bruin" Commodore Matthew C. Perry 1794–1858* (Boston: Little, Brown and Co., 1967), 118. His guess was correct. In the Beinecke Rare Book and Manuscript Library at Yale is an album of watercolors and drawings, most of them made by Italian artists of landscapes, monuments, and costumes. But four of them show portraits of members of the crew of the *Concord*: one of these depicts a messenger boy with one of the pet bears originally received in St. Petersburg.

24 Mrs. John T. Kirkland mentioned the shawls in one of her letters and Matthew Perry did also in a letter to Gliddon of April 3, 1832. Captain Kennedy is not further identified, but perhaps is Edmund P. Kennedy.

25 Reported in a letter of Lady Franklin: D.D. Traill, *The Life of Sir John Franklin, R.N.* (London: John Murray, 1896), 291.

26 From a second album of watercolors, also once belonging to Perry, with sketches of Mediterranean costumes done by Edward C. Young, a marine sergeant on the *Concord*; now in the library at Mystic Seaport. On the top of the sheet, John H. Hill, the missionary head of the American school in Athens wrote, "having had frequent opportunities of seeing Mohammed Ali the undersigned can testify and confirm that this is an excellent likeness of the Pasha. The costume is perfectly correct. John H. Hill of Athens, Greece." Thanks to Nancy Micklewright of the Freer and Sackler Galleries in Washington DC for assistance in describing the dress of the Pasha.

27 W.M. Paxton, *The Marshall Family* (Cincinnati: Robert Clarke & Co, 1885), 141.

28 23rd Congress, no. 531, 1st session, p. 492.

29 "Letters of Mrs. John T. Kirkland," 493.

30 "Letters of Mrs. John T. Kirkland," 494–95.

31 A. Francis Steuart, *A Short Sketch of the Lives of Francis and William Light the Founders of Penang and Adelaide* (London, 1901), 70, 1n.

32 "Letters of Mrs. John. T. Kirkland," 464, where she speaks of meeting Miss Caton, namely Elizabeth, a sister of the Marchioness Wellesley. On the Wellesley family, see Iris Butler, *The Eldest Brother: The Marquess Wellesley, the Duke of Wellington's Eldest Brother* (London: Hodder and Stoughton, 1973) and Jehanne Wake, *Sisters of Fortune* (London: Chatto and Windus, 2010). Also the catalogue notes on the portrait of Gerald Wellesley by Thomas Lawrence sold at Sotheby's London, *Early British & Irish Paintings*, December 4, 2008, lot 44.

33 "Mr. Kirkland's Letter on the Holy Land," *Christian Examiner and General Review* (November 1837), 261–69.

34 George Jones, *Excursions to Cairo, Jerusalem, Damascus and Balbec, from the United States Ship Delaware, during Her Recent Cruise* (New York: Sampson Low, Marston & Company, 1836).

35   "Letters from an Officer in the U.S. Navy (United States Schooner
     Shark)," *New-York Spectator*, December 29, 1834; [Harriet Patterson], "Visit
     to a Harem," *Albany Argus*, January 1835; [Lieut. David R. Stewart?] *New
     York Gazette*, March 1835; Lieut. David R. Stewart, "Cairo, Jerusalem, and
     Damascus," *The Naval Magazine*, January 1836; Samuel T. Gillett, "Letters
     from the Mediterranean," *Western Christian Advocate*, March 31, April 7,
     April 14, 1837; Omer T. Gillett, *How I Became a Preacher* (Cincinnati: Van
     Nostrand and Dwight, 1893) (a conversational account based on the jour-
     nal of Samuel T. Gillett by one of his sons). David D. Porter's letter in the
     papers of David Porter at the Library of Congress.

36   Now in the Nimitz Library at the United States Naval Academy at Annap-
     olis: Papers of George Mifflin Bache Who Married Eliza Patterson; Ms
     212, nos. 20 and 22.

37   Oil on canvas. Chrysler Art Museum, Norfolk, Virginia, 65.34.6. Martha N.
     Hapgood and Jefferson C. Harrison, *American Art at the Chrysler Museum:
     Selected Paintings, Sculpture, and Drawings* (Norfolk: Chrysler Museum of
     Art, 2005) 31, no. 10; Bryan John Zygmont, "Portraiture and Politics in
     New York City, 1790–1825: Stuart, Vanderlyn, Trumbull, and Jarvis," diss.,
     University of Maryland College Park, 2006, 263, fig. 160.

38   Preserved among the Patterson papers in the Library of Congress. See John
     Ruffle, "The Journeys of Lord Prudhoe and Major Orlando Felix in Egypt,
     Nubia and the Levant 1826–1829," in *Travellers in Egypt*, eds. Paul and Janet
     Starkey (London: I.B.Tauris, 1998), 75–84, esp 77–79; John Ruffle, "Lord
     Prudhoe and Major Felix, *Hiéroglyphiseurs Décidés*," in *Egyptian Encounters*, ed.
     Jason Thompson, *Cairo Papers in Social Science* 23, no. 3 (2000), 80–89, esp. 84.

39   Eliza C. Patterson's journal, among the George Mifflin Bache Papers, MS
     212, Special Collections & Archives Department, Nimitz Library, US
     Naval Academy, Annapolis.

40   Mary E.I. Frere, "[Obituary Notice] The Right Hon, Sir Bartle Frere . . ."
     in *Transactions of the Royal Historical Society*, n.s. 3 (1886), 293–302, at 298.

41   Nathalie Coilly and Philippe Régnier, eds., *Le siècle des saint-simoniens du
     Nouveau christianisme au canal de Suez* (Paris: Bibliothèque nationale de
     France, 2006), 102–21; and the concise summary in Zachary Karabell, *Part-
     ing the Desert: The Creation of the Suez Canal* (New York: Alfred A. Knopf,
     2003), 25–37.

42   *Norfolk Beacon*, early January, 1830.

43   Letter in the Maryland Historical Society.

44   John Brockenbrough Offley, ed., *Diary of John Holmes Offley: An Account of
     His Voyage from New York to Trieste on the Ship "Prudence" from August 20th
     to October 17th 1826, to Which Is Appended Additional Memoirs and Correspon-
     dence* (Williamsburg, Virginia: J.B. Offley, 1993), 81–82.

45   F.V.J. Arundell, *Discoveries in Asia Minor* (London: Richard Bentley, 1834),
     vol. 1, 18–19, n; W.H. Yates, "Brusa and Magnesia in Asia Minor, With

Observations on the Phenomena of Magnetic Influence," *The Athenaeum*, January 4, 1834, 13. Arundell says that the date was January 1830, but he meant 1831, as Yates' and Moores' itineraries allow no other year.

46   The Brooklyn Museum 48.29: Elizabeth Riefstahl, *Ancient Egyptian Glass and Glazes* (Brooklyn: The Brooklyn Museum, 1968) 107, no. 61, illustrated p. 63; Andrew Oliver Jr., *Beyond the Shores of Tripoli* (Washington, DC: Washington Society of the Archaeological Institute of America, 1979), 24.

47   Annie Caubet and Geneviève Pierrat-Bonnefois, eds., *Faïences de l'Antiquité. De l'Égypte à l'Iran* (Paris: Musée du Louvre Éditions, 2005), 156–58, nos. 415, 416, 418, 423.

48   *The Military and Naval Magazine of the United States* (November 1835), vol. 6, 235.

49   James E. Valle, *Rocks and Shoals: Naval Discipline in the Age of Fighting Sail* (Annapolis: United States Naval Institute Press, 1980), 167–68.

50   Letter from John Gliddon to Eli Smith, dated May 26th, 1836, in the papers of the ABCFM on deposit at the Houghton Library, Harvard.

51   Letters to the Secretary of the Navy, Roll 118, vol. 2, October 12, 1838, from Lt. G.F. Pearson, "When I was a first lieutenant of the U.S. Ship *Constitution*, under the command of Commodore Elliott, I received, through him, a Turkish sabre, which he informed me had been presented by Mehemet Ali while at Alexandria in Egypt and which he had received together with one for himself, through the American Consul of the place. Commodore Elliott also informed me that he had received these sabres subjected to the orders of the Navy Department. The sabre which I received is a plain one of little value, and is still in my possession ready for any disposition the Department may require."

52   George W. Cullum, *Biographical Register of the Officers and Graduates of the U.S. Military Academy at West Point, N.Y.* (New York: D. Van Nostrand, 1868), vol. 1, 365.

53   Cass kept a diary of the whole cruise, unpublished, today preserved in the William L. Clements Library at the University of Michigan, Ann Arbor. He published their visits to Crete and Cyprus within a few years of his return to Paris: [Cass], "The Island of Candia," *Southern Literary Messenger* 5 (1839), 709–20; [Cass], "The Island of Cyprus," *Southern Literary Messenger* 7 (1841), 93.

54   W. Stanley Hoole, ed., "A Visit to the Holy Land in 1837," *Journal of the American Oriental Society* 95 (1975), 633–44.

55   The account by Cass of the visit, originally printed in *The United States Magazine and Democratic Review* (May 1838), has been reprinted in T.J. Gorton and A. Féghali Gorton, eds., *Lebanon through Writers' Eyes* (London: Eland, 2009), 129–34.

56   Letter from John Gliddon to Eli Smith, dated March 30, 1837, in the papers of the ABCFM on deposit at the Houghton Library, Harvard.

57 Rita C. Severis, ed., *The Diaries of Lorenzo Warriner Pease 1834–1839* (Aldershot, UK, and Burlington, Vermont: Ashgate, 2002), 702. Regrettably all three midshipmen are erroneously identified in the footnotes. The governor in question is Enos T. Throop (pronounced Troop), Governor of New York from 1829 to 1832, whose brother George was married to Frances Hunt, sister of Montgomery Hunt.

58 Lamont Gallery, Phillips Exeter Academy. Gift of the children of Lewis Cass. Frank H. Cunningham, *Familiar Sketches of The Phillips Exeter Academy* (Boston: James R. Osgood, 1883), 118. A copy, signed by Healy and dated 1840, is owned by the Detroit Historical Society, the gift of Matilda Cass Ledyard, his granddaughter.

59 David McCullough, *The Greater Journey: Americans in Paris* (New York: Simon and Schuster, 2011), 143.

60 Swann Galleries, Inc., New York, *Photographs*, April 4, 1995, lot 102; Dr. William J. Schultz, "Silver Shadows before the Storm: The American Military Daguerreotype," *The Daguerreian Annual* (2002–2003), 264, pl. 114. Dr. Schultz, the owner, provided the date.

61 *A Metrical Description of a Fancy Dress Ball Given at Washington, 9th April 1858, dedicated to Mrs. Senator Gwin* by John Van Sonntag Haviland, Washington, 1858.

62 S.J. Wolfe with Robert Singerman, *Mummies in Nineteenth-Century America* (Jefferson, NC: McFarland & Company, Inc., 2009), 140.

63 "Antiquities," *Army and Navy Chronicle*, vol. 7 (August 16, 1838), 110, and "Present by Commodore Elliott to Girard College," in *Army and Navy Chronicle*, vol. 1 (November 15, 1838), 318–19; E[dwin] A. B[arber], "An Ancient Sarcophagus," *Bulletin of the Pennsylvania Museum* 12 (January 1919), 1–5; Oliver, *Beyond the Shores of Tripoli*, 11; John Roth, "The Elliott Marbles," *American Journal of Archaeology* 89 (1985), 692–93.

64 *Speech of Com. Jesse Duncan Elliott, U.S.N. delivered in Hagerstown, MD on 14th November, 1843* (Philadelphia: G.B. Zieber & Co, 1844), esp. 32–46, and J.D. Elliott, "Letter, Mahon, November 10, 1837," in *Speech of Com. Jesse Duncan Elliott*, appendix, 65–68.

65 A. Slidell (and M.C. Perry), "Thoughts on the Navy," *The Naval Magazine* (1837), 1–42.

Chapter 11

1 Edward W. Hooker, *Memoir of Mrs. Sarah Lanman Smith*, 2nd ed. (Boston: American Tract Society, 1840), 172.

2 C. Rochfort Scott, *Rambles in Egypt and Candia* (London: Henry Colburn, 1837), vol. 1, 7.

3 "Extracts from a Communication of Mr. Smith," *The Missionary Herald*, April 1835.

4 National Archives, record Group 84, vol. 36, Cairo, Egypt, letter of October 23, 1834, from Alexandria.

5   Ken McGoogan, *Lady Franklin's Revenge: A True Story of Ambition, Obsession and the Remaking of Arctic History* (Toronto: HarperCollins Canada, 2005), 117.

6   Hooker, *Memoir of Mrs. Sarah Lanman Smith*, 172.

7   LaVerne Kuhnke, *Lives at Risk: Public Health in Nineteenth-century Egypt* (Berkeley: University of California Press, 1990), 95.

8   Henry, born in 1806, was the son of Dr. Henry Somerville of Stafford. He went to Charterhouse School, then Caius College, Cambridge. His father died in January 1830. In 1837 young Henry had completed medical training and became a Member of the Royal College of Surgeons and opened a practice at Cannock. See John Vann, *Biographical Histories of Gonville and Caius College, 1349–1897*, vol. 2, *admissions 1713–1897* (Cambridge, 1898), 196. He married Frances Rogers in January 1839.

9   This and other statements by Hamersley are taken from his manuscript diary.

10   Edward William Lane, *An Account of the Manners and Customs of the Modern Egyptians*, 5th ed., Stanley Poole, ed. (London: John Murray, 1860), 480–87. Hamersley saw the procession on March 3, Lane says February 15.

11   Dieter Arnold, *Temples of the Last Pharaohs* (Oxford and New York: Oxford University Press, 1999), 222, fig. 178.

12   Johann Rudolph Theophilus Lieder (1798–1865) remained in Egypt until his death.

13   Andrew Hilen, ed., *The Letters of Henry Wadsworth Longfellow*, vol. 1, *1814–1836* (Cambridge, MA: Harvard University Press, 1966), 263–64 (translation of the Italian phrase Longfellow wrote at the time).

14   Marchebeus, *Voyage de Paris à Constantinople par bateau à vapeur* (Paris: Artus Bertrand, 1839), xvi.

15   "Extracts from the Journal of Mr. Thomson," *The Missionary Herald*, March 1835.

16   Diane Harlé and Jean Lefebvre, eds., *Sur le Nil avec Champollion: Lettres, journaux et dessins inédits de Nestor L'Hôte premier voyage en Égypte—1828– 1830* (Orléans-Caen: Éditions Paradigme, 1993), 276.

17   Victor V. Solkin, "The Sphinxes of Amenhotep III in St. Petersburg: Unique Monuments and their Restoration," *Proceedings of the Ninth International Congress of Egyptologists*, Jean-Claude Guyon and Christine Cardin, eds. (Leuven: Peeters, 2007), vol. 2 (1713–1716), figs. 1–2.

18   Gardner Wilkinson, *Modern Egypt and Thebes: Being a Description of Egypt; Including the Information Required for Travellers in that Country* (London: John Murray, 1843), vol. 1, 284.

19   Edward Robinson, *Biblical Researches in Palestine, Mount Sinai and Arabia Petræa: A Journal of Travels in the Year 1838* (Boston: Crocker & Brewster, 1841), vol. 1, 339.

20   In one of Thomson's letters serialized in *The Missionary Herald* (March 1835).

21 John W. Hamersley, "Lady Hester Stanhope: From the Journal of a Travel-ler," *The United States Magazine and Democratic Review*, vol. 13 (November 1843), 536–41.

22 W.H. Bartlett, *Footsteps of Our Lord and His Apostles in Syria, Greece, and Italy: A Succession of Visits to the Scenes of New Testament Narrative* (London: Arthur Hall, Virtue & Co., 1851), 27 and 34.

23 Excerpts from DeKay's diary were published by Phyllis DeKay Wheelock, "The Levant Journal of Capt. George C. DeKay," *Lands East*, vol. 1 (1956), no. 9, 19–23, and no. 10, 20–26.

24 Lady Hester's letters to Dundas are among his papers in the National Library of Scotland, acc. 10719/26: Noel Matthews and M. Doreen Wain-wright, *A Guide to Manuscripts and Documents in the British Isles Relating to the Middle East and North Africa* (Oxford: Oxford University Press, 1980), 370. Henry Dundas (1742–1811) was first Viscount Melville.

25 At one time I thought that Mr. Dodge was Pickering Dodge (1804–1863), Harvard class of 1823. But in 1834 Pickering Dodge was married, had three young children, and was settling the estate of his father who had died the previous year, which involved selling ships and contending with an elephant (named Romeo) that his father had imported from Cal-cutta in 1832: *Salem Gazette*, November 28, 1834. Moreover Pickering Dodge is known to have gone abroad with his wife and at least one child in July 1835. The gentleman is surely John C. Dodge of Salem (John Crowninshield Dodge), age about twenty-five, a merchant with business in Smyrna, who had left Smyrna on March 21, 1833, and had reached Boston in late May only to turn right around and ship out on the Brig *Ceres* for Gibraltar in early July. This puts him back in the Mediterranean more than a year before Hamerlsey encountered him, but he may well have made additional trips or have stayed on in Smyrna and points east until November 1834. We know he was in Alexandria in late Decem-ber 1833 where he met Eli and Sarah Smith at the Gliddons. (National Archives, record group 84, volume 36 Cairo, Egypt, letter of October 23, 1834 from Alexandria.)

26 John Watts de Peyster, "Tribute to John William Hamersley," *Magazine of American History with Notes and Queries*, vol. 22 (September 1889), 224–28.

27 *Boston Commercial Gazette* (August 26, 1824).

28 Sherman Hoar, "The Ripley School," *Papers Read before the Citizens' Club of Waltham: Season of 1891–92* (Waltham, 1891), 38–39, cited in Jane W. Goodwin, *The Remarkable Mrs. Ripley: The Life of Sarah Alden Bradford Ripley* (Boston: Northeastern University Press, 1998), 132. Stackpole must have been suspended for some weeks from Harvard for mischievous behavior or the like, during which times of absence it was traditional for such students to be tutored by Samuel Ripley at his school in Waltham.

29 *American Jurist*, vol. 4 (July 1830), 28–63.

30 *New-York Spectator* (September 9, 1831).

31 Alfred R. Ferguson, ed., *The Journals and Miscellaneous Notebooks of Ralph Waldo Emerson* (Cambridge, MA: The Belknap Press of Harvard University Press, 1964), vol. iv, 151; Ralph L. Rusk, ed., *The Letters of Ralph Waldo Emerson*, vol. 1 (New York: Columbia University Press, 1939), vol. 1, 381.

32 Langdon Cheves, "Izard of South Carolina," *South Carolina Historical and Genealogical Magazine* 2, no. 3 (July 1901), 236–39.

33 Maurie D. McInnis and Angela D. Mack, eds., *In Pursuit of Refinement: Charlestonians Abroad 1740–1860* (Charleston: University of South Carolina Press, 1999), 140, no. 22.

34 Lady Franklin's diary in the Scott Polar Research Institute, Cambridge, UK. John Lieder, with whom Franklin was traveling, also kept a diary, but I have not seen it: Matthews and Wainwright, *A Guide to Manuscripts and Documents*, 76.

35 [Sarah Haight], *Letters from the Old World by a Lady of New York* (New York: Harper & Brothers, 1840), vol. 1, 158.

36 Roger O. De Keersmaecker, *Travellers' Graffiti from Egypt and the Sudan: The Temples of Abu Simbel, Additional Volume* (Mortsel, Antwerp, 2012), 48.

37 De Keersmaecker, *Travellers' Graffiti, The Temple of Abu Simbel*, 46, where a close reading of the grafitto reveals that the date is 1834. The other Poupillier in the grafitto is Jules, a relative who was in Egypt in 1837: Gustave Schlumberger, ed., *Mémoirs du commandant Persat 1806 à 1844* (Paris: Plon-Nourrit et Cie, 1910), 314, a report of Poupillier in Syra in 1836 on his way to Egypt.

38 Paul Santi and Richard Hill, eds., *The Europeans in the Sudan 1834–1878* (Oxford: The Clarendon Press, 1980), 39.

39 *Boston Journal of Natural History* (January 1836), 255.

40 Oliver Wendell Holmes, *John Lothrop Motley: A Memoir* (Boston: Houghton, Osgood and Company, 1879), 55.

41 This must have been Robert Goff (1801–1866) who spent some time in Egypt, becoming a member of the Egyptian Society of Cairo in 1836 and forming a small collection of antiquities that he presented to the British Museum in 1847.

42 Hodgson's diplomatic career at Constantinople and in Egypt is well covered in the biography by Thomas A. Bryson, *An American Consular Officer in the Middle East in the Jacksonian Era: A Biography of William Brown Hodgson, 1801–1871* (Atlanta: Resurgens Publications, 1979), 49–98.

43 Bryson, *An American Consular Officer*, 91 .

44 For Hodgson's dispatches to the secretary of state see National Archives, Diplomatic dispatches, M46, roll 8, with the letters dated Dec. 2, 1834; Dec. 13, 1834; Aug. 25, 1834; Sept. 28, 1834; and March 2, 1835.

45 William L. Whitwell, *The Heritage of Longwood* (Jackson, MS: University Press of Mississippi, 1975), 19.

46 *New-York Spectator* (May 8, 1834).

47 Now in the possession of Woodbury Butler Gates, Shreveport, Louisiana; a typed copy is in the Huntington Library, San Marino, California.

48 Frank Allaben, *John Watts de Peyster* (New York: Frank Allaben Genealogical Company, 1908), vol. 1, 145. De Peyster or Allaben, or both, confused Rush Nutt with Dr. J.C. Nott (as he is elsewhere identified in this book), namely Josiah Clark Nott (1804–1873), who, after studying at the University of Pennsylvania, went to Europe in 1835 and 1836, not this year. The *Utica* passenger list confirms that Dr. Nutt and Rittenhouse Nutt were on board with the de Peysters.

49 Leo Francis Stock, ed., *Consular Relations between the United States and the Papal States: Instructions and Despatches* (Washington, DC: American Catholic Historical Association, 1945), 44.

50 Letters of Rittenhouse Nutt to his brother Haller and to his sister Mary in the Mississippi Department of Archives and History in Jackson, Mississippi.

51 This and the following quotes by Rittenhouse Nutt are taken from his unpublished diary.

52 National Archives, record group 84, volume 36, Cairo Egypt, letter of October 23, 1834, from Alexandria.

53 One presented to the Cottonlandia Museum (now known as the Museum of the Mississippi Delta) in Greenwood, Mississippi; another still in the possession of a descendant, Gregory R. Johnson of Arlington, Tennessee.

54 Typed copy in the Huntington Library, San Marino.

55 "Letter from Mr. Whiting, February 3, 1835," *The Missionary Herald*, November 1835.

56 Diary in Union Theological Seminary, New York City; Rita C. Severis, ed., *The Diaries of Lorenzo Warriner Pease 1834–1839* (Aldershot and Burlington, Vermont: Ashgate, 2002), vol. 1, 255 (father's name incorrectly given in 359n).

57 [John L. Stephens], *Incidents of Travel in Greece, Turkey, Russia, and Poland* (New York: Harper & Brothers, 1838), vol. 1, 203-206, 219, 236.

58 Letter among the Dallam Papers, MS 1250, at the Maryland Historical Society, Baltimore.

59 *New-York Spectator*, November 5, 1835, "Mr. Nutt . . . of Mississippi." The ship's manifest, preserved in the National Archives in Washington, DC, gives his name as Robt Nutt, a scribe's misreading of Ritt. His age is given as twenty-five.

60 "Remarks of a Late American Traveller in the East," reprinted in the *Daily National Intelligencer*, Washington, DC, December 10, 1835.

61 George Sandys, *A Relation of a Journey begun An: Dom: 1610, Foure Bookes* (London, 1615), 127.

62 David Roberts, *Egypt & Nubia* (London: F. G. Moon & Sons, 1849), vol. 3.

63 Samuel Sloan, *The Model Architect: A Series of Original Designs for Cottages, Villas, Suburban Residences, Etc.* (Philadelphia: E.S. Jones & Co., 1852), pl. lxiii.

64   Harold Cooledge, "The Landscape and Architecture of Longwood: A Romantic Exercise in Hubris," *Arris: Journal of the Southeast Chapter of the Society of Architectural Historians* (1992), vol. 3, 4–22.

65   Robert F. Dalzell Jr., *Enterprising Elite: The Boston Associates and the World They Made* (Cambridge, MA: Harvard University Press, 1987), 5–44; Dan Yaeger, "Francis Cabot Lowell: Brief Life of an American Entrepreneur, 1775–1817," *Harvard Magazine* (September–October 2010), 30–31.

66   Quoted in Ferris Greenslet, *The Lowells and Their Seven Worlds* (London and Boston: Ernest Benn Ltd. and Houghton Mifflin Co., 1947), 179.

67   Summarized in William Hauptman, *Charles Gleyre 1806–1874* (Princeton: Swiss Institute for Art Research, Zurich, and Princeton University Press, 1996), vol. 1, *Life and Works*, 77–106.

68   Jason Thompson, *Edward William Lane 1801–1876: The Life of the Pioneering Egyptologist and Orientalist* (London: Haus Publishing, 2010), 345–65.

69   Edward Everett, *A Memoir of Mr. John Lowell, Jun.* (Boston: Charles C. Little and James Brown, 1840), 41. These observations appear verbatim in his diary as if part of it functioned as a letter book.

70   Bernard V. Bothmer, "A Granite Block of Philip Arrhidaeus," *Bulletin of the Museum of Fine Arts* 50 (1952), 19–27.

71   Sekhmet: William Stevenson Smith, *Ancient Egypt as Represented in the Museum of Fine Arts, Boston* (Boston, 1960), 130, fig. 81; obelisk fragment, Joyce L. Haynes in Nancy Thomas, ed., *The American Discovery of Ancient Egypt* (Los Angeles: Los Angeles County Museum of Art, 1995), 175.

72   Philippe Mainterot, *Aus origins de l'égyptologie: Voyages et collections de Frédéric Cailliaud (1787–1869)* (Rennes: Presses Universitaires de Rennes, 2011), 43–47.

73   Archibald Edmonstone, *A Journey to Two of the Oases of Upper Egypt* (London: John Murray, 1822).

74   G.A. Hoskins, *Visit to the Great Oasis of the Libyan Desert* (London: Longman, Rees, Orme, Brown, Green, & Longman, 1837).

75   *Asiatic Register* (1836), part 2, 184.

76   Hauptman, *Charles Gleyre*, vol. 1, 79, 192n.

77   Warren R. Dawson and Eric P. Uphill, *Who Was Who in Egyptology*, 2nd ed. (London: Egypt Exploration Society, 1972), 177, 77, and 196 respectively.

78   [William D. Phelps], *Fore & Aft: Or Leaves from the Life of an Old Sailor* (Boston: Nichols & Hall, 1871), 214–27.

Chapter 12

1   Harvey Levenstein, *Seductive Journey: American Tourists in France from Jefferson to the Jazz Age* (Chicago: University of Chicago Press, 1998), 23.

2   *New York American*, May 28, 1830, picked up by the *Daily National Journal* (Washington, DC, June 9, 1830).

3 Leo Francis Stock, ed., *Consular Relations between the United States and the Papal States: Instructions and Despatches* (Washington, DC: American Catholic Historical Association, 1945).

4 Cited in Rosemary Sweet, *Cities and the Grand Tour: The British in Italy, c. 1690–1820* (Cambridge, UK: Cambridge University Press, 2012), 11, 34n.

5 Craig Robertson, *The Passport in America: The History of a Document* (Oxford and New York: Oxford University Press, 2010), 66–67.

6 Andrew Oliver, *Portraits of John Quincy Adams and His Wife* (Cambridge, MA: The Belknap Press of Harvard University Press, 1970), 9–11. On the lyre is the motto *Nunc sidera ducit*, taken from book 1, line 329 of the *Astronomica* of the Latin poet Manilius.

7 The website Ancestry Library Edition lists many of the Americans applying for passports for the period from October 1810 into October 1817, and from November 1834 on. Photographic images of many of the actual letters of application (in the National Archives) are available for the 1830s and thereafter with the exception of the year 1832.

8 Offered for sale in 2010 by Alexander Historical Auctions. Another Massachusetts passport of the same date was sold, also in 2010, by PBA Galleries of San Francisco.

9 Now in the collection of the Museum of the City of New York.

10 Robert Richardson, *Travels along the Mediterranean, and Parts Adjacent in Company with the Earl of Belmore during the Years 1816–17–18*, 2 vols. (London: T. Cadell, 1822).

11 Jason Thompson, *Sir Gardner Wilkinson and His Circle* (Austin: University of Texas Press, 1992).

12 Gardner Wilkinson, *Modern Egypt and Thebes: Being a Description of Egypt; Including the Information Required for Travellers in that Country*, 2 vols. (London: John Murray, 1843).

13 George Rapelje, *A Narrative of Excursions, Voyages, and Travels Performed at Different Periods in America, Europe, Asia, and Africa* (New York: West & Trow, 1834), 293 and 316.

14 Rapelje, *Narrative of Excursions*, 293–94.

15 "Extracts from a Communication of Mr. Smith," *The Missionary Herald* (April 1835).

16 Rapelje, *Narrative of Excursions*, 316.

17 Douglas R. Nickel, *Francis Frith in Egypt and Palestine: A Victorian Photographer Abroad* (Princeton: Princeton University Press, 2004), 149–57.

18 J.G. Wilkinson, *Topography of Thebes, and General View of Egypt* (London: John Murray, 1835), 562.

19 Wilkinson, *Modern Egypt and Thebes*, vol. 1, 100.

20 C. Rochfort Scott, *Rambles in Egypt and Candia* (London: Henry Colburn, 1837), vol. 1, 50.

21 Sotheby's, London, *British Drawings and Watercolours* (November 25, 1999), lot 155A. Baldwin Leighton's journal is in the National Library of Wales, Aberystwyth.

22 Rapelje, *Narrative of Excursions*, 331.

23 [[John L. Stephens], *Incidents of Travel in Egypt, Arabia Petræa, and the Holy Land* (New York: Harper & Brothers, 1837), vol. 1, 52.

24 [Stephens], *Incidents of Travel in Egypt*, vol. 1, 178.

25 Hector Horeau, *Panorama d'Égypte et de Nubie* (Paris: Chez l'Auteur, 1841), folio 10 recto, 1n.

26 "Cheever's Letters from Egypt," *New-York Observer and Chronicle*, March 21, 1840.

27 Eliza C. Patterson's journal among the George Mifflin Bache Papers, MS 212, Special Collections & Archives Department, Nimitz Library, United States Naval Academy, Annapolis.

28 Rapelje, *Narrative of Excursions*, 304 and 322.

29 William Holt Yates, *The Modern History and Condition of Egypt* (London: Smith, Elder and Co., 1843), vol. 1, 65–66.

30 Edward W. Hooker, *Memoir of Mrs. Sarah Lanman Smith*, 2nd ed. (Boston: American Tract Society, 1840), 88.

31 Edward C. Young, an artist on the *Concord*, made a watercolor sketch of "Achmet, an Arab servant to Dr. Kirkland," now in his album at Mystic Seaport.

32 [Stephens], *Incidents of Travel in Egypt*, vol. 1, 52–53.

33 [Sarah R. Haight], *Letters from the Old World* (New York: Harper & Brothers, 1840), vol. 1, 302–305, vol. 2, 304–305.

34 [Stephens], *Incidents of Travel in Egypt*, vol. 1, 54.

35 A relatively recent introduction to the subject is LaVerne Kuhnke, *Lives at Risk: Public Health in Nineteenth-Century Egypt* (Berkeley: University of California Press, 1990).

36 Alan Mikhail, *Nature and Empire in Ottoman Egypt: An Environmental History* (Cambridge, UK: Cambridge University Press, 2011); Enid M. Slatter, "Illustrations from the Wellcome Institute Library: The New Lazaretto at Siros (Syra), Greece, in 1840," *Medical History* 28 (1984), 73–80.

37 Janet Starkey, "'The Contagion Followed, and Vanquish'd Them': Plague, Travellers and Lazarettos," in Deborah Manley and Diane Fortenbury, eds., *Saddling the Dogs* (Oxford: Astene and Oxbow Books, 2009), 113–25; Alan Mikhail, "The Nature of Plague in Late Eighteenth-Century Egypt," *Bulletin of the History of Medicine* 82 (2008), 249–75; Kuhnke, *Lives at Risk*, 78–91 (the plague epidemic of 1835).

38 Kuhnke, *Lives at Risk*, 51–64 (the cholera epidemic of 1831).

39 Kuhnke, *Lives at Risk*, 111–21.

40 Robert Halsband, *The Life of Lady Mary Wortley Montagu* (Oxford: Clarendon Press, 1956), 80–81.

41   Amalie M. Kass, "Boston's Historic Smallpox Epidemic," *The Massachusetts Historical Review* 14 (2012), 1–50.

42   Robert Blake, *Disraeli's Grand Tour: Benjamin Disraeli and the Holy Land 1830–31* (London: Weidenfeld and Nicolson, 1982), 99.

43   Wilkinson, *Topography of Thebes*, 560.

Chapter 13

1   [John L. Stephens], *Incidents of Travel in Egypt, Arabia Petræa, and the Holy Land* (New York: Harper & Brothers, 1837), vol. 1, 160.

2   For Stephens' early career see "The late John L. Stephens," *Putnam's Magazine* 1, no. 1 (1853), 64–68, and Harvey E. Mole, "John L. Stephens, Traveler," *Proceedings of the New Jersey Historical Society* 61 (1943), 98–114. Admission as attorney, *New-York Spectator*, March 16, 1827.

3   Class of 1819 at Columbia and MD, College of Physicians and Surgeons, 1823.

4   [John L. Stephens], *Incidents of Travel in Greece, Turkey, Russia, and Poland* (New York: Harper & Brothers, 1838), vol. 1, 13.

5   [Stephens], *Incidents of Travel in Egypt*, vol. 2, 77 and 269.

6   Roger O. De Keersmaecker, *Travellers' Graffiti from Egypt and the Sudan*, IX, *Thebes* (Mortsel, Antwerp, 2010), 78.

7   [Stephens], *Incidents of Travel in Egypt*, vol. 1, 116.

8   Peter Rowley-Conwy, John Rowley-Conwy, Deborah Rowley-Conwy, "A Honeymoon in Egypt and the Sudan: Charlotte Rowley, 1835–1836," in Paul and Janet Starkey, eds., *Travellers in Egypt* (London: I.B.Tauris, 1998), 108–17.

9   [Stephens], *Incidents of Travel in Egypt*, vol. 1, 93–95.

10   Roger O. De Keersmaeker, *Travellers' Graffiti from Egypt and the Sudan*, V, *Thebes: The Temples of Medinet Habu* (Mortsel, Antwerp, 2006), 26.

11   De Keersmaecker, *Travellers' Graffiti, Medinet Habu*, 27.

12   [Stephens], *Incidents of Travel in Egypt*, vol. 1, 87, 93–94.

13   *Asiatic Journal and Monthly Miscellany* (1842), 161–62.

14   Alan Pryce-Jones, *The Spring Journey* (London: Cobden-Sanderson, 1931), 168–79.

15   James A. Harris, ed., *The Complete Works of Edgar Allan Poe* (New York: Crowell, 1902, reprinted New York: AMS Press Inc., 1965), vol. 10, 1-25.

16   Jason Thompson and Angela T. Thompson, "Between Two Lost Worlds: Frederick Catherwood," in Starkey and Starkey, *Travellers in Egypt*, 130–39.

17   *Description of a View of the Great Temple of Karnak, and the Surrounding City of Thebes, Now Exhibiting at the Panorama, Broadway, Corner of Prince and Mercer Streets, New York. Painted by Robert Burford, from Drawings Taken in 1834, by F. Catherwood* (New York, 1839).

18   Also shown later in the United States, for example, *Description of a View of the City of Jerusalem and the Surrounding Country, Now Exhibiting at the Panorama, Corner of Ninth and George Streets, Philadelphia. Painted by Robert Burford, from Drawings taken in 1834, by F. Catherwood, architect* [Philadelphia, 1842].

19   Later shown in New York in 1839 in a circular exhibition hall at the corner of Prince and Mercer streets (now Soho) in New York City. This was the closest most Americans would get to the great ruins at Thebes. Admission was 25 cents.

20   John L. Stephens, *Incidents of Travel in Central America, Chiapas, and Yucatan* (New York: Harper & Brothers, 1841); John L. Stephens, *Incidents of Travel in Yucatan* (New York: Harper & Brothers, 1843); F. Catherwood, *Views of Ancient Monuments in Central America, Chiapas, and Yucatan* (London: Vizetelly Brothers, 1844).

21   Henry Wikoff, *The Reminiscences of an Idler* (New York: Fords, Howard & Hurlbert, 1880), 97.

22   *The Travels of Sarah R. Haight through Switzerland, Austria-Hungary, Bohemia, Bavaria, Prussia, Holland, Denmark, Norway, Sweden, Finland, and Russia as Published in the New York American, 1839–1840*; owned by the New York Public Library (BTYA, Haight, S.R. Travels of Sarah R. Haight).

23   *Franklin Gazette*, Philadelphia, November 23, 1820.

24   *The Friend: A Religious and Literary Journal* 5, no. 2 (October 1831), 16; Jane W. T. Brey, *A Quaker Saga* (repr. Philadelphia: Dorrance, 1967), 358.

25   J.H. Battle, ed., *History of Bucks County, Pennsylvania* (Philadelphia, 1887; repr. Spartanburg, SC: The Reprint Company, 1985), 1090.

26   Notebook in the Joseph Downs Collection of Manuscripts and Printed Ephemera in the Winterthur Library in Wilmington, kindly photocopied for me by the staff of the library.

27   E.g., *Daily National Intelligencer*, Washington, DC, October 31, 1836; *United States' Telegraph*, Washington, DC, November 9, 1836.

28   [Sarah R. Haight], *Letters from the Old World by a Lady of New York* (New York: Harper & Brothers, 1840).

29   *Daily National Intelligencer*, Washington, DC October 31, 1836.

30   *United States' Telegraph*, Washington, DC November 9, 1836.

31   [Haight], *Letters from the Old World*, vol. 1, 207. In a note she added, "The French, by permission of the pacha, have taken one of the beautiful obelisks to Paris, where I saw it lying on the quay."

32   Letters from John Gliddon to Eli Smith in papers of the ABCFM on deposit at the Houghton Library, Harvard College; [Haight], *Letters from the Old World*, vol. 1, 293.

33   Richard Randolph on the *Garrick* from Liverpool, Richard Haight on the *Independence* from Liverpool, Sarah Haight and her children on the *Ville de Lyon* from Havre.

34   Preserved in the South Carolina Historical Society, Charleston, which kindly made available to me photocopies of both the original manuscript and a typescript version.

35   Owned in the 1930s by Allen's granddaughter, Mrs. Russell D. Lewis of Orange, New Jersey. Present whereabouts not known. *A Century of Progress:*

History of the Delaware and Hudson Company 1823-1923 (Albany: J.B. Lyon Company, 1925), 47, illustrated; *The Story of Anthracite* (New York: Prepared by the Hudson Coal Company, 1932), 89, illustrated. The New York Chapter of the Railway and Locomotive Historical Society presented a photograph of the miniature to the Smithsonian Institution in 1936: Alexander Wetmore, *Report on the Progress and Condition of the United States National Museum for the Fiscal Year ended June 30, 1936* (Washington, DC, 1936), 56. Amélie d'Aubigny (1795–1861) painted portrait miniatures in the 1830s and 1840s.

36   Longfellow describes the same excursion in his journal but without mentioning the Allens: Samuel Longfellow, ed., *Life of Henry Wadsworth Longfellow with Extracts from his Journals and Correspondence* (Boston: Ticknor and Company, 1886), vol. 1, 228.

37   David James, "An Irish Visitor to the Court of the Shah of Persia in 1835," *Studies: An Irish Quarterly Review* 60 (1971), 139–54.

38   Deborah Manley and Peta Rée, *Henry Salt: Artist, Traveller, Diplomat, Egyptologist* (London: Libri Publications Limited, 2001), 100–108.

39   Lord Lindsay, *Letters on Egypt, Edom, and the Holy Land* (London: Henry Colburn, 1838), vol. 1, 114–202.

40   Gardner Wilkinson, *Modern Egypt and Thebes: Being a Description of Egypt; Including the Information Required for Travellers in that Country* (London: John Murray, 1843), vol. 2, 274.

41   Gerard T. Koeppel, *Water for Gotham* (Princeton: Princeton University Press, 2000), 204, 225.

42   George Cochrane, *Wanderings in Greece* (London: Henry Colburn, 1837), vol. 2, 222–23. But Baghdad must be a mistake.

43   Leo Francis Stock, ed., *Consular Relations between the United States and the Papal States: Instructions and Despatches* (Washington, DC: American Catholic Historical Association, 1945), 46.

44   "The Will of Ambrose S. Courtis," *Daily National Intelligencer*, Washington DC, November 1, 1838.

45   Stock, *Consular Relations*, 44.

46   [Haight], *Letters from the Old World*, vol. 2, 325.

47   Cochrane, *Wanderings in Greece*, vol. 2, 222–23.

48   *Boston Post*, October 1836, picked up by the *New-York Spectator* October 31, 1836.

49   *Boston Courier* and *Salem Gazette*, November 18, 1836.

50   [Haight], *Letters from the Old World*, vol. 2, 325.

51   "The Will of Ambrose S. Courtis," *Daily National Intelligencer*, Washington, DC, November 1, 1838.

52   Stephen McAuliffe of Mount Auburn Cemetery forwarded to me the text of the inscription on his stone, *In memory of Ambrose Stacy Courtis Born in Marblehead March 6, 1775 died in Nauplia Greece August 26, 1835.*

53   Stock, *Consular Relations*, 51.

54   [Haight], *Letters from the Old World*, vol. 2, 149.

55   Franklin Bowditch Parker, *Biographical Notices of the Graduates of Yale College, Including those Graduated in Classes Later than 1815, Who Are Not Commemorated in the Annual Obituary Records* (New Haven: [Yale University Press], 1913), 217.

56   James A. Dorr, trans., *Napoleonic Ideas: Des idées napoléoniennes par le prince Napoléon-Louis Bonaparte, Brussels 1839* (New York: D. Appleton & Company, 1859).

57   There are some clues. Joe Attard Tabone, a resident of Malta, kindly furnished me with the following information about steamers from Malta to Alexandria and their passengers in the fall of 1837, as listed in the *Malta Government Gazette*. The steamer *Hermes* left for Alexandria on September 27 with Miss Dudley and Sig. G. Sevastopulo as passengers. Neither of them is a candidate. The steamer *Volcano* left for Alexandria on October 25 with three passengers: Mr. Lancaster, Mr. Nott, and Mr. Alpen or MacAlpine. From other sources we know that H. Lancaster Esq. soon took passage on the steamer *Atalanta*, leaving Suez on November first for Bombay, and that Lt. Anthony H. Nott of the Indian navy took passage on the steamer *Hugh Lindsay* about a month later, leaving Suez on November 29 for Bombay. The name Alpen or MacAlpine does not reappear in subsequent passenger lists. He may have been the American. No corresponding individual of that name shows up in passport records or in transatlantic passenger lists. The closest match is Alexander McAlpin, a American gentleman aged 30, who arrived in New York on November 15, 1838, on the *Great Western* from Bristol. But there is no positive identification.

58   Excerpted in the *Maryland Gazette* of April 22, 1830.

59   Felix E. Hirsch, "The Bard Family," *Columbia University Quarterly* (October 1941), 222–41.

60   John Brett Langstaff, *The Enterprising Life: John McVickar* (New York: St Martin's Press, 1961), 255.

61   Georges Goyon, *Les inscriptions et graffiti des voyageurs sur la Grande Pyramide* (Cairo: Société Royale de Géographie, 1944), 87, pl. xxvii.

62   Roger O. De Keersmaecker, *Travellers' Graffiti, Medinet Habu*, 33.

Chapter 14

1   *New York Farmer*, issue published March 4, 1838, picked up from the *New York Daily Express*; also *American Railroad Journal*, issue published February 18, 1838.

2   Charles Colville Frankland, *Travels to and from Constantinople in 1827 and 1828* (London: Henry Colburn, 1830), vol. 2, 215.

3   Alfred R. Ferguson, ed., *Journals and Miscellaneous Notebooks of Ralph Waldo Emerson*, vol. 4, 1832–1834 (Cambridge, MA: Harvard University Press, 1964), 138–40; William H. Gilman, ed., *Journals and Miscellaneous*

Notebooks 1832–1834 (Cambridge, MA: The Belknap Press of Harvard University Press, 1982), vol. 3, 140.

4   Charles MacFarlane, *Constantinople in 1828* (London: Sander and Otley, 1829), 245–46, and 372.

5   *Journal of Commerce*, picked up by the *Daily National Intelligencer*, Washington DC, January 5, 1833.

6   *Memorials of Peter A. Jay, Compiled for his Descendants by his Great-grandson, John Jay* (New York: The DeVinne Press, 1905), 135.

7   Marchebeus, *Voyage de Paris à Constantinople par bateau à vapeur* (Paris: Artus Bertrand, 1839).

8   John Auldjo, *Journal of a Visit to Constantinople and Some of the Greek Islands in the Spring and Summer of 1833* (London: Longman, Rees, Orme, Brown, Green, & Longman, 1835), 192.

9   Harrison Wilkinson, "Proposal for an East-India Steam-mail," *The Monthly Magazine*, January 1, 1824, 431–35.

10 R.T. Claridge, *A Guide along the Danube, from Vienna to Constantinople, Smyrna, Athens, The Morea, The Ionian Islands, and Venice, from Notes of a Journey Made in the Year 1836* (London: F.C. Westley, 1837), 5–6.

11 The illustration, entitled *Vue de Smyrne, prise de la Rade* (View of Smyrna, taken from the roadstead) and dated 1836, is one of a set of some twenty-five plates showing costumes and scenes of Smyrna done between 1836 and 1838 in an album in the Fine Arts Library Collection at Harvard University, an album once owned by an American expatriate merchant, long resident in Smyrna, Thomas Walley Langdon.

12 Charles G. Addison, *Damascus and Palmyra: A Journey to the East; With a Sketch of the State and Prospects of Syria, under Ibrahim Pasha* (London: Richard Bentley, 1838), vol. 1, 406–407.

13 *Vermont Chronicle*, January 7, 1836.

14 Forrest's diary, preserved in the Harvard Theater Collection in the Pusey Library in Cambridge, MA, ends before they reached Turkey. The story is told in Henry Wikoff, *The Reminiscences of an Idler* (New York: Fords, Howard & Hurlbert, 1880), 299–300. On Forrest's career, which includes his tour with Wikoff, see Richard Moody, *Edwin Forrest: First Star of the American Stage* (New York: Alfred A. Knopf, 1960).

15 Xavier Daumalin and Marcel Courdurié, *Vapeur et révolution industrielle à Marseille 1831–1857* (Marseilles: Chambre de commerce et d'industrie Marseille-Provence, 1997), 185.

16 Fanny W. Hall, *Rambles in Europe: Or, a Tour through France, Italy, Switzerland, Great Britain, and Ireland, in 1836* (New York: E. French, 1838).

17 For a description of the cruise see "Voyage de Phocéen," *Revue de Paris* 28 (1836), 256–59.

18 Daniel Panzac, *La marine ottoman: De l'apogée à la chute de l'Empire (1572–1923)* (Paris: CNRS Editions, 2012), 295.

19   Paul Bois, *Histore du commerce et de l'industrie de Marseille xixe–xxe siècles, tome vii. Le grand siècle des messageries maritime* (Marseilles: Chambre de commerce et d'industrie Marseille-Provence, 1991), 162–64.

20   Ronald E. Coons, *Steamships, Statesmen, and Bureaucrats: Austrian Policy towards the Steam Navigation Company of the Austrian Lloyd, 1836–1846* (Wiesbaden: Franz Steiner, 1975).

21   Edward Robinson, *Biblical Researches in Palestine, Mount Sinai and Arabia Petræa: A Journal of Travels in the Year 1838* (Boston: Crocker & Brewster, 1841), vol. 1, 4.

Chapter 15

1   Henry B. Smith and Roswell D. Hitchcock, *The Life, Writings, and Character of Edward Robinson, D.D., LL.D. Read before the N.Y. Historical Society* (New York: Anson D.F. Randolph, 1863); Jay G. Williams, *The Times and Life of Edward Robinson* (Atlanta: Society of Biblical Literature, 1999).

2   Professor Jay Williams of Hamilton College kindly made available to me a typescript of the unpublished document recounting Robinson's first trip to Europe, "Robinson's Letter—Journal (1826–1829), Written from Europe by Edward Robinson to His Sister Elizabeth."

3   *New-York Spectator*, July 20, 1837.

4   Dorothy Rogers and Alexandra Perry, "George Barrell Cheever (1797–1890)," in John R. Shook, ed., *Dictionary of Early American Philosophers* (New York: Continuum 2012), 212–217.

5   Records in the National Archives show that their passports were issued on July 19, 1837.

6   Edward Robinson, *Biblical Researches in Palestine, Mount Sinai, and Arabia Petræa: A Journal of Travels in the Year 1838* (Boston: Crocker & Brewster, 1841), vol. 1, 1–48.

7   *New York Observer and Chronicle*, April 11, 1840.

8   William Jowett, *Christian Researches in the Mediterranean, from MDCCCXV to MDCCCXX* (London: L.B. Seeley and J. Hatchard & Son, 1822).

9   Manuscript diary of Mary Allen in the South Carolina Historical Society, Charleston.

10   The diary of Rittenhouse Nutt, original in a private collection, transcript in the Huntington Library, San Marino, California.

11   *New York Observer and Chronicle*, April 11, 1840.

12   *New York Observer and Chronicle*, May 2, 1840.

13   *New-York Spectator*, June 6, 1839.

14   Edward Robinson, letter to the *Biblical Repository*, repr. in *Christian Register and Boston Observer*, November 3, 1838, and *Daily National Intelligence*, Washington, DC, November 16, 1838.

15   Robinson, *Biblical Researches*, vol. 1, 338, and map at the end of the volume, derived from the map of Frederick Catherwood.

16 J.D. Paxton, *A Memoir of J.D. Paxton DD: Late of Princeton, Indiana* (Philadelphia: J.B. Lippincott & Co, 1870).

17 J.D. Paxton, *Letters from Palestine: Written during a Residence There in the Years 1836, 7, and 8* (London: Charles Tilt, 1839).

18 Robinson, *Biblical Researches*, vol. 3, 448–51; Karl Eduard Zachariä von Lingenthal, *Reise in den Orient in den Jahren 1837 und 1838* (Heidelberg: J. C. B. Mohr, 1840), 322–34.

19 John B. Adger, *My Life and Times, 1810–1899* (Richmond: The Presbyterian Committee of Publications, 1899), 111.

20 William H. Gerdts and Carrie Rebora, *The Art of Henry Inman* (Washington, DC: The National Portrait Gallery, 1987), 101, no. 37.

21 Leo Francis Stock, ed., *Consular Relations between the United States and the Papal States: Instructions and Despatches* (Washington, DC: American Catholic Historical Association, 1945), 50.

22 Valentine Mott, *Travels in Europe and the East, Embracing Observations Made During a Tour through Great Britain, Ireland, France, Belgium, Holland, Prussia, Saxony, Bohemia, Austria, Bavaria, Switzerland, Lombardy, Tuscany, the Papal States, the Neapolitan Dominions, Malta, the Islands of the Archipelago, Greece, Egypt, Asia Minor, Turkey, Moldavia, Wallachia, and Hungary, in the years 1834, '35, '36, '37, '38, '39, '40, and '41* (New York: Harper & Brothers, 1842).

23 Hopper Striker Mott, "The Ancestors and Descendants of the Rev. John Frelinghuysen Jackson," *The New York Genealogical and Biographical Record*, vol. 37 (1906), 81–91.

24 Russell M. Jones, "American Doctors in Paris, 1820–1861: A Statistical Profile," *Journal of the History of Medicine* (1970), 143–57.

25 Letter preserved among Mott's papers in the Library of Medicine, Bethesda, Maryland.

26 King's letter to Lady Hester Stanhope, dated May 9, 1838, is preserved in the Beinecke Library, Yale University, Hebrew MS. 64.

27 Mott, *Travels in Europe and the East*, 387.

28 Valentine Mott, "The Gleanings in the East of a ci-devant Invalid, in 1838," *The American Journal of Medical Sciences* (August 1839), 367ff.

29 *The New York Herald*, May 17, 1841.

30 Later in 1838, the year of Mott's visit, an English scholar, the Rev. Henry Tattum, arrived in Egypt with his stepdaughter, Miss Platt, to search for Coptic manuscripts with a view of editing and publishing proper texts of some of the scriptures: [Eliza Platt], *Journal of a Tour through Egypt, the Peninsula of Sinai and the Holy Land in 1838, 1839*, 2 vols. (London: Richard Watts, 1841, 1842). The venture had started ten years earlier, in 1828, when the English collector Algernon Percy (Lord Prudhoe) began to make inquiries for Coptic works having Arabic translations, in order to assist Mr. Tattum in his Coptic and Arabic Dictionary. Pursuing this venture, Lord Prudhoe, traveling with the French engineer and explorer Linant de Bellefonds, purchased

several manuscripts from the monastery of Deir al-Suryan (Monastery of the Syrians) in Wadi al-Natrun in the Saharan desert west of the Nile Delta, and from another monastery in the same region, which he presented to Tattum: Robert Curzon, *A Visit to Monasteries in the Levant* (London, 1849). In 1837, another English scholar, Robert Curzon, traveling for the second time in the East in search of manuscripts, again visited the monastery of Deir al-Suryan where, among boxes of manuscripts, he managed to acquire three books, leaving behind a fourth that he also wanted: xxxx begin *Quarterly Review* . . . A letter of April 3, 1838, addressed to the Rev. Walter Sneyd, preserved at Keele University, Staffordshire, gives a list of manuscripts in Arabic, Persian, Coptic, Syriac, and Abyssinian that Curzon had acquired: Noel Matthews and M. Doreen Wainwright, *A Guide to Manuscripts and Documents in the British Isles Relating to the Middle East and North Africa* (Oxford: Oxford University Press, 1980), 174. In early 1839 Tattum toured a number of monasteries, including Deir al-Suryan, where he purchased the book left behind by Curzon (a treatise of Titus of Bostra against the Manicheans, datable to AD 411), and successfully acquired elsewhere nearly fifty Coptic, Syrian, and Arabic texts. Tattum returned to Egypt a year later to purchase more than a hundred additional manuscripts, and in 1845 the British Museum sponsored a final search of Deir al-Suryan by Auguste Pacho of Alexandria in the course of which another two hundred volumes, many fragmentary, were acquired: William Wright, *Catalogue of the Syrian Manuscripts in the British Museum* (1872), vol. 3, xiv. Most of these texts, all now in the British Library, are ecclesiastical, but one is a Syriac translation of a work of the second century AD Greek medical writer Galen: "Manuscripts from the Egyptian Monasteries," *Quarterly Review* (December 1845–March 1846), 39–69; reprinted in *The Eclectic Magazine of Foreign Literature*, March 1846. A postscript to the story came in 2005 when two Syriac scholars discovered at Deir al-Suryan additional fragments of some of the key manuscripts found more than 150 years earlier: Martin Bailey, "Fragments of the World's Oldest Christian Manuscript Found in Monastery," *The Art Newspaper*, no. 188 (February 2008), 8–9.

31 S.D. Gross, *Memoir of Valentine Mott, D.C. LL.D.* (New York: D. Appleton and Co., 1868), 73.

32 *New York Times*, January 28, 1912.

33 www.loc.gov/rr/amed/guide/images/nes_p23tops.jpg.

34 Library of Congress call no: R126.H6A844 1300z. Forty manuscript copies of the work have been identified in libraries, three of which, including this one, are in the United States: Peter E. Pormann, and N. Peter Joosse, "Commentaries on the Hippocratic *Aphorisms* in the Arabic Tradition: The Example of Melancholy," in P.E. Pormann, ed., *Epidemics in Context: Greek Commentaries on Hippocrates in the Arabic Tradition* (Berlin: de Gruyter, 2012), 211ff, at 222–23.

35 *National Intelligencer*, Washington, DC, March 2, 1830.

36 Sami Khalaf Hamarneh, *Catalogue of Arabic Manuscripts on Medicine and Pharmacy at the British Library* (Cairo: Les Éditions Universitaire d'Égypte in collaboration with the Smithsonian Institution, 1975), x (224 vols. press marked Add. 9451 to 9675).

37 W.B. Llewellyn in *The Naval Magazine*, vol. 1 (1836), 195–96; *Army and Navy Chronicle*, vols. 8–9 (1839), 398.

38 Meredith M. Quinn, "Making Sense of Miscellanies: Houghton Library MS Turk 11, an Ottoman *Mecmus*," *Harvard Library Bulletin* 24 (Spring 2013), 27–44.

39 Edward Everett, "An Account of Some Greek Manuscripts," *Memoirs of the American Academy of Arts and Sciences*, vol. 4 (1820), 409ff; Gary Vikan, ed., *Illuminated Greek Manuscripts from American Collections: An Exhibition in Honor of Kurt Weitzmann* (Princeton: Princeton University Art Museum, 1973), 128–29 (Ms Gr. 3). Nadezhda Kavrus-Hoffmann, "Catalogue of Greek Medieval and Renaissance Manuscripts in the Collections of the United States of America, Part V:1: Harvard University, The Houghton Library," in *Manuscripta*, vol. 54.1, 2010, 64–141, Mss. Gr. 3, 4, 6, 7.1–2, 8, 12; and the online catalogue with bibliographies and selected images at http://hcl.harvard.edu/libraries/houghton/collections/early_manuscripts/bibliographies/Greek.cfm.

40 *New-York Spectator*, March 15, 1838.

41 Preserved in the Museum of the City of New York; gift of his daughter Cornelia E. Marshall, 1931.

42 *Oriental Herald* 1839; *Asiatic Register* 1839, 166.

43 Stewart Brown, a cousin of the founding family of Brown Brothers, who had joined the firm in 1827, married Mary Ann Abbott (1812–1874) on May 6, 1830.

44 Gift of Mr. Marshall's daughter, Cornelia E. Marshall 1931; 31.193.43.

Chapter 16

1 Colonel Howard Vyse, *Operations Carried out at the Pyramids of Gizeh in 1837: with an Account of a Voyage into Upper Egypt* (London: James Fraser, 1840), vol. 1, 208; C. Rochfort Scott, *Rambles in Egypt and Candia* (London: Henry Colburn, 1837), vol. 1, 65, reporting on a visit of 1834; [Joseph Wolff], *Journal of the Rev. Joseph Wolff* (London: James Burns, 1839), 300, reporting on a visit of February 17, 1836.

2 George R. Gliddon, *A Memoir on the Cotton of Egypt* (London: James Madden & Co., 1841), 20. Mr. Brown was probably the Charles Brown of New York cited in John Gliddon's list of American visitors to Alexandria from 1832 to 1834.

3 As reported in Mary Allen's journal owned by the South Carolina Historical Society.

4   As reported in a letter from John Gliddon to Eli Smith of March 30, 1837 in the papers of the ABCFM on deposit at the Houghton Library, Harvard College.

5   *Rhode-Island Republican*, Newport, January 25, 1837.

6   Frederick Brown, ed. and trans., *Alexis de Tocqueville: Letters from America* (New Haven: Yale University Press, 2010), 20–21.

7   [John L. Stephens], *Egypt, Arabia Petræa, and the Holy Land* (New York: Harper & Brothers, 1838), vol. 2, 283–85. A list of the society's first members is printed in *The Foreign Quarterly Review* (London), vol. 12 (1838), 473 ff.

8   "Transactions of the American Lyceum," *American Annals of Education* (July 1837).

9   *The Globe*, Washington, DC, October 6, 1837.

10   Henry S. Patterson, "Memoir of the Life and Scientific Labors of Samuel George Morton," in J.C. Nott and George R. Gliddon, *Types of Mankind: Or Ethnographical Researches* (Philadelphia: Lippincott, Grambo & Co., 1854), xvii–lvii at xxxv–xxxvi.

11   Ann Fabian, *The Skull Collectors: Race, Science, and America's Unburied Dead* (Chicago: University of Chicago Press, 2010), 9–36 and 103–12. After Morton's death in 1851, some of his work was used selectively by those anxious to prove the inferiority of negroes. Morton's reputation suffered further at the hands of Stephen Jay Gould who in 1981, as reported in *The New York Times* of June 14, 2011, "asserted that Morton, believing that brain size was a measure of intelligence, had subconsciously manipulated the brain volumes of European, Asian and African skulls to favor his bias that Europeans had larger brains and Africans smaller ones." And that Gould "based his attack on the premise that Morton believed that brain size was correlated with intelligence. But there is no evidence that Morton believed this or was trying to prove it." As reported in the *Times*, a team of anthropologists writing in *PLoS Biology* for June 7, 2011, demonstrated that Gould's observations on Morton's skull measurement were erroneous.

12   On Palmer see Jessica Lepler's article in the *Rothschild Archive, Annual Review of the Year (April 2007–March 2008)*, 14–20.

13   E.g., *Journal of the American Institute* (1837), vol. 2, 112.

14   Richard Cowling Taylor, *Statistics of Coal: The Geographical and Geological Distribution of Mineral Combustible or Fossil Fuel* (Philadelphia: J.W. Moore, 1848), 633.

15   See the account in Daniel Walker Howe, *What Hath God Wrought* (Oxford: Oxford University Press, 2007), 501–508; and Jessica M. Lepler, *The Many Panics of 1837: People, Politics, and the Creation of a Transatlantic Financial Crisis* (Cambridge: Cambridge University Press, 2013).

16   Preserved among the John L. Stephens papers in the Bancroft Library, University of California, Berkeley.

17 From a letter in J.L. Stephens' papers at the Bancroft Library, University of California, Berkeley.

18 Oil on canvas, private collection.

19 National Archives records of passports issued.

20 *The New York Sunday News*, March 21, 1838; see also the *Hudson River Chronicle*, April 10, 1838.

21 Information courtesy of Joan Wood, one of Marshall's many descendants.

22 [Andrew A. Bonar], *Narrative of a Mission of Inquiry to the Jews from the Church of Scotland in 1839* (Philadelphia: Presbyterian Board of Publications, 1842), 58.

23 *The Times*, October 24, 1839.

24 This and the following extracts in French are from Pierre Nicolas Hamont, *L'Égypte sous Méhémet-Ali* (Paris: Leautey et Leconte, 1843), vol. 1, 182–83.

25 Letter in the Bancroft Library, University of California, Berkeley.

26 *Commerical Advertiser* (May 15, 1840), *The American Repertory of Arts, Sciences, and Manufactures*, vol. 2 (1841), 252. The Lyceum, founded in 1817, has now become the New York Academy of Sciences.

27 *The Oriental Herald and Colonial Review* 1 (1824), 368; Robert Walsh, *A Residence at Constantinople* (London: Frederick Westley and A.H. David, 1826), vol. 2, 223–24. This was not the very first giraffe to reach Constantinople. Two Italian travelers saw one there, in a converted church near the hippodrome, in 1497: Eve Borsook, "The travels of Bernardo Michelozzi and Bonsignore Bonsignori in the Levant (1497–98)," *Journal of the Warburg and Courtauld Institutes*, vol. 36 (1973), 160. The Mamluk ruler of Egypt had presented a giraffe to Lorenzo de Medici some ten years earlier in 1486.

28 Gabriel Dardaud, "L'extraordinaire aventure de la girafe du pacha d'Égypte," *Revue des conférences françaises en Orient* 14 (1951), 1–72; Gabriel Dardaud, *Une girafe pour le roi* (Paris: Dumerchez-Naoum, 1985). The French giraffe: Olivier Lagueux, "Geoffrey's Giraffe: The Hagiography of a Charismatic Mammal," *Journal of the History of Biology* 36 (2003), 225–47; Erik Ringmar, "Audience for a Giraffe: European Expansionism and the Quest for the Exotic" *Journal of World History*, vol. 17, no. 4 (2006), 375–97, esp. 383–89; Nancy Milton, *The Giraffe that Walked to Paris* (New York: Crown, 1992); Michael Allin, *Zarafa: A Giraffe's True Story, from Deep in Africa to the Heart of Paris* (New York: Walker, 1998). Olivier Lebleu, *Les Avatars de Zarafa: Première girafe de France; Chronique d'une girofomania 1826–1845* (Paris: Arléa, 2006).

29 Andrew Bigelow, *Travels in Malta and Sicily, with Sketches of Gibraltar in MDCCCXXVII* (Boston: Carter, Hendee & Babcock, 1831), 226–27. The giraffe arrived in England in August 1827, and was soon painted by Jacques-Laurent Agasse (Royal Collections at Windsor). But she lived little more than two years: *The Morning Post*, London, October 26, 1829.

30 James Franklin Beard, ed., *The Letters and Journals of James Fenimore Cooper* (Cambridge, MA: The Belknap Press of Harvard University Press, 1960), vol. 1, 229.

31 Neil Cooke, "James Burton's Giraffe," *Astene Bulletin* 57 (Autumn 2013), 16–21.

32 Paul Santi and Richard Hill, trans. and eds., "A Saint-Simonian in Kordofan: Reboul's Journal of an Expedition to Collect Live Animals, 1834–5," *The Europeans in the Sudan 1834–1878* (Oxford: Clarendon Press, 1980), 35–51.

33 *Transactions of the Zoological Society*. The story was reprinted in many American papers: *United States' Telegraph*, Washington DC, July 27, 1836; *Boston Courier*, September 22, 1836; *Farmer's Cabinet*, October 7, 1836. And see G. Scharf, *Six Views in the Zoological Gardens, Regent's Park* (London: The Artist, 1835).

34 Also in *Bell's Life in London and Sporting Chronicle*, London, May 29, 1836; *The Mirror of Literature, Amusement, and Instruction*, Saturday, June 11, 1836.

35 Ann Lucas Birle and Lisa A. Francavilla, eds., *Thomas Jefferson's Granddaughter in Queen Victoria's England: The Travel Diary of Ellen Wayles Coolidge 1838–1839* (Boston and Charlottesville: Massachusetts Historical Society and the Thomas Jefferson Foundation, 2011), 32.

36 *New York American*, reprinted in *Daily National Intelligencer*, Washington DC, October 31, 1836.

37 *London Morning Herald*, May 3, 1836, reprinted in American newspapers; repeated by William Holt Yates, *The Modern History and Condition of Egypt* (London: Smith, Elder and Co., 1843), vol. 2, 244.

38 [Sarah R. Haight], *Letters from the Old World* (New York: Harper & Brothers, 1840), vol. 1, 289.

39 J.E. Warwick, *Description and History, with Anecdotes, of the Giraffes (Camelopardalis giraffa, Gmel.): Now Exhibiting at the Surrey Zoological Gardens, With an Account of Their Capture and Voyage* (London: J. King, 1836).

40 *Boston Daily Times*, April 1837, reprinted in *Rhode-Island Republican*, April 5, 1837.

41 Allan Nevins, ed., *The Diary of Philip Hone 1828–1851* (New York: Dodd, Mead & Company, 1936), 336; Newspapers reported their exhibition the following day: *Morning Herald*, New York, July 4, 1838.

42 J.D. Paxton, *Letters from Palestine: Written during a Residence There in the Years 1836, 7, and 8* (London: Charles Tilt, 1839), 260–61.

43 J.D. Paxton, *A Memoir of J.D. Paxton, DD: Late of Princeton, Indiana* (Philadelphia: J.B. Lippincott & Co, 1870), 299.

44 James Shepard, *History of Saint Mark's Church, New Britain, Conn., and of Its Predecessor Christ Church, Wethersfield and Berlin* (New Britain, CT: Tuttle, Morehouse & Taylor, 1907), 460.

45   *Morning Herald*, New York, October 6, 1838.
46   *New York Era*, early November, reprinted in *Daily National Intelligence*, Washington, DC, November 8, 1838.
47   [P. Cator], *Up the Red Sea and Down the Nile in 1839* (London: Smith, Elder and Co., 1841) 92.
48   Stephen Olin, *Travels in Egypt, Arabia Petræa, and the Holy Land* (New York: Harper & Brothers, 1843), vol. 1, 131.
49   George R. Gliddon, *An Appeal to the Antiquaries of Europe on the Destruction of the Monuments of Egypt* (London: James Madden & Co., 1841), 55n; Norman de G. Davis, *The Rock Tombs of El Amarna: Smaller Tombs and Boundary Stelae* (London: Egypt Exploration Fund, 1908), 27. On the boundary stelae in general: Cyril Aldred, *Akhenaten: King of Egypt* (London and New York: Thames and Hudson, 1988), 44–50; William J. Murnane and Charles C. Van Siclen III, *The Boundary Stelae of Akhenaten* (London and New York: Kegan Paul International, 1993) (brought to my attention by Lawrence Berman).
50   Richard Hill, ed. and trans., "A Journey to Sinnar and the Hijaz, 1837– 1840," *On the Froniers of Islam: Two Manuscripts Concerning the Sudan under Turco-Egyptian rule 1822–1845* (Oxford: Clarendon Press, 1970), 203, 205.
51   From a letter in the Morton Collection at the American Philosophical Society, Philadelphia.
52   Letters in the Morton papers at the American Philosophical Society, March 21, 1839; May 21–24, 1840; Samuel George Morton, "Observations on Egyptian Ethnology, Derived from Anatomy, History and the Monuments, Read December 16, 1842, January 6, April 6 1843," *Transactions of the American Philosophical Society*, vol. 9 (1846), 93–159; Ann Fabian, *The Skull Collectors*, 105–106.
53   Malcolm Daniel, "Daguerre (1787–1851) and the Invention of Photography," *Heilbrunn Timeline of Art History* (New York: The Metropolitan Museum of Art, 2000), www.metmuseum.org/toah/hd/dagu/hd_dagu.htm.
54   *100th Anniversary of the Caledonia County Grammar School, Peacham, VT* (Peacham, VT, 1900), 17–18, with biography and a letter from Chamberlain to his sister dated Paris, September 19, 1838.
55   Yakup Bektas, "Displaying the American Genius: The Electromagnetic Telegraph in the Wider World," *British Journal for the History of Science* 34 (2001), 199–232, esp. 207–11.
56   Samuel Irenæus Prime, *The Life of Samuel F.B. Morse, LL.D.: Inventor of the Electro-magnetic Recording Telegraph* (New York: D. Appleton and Company, 1875), 411, letter from Athens, January 5, 1839, letter from Syra, January 9, 1839.
57   Dated August 31, 1853, in the Morse papers at the Library of Congress, digital archive: http://memory.loc.gov/mss/mmorse/032/032001/0122d.jpg.
58   *Boston Courier*, first set of seventeen letters, December 29, 1839 to March 30, 1840; second set of twenty letters, October 12, 1840 to January 4, 1841.

59 "Sketches of Foreign Travel, Letter xvii," *Boston Courier*, March 30, 1840.

60 Cass was the American minister in Paris who had visited ports all around the Mediterranean while on board the *Constitution* in 1837; Dr. J. was Dr. William H. Jackson who had traveled with Dr. Valentine Mott the previous year, Mr. C. is unidentified—he cannot have been Mellen Chamberlain.

61 "Sketches of Foreign Travel, letter xvii," *Boston Courier*, March 30, 1840.

62 *Philadelphia North American*, picked up by the *New-York Spectator*, June 20, 1839.

63 Andrew Hilen, ed., *The Letters of Henry Wadsworth Longfellow, vol. 2, 1837–1843* (Cambridge, MA: The Belknap Press of Harvard University Press, 1966), 83–84 (letter in the Berg Collection at the New York Public Library). Greene (1811–1883) was American consul in Rome from 1837 to 1845.

Chapter 17

1 "Journal of a Lady during Her Travels in Egypt," *The Courier*, August 27, 1839.

2 This and the following three extracts are from "Journal of a Lady, during her Travels in Egypt," *The Courier*, Charleston, August 27, 1839.

3 *The Age*, London, July 28, 1839: "On the 22nd inst., at the British Embassy, Paris, William Young, Esq., youngest son of Rear-Admiral Young, to Harriet Elizabeth, only child of A.S. Wellington, Esq., of Charleston, South Carolina." Also *The Gentleman's Magazine*, vol. 166, September 1839, 308 (Willington's name correctly spelled).

4 Handwritten ship's manifest in the National Archives, Washington DC.

5 *New-York Spectator*, May 3, 1838.

6 Adolphus Slade, *Travels in Germany and Russia: Including a Steam Voyage by the Danube and the Euxine from Vienna to Constantinople, in 1838–39* (London: Longman, Orme, Brown, Green, and Longman, 1840), 213.

7 F.E.H. Haines, *Jonas King: Missionary to Syria and Greece* (New York: American Tract Society, 1879), 279.

8 *Gentleman's Magazine* 1839, 437.

9 *New-Hampshire Statesman and State Journal*, Concord, March 3, 1838.

10 I am grateful to Elizabeth Call, special collections librarian at the society, for providing me with a photocopy of an existing typescript of the diary.

11 Slade called Madame Ruthvin, Mme Rochstein; he said that Barton was deputy lieutenant for County Fermanagh in Ireland, and that he (Slade) was traveling with Col. Knox, of the Guards. Baron Stürmer (1787–1863) was internuncio from 1834 to 1850.

12 Manuscript diary of Susan Holmes in the Brooklyn Historical Society.

13 Salome Danforth had arrived in Smyrna in March 1837 on board the brig *Banian*, together with three American missionary couples, one bound for the island of Syros, the other two for Persia: *The Pittsfield Sun*, January 12, 1837; *Salem Gazette*, January 6, 1837.

14 N. Neal Solly, *Memoir of the Life of William James Müller, a Native of Bristol, Landscape and Figure Painter* (London: Chapman and Hall, 1875), 64–85; Francis Greenacre and Sheena Stoddard, *W.J. Müller 1812–1845* (Bristol: Bristol Museums and Art Gallery, 1991); Sotheby's London, 25 November 1999, *The Bill Thomson Collection of Paintings, Watercolours and Drawings by William James Müller 1812–1845*, lots 53–57.

15 *The Spirit of Missions*, vol. 7 (1842), 210; *Historical Magazine of the Protestant Episcopal Church* 31 (1962). Susan Holmes' diary is one of the few records for his presence in Egypt.

16 This and the following three extracts are from the manuscript diary of Susan Holmes at the Brooklyn Historical Society.

17 They had arrived in Egypt from Bombay on the steamer *Berenice*: *Asiatic Register* 1839, 166; *Oriental Herald* 1839.

18 Francis Hovey Stoddard, *The Life and Letters of Charles Butler* (New York: Charles Scribner's Sons, 1903), 175–82; William Allen Butler, *A Retrospect of Forty Years 1825–1865* (New York: Charles Scribner's Sons, 1911), 101–104, where it is stated that the journal of his 1839 Italian trip survives.

19 [George Gliddon], *Appendix to "The American in Egypt"* (Philadelphia: Merrihew & Thompson, 1842), 29; David H. Finnie, *Pioneers East: The Early American Experience in the Middle East* (Cambridge, MA: Harvard University Press, 1967), 283–84.

20 Peter J. Wosh, *Spreading the Word: The Bible Business in Nineteenth-century America* (Ithaca: Cornell University Press, 1994), 164ff.

21 *New-York Spectator*, November 21, 1836.

22 Excerpts of his journal in a letter to the corresponding secretary of the American Bible Society in New York: *The North American and Daily Advertiser* (Philadelphia), June 3, 1840; *New York Evangelist*, June 13, 1840.

23 *Oeuvres complete de Voltaire avec des remarques et des notes historiques, scientifiques et littéraires* (Paris: Baudouin frères, 1825–1828).

24 [Eliza Platt], *Journal of a tour through Egypt, the peninsula of Sinai and the Holy Land, in 1838, 1839* (London: Richard Watts, 1842), vol. 2, 71.

25 "Tour through Egypt and Palestine," *The New-York Mirror*, October 17, 1840.

Chapter 18

1 Martha V. Pike and Janice Gray Armstrong, *A Time to Mourn: Expressions of Grief in Nineteenth-Century America* (Stony Brook, NY: The Museums at Stony Brook, 1981), 179, no. 207. Some of this information, including the catalogue reference, was brought to my attention by Jeanne Rhinelander.

2 Carl C. Cutler, *Queens of the Western Ocean: The Story of America's Mail and Passenger Sailing Lines* (Annapolis: United States Naval Institute, 1961), 160–61.

3 Moses Yale Beach, ed., *Wealth and Pedigree of the Wealthy Citizens of New York Comprising an Alphabetical Arrangement of Persons Estimated to be Worth $100,000 and Upwards*, 3rd. ed. (New York: The Sun Office, 1842), 32.

4 Thomas Lawrence, *Historical Genealogy of the Lawrence Family, from Their First Landing in This Country* (New York: Edward O. Jenkins, 1858), 105–106.

5 Allan Nevins and Milton Halsey Thomas, eds., *The Diary of George Templeton Strong* (New York: The Macmillan Company, 1952), vol. 1, 85.

6 *New-York Spectator*, May 3, 1838.

7 Allan Nevins, ed., *The Diary of Philip Hone 1828–1851* (New York: The Macmillan Company, 1936), 316–17.

8 *Morning Herald*, March 31, 1838. The couple sailed with their servants on the packet ship *Cambridge* in early April: *New-York Spectator*, April 5, 1838. Henry's younger siblings were Edward Payson (born 1824), Laura Virginia (born 1826), and George Clarence (born 1830).

9 Christopher W. Knauff, *Doctor Tucker: Priest-Musician, A Sketch which concerns the doings and thinkings of the Rev. John Ireland Tucker, S.T.D.* (New York: A.D.F. Randolph Company, 1897), 37–97.

10 Andrew Oliver, "An American Tourist in 1839: Philip Rhinelander Visits the Mediterranean," in Deborah Manley and Diane Fortenbury, eds., *Saddling the Dogs* (Oxford: ASTENE and Oxbow Books, 2009), 95–109.

11 *The Evening Post*, New York, July 14, 1854, quoted in Hatzidimitriou, *Christodoulos*, 230. The twenty-franc gold piece in the 1830s featured the head of Louis Philippe.

12 The quotes in this chapter from Philip Rhinelander are from his manuscript diary, in the author's possession.

13 Eliot Warburton, *The Crescent and the Cross: Or Romance and Realities of Eastern Travel* (London: Henry Colburn, 1845), vol. 1, 291.

14 Knauff, *Doctor Tucker*, 41.

15 [Peter Cator], *Up the Red Sea and Down the Nile in 1839* (London: Smith, Elder and Co., 1841), 95.

16 The identity of some of the Europeans is not certain because the three sources naming them offer variant lists. In his manuscript diary (in a private collection) David Roberts says, "our party consisted of Mr. Dunlop one of the Council of Directors at Bombay – Dr Tatham [*sic*] a gentleman celebrated for his learning in the early Coptic Gospels [the manuscript reads "Conquest" but "Gospels" was surely intended] and who has visited Egypt for that purpose, Leut Goldsmith and Mr. Pell." Dunlop was the Hon. John A. Dunlop who had just arrived by steamer from India, and Pell was John Pell who had accompanied Roberts to Palestine and Syria. The letterpress accompanying the lithograph names Campbell, Waghorn, Tattam, Roberts, and Pell. The third source is an oil painting by Roberts of the same subject in which all of the figures, Egyptian and European, are slightly differently posed: Sotheby's London, *The British Sale: Paintings, Drawings and Watercolors*, March 26, 2004, lot 50. Despite the presence of only five Europeans in the oil painting, an inscription on the back of the panel names eight: Campbell, Goldsmith, Waghorn, Tattam, Dunlop, Pell, Roberts, and Walne.

17 David Roberts, *Egypt & Nubia* (London: F. G. Moon & Sons, 1849), vol. 3, pl. 1. The caption for the lithograph reads, "Interview with the Viceroy of Egypt, at his Palace, Alexandria, May 12th 1839." But that date is incorrect. The transcript of David Roberts' diary published by his biographer, James Ballantine, states, "On the morning of the 13th took leave of Palestine (meaning Beirut) and embarked on board the "Majorca" [*sic*, meaning *Megara*] for Alexandria where we landed after a voyage of three days. During my stay here I was presented by Colonel Campbell to Mehemet Ali, who, at the request of his son, Said Bey, sat to me for his portrait." See James Ballantine, *The Life of David Roberts, R.A.: Compiled from His Journals and Other Sources* (Edinburgh: Adam and Charles Black, 1866), 140. The correct date must be May 20, the day that the Rev. Henry Tattam accompanied Colonel Campbell for an interview, surely in the company of David Roberts and others: [Eliza Platt], *Journal of a Tour through Egypt, the Peninsula of Sinai and the Holy Land in 1838, 1839* (London: Richard Watts, 1842) vol. 2, 365.

18 Clot Bey's menagerie was destined for the Jardin des Plantes in Paris by way of Marseilles: *The Morning Post* (London), July 2, 1839, picking up a report from a Marseilles paper.

19 The *Marmoudie*, built by Henry Eckford, at 3,932 tons, was indeed said by many observers to be the largest vessel of its day. She carried 120 cannon.

20 R.C. Anderson, *Naval Wars in the Levant 1559–1853* (Princeton: Princeton University Press, 1952), 553–54. For the background to the events, see P.E. Caquet, "The Napoleonic Legend and the War Scare of 1840," *The International History Review* 35, no. 4 (2013), 702–22.

21 Jean-Michel Casa, *Le Palais de France à Istanbul* (Istanbul: Yapi Kredi Yayinlari, 1995), 34–37.

22 Charles Lowell (1782–1861), class of 1800 at Harvard, was the father of the poet James Russell Lowell, and the great-great-grandfather of the twentieth-century poet Robert Lowell.

23 Names at the Ramesseum at Thebes: Roger O. De Keersmaecker, *Travellers' Graffiti from Egypt and the Sudan. IX Thebes, the Ramesseum* (Mortsel, Antwerp, 2010), 64; Pirie's obituary in *The Gentleman's Magazine* 12 (December, 1839), 668.

24 *Boston Recorder*, August 16, 1839. A few more details were published in the *Daily National Intelligencer*, Washington, DC, August 7, 1839.

25 Ida Pfeiffer, *Visit to the Holy Land, Egypt, and Italy* (London: Ingram, Cooke, and Co., 1852), 27.

26 Perhaps, since Tucker says that one of the Englishmen had been a fine classical scholar at Cambridge: Theodore Thring, eldest son of the Rev. John Gale Dalton Thring, Eton 1835, entered Trinity College Cambridge the same year; and Edward Rawnsley, a former classmate of Theodore Thring at Eton. Less likely they were John Walker Thring and Robert Drummond Burrell Rawnsley, both in their early twenties and recent classmates at Rugby.

27 Knauff, *Doctor Tucker*, 80.

28 *House Documents Otherwise Published as Executive Documents by the United States Congress*, 13th Congress 2nd . . . Document no. 71, Report # xviii, Washington, DC, 1850, 49.

29 *House Documents Otherwise Published as Executive Documents by the United States Congress*, 13th Congress 2nd . . . Document no. 71, Report # xix, 56.

Chapter 19

1 Christopher W. Knauff, *Doctor Tucker: Priest-Musician, A Sketch which concerns the doings and thinkings of the Rev. John Ireland Tucker, S.T.D.* (New York: A.D.F. Randolph Company, 1897), 80–81.

2 Knauff, *Doctor Tucker*, 114–351.

3 Clarence E. Walworth, *The Oxford Movement in America: Or, Glimpses of Life in an Anglican Seminary* (New York: The Catholic Book Exchange, 1895), 136ff.

4 James Shepard, *History of Saint Mark's Church, New Britain, Conn., and of its Predecessor Christ Church, Wethersfield and Berlin* (New Britain, CT: Tuttle, Morehouse & Taylor, 1907), 460. Allan Nevins and Milton Halsey Thomas, eds., *The Diary of George Templeton Strong* (New York: The Macmillan Company, 1952), vol. 4, 539. Strong remembered him as a Columbia classmate.

5 Nevins and Thomas, *The Diary of George Templeton Strong*, vol. 1, 139.

6 Nevins and Thomas, *The Diary of George Templeton Strong*, vol. 1, 148.

7 Nevins and Thomas, *The Diary of George Templeton Strong*, vol. 4, 248.

8 R. Ormand and E. Kilmurray, *John Singer Sargent: Portraits of the 1890s; Complete Paintings*, vol. 2 (New Haven: Yale University Press for the Paul Mellon Centre for Studies in British Art, 2002), 72, no. 292.

9 Eleanor Dwight, *Edith Wharton: An Extraordinary Life* (New York: Harry N. Abrams, 1994), 97, 99; Hermione Lee, *Edith Wharton* (New York: Alfred A. Knopf, 2008), 152.

10 Nevins and Thomas, *The Diary of George Templeton Strong*, vol. 1, 139.

11 *New York Evening Post*, February 22, 1850.

12 Nevins and Thomas, *The Diary of George Templeton Strong*, vol. 2, 273.

13 Nevins and Thomas, *The Diary of George Templeton Strong*, vol. 4, 485–86.

14 M.V. Pike and J.G. Armstrong, *A Time to Mourn: Expressions of Grief in Nineteenth-century America* (Stony Brook, NY: The Museums at Stony Brook, 1981), 179, no. 207.

15 New-York Historical Society, nos. 1909.26 and 1909.21, bequest of Mary Rhinelander King.

16 The portrait: William C. Rhinelander (1790–1878), to his daughter Mary Rhinelander Stewart (1821–1893), to her daughter Mary Stewart Witherbee (died 1949), to her daughter Evelyn Witherbee Miller, to her son and daughter-in-law, Mr. and Mrs. Charles Duncan Miller (died 1994 and 1999), and to their children. The diary: prior to appearing in the book

trade in 1978, the diary had belonged to George S. Hellman (1878–1958), literary scholar, and rare book and manuscript dealer and collector, and then to his son, Geoffrey T. Hellman (1907–1977), writer and long-time staff member of the *The New Yorker*. It is likely that it had been inherited by Mary Rhinelander King's eldest daughter, Mary R. King, and had come into the market at the time of her death in 1909.

17   Moses Yale Beach, ed., *Wealth and Pedigree of the Wealthy Citizens of New York, Comprising an Alphabetical Arrangement of Persons Estimated to Be Worth $100,000 and Upwards*, 3rd ed. (New York: The Sun Office, 1842), 10.

18   Benson J. Lossing, *The Hudson from the Wilderness to the Sea* (New York: Virtue and Yorston, 1866), chap. 3, pt. 2.

19   [Isaac McLellan], "Sketches of Foreign Travel," *Boston Courier*, December 17, 1840.

20   Mary married James F. Bacon; Charles married Helen Jacquilin in 1902.

21   S. Herbert Lancey, *Native Poets of Maine* (Bangor: David Bugbee Co., 1854), 117–18.

22   *Memorial of Samuel Gilman Brown, D.D., LL.D* (New York, 1886).

23   Nevins and Thomas, *The Diary of George Templeton Strong*, vol. 1, 343. The footnote to this statement includes the observation that Margaret Johnston was the daughter of John Johnston of New York, ironfounder, and sister of John Taylor Johnston, railroad executive, art collector, and first president of the Metropolitan Museum of Art.

24   And where my great-grandfather, the Rev. Andrew Oliver, was professor of Greek and Hebrew from 1864 to 1873.

25   Peter J. Schlinger, *Kentucky's Last Cavalier: General William Preston 1816–1887* (Frankfurt: Kentucky Historical Society, 2004), 279.

26   Library Company of Philadelphia 8259.F.8.

27   *The Albion, A Journal of News, Politics and Literature*, May 6, 1848: "With the last number of the Albion terminated the editorial labours of the writer, after a period of twenty-five years. The sale and transfer of the journal have been made to Mr. William Young, an English gentleman of good literary attainment and family connexions, in whose hands he feels assured that the general conduct of the paper will not deteriorate."

28   *Boston Evening Transcript*, October 11, 1843. A second set of the work was in Columbia College. Haight's set came to the New-York Historical Society in the late 1850s and was there as late as the 1920s: *The New-York Historical Society Quarterly Bulletin*, vol. 4 (1920–1921), 8.

29   Bayard Tuckerman, ed., *The Diary of Philip Hone, 1828–1851* (New York: Dodd, Mead and Company, 1889), vol. 2, 14.

30   Gouache on paper in the Museum of the City of New York, 74.97.2. Wendy A. Cooper, *Classical Taste in America, 1800–1840* (Baltimore: The Baltimore Museum of Art, 1993), 100–101, there dated to 1848. In a perceptive analysis, Lauren Lessing has convincingly dated the gouache

to 1842 based on the style of clothing, the age of the children, and other circumstantial evidence: Lauren Keach Lessing, "Presiding Divinities: Ideal Sculpture in Nineteenth-century American Domestic Interiors," diss., Indiana University, 2006. And she has more recently suggested that the portrait was the work of Thomas Seir Cummings, a partner of Henry Inman. The gouache was left to the Museum by Elizabeth Cushing Iselin. It had belonged to her husband, William O'Donnell Iselin (1883–1956), who had inherited it from his mother, Alice Iselin (née Jones), who in turn had received it from her mother, Lydia Haight Jones.

31 Lydia Beekman Haight was with her parents in Paris in 1834 and 1835. She married William Henry Jones in 1849 and had several children. Richard Haight was lost at sea in early 1856 when the steamship *Pacific* disappeared on a run from England to New York. David Haight went to Yale, class of 1860, became a doctor with a degree from the Columbia College of Physicians and Surgeons, class of 1864, and died unmarried in 1918.

32 Charles Lockwood, "The Italianate Dwelling House in New York City," *The Journal of the Society of Architectural Historians* 31 (1972), 145–51, at 148–49, fig. 7.

33 *Evening Post*, New York, August 27, 1835.

34 Henry Robert Abbott and his wife Mary Ann arrived in New York with their family on board the ship *Charlemagne* from Havre. A note in the *Commercial Advertiser* of New York, September 19, 1828, lists them as passengers: "Henry Abbott, Esq. lady four children and servant, Miss Mary Ann Abbott, Miss Emma Abbott, Frederick Abbott, Esq., Miss Maria Abbott, Miss Clara Abbott, Mr. Alfred Abbott, all of England." The family eventually settled in Auburn, New York State.

35 In a letter in the New-York Historical Society of February 1, 1852, to Robert Minturn, a leading merchant and shipper, whom Abbott had met in Cairo in 1849, he reported that "I think they will reach N. York in safety & that I shall have the pleasure of forming the nucleus of a National Museum, which will be an honor to the Great Nation America is destined to be."

36 As revealed in newspaper accounts of early May: "Egyptian Antiquities. – Twenty five thousand dollars worth of Egyptian antiquities were on Tuesday entered at the Custom House at Boston."

37 The passenger list names him Henry W.C. Abbott, age 42, physician, English and a resident of Egypt. His full name was Henry William Charles Abbott.

38 Owned by a descendant.

39 *The Literary World*, November 5, 1853, 234.

40 In 1937 the Historical Society transferred it on long-term loan to the Brooklyn Museum, and in 1948 the Brooklyn Museum purchased it from the Society: John D. Cooney, "Acquisition of the Abbott Collection," *Brooklyn Museum Bulletin* 10 (Spring 1949). The Historical Society presented Hick's portrait of Abbott to the museum.

41   The Brooklyn Museum. Illustrated in Nancy Thomas, ed., *The American Discovery of Ancient Egypt* (Los Angeles: The Los Angeles County Museum of Art, 1995), 41, fig. 15.

42   Most recently by Cassandra Vivian in *Americans in Egypt* (Jefferson, NC: McFarland, 2012, 105–11), a fine and sympathetic account which avoids unnecessary and unwarranted comments about Gliddon's ideas of race brought out in other tellings of the story.

43   Curtis Runnels, "Eureka in a Box," *Bostonia* (Winter 2003–2004).

44   Ephraim George Squier, *Peru: Incidents of Travel and Exploration in the Land of the Incas* (New York: Henry Holt, 1877), 18–19.

INDEX

al-Arish, 32
Armansperg, Count Joseph von, 114
Armant, temple at, 32, 121, 172–73, *plate 5*
Armstrong, General John (US minister to
France), 54
Artaud (French traveler), 191
Artin Bey (interpreter), 298, *plate 30*
artists accompanying Egyptian travelers, 192
Arundale, Francis, 135, 136, 148, 215
Arundell, Rev. Francis Vyvyan Jago, 160, 354n45
Ashby family, Charleston, SC, 49
Asselin de Cherville, Jean-Louis (French consul),
94, 96
asses and donkeys, Christians required to ride, 12,
22, 23, 42, 155
Aswan, 30, 32, 65, 98–99, 173, 212, 238, 263, 282
Asyut, 30, 98, 191, 212, 294
Atalanta (steamship), 226, 231, 270, 366n57
Atfih, 38, 86, 155, 162, 271, 276, 277, 282, 291, 297
d'Athanasi, Giovanni (Yanni), 65, 102–3, 142, 174
Athens: American travelers before and during
War of 1812 in, 54, 58, 59; American travelers
1829–1832 in, 131, 132, 139; American travelers 1833–1835 in, 187, 189; American travelers 1835–1839 in, 212, 219, 220, 223–25, 236,
237, 242, 244, 250, 265, 268, 272, 275, 280,
289–91, 292, 299; Belmore party in, 68; Cass
party in, 162; in Greek War of Independence,
111, 112, 115; panorama of, 59; steamship
service at, 231, 233
d'Aubigny, Amélie, 220, 365n35, *plate 19*
Audubon, John James, 236
Audubon, John W. (son of John James), 236
Augustus (Roman emperor), 84, 133, 173, 348n50
Auldjo, John, 230
Austria: diplomacy of, 61, 115; in Napoleonic wars,
50; Rhinelander's death in Vienna, 302–4, 305;
steamer accident on Danube (1839), 301–2,
309; steamer service to and from, 196, 233–34
Avicenna, 243
Avignon, 53, 183

B
Baalbek, 9, 27, 160, 161, 162, 215, 216
Baffi, Giovanni, 40–41, 62
Baillie, David, 64
Bainbridge, Commodore William (US Navy), 46,
47, 79, 143
Baird, Rev. Robert, 242
Baldwin, George (British consul), 9, 17, 21, 29
Baldwin, Jane (née Maltass), 9
Baldwin, Mary, 224
Baldwin, Miss (of Virginia), 275
Ball, Sir Alexander, 47
Balugani, Luigi, 24
Balzac, Charles-Louis, 33, 213
Bancroft, George, 58
Bancroft, Thomas, 51
Bankes, William John, 43, 63, 64–65, 76–77,
340n27
banking. *See* funds and banking
Banks, Joseph, 19, 23, 25–26
Barbary pirates, 45–48, 143

Barbie du Bocage, Guillaume, 67
Barclay (English traveler), 98
Bard, Eliza (later McVickar), 227
Bard, John, 227–28, 261–62, 278–79, 305, 310
Bard, Margaret (née Johnston; wife of John), 310,
381n23
Bard, Dr. Samuel (grandfather of John), 227
Bard, William (father of John), 227
Bard College (formerly St. Stephens College), 310
Barker, Hester Elizabeth (later Peach), 214
Barker, John (British consul-general), 115, 132,
151, 174, 214, 226, 341n27
Barker, Robert, 59
Barnum, P.T., 259
Baron Eichhof (Austrian steamer), 233
Barral, Joseph-Napoléon-Paul, Comte de, 180, 191
Barrell, George, 70
Barrett, Elizabeth, 228
Barry, Charles, 64
Bartholomew, Captain (of brig *Free-ocean*), 70
Barthow, Francis (François Barthou), 42–43, 63, 99
Bartlett, John Russell, 123
Bartlett, William Henry, 174–76
Barton (deputy lieutenant for County Ferman-
agh, Ireland), 273, 376n11
Bassano, Duc de, 52
bastinado, 41
Batavia (modern Jakarta), 51
baths, 16, 95, 170, 270
Baudelaire, Charles, *Le voyage* (1859), v, 3
Baybars (sultan), 133
bears presented to Mehmet Ali, 150, 353n23,
plate 13
Beaufoy, Henry, 21, 23, 26
Beaumont, Gustave de, 250
Bee, John P., 254
Beechey, Henry William, 64
Beirut: Allen, Oakley, and Ferguson in, 132; Amer-
ican travelers after War of 1812 in, 87, 97, 105,
106, 114; American navy in, 161, 165; American
travelers 1833–1835 in, 169, 174, 175, 176, 177;
American travelers 1835–1839 in, 215, 219, 236,
240, 266, 281, 299, 301; Belmore party in, 68;
Boylston in, 9; coal from outside of, 252; Russian navy in, 8; steamship service at, 231, 232;
on travel itineraries of Americans, 197
Bellerophon (Greek brig), 189
Belliard, General Auguste-Daniel (French army),
31, 32
Belmore, Somerset Lowry-Corry, second Earl of,
and family, 68, 71, 72, 103, 145–46, 199, 213,
222, 340n27
Belzoni, Giovanni Battista: employed by Salt to
collect antiquities, 63–66, 340n27; exhibition
in Egyptian Hall, London, 120, 145; Fisk's
reading of travels of, 94; Karnak, excavations
at, 102; on Sekhmet, 102, 340–41n27; *shabtis*
from tomb of Seti I and, 144–45; tomb of Seti
I, discovery of, 64, 68, 103, 120, 144–45, 239;
travel account of, 94, 199
Belzoni, Sarah, 63
Benet, Louis, 233
Beni Hasan, 239

Beni Suef, 292
Benjamin, Nathan, 265, 275
Bennet, Mary (later Light), 152–53
Bennett, William, 266, 268, 269, 301, 302, 309
Berenice (steamship), 231, 247, 377n17
Beresford, Henry, third Marquess of Waterford, 171
Berthollet, Claude-Louis, 31, 33, 35
Besson, Victor, 43
Betancourt, Manuel de, 291, 292, 301–2, 309
biblical scholarship: of Everett and English, 72–73, 246; of Robinson, Rev. Edward, 40, 233, 235–41, 273, 327n7
Biddle, Commodore James (US Mediterranean Squadron), 113, 124–25, 151, *plate 3*
Biddle, Nicholas, 17, 54–55, *plate 3*
Bienvenu de Clairambault, Bernard, 43
Bigelow, Andrew, 259
Bigelow, Jacob, 121
Bilotti, Carlo, 39
Bird, Isaac, 132
Bishop, Alexander Hamilton, 310
Bishop, Susan (née Holmes), 228, 271, 273–75, 285, 288, 290, 299, 310, 312
Black Ball Line, 83
Blazer (steamer), 231
Boardman, Margaret (née Willett), 216
Boddington, George, 8, 320n17
Boddington, John (British consul), 9
Boerum, William (US naval officer), 161
Boghos, Youssef, 40, 73, 150, 151, 162, 182, 298, *plate 30*
Boislecomte, Baron de (French special envoy), 115
Bona Santa (Venetian vessel), 8
Bonaparte, Louis, 226
Bonaparte, Napoleon, 29–35, 50, 52, 56, 58, 72
Bonar, Andrew A., 255–56
Bonomi, Joseph, 215
Booth, George, 223
Boriès, Jean-Paul (French vice-consul), 17
Bosc (companion of Pariset), 142
Boston Athenaeum, 27, 131, 223, 225
Boston Courier (newspaper), 193, 265
Boston Evening Gazette (newspaper), 70–71
Boston Naval Library and Institute, 160
Boston Patriot (newspaper), 69
Boston Register and Recorder (newspaper), 226
Boston Society of Natural History, 180, 224, 225
Boston tea party, 6
Botzaris, Dimitrio, 75–76
Bové, Nicolas, 157
Bowditch, Henry Ingersoll, 223
Bowditch, Nathaniel, 223
Bowdoin, James (Jemmy), 6, 7, 72
Bowdoin, James (Sr.; father of Jemmy), 6
Bowdoin College, 236, 265
Bowdoin Prize, 72
Bowen, Capt. Hugh A., 153
Boyd, James McHenry ("Henry"), 225–26
Boylston, Ann (née Molineux; first wife of Ward Nicholas), 5–6, 27
Boylston, Mary (later Hallowell; mother of Ward Nicholas), 5, 10, 319n3
Boylston, Nicholas (son of Ward Nicholas), 6

Boylston, Nicholas (uncle of Ward Nicholas), 5, 6, 27
Boylston, Thomas (uncle of Ward Nicholas), 6, 319n3
Boylston, Ward Nicholas (born Ward Hallowell), 5–19; account book, on Egyptian travels, 10, 16–17; birth, family, marriage, and career, 5–6; diary on Egyptian travels, 9–10, 13, 14–15, 27; East, decision to travel to, 8–9, 18–19; on egg hatchery, 12, 295; in Egypt, 9–18; as first American to visit East, 18–19, 27; Italy, travel to, 6–8; letter to mother on Egyptian travels, 10–14, 19, 27; letters of introduction used by, 7, 8, 198; in London, 18–19, 25–27; as loyalist, 6, 19; return to Boston, 27; souvenirs of, 16, 18
Boylston, Zabdiel (great-uncle of Ward Nicholas), 206
Boylston Medical Library, 27
Boylston Prize for Elocution, Harvard, 27
Bradford, Cornelius (US consul in Lyons), 125–31; background and career, 125–26; bust of, 126, 131; death and burial in Jerusalem, 129–31, 186, 214, 239–40, 347n42; graffiti left by, 135, 212, 218; purported conversion to Catholicism, 130–31, 239–40, 348n44; unpleasant impressions of, 126, 127
Bradish, Alvah (artist and second cousin of Luther), 81, *plate 26*
Bradish, Helen Elizabeth (née Gibbs; wife of Luther), 78
Bradish, Luther, 78–82; commercial treaty with Ottoman empire, efforts to negotiate, 79, 114, 132; Goodell's memoirs, omitted from, 336n29; on Greek War of Independence, 79, 108; Ismail Djebel Akhdar and, 104; later career of, 81; New-York Historical Society, as president of, 313; portrait of, 81, *plate 26*; return of American visitors to Egypt after War of 1812 and, 72; Stanhope, Lady Hester, visited by, 80, 82, 87; Stuyvesant Institute petition to purchase Abbott collection signed by, 313; Thebes never described by, 99
Bradlee, Edmond F., 187
Brayton, Agnes A., 274
Breck, Samuel, 26
Brennan (Irish traveler in Egypt), 275–76
Brent, Daniel (US consul in Paris), 183
Brent, John Carroll (nephew of Daniel), 183
Brescia, 7, 133, 273
Bretell, James, 252
Breuvery, Jules de, 127, 129–30
Brewer, Eliot (nephew of Josiah), 274
Brewer, Rev. Josiah, 232, 274
Brewton, Miles, 49, 329n16
Briggs, Samuel (acting British consul), and Briggs firm, 47, 62, 137, 153, 211, 226
Brine, Charles, 39, 62
Brinton, Hugh P., 272
Brisbane, Albert, 139–40
Britain: consular offices in Egypt, 61; Greek War of Independence and, 111, 113, 114–16; India, passage to, 66, 99, 119, 231; Napoleonic wars, 29–30, 33, 37.56; naval squadron

in Mediterranean, 45; postal service between
India and, 211, 221; regiment marching to
Rosetta from Alexandria (1807), 94; steamer
service in Mediterranean provided by,
229–30, 231–32; support for Mamluks over
Mehmet Ali, 37; War of 1812, 56–57; with-
drawal from Egypt, 37, 47. *See also* London
British Museum, 26, 68, 120, 145, 146, 245,
340n27, 358n41, 370n30
British Queen (ship), 241
Britton, Lloyd L., 246
Brocchi, Giambattista, 66
Broglie, Victor de, 115
Bronson, Frederic, 250, 258–59, 262
Brown, Benjamin F., 262, 263, 264, 267
Brown, Charles, 184, 249, 371n2
Brown, John Porter, 220
Brown, Mary Ann (née Abbott; wife of Stewart),
247, 312, 371n43, 382n34
Brown, Samuel Gilman, 265, 266, 309–10
Brown, Stewart, 247, 312, 371n43
Browne, William George, 26
Browning, Robert, 228
Bruce, James (British consul in Algiers), *Travels to
Discover the Source of the Nile* (1767–1773), 24–25
Bruce, Michael, 80
Bryant, William Cullen, "The Greek Boy"
(poem), 112
Bryce, John W., 163
bubonic plague. *See* plague
Buffon, Georges-Lewis Leclerc, Comte de, 24
Bulaq: American naval parties in, 155, 160, 162;
anonymous American in (1839), 282; Firmin
Didot in, 67; Fisk in, 95; Littlefield party in,
276; as port of Cairo, 86, 95, 155, 211, 291;
Rapelje in, 86; Rhinelander party in, 291;
school and printing press at, 39, 95, 239;
Stephens in, 211; Willingtons in, 269
Bullus, Lt. Oscar (US Navy), 163
Bunker Hill, Battle of (1775), 18
Burckhardt, John Lewis (Sheik Ibrahim), 43, 73
Burford, Robert, 59, 215–16
Burns, Lt. Owen (US Navy), 160–61
Burton, James, 85, 86, 259, 337n43
Butenov (Russian ambassador to Constantinople),
115
Butler, Charles, and Eliza, 278
Butler, Frances, 228, 271, 272, 278, 279, 310
Butler, Henrietta (later Littlefield; sister of Fran-
ces), 271–80, 285, 287, 288
Byron, George Gordon, Lord, 55, 58, 80, 111,
143–44, 164, 290, *plate 9*; *Childe Harold's
Pilgrimage* (1812–1818), 55

C

Cabot, Elizabeth. *See* Kirkland, Elizabeth (née
Cabot), and John Thornton
Cadalvène, Edmond de, 127–28, 130
Cadmus (packet ship), 286
Caesareum, Alexandria, 84, 133
Cailliaud, Frédéric, 63, 75–76, 191
Cairo: American naval parties in, 47, 151–52,
154–56, 158, 159, 160–61, 162–63; American

travelers after War of 1812 in, 73, 74, 75, 76,
79, 80, 81, 82, 84, 86, 87, 88; American travelers
1829–1832 in, 119, 124, 127–29, 131–34, 136,
137, 142; American travelers 1833–1835 in,
169–71, 174, 177, 179–80, 182, 184–86, 188–91;
American travelers 1835–1839 in, 210–15, 218,
219, 221–24, 226, 227, 235, 237–41, 243–47,
251, 255, 260–64, 266, 268–71, 276–78, 281–82,
291–92, 294–99, 304, 312; Boylston in, 10–16,
17, 26, 27; European presence in, 61, 63, 66,
67, 68; Feast of the Circumcision, 226–27; Fisk,
King, Parsons, and Smith in, 94–98, 104, 106;
Ledyard in, 20–23; Legh, Barthow, and Smelt
in, 43; mummies shipped from, 88, 89; Napoleonic expedition in, 29–30, 32; panorama of,
64; as part of Americans' European tour, 196,
197; reforms of Mehmet Ali and, 38–39, 41–42;
steamship service at, 232; westerners wearing
eastern clothing in, 202
Caldecott, John, 295, 299
Calhoun, Rev. Simeon Howard, 280–81, 299
caliphs, tombs of, Cairo, 95, 156, 163, 269, 295, 313
Cambridge (packet ship), 378n8
Campbell, Colonel Patrick (British consul-gener-
al), 115, 171, 189, 298, 378n16, 379n17, *plate 30*
Canadian border, US dispute with Britain over, 56
Candia (Crete), 56, 116, 162, 354n53
*canjiah*s, 86, 127, 155, 190, 291
Canning, Stratford (British ambassador to Con-
stantinople), 115
Cape of Good Hope, 51, 66, 211, 311
Carew, Sir Benjamin Hallowell, 325n3
Carey, Matthew, 35
Carlo Felice (duke of Savoy and king of Sardinia),
65
Carnarvon, Henry Herbert, Lord, 301
Caroline Augusta (ship), 88
Carroll (American brig), 243, 255, 258–62, 306
Carter, William, 49, 329–30n16
Cartwright, John (British consul-general in
Constantinople), 246
Cass, Lewis (US secretary of war and minister
to France), and family, 162–65 266, 354n53,
354n55, 376n60, *plate 16*
Cass, Matilida Francis (later Ledyard), 162, 164
Castex, Jean-Jacques, 31, 32, 33
Castro Gonsales (Spanish priest and mission-
ary), 136
Catel, Franz Ludwig, 110
Cathalan, Stephen/Étienne (American consul in
Marseilles), 20
Catherine II the Great (empress of Russia), 19, 26
Catherwood, Frederick, 123, 136, 191, 215–16,
368n15
Catherwood, Gertrude (née Abbott), 215
Catholicism, 8, 18, 79, 93, 97, 130, 240, 279, 303,
306, 348n44
Caton, Elizabeth, 352n32
Cator, Peter, and wife, 262, 298
Caussin de Perceval, Armand-Pierre, 67, 97,
339n14
Caviglia, Giovanni Battista, 221
Cécile, François-Charles, 33, 134

Denon, Dominique Vivant, 31–34, 35, 79; *Voyage dans la basse et la haute Égypte*, 34, 120, 199, 324n1, 345n11
Derby, Elias Hasket (father of John), 51
Derby, John, 50
Desaix de Veygoux, General Louis (French army), 30, 31, 33
Description de l'Égypte (1809–1828), 34–35, 121–23, 172, 213, 222
Despatch (British brig), 96
Detmold, Christian Edward and Phoebe, 220
Dick, Sir John (British consul in Leghorn), 7
Dinsmore, Silas, 46–47, 329n5
Diocletian (Roman emperor), 84–85
diplomacy: American naval presence in Mediterranean and, 147; European, 61–62; Greek War of Independence, American neutrality and diplomacy in, 111, 112–14; Greek War of Independence, European efforts to resolve, 111, 113, 114–16; Ottoman empire, European opposition to American diplomatic presence in, 79, 113. *See also specific consuls, ambassadors, etc.*
Dispatch (brig), 76
Disraeli, Benjamin, 206
Djiddeh, 212
Dodge, Asa, 186, 240
Dodge, John Crowninshield, 169, 177, 357n25
Dodge, Martha W. (née Merrill; widow of Asa, later married John D. Paxton), 240, 261
Dodge, Mary and Martha (daughters of Asa and Martha), 240, 261
Dodge, Pickering, 357n25
Donald, Captain (Khalil Aga), 74–77
Donati, Vitaliano, 340n27
Dongola, 65, 77, 98–99, 185, 259, 263
Donizetti, Giuseppe, 301
donkeys and asses, Christians required to ride, 12, 22, 23, 42, 155
Dorr, James Augustus, 223–26; *Napoleonic ideas* (1859), 226
Douglass, Sarah, 112
Drayton, Lt. Percival (US Navy), 163
Drovetti, Bernardino (French consul): British troops released under influence of, 94; Cailliaud and, 63, 75; diplomatic career of, 61–62, 63; Egyptian antiquities collected by, 65, 99, 146, 341n27; English, George Bethune, and, 77; Fisk and King calling on, 97; Greek War of Independence and, 111; at Khargeh Oasis, 191; Lowell and, 189; Mehmet Ali's reforms and, 37, 38, 40, 43; Rifaud and, 63
Du Camp, Maxime, 172, 206
Dubois-Aymé, Jean-Marie, 32
Duchesse d'Orleans (packet ship), 286
duels and duelling, 160, 279, 310
Duhamel, Alexander (Russian consul), 171, 190
Dumont (companion of Pariset), 142
Dumreicher, Daniel (Danish consul), 148
Dundas, Henry, Viscount Melville, 177, 357n24
Dundas, William, 173–77
Dunlop, John A., 298, 378n16
Durand, Asher B., 112
Dutertre, André, 33, 172, 222

Dwight, Harrison Gray Otis, 124, 167
Dwight, Theodore, 250
dysentery, 190, 205, 207

E
East India Company, 291
East India Marine Society, 145
"Eastern Question," 115
Eastern/Turkish clothing, 201–2; Abbott, Henry, portrait of, 313; of Ahmed (servant of Eli and Sarah Smith), 167, 204; of Almeh, 282–83; Boylston wearing, 9; Cohen's portrait wearing, 136, *plate 14*; Margaret Kemble Gage wearing, 322n40; Haight, Richard, wearing, 311; Ledyard, Henry, wearing, 164; Ledyard, John, wearing, 23; Lowell wearing, 191, *plate 21*; Maltass family of Smyrna wearing, 9, 128; Mott party member wearing, 243; from Nubia, 299; Prissick wearing, 150; Rhinelander party purchasing/wearing, 291, 292–93, 299; Robinson and Cadalvène adopting, 128; Smith, Eli, adopting, 106; Willington, Harriet, donning, 270
Eaton, William (US naval officer), 47–48, 53, 143
Eckford, Henry, 76, 114, 176, 300, 379n19
École des Ponts et Chaussées, 133
Edes, Abigail (later Clark), 117
Edes, Robert B., 88
Edfu, 32, 173, 191, 212–13, 222, 283, 294
Edmonstone, Sir Archibald, 191
egg incubation in Egypt, 12, 269, 295
Egypt: European commerce in eighteenth century, discouragement of, 17; European presence in (1815–1825), 61–68; increasing European and American interest in, 119–20; Napoleonic expedition to, 24, 29–35; Palestine and Syria seized by Mehmet Ali, 116, 175; reforms of Mehmet Ali in, 10, 37–43, 281; slave trade in, 41–42; wedding processions in, 11–12. *See also* American travelers in Mediterranean, Middle East, and Egypt; Ibrahim Pasha; Mehmet Ali; *specific cities and sites*
Egyptian antiquities: Abbott's collection of, 81, 312–13, 314, 382n35; Barthow trading in, 43; Boylston, souvenirs of, 16, 18; Champollion's purchases, 142; Cohen's collection of, 136; colossal head and torso from Ramesseum, Thebes, 63–64; Drovetti's collection of, 65, 99, 146, 341n27; of Elliott, Jesse, 164; English, George Bethune, collecting, 75; European collectors and researchers, 62–66; European tourists digging for, 68; faience rhyton or drinking horn in shape of lion, 160, *plate 7*; Fisk's collection of, 103–4; Gliddon's pharaoh statue from Tanis, 239; Goff's collection of, 358n41; Karomana, statuette of, 142; Louvre and British Museum collections, beginning of, 120, 146; Lowell acquiring, 190–91, 192, 193; manuscripts, 31, 39, 73, 171, 244–46, 281, 292, 298, 369–70n30, 370n34; Moores collecting, 160; Napoleonic expedition and, 33, 35; New-York Historical Society collection, 81; Salt's collection of, 63–65, 120, 136, 142, 145–46, 340n27, 341n27; Sekhmet, statues of, Karnak,

102, 340–41n27, *plate 22B*; Senwosret Sunbefni, Egyptian quartzite statue of, 35, *plate 6*; *shabti*s or *ushabti*s, 65, 144–47, 163, 350n5; skulls, Morton's acquisition of, 251, 263–64, 372n11. *See also specific objects and monuments, e.g.* Rosetta Stone, Pompey's Pillar, mummies
Egyptian/Oriental Revival style, 120–22, 123, 188
Egyptian Society of Cairo, 219, 250, 358n41
Ehrenberg, Christian Gottfried, 65
eighteenth century American travelers, 5–27; European travelers, influence of accounts of, 23–25; in Italy, 6–7; Ledyard, 19–23, 24, 25, 26, 45, 94, 128, 163, 319n2; letters of introduction used by, 7, 20. *See also* Boylston, Ward Nicholas
El Kab, 173
Elba, 58, 72
Eleanor (brig), 55
elephants, 51, 183, 282, 291, 357n25
Elgin, Lord (British ambassador to Constantinople), 33, 55
Eliot, William H., 35, 121
Eliso (Austrian brig), 93
Elliott, Commodore Jesse D. (US Navy), 161, 162–65, 354n51
Elliott, Mary, 97
Ellis, Henry (British ambassador to shah of Persia), 220
Ellis, William, 261
Ely, Elizabeth (later Randolph), 217
Emerald (packet ship), 265
Emerson, Edward and William (brothers of Ralph), 178
Emerson, Ralph Waldo, 178, 229
Enfantin, Barthélemy Prosper (Le Père), 158–59, 189, 191
England. *See* Britain
England (packet ship), 236
English, George Bethune (Muhammad Effendi), 72–78, 96, 99, 114, 119, 148, 206, 281; *The Grounds of Christianity Examined by Comparing the New Testament with the Old* (1813), 72–73; *A Narrative of the Expedition to Dongola and Sennaar* (1822), 77
Enterprise (British steamer), 229
Ephesus, 55, 69, 70, 92, 300, 331–32n40
Episcopal Theological Seminary (now General Theological Seminary), 305–6
Episcopalians/Anglicans, 82, 97, 131, 132, 275, 280, 290, 305–6, 310
USS *Erie*, 145
Erin (brig), 110–11, 117, 193
Erving, George W. (US minister in Madrid), 58
Esna, 32, 213, 282, 293
Esperance (French corsair), 56
Europe: American travelers in, 195–97; collectors and researchers of Egyptian antiquities from, 62–66; commerce in eighteenth century, Ottoman discouragement of, 17; Egypt, European presence in, 61–68; Greek War of Independence, efforts to resolve, 111, 113, 114–16; opposition to American diplomatic presence in Ottoman empire, 79, 113. *See also specific countries*
Eurotas (French postal steamer), 233

Evangeles, Christopher (Christy, later Christodoulos Leonídas Miltiades Evangeles; "the Greek Boy"), 111–12, 250, 275, 290–91, 343n23, 343n26
Evans, Estwick, 110, 343n15
Everett, Edward, 58–59, 69, 72–73, 74, 78, 110, 122, 246, 333n46, *plate 4*; *A Defense of Christianity against the Work of George B. English* (1814), 73

F
Fabre, François Xavier, 53, 331n29, *plate 2*
Farris, Captain (of brig *Alligator*), 70
Fauvel, Louis-François-Sébastien (French consul in Athens), 54–55, 58, 85, 331n33, 337n39–40
Favray, Antoine de, 320n18, *plate 1*
Felix, Major Orlando, *Notes on Hieroglyphics* (1830), 156
Fenelon (ship), 88
Ferdinand (steamboat), 273
Ferdinando Primo (Austrian steamer), 234, 301–2
Ferguson (from Natchez, Mississippi), 131–34, 135, 148, 204
Finati, Giovanni, 43, 63
Finlay, George, 275
Finley, John, 76
firearms carried by American travelers, 204, 250–51, 263, 291
firman, 92, 198, 239
Firmin Didot, Ambroise, 67, 339n14
Fisk, Pliny, 91–105; Bradish and, 79, 80, 82; death of, 105; English, George Bethune and, 76; on Greek War of Independence, 92, 107, 113; journals of, 93, 94, 95–96, 98–104, 339n16; on Khalil Aga, 74; King, Jonas, travels with, 96–105; Parsons, travels with, 91–93; preaching aboard frigate *United States* in Smyrna harbor, 113, 143; Rapelje and, 87; return of American visitors to Egypt after War of 1812 and, 72; solo travels after Parson's death, 94–96; Thompson, William (Osman Effendi) and, 94–95, 152
Fitzclarence, Lt.-Col. George Augustus Frederick (British army; natural son of William IV of England), 66
flag, American, 48, 49, 136, 250, 277, 281, 291, 300
Flaubert, Gustave, 172, 206
Fleming (American traveler from South Carolina), 290, 305
Florence: American travel to, 196; Boylston in, 7; Brown, Chamberlain, and McLellan in, 265; Cass party in, 162; *Cleopatra's Barge*, voyage of, 72; Kirklands and Bradford in, 126; Littlefield party in, 279; Lowell, John, in, 183; Nutts in, 183; Poinsett in, 52; on steamship cruise itinerary, 230
Folsom, Charles, 79, 114, 143
food eaten by American travelers, 202–4, 209, 239, 292, 294–95, 296
Forbes, Col. (British army), 171
Forbes, Dr. John, 171, 281
Forbes, Margaret (née Perkins; wife of Ralph), 57
Forbes, Ralph Bennet, 57
Forbin, Comte Auguste de, 64, 341n27

arrangements with, 137, 201; Calhoun and, 281; Dodge, John C., and, 357n25; Dorr and, 223; Fisk and, 93; giraffe speculation and, 258, 261; Haights and, 219; Hamersley, John W., and, 170; Hodgson and, 182; Littlefield and Holmes met by, 275; Lowell and, 189; Marshall, Henry P., and, 246, 247; McVickar and, 228; as merchant, 62; Mott party and, 243; Nutts and, 184; Rhinelander party and, 291; Robinson party and, 237, 239; Smith, Eli and Sarah, and, 169; Stackpole and Lewis meeting, 179; statue of pharaoh acquired at Tanis by, 239; Stephens and, 211; US trip of son George and, 249, 251
Gliddon, Mrs. (wife of John), 174, 177
Gliddon, William (son of John), 137, 249–50, 255
Glover, Russell E., 112, 290
Gobat, Samuel, 106
Goethe, Johann Wolfgang, 331n29
Goff, Robert, 181, 358n41
Goldsmith, Lt. (commander of *Megara*), 298, 378n16, *plate 30*
Goodell, Rev. William, 81–82, 138, 220, 242, 336n29
Gordon (duelist), 279
Gordon, Robert (British envoy in Constantinople), 115
Gordon, Captain Robert James (Royal Navy), 86–87, 96
Gordon, Captain William L. (US Navy), 143
Gorham, Dr. (of Massachusetts General Hospital), 88
Gosset, John, 174, 185–86, 190
Göttingen, Americans studying at, 58, 70, 122, 181, 235
Gould, Steven Jay, 372n11
Gouverneur, Samuel Laurence, 80, 336n26
graffiti: at Abu Simbel, 82, 180, 340n18, 358n37; at Abusir, 128, 135; at Dendur, 82, 135; at Esna, 293; at Gabal al-Silsila, 82; at Karnak, 214; on Kiosk of Trajan, Philae, 340n20; at Luxor, 124; at Medinet Habu, 214, 228; from Napoleonic expedition, 30–31, 101; at Petra, 214; on Pompey's Pillar, Alexandria, 85; at Pyramids, Giza, 79, 124, 135, 152, 157, 228, 239, 243; at Ramesseum, Thebes, 82, 211, 379n23; scholarly study of, 135; at Temple of Isis, Philae, 30–31, 135, 212, 218–19
Graham, Jorie, 27
Grant, Lady (widow of Governor of Bombay) and children, 278
Great Britain. *See* Britain
Great Pyramid. *See* Pyramids
Great Western (transatlantic steamer), 234, 244, 262, 271, 288, 309, 366n57
Greece: American visitors before 1820, 53–55, 58–59; American visitors 1829–1832 in, 132, 139, 140; American visitors 1833–1835 in, 170, 177, 189; American visitors 1835–1839 in, 210, 215, 224, 225, 240, 265, 268, 273, 275, 280, 290–91; as part of Americans' European tour, 196; pirates in, 147. *See also specific cities and sites*
"the Greek Boy" (Christopher Evangeles), 111–12, 250, 275, 290, 343n23, 343n26

Greek Orthodox, 92, 107
Greek War of Independence, 107–18; American merchants and shipping in Eastern Mediterranean during, 116–18; American neutrality and diplomacy in, 111, 112–14; American witnesses to, 107–11; atrocities during, 92, 107–8; Bradish on, 79, 108; European efforts to resolve, 111, 113, 114–16; Fisk's account of, 92, 107, 113; Mavromichalis, Petro, Americans visiting, 275, 290; Navarino, Battle of (1827), 41, 111, 113, 114, 116; Philhellenism in response to, 110; Rapelje on, 108; refugee children brought to United States, 111–12
Green, Dr. James M. (US naval surgeon), 351n22
Greene, George Washington (US consul in Rome), 266
Greene, Joseph, 18
Greenough, Horatio, 126, 131, 188, *plate 11*
Greenwood, Ethan Allen, 89
Greig, Rear Admiral Samuel (Scots naval officer in Russian navy), 7–8
Grenier, Joseph, 98, 340n20
Grey, Charles, 115
Griffin, Francis, 250, 254, 258–59, 262, 264
guidebooks, 39, 99, 103, 175, 184, 195, 198–200, 201–2, 207, 222, 232
guides, 95, 105, 129, 156, 204, 210, 211, 218, 228, 276
Guilhon (companion of Pariset), 142
Guilleminot, Armand-Charles de (French ambassador to Constantinople), 115

H
Hague, Louis, *plate 30*
Haight, David (son of Richard and Sarah), 311, 382n31
Haight, Lydia Beekman (daughter of Richard and Sarah Haight; later Jones), 217, 219, 311, 382n31
Haight, Richard (son of Richard and Sarah), 217, 219, 311, 382n31
Haight, Richard Kip and Sarah (née Rogers), 216–19; Boyd met by, 225; career and previous travels of Richard, 216; Chasseaud and, 82; continuing interest in Egypt after trip, 311–12; Courtis, Sarah on, 224, 225; diaries and letters of Sarah, 216, 217, 218, 219; giraffes, Sarah on, 260; Gliddon, George, and, 218, 250, 312, 313; obelisk moved to Paris, Sarah on, 219, 364n31; in quarantine in Athens, 224, 225; Randolph and, 217–19, 224, 250, 364n33; Rapelje and Richard, 83, 87, 216; return to US, 219, 364n33; riverboat chartered by, 292; servants of, 204, 217; slavery in Egypt observed by, 237; smallpox, Sarah on, 180
Haight family portrait, 311, 381–82n30, *plate 31*
Haines, Francina Eglée Hannah, 339n13
Haitian Revolution (1804), 42
Hall, Fanny W., 233
Hall, Frederick, 92, 103, 233, 328, 341n29
Hallock, Homan, 187
Hallowell, Benjamin (father of Ward Nicholas Boylston), 5, 319n3

Hallowell, Captain Benjamin (Royal Navy; brother of Ward Nicholas Boylston), 30
Hallowell, Mary (née Boylston; mother of Ward Nicholas Boylston), 5, 10, 319n3
Hallowell, Ward. *See* Boylston, Ward Nicholas
Halls of Justice, New York ("The Tombs"), 121–22
Hamersley, Andrew Gordon (brother of John), 169
Hamersley, Andrew S. (first cousin of John), 287
Hamersley, John W., 169–77; banking arrangements, 201; Boyd and Scoville met by, 225; career after Egyptian travels, 177; Catherwoods met by, 215–16; Costigan and Gosset met by, 174, 185, 190, 215; first full surviving account of American in Egypt and on Nile, 170; on food eaten in Egypt, 202; giraffe speculation and, 258–59, 262; Gliddon brothers in New York and, 250; guidebooks used by, 175, 199; Hedenborg met by, 171, 191; Heijkenskjöld and, 173, 230; Hodgson and, 181; Inglis and, 228; Stackpole and Izard, interactions with, 177, 179–81; Stephens compared, 211; on sycamore at Heliopolis, 187–88; on Wolff and Rapelje, 87
Hamet of Tripoli, 47–48
Hamilton (of Foreign Office), 76, 77
Hamilton, Lady Catherine, 7
Hamilton, Captain Gawen William (Royal Navy), 79, 92
Hamilton, Sir William, 7
Hamilton, William R. (Scottish artist), 254, *plate 27*
Hamilton, William Richard, *Aegyptiaca* (1810), 33, 93, 94, 103, 199
Hamilton College, 235, 287, 309, 310
Hamont, Pierre Nicolas, 256–58
Hanbury, Rev. Bernard, 74
Hancock, John, 6
Hanson, Captain John (British army), 66
Harmer, Thomas, 25
Harriet (schooner), 112, 117
Harris, Anthony Charles, 263
Harris, Levett (American consul in St. Petersburg), 331n30
Harris, Richard (British consul), 17
Harvard: bequests to, 7, 27, 35, 59, 246, 324n65; graduates of, 6, 53, 58, 72, 110, 177–78, 223; library of, 7, 35, 121; Medical School, 206, 242; professors at, 58, 121, 122, 246. *See also* Kirkland, John Thornton (president of Harvard)
Hasselquist, Frederick, 23, 321n26
Hastings, Warren, Lord (governor-general of Bengal), 17, 66
Hathaway, Harriet (née Moores), 159–60
Hathorne, Nathaniel (father of novelist), 330n21
Hatshepsut (pharaoh), fallen obelisk of, 101, 191, *plate 22A*
Haviland, John, 35, 121–22
Hay, Robert, 135–36, 146, 148, 191, 215
Haydon, Anna (née Gillespie; wife of Dudley), 310
Haydon, Dudley M., 242–44, 310
Hayes, Anthony (British consul in Smyrna), 8, 320n17
Hazard, Samuel, 56–57
health issues, 204–7; cholera, 40, 114, 148, 162, 171, 204–5, 240, 244, 303; dysentery, 190,

205, 207; ipecacuanha, 207; laudanum, 190, 206–7; Mott as medical professional in Egypt, 241–44; ophthalmia, 74, 185, 190, 205, 206, 207; Pariset as medical professional in Egypt, 140–42; scarlet fever, 188, 240; smallpox and smallpox vaccinations, 30, 180, 205–6; sulphate of zinc, 207; syphilis, 204, 206; Syrup of Capillaire, 11, 321n22; typhoid, 225; yellow fever, 140, 177, 217, 313. *See also* deaths abroad; plague; quarantines
Healy, George P. A., 164, *plate 16*
Heaney, Seamus, 27
Heap, James Lawrence, 154
Heap, Samuel D. (US consul at Tunis; father of James Lawrence), 154
Heard (American in Rome and Naples), 278–79
Hebron, 116, 175
Hedenborg, Johan, 171, 191
Heideck, General Karl (Bavarian army), 114
Heijkenskjöld (Heiskinkioll), Margareta Charlotta, 173, 230
Heliopolis: Cass/Elliott party visiting, 163; Fisk in, 95; Indian cotton grown at, 39; obelisks, 84, 95, 133, 239, 243, 269, 348n50; Rhinelander party visiting, 295; sycamore tree, 95, 187–88, 239, 243
Helme (British brig), 263, 264
Hely-Hutchinson, General John (British army), 33
Hemprich, Friedrich Wilhelm, 65
Hendrickson, Charles, 210
Herald (brig), 77
Herbert, Henry, Lord Carnarvon, 301
Herculaneum, 7, 53
Hermes (steamer), 231, 277, 366n57
Herodotus, 24
Hey, Michael, 66
Hibernia (ship), 215
Hicks, Thomas, 313, 382n40, *plate 32*
Hill, Mrs. John H. (née Mulligan), 224, 242, 275, 290
Hill, Rev. John H., 132, 224, 242, 265, 275, 290, 352n26
Hippocrates, commentary of Abd al-Rahman ibn Abi Sadiq on aphorisms of, 244–46
Hobhouse, John Cam, 55
Hodge, James L., 89
Hodgson, William B., 181–82, 184, 245, *plate 20*
Hoffman, Judge Josiah Ogden (father of Mary and Matilda), 285
Hoffman, Mary Colden (later Rhinelander), 285
Hoffman, Matilda (fiancée of Washington Irving), 285, 308
Hoffman, Ogden (brother of Mary and Matilda), 285
Hoghton, Captain Henry (British army), 191
Holland, Henry, 58
Holmes, Obadiah (father of Susan), 271, 279
Holmes, Oliver Wendell, 181
Holmes, Susan (later Bishop), 228, 271–80, 285, 288, 290, 299, 310, 312
Holy Family, sites associated with, 13, 187, 269, 321n25
Homer, 67, 70; *Iliad*, 235

Homes, Rev., 232
homosexuality, 161
Hone, John, Emily, and Maria (siblings), 287
Hone, Philip (mayor of New York; uncle of Hone siblings), 125, 126, 260–61, 287–88, 311, 343n26
honeymooning in Egypt, 169, 213–14, 220, 236
Hopkins, Sir Francis, 220
Horeau, Hector, 203; *Panorama d'Égypte et de Nubie* (1841), 233
Horemheb (pharaoh), 100
Hoskins, George Alexander, 136, 191
hotels, 97, 119, 140, 200, 201, 220, 266, 291, 298, 300
Howe, Dr. Samuel Gridley, 110
Hüet, Nicholas, *plate 28*
Hügel, K.A.A. von, 192
Hugh Lindsay (British steamer), 153, 191, 231, 366n57
Hull, Captain Isaac (US Navy), 47–48
Humphries, Charles, 259, 337n43
Hunt, Montgomery, 163, 355n57
Hunter (English merchant and friend of John Ledyard), 21
Hunter, Lt. Bushrod W. (US Navy), 21, 163
hunting by American travelers, 204
Huntingdon, Sarah (later Smith), 167–69, 201, 204, 236, 357n25
Hurd, John R., 55
Hutchinson, Thomas (last civilian royal governor of Massachusetts), 18
Huyot, Jean Nicholas, 64–65
Hyacinthe (mistress and later wife of Richard Wellesley), 153
Hyde de Neuville, Jean-Guillaume (French minister of the Marine), 141
Hylton Joliffe (steamer), 230

I
Iavaja, Jacob, 16
Ibn al-Wahhab, 38
Ibrahim (Mamluk bey), 17, 30
Sheik Ibrahim (John Lewis Burckhardt), 43, 73
Ibrahim Pasha (son of Mehmet Ali): Abbott and, 312; American audiences with, 1833–1835, 175, 189; Americans naval visits to Egypt and, 148, 156, 163; Bradford's audience with, 211, 212; career of father and, 37, 38; Feast of the Circumcision, Cairo, 226, 227; giraffes acquired by, 259; Greek War of Independence and, 110, 116; Roda, garden and palace on island of, 156, 174, 221, 239, 243, 247, 269; in Syria and Palestine, 175
incubation of eggs in Egypt, 12, 269, 295
Independence (ship), 364n33
USS *Independence*, 145
India: American missionaries in, 91, 94; American ships first reaching, 51; British passage to, 66, 99, 119, 231; Marshall, Henry P., in, 246, 247; postal service between Britain and, 211, 221; steamships running between Bombay and Suez, 226, 231, 246–47, 255, 270, 292, 366n57
Inglis, Sir Robert, 228
Inman, Henry, 241, 382n30, *plate 25*
Ioannina, 58, 59, 107

ipecacuanha, 207
Irby, Charles Leonard, 64
Ireland, Andrew Lawrence, 285, 287–89, 291, 292, 301–4, 309
Ireland, John (father of Andrew), 287, 309
Irving, Washington, 53, 81, 285, 308
Isfording (Austrian attaché), 273
Isis, temples of: Medinet Habu, 103; Philae, 30–31, 135, 212, 218–19
Islam: Feast of the Circumcision, Cairo, 226–27; Koran purchased by Richard Randolph, 219; missionaries and, 91. *See also* converts to Islam; Mecca
Ismail Djebel Akhdar (Ismail Gibraltar; admiral of pasha's fleet), 104
Ismail Pasha (youngest son of Mehmet Ali), 74, 75, 76, 78
Isserverdens Stith & Co., 182
Italinski, Count Andrei (Russian envoy in Constantinople), 54, 331n33
Italy: American visitors in eighteenth century, 6–8; American visitors before and during War of 1812, 52–53, 58–59; American visitors after War of 1812, 72, 80, 83; American visitors 1829–1832 in, 126, 133, 134, 139; American visitors 1833–1835 in, 170, 178, 179, 183–84, 188; American visitors 1835–1839 in, 210, 216, 222, 225, 265, 266, 269. *See also specific cities and sites*
Izard, Elizabeth (later Pinckney; aunt of Ralph), 179
Izard, Mary (later Pringle, then Poinsett; aunt of Ralph), 179
Izard, Ralph Stead, Jr., 178–81, 184, 259
Izard, Rosetta Ella (née Pinckney; wife and first cousin of Ralph), 179

J
Jackson, Dr. (Massachusetts General Hospital), 88
Jackson, Andrew, 113, 125, 155, 162, 165
Jackson, Rev. John Frelinghuysen, 242
Jackson, Dr. William Henry, 242–44, 278, 376n60
Jaffa: American navy in, 154, 159, 161, 162; Ward Nicholas Boylston in, 9; Bradford and companions visiting, 129–30; captured in Napoleonic invasion, 32; Cohen in, 134; European tourists in early nineteenth century in, 67, 68; Fisk, Parsons, King, and Smith in, 92, 106; Hamersley in, 175; Paxtons in, 240; Rapelje in, 87; steamship service at, 232
Jakob, Therese Albertine Louise von (later Robinson), 235, 236
James Monroe (packet), 83
Jarvis, George, 110
Jarvis, John Wesley, 155, *plate 15*
Java (US frigate), 113
Jay, Peter Augustus, 230
Jedda, 38
Jefferson, Thomas, 19, 20–21, 23, 24, 49, 54, 58, 122, 163, 206, 260
Jem (yacht of third Marquess of Waterford), 171
Jenks, Joseph William, 351n22
Jenner, Edward, 206
Jenney, Captain (of brig *Fortune*), 117
Jepson, Daniel, 343n23

Lagasquie, Auguste, 142
Laidlaw, Dr. James, 171
Lake Mareotis, 168
Lake Mariout, 86
Lake Moeris, 86
Lampi, Giovanni-Battista, 24
Lancaster, H., 366n57
Lane, Edward William, 11–12, 13, 41, 172, 189, 190, 326n4
Lang, Mr. and Mrs. William, 242
Langdon, John (brother of Thomas Walley), 116
Langdon, Joseph (son of John), 92, 116–17
Langdon, Thomas Walley, 92, 116–17, 367n11
Larkin, Charles, 198
Larking, John Wingfield (British consul), 212
Larking, Rosina (née Pellegrini de Tibaldi), 212
Larnaca, 9, 68, 169
laudanum, 190, 206–7
Laurel Hill Cemetery, Philadelphia, 313
Lavison, Édouard, 171
Lawrence, Captain (of brig *Erin*), 110, 117
lazarettos. *See* quarantines
Leake, William Martin, 76, 77
Lebas, Apollinaire, 133–34
Lebolo, Antonio, 65
Leclerc, Georges-Louis, Comte de Buffon, 24
Ledyard, Henry, 162–65, *plate 17*
Ledyard, Dr. Isaac (first cousin of John), 22, 163
Ledyard, John, 19–23, 24, 25, 26, 45, 94, 128, 163, 319n2
Ledyard, Matilida (née Cass; wife of Henry), 162, 164
Lee, Edward (brother of Peter), 88
Lee, Hester Maria (née Van Lennep; wife of Edward), 88
Lee, John (brother of Peter), 48, 329n14
Lee, Larkin T., 88
Lee, Peter (British consul), 62, 74, 77, 88, 93–94, 103
Lefebvre de Cerisy, Charles, 41, 148
Legh, Thomas, 43
Leghorn (Livorno): American merchants in, before War of 1812, 50; American navy in, 126, 143, 145; American travelers after War of 1812 in, 72, 88; American travelers 1838–1839 in, 244, 265, 278, 280; Boylston in, 7–8, 9, 18; collections of Egyptian antiquities passing through, 146–47; giraffes shipped through, 259; Nutts in, 183; steamer service at, 230, 233
Leighton, Sir Baldwin, 202
Lelorrain, Jean Baptiste, 79
Leonidas (French postal steamer), 233, 299
Lesseps, Ferdinand de, 243
Lesseps, Theodore de, 98, 340n18
Lessing, Lauren, 381–82n30
Letorzec, Pierre Constant, 75
letters of credit, 92, 200–201, 251–52, 291
letters of introduction, 7, 198; American travelers in eighteenth century using, 7, 8, 20, 23; American travelers before and during War of 1812 using, 47, 50, 54, 58; American travelers after War of 1812 using, 71, 73, 79, 92, 93, 94, 97, 98, 105; American travelers 1829–1832

using, 71, 73, 79, 92, 93, 94, 97, 98, 105, 126; American travelers 1833–1835 using, 170, 189; American travelers 1835–1839 using, 219, 223, 228, 237, 239, 242, 266
Levant (British frigate), 8
Levant (steamship), 232
Levant Company, 48, 49, 50, 320n17
Lexington (US ship), 124, 159
L'Hôte, Nestor, 141, 174, 192
Library of Congress, 35, 122, 245
Lidman, Swen Frederick, 62–63
Lieder, Rev. Johann Rudolph Theophilus, 106, 173, 281, 292, 356n12, 358n35
Lieven, Christopher and Dorothea, 115
Light, Colonel William, 152–53
Light, Mrs. Col. William (née Mary Bennet), 152–53
Linant de Bellefonds, Louis Maurice Adolphe, 64, 158, 298, 369n30, *plate 30*
Lincoln, Charles R. and Lucretia, 280
Lincoln, Levi (governor of Massachusetts), 198
Lindsay, Alexander Crawford, Earl of, 221, 326n5
Linnaeus, Charles, 23
Lisbon, 54, 57, 217, 246
Liston, Robert (British ambassador to Constantinople), 59, 73
Litchfield Law School, Connecticut, 124
Littlefield, Henrietta (née Butler; wife of Nathaniel), 271–73, 285, 287, 288
Littlefield, Nathaniel, 271–80, 285, 287, 288, 299, 310
Livingston, Edward (mayor of New York City), 34
Livingston, Henry Brockholst, 163
Livingston, Robert R. (US minister to France), 34, 53
Livorno. *See* Leghorn
Llewellyn, William B. (US consul in Salonica), 246
Lock, Captain (of brig *Alligator*), 70
London: Adgers in, 241; Boyd's diplomatic career in, 226; Boylston in, 18–19, 25–27; Curtis in, 224; Egyptian Hall, 120–21; giraffes in, 259–60, 272, 373n29; Gliddon, George, in, 258; Ledyard, John, in, 19; Littlefield party in, 272; obelisk moved to, 84, 133, 134; Rhinelander party in, 288; Stephens in, 210; Victoria, Americans witnessing coronation of, 164, 272, 279, 288, 289, 290
Longfellow, Henry Wadsworth, 173, 220, 266, 365n36
Longinus, Dr. (traveler with Parthey), 98
Longwood (mansion, Natchez), 188
Louis Philippe (king of France), 115
Louis Philippe (packet ship), 164
Louvre Museum, 64, 79, 120, 142, 146, 160, 341n27
Lowell, Rev. Dr. Charles Russell, 301, 379n22
Lowell, Francis Cabot (father of John, 1830s traveler), 188
Lowell, James Russell (poet; son of Charles), 379n22
Lowell, John (1830s traveler), 101, 102, 188–92, 193, 206, 207, 215, 312, *plate 21*
Lowell, John (1804 traveler), and Rebecca (née Amory), 53

McAlpin, Alexander, 366n57
McCall, Richard (US consul in Barcelona), 86, 108
McEvers, Jeannette Emmet (later Whitlock), 307
McGill (Catholic bishop of Philadelphia), 279
McLean Asylum, Boston, 139
McLellan, Isaac, 265–66, 268, 301, 309
McLeod, Dr. Daniel C. (US naval surgeon), 163
McMurtrie, William (US navy purser), 351n22
McVickar, Eliza (née Bard; mother of Henry), 227
McVickar, Henry ("Harry"), 227–28, 261–62, 278, 305–6, 310
McVickar, John (father of Henry), 227–28
McVickar, Samuel Bard (brother of Henry), 227–28
Mecca: carpet sent to, 171–72; cholera introduced by pilgrims returning from, 205; departure of caravan for, 13–14; purge of Wahhabis in, 38
Medem, Count Peter von, 98
medical issues. See health issues
Medici, Lorenzo de, giraffe presented to, 373n27
Medina, 38
Medinet Habu, 32, 103, 136, 214, 228
Mediterranean, US naval squadron in. See navy, US
Megara (British steamer), 240, 298, 379n19
Mehmet Ali (viceroy of Egypt): American steam-driven cotton and rice processing machines, efforts to obtain, 249–58; Americans naval visits to Egypt and, 148, 150–51, 152, 156, 158, 159, 161, 162, 163; Americans working for, 74, 77; audiences with, 171, 179, 182, 212, 298–99, 378–79n16–17, plate 30; background and family, 37; British regiment marching to Rosetta from Alexandria (1807) and, 94; coal, Syrian, 252; consolidation of power under, 37–38; defection of sultan's fleet to, 300; Europeans working for, 62, 63, 75; Feast of the Circumcision, Cairo, 226, 227; gifts exchanged with American naval officers, 150–51, 354n51; giraffes presented to foreign rulers by, 259, plate 28; Greek War of Independence and, 110, 114, 115–16; guidebooks on, 199; invasion of Syria and Palestine by, 116; inventions presented to, 63, 73; letters of introduction from, 98; menagerie of, 291, 295; obelisks ceded to France and Britain by, 133; palace and gardens at Shubra, 95–96, 104–5, 152, 157, 221, 247, 259, 269, 276, 295; Palestine and Syria seized by, 116, 175; Pellegrini de Tibaldi poisoned by, 212; quarantine established by, 40, 170; Rapelje's interview with, 85–86; reforms of, 10, 37–43, 281; representations of, 10, 37–43, 298–99, 352n26, 378–79n16–17, plate 12, plate 30; telegraph demonstrated to, 264–66, 267; tombs of family of, 295
Melos, 69, 145
Melville, Captain (British army), 153
Melville, Henry Dundas, Viscount, 177, 357n24
Memnon, colossi of, 103, 174
Memnon, Temple of, Qurna, 103
Memphis, 15, 163, 239, 310
Memphis Daily Appeal (newspaper), 310
Menou, General Jacques (French army), 33
Mentor (French postal steamer), 233, 290

merchants and commerce: American merchants in Mediterranean, before War of 1812, 48–52; American merchants in Mediterranean, during Greek War of Independence, 116–18; American naval presence in Mediterranean and, 147; European commerce in eighteenth century, discouragement of, 17; European merchants in nineteenth century, 62
Meredith, William, 206
Meroe, 74, 75, 191
Merrill, Martha W. (later Dodge, then Paxton), 240, 261
Meryon, Charles, 80
Messina, 45, 50, 52, 53, 68, 83, 143, 144, 145, 229, 268
Messolonghi, 110, 111, 116
Metamora (ship), 280
Meteor (steamer), 231
Metternich, Klemens von, 115
Middlebury College, 91, 92, 103, 233, 263
Middleton, Henry (US minister to Russia), 122–23, 125
Middleton, John Izard, 110
Milan, 7, 133, 273, 282, 309
Miller, Dr. James H., 164
Miller, Jonathan Peckham, 110
Miller, Ralph Willett (American officer in British Navy), 325n3
Mimaut, Jean-François (French consul), 115, 137, 158
Minassian, Kirkor, 245
Minerva, colossal foot of, 56–57
Minos (French postal steamer), 233, 289
Mintum, Robert, 382n35
Minutoli, Menu von, 65
Minya, 180, 212
Missett, Ernest (British consul-general), 47
missionaries: ABCFM (American Board of Commissioners for Foreign Missions), 91, 96, 106, 239; American and European travelers sheltering with, 22–23; American Bible Society, 267, 280, 299; Church Missionary Society, 106, 171, 240; in India, 91, 94; Lutheran, 106; Moravian, 16; no American posts in Egypt, 274; Paris Missionary Society, 105, 339n13; Saint Simoniens, 158–89, 191; Wesleyan Missionary Society, 106. See also specific individuals
The Missionary Herald (periodical), 81, 175–76
Mitchell, Dr. Samuel L., 88
Mocha, 42, 51, 71, 99, 191, 350n5
The Modern Traveller, 152, 175, 198–99
Mokattam mountains, 190, 221
Moldavia, 7, 108, 113, 223
Molineux, Ann (later Boylston), 5–6, 27
Molineux, William, 5, 6
Monge, Gaspard, 31, 33, 35
Monroe, James, 56, 73, 78, 286, 336n26
Montagu, Edward Wortley (son of Lady Mary), 206, 322n34
Montagu, Lady Mary Wortley, 206, 322n34
Montague (British traveler), 174, 177
Moores, Frederick W. (US navy sailing master), 159–60, 354n45

Ney, Marshall (French army), 127
Nice, 53, 183
Nicholas I (tsar), 115, 178
Niebuhr, Carsten, 23–24, 321n26
Nightingall, Sir Miles and Florentia, 66
Nile: American impressions of, 22–23, 94, 128, 185, 240; barrage at Delta, 158; source of, 24, 87
Nile, Battle of the (1798), 17, 30, 325n3
Nile Valley, Americans in. *See* American travelers in Mediterranean, Middle East, and Egypt
Nilometer, Roda, 14, 15, 41, 86, 174, 239, 327n11
Nonsuch (US schooner), 109, 144
Normandie (packet ship), 180–81
North America (ship), 287
North American Review (magazine), 120
USS *North Carolina*, 77, 110
Nott, Lt. Anthony H. (Indian navy), 366n57
Nott, Josiah Clark, 359n48
Nourredin, Osman, 148
Nubia: attendants from, 260, 269; Barthow in, 43; English, George Bethune, on military expedition to, 74; European researchers and collectors in, 63; increasing interest in Egypt (1829–1832) and, 124, 128, 136; Rhinelander's souvenirs from, 299; slaves from, 74, 268
Nubian club owned by Rhinelander, 294, 299
Nuozzo, Paolo, 185, 203, 204, 210–11, 212
Nutt, Haller (son of Rush), 188, 359n56
Nutt, Dr. Rush and Rittenhouse (father and son), 182–88, 189, 190, 204, 206, 210, 238, 240, 249, 359n48, 359n59

O
Oakley, Robert W., 131–34, 135, 148, 204
O'Bannon, Lt. Presley Neville (US marine), 47, 48
obelisks: Cleopatra's Needles, Alexandria, 20, 23, 83–84, 93, 95, 133, 211, 246, 275, 291; Hatshepsut (pharaoh), fallen obelisk of, 101, 191, *plate 22A*; Heliopolis, 84, 95, 133, 239, 243, 269, 348n50; in Karnak, 212, 221, 348n50; in London, 84, 133, 134; in New York City, 84, 134; in Paris, 99, 133–34, 135, 136, 173, 219, 230, 364n31; remaining in Luxor, 173, 219; Roman removals of, 348n50
Odeon (brig), 250
Offley, Catherine H., 160
Offley, David (US Consul in Smyrna), 50, 79, 113, 114, 116, 124–25, 300
Offley, David Washington (US consul in Smyrna; son of David), 300
Offley, James Holmes (son of David), 353n44
Offley, Richard Jones (son of David), 159–60
Old South Church, Boston, 91
Olin, Stephen, 263
Oliver, Charles (brother of Henry), 125
Oliver, Henry, 124–25, 127, 135, 142, 148, 202, 204, 219
Oliver, Robert (father of Henry), 125
Oliver, Thomas (brother of Henry), 125
Oman (Muscat), Henry P. Marshall as US consul in, 198, 246–47, 255, 289, 290, 292, 311, 312
Ombrosi, James (US consul in Florence), 126, 347n36

Ontario (US corvette), 109, 143–44
ophthalmia, 74, 185, 190, 205, 206, 207
Oren, Michael B., 327n14
Orient (Napoleonic flagship), 30
Oriental/Egyptian Revival style, 120–22, 123, 188
d'Orléans, Duc, 97, 123
Orlov, Count (of Russia), 113
Orpheus (ship), 224
Osman Effendi (William Thompson), 94–96, 152
Osprey (schooner), 68
Otho (first king of independent Greece), 114, 265
Ottoman empire: American diplomatic relations with, 79, 112–14; American shipbuilders for, 114; defection of fleet to Mehmet Ali, 300; early nineteenth century American visitors to (before 1820), 53–55; European commerce not encouraged by, 17; European opposition to American diplomatic presence in, 79, 113; invaded by Mehmet Ali, 116; rise of Mehmet Ali, 37–38; Russia, war with, 7–8; sale of Carolina rice in, 49, 329n16. *See also* Constantinople; Greek War of Independence
Ovans, Major Charles (British army), 153
Oxford Movement, 306

P
Pacho, Auguste, 370n30
Pacific (steamship), 382n31
packet ships, translatlantic travel on, 83, 119
Padang (ship), 187
Padua, 7, 102, 273, 341n27
Paine, Thomas, 21–22, 23
Palermo, 45, 52, 53, 68, 162, 229, 230, 244
Palestine. *See specific cities*
Palmer, Aaron Haight, 251–54
Palmer, Charles, 254, 258
Palmer, John, 54
Palmer, Thomas, 6–7
Palmerston, Lord, 115
Panckoucke, Charles-Louis, 35, 122
Panic of 1837, 228, 252–53
Pannonia (steamboat), 273
panoramas, 59, 64, 215–16, 364n19
Paphos, 92, 93
Paris: Egyptian scholars in, 40, 281; giraffes in, 183, 259, *plate 28*; Jardin des Plantes, 31, 183, 259, 379n18; Place de la Concorde, obelisk erected in, 99, 133–34, 135, 136, 173, 219, 230, 364n31; statistics on American travelers to, 195
Paris, Treaty of (1783), 45
Paris Missionary Society, 105, 339n13
Pariset, Dr. Étienne, 140–42
Park Street Church, Boston, 91
Parsons, Rev. Levi, 72, 74, 91–94, 96, 103, 107, 110, 168
Parthey, Gustav, 98–99
Partridge, Martha, 274
Pasley, John, 66
passports, 196–97, 286, 361n7, *plate 23*
Patmos, 132, 221
Patterson, Commodore Daniel T. (US Navy), 154–61, 162, 165, 181, 203, *plate 15*

Patterson, Eliza (daugher of Daniel), 154, 155–56, 158, 203–4
Patterson, George Ann (Georgy; daughter of Daniel; later Porter), 154, 155, 157, 161, 203
Patterson, George Ann (née Pollock; wife of Daniel), 154, 156, 203
Patterson, Harriet (daughter of Daniel), 154, 155, 161, 203
Patterson, Marianne Caton (later Wellesley), 153
Paxton, Rev. John D., 240, 241, 261–62, 306
Paxton, Martha (daughter of Martha and John), 261
Paxton, Martha W. Dodge (née Merrill; married to John D.), 240, 241, 261
Peabody Museum, Salem (now Peabody Essex Museum), 144
Peach, Hester Elizabeth (née Barker), 214
Peach, William Nathaniel, 214
Peacock (US sloop of war), 73
Peale, Rubens, 89, 129
Pearson, Lt. George F. (US Navy), 354n51
Pease, Lorenzo Warriner, 163, 186
Pell, John, 298, 378n16
Pellegrini de Tibaldi, Mary (widow of Pierre Anthony; later Thurburn), 212
Pellegrini de Tibaldi, Pierre Anthony, 212
Pellegrini de Tibaldi, Rosina (daugher of Mary and Pierre Anthony; later Larking), 212
Pendleton, N., 193
Pennsylvania (packet ship), 246
Pennsylvania Academy of Natural Sciences, 89
Pera, 81, 300
Percy, Algernon, Lord Prudhoe, 369n30
Le Père (Barthélemy Prosper Enfantin), 158–59, 189, 191
Peregrine (brig), 89
Pergamon, 67, 92
Périer, Casimir Pierre, 115
Perkins, George (cousin of James, Thomas, and Margaret), 48, 50, 57, 92, 330n20
Perkins, James, 48, 50, 57, 92
Perkins, Margaret (later Forbes; sister of Thomas and James), 57
Perkins, Samuel Gardner, and wife, 58
Perkins, Stephen Higginson (son of Samuel), 58
Perkins, Thomas Handasyd, Jr. (son of Thomas Handasyd Perkins Sr.), 59
Perkins, Thomas Handasyd, Sr. (brother of James and Margaret), 48, 50, 57, 92, 149
Perry, Matthew Calbraith (US naval officer), 148, 149–51, 165, 352n24, 352n26, *plate 10*
Perry, Oliver Hazard, Jr. (nephew of Matthew), 351n22
Perseverance (British steamer), 229
Petra, 214, 277
petrified wood, 16, 247, 269
Peysonnel, Claude-Charles de (French consul in Smyrna), 320n17
Pharsalus, Battle of (1st century BC), 84
Phelps, William D., 193
USS *Philadelphia*, 47
Philae: Belmore party at, 68; Bradford and companions at, 128, 218; European researchers

and collectors at, 63, 64; Haights at, 218–19; Hamersley at, 173; Lowell at, 191; Napoleonic expedition at, 30–31, 32–33; Rhinelander party at, 293; skulls shipped to Morton from, 264; Stephens at, 212; Temple of Isis at, 30–31, 135, 212, 218–19; Trajan, Kiosk of, 340n20
Philhellenism, 110
Philip Arrhidaeus, sanctuary of, Karnak, 190, 221
Phocéen (steamer; later *Peyk-i Sevket*), 233
Pickman, Benjamin, 50
Pilgrim (brig), 114
Pillavoine, Alexandre (acting French consul), 61
Pinckney, Elizabeth (née Izard; daughter of Rosetta and Thomas), 179
Pinckney, Rosetta Ella (later Izard), 179
Pinckney, Thomas, Jr., 179
piracy in Mediterranean, 45–48, 147
Piraeus, 197, 205, 231–33, 275, 290, 299
Piranesi, Giovanni Battista, *Le Antichità Romane* (1756), 7
Pirie, Lt. Duncan (British army), 302
Pitt, William, 80
plague, 204–5; American travelers after War of 1812 and, 69, 70, 72, 94; American travelers 1829–1832 and, 138, 140, 142; American travelers 1833–1835 and, 170, 189–91; American travelers 1835–1839 and, 210, 217, 244, 273; Mahmoudiya Canal, construction of, 39; Napoleonic expedition and, 34; Nile barrage halted by, 158
Platt, Eliza, 281, 292, 369n30
Pocahontas (packet ship), 242
Pococke, Richard, 70
Poe, Edgar Allan, 215
Poinsett, Joel Roberts, 52–53, 54, 179
Poinsett, Mary Izard Pringle (wife of Joel), 179
Polignac, Jules-Armand, Prince de, 123
Pollock, George Ann (later Patterson), 154, 156, 203
Pomo (Austrian trabaccolo), 169
Pomona (brig), 52
Pompeii, 7, 53, 196, 230, 278
Pompey (Roman general), 84
Pompey's Pillar, Alexandria: fragments taken from, 46–47, 104, 328–29n5; Ledyard on, 20, 23; Littlefield and Holmes visiting, 275; Marshall, Henry P., at, 246; missionaries visiting, 93, 104; Nutts viewing, 184; origins and history, 84–85; Rapelje on, 83, 84–85; Rhinelander party at, 291; Smith, Eli and Sarah, on, 168, 169; Stephens visiting, 211; tourists climbing, 85, 337n39; *Warren* officers visiting, 148
Ponsonby, Lord (British ambassador to Constantinople), 115
Ponsonby, Miles (British traveler in Egypt), 136
Porpoise (schooner), 147
Port Mahon, Minorca, 43, 71, 109, 113, 143, 145
Portalis (French traveler), 191
Porter, Commodore David (US chargé d'affaires in Constantinople), 113, 114, 154, 155, 157, 161, 181, 215, 220, 246
Porter, David Dixon (son of Commodore David), 154–57, 161, 181

Reed, Catherine (later Allen), 133
Reed, Howard, 52
Reed, Luman (father of Catherine), 133
Reeve, Tapping, 210
Regulator (brig), 193
Reinlein (Dutch consul), 189
Renwick, James, 252
Revolutionary War, 6, 17, 18–19, 30, 45, 48, 325n3
Reynolds, Joshua, 9
Rhazes, 244
Rhind, Charles, 113, 124
Rhinelander, Frederick William (uncle of Philip Jr.), 285
Rhinelander, John R. (uncle of Philip Jr.), 285
Rhinelander, Mary (later King; sister of Philip Jr.), 285, 303, 304, 308
Rhinelander, Mary Colden (née Hoffman; mother of Philip Jr.), 285
Rhinelander, Philip (Sr.; father of Philip Jr.), 285
Rhinelander, Philip (Jr.): in Alexandria and Cairo, 291–92, 295–99; death in Vienna, 302–4, 305; diary kept by, 289, 308, 380–81n16; in Europe, 288–91; family, background, and education, 285–86; on French and British interest in Egypt, 119; guidebook carried by, 199; on languages, 289–90, 293; Nile cruise, 292–95; portrait of, 285, 308, 380n16, *plate 29*; in Smyrna and Constantinople, 200–301
Rhinelander, Philip Jacob (ancestor of Philip Jr.), 285
Rhinelander, William C. (uncle of Philip Jr.), 285, 308
rhinoceroses, 264, 282, 295
Rhodes, 9, 67, 68, 107, 132, 154, 180, 181, 189, 193, 232, 301
Rhodes, Foster, 114, 187, 300, 301
rhyton or drinking horn in shape of lion, faience, 160, *plate 7*
Ricci, Alessandro, 64
rice: American observation of Egyptian cultivation of, 133; American sales of, 49, 51, 329n16; milling, 249–58, 264
Richardson, Robert, *Travels along the Mediterranean*, 199, 213
Richter, Otto Friedrich von, 62–63
Rifaud, Jean-Jacques, 63, 65, 68, 79, 99, 102, 341n27; *Tableau de l'Égypte* (1830), 175, 199
Riggs, Rev. Elias, 274–75
Rigo, Nicola (Nicola il Conte Rigo; Venetian consul), 16
Ringgold, Lt. William S. (US Navy), 163
Ripley, Samuel, 177–78, 357n28
Rittenhouse, David, 183
Rivière, Marquis de (French ambassador to Constantinople), 67, 73
Roberts (Englishman living in Alexandria), 292
Roberts, David, 292, 298, 378–79n16–17, *plate 30*; *Egypt & Nubia*, 188
Robertson, Rev. John J., 131, 132, 274–75, 276, 280
Robinson, Rev. Edward, 40, 233, 235–41, 273, 327n7; *Biblical Researches*, 237
Robinson, Eliza (née Kirkland; first wife of Edward), 235

Robinson, George, 127, 128, 130
Robinson, Therese Albertine Louise (née von Jakob; second wife of Edward), 235, 236
Rochfort Scott, Charles, 167–68, 202
Roda: American naval parties visiting, 156, 157; Ward Nicholas Boylston on, 13, 14, 15; garden and palace of Ibrahim Pasha on, 156, 174, 221, 239, 243, 247, 269; gunpowder factory, 41, 86; Nilometer, 14, 15, 41, 86, 174, 239, 327n11
Rodgers, Commodore (US Navy), 77, 78, 114
Rodgers, Eugene E., 163
Rodgers, John, 351n22
Roenne, Baron von, 98
Rogers, Sarah (later Haight). *See* Haight, Richard Kip and Sarah
Roman Catholicism, 8, 18, 79, 93, 97, 130–31, 240, 279, 303, 306, 348n44
Roman sarcophagi from near Beirut, 165
Romanism, 306
Rome: American travelers in eighteenth century, 6, 7; American travelers before and during War of 1812 in, 52, 53, 58; American travelers after War of 1812 in, 72, 81; American travelers 1829–1832 in, 125, 131, 132; American travelers 1833–1835 in, 177, 178, 179, 183, 188; American travelers 1835–1839 in, 210, 223, 224, 228, 241, 242, 247, 266, 268, 270, 271, 278, 279, 289, 301; Cass party in, 162; English-speaking travelers in, 196; Middleton, John Izard, in, 110; Napoleonic appropriations from, 31; obelisks transported to, 348n50; statistics on American travelers to, 195; on steamship cruise itinerary, 230
Romney, George, 322n34
Ropes, George, *plate 8*
Roscoe (packet ship), 222
Rosellini, Gaetano, 141
Rosellini, Ippolito, 141, 142; *I Monumenti dell'Egitto e della Nubia* (from 1832), 311
Rosetta: American naval parties in, 47–48, 148, 150, 152, 158, 159; Ward Nicholas Boylston in, 10–11, 16; British regiment marching from Alexandria to (1807), 94; Firmin Didot in, 67; Fisk and King in, 97; Napoleonic invasion and, 29, 37; obelisk shipped to Paris through, 134; as port, 38; steam-driven rice and cotton mills at, 249, 255–58
Rosetta Stone, 33, 34, 120
Rossetti, Carlo (Venetian consul in Egypt), 17, 22, 193
Rossignana, Joseph, 63, 65
Rothschild, Baron Salomon, 233
Rotterdam, 51
Rouen, Baron de, 115
Roussel, Joseph Jean-Baptiste (French consul), 61, 67, 73, 77, 78
Roussin, Albin-Reine (French ambassador to Constantinople), 115
Roux, Polydore, 192
Rowe, Samuel, 56
Rowley, Charlotte and Richard, 213, 214
Ruckmann, Baron, 115
Rüppell, Edouard, 66
Rush, Benjamin, 183

Russell, Rev. Michael, *View of Ancient and Modern Egypt: With an Outline of Its Natural History* (1830 and 1831), 199
Russia: British naval officers serving in navy of, 7–8; Greek War of Independence and, 111, 113, 114–16; Ottomans, war with, 7–8; Poland, partition of, 178; steamers operated by, 234
Rutherford, Robert, 7
Ruthvin, Madame (French traveler), 273, 376n11
Rutledge, Edward, 49
Rutledge, Henry Middleton, 179
Ryme, Amedée, 263

S
sabers and swords presented to American naval and marine officers, 48, 150–51, 161, 354n51
Sack, Albert von, 64, 65
St. Catherine's monastery, Sinai, 128–29, 136, 214, 239
Saint-Elme, Ida (Maria Johanna Elselina Versfelt; Elzelina Tolstoy can Aylde Jonghe; "La Contemporaine"), 127, 128
Saint-Elme, Leopold, 127
Saint-Hilaire, Étienne Geoffroy, 33
St. James (ship), 287
Saint-Marcel, Pierre-Emmanuel Mazières de (French vice-consul), 52
St. Sergius (Abu Sarga), Cairo, 13, 321n25
Saint Simoniens, 158–89, 191
St. Stephens College (now Bard College), 310
Saladin, well of, 95, 269
Salavatore (acting for British consul Salt), 94
Salem Gazette (newspaper), 71
HMS *Salisbury*, 5–6
Sally Anne (brig), 88, 92, 343n15
Salonica, 49, 82, 108, 246, 302
Salt, Henry (British consul-general): Caviglia and, 221; diplomatic career, 62; Egyptian antiquities collected by, 63–65, 120, 136, 142, 145–46, 340n27, 341n27; English, George Bethune, and, 73, 74, 76–77; Firmin Didot and, 67; India passage and, 66; missionaries in Egypt and, 94, 95, 97, 103, 105; Thompson, William (Osman Effendi) and, 95, 152
Samos, 93, 108
Sandys, George, 188
Santoni, Pietro, 146
Saqqara, 15, 163, 190, 239, 243, 264
Sargent, John Singer, 307
The Saturday Magazine, 260
Savary, Claude Étienne, 24–25
Sawyer (or Savage), Daniel, 49
Scagliotti (Piedmontese teacher in Bulaq), 39
Scamandre (French postal steamer), 233, 300
scarlet fever, 188, 240
Schmidt, Dr. John W., Jr., 241, 242
Schütz, Henriette Helene (later Van Lennep), 93
Schutz, Pierre Ambroise (Dutch consul), 93, 137, 189
Schwarz, John George (US consul in Vienna), 303
Scott, Charles (son of Sir Walter), 58
Scott, Sir Walter, 58, 273
Scotto, Dr. Antonio, 76

Scoville, Charles Elliott, 225
Scoville & Britton (East India traders), 246, 247, 311
scythe chariot (invention of George Bethune English), 73–74, 78
Sébastiani, Horace, 115, 137
Seguera, Antonio de, 41, 157
Sekhmet, statues of, Karnak, 102, 190, 340–41n27, *plate 22B*
Sennar, 21, 41, 66, 75–77, 87, 213, 259, 282
Senno, Alessandro del, 16
Senwosret Sunbefni, Egyptian quartzite statue of, 35, *plate 6*
Sergeant, Katherine (later Cram), 307
Serigo (now Kythera), 56
servants, 204; of Abbott family, 382n34; Achmet (of Kirklands), 189, 204, 362n31; Ahmed (of Eli and Sarah Smith), 167, 204; Ali and Abdella (animal handlers with giraffes sent to New York), 259, 261, 262; of Allen, Oakley, and Ferguson, 132; Antonio (of Hamersley), 175, 176; Antonio (of Rhinelander party), 289, 292; Antonio (of Willingtons), 270; of Belmore party, 67, 68, 145; of Cass party, 162; of Cohen, 136; of Crams, 378n8; Curtin, James (of Belzoni), 63; da Costa, Antonio (of Bankes), 63; in Danube steamer accident (1839), 301, 302; Deri (of Benjamin F. Brown), 263; of Eaton, 47; François (of Haights), 204; of Lady Franklin, 149; Giovanni (of Haights), 204; Grenier, Joseph (of Parthey party), 98, 340n20; guidebooks on, 200; of Haights, 204, 217; Haroum (of Benjamin F. Brown), 263; Hassan (dragoman of anonymous American in Egypt 1839), 282; Henry (of Mott), 242; Jeffrey or Geffrey-Boni (dragoman of Benjamin F. Brown), 263; John (of Littlefields), 279; of Littlefield and Holmes, 276, 279; Mahomet (of Bradford), 129; Mohammed Abdini (dragoman for Yates), 204; Mustapha (caravan guide of Fisk, King, and Wolff), 105; Nubian, 260, 269; Nuozzo, Paolo (of Nutts and Stephens), 185, 203, 204, 210–11, 212; of Nutts, 185; O'Neale, Ellen (of Ellen Purdie), 187; of Patterson party, 155, 156; price of steamer passage for, 231; in quarantine, 299; of Rhinelander party, 289, 291, 292, 294, 299; of Robinson, Edward, 236, 239; Selim (of Peter Haights), 204; Selim (of Peter Lee), 93; of Lady Hester Stanhope, 80; of Turtons, 222; Vicenzo (to Burton), 337n43; of Willingtons, 266, 269, 270
Sésostris (French steamer), 233, 247
Seti I (pharaoh), 64, 65, 68, 100, 103, 120, 144–46, 199, 239
Sève, Joseph (Suleiman Pasha or Suleiman Bey), 41, 127, 189
Seyd Bey (admiral of the Egyptian fleet), 298, 379n17, *plate 30*
Seymer, Henry Ker, 213
Seymour (American traveler from Georgia), 289, 290
*shabti*s or *ushabti*s, 65, 144–47, 163, 350n5
Shaler, William (US consul in Algiers), 245
Shark (US schooner), 154–61, 162

Sparks, Jared, 163
Sparta, 59, 224
Spencer, James, 161
Sphinx (steamship), 134, 230
Sphinx , Giza, 14, 15, 190, 221, 313
sphinxes, Karnak, 43, 100, 102, 174, 191, 221, 295
Sprague, Horatio (US consul in Gibraltar), 255
Sprague, Seth, 147
Springfield Gazette (newspaper), 280
Sproule (British traveler), 171
Spurrier (traveler and friend of Fisk), 96
Squier, Ephraim George, 313, 314
Stackpole, J. Lewis, 177–81, 184, 206, 259, 357n28, *plate 18*
Stackpole, Roxana (later Dabney; sister of J. Lewis), 180
Stackpole, William (falther of J. Lewis), 177
Stael, Anna Louise Germain de (Madame de Stael), 53
Stanhope, Lady Hester: background and life of, 80; Bradish visiting, 80, 82, 87; Cass party calling on, 162; Chasseaud and, 82, 336n32; on Cohen, 176; Courtis and Dorr visiting, 223, 224; DeKay brothers calling on, 114, 176; Firmin Didot calling on, 67; Hamersley party calling on, 176–77; King, Jonas, and, 97, 105, 243; Mott party and, 243, 244; Rapelje visiting, 87
Stark's Italy, 184
steam-driven cotton and rice processing machines, 156, 184, 249–58, 264
steam locomotives in US, 216–17, 220, 222
steamer accident on Danube (1839), 301–2
steamship travel, 196–97, 229–34, *plate 24*
Steele, Lt. Henry A. (US Navy), 163
Steinberg, Chevalier (Austrian consul, at Salonica), 302
Stephens, Amelia Ann (later Willett; sister of John L.), 216
Stephens, John L., 210–16; Catherwood and, 215–16; education, career, and travels before Egyptian trip, 210; Egyptian Society of Cairo and, 250; at Esna, 213, 293; on food eaten in Egypt, 202–3; giraffe speculation and, 215, 258–59, 262; guidebook used by, 199; hotel in Alexandria, 201; *Incidents of Travel in Egypt, Arabia Petræa, and the Holy Land*, 215, 217, 275, 293; *Incidents of Travel in Greece, Turkey, Russia, and Poland*, 215, 217; Nuozzo as servant of, 203, 204; Nutts and, 186–87; on pleasures of travel, 209; portrait of, 216; Waghorn and, 211, 221
Stewart, Lt. David R., 154, 156, 160
Stewart, Deborah (mother of William), 49
Stewart, William (US representative in Smyrna), 49–50
Stith, Griffin, 117, 159, 182, 186
Stith, Thorowgood S. (son of Griffin), 117, 186–87
Stone (Irish traveler in Egypt), 275–76
Stourbridge Lion (steam locomotive), 217, 220
Strickland, William, 123
Stringham, Silas H. (US naval officer), 161

Strong, George Templeton, 122, 287, 306–8, 310, 380n4
Strong, George W., 210
Stuart, Sir Charles (British ambassador to France), 97
Stuart, Gilbert, 27, 59, *plate 4*
Stürmer, Baron (Austrian internuncio in Constantinople) and Baroness, 115, 273, 376n11
Stuyvesant Institute, New York, 313
Sudan, 24, 41, 63, 74, 87, 99, 180, 191, 259, 263
Suez: Barthow in, 42; Bradford and companions in, 128–29; Champollion and Pariset in, 142; coal for steamships at, 252; Cohen in, 136; discouragement of European commerce via, 17; Egyptian antiquities shipped through, 312; food provisions for, 202; India passage across, 119; Marshall, Henry P., in, 246–47, 292; postal service using, 211, 221; Rowley party in, 213; steamships running between Bombay and, 226, 231, 246–47, 255, 270, 292, 366n57
Suez Canal, 64, 158–59
Suleiman Pasha/Bey (Joseph Sève), 41, 127, 189
sulphate of zinc, 207
Sultan Hasan, Mosque of, Cairo, 295, 296–97
Swift (British steamer), 229–30
Swiftsure (Nelson's flagship), 30
Swords, Charles R., 266, 268, 269, 301, 302, 309
Swords, Sarah (née Willis), 309
sycamore, Heliopolis, 95, 187–88, 239, 243
Syene (Aswan), 30, 32, 65, 98–99, 173, 212, 238, 263, 282
Sylvestre de Sacy, Antoine Isaac, 97
syphilis, 204, 206
Syra (Syros): American travelers 1835–1839 in, 220, 221, 236, 240, 247, 258, 268, 274, 276, 280–82, 289, 290–92, 299, 300, 376n13; Cass party in, 162; Evangeles as educator on, 112; Parsons at, 93; quarantine in, 205; steamer service at, 233, 311; on travel itineraries of Americans, 197, 200
Syracuse, 52, 53, 143, 145, 184
Syria. *See specific cities*
Syrup of Capillaire, 11, 321n22

T
Talleyrand-Périgord, Charles Maurice de, 115
Tancrède (French postal steamer), 233
Tanis, 239
Tanner, Lt. T. (US Navy), 144–45, 147
Tanner, Lt. Thomas (British Navy), 350n5
Tasburgh, George, 8, 9, 18–19, 322n39–40
Tasburgh, Theresa (née Gage), 8, 18, 322n39–40
Tattam, Rev. Henry, 281, 292, 298, 369–70n30, 378–79n16–17
Taylor, Baron Isadore Justin Séverin, 133, 192
Taylor, John H., 341n27
Taylor, Peter, 211
telegraph, 264–66, 267, 301
Temple, Rev. Daniel, 87, 96, 106, 274
Temple, Rachel, 96
Terry, Sidney, 211
Tessier, Jean-Joseph, 123
Teynard, Félix, 172